Handbook of career theory

Edited by

MICHAEL B. ARTHUR
Suffolk University

DOUGLAS T. HALL
Boston University

BARBARA S. LAWRENCE
University of California at Los Angeles

 CAMBRIDGE
UNIVERSITY PRESS

Published by the Press Syndicate of the University of Cambridge
The Pitt Building, Trumpington Street, Cambridge CB2 1RP
40 West 20th Street, New York, NY 10011-4211, USA
10 Stamford Road, Oakleigh, Melbourne 3166, Australia

© Cambridge University Press 1989

First published 1989
Reprinted 1991, 1993, 1995, 1996

Printed in the United States of America

Library of Congress Cataloging-in-Publication Data is available.

A catalogue record for this book is available from the British Library.

ISBN 0-521-33015-7 hardback
ISBN 0-521-38944-5 paperback

Contents

v   101054

Contributors

Clayton P. Alderfer is a professor of organizational behavior at the Yale School of Organization and Management. A fellow of the American Psychological Association and the Society for Applied Anthropology, he serves on the editorial board of the *Journal of Applied Behavioral Science*, the *Family Business Review*, and the *Journal of Organizational Behavior*. Professor Alderfer is a diplomate of the American Board of Professional Psychology and a winner of the Cattell and MacGregor Awards for research contributions; he is a consultant to a variety of business, government, and nonprofit organizations.

Michael B. Arthur is an associate professor at the School of Management, Suffolk University, and holds a Ph.D. in management from Cranfield Institute of Technology, United Kingdom. Arthur is first author of the text "Working with Careers" (1984) and joint editor of "Environment and Career" (1984, with Barbara S. Lawrence), a special issue of the *Journal of Occupational Behaviour*. His further journal articles span the topics of career development and employee participation and their implications at both individual and organizational levels of analysis.

Lotte Bailyn is a professor at the Sloan School of Management, Massachusetts Institute of Technology. She holds a Ph.D. in social psychology from Harvard University, an M.A. from Harvard University, and a BA from Swarthmore College. Her recent books include *Living with Technology* (1980), a study of engineers in midcareer, and the co-authored text *Working with Careers* (1984). She has written and consulted extensively on career-related issues for more than twenty years and been a visiting scholar in the United Kingdom, Italy, New Zealand, and most recently Australia.

Stephen R. Barley serves as an assistant professor of organizational behavior at Cornell University's School of Industrial and Labor Relations. He received his doctorate in organization studies from the Massachusetts Institute of Technology. Barley's research and writing have centered on organizational culture and the implications of technological change for the social organization of work. He is currently involved in a longitudinal study of the commercialization of molecular biology.

Jay B. Barney is an assistant professor in the Department of Management at Texas A&M University and holds a Ph.D. from Yale University in sociology and administrative sciences. Professor Barney's research and teaching interests have been in the areas of organizational economics and strategic management. He has written a book with William G. Ouchi, titled *Organizational Economics* (1986), along with several articles that examine the role of idiosyncratic firm attributes in creating sustained competitive advantage.

Nancy E. Bell is an assistant professor of behavioral and organizational science at Cornell University's Johnson Graduate School of Management. Her current research interests include the assignment of blame and credit in organizations as well as the relationship of both stable dispositions (personality) and transitory dispositions (mood) to job attitudes and behaviors. Her Ph.D. is in organizational behavior and industrial relations, from the University of California, Berkeley.

Lisa R. Berlinger is a doctoral candidate and assistant instructor of management at the University of Texas at Austin. She received her A.B. degree (1979) from Georgetown University in political theory. Her research and writing span the areas of employee commitment, work design, and organizational design, with a particular interest in the relationship between the nature of work roles and organizational adaptation to the external environment.

Nancy E. Betz is a professor in the Department of Psychology at the Ohio State University. She received her Ph.D. in psychology from the University of Minnesota in 1976, and her subsequent research and writing span topics ranging from gender differences in career development to ethics in psychological testing. She has written two books: *Tests and Assessment* (1985, with W. Bruce Walsh) and *The Career Psychology of Women* (1987, with Louise F. Fitzgerald). She has been the editor of the *Journal of Vocational Behavior* since 1984 and is a fellow of the American Psychological Association.

John O. Crites is currently a professor in the School of Educational and Social Policy and Director of the Career Development Center at Northwestern University. His publications include *Vocational Psychology* (1969), *Career Counseling* (1981), *The Career Maturity Inventory* (1978), and over 100 journal articles, monographs, and book chapters. A former president of the American Psychological Association's Division of Counseling Psychology, he also holds the Diplomate in Counseling Psychology. He took his undergraduate degree at Princeton University and his Ph.D. at Columbia University.

Solomon Cytrynbaum is a professor at the School of Education and Social Policy and the Institute of Psychiatry and Behavioral Sciences, and a coordinator of the Counseling Psychology Program, Northwestern University. He is also a research fellow and faculty member, Doctor of Psychotherapy Program, Institute for Psychoanalysis in Chicago. Cytrynbaum received his Ph.D. in psychology from the University of Michigan in 1971, and his current research interests focus on adult development and aging, psychopathology and transference, and authority relations in group and organizational life.

Gene W. Dalton (D.B.A., Harvard) is the former Chairman of the Organizational Behavior Department, Brigham Young University, where he has taught and done research for 16 years. He has authored five books, one of which won the Academy of Management Best Book Award in Management, plus a number of articles on organizational change and employment practices. Much of his recent research has focused on the management and careers of professional employees – engineers, scientists, accountants, bankers, and so on – and is reported in the book *Novations: Strategies for Career Management* (1986, co-authored with Paul Thompson).

C. Brooklyn Derr is a professor of organizational behavior at the Graduate School of Business and Director of the Institute for Human Resource Management at the University of Utah. He is currently also a visiting professor at the International Management Institute (IMI) in Geneva, Switzerland. Derr received his doctorate in 1971 from Harvard and his B.A. from the University of California at Berkeley in 1967. His most recent book is *Managing the New Careerists: The Diverse Career Success Orientations of Today's Workers* (1986).

Louise F. Fitzgerald is an associate professor of educational psychology and psychology at the University of Illinois at Champaign. She received her Ph.D. in psychology from the Ohio State University. She is co-author, with Nancy E. Betz, of *The Career Psychology of Women* (1987) and has published extensively in the areas of vocational psychology and women's career development. Her current research addresses the issue of sexual harassment in higher education and the workplace.

Joan V. Gallos has a B.A. from Princeton University and a doctorate in organizational behavior from the Harvard Graduate School of Education. She is an instructor of management at Harvard University, where she teaches courses in power and leadership, and organizational behavior, at the Radcliffe Seminars. She is a consultant/educator on issues of professional effectiveness and the design and management of collaborative work systems. Her present research and writing interests focus on issues of gender and power and their implications for individual learning and performance.

Dan Gowler, M.A. (cantab.), is a lecturer in management studies and a fellow in organizational behavior at the Oxford Centre for Management Studies, Templeton College, Oxford University. His interests are in evaluation research, with special reference to interpretive methods, and in the social anthropology of management, with special reference to cultural analysis. His publications include contributions to management journals and books and to specialist publications in the social sciences.

Douglas T. (Tim) Hall is a professor of organizational behavior in the School of Management at Boston University. He received his B.S. degree from the School of Engineering at Yale University and his M.S. and Ph.D. degrees from the Sloan School of Management at the Massachusetts Institute of Technology. He is the author of *Careers in Organizations* (1976), editor of *Career Development in Organizations* (1986), and co-author of books on organizational behavior and human resource management. He is a recipient of the American Psychological Association's James McKeen Cattell Award (now called the Ghiselli Award) for research design. He is a fellow of the American Psychological Association and of the Academy of Management.

Raymond E. Hill is an associate professor of organizational behavior in the School of Business Administration, the University of Michigan. He is a member of the American Psychological Association and the Academy of Management. His research interests are focused on the career transition from scientist to manager within research and development departments in organizations. He has published several articles in professional journals, and recently co-authored (with Trudy Somers) a book entitled *The Transformation from Technical Specialist to Technical Manager* (1988).

Rosabeth Moss Kanter is Class of 1960 Professor at the Harvard Business School, a tenured full professorship dedicated to innovation and entrepreneurship. Doctor Kanter is the author of ten books, and she has published over 100 articles in books and scholarly journals. Her newest book, tentatively entitled *The Great Corporate Balancing Act*, will be published early in 1989. Her recent best selling titles are *The Change Masters: Innovation and Entrepreneurship in the American Corporation* (1983) and *Men and Women of the Corporation* (1977), which received the C. Wright Mills Award for the best book of that year on social issues.

Kathy E. Kram, Ph.D., is an associate professor in the Department of Organizational Behavior at the Boston University School of Management. She holds B.S. and M.S. degrees from the Massachusetts Institute of Technology Sloan School of Management and a Ph.D. from Yale University. Her primary interests are in the areas of adult development and career dynamics, values and ethics in corporate decision making, organizational change processes, and gender dynamics in organizations. Her book, *Mentoring at Work*, was published in 1985.

Janina C. Latack is an associate professor in the Faculty of Management and Human Resources at the Ohio State University. Professor Latack earned her Ph.D. in organizational behavior from Michigan State University after a background in career counseling. Her research and publications focus on career development, stress, job loss, and outplacement. She has published multiple journal articles, and her most recent contributed chapter, "Termination and Outplacement Strategies," appears in M. London and E. M. Mone (eds.), *Career Growth and Human Resource Strategies* (1988).

André Laurent is a professor of organizational behavior at INSEAD, the European Institute of Business Administration, Fontainebleau, France. He is a graduate of the Ecole de Psychologues Praticiens de Paris and holds a doctorate in psychology from the University of Paris, Sorbonne. Laurent is also a graduate of Harvard University's International Teachers Program and a former study director at the Survey Research Center, Institute for Social Research, University of Michigan. His major publications have covered survey interviewing methodology, managerial subordinacy, organizational change, and comparative management.

Barbara S. Lawrence is an assistant professor at the John E. Anderson Graduate School of Management, University of California at Los Angeles. She holds a Ph.D. from the Massachusetts Institute of Technology. Lawrence has developed a theory of age effects in organizations and has written extensively on this topic in journals and anthologies. Her work has been funded by the National Institute on Aging. She is joint editor of "Environment and Career" (1984, with Michael B. Arthur), a special issue of the *Journal of Occupational Behaviour*.

Karen Legge, Ph.D., is a reader in organizational behavior at the newly formed School of Management at Imperial College, London. She is the editor of *Personnel Review* and a joint editor of the *Journal of Management Studies*. Her major publications include *Power, Innovation and Problem Solving in Personnel Management* (1978), *Evaluating Planned Organizational Change* (1982), and (as co-editor)

Cases in Organizational Behavior (1985). Presently Dr. Legge is continuing conceptual work in the areas of human resource management and organizational change.

Angeline W. McArthur is an assistant professor of organizations and strategic management in the School of Business Administration at the University of Wisconsin – Milwaukee. She earned her Ph.D. in organizational studies from the University of Oregon in 1983. Her current research develops a model of organizational adaptation in the U.S. airline industry. This research examines organizational characteristics and the environment as predictors of strategic changes.

Judi Marshall, Ph.D., is a senior lecturer in organizational behavior in the School of Management, University of Bath, United Kingdom. Her main areas of research and publication have been managerial job stress (the topic of her Ph.D. thesis), women in management, organizational cultures and change, and "new paradigm" approaches to inquiry. Her publications include *Understanding Executive Stress*, (1978, with Cary Cooper) and *Women Managers: Travellers in a Male World* (1984).

David A. Morand has a Master of Industrial and Labor Relations from Indiana University of Pennsylvania. He is presently a Ph.D. candidate in organizational behavior at the New York State School of Industrial and Labor Relations, Cornell University. His research interests include organizational culture and subculture, systems of workplace participation, and the sociolinguistics of deference behavior in organizations. His dissertation research is a study of how the need for efficiency and authority in communication can conflict with the need for social consideration and politeness.

Nigel Nicholson received his Ph.D. from the University of Wales. Since 1972 he has been at the MRC/ESRC Social and Applied Psychology Unit, University of Sheffield, where he is a senior research fellow and research team leader. His research has been in three areas: absenteeism, industrial relations, and work role transitions, and in 1983 he was co-recipient of the Academy of Management New Concept Award for theoretical developments on absence. He has been a visiting scholar at universities in the United States, Canada, and West Germany and is currently co-editing *European Handbook of Work and Organizational Psychology*.

Paul C. Nystrom is a research professor of organizations and strategic management in the School of Business Administration at the University of Wisconsin – Milwaukee. He earned his Ph.D. in industrial relations from the University of Minnesota in 1970. He co-edited the two-volume *Handbook of Organizational Design* (1981), which received the Academy of Management's best-book award. Professor Nystrom's current research focuses on managers' beliefs and values.

Jeffrey Pfeffer is Thomas D. Dee II Professor of Organizational Behavior at the Graduate School of Business, Stanford University, and holds a courtesy appointment in the Department of Sociology. He received his B.S. and M.S. degrees from Carnegie-Mellon University and his Ph.D. from Stanford. He is the author of *Power in Organizations* (1981), *Organizations and Organization Theory* (1982), and *Organizational Design* (1978), co-author of *The External Control of Organizations* (1978), and author of more than 70 articles and chapters.

James E. Rosenbaum is a professor of sociology, education, and social policy at Northwestern University. He holds a Ph.D. in social relations from Harvard

University. He specializes in research on stratification, organizations, and education. In addition to studying how organizational structures affect employees, he has also studied how schools affect the careers and the development of students. He is author of *Career Mobility in a Corporate Hierarchy* (1984), *Making Inequality* (1986), and many articles on these topics. Most recently, he has begun research on the school-to-work transition in the United States and Japan.

Uma Sekaran is the chairperson and a professor in the Department of Management at Southern Illinois University in Carbondale. She obtained her Ph.D. in management from the University of California at Los Angeles. Sekaran is the author of four books and several articles in the areas of careers and international management. Her book *Dual Career Families* (1986) was selected as one of the three best books of the year by Macmillan's Behavioral Science Book Club, and she has been awarded the Distinguished Research Leadership Award by the International and American Biographical Institutes.

Jeffrey A. Sonnenfeld (D.B.A., Harvard) is an associate professor at the Harvard Business School. He has published 45 articles and 5 books on such topics as career management, executive training and development, and the management of corporate and public affairs. His newest book, *The Hero's Farewell: What Happens When CEO's Retire* (1988), examines the impact of late career leaders on their firms. Sonnenfeld serves on the editorial board of the *Academy of Management Executive* and is a member of the Academy of Management Board of Governors.

Barry M. Staw holds the Mitchell Chair in Leadership and Communication at the University of California, Berkeley. He is also the chairperson of the Organizational and Industrial Relations Group at the Berkeley Business School. He is co-editor of *Research in Organizational Behavior*, an annual series of analytical essays and critical reviews, and serves on the editorial boards of *Administrative Science Quarterly*, *Organizational Behavior and Human Performance*, the *Journal of Applied Psychology*, and the *Academy of Management Journal*. Currently, Professor Staw's research focuses on the issues of organizational commitment, job attitudes, and work performance.

David A. Thomas is Atlantic Richfield Foundation Term Assistant Professor of Management at the Wharton School of the University of Pennsylvania. He has written several articles on organizational change, intergroup, and cross-race relations and recently completed a study of the impact of race on mentor–protégé relationships. He received his B.S. from Yale College and an M.Phil. and Ph.D. from Yale University, both in organizational behavior. He also earned an M.A. in organizational psychology from Columbia University.

Robert J. Thomas holds a Ph.D. in sociology from Northwestern University and is Leaders for Manufacturing Chair in Organization Studies, Sloan School of Management, Massachusetts Institute of Technology. He has authored two books on technological change in agriculture: *Manufacturing Green Gold* (1981) and *Citizenship, Gender and Work* (1985). He has also written about labor–management relations in the U.S. and Japanese auto industries and the problems and prospects of quality control circles. He is presently completing several articles on the relationship between choices about production technology and power relations in aerospace and other manufacturing firms.

Harrison M. Trice, Ph.D., is a professor in the Department of Organizational Behavior, School of Industrial and Labor Relations, Cornell University. He teaches courses in organizational and occupational cultures and has done research and published widely on the role of rites and ceremonies in the behavior of work organizations. He currently is involved in using a cultural framework for a study of occupations and their interrelationships with organizations.

Karl E. Weick is Rensis Likert Collegiate Professor of Organizational Behavior and Psychology at the University of Michigan. He received his Ph.D. in psychology from Ohio State University in 1962. He has written four books and numerous articles on behavior and sense-making in organizations, including the highly acclaimed *The Social Psychology of Organizing* (Second Edition, 1979). Weick is a former editor of the *Administrative Science Quarterly* and a member of the editorial boards of *Contemporary Psychology, Small Group Behavior*, the *Organizational Behavior Teaching Review*, the *Journal for the Theory of Social Behavior*, and *Accounting, Organizations and Society*.

Michael West is currently a lecturer at the psychology department and Research Officer at the MRC/ESRC Social and Applied Psychology Unit, University of Sheffield. He gained his Ph.D. from the University of Wales and his current research is focusing on innovation in work groups. He has authored and edited a number of books, including *The Psychology of Meditation* (1987), *Managerial Job Change* (1988, with Nigel Nicholson), and *Innovation at Work* (in press).

Preface

Back in the early 1970s, there was no established "field" of careers in organization and management studies. Tim Hall recalls that it was fun when he and a small band of organizational scholars, who viewed themselves as being on the cutting edge of theory, who liked to work on somewhat offbeat topics, and who would rather challenge than defend the academic "establishment," embarked on their career studies. Anyone interested in examining the long-term issues associated with working in organizations was really on his or her own to find useful theory and research in a number of relevant social science disciplines, such as psychology, sociology, political science, economics, and anthropology. To do good research, you had to scan and learn from a number of disciplines and you had to develop your own theoretical ideas. In organizational terms, the scholarly environment in which we operated was complex, dynamic, and nonroutine.

The down side of all this was that sometimes you wondered who your audience was. Many questions gnawed away at you: Is anyone out there interested in this "career stuff?" What journals would possibly publish papers on careers? Who is in my reference group? Everyone I trade papers with is in a psychology, sociology, or education department. Yet I work in a business school. Am I in the right place? But you had a sense that it was all new. And you *knew* it was important as you saw more and more evidence of the long-term influence of careers on individuals, the institutions in which they worked, and the societies to which they belonged. There was a sense of being on the "ground floor" of something important.

This sense was confirmed by interactions with scholars looking at careers from other vantage points. Psychologists and sociologists were interested in outside perspectives that would complement and enrich their own disciplinary views. Educationalists were anxious to look beyond consideration of "vocational choice" that so dominated their inquiries but only represented the starting point of people's careers. But there was no accepted meeting place for views to be exchanged, and the exchanges that did take place tended to be fragmentary or to represent one-shot attempts at interdisciplinary theory.

So, what has changed? In a word (or two), career theory has "gone legitimate." We (people who study careers) have become established. We have become a *field*. In the immortal words of Yvette Mimieux in the classic movie *Where the Boys Are*, "Who'd 'a thunk it?"

The groundwork was laid by vocational psychologists and sociologists. Each of these groups, inspired by writers such as Don Super (1957) and Everett Hughes (1958), had already had their "fun" with the career concept. But although their definitions of career were similar, the two groups stayed largely apart. By the late 1970s organizational scholars' observations about career outcomes paved the way for new initiatives.

Three key books appeared (Hall, 1976; Schein, 1978; Van Maanen, 1977) that helped focus applied work on careers. Don Super organized what he called the "Mobile Career Seminar," which met in different locations semiannually, and which, significantly, reached out beyond counseling psychologists and educational researchers to those studying organizational behavior. Those of us who sat around the ornate living room at MIT's Endicott House in 1978 and began to discuss forming some sort of professional society devoted to careers had a sense that it probably would happen some day. This was followed up by a similar meeting in Asilomar in 1980 as well as by organizing meetings at the Academy of Management. Very rapidly, this loosely connected group of career enthusiasts became an interest group in the academy and then a full-fledged division. And the coverage of career issues in books and journals also grew in exponential fashion.

An important parallel initiative involved the development of teaching materials about careers for present and future managers in graduate and management development classes (Kotter, Faux, and McArthur, 1978; Sonnenfeld, 1984). This "career management" perspective prompted major changes in organizational practice. Careers came to be looked on as the products of individual–organization negotiation instead of as paths preordained by high-level "human resource planners." These changes were further recognition for the career theory behind them and provided fertile ground for new research. We joined and identified with these attempts to gain more effective application of our own ideas (Arthur et al., 1984; Hall and Associates, 1986).

However, as we become "legit," we established our own theories and paradigms related to careers. People studying careers now had a body of career literature to turn to in formulating their research designs. There was less need to discover or invent useful, relevant theory and research in various social science disciplines. We began talking to ourselves and writing for each other.

As we turned inward, our work took the form of processing and debating and applying existing theory. Less energy went into discovery. As a result, we soon reached a point where career practice threatened to catch up with the career theory that inspired it. Career counselors and organizational career program designers were putting into practice the latest ideas on adult development, internal labor markets, sense making, and so forth. Career academics were investing much more in theory testing than in theory development. Our recently formed field, which had seemed so open and welcoming, was beginning to appear closed.

So, we needed new blood – or rather, new theory – which is the lifeblood of any scholarly field. And that is what this handbook of career theory is all about.

What was our plan for infusing new blood into the field? Our first tentative explorations (Arthur and Lawrence, 1984) convinced us we should return to our original scholarly "home," the basic social science disciplines. We felt that some of our best resources were people who would not claim to be associated with the field of careers in any way. We wanted to enlist the finest minds – from both career theory and beyond – in a number of relevant social science disciplines and have them join us to "think careers." As you look at the table of contents, you will understand our pride at having these particular contributors together between the covers of a volume devoted to career theory.

That is how this project began. Next, we came up with a design for the handbook that would highlight the contrast between current approaches and new ideas in career theory, and we set out to find our authors. We enlisted the cooperation of a group of people who are leaders in the careers field to write what we call "review chapters with a point of view." These chapters provide an overview of the very best the field has to offer today and generate new questions for exploration. The chapters represent Part I.

We next identified a number of intellectual leaders in their particular social science fields who expressed interest in the long-term effects of work on people but were not "career people." We asked them simply to think out loud about concepts from their field that potentially would be useful to people studying careers. Very few of those we approached turned us down. Their chapters make up Part II. Parts I and II together represent the fertile ground that we hope will nourish a decade or two of career research and theoretical debate.

Finally, we asked four leading scholars of organizations to take the rich harvest of ideas in Parts I and II and simply "play" with them. Apart from requesting that these authors focus on different levels of analysis, we left their assignments quite unstructured. We wanted them to do what we hope every reader will do, namely, to become immersed in the diverse contributions from Parts I and II and come up with their own ideas about new potential directions and theoretical approaches for the study of careers. We think you will be intrigued with their thoughts.

In fairness to all our authors we should stress that this handbook is no mere anthology. Not only were they all asked to fall in with the handbook design as outlined, but also their work was subject to an exacting review schedule that would have driven lesser academics to despair! First, most authors joined a workshop that Barbara Lawrence organized for the 1986 Academy of Management meeting. The authors' drafts were read in advance by six to eight other scholars. Each paper was then the subject of a ninety-minute discussion among the readers during which the authors received feedback. To illustrate the intensity of these sessions, we can recall that Harrison Trice commented he had never had to work so hard for his living at a workshop in his life! After submitting drafts that accommodated workshop feedback, all authors received three lengthy and unsparingly critical reviews from the editors. A further draft of each chapter was read by an independent reader from Cambridge University Press, after which both the reader's and the editors' further comments were relayed back to the authors. All of this occurred before the usual copy-editing procedures for the handbook began. We deeply and sincerely appreciate the efforts all handbook contributors made in sticking to the task. We hope that they, and every other reader, will see these efforts fully reflected in their final product, this handbook.

We owe a great intellectual debt to Lotte Bailyn, Ed Schein, Don Super, and John Van Maanen, who did so much to demonstrate the potential of career studies during the 1970s. And as this project wended its way from a vague itch in the back of Mike Arthur's head, the early support of Lotte Bailyn, Gene Dalton, Dan Gowler, Dan Levinson, and Paul Nystrom was crucial. We humbly thank them, and other trusted friends and publishers in whom we confided, for believing in us when we most needed their assurance. Francis Brooke, then of Cambridge University Press, also shared both our vision and our enthusiasm for what the handbook could become.

We have already mentioned the Academy of Management, whose officers graciously supported our endeavors in career studies within the academy's Careers Division. However, we have yet to acknowledge the extent of intellectual and interpersonal support we received from that quarter. The long list of Careers Division members who helped in some way with this enterprise, but who are not authors here, includes Don Bowen, Jim Clawson, Marcy Crary, Tom DeLong, Mike Driver, Mary Ann Von Glinow, Jeff Greenhaus, Tom Gutteridge, Meryl Louis, Bob Morrison, Suzyn Ornstein, Sam Rabinowitz, Jim Stoner, and Paul Thompson. We have also enjoyed productive links both directly and through handbook contributors with the Industrial and Organizational Psychology Division (Division 14) of the American Psychological Association and the Organizations and Occupations Section of the American Sociological Association.

We each owe thanks to our host institutions, Suffolk University, Boston University, and the University of California at Los Angeles, for granting us the necessary time and support services to undertake this venture. Rosemary Carroll, Nancy Croll, Mary Kelly, and Paula Rauschl (at Suffolk University), Marie Jean Curtenaz, Vince Mahler, and Victoria Selden (at Boston University), and Alice Hirata and Lucy Wallen (at the University of California at Los Angeles) all went out of their way to help us complete our task. We editors would also like to thank each other for the distinct contributions that made this handbook possible, for picking up the slack when one or another of us got bogged down, and for pressing forward in the face of the numerous trials and tribulations of shepherding a book such as this from idea to publication.

From Cambridge University Press, we were most ably helped through the publisher's editorial cycle by Ina Isobe, Andrew Schwartz, Janis Bolster, Ernestine Franco, Beatrice Ruberto, and an insightful anonymous academic reader. As this book goes to press, we are indebted to Linda Hollick for helping us reach our intended audience. Our association with Cambridge University Press has been, and continues to be, everything we could have wanted.

Finally, our spouses – Cia, Marcy, and Charlie – and our children have accepted, almost always with good grace, the impositions and demands the handbook has made upon them.

Michael B. Arthur
Douglas T. (Tim) Hall
Barbara S. Lawrence

Boston, Massachusetts
and
Los Angeles, California
January 1989

REFERENCES

Arthur, M. B., Bailyn, L., Levinson, D. J., and Shepard, H. A. (1984). *Working with Careers.* New York: Columbia University Graduate School of Business.
Arthur, M. B., and Lawrence, B. S. (1984). *Environment and Career.* Special Issue of the *Journal of Occupational Behaviour,* 5(1), 1–81.
Hall, D. T. (1976). *Careers in Organizations.* Pacific Palisades, CA: Goodyear.
Hall, D. T., and Associates (1986). *Career Development in Organizations.* San Francisco: Jossey-Bass.

Hughes, E. C. (1958). *Men and Their Work*. Glencoe, IL: Free Press.

Kotter, J. P., Faux, V. A., and McArthur, C. C. (1978). *Self-Assessment and Career Development*. Englewood Cliffs, NJ: Prentice-Hall.

Schein, E. H. (1978). *Career Dynamics: Matching Individual and Organizational Needs*. Reading, MA: Addison-Wesley.

Sonnenfeld, J. A. (1984). *Managing Career Systems: Channeling the Flow of Executive Careers*. Homewood, IL: Irwin.

Super, D. E. (1957). *The Psychology of Careers*. New York: Harper and Row.

Van Maanen, J. (ed.) (1977). *Organizational Careers: Some New Perspectives*. New York: Wiley.

PART I

Current approaches to the study of careers

Introduction to Part I

Our Preface offers some general comments about the way career theory has evolved. Now it is time to get down to specifics and consider the various theoretical approaches to careers extant in the literature today. In Part I we review the current "state of the art" of career theory, based upon the major lines of inquiry that have thus far emerged. Underlying all Part I chapters is a belief that before we can add to the theoretical landscape about careers, we must first have a good sense for its present contours.

To set the scene for the review that follows, a preliminary chapter by Arthur, Hall, and Lawrence explores how the diversity of theoretical perspectives that share the career concept can be brought together to promote cross-fertilization and new career theory development. First, the authors discuss definitions of career and career theory, the range of social science perspectives relevant to career studies, and the characteristics that guide career theory to highlight how career theory can serve as a nexus for transdisciplinary study. They then move on to consider how new career theory develops, by describing a cycle of new theory generation and mapping out the mix of philosophies of knowledge that career theory reflects. The authors conclude, and extend the thesis of the handbook, by claiming that debate at both these levels of analysis can promote "transformational" career theory that gains new relevance in a changing world.

Each subsequent chapter takes responsibility for an established perspective in career theory and covers both the historical emergence and the current relevance of that particular stream of thought. However, these chapters represent more than mere reviews of the literature; they also propose fresh ways for viewing the issues they cover. The charge to each author was to produce "a literature review with a point of view," that is, to reflect the writer's own judgment about what was noteworthy. Moreover, authors were encouraged to project what could still be done with the adopted perspective and thus to help prepare the ground for future inquiries.

The flow of Part I is an *evolutionary* one. The chapters are arranged in the order in which each stream of theory and research has emerged. Thus, we begin with the two most established lines of career inquiry stemming from psychology, on personality–occupation matching, and sociology, on careers as social roles. Then we turn to the more recent literature on adult development and its implications for individual careers and for the organizational processes to which careers connect. The adult development theme is also a component of what can be seen as three sets of responses to the early research emphasis on white males; responses that have women's careers, minorities' careers, and dual careers as their respective foci. The final two chapters in Part I cover the most recently emerging, but now clearly visible, topics in the field: the first focusing on career transitions and the second on organizational career systems. These ten chapters that make up Part I, then, are offered as a set that reflects the best of what career theory has come to be and serve as reference points for further activity within each line of inquiry.

Our survey of established lines of career inquiry begins with the traditional cornerstone of career theory, namely, the vocational psychology perspective on personality–occupation matching. The second chapter, by Betz, Fitzgerald, and Hill, examines the theory and research on individual differences as they affect career outcomes. However, the chapter points out that traditional vocational psychology has often overlooked the effects of organizational variables as well as the interactions between the individual and the environment. The chapter provides first a brief historical overview, after which it summarizes the basic trait-factor theories of vocational behavior, discussing their current status, strengths, and limitations. It concludes with recommendations for future work in theory and research.

Next, Barley presents a historical overview of the Chicago School of Sociology and its contribution to current ideas about careers. The author argues that the Chicago School did not tie the meaning of career to currently popular notions in career theory: for instance, the succession of jobs, vertical mobility, or formally organized contexts. Instead, careers were viewed as social constructions woven together by four themes: (1) status passages, (2) the objective and subjective, (3) properties of collectives, and (4) social structures. Barley suggests that, again in contrast to more recent sociological thought, the Chicago School advocated theory development rather than theory testing. While this approach led to an important body of empirical work that expanded our view of how individuals both construct and are socialized into society, it focused on the particulars of each situation and never provided generalizable theory. The author argues that Gidden's work on structuration might provide such a theory and presents examples of how this theory might be applied.

Chapter 4, by Cytrynbaum and Crites, examines the different historical approaches to adult development (remember that before the work of Erik Erikson, "development" in psychology was assumed to mean "child development") and shows how this work can help explain previously uninterpretable findings in research on occupational behavior. Several chapters in this volume employ adult development theory as a point of departure (e.g., Gallos, Chapter 6; Sekaran and Hall, Chapter 8; Marshall, Chapter 13; and Arthur and Kram, Chapter 14) as does much of contemporary work on careers, and a clear presentation of what we know in this area is critical foundation work for this handbook. Similarly, contemporary careers are impacted primarily by the experience of individuals in organizational settings, and it is these processes that form the basis for the chapter by Dalton (Chapter 5). Thus, Chapter 4 provides a crucial conceptual foundation on adult development for later work in the handbook.

Dalton raises the specter of modern society's ambivalence toward organizations. On the one hand, people feel angered by the control that organizations exert over their lives; on the other hand, they seek the stability and companionship provided within organizations. The author discusses this ambivalence from the perspective of career development theories, examining how organizations influence, enhance, and constrain individual growth. Individually and organizationally based models of career development are summarized. The author then utilizes Dalton and Thompson's four stage model – identity, competence, interdependence, and leadership – to explicate both the positive possibilities and negative consequences that exist for an individual's development within organizational contexts. Dalton concludes by raising questions concerning who bears the responsibility for these consequences and what individuals and organizations can do about them.

Next, we move to a critical career issue in contemporary work settings, namely, that of gender. To what extent do our theories and practices encompass the experiences of women as opposed to being primarily oriented toward the male experience? Gallos (Chapter 6) examines this issue with an in-depth analysis of adult development in women. The purpose of this chapter is, in her words, "to explore the different vision of reality that women can bring to work, love, and career." She starts by reviewing the literature on women's development, to provide more context about women's lives, contrasting women's development with that of men. She raises and examines the models of career and career success implicit in male and female views of development and concludes with the need for new career directions for both men and women. Thus, her chapter speaks not just to a theory of women's development but to the wider body of career theory.

A similar question regarding diversity versus the traditional views of career could be asked in relation to the influence of race on career dynamics, a minority topic in career research (pun intended). Thomas and Alderfer (Chapter 7) reflect on the very limited set of descriptive and research studies into the dynamics of race in organizations. Drawing principally on available studies of the black American experience, they identify and explore a number of themes – biculturation, racial identity, cross-race developmental relationships, and gender–race interaction – that affect the career development of minorities. The authors then move to offer an intergroup perspective on race and career dynamics, concerned with the embeddedness of intergroup phenomena in organizational life and the extra barriers minorities face in the progress of their own careers. A series of recommendations for organizational research ends with the poignant observation that researchers need to take an introspective look at their own (professional) organizations to learn why greater progress on racial issues has yet to be made.

The problem of combining career and family, a critical and still-growing one in our society, is reviewed and examined by Sekaran and Hall (Chapter 8). Their review of work done on spouse attitudes and behavior, boundary differences between spouses, and organizational accommodation to family points to a missing element in past research, synchronism, or its counterpart asynchronism, between the partner's careers. Themes of asynchronism, male development, and female development are explored as background to a stage-based model of the dual-career *couple* that combines separate strands of previous inquiry. The model informs an implications section encouraging organizations to pay attention to late career development for men and women, to reconsider the "bailing-out" tag applied to women who quit established careers for motherhood, to confront organizational definitions of success, and to consider cultural barriers for what they are. The authors predict that through such efforts greater synchronization can be achieved, not only between partners but also between the work force and organizations generally.

The final two chapters present recent views that show much potential for our understanding of the interconnectedness of individual career processes and organizational career dynamics. At the individual level, an important stream of research has been concerned with transitions, which provide a way of treating the all important time dimension in a bounded, practical way. Nicholson and West (Chapter 9) present an overview as well as new approaches on transitions. After reviewing work on stages of transitions, they turn to the body of the chapter, an examination of four interconnected themes they have identified in relation to the outcomes of transitions: (1) experiential content of antecedents and consequences of the change event; (2) how different adjustment strategies originate; (3) linkages between transitions cycles to explain their life-long patterning; and (4) how influences within the person and the organization interact to affect job mobility. The authors conclude with a call for researchers from different disciplinary perspectives to utilize transitions concepts to help integrate their related fields in relation to the study of careers.

Finally, at the organization level, concepts of large-scale human resource management systems have provided employers with ways of linking the development of individuals to the achievement of organizational objectives. Chapter 10, by Sonnenfeld, focuses on this process of strategic staffing and its implications. Noting the wide variations in human resource management approaches to people's careers, he highlights a "missing link" in the research that fails to relate this variation to strategic differences among firms. For Sonnenfeld, organizational career systems reflect strategic staffing choices that can be categorized according to two critical dimensions of career movement: "supply flow" into the organization and "assignment flow" across jobs. The resultant typology of implicit career systems can be used to reinterpret previous labor market research and to describe and predict an organization's work force composition. Sonnenfeld concludes by relating his typology to Miles and Snow's alternative strategic orientations and presenting coherent sets of staffing policies to match selected strategic postures.

In sum, the chapters in Part I represent the central concepts and issues stemming from career theory as we know it. With this work as a foundation, we shall later consider possible new theoretical directions in Part II.

1 Generating new directions in career theory: the case for a transdisciplinary approach

MICHAEL B. ARTHUR, DOUGLAS T. HALL, AND BARBARA S. LAWRENCE

> The limitation of social organization is found in the inability of individuals to place themselves in the perspectives of others, to take their points of view.
>
> *George Herbert Mead, 1927*

> When we pause in our studies to reflect on theory and method, the greatest yield is a restatement of our problems.
>
> *C. Wright Mills, 1959*

The concept of the career has never been more popular. Once viewed mainly as a synonym for initial job choice, it is now widely accepted as a central feature in employment arrangements. Career development and human resource management programs are not only widely accepted but also seen as critical to both individuals and organizations. Such programs cover a wide range of issues, from individual careers and work–family accommodation, to policy and strategic concerns such as the aging of the work force, adaptation to new technology, and organizational productivity (Gutteridge, 1986; Mills, 1985). However, these trends mean that much of the practice of managing careers has come close to catching up with the body of theory that inspired it (Hall and Associates, 1986). Either career theory has served its purpose and should be laid to rest or it needs a good shot in the arm.

We believe this state of affairs exists not because we are done explaining careers, but because work on the topic has moved away from its conceptually rich heritage. As a result, career studies are at risk of addressing increasingly narrow and decreasingly innovative questions. Our view is that a good shot in the arm will help rejuvenate career theory and also help us adapt to the dynamic character of modern industrial society. But where do we go from here and how do we get there?

Our point of departure is that, unlike many social science concepts, the concept of the career is not the property of any one theoretical or disciplinary view. From psychological notions of how dispositional differences affect job adaptation (Holland, 1973), to sociological interpretations of role behavior in organizational settings (Glaser, 1968), to economic views on how human capital accrues through education and experience (Becker, 1975), the career concept is shared among a diversity of perspectives. We believe that exploring this diversity will help us uncover new theoretical questions as well as new answers. Thus, our purpose is to re-establish the importance of this shared view of the career concept and to examine the process by which disciplinary cross-fertilization may help move career theory in new directions. In sum, while this chapter represents a pause in our studies to reflect on the heritage of career theory, we hope that the yield is not just a restatement of problems but a statement of possibilities that will prod us to pursue new theoretical developments.

These notes are divided into two main sections. In the first section, we examine what makes career theory a nexus for transdisciplinary study. How do we define the term "career," what do we mean by career theory, and more particularly, what characteristics make career theory useful to study from multiple disciplinary perspectives? We then discuss the kinds of contributions that can aid further development of the field. In the second section, we explore how the substance of career theory evolves. By what process do new ideas about careers emerge and stand or fall through comparison with previous explanations? At a broader level, how do the different philosophies behind career theory support or challenge one another and with what implications for our debate at both theoretical and practical levels? We conclude by suggesting that scholars should join in the continuing pursuit of transformational career theory, which can serve to improve both theory and practice as they are applied to careers.

CAREER THEORY AS A NEXUS FOR TRANSDISCIPLINARY STUDY

To consider theory building across social science disciplines, we need to establish a joint frame of reference. A fundamental, although not necessarily straightforward, task is to establish shared definitions of *career* and *career theory* and the meanings they convey. Related to this is a need to appreciate why the career concept stemming from the definition should be viewed from a range of disciplinary perspectives. And, beyond these basics lies a vital but neglected question: What makes the body of career theory so valuable, and why do we need such theory in addition to – and therefore separately cultivated from – other studies of work within the organizational and social sciences?

The definitions of career and career theory

Our adopted definition of career is *the evolving sequence of a person's work experiences over time*. A central theme in this definition is that of work and all that work can mean for the ways in which we see and experience other people, organizations, and society. However, equally central to this definition is the theme of time, along which the career provides a "moving perspective" (Hughes, 1958, p. 67) on the unfolding interaction between a person and society. This moving perspective offers a link, in Erikson's terms, between an individual's initial identity and final integrity over the course of his or her adult life (Arthur, 1984, p. 5). Yet, the notion of a career also links matters internal to the individual with matters external, such as those concerning official position (Goffman, 1961, p. 127). Thus, careers reflect the relationships between people and the providers of official position, namely, institutions or organizations, and how these relationships fluctuate over time. Seen in this way, the study of careers is the study of both individual and organizational change (Van Maanen, 1977) as well as of societal change (Kanter, Chapter 25).

While the preceding or a similar definition of career is well established in previous literature (e.g., Arthur and Lawrence, 1984; Hall, 1976; Schein, 1978; Super, 1957), it differs from certain popular conceptions of the term. For instance, the Oxford English Dictionary (1961, Vol. II, p. 117) defines career as "a person's course or progress through life (or distinct portion of life)" and adds the qualifier "esp. when publicly conspicuous, or abounding in remarkable incidents." This selectivity about what qualifies as a career recurs in a later definition implying that careers include only those aspects of work in which "a course of professional life or employment . . . affords opportunity for progress or advancement in the world."

Unfortunately, this restrictive definition and others like it (Arthur and Lawrence, 1984) have led some scholars to avoid the term and adopt alternatives such as "working lives" (e.g., Shamir and Salomon, 1985; Thomas, Chapter 17) or "work histories" (Nicholson and West, 1985, Chapter 9). Yet, we believe the term "career" better captures the focal relationship between work and time that we seek to study. Moreover, to abandon the term would be to abandon a rich vein of theoretical endeavors that use the term as we do, and which we support. But let us be clear about the view adopted here: Everyone who works has a career.

This leads us to a definition of career theory. Career theory, for us, is the body of all generalizable attempts to explain career phenomena. We use the qualifier "generalizable" to distinguish what we mean by career theory from the more situation-specific explanations of career outcomes derived from personal experience or local practice (cf. Kaplan, 1964). However, we proclaim a vital interest in the link between theory and practice. Our interest is both to learn from and contribute to practice, so that the multiple individual, institutional, and societal parties affected by careers can be better served by the career theory we hold.

Career theory and the social sciences

Over the past fifteen years, reviews of career theory consistently suggest that the field is composed predominantly of psychological and secondarily of sociological views. For instance, Sonnenfeld and Kotter (1982) identify four types of career theory. The first type is sociological and concerned with social class determinants of career outcomes (e.g., Blau and Duncan, 1967; Chinoy, 1955). The second type is psychological and concerned with static dispositional differences and their occupational implications (e.g., Holland, 1973; Strong, 1943). The third, newer type is of mixed psychological–sociological origins, focusing on the career stages that surround occupational choice and development (Crites, 1981; Dalton and Thompson, 1986; Super, 1957).[1] The final and most recent type is principally psychological and focuses on the broader notion of the adult life course and the relationship of the career to other major life activities (e.g., Levinson, 1978; Vaillant, 1977).

This emphasis on psychology and sociology does little justice to the range of social science perspectives that can contribute to our understanding of careers. What, for example, of a political science perspective, which might approach the career as a vehicle for accumulating power or influence regardless of an individual's personality disposition? Or what of an economics perspective, which might examine the career as an outcome of the overall distribution of jobs and wealth? As Table 1.1 attests, the career concept can appeal to just about every social science discipline.

The diversity of social science perspectives that can engage in the study of

Table 1.1. *Examples of social science viewpoints on the career concept*

Psychology
Career as vocation: a viewpoint accepting the traditional psychological position on stability of personality in adulthood; associated theory is intended to help guide individuals and organizations fill job openings in a mutually satisfactory way (e.g., Holland, 1985).

Career as a vehicle for self-realization: a humanistic viewpoint focusing on the opportunities a career can provide for further individual growth and how that growth can in turn benefit organizations and society (e.g., Shepard, 1984).

Career as a component of the individual life structure: from this viewpoint eras and transitions throughout the career are predictable and are to be accommodated in the work arrangements made (e.g., Levinson, 1984).

Social psychology
Career as an individually mediated response to outside role messages: a viewpoint that studies particular occupational circumstances, such as those of priests (Schneider and Hall, 1972) or scientists and engineers (Bailyn, 1980), for their psychological effects.

Sociology
Career as the unfolding of social roles: this viewpoint overlaps with social psychology but places greater emphasis on the individual's reciprocal contribution to the social order (e.g., Hughes, 1958; Van Maanen and Barley, 1984).

Career as social mobility: seeing a person's title as an indicator of social position (e.g., Blau and Duncan, 1967; Featherman and Hauser, 1978; Warner and Abegglen, 1955).

Anthropology
Career as status passages: a viewpoint overlapping with functional sociology about how rites and ceremonies serve to maintain a society or culture over time (e.g., Glaser and Strauss, 1971).

Economics
Career as a response to market forces: a viewpoint emphasizing the near-term distribution of employment opportunities and the long-term accumulation of human capital (e.g., Becker, 1975; Doeringer and Piore, 1971).

Political science
Career as the enactment of self-interest: this views individual needs such as power, wealth, prestige, or autonomy as prominent objects of self-interested behavior in the context of institutional political realities (e.g., Kaufman, 1960).

History
Career as a correlate of historical outcomes: looking at the reciprocal influence of prominent people and period events on each other (e.g., Schlesinger, 1965).

Geography
Career as a response to geographic circumstances: focusing on variables such as availability of raw materials, a natural harbor, or a population ready for work or trade as they affect the way working lives unfold (e.g., Van Maanen, 1982).

---

careers suggests that the career concept provides an excellent nexus for trans-disciplinary debate. In other words, career theory provides a forum for "taking us beyond the limitations and confines of disciplines as we currently conceive them" (Mitroff and Kilmann, 1978, p. viii). However, scholars have only recently recognized the value of this debate. Van Maanen's (1977) plea for a shared focus on the career laments the lack of previous multi-disciplinary activity. Sonnenfeld and Kotter (1982) observe that the habit of people working within traditional disciplinary boundaries still "retards the maturation of career theory." And, Collin and Young (1986) struggle to identify an "accepted corpus of theory" about careers and claim the theory that does exist lacks organizing principles. Yet, despite such calls for integrating different disciplinary views, much of the work has yet to be done.

Why have diverse perspectives not been brought together earlier, or more substantially, in studies of careers? One answer is that studies spanning disciplinary boundaries are difficult to perform and do not easily gain acceptance. The ideas and language in such studies are borrowed from several disciplines; further, building theoretical bridges across these disciplines frequently requires a middle-range or grand theory. Consequently, the reviewers who serve as disciplinary gatekeepers often find these studies wanting. The ideas and language fit neither here nor there, and the work itself lacks the same depth and specificity of within-discipline studies that mine existing ideas. These difficulties make it easy to see why contributions to career theory tend to revert to their disciplinary backgrounds. For these reasons, we believe it is critical to maintain career theory as a forum separate from, but integrated with, the organizational and social sciences.

Characteristics that guide career theory

In this section, we discuss two guiding characteristics that make career theory an appropriate nexus for transdisciplinary debate. As suggested by our definition of the career, career theory provides a view of work situations that (I) encourages study of both *individuals and institutions* and (II) incorporates properties of both *emergence and relativity*, as we define them in what follows.

The individual and the institution. The first characteristic of career theory is that it encourages study of both individuals and institutions. This characteristic flows from the definition of career, which speaks directly to the individuals who work and indirectly – through the notion of work – to the institutions in which work gets performed. This characteristic brackets theoretical approaches that explicitly address the career concept as well as other approaches in which the concept is implicit (e.g., Giddens, 1984).

For the individual, work can provide a potent influence on both personal adjustment (Evans and Bartolome, 1981; Hall and Hall, 1979) and development in life (Levinson, 1984; Mortimer and Borman, 1987). Thus, an "added value" of career theory – in contrast to many theories of organizational behavior – is this focus on the whole person as he or she relates to the work situation. Whereas early theories of organizational behavior (Argyris, 1957; McGregor, 1960) did have this wholistic view of the person, the field later became fragmented into theories of variables and processes, not people (cf. Schneider, 1985). The notion of the career, on the other hand, promotes consideration of both the whole person and the organization, or institution, for which work is being performed.

The term "institution" refers to a social phenomenon in which the form of collective behavior is relatively established and permanent (Hughes, 1971, p. 6). Most prominently, in our case, institutions are public and private organizations in which the required collective behaviors include the work roles out of which careers are made. In our view a career theory – in contrast to basic psychological theories of individual differences – needs to attend to the institutional dimension.

It is also important to note that occupations too are institutions. For instance, artists may not belong to any formal organization; however, collective behavior in the art world provides an artist's career with a relatively established form. This view of institutions accommodates a broad view of work settings. For instance, the institution of the professional association affects the work its members perform; the institution of the education system affects the work for teachers; the institution of the family affects the work for homemakers, and so on. Not least, the institution of society affects what work gets called for, through society's consumption of goods and services, and how work gets viewed, through the occupational status that society assigns. All of these institutions and forms of work are embraced in the way we view careers and career theory.

The interaction of individuals and institutions is often captured through sets of concepts that juxtapose psychological and sociological ideas. For instance, identity and role provide one set of individual–institution concepts. Identity refers to how a person sees him or herself and incorporates how work is viewed by the person as performer (e.g., Hall, 1986). Role refers to a set of behaviors expected by those affected (role senders) and incorporates how work is viewed by the institution as sponsor (e.g., Katz and Kahn, 1966). These concepts are related closely to other sets of individual–institution concepts, for instance, the subjective (individually perceived) and objective (organizationally prescribed) views of the career (e.g., Van Maanen and Schein, 1977), the psychological versus situational determinants of individual work attitudes and behaviors (e.g., Joyce, Slocum, and Von Glinow, 1982), the distinctions between micro- and macro-levels of analysis (e.g., Hall, 1986), and earlier philosophical ideas on individual–organization interaction (Mead, 1956; Simmel, 1950). All of these concepts can serve career theory's parallel interests in individual and institutional levels of analysis.

Emergence and relativity. The second characteristic of career theory that invites trans-disciplinary study is that it incorporates the interconnected properties of emergence and relativity. Emergence and relativity are terms concerned with people's interpretation of time and social space, respectively (McHugh, 1968; Mead, 1932), which we use here to describe properties of theory. In this sense, the property of emergence means that theory makes some attempt to explain the way people experience time; the property of relativity means that theory makes some attempt to explain the way people experience social space. Thus, we are saying that the study of both time and social space is inherent to career theory.

Our interest in time is explicit in the definition of career, that is, in how work experiences emerge or evolve over time. Thus, contributions to career theory with the property of emergence attempt to explain something of the link between time and work. For example, such contributions – in contrast to many explanations of job satisfaction or motivation to work – may suggest why people respond differently to the same job situation at different points in their lives. Alternatively, such contributions – in contrast to many popular explanations of organizational efficiency – may suggest why organizations should make inefficient short-run job assignments in pursuit of long-term benefits. Further, the property of emergence encourages the use of historical perspective (Lawrence, 1984a) in examining work experiences. In other words, career theory – in contrast to much static theory – may suggest how to interpret an organization's promotion system by examining its demographic past (cf. Rosenbaum, 1984; Stewman and Konda, 1983).

Our interest in social space focuses on the person's work role in a larger occupational setting. Social space is defined as some dimension of social significance, for example, a communication network or an organizational hierarchy, along which individuals are arrayed by their relative positions. Contributions to career theory with the property of relativity attempt to explain something of the link between social space and work. For example, such contributions – in contrast to trait-based explanations of leadership – could suggest why organizational position may make a difference to the kind of behavior a person exhibits. Alternatively, such contributions – in contrast to some explanations of organizational structure – could suggest how organization redesign may promote more effective interpersonal mentoring.

Although we have discussed emergence and relativity as distinct properties within the domain of career theory, these characteristics should work "in tandem" with one another as "two faces of a dialectic" (McHugh, 1968, p. 136). Projections about careers along the time dimension have an immediate effect on how careers are viewed across social space. One example of this interdependence is when an individual becomes alienated from an organization (social space) because he or she perceives a lack of future career opportunity (time). Conversely, projections about careers along social space have an immediate effect on how careers are viewed across time, for example, when we observe segmentalism among an organization's various departments and derive a sense of stagnation about the organization as a whole (Kanter, 1983). The theoretical tension created by these two faces of the dialectic – that is, of how interpretations of time and social space affect people's work experiences – calls for a diversity of viewpoints to contribute to the ensuing debate. Since this diversity can be fueled by multiple social science disciplines, it reinforces the case for career theory to foster transdisciplinary debate.

The implications of transdisciplinary debate for career theory

If we accept Dewey's (1933) point that the problems of social science should define the investigative approaches to be adopted, then problems concerned with the careers of individuals in organizations and society will often call for a mix of disciplinary views. The implications of such an observation for the study of careers are several. Not only do we get multiple perspectives on the career, but we also get multiple views on the environment surrounding the career, which, as a chameleon, changes color depending on the context in which it is viewed (Arthur and Lawrence, 1984). Moreover, the knowledge garnered from diverse perspectives may not be simply additive (Argyris, 1980). Similar to the pieces of a jigsaw puzzle, separate perspectives on the career may together suggest new properties (Broad, 1969) when viewed together. Or the pieces may not fit together at all, thus obliging us to rethink our approach to the overall puzzle (Burrell and Morgan, 1979).

We can benefit from these diverse viewpoints and differing environmental assumptions. However, the question arises, do we build our theory in a way that allows us to benefit; do we build our theory in a spirit of transdisciplinary debate? It is easy to find critiques of the career literature in particular (e.g., Van Maanen, 1977) or of social science more generally (e.g., Burrell and Morgan, 1979; Mitroff and Kilmann, 1978; Roberts, Hulin, and Rousseau, 1978) that suggest we have traditionally failed to do so. However, if we are to build a body of theory that takes advantage of the central concept career, we need help from a variety of theoretical endeavors.

First, we need efforts grounded in a single disciplinary viewpoint that acknowledge other viewpoints. An example is Rosenbaum's (1984) sociological perspective on career mobility, which provides an alternate explanation for Berlew and Hall's (1966) psychologically grounded ideas on early career experience. Such efforts demonstrate an openness to, and invite a response from, the other viewpoints they cite (Van Maanen, 1977). Second, we need contributions that reinterpret the findings of one viewpoint from another perspective. Herriot's (1984) review, reinterpreting the work of vocational psychology from a social psychological perspective, falls into this category.

Third, we need works that acknowledge different assumptions across viewpoints. For instance, a "mating" approach to inquiry (Cyert and March, 1963) can spur us to see new barriers to progress, such as when the guiding assumptions of corporate career development programs are challenged by the different assumptions of simultaneous employee participation efforts (Arthur, 1988). Finally, we need the kind of interdisciplinary theory that spans previously separate levels of analysis. An example is the work of Slocum and his colleagues linking psychologically grounded ideas about individual career development to organization-level views of corporate strategy (Slocum, Cron, Hansen, and Rawlings, 1985).

In sum, the definitions of career and career theory, the range of possible viewpoints on the career, and the characteristics that make career theory distinctive can all contribute to a shared frame of reference for career scholars. And within this shared frame of reference, various kinds of theoretical endeavor can contribute to transdisciplinary debate. But how can we keep the debate going? And how can the debate be kept lively enough to promote new and better career theory? It is to these questions that we now turn.

THE PROCESS OF DEVELOPING CAREER THEORY

Good debate will promote a range of activities from the introduction of new ideas to the affirmation of existing theory. But if the debate is to be productive, it is important to know both where we are in the debate and what we are doing. In the following sections we offer two frameworks to guide this debate. We invite career scholars to use these frameworks to identify both their own and other people's roles in the debate and in turn to challenge one another to new levels of achievement. Such further achievement, and through it the development of better career theory, is a goal that we all share.

We discuss the value of transdisciplinary debate at two levels of analysis. First, we consider what such debate can mean for the evolution of new ideas within career theory. Second, we consider what debate can mean at a broader level of analysis for the evolution of the body of knowledge that career theory claims to hold.

A cycle of new career theory generation

Theory generation in the social sciences involves an iterative and ongoing relationship among contributors to a field of inquiry. Accordingly, social science in general and career theory in particular can be regarded as in a state of continuing evolution (e.g., Kuhn, 1970; Popper, 1959). Career theory needs to attempt new forms of adaptation while sustaining the explanations that have stood the test of time.

We draw here on the work of Quinn (1988; Quinn and Cameron, 1985), applying his discussion of excellence in human endeavor to excellence in contributing to career theory. Excellence is "the fact or condition of excelling, of going beyond some norm or criterion of performance" (Quinn, 1988, p. 13). Thus, when applied to work in career theory, excellence refers to contributing fresh insights that extend our previous understanding about "the evolving sequence of a person's work experiences over time." Quinn's work suggests that this progress occurs through a four-stage process that repeats for each emergent contribution to new theory: initiation, uncertainty, transformation, and routinization. We would add that fresh insights can be achieved either when new theory emerges or when established theory proves itself against new challenges.

The cycle begins when one or more individuals conclude that current theory routinely in use will not explain the phenomena they are observing. There is a felt need for change, the system is unfrozen, and a stage of initiation begins during which these individuals explore new explanations. This exploration inevitably involves risk that leads to uncertainty, the second stage in the cycle. Uncertainty comes from several sources. First, any new idea that disconfirms old ones is rarely welcomed by those already invested in established work. Second, a new idea may or may not succeed in providing improved explanation. If the idea proves successful, that is, the idea becomes sufficiently developed and supported by empirical evidence that at least some people are convinced of its value to the field, then this uncertainty dissipates. The idea then enters the stage of transformation into an acknowledged contribution to theory. If and when the contribution becomes more generally accepted by the field, we can say that further routinization has taken place, from which other scholars can take their cue to begin the cycle all over again. In the following sections, we use this four-stage cycle to illustrate the current state of certain career theory efforts.

Routinization. Routinization, representing both the beginning and the end of the cycle, has some distinctly positive features. It tells us we have been successful, in that people are finding established theory to be useful in explaining career behavior. Routinization often also means that theory has been successfully converted to practice. For example, much current career theory based on psychology and social psychology has already been subjected to considerable empirical inquiry and has been put into practice in organizational career programs (Brown, Brooks, and Associates, 1984; Gysbers et al., 1984; Hall and Associates, 1986; Miller, 1986). The person–environment fit model of Holland (1973) now provides the basis for the Strong–Campbell interest inventory that is widely used for career counseling and placement. Explanations of adult development are reflected in Super's (1988) career concerns inventory and Schein's (1985) career anchors questionnaire, which are now available in commercial test form. Such applications reflect a common phenomenon of career practice following on from career theory.

However, while routinization represents progress of a sort, it can raise barriers to further progress. People become comfortable with and accustomed to an established literature, and it takes more persuasion for them to perceive the potential value added of other literatures. Thus, the barriers to the entry of fresh ideas also protect established theory from the new challenges needed to sustain its legitimacy. As a result, although routinization is a tribute to career theorists and practitioners alike, it also signals an urgency for re-evaluation.

Initiation and uncertainty. Career researchers have moved in a multiplicity of directions, and social science has developed along a range of different fronts. As Quinn suggests, some of these further explorations will prove inappropriate, and it is understandable that such deviations from established theory will come in for criticism. Schein, for instance, suggests that recent explorations around the career concept are fractionated, ignore related subfields of activity, exhibit cultural biases, lack integrative constructs, and emphasize content rather than process in their solutions (Schein, 1986). However, we would offer a more optimistic and evolutionary view of some of the same explorations. Some of this fractionation and diversification of efforts may be seen as risk taking – risk taking that represents sincere attempts to generate more developed theory. The risk taking may also represent creative attempts to reach out to more developed social science perspectives that can add to our appreciation about the nature of careers. Such trends would be consistent with the activity associated with the initiation stage of new theory development. And we would agree with Schein's (1986) proposed remedy for fractionation: escalated cross-disciplinary debate.

The possibilities in uncertainty. If uncertainty is the wellspring for new theory generation, we should be able to spot new initiatives that both respond to uncertainty and have the potential to move forward to the next stage of the cycle. For example, within the current boundaries of career theory there is uncertainty about whether to view organizations as lifelong providers of careers (Kerr and Slocum, 1987) or, instead, as short-term providers of current jobs (Miller-Tiedeman and Tiedeman, 1984). Two new directions suggested by this uncertainty involve studies of transitions and minority careers.

The study of job and role transitions is akin to studying mini-careers, since transitions involve processes of exploration, decision, entry/establishment, and stability/maintenance. Several advances have been made over the last few years in understanding stages in the transition process (e.g., Feldman 1981; Louis, 1980), exchanges with role senders (Nicholson, 1984), career shifts (Latack, 1984; Stout, Slocum and Cron, 1987), the effects of periods of unemployment (Shamir and Arthur, in press), and the fabric of social diversity (Bailyn, 1984). Because much career change and growth is represented by critical job and role transitions, this recent work may help us to link between short-term and long-term organizational effects and so address the uncertainty that currently exists.

In a similar fashion, work on minority careers – although more in its infancy than work on transitions – also promises to address the uncertainty described in the preceding. The writing of Alderfer and his colleagues (Alderfer, 1982, 1986; Thomas and Alderfer, Chapter 7) provides rich detail on how short-term group and intergroup dynamics within an organization can interact with long-term individual development processes to affect minority career outcomes. As we learn from these efforts, we may not only add to our understanding of organizational group and individual career effects on one another, but also prepare the ground for better accommodation of cross-cultural and international career processes as well.

Beyond the boundaries of existing career theory, further uncertainty stems from the advancement of other social science inquiries. In this vein, a range of recent ideas about an organization's adjustment to its environment may have consequences for the way we think about work experiences over time and so about careers.

For instance, some of these ideas examine the constraining effects of organizational stability on mobility and so the implicit rules that govern employees' careers. Thus, the work on internal labor markets (Doerlinger and Piore, 1971), career timetables (Lawrence, 1984b, In press; Roth, 1963) or tournaments (Rosenbaum, Chapter 16), and the complexities of informal and formal mobility paths (Davis-Blake and Mittman, 1988; Markham, Harlan and Hackett, 1987; Mittman, 1986) can appeal to career theory as ways to better understand the pervasive effect of organization structure on career outcomes.

Meanwhile, other writers have challenged the appropriateness of stability from the organization's standpoint and promoted a new vision of organizational adaptation and evolution (e.g., Wholey and Brittain, 1986). Among these, the notion of the self-designing organization has been developed to help us imagine how organizations can be "chronically unfrozen" (Weick, 1977) in the face of a changing environment. However, as we strive for organizational models that are more flexible and adaptive, we are creating forces that oblige their members to be equally flexible and adaptive in their career responses (Nystrom, 1981). We are only beginning to see the implications of the self-designing organization model for the career theory that we espouse (Hedberg, 1984; Weick and Berlinger, Chapter 15).

Towards further transformation. The preceding ideas all represent initiatives that need further testing and development, but each has the potential to transform career theory as we know it. And, as any new contribution to theory becomes accommodated through routinization, it will change the starting point for new rounds of uncertainty and initiation, on which the fate of subsequent ideas will depend. Thus, prodding career theory toward further transformation is an important challenge for career scholars. The challenge involves supporting new ideas on the one hand and re-evaluating established theory on the other hand. Only through excellence in both these endeavors can we ensure that career theory continues to evolve and sustains its relevance in a changing world.

Philosophical differences in career theory debate

There is more to the development of career theory than the testing of new ideas. New ideas, as established social science viewpoints, will vary in their assumptions about how knowledge is formed and how it should be applied. For instance, our own assumptions have guided the development of this chapter. By now, it should be apparent that we believe "progress" in career theory, representing a variety of meanings not necessarily linear or additive, is both possible and desirable. And further, that we believe it is critical to encourage new contributions to challenge existing career theory. This leads us to address a further set of questions that add to the complexity of transdisciplinary debate and concern the philosophical differences that underlie career theory.

Social scientists assume a variety of philosophical positions in their work. We suggest here two sets of distinctions as particularly helpful to the way we think about work on careers. One set examines abstract views on career theory itself, the other set is concerned with applied views on career theory's practical effects. The value of considering these sets is not so much to force any particular approach into one category or another, but rather to establish two dimensions along which multiple approaches within career theory can be interpreted.[2]

Looking first at career theory in the abstract, we can ask what view of social science does a contribution to career theory imply? Here, two competing views can be contrasted: (1) career theory as social science orthodoxy and (2) career theory as social science reform.

1. *Career theory as social science orthodoxy.* This traditionally dominant view of career theory ties it to the main thrust of the scientific method. The social world is seen as analogous to the physical world, the distinctions between independent and dependent variables are emphasized, and support is drawn from empirical, objective evidence, usually within a single social science discipline. An example is the thinking behind the classical "vocational" view of occupational stability. The independent variable of individual dispositions (which according to traditional personality theory are largely established before people start their careers) is seen as responsible for the dependent variable of occupational stability (the phenomenon that those reporting most satisfaction with their careers cluster by occupation according to the dispositions they report). A related idea in this orthodox view is that knowledge is additive. We can debate the separate influences of, say, individual dispositions and social background in determining career outcomes while believing each has a separate place in a given web of cause–effect relationships. This kind of thinking reflects a philosophical system of logic tracing back to Mill (1965), which some argue still dominates the social sciences today (Argyris, 1980; Burrell and Morgan, 1979).

2. *Career theory as social science reform.* A counterview to the preceding argues that the scientific method promotes an "obsessive quest for certainty" (Dewey, 1960) and deflects inquirers away from less quantifiable concerns. In this counterview, the social world is seen as less orderly, so that we should draw on multiple disciplines according to the problem at hand and emphasize the interdependence of variables (Gowler and Legge, Chapter 21; Van Maanen, 1977). An example is the "interactionist" thinking about careers that rejects orthodox cause–effect explanations but instead sees occupational members – be they doctors, schoolteachers, or hobos – in tacit collaboration with their environments to produce career effects (Barley, Chapter 3; Strauss, 1959). According to this reform view, all knowledge is relative, and the web of knowledge is not predetermined but must necessarily change as new insights are gained. Such thinking draws on a philosophical system of relativism, such as that of Russell (1927), holding that any knowledge claimed according to Mill's style of logic will prove temporary.

Turning our attention to the application of career theory, we can ask what practical outcomes does a contribution to career theory suggest? Once more, two competing views can be identified, this time allowing us to contrast the direct implications for practice of different theoretical positions. Here again, our purpose is to provide a spectrum for interpretation rather than to force diverse theories into two extremes.

3. *Career theory as functionalism.* This view of career theory includes formulations that emphasize a "functionalist" view of the career environment by supporting systems already in place (Burrell and Morgan, 1979) An example is the career theory associated with conventional ideas on human resource planning. Established patterns of organization structure are assumed to be effective, and the goal of human resource planning is to keep a structure staffed with appropriately qualified people (Arthur, 1984). This goal gives rise to further developments, such as programs to accelerate "high-potential" employees toward top positions (Miller, 1984) or assessment centers where an individual's talents are tested against those sought in predefined managerial positions (Bray, 1982; Bray, Campbell, and Grant, 1974). While the effective merits of different ideas can be debated, there is the prospect of additive effects, such as high-potential employee programs and assessment centers both proving useful so long as the underlying assumptions about an organization's structure are retained. This functionalist line of thought traces back to Comte (1853), who envisioned the "human and social unity" that could evolve from such programmatic developments.

4. *Career theory as criticism.* Our final type of career theory is again focused on practical outcomes, but this time serves to challenge rather than service the systems in place. In pure form, "human potential" (Shepard, 1984) or "protean" (Hall, 1976) models of the individual career fit here since each of these lines of thought calls into question the relevance of predetermined job positions to individual growth. Similarly, images of blue-collar "careers at work" (Sabel, 1982; Thomas, Chapter 17) that highlight the strategic choices underlying worker behavior can challenge the assumptions behind the ongoing management of worker careers. Critical theory contributions stand in contrast to, rather than in support of, established views. The philosophical underpinnings of this line of reasoning trace back to Hegel's (1931) "universal principle" that knowledge advances only through dialectical inquiry.[3]

Abstract theoretical views, of course, cannot be separated from their practical effects, so that the two dimensions described in the preceding must necessarily overlap. Nevertheless, these four philosophies of knowledge allow us to ask two distinct questions about any particular contribution to career theory. First, regarding the focus of the contribution itself, does it attempt to add incrementally to our understanding of the world, or does it directly challenge existing knowledge that is claimed? Second, regarding the use or purpose of the contribution, does it refine or does it refute existing applications or practice? We wish to emphasize that our purpose here is neither to take sides in promoting one view over another nor to suggest false simplification or categorization of any theoretical contribution. Rather, we firmly believe that views along the length of both dimensions need to be represented and that their coexistence is healthy. We can continue to draw on the scientific method while experimenting with alternatives. We can continue to serve institutional life while asking how it might be productively changed. When it comes to philosophical debate about the relative merits of different career theories, the two dimensions can serve as reference points for where we stand.

The previous discussion adds to the sense in which we can aspire for work on

career theory to be transformational. Earlier in the chapter we described transformation in the sense of developing and testing new explanations. Now we have
extended this view to address the philosophies of knowledge that can underlie
competing explanations.

In this broader sense, transformation depends on the spirit in which views are
shared. We need to consider the implications that theory and practice have for
one another. We need to consider the debate that a diversity of perspectives brings.
The assumption of competing positions is a virtue if the relative merits of each
position are to be fully explored. However, to take full advantage of such contrasting insights calls for an open, self-critical community of inquiry (Torbert,
1983). To engage in the pursuit of transformational career theory involves finding
pleasure in uncertainty and gratitude in not knowing where the journey will
ultimately lead.[4]

CONCLUSION

It is in the spirit of pursuing transformational career theory in its fullest sense
that we call for social scientists of diverse persuasions to come together around
the concept of career, not only to offer their own perspectives, but also to "place
themselves in the perspectives of others" (Mead, 1927). We have proposed that
the field of career theory provides an important forum for the transdisciplinary
study of people at work because of two characteristics. First, the career concept
encourages theories to examine both individuals and institutions and, second, it
encourages theories to consider emergence and relativity. Given this forum, the
process of career theory development can be viewed as a continuing one, with
disparate excursions into new territory coming together as theoretical transformation takes place. And as new theory gets formed, we can include it in constructive debate spanning both our theories themselves and the consequences of
their practical application.

We believe that if scholars are serious about understanding people at work,
then career theory remains a critical forum for developing both abstract and
practical ideas about this subject. Career theory, as a subfield of social science
inquiry, will always be engaged in a struggle for viewpoints (Mills, 1959). However, there is merit in a struggle that looks to build more constructive dialogue
about the condition and development of individual and institutional lives that
career theory connects. To pursue helpful application of career theory from this
dialogue is a worthy goal. Yet any goal must be transient, as progressive transformation through new career theory leads us on to different problems and possibilities. Only the spirit behind the development of career theory can remain
constant.

NOTES

We are indebted to Lotte Bailyn, Suzyn Ornstein, and Boas Shamir for their comments on
an earlier draft of this chapter.
1 We would prefer to separate from Sonnenfeld and Kotter's career stage classification the
   highly significant work of the Chicago sociologists, which does not emphasize stages but
   does focus on person–role interaction over time (see Barley, Chapter 3).
2 Our presentation of the four philosophical positions behind career theory owes much to
   the earlier work of Burrell and Morgan (1979).

3 Argyris and his colleagues propose three exemplary lines of critical theory, each of them relevant to the discussion here. The first, inspired by Freud, pushes people to more fully understand themselves; the second, after Marx, pushes people to more fully understand the nature of institutional life; and the third, after Lewin, pushes people to more fully understand their roles as agents for or against change (Argyris, Putnam, and Smith, 1985). The influence of each of these is discernible in certain work or careers: for example, the Freudian view in work on vocational choice (e.g., Holland, 1985); the Marxian view in work on organizational career structures (e.g., Rosenbaum, 1984); and the Lewinian view in efforts to link career development and participation at work activities (Arthur, 1988; Hedberg, 1984). Career theory therefore provides an ideal crucible for critical inquiry, in contrast to the way it is sometimes perceived.

4 Critical theorists use the term "emancipatory" in a similar way to our use of the term "transformational." However, we wish to emphasize our belief that emancipation or transformation stems from the quality of debate across *different* philosophies and not just from critical theory. People's starting points in this debate are secondary provided diverse starting points are represented. The efforts of Bailyn, Nystrom and McArthur, and Kanter in Part III of this handbook represent early responses to our call for transformational activity.

REFERENCES

Alderfer, C. P. (1982). The problem of changing white males' beliefs and behavior in race relations. In P. Goodman (ed.), *Change in Organizations*. San Francisco: Jossey-Bass.
Alderfer, C. P. (1986). An intergroup perspective on group dynamics. In J. Lorsch (ed.), *Handbook of Organizational Behavior*. Englewood Cliffs, NJ: Prentice-Hall, pp. 190–222.
Argyris, C. (1957). *Personality and Organization*. New York: Harper.
Argyris, C. (1980). *Inner Contradictions of Rigorous Research*. New York: Academic.
Argyris, C., Putnam, R., and Smith, D. M. (1985). *Action Science*. San Francisco: Jossey-Bass.
Arthur, M. B. (1984). The career concept; challenge and opportunity for its further application. In M. B. Arthur, L. Bailyn, D. J. Levinson, and H. A. Shepard, *Working with Careers*. New York: Graduate School of Business, Columbia University, pp. 3–24.
Arthur, M. B. (1988). Career development and participation at work: time for mating?" *Human Resource Management, 27*, 181–199.
Arthur, M. B., and Lawrence, B. S. (1984). Perspectives on environment and career: an introduction. *Journal of Occupational Behaviour, 5*(1), 1–8.
Bailyn, L. (1980). *Living with Technology: Issues at Mid-Career*. Cambridge, MA: MIT Press.
Bailyn, L. (1984). Issues of work and family in organizations: responding to social diversity. In M. B. Arthur, L. Bailyn, H. A. Shepard, and D. J. Levinson, *Working with Careers*. New York: Graduate School of Business, Columbia University, pp. 75–98.
Becker, G. S. (1975). *Human Capital*, 2nd ed. New York: Columbia University Press.
Berlew, D. E., and Hall, D. T. (1966). The socialization of managers: effects of expectations on performance. *Administrative Science Quarterly, 11*, 207–223.
Blau, P. M., and Duncan, O. D. (1967). *The American Occupational Structure*. New York: Wiley.
Bray, D. W. (1982). The assessment center and the study of lives. *American Psychologist, 37*, 180–189.
Bray, D. W., Campbell, R. J., and Grant, D. L. (1974). *Formative Years in Business: A Long-Term AT&T Study of Managerial Lives*. New York: Wiley.
Broad, C. D. (1969). *Scientific Thought*. New York: Humanities.
Brown, D., Brooks, L., and Associates (1984). *Career Choice and Development: Applying Contemporary Theories to Practice*. San Francisco: Jossey-Bass.
Burrell, G., and Morgan, G. (1979). *Sociological Paradigms and Organisational Analysis*. London: Heinemann.
Chinoy, E. (1955). *Automobile Workers and the American Dream*. New York: Doubleday.
Collin, A., and Young, R. A. (1986). New directions for theories of career. *Human Relations, 39*, 837–853.

Comte, A. (1853). *The Positivist Philosophy* (translated by H. Martineau). London: Chapman.

Crites, J. O. (1981). *Career Counseling: Models, Methods and Materials*. New York: McGraw-Hill.

Cyert, R. M., and March, J. G. (1963). *A Behavioral Theory of The Firm*. Englewood Cliffs, NJ: Prentice-Hall.

Dalton, G. W., and Thompson, P. H. (1986). *Novations: Strategies for Career Management*. Glenview, IL: Scott Foresman.

Davis-Blake, A., and Mittman, B. (1988). Job ladders in organizations: a typology and conceptual analysis. Unpublished manuscript, Graduate School of Industrial Administration, Carnegie-Mellon University.

Dewey, J. (1933). *How People Think*. Boston: Heath.

Dewey, J. (1960). *The Quest for Certainty: A Study of the Relation of Knowledge and Action*. New York: Capricorn.

Doeringer, P. B., and Piore, M. J. (1971). *Internal Labor Markets and Manpower Analysis*. Lexington, MA: Heath.

Evans, P. A. L., and Bartolomé, F. (1981). *Must Success Cost So Much?* New York: Basic.

Featherman, D. L., and Hauser, R. M. (1978). *Opportunity and Change*. New York: Academic.

Feldman, D. C. (1981). The multiple socialization of organizational members. *Academy of Management Review*, 6, 309–318.

Giddens, A. (1984). *The Constitution of Society*. Berkeley, CA: University of California Press.

Glaser, B. G. (ed.) (1968). *Organizational Careers: A Sourcebook for Theory*. Chicago: Aldine.

Glaser, B. G., and Strauss, A. (1971). *Status Passage: A Formal Theory*. Chicago: Aldine.

Goffman, E. (1961). The moral career of the mental patient. In E. Goffman (ed.), *Asylums*. New York: Anchor.

Gutteridge, T. G. (1986). Organizational career development systems: the state of the practice. In D. T. Hall and Associates, *Career Development in Organizations*. San Francisco: Jossey-Bass, pp. 50–94.

Gysbers, N. C., and Associates (1984). *Designing Careers: Counseling to Enhance Education, Work, and Leisure*. San Francisco: Jossey-Bass.

Hall, D. T. (1976). *Careers in Organizations*. Pacific Palisades, CA: Goodyear.

Hall, D. T. (1986). Breaking career routines: midcareer choice and identity development. In D. T. Hall and Associates, *Career Development in Organizations*. San Francisco: Jossey-Bass.

Hall, D. T., and Associates (1986). *Career Development in Organizations*. San Francisco: Jossey-Bass.

Hall, F. S., and Hall, D. T. (1979). *The Two-Career Couple*. Reading, MA: Addison-Wesley.

Hedberg, B. (1984). Career dynamics in a steelworks of the future. *Journal of Occupational Behaviour*, 5(1), 53–69.

Hegel, G. (1931). *The Phenomenology of the Mind*. London: Allen & Unwin.

Herriot, P. (1984). *Down from the Ivory Tower*. Chichester: Wiley.

Holland, J. L. (1973). *Making Vocational Choices: A Theory of Careers*. Englewood Cliffs, NJ: Prentice-Hall.

Holland, J. L. (1985). *Making Vocational Choices: A Theory of Personality and Work Environments*, 2nd ed. Englewood Cliffs, NJ: Prentice-Hall.

Hughes, E. C. (1958) *Men and their Work*. Glencoe, IL: Free Press.

Hughes, E. C. (1971). *The Sociological Eye*. Chicago: Aldine.

Joyce, W. F., Slocum, J. W. Jr., and Von Glinow, M. A. (1982). Person–situation interaction: competing models of fit. *Journal of Occupational Behaviour*, 3, 265–280.

Kanter, R. M. (1983). *The Change Masters*. New York: Simon & Schuster.

Kaplan, A. (1964). *The Conduct of Inquiry*. New York: Intext.

Katz, D., and Kahn, R. L. (1966). *The Social Psychology of Organizations*. New York: Wiley.

Kaufman, H. (1960). *The Forest Ranger: A Study in Administrative Behavior*. Baltimore, MD: Johns Hopkins University Press.

Kerr, L., and Slocum, J. W. Jr. (1987). Managing corporate culture through reward systems. *Academy of Management Executive*, 1, 99–108.

Kuhn, T. S. (1970). *The Structure of Scientific Revolutions*, 2nd ed. Chicago: University of Chicago Press.

Latack, J. C. (1984). Career transitions within organizations: an exploratory study of work, non-work and coping strategies. *Organizational Behavior and Human Performance, 32,* 296–322.

Lawrence, B. S. (1984a). Historical perspective: using the past to study the present. *Academy of Management Review, 9,* 307–312.

Lawrence, B. S. (1984b). Age grading: the implicit organizational timetable. *Journal of Occupational Behaviour, 5*(1), 23–35.

Lawrence, B. S. (in press). At the crossroads: a multiple level explanation of individual attainment. *Organization Science.*

Levinson, D. J. (1984). The career is in the life structure, the life structure is in the career: an adult development perspective. In M. B. Arthur, L. Bailyn, D. J. Levinson, and H. A. Shepard, *Working With Careers.* New York: Graduate School of Business, Columbia University, pp. 49–74.

Levinson, D. J., with C. N. Darrow, E. B. Klein, M. H. Levinson, and B. McKee, (1978). *The Seasons of a Man's Life.* New York: Knopf.

Louis, M. R. (1980). Surprise and sense making: what newcomers experience in unfamiliar organizational settings. *Administrative Science Quarterly, 25,* 226–251.

McGregor, D. (1960). *The Human Side of Enterprise.* New York: McGraw-Hill.

McHugh, P. (1968). *Defining the Situation: The Organization of Meaning in Everyday Interaction.* Indianapolis: Bobbs-Merrill.

Markham, W. T., Harlan, L., and Hackett, J. (1987). Promotion opportunity in organizations: causes and consequences. In G. Ferris (ed.), *Research on Personnel and Human Resource Management,* Vol. 5. Greenwich, CT: JAI, pp. 223–289.

Mead, G. H. (1927). The objective reality of perspectives. Reprinted in G. H. Mead (1934). *Selected Writings.* Indianapolis: Bobbs-Merrill, p. 310.

Mead, G. H. (1932). *The Philosophy of the Present.* Chicago: Open Court.

Mead, G. H. (1956). *The Social Psychology of George Herbert Mead* (edited by A. M. Strauss). Chicago: University of Chicago Press.

Mill, J. S. (1965). *On the Logic of the Moral Sciences.* Indianapolis: Bobbs-Merrill.

Miller, D. B. (1986). *Managing Professionals in Research and Development.* San Francisco: Jossey-Bass.

Miller, E. (1984). Strategic staffing. In C. J. Fombrun, N. J. Tichy, and M. A. Devanna (eds.), *Strategic Human Resource Management.* New York: Wiley.

Miller-Tiedeman. A., and Tiedeman, D. V. (1984). To be in work: on furthering the development of careers and career development specialists. In N. C. Gysbers and Associates, *Designing Careers: Counseling to Enhance Work and Leisure.* San Francisco: Jossey-Bass, pp. 91–192.

Mills, C. W. (1959). *The Sociological Imagination.* New York: Oxford University Press.

Mills, D. Q. (1985). Planning with people in mind. *Harvard Business Review, 63*(4), 97–105.

Mitroff, I. J., and Kilmann, R. H. (1978). *Methodological Approaches to the Social Sciences.* San Francisco: Jossey-Bass.

Mittman, B. (1986). Mobility and inequality in the civil service: Job ladders and vacancy chains in bureaucratic labor markets. Ph.D. dissertation. Stanford University.

Mortimer, T., and Borman, M. (eds.) (1987). *Work Experience and Psychological Development Through the Life Span.* Boulder, CO: Westview.

Nicholson, N. (1984). A theory of work role transitions. *Administrative Science Quarterly, 29,* 172–191.

Nicholson, N., and West, M. A. (1985). Life Stories. *New Society, 70,* 1146.

Nystrom, P. C. (1981). Designing jobs and assigning employees. In P. C. Nystrom and W. H. Starbuck (eds.), *Handbook of Organizational Design,* Vol. 2. New York: Oxford University Press, pp. 272–301.

Oxford English Dictionary (1961). Oxford: Oxford University Press.

Popper, K. E. (1959). *The Logic of Scientific Discovery.* New York: Basic.

Quinn, R. E. (1988). *Beyond Rational Management: Mastering the Paradoxes and Competing Demands of High Performance.* San Francisco: Jossey-Bass.

Quinn, R. E., and Cameron, K. S. (1985). The transformational cycle: a dynamic theory of excellence. Working paper, Rockefeller College of Public Affairs and Policy, State University of New York at Albany, Albany, NY.

Roberts, K. H., Hulin, C. L., and Rousseau, D. M. (1978). *Developing an Interdisciplinary Science of Organizations.* San Francisco: Jossey-Bass.

Rosenbaum, J. E. (1984). *Career Mobility in a Corporate Hierarchy.* Orlando, FL: Academic.

Roth, J. A. (1963). *Timetables: Structuring the Passage of Time in Hospital Treatment and Other Careers.* Indianapolis: Bobbs-Merrill.

Russell, B. (1927). *Philosophy.* New York: Norton.

Sabel, C. (1982). *Work and Politics: The Division of Labor in Industry.* New York: Cambridge University Press.

Schein, E. H. (1978). *Career Dynamics: Matching Individual and Organizational Needs.* Reading, MA: Addison-Wesley.

Schein, E. H. (1985). *Career Anchors: Discovering Your Real Values.* San Diego, CA: University Associates.

Schein, E. H. (1986). A critical look at current career development theory and research. In D. T. Hall and Associates, *Career Development in Organizations.* San Francisco: Jossey-Bass.

Schlesinger, A. M. Jr. (1965). *A Thousand Days: John F. Kennedy in the White House.* Boston: Houghton-Mifflin.

Schneider, B. (1985). Organizational behavior. *Annual Review of Psychology, 36,* 573–611.

Schneider, B., and Hall, D. T. (1972). Toward specifying the concept of work climate: a study of Roman Catholic diocese priests. *Journal of Applied Psychology, 56,* 447–455.

Shamir, B., and Arthur, M. B. (in press). An exploratory study of perceived career change and job attitudes among job changers. *Journal of Applied Psychology.*

Shamir, B., and Salomon, I. (1985). Work-at-home and the quality-of-working life. *Academy of Management Review, 10,* 455–464.

Shepard, H. A. (1984). On the realization of human potential: a path with a heart. In M. B. Arthur, L. Bailyn, D. J. Levinson, and H. A. Shepard, *Working With Careers.* New York: Graduate School of Business, Columbia University, pp. 25–46.

Simmel, G. (1950). *The Sociology of George Simmel* (edited by K. H. Wolff). Glencoe, IL: Free Press.

Slocum, J. W., Jr., Cron, W. L., Hansen, W., and Rawlings, S. (1985). Business strategy and the management of plateaued employees. *Academy of Management Journal, 28,* 133–154.

Sonnenfeld, J., and Kotter, J. P. (1982). The maturation of career theory. *Human Relations, 35,* 19–46.

Stewman, S., and Konda, S. L. (1983). Careers and organizational labor markets: demographic models of organizational behavior. *American Journal of Sociology, 88,* 637–685.

Stout, S. K., Slocum, J. W., Jr., and Cron, L. (1987). Career transitions of superiors and subordinates. *Journal of Vocational Behavior, 30,* 124–147.

Strauss, A. L. (1959). *Mirrors and Masks.* New York: Free Press.

Strong, E. K., Jr. (1943). *Vocational Interests of Men and Women.* Stanford, Stanford University Press.

Super, D. E. (1957). *The Psychology of Careers.* New York: Harper & Row.

Super, D. E. (1988). *Adult Career Concerns Inventory.* Palo Alto, CA: Consulting Psychologists Press.

Torbert, W. (1983). Initiating collaborate inquiry. In G. Morgan (ed.), *Beyond Method: Strategies for Social Research.* New York: Sage.

Valliant, G. E. (1977). *Adaptation to Life.* Boston, MA: Little-Brown.

Van Maanen, J. (1977). Introduction: the promise of career studies. In J. Van Maanen (ed.), *Organizational Careers: Some New Perspectives.* New York: Wiley, pp. 1–12.

Van Maanen, J. (1982). Getting into fishing: observations on the social identities of New England fishermen. *Urban Life, 11*(1), pp. 27–54.

Van Maanen, J., and Barley, S. (1984). Occupational communities: culture and control in organizations. In B. Staw and L. Cummings (eds.), *Research in Organizational Behavior,* Vol. 6. Greenwich, CT: JAI, pp. 287–365.

Van Maanen, J., and Schein, E. H. (1977). Career development. In J. R. Hackman and J. L. Suttle (eds.), *Improving Life at Work.* Santa Monica, CA: Goodyear, pp. 30–95.

Warner, W. L., and Abegglen, J. (1955). *Occupational Mobility in American Business and Industry.* Minneapolis, MN: University of Minnesota Press.

Weick, K. E. (1977). Organization design: organizations as self-designing systems. *Organizational Dynamics*, 6(2), 30–46.

Wholey, D. R., and Brittain, J. W. (1986). Organizational ecology: findings and implications. *Academy of Management Review*, *1*, 513–533.

2 Trait-factor theories: traditional cornerstone of career theory

NANCY E. BETZ, LOUISE F. FITZGERALD, AND
RAYMOND E. HILL

INTRODUCTION

Researchers interested in career development must begin by addressing the fact that occupational and organizational choice, adjustment, and success are products of two distinct but interactive forces: the individual and the environment in which that individual functions. That they are distinct is evident in the vast amount of research amassed relevant to the dimensions separately – individual characteristics on the one hand (the domain of traditional psychology) and the organization on the other hand [the domain of the organizational behaviorist, individual–organization (I/O) psychologist, and human resource specialist]. That they are interactive is the focus of this book.

This chapter will review theory and research based on the assumption that optimal career outcomes for both the individual and the organization can best be facilitated through a congruence between the individual's characteristics and the demands, requirements, and rewards of the organizational environment. This body of theory and research stems historically from two areas of psychology – first, the study and measurement of individual differences and, second, Parsons's (1909) "matching men and jobs" approach to career choice and guidance. The joining of the concepts and technology of individual differences with matching models of career choice led to "trait-factor" approaches to career development and adjustment. These approaches range from a general emphasis on the use of tests of individual differences variables in selection, placement, and counseling to theories that focus specifically on ways in which the correspondence between individuals and environments leads to outcomes such as successful job performance and job satisfaction. More recently, widespread interest in interactionist (person–environment) models of behavior (e.g., Magnusson and Endler, 1977; Pervin and Lewis, 1978; Schneider, 1987) has served to continue and broaden this tradition.

Trait-factor theories have focused primarily on describing and measuring individual characteristics rather than organizational variables. Although this chapter will focus on the importance of individual differences to the understanding and facilitation of organizational career development, it also acknowledges that traditional vocational psychology often overlooked both the effects of organizational variables and, most important, the interactive, dynamic qualities of both people and environments. Fortunately, many new directions in career theory, to be mentioned later in this chapter, take an explicitly dynamic rather than static approach to the description of behavior. Following a brief historical overview, the basic trait-factor theories will be summarized, and their strengths and limitations will be discussed.

26

The chapter ends with mention of recent theoretical and empirical directions and recommendations for further theory development and research.

The measurement and study of individual differences in mental faculties began in the late-nineteenth century with the work of Sir Francis Galton in England and the first experimental psychologists in Germany. Galton postulated the existence of a general mental ability in humans and further postulated that mental functioning was the sum of its component parts of sensory functioning. James McKeen Cattell, after completing his doctoral work in sensation and perception under Wilhelm Wundt in Germany, joined Galton in England. Galton and Cattell developed numerous laboratory devices (termed "mental tests" by Cattell in 1890) for measuring the sensory capacities they thought were the component parts of human intellect. Tests were developed to assess capacity to discriminate sizes, colors, weights, and pitch and to measure visual and hearing acuity, reaction time, memory span, and numerous other sensory and motor capabilities. Their work and the subsequent work of Hugo Munsterberg were the forerunners of our modern testing programs for occupational selection. The French developmental psychologists Alfred Binet and Theodore Simon developed the first practically useful, valid test of mental abilities, the Binet–Simon scale (later adapted for use in the United States as the Stanford–Binet). Although intellectual abilities were the first "mental" variables measured, the Woodworth Personal Data Sheet, the first personality inventory, appeared in 1920, and the first vocational interest inventory, Strong's Vocational Interest Blank, appeared in 1927. Thus, by the late 1920s, technology for measuring individual differences in psychological characteristics was in place.

The second major development that shaped the emergence of trait-factor theory was Parsons's "matching model" of career choice and counseling. Parsons, a pioneer in the field of vocational psychology, postulated, in his 1909 book *Choosing a Vocation*, that optimal career choices required three steps: knowledge of self, knowledge of work environments, and some method of matching the characteristics of one's self to those of the work environment. More specifically, Parsons postulated that (a) individuals differ in their job-related interests, needs, and values; (b) jobs differ in the amount and nature of the rewards they offer and in the kinds of demands they make of the employee; and (c) vocational adjustment (operationalized as success and satisfaction) is directly proportional to the "match," or "goodness of fit," between the characteristics of the worker and the characteristics of the environment.

Thus, the means for measurement of individual differences and a useful postulate relating these differences to important career outcomes were in place early in this century. Practical uses for the developing knowledge emerged quickly. The Binet tests and successors such as the Stanford–Binet were widely used in the diagnosis of retardation and in educational selection and placement. The two world wars required mass testing for the selection and placement of recruits to the armed services, and the Great Depression stimulated programs to assist unemployed workers. Among the government programs of the 1930s was the Minnesota Employment Stabilization Research Institute at the University of Minnesota, charged with the development of numerous aptitude tests to be used in the assessment of unemployed workers; hence the university's identification with "trait-factor" theory, so called because of its emphasis on trait measurement and extensive use of factor analysis to derive fundamental dimensions of ability. The following discussion provides an overview of trait-factor theoretical concepts, with emphasis on individual differences characteristics, followed by a presentation of several specific trait-factor theories.

GENERAL TRAIT-FACTOR THEORY

Trait-factor theory has as its bases the characteristics of the individual, those of the work environment, and the match or fit between the two sets of characteristics, often called the degree of congruence or correspondence. In the following section, the major psychological variables that have been used to describe the individual will be summarized. These variables are abilities, theoretically related to job performance, and interests, needs, and values, theoretically related to job satisfaction and motivation.

Abilities

One of the most influential individual characteristics is job-related abilities. Abilities, which describe what the person can do now or will be potentially able to do in the future, range in specificity from general cognitive ability (also sometimes called general intelligence, or g) to more specific job-related abilities such as clerical, mechanical, and manual abilities. General cognitive ability can be defined as the capacity for inductive and deductive reasoning and for insight, that is, the ability to discover patterns and interrelationships. It is indicated statistically by the first general factor resulting from factor analyses of several ability tests. Commonly used measures include the composite of verbal, quantitative, and sometimes spatial reasoning or technical aptitude scores from multiple aptitude batteries such as the General Aptitude Test Battery (GATB), the Differential Aptitude Tests (DAT), and the Employee Aptitude Survey.

In general, it may be concluded that possession of adequate job-related abilities is necessary but not sufficient for acceptable job performance. For example, Ghiselli's (1966, 1973) reviews of research studying the effects of ability–job requirement correspondence on job training and on-the-job performance indicated an average correlation of 0.39 for training success and 0.22 for job performance. Correlations of this magnitude account for 15 and 5% of the variance in performance, clearly implicating other factors (such as motivation). Interestingly, being overqualified may be as detrimental to performance as being underqualified (Wanous, 1980).

Because Ghiselli's reviews included measures of specific as well as general ability, their conclusions regarding the importance of ability are not entirely consistent with findings from research on "validity generalization" (Hunter, 1986; Schmidt and Hunter, 1977, 1981). Validity generalization refers to the consistent finding of the high predictive validities of general cognitive (rather than specific) ability tests both in training and on the job across a variety of jobs and job settings and for both majority and minority applicants. Hunter (1986) reviewed hundreds of studies, including the work of Ghiselli (whose validity studies covered the period 1949–1973), the 515 validation studies carried out by the U.S. Employment Service, and the 30 years of validation research carried out by the U.S. military. Based on this massive body of research, Hunter (1986) concluded that general cognitive ability predicts supervisors' ratings and training success as well as objective, rigorously content-valid work sample performance and that the average ability performance correlation is 0.80 (versus the 0.22 shown when specific abilities are included). Hunter (1986) concludes that general ability is related not only to level of job knowledge but also to the ability to solve new job-related problems that are beyond basic job knowledge. Gottfredson (1986b) martials an impressive array of evidence supporting the role of general intelligence in job performance even when levels of education are controlled – in other words, although intelligence is related to level of attained education, it further predicts level of performance even within groups of employees who have attained the same educational level.

Thus, evidence clearly indicates that abilities, particularly general cognitive ability, are related to job performance. There is most likely a range of ability that constitutes a "match" with the occupation in the organization – too little ability mitigates against attaining sufficient job knowledge and limits problem solving in novel situations, but too much ability leads to decrements in job satisfaction through boredom, frustration, and so forth. Gottfredson (1986b) has provided a table showing the ranges of IQs in a variety of occupations. However, the size of the ability–performance correlations, while respectable given problems of unreliability in the measurement of both predictors and criteria, leaves considerable room for other factors potentially influencing job performance.

Although not the focus of this chapter, the topic of abilities cannot be covered responsibly without mention of the well-known problem of "adverse impact." Adverse impact refers to the fact that standardized cognitive ability tests lead to the hiring of fewer minority group members because minorities obtain lower average scores on such tests. Although poorer performance of blacks, Hispanics, and other minorities on cognitive ability tests can be attributed partially to socioeconomic disadvantage, the fact of lower performance has an adverse impact even in the absence of discriminatory intent as long as the same selection criteria are used for majority and minority groups. Since studies show that test validity is at least as high for minority as majority groups, we are left not with issues of test validity but with the question of how selection decisions should be made. Selection procedures continuing to include test scores may also need to incorporate decision rules that account for the effects of socioeconomic disadvantage upon performance and incorporate the values of equal opportunity and racial and ethnic diversity in all settings. These comments are necessarily too brief to adequately discuss the issues, but more extensive discussions may be found in Cole (1981), Gottfredson (1986a,b), Hunter and Schmidt (1983), Messick (1980), and Walsh and Betz (1985).

Vocational interests, needs, and values

While the individual differences variable of abilities has been most closely connected to job performance, the concepts of interests, needs, and values have been more closely associated with the prediction of job satisfaction and motivation. Interests refer to a person's likes, dislikes, and preferences for activities, people, or events and are postulated in trait-factor theory to affect career adjustment and functioning. For example, Kuder, in the development of the Kuder Preference Record (KPR) (Kuder, 1946), postulated that job satisfaction is related to the extent to which the job content includes the kind of activities a person likes to do and does not emphasize disliked activities; inventories such as the KPR measured liked and disliked activities using this "rational" method of interest inventory construction. Other rationally constructed scales include the Basic Interest Scales of the Strong–Campbell Interest Inventory (SCII) and various measures of the Holland (1973) themes, measures such as the Self-Directed Search, Vocational Preference Inventory, and the SCII General Occupational Theme scores.

On the other hand, Strong postulated that job satisfaction is related to the extent that a person has interests similar to those of people already employed in the occupation; his occupational scales (originally in the Strong Vocational Interest Blank and now in the SCII) were developed to assess similarity of interest to those members of various occupational groups. This "empirical" method is also used in the Kuder Occupational Interest Survey (Kuder, 1966) and the occupational scales of the Career Assessment Inventory (Johansson, 1976).

Regardless of the method used to construct interest inventories, there is evidence that the congruence of interests with career choice is related to subsequent satisfaction and tenure in the job. And interest inventories can be particularly useful for career counseling, both with young people making initial career choices and with adults dissatisfied with their present work and/or considering career change. The utility of interest inventories with employed individuals has only begun to be explored; researchers such as Hill and Roselle (1985) and Sedge (1985) have explored the use of interest inventories in the prediction of changes from engineering and R&D technical positions to management, but considerably more research on topics related to career development in adulthood is needed.

Also believed to be important in an individual's potential for job satisfaction are the concepts of work needs, values, preferences, and motives. Although the psychological and organizational literatures contain several related concepts, some distinctions can be made. Needs, values, and preferences refer to individual differences in preferences for the rewards, payoffs, or outcomes of a job or career (e.g., intellectual stimulation or creativity). These concepts are similar to that of a motive, but the concept of "motive" is associated with goal-directed activity toward the desired reward; the incentive value of the reward is its valence.

There are many systems for describing and categorizing work needs. A basic distinction which can be made is that between "intrinsic" and "extrinsic." Intrinsic work needs are those fulfilled by actually engaging in the work; creativity, the opportunity to use one's abilities, and intellectual stimulation are examples. The concept emphasizes the contribution of work to self-esteem, self-actualization, and enjoyment of life (Dawis and Lofquist, 1984). Extrinsic needs are for the rewards work brings after it is done (including the pay, promotion, fringe benefits, security) or for the external conditions of the work (e.g., the surroundings, co-workers, and supervision). Other well-known theoretical systems are Alderfer's (1972) ERG (Existence, Relatedness, Growth) model, Maslow's (1943) need theory, and Hackman and Oldham's (1976) job characteristics theory.

Measures of work needs and values include Porter's (1961) Need Satisfaction Questionnaire, the Minnesota Importance Questionnaire (MIQ; Rounds et al., 1981), Super's (1968) Work Values Inventory (WVI), the Values Scale (Fitzsimmons, Macnab, and Casserly, 1986), the Work Aspects Preference Schedule

(WAPS; Pryor, 1979), and Manhardt's (1972) 25-item scale assessing the importance of 25 different work outcomes. The overlapping nature of these concepts was shown recently in a study by Macnab and Fitzsimmons (1987). They used multitrait–multimethod methodology and confirmatory factor analysis to examine the relationships among eight traits, each of which was measured in four different instruments. The traits, including authority, co-workers, creativity, security, independence, altruism, working conditions, and prestige, were contained in one measure of "needs" (the MIQ), two of "values" (the WVI and Value Scale), and one of "preferences (the WAPS). On the basis of strong evidence for convergent and discriminant validity, the researchers concluded that the four measures were measuring highly similar constructs.

There is considerable evidence that the correspondence between individual needs and the characteristics of the job are related to job satisfaction (see Dawis and Lofquist, 1984; Mobley et al., 1979; Osipow, 1983; Porter and Steers, 1973). Mismatches between one's needs and the work environment lead to dissatisfaction and, frequently, quitting the organization (Wanous, 1980) and are thus especially serious problems.

Summary

Although abilities, interests, and needs are important individual variables, traditional psychometric and vocational theories failed to include in this description of the "structure" of individual differences (Herriot, 1984) some important variables. The self-concept, including self-esteem and sex stereotypes, perceptions of the social environment, and social and leadership skills warrant additional attention. Also receiving insufficient attention are background variables such as gender, race, and socioeconomic status. For example, we know that the development of vocational interests is strongly influenced by sex role socialization but that interests can be modified in adulthood given appropriate learning experiences. Sex and race differences in work values (e.g., Brenner, Blazini, and Greenhaus, 1988) have important implications for both individuals and organizations. Finally, the fact that traditional psychometric theory emphasized the view of traits as fixed rather than as modifiable slowed the incorporation of organizational interventions into models of the interaction of person and environment. Thus, although existing concepts and measures of abilities, interests, and needs can be very useful in the facilitation of organizational careers, emphases on a broader range of variables (see Herriot, 1984) and on patterns of change in individual variables should characterize future research.

SPECIFIC TRAIT-FACTOR THEORIES

The following section will describe specific trait-factor theories, emphasizing the theory of work adjustment and Holland's theory of person–environment types. Several other theories will also be mentioned.

Theory of work adjustment

Probably the most comprehensive trait-factor theory is the theory of work adjustment (Dawis, England, and Lofquist, 1964; Dawis and Lofquist, 1984; Dawis, Lofquist, and Weiss, 1968), developed as part of the Minnesota Studies in Vocational Rehabilitation. The theory describes the key components of the individual and the work environment and specifies how the correspondence between the two is related to subsequent outcomes.

The first major concept of the theory is that of work adjustment, defined operationally as tenure on the job. Work adjustment is postulated to be a function of two characteristics of the employee in interaction with his or her work environment, that is, *satisfactoriness* and *satisfaction*. Satisfactoriness, the extent to which the worker is able to successfully perform job responsibilities, is postulated to be a function of the correspondence between an individual's *abilities* and the *ability requirements* of the job. Satisfaction is postulated to be a function of the correspondence between the individual's vocational *needs* or *values* and the *reinforcer systems* of the work environment.

In this theory the relevant individual characteristics are abilities and values and those of the job are ability requirements and reinforcer patterns; the ability–ability requirement interaction leads to satisfactoriness or lack thereof, while the value–reinforcer pattern leads to satisfaction or dissatisfaction. The outcomes that may follow from different combinations of satisfactoriness and satisfaction include the "adjusted" worker, as indicated by tenure on the job, who is both satisfactory and satisfied. Cases of dissatisfactoriness may be resolved in several ways, as can cases of dissatisfaction. For example, an unsatisfactory employee may be fired, while a dissatisfied one may quit.

One of the particularly noteworthy features of the theory is the precision with which the concepts have been operationalized, or measured. Abilities are assessed by the General Aptitude Test Battery (GATB), while ability requirements are described by Occupational Aptitude Patterns. Needs are assessed by the Minnesota Importance Questionnaire, and reinforcer systems by the Occupational Aptitude Patterns mentioned earlier. The satisfactoriness of the worker is assessed by supervisors' responses to the Minnesota Satisfactoriness Scales, and job satisfaction is assessed by the Minnesota Satisfaction Questionnaire. Tenure, the criterion of work adjustment, is the number of years employed in that occupation.

In addition to the major individual difference variables, the theory also postulates aspects of personality style that moderate the influence of lack of correspondence on work adjustment. In other words, although lack of congruence between abilities and ability requirements and/or between needs and reinforcers is always undesirable, there will be differences in both the nature and timing of individual responses to the discorrespondence. There are, first, individual differences in tolerance for discorrespondence before doing something to reduce it; this characteristic is termed "flexibility." Second, the extent to which an individual reacts to discorrespondence by attempting to act upon the environment is called "activeness," while the extent to which he or she attempts to change self to reduce discorrespondence is called "reactiveness." Finally, "perseverance" is the length of time an individual will remain in a situation of discorrespondence. Instruments to measure these aspects of response style are currently under development (S. Osipow and J. Madden, personal communication, May 1988).

Research on the theory of work adjustment is reviewed by Dawis and Lofquist (1984), Osipow (1983), and Rounds, Dawis, and Lofquist (1987). Generally, the research is supportive of the postulates of the theory, suggesting the importance of person–environment congruence to both satisfactoriness and satisfaction and the importance of these, in turn, to job tenure. Current issues in research have concerned the need for "commensurate measurement," that is, methods by which the same dimensions and units of measurement are used in the assessment of both persons and environments (Rounds et al., 1987) and the comparative utility for predictive purposes of different ways of operationalizing the concept of congruence (Kahana, 1982; Rounds et al., 1987). In a recent study of the former issue, Doering, Rhodes, and Kaspin (1988) reported that the factor structures of the theoretically parallel measures of work needs (the MIQ) and environmental reinforcers (the Minnesota Job Description Questionnaire) were not completely parallel, thus failing to completely meet the requirement of commensurate measurement.

Holland's theory

One of the most widely studied trait-factor theories is that of Holland (1973, 1985). The central postulate of Holland's theory is that vocational satisfaction, stability, and achievement depend on the congruence between one's personality and the environment in which one works (Holland, 1973). The variable for which congruence is sought in this theory is a personality *type*, by which both persons and environments can be characterized. The six personality types, along with salient associated characteristics, are as follows: (1) realistic (related to outdoor and technical interests), (2) investigative (intellectual, scientific), (3) artistic (creative, expressive in literary, artistic, musical, or other areas), (4) social (interest in working with people), (5) enterprising (interest in persuasion, leadership), and (6) conventional (enjoyment of detail, computational activity, high degree of structure). The types can be arranged hexagonally in the order presented in the preceding to indicate their similarity to each other. Similarities between the types can also be described in terms of basic dimensions such as people oriented (social, enterprising) versus non-people-oriented (realistic, investigative) and intellectually oriented (investigative, artistic) versus practically oriented (conventional, realistic).

There are numerous methods of measuring the Holland types of individuals. Inventories include the Vocational Preference Inventory (VPI) (Holland, 1978), the Self-Directed Search (SDS) (Holland, 1979), and the Strong–Campbell Interest Inventory (Hansen and Campbell, 1985). There has been less attention to assessing environments, although techniques available include the Environmental Assessment Technique (Astin and Holland, 1961), rationally derived codes such as those of the Occupations Finder from the SDS, and the empirically derived occupational code types of people actually employed in the occupation from the normative work on the SCII (Hansen and Campbell, 1985).

Using these concepts, two important predictions of the theory are the following:

1. Congruent individuals will be more satisfied and less likely to change environments than will incongruent persons.
2. Incongruent persons will be influenced by the dominant environment (that in which they are employed) toward congruence.

Research investigating these postulates has been summarized by Herriot (1984), Muchinsky (1987), Osipow (1983), Spokane (1985), and Weinrach (1984), among others. The first proposition, that of congruence versus incongruence, has been the subject of numerous correlational studies that have, in sum, shown positive relationships between congruence and academic performance, persistence in school, job satisfaction, stability of choice, and perceived congruence. For example, Mount and Muchinsky (1978) classified 362 subjects using first-letter codes from the SDS and an occupational code. Congruence of personality and occupational type was found to be related to job satisfaction, as measured by the Job Descriptive Index; means for congruent subjects were higher than those for incongruent subjects across all five environments.

Spokane (1985) reviewed 63 studies of Holland's congruence hypothesis and found support for the relationship of congruence to satisfaction with and stability in the job and to achievement. Assouline and Meir (1987) extended the Spokane review and performed a meta-analysis of 41 studies yielding 77 correlation coefficients; again there was substantial support for Holland's theory. Some recent research has investigated the degree to which gender and race moderate the validity of the theory. For example, Walsh and his colleagues (Greenlee, Damarin, and Walsh, 1988; Walsh and Huston, 1988) have continued their program of research investigating the applicability of the theory to employed women and minorities, and Elton and Smart (1988) reported interactions among sex, congruence, and Holland type in the prediction of extrinsic job satisfaction.

Although these studies show the importance of congruence to positive career outcomes, the second hypothesis having to do with changes in congruence over time has received considerably less attention. In other words, the question of what happens to the large number of incongruent workers is not well understood. As an example of the issue, Aranya, Barak, and Amernic (1981) found that only 27% of their sample of accountants had Holland code types congruent with their occupational choice. Accountants who did have the conventional–enterprising–social (CES) code type were significantly more satisfied than were other accountants, but the variety of the accountants' incongruent code types was striking; it is the 73% of incongruent accountants in this sample and large proportions of incongruent employees more generally who present an extremely important and interesting challenge to career theorists, researchers, and practitioners.

Although research on changes in congruence is limited in amount (Spokane, 1985), early results are intriguing. For example, Gottfredson (1979) reported that the 3,730 white men in the 1973 National Longitudinal Study changed over time in the direction of greater congruence of aspirations and actual jobs and that most men adjusted their aspirations to the realities of the marketplace by age 30. Gottfredson and Becker (1981) found that while changes in both aspiration and actual job were used to resolve incongruence, it was more common for men to change their aspirations than to change their jobs in this resolution. It is likely that processes of organizational socialization (e.g., Wanous, 1980) were influential in the movement toward congruence.

Thus, although there has been some work on change over time, this is the most important direction for future research. Research on Holland's theory has taken a primarily static rather than dynamic approach. It is now vital to more fully investigate the question of what happens to incongruent people over time. Does time itself resolve or lessen incongruence? What effects does organizational socialization have on incongruence? How general is the phenomenon of "progressive conformity" (Herriott, 1984)? How should management assess and respond to incongruence and what strategies maximize organizational commitment and productivity? In a closely related vein, Super and Hall (1978) strongly suggested the need for studies of Holland's theory in relation to adult career change, turnover, and the outcomes of midcareer crises.

Other trait-factor theories

Although space does not permit detailed discussion, several other trait-factor theories deserve brief mention. First, the theory of Roe (1956) was based on her extensive studies of the personality characteristics of eminent scientists. Roe's basic individual differences variable, described using traditional psychoanalytic concepts, is that of psychological needs that differ primarily along a dimension of orientation toward versus away from people. Although Roe's theory has received insufficient research attention, her occupational classification system of eight fields and six levels is widely used. Because of the lack of research interest and problems with Roe's theory (see Osipow, 1983), it is in need of both extensive research attention and revision if it is to contribute to career theory.

Another major career theorist is Super. His (1963) postulate that career choices require a process of self-concept implementation, while not expressly a trait-factor approach, is important because it notes the salience of self-perceptions as well as of objectively measurable psychological characteristics. The research of Betz and Hackett (1981), showing that career-related expectations of personal efficacy influence perceived career options, and Herriot's (1984) book *Down the Ivory Tower* illustrate the role of the self-concept in career development. Thus, the work of Super is a basis for integrating the extensive work in social psychology on self-perception theory into the traditional domain of trait-factor theories.

SUMMARY

This chapter has reviewed the foundations of career theory related to the concepts of person–environment matching. The concept of individual differences and the idea that individuals will perform and feel best when their unique characteristics are correspondent with those of the work environment are both logically and empirically grounded.

However, although trait-factor theories have had much to contribute to career theory, their potential contribution has not been fully realized because of some major limitations alluded to throughout this chapter. These limitations include the static rather than dynamic nature of most of the trait-factor research, limited views of the range of important individual variables, and insufficient attention to sex, race, and socioeconomic status. Fortunately, even though concepts related to person–environment matching are among the early foundations of career theory, they continue to provide an active area for new developments on both theoretical and empirical levels.

First, several recent works represent the attempt to integrate the vocational and organizational approaches to fit. A particularly important paper was that of Muchinsky and Monahan (1987), who distinguished "supplementary" versus "complementary" congruence. In supplementary congruence, individuals are matched to environments in which they are similar to the people already in those environments; this is the classic vocational counseling approach exemplified by Holland's theory. In complementary congruence, on the other hand, the characteristics of the individual serve to "make whole," or complement, the characteristics or needs of the work environment; gaps in the work group are filled by individuals who, rather than being similar to others in the group, are different from them in ways that will enhance the group's ability to meet its objectives. This is the classic personnel selection approach. Muchinsky and Monahan discuss the advantages and the disadvantages of each kind of congruence from a long-term perspective; for example, complementary fit may lead to problems for the employee when his or her particular strengths are no longer needed, but using a supplementary model of fit to select employees may well lead to collective stagnation.

Another integrative work was that of Kulik, Oldham, and Hackman (1987), who discussed how Hackman and Oldham's (1976, 1980) well-known job characteristics theory of employee motivation can be integrated with person–environment fit theories. Job characteristics theory can be viewed as a means of analyzing the fit between the characteristics of jobs and the needs of job holders. In a related vein, Naughton and Outcalt (1988) developed and tested an occupational classification system based on the motivational components of job characteristics theory; they suggest that the resulting taxonomy may supplement, although not replace, existing classification systems such as those of Roe and Holland.

A final integrative effort worthy of mention is that integrating Holland's theory with Owens and Schoenfeldt's (1979) work on biodata. Research by Eberhardt and Muchinsky (1982, 1984) demonstrated significant relationships between life history experiences and vocational interests. Most recently, Smart (1989) has used biodata as a means to examine the development of Holland types within individuals. Smart's finding that family background experiences were particularly influential in Holland-type development raises the interesting possibility that Roe's theory (based heavily on early family experiences) could be integrated within a larger theoretical framework explaining vocational interest and personality development.

Several other researchers have addressed the dynamic, rather than static, nature of person–environment interactions. As so well discussed by Herriot (1984), trait-factor theories emphasized the *structure* of personality but overlooked the important *process* of social negotiation by which individuals and organizations adjust their expectations of each other to achieve a workable level of congruence. Some potentially important yet not well-understood parts of the negotiation process include the employee's own objectives and goals (Pervin, 1987), the standards he or she uses in assessing and reacting to the environment (Kulik et al., 1987), and memories of past fit and anticipations and/or expectations of future fit (Caplan, 1983, 1987).

Also receiving more attention recently are the effects of growth, experience, and organizational interventions on congruence. Job redesign as a means of addressing incongruence is addressed by Hackman and Oldman (1980) and Kulik et al. (1987), among others. A more radical approach is that of Schneider (1983, 1987), who, in his attraction–selection–attrition model, has proposed that environments are a function of the people behaving in them. That is, at some level persons "cause" environments. The implications of this idea for concepts of congruence are potentially significant and in need of further exploration.

An additional area of new research with potentially important implications is that of congruence within occupations and work environments. For example,

Hesketh and Shouksmith (1986) studied congruence among different veterinary specialties. Meir and Yaari (1988) examined the hypothesis that the relationship between congruent specialty choice within occupations and satisfaction exceeds the relationship between congruent occupational choice and job satisfaction. Using a sample of 324 subjects representing several occupations that could be categorized by subspecialties (e.g., engineers, physicians, psychologists, and lawyers), the hypothesis was supported by a median congruence–satisfaction correlation of 0.41 versus that of 0.30 reported by Spokane (1985) for occupational congruence–satisfaction.

Finally, additional research needs alluded to throughout this chapter include focus on variables related to self-perception, including the self-concept, and perceptual variables such as causal attributions, expectations of self-efficacy, social skills, and social perception. Herriot's (1984) postulate that self-concept is more predictive of occupational outcomes than personality warrants empirical attention. Also, more attention to the impact of gender, race, and socioeconomic status is needed.

To summarize, we now need more complex research designs (e.g., time series designs, longitudinal studies, and treatment studies), a dynamic rather than static approach to theory and research, and greater attention to a wider variety of individual difference and demographic variables. It is hoped that this chapter will provide a foundation for career theorists and stimulate interest in further research and theory development.

NOTE

Louise Fitzgerald and Raymond Hill would like to express appreciation to Nancy Betz for doing the majority of the work on this chapter. She is the lead author because of her contribution, not because of the alphabetic order of her last name.

REFERENCES

Alderfer, C. P. (1972). *Existence, Relatedness, and Growth Human Needs in Organizational Settings.* New York: Free Press.
Aranya, N., Barak, A., and Amernic, J. (1981). A test of Holland's theory in a population of accountants. *Journal of Vocational Behavior, 19,* 15–24.
Assouline, M., and Meir, E. I. (1987). Meta-analysis of the relationship between congruence and well-being measures. *Journal of Vocational Behavior, 31,* 319–332.
Astin, A. W., and Holland, J. L. (1961). The environmental assessment technique. *Journal of Educational Psychology, 54,* 217–226.
Betz, N. E., and Hackett, G. (1981). Relationships of career related self-efficacy expectations to perceived career options. *Journal of Counseling Psychology, 28,* 399–410.
Brenner, O. C., Blazini, A. P., and Greenhaus, J. H. (1988). An examination of race and sex differences in managerial work values. *Journal of Vocational Behavior. 32,* 336–344.
Caplan, R. D. (1983). Person–environment fit: past, present, and future. In C. L. Cooper (ed.), *Stress research.* New York: Wiley.
Caplan, R. D. (1987). Person–environment fit theory and organizations: commensurate dimensions, time perspectives, and mechanisms. *Journal of Vocational Behavior, 31,* 231–247.
Cattell, J. M. (1890). Mental tests and measurements. *Mind, 15,* 373–380.
Cole, N. S. (1981). Bias in testing. *American Psychologist, 376,* 1067–1077.
Dawis, R. V., England, G. W., and Lofquist, L. H. (1964). A theory of work adjustment. *Minnesota Studies in Vocational Rehabilitation, XV.*
Dawis, R. V., and Lofquist, L. H. (1984). *A Psychological Theory of Work Adjustment.* Minneapolis: University of Minnesota Press.

Dawis, R. V., Lofquist, L. H., and Weiss, D. J. (1968). A theory of work adjustment (a revision). *Minnesota Studies in Vocational Rehabilitation, XXIII, 47*, 1–14.

Doering, M., Rhodes, S. R., and Kaspin, J. (1988). Factor structure comparison of occupational needs and reinforcers. *Journal of Vocational Behavior, 32*, 127–138.

Eberhardt, B. J., and Muchinsky, P. M. 1982). Biodata determinants of vocational typology: an integration of two paradigms. *Journal of Applied Psychology, 67*, 714–727.

Eberhardt, B. J., and Muchinsky, P. M. (1984). Structural validation of Holland's hexagonal model: vocational classification through the use of biodata. *Journal of Applied Psychology, 69*, 174–181.

Elton, C. F., and Smart, J. C. (1988). Extrinsic job satisfaction and person–environment congruence. *Journal of Vocational Behavior, 32*, 226–238.

Fitzsimmons, G. W., Macnab, D., and Casserly, C. (1986). *Life Roles Inventory: Technical Manual for the Values Scale and Salience Inventory.* Edmonton, Canada: Ps: Can Consulting.

Ghiselli, E. E. (1966). *The Validity of Occupational Aptitude Tests.* New York: Wiley.

Ghiselli, E. E. (1973). The validity of aptitude tests in personnel selection. *Personal Psychology, 26*, 461–478.

Gottfredson, L. S. (1979). Aspiration–job match: age trends in a large, nationally representative sample of young, white men. *Journal of Counseling Psychology, 26*, 319–328.

Gottfredson, L. S. (ed.) (1986a). The "g" factor in employment. *Journal of Vocational Behavior* (Special issue), *29*(3), 293–296.

Gottfredson, L. S. (1986b). Societal consequences of the "g" factor in employment. *Journal of Vocational Behavior, 29*, 379–410.

Gottfredson, L. S., and Becker, H. J. (1981). A challenge to vocational psyychology: how important are aspirations in determining male career development? *Journal of Vocational Behavior, 18*, 121–137.

Greenlee, S. P., Damarin, F. L., and Walsh, W. B. (1988). Holland's theory in black and white males in non-college degreed occupations. *Journal of Vocational Behavior, 32*, 298–306.

Hackman, J. R., and Oldham, G. R. (1976). Motivation through the design of work: test of a theory. *Organizational Behavior and Human Performance, 16*, 250–279.

Hackman, J. R., and Oldham, G. R. (1980). *Work Redesign.* Reading, MA: Addison-Wesley.

Hansen, J. C., and Campbell, D. P. (1985). *Manual for the SVIB-SCII*, 4th ed. Palo Alto, CA: Consulting Psychologists Press.

Herriot, P. (1984). *Down from the Ivory Tower.* New York: Wiley.

Hesketh, B., and Shouksmith, G. (1986). Job and nonjob activities, job satisfaction, and mental health among veterinarians. *Journal of Occupational Behavior, 7*, 325–339.

Hill, R. E., and Roselle, P. F. (1985). Differences in the vocational interests of research and development managers versus technical specialists. *Journal of Vocational Behavior, 26*, 92–105.

Holland, J. L. (1973). *Making Vocational Choices.* Englewood Cliffs, NJ: Prentice-Hall.

Hoiland, J. L. (1978). *The Occupations Finder.* Palo Alto, CA: Consulting Psychologists Press.

Holland, J. L. (1979). *Professional Manual for the Self-Directed Search.* Palo Alto, CA: Consulting Psychologists Press.

Holland, J. L. (1985). *Making Vocational Choices*, 2nd ed. Englewood Cliffs, NJ: Prentice-Hall.

Hunter, J. E. (1986). Cognitive ability, cognitive aptitudes, job knowledge, and job performance. *Journal of Vocational Behavior, 29*, 340–362.

Hunter, J. E., and Schmidt, F. L. (1983). Quantifying the effects of psychological interventions on employee job performance and work force productivity. *American Psychologist, 38*, 473–477.

Johansson, C. B. (1976). *Manual: The Career Assessment Inventory.* Minneapolis: National Computer Systems Interpretive Scoring Systems.

Kahana, E. (1982). A congruence model of person–environment interaction. In M. P. Lawton, P. G. Windley, and T. O. Byerts (eds.), *Aging and the environment.* New York: Springer, pp. 97–121.

Kuder, G. F. (1946). *Manual, Kuder Preference Record, Vocational.* Chicago: Science Research Associates.

Kuder, G. F. (1966). The Occupational interest survey. *Personnel and Guidance Journal, 45*, 72–77.
Kulik, C. T., Oldham, G. R., and Hackman, J. R. (1987). Work design as an approach to person–environment fit. *Journal of Vocational Behavior, 31*, 278–296.
Macnab, D., and Fitzsimmons, G. W. (1987). A multitrait multimethod study of work-related needs, values, and preferences. *Journal of Vocational Behavior, 30*, 1–15.
Magnusson, D., and Endler, N. S. (eds.) (1977) *Personality at the Crossroads*. Hillsdale, NJ: Lawrence Erlbaum Associates.
Manhardt, P. J. (1972). Job orientation among male and female college graduates in business. *Personnel Psychology, 25*, 361–368.
Maslow, A. H. (1943). A theory of human motivation. *Psychological Review, 50*, 370–396.
Meir, E. I., and Yaari, Y. (1988). The relationship between congruent specialty choice within occupations and satisfaction. *Journal of Vocational Behavior, 33*, 99–117.
Messick, S. (1980). Test validity and the ethics of assessment. *American Psychologist, 35*, 1012–1037.
Mobley, W. H., Griffeth, R. W., Hand, H. H., Meglino, B. M. (1979). Review and conceptual analysis of the employee turnover process. *Psychological Bulletin, 86*, 493–522.
Mount, M. K., and Muchinsky, P. M. (1978). Person–environment congruence and employee job satisfaction: a test of Holland's theory. *Journal of Vocational Behavior, 13*, 84–100.
Muchinsky, P. M. (1987). *Psychology Applied to Work: An Introduction to Industrial and Organizational Psychology*. Chicago: Dorsey.
Muchinsky, P. M., and Monahan, C. J. (1987). What is person–environment congruence? Supplementary versus complementary models of fit. *Journal of Vocational Behavior, 31*, 268–277.
Naughton, T. J., and Outcalt, D. (1988). Development and test of an occupational taxonomy based on job characteristics theory. *Journal of Vocational Behavior, 32*, 16–36.
Osipow, S. H. (1983). *Theories of Career Development*, 3rd ed. Englewood Cliffs, NJ: Prentice-Hall.
Owens, W. A., and Schoenfeldt, L. F. (1979). Toward a classification of persons. *Journal of Applied Psychology, 65*, 569–607.
Parsons, F. (1909). *Choosing a Vocation*. Boston: Houghton Mifflin.
Pervin, L. A. (1987). Person–environment congruence in the light of the person situation controversy. *Journal of Vocational Behavior, 31*, 222–230.
Pervin, L. A., and Lewis, M. (eds.) (1978). *Perspectives in Interactional Psychology*. New York: Plenum.
Porter, L. W. (1961). A study of perceived need satisfaction in bottom and middle management jobs. *Journal of Applied Psychology, 45*, 1–10.
Porter, L. W., and Steers, R. M. (1973). Organizational, work, and personal factors in employee turnover and absenteeism. *Psychological Bulletin, 80*, 151–176.
Pryor, R. G. L. (1979). In search of a concept: work values. *Vocational Guidance Quarterly, 27*, 250–258.
Roe, A. (1956). *The Psychology of Occupations*. New York: Wiley.
Rounds, J. B., Dawis, R. V., and Lofquist, L. L. (1987). Measurement of person–environment fit and prediction of satisfaction in the theory of work adjustment. *Journal of Vocational Behavior, 31*, 297–318.
Rounds, J. B., Jr., Henley, G. A., Dawis, R. V., Lofquist, L. H., and Weiss, D. J. (1981). *Manual for the Minnesota Importance Questionnaire*. Minneapolis, MN: Vocational Psychology Research, Department of Psychology, University of Minnesota.
Schmidt, F. L., and Hunter, J. E. (1977). Development of a general solution to the problem of validity generalization. *Journal of Applied Psychology, 62*, 529–540.
Schmidt, F. L., and Hunter, J. E. (1981). Employment testing: old theories and new research findings. *American Psychologist, 36*, 1128–1137.
Schneider, B. (1983). Interactional psychology and organizational behavior. In L. L. Cummings and B. M. Staw (eds.), *Research in Organizational Behavior*, Vol. 5. Greenwich, CT: JAI.
Schneider, B. (1987). $E = f(P, B)$: the road to a radical approach to person–environment fit. *Journal of Vocational Behavior, 31*, 353–361.
Sedge, S. K. (1985). A comparison of engineers exploring alternate career paths. *Journal of Vocational Behavior, 27*, 56–70.

Smart, J. C. (1989). Life history influences on Holland vocational type development. *Journal of Vocational Behavior, 34,* 69–87.

Spokane, A. R. (1985). A review of research on person–environment congruence in Holland's theory of careers. *Journal of Vocational Behavior, 26,* 306–343.

Super, D. E. (1963). *Career Development: Self-concept Theory.* New York: CEEB.

Super, D. E. (1968). *Work Values Inventory.* Lombard, IL: Riverside.

Super, D. E., and Hall, D. T. (1978). Career development: exploration and planning. *Annual Review of Psychology, 29,* 333–372.

Walsh, W. B., and Betz, N. E. (1985). *Tests and Assessment.* Englewood Cliffs, NJ: Prentice-Hall.

Walsh, W. B., and Huston, R. E. (1988). Traditional female occupations and Holland's theory for employed men and women. *Journal of Vocational Behavior, 32,* 358–365.

Wanous, J. P. (1980). *Organizational Entry.* Reading MA: Addison-Wesley.

Weinrach, S. G. (1984). Determinants of vocational choice: Holland's theory. In D. Brown and L. Brooks (eds.), *Career Choice and Development.* San Francisco: Jossey-Bass.

3   Careers, identities, and institutions: the legacy of the Chicago School of Sociology

STEPHEN R. BARLEY

> A sociology which forgets its past may be committed to the continuous rediscovery of old ideas. When the provenance of thought is unknown, authorship can be claimed by those who lack any proper title to it. Old issues are proclaimed innovations, only to recede again into the limbo from which they were retrieved. The unstated component...is a fertile culture for the emergence of a cyclical pattern of recovery and loss.
>
> *Paul Rock, 1979*

Specialization rarely proceeds by simply redistributing tasks. Instead, most specialties evolve gradually by pruning back an initially broader set of interests. By sloughing off the fuzzier elements of earlier thought in favor of more developed concepts, nascent specialties ostensibly select more precise tools for roughing out a cumulative line of inquiry. In the process, however, fruitful but less articulate ideas may fall through the discipline's cracks. Consequently, when specialists stop to take stock of their progress, as is the partial function of a handbook such as this, they should not only seek to consolidate their hard-won treasures but also attempt to uncover long-neglected paths once blazed by their forebears. By so doing, specialists may reclaim realms of inquiry that might now be more profitably explored. Thus, it is with an eye to enriching career theory that this essay deals in what may seem the all-too-distant past.

My intent, however, is neither to write a history of career theory nor to lead modern scholars on a pilgrimage to their roots. Though such a trek might prove enlightening, it begs for a focus broader than my own.[1] Rather, I wish merely to indicate how current conceptions of career differ from those found in the writings of a small group of sociologists from which modern career theory, in part, descends. I shall argue that these differences inscribe neglected insights whose nurture might enable theorists to grapple once again with what should be the central problem of any sociologically informed social psychology: the link between structure and action.

This grail-like quest requires a return to Chicago at the turn of the century, the intellectual crucible where American sociology and the sociological notion of career were first forged. There, we shall retrace the circumstances that encouraged early sociologists to study careers. After briefly reviewing how sociological investigations of careers began, the essay then explicates more fully the concept of career as it was employed by sociologists of work trained by Everett C. Hughes. The discussion aims not only to consolidate the ideas formulated by Hughes and his students but also to distinguish their notions from current ideas. The essay concludes by showing how one might reformulate career studies in order to amass the conceptual leverage necessary for building an empirical account of how social action and social structure entwine.

THE EMERGENCE OF A SOCIOLOGY OF CAREERS

The University of Chicago bears distinction as the first American university to establish a department of sociology.[2] At the invitation of William R. Harper, Chicago's first president, Albion W. Small came to the university in 1892 from his presidency at Colby College to serve as the sociology department's head professor. Over the next three decades Small gradually assembled a faculty widely credited with transforming what was, at the time, a branch of social philosophy into an independent empirical discipline (Faris 1967). The most influential members of the early faculty were W. I. Thomas, Robert Park, and Ernest Burgess.

Two intellectual traditions, *German formalism* and *American pragmatism*, fed sociology's transformation at Chicago. Formalism entered Chicago's curriculum through the writings of Georg Simmel, under whom Park had once studied (Rock 1979). From Simmel, Park's students acquired the notion that sociology's business is to discover and depict "social forms." Social forms were conceived as patterns of interaction whose repetition accounts for the coherence and reproduction of bounded social worlds. But while social forms were thought to constrain social life, they were also held to be abstractions with no existence independent of the actions that give them substance. The Chicago sociologists' notion of social structure therefore differed from Durkheim's. Rather than impute to structure the status of a "social fact," Park and Burgess taught their students to treat structures as grammars composed of rules that can vary across time and from situation to situation.[3]

From the American pragmatists, especially John Dewey and George Herbert Mead, who taught at Chicago during the same era, Chicago sociology absorbed a strain of nominalism that conflicted with, and yet ironically complemented, Simmel's formalism (Lewis and Smith 1980; Rock 1979). By definition, nominalists claim that only particulars have empirical substance. Theoretical abstractions are understood to be mere emanations of an analyst's mind that have no referent outside the conceptual scheme that contains them. But while Dewey and other pragmatists adopted a nominalist ontology, they also posited the claim that humans must devise abstractions in order to impute coherence to what would otherwise be a world of chaotic detail. Because construing was therefore held to be a practical but situated activity, the pragmatists argued that academics should turn "away from ... verbal solutions ... from fixed principles, closed systems, and pretended absolutes ... towards concreteness and adequacy, towards action and power" (James 1949:51). Thus, it was from the pragmatists that Chicago sociologists acquired the conviction that knowledge of social worlds must entail an understanding of how members construe the problems they face.

Out of the fusion of German formalism and American pragmatism grew a sociological stance that remains unique in its tendency to eschew formal theory in favor of knowledge of social particulars. Chicago sociologists sought to bridge the two traditions by arguing that one cannot adduce social forms without first understanding the details of daily life. Thus, the melding of formalism and pragmatism underwrote the Chicago sociologists' commitment to empiricism. For although formalism and pragmatism posit conflicting ontologies (Rock 1979), both reject formal theories developed in an empirical vacuum.

By the 1920s, sociologists at Chicago had begun to turn routinely to the surrounding city to study forms of social life at close range. The substance of these early investigations clustered around topics now known as social ecology, demography, urbanization, and social deviance. Of these, the latter was particularly influential in the development of a sociology of careers.

Life histories and the study of deviance. At one time or another, most of the faculty and many of the graduate students at Chicago studied areas of the city marked by high rates of prostitution, delinquency, and homelessness. Although much of the work consisted of mapping the distribution and incidence of social problems (Shaw, Zorbough, McKay, and Cottrell 1929), this ecological agenda was bolstered by a second type of research aimed at documenting the deviants' own perspectives. Crucial to this second agenda was the development of a methodology known as the "life history."

Thomas and Znaniecki (1918) pioneered the use of life histories in their research on social disorganization among Polish immigrants. Thomas later employed the technique to study the chain of events by which young girls became juvenile delinquents (Thomas 1923). Like modern social scientists, Thomas defended the life history and other types of case study as techniques for generating "realistic hypotheses" (Thomas 1931). However, Thomas's vision of the method's propriety went beyond its utility as a preliminary to hypothesis testing. Like the pragmatists under whom he studied, Thomas gave priority to the researcher's ability to comprehend how members of a social group construe their lives. "If men define situations as real," he wrote, "they are real in their consequences" (Thomas and Thomas 1928:572). Life histories represented one means of gathering data on how people construed their lives. Yet, Thomas's interest in life histories entailed more than the pragmatist's valuing of situated knowing. Echoing the strains of a formalist sociology, Thomas also argued that life histories provided evidence for how specific institutions drew their very sustenance from the patterning of peoples' lives:

A social institution can be fully understood only if we do not limit ourselves to the abstract study of its formal organization, but analyze the way in which it appears in the personal experience of various members of the group and follow the influence it has upon their lives. (Thomas and Znaniecki, 1918:1832)

Following Thomas's lead, throughout the 1930s Chicago sociologists published numerous ethnographies of deviant subcultures based on the life histories of people who partook of the subculture. Notable among these were Anderson's (1923) study of hobo life, Cressey's (1932) description of taxi-dance halls, and Sutherland's (1937) work on professional thieves.[4] But although many Chicago sociologists employed life history data, the technique was most extensively developed by Clifford Shaw. In the late 1920s, Shaw and other investigators at the Illinois Institute of Juvenile Research joined with Burgess's students to collect the life histories of thousands of juvenile delinquents serving time in correctional institutions. The investigators invited the juveniles to write their life stories and then, in a series of subsequent interviews, encouraged the authors to clarify the details of their accounts. These autobiographies were almost always preserved in the first person with little attempt to edit the juvenile's words.[5] Whatever analysis the researchers chose to provide appeared in preliminary or concluding chapters clearly set apart from the main body of the text which was treated as data. Shaw published three of the case studies as books: *The Jack-Roller: A Delinquent Boy's Own Story* (1930), *The Natural History of a Delinquent Career* (1931), and *Brothers in Crime* (1938).

As the second volume's title indicates, Shaw viewed life histories as documents of "careers." But although Shaw and other early Chicago sociologists spoke frequently of careers, they used the term casually. Shaw, for instance, penned no formal explication of career's utility as a sociological construct. Nevertheless, in the context of his discussions one detects a recognition of career's sociological value. As an example, consider Shaw's first mention of career in the *Jackroller*:

An important initial step in the study of a delinquent child is to procure a rather complete and accurate description of his delinquencies and other behavioral difficulties. Among other things, this description should show the specific offenses in the order of their occurrence, the chronological age of the child at the time of each offense, the immediate circumstances in which each offense occurred, and the number of persons involved. It is especially important to know also the age of the child at the time of the onset of the delinquent career and the immediate circumstances surrounding the initial experience of delinquency. (Shaw 1930:25)

The passage's emphasis on the situational, the relational, and the chronological foreshadows themes later associated with career's emergence as a formal sociological concept. Shaw and other analysts of life histories held that a life's unfolding was bound to the contingencies of the social situation in which the person lived. Shaw insisted that incidents of delinquency, for example, could be traced to the dynamics of a troubled family that had taken up residency in a neighborhood characterized by a high degree of social disorganization. Moreover, the unfolding of the delinquent's life was thought to be intimately tied to a patterned series of relationships that gradually defined the delinquent's sense of self. To have a deviant career was thus tantamount to being socialized into the ways of a subculture. Finally, the comparative study of life histories led analysts to argue that deviant careers emerged in a series of typical "stages," a point that received its clearest formulation in Cressey's (1932:94–106) account of how a taxi-dancer's experience was organized by a sequence of "periods" that defined the "life-cycle" of dancehall work. Cressey depicted each period as a "turning point," a set of experiences and interpretations that led the dancer to either exit the career's trajectory or else move deeper into the dancehall world toward the life of a prostitute.

Hughes and the sociology of work and careers. Explicit recognition that career could be fruitfully employed as a formal concept in studies of social organization first appeared in the work of Everett C. Hughes (see Hughes 1958a, 1971). Although Park had been interested in formal organizations (Faris 1967), no systematic studies of organized institutions were undertaken at Chicago until Hughes began his dissertation on the Chicago Real Estate Board (Hughes 1928). Hughes retained an acute interest in organizations and occupations throughout the remainder of his career, and it was largely during his tenure on the faculty from 1938 to 1961 that the sociology of work flowered at Chicago. Hughes and his students approached the study of work as a thoroughly ethnographic affair. Yet, each individual ethnography also contributed in piecemeal fashion to the formulation of a theoretical framework. This framework was composed of a constellation of concepts that were understood to be closely entwined: role, self, identity, institution, and most important for present purposes, career.

During the 1940s and 1950s students under Hughes's tutelage investigated the careers of individuals in a wide variety of occupations and organizations. Representative dissertations were Hall's (1944) and Solomon's (1952) studies of medical careers, Becker's (1951) analysis of the career problems of public school teachers, Habenstein's (1954) study of funeral directors, and Wager's (1959) work on airline pilots. Theoretical and empirical papers derived from these and other studies accumulated in the sociology journals during the mid-1950s. From these studies came many analytic terms still in vogue among career researchers: for instance, career contingencies (Becker 1953b), career timetables (Roth 1963), and career lines (Hughes 1937, 1958b).

But although the lexicon of modern career theory may descend from terms coined by Hughes and his students, it is important to realize that the Chicago sociologists treated career as a heuristic applicable to a much wider range of situations than is typical of current usage. For example, Hughes and his students were just as willing to talk about the careers of marijuana users (Becker 1953a) as they were about the careers of doctors (Hall 1948) and executives (Dalton 1951). One suspects, then, that Wilensky (1960:554) had Chicago sociologists firmly in mind when he wrote:

Just as the concept of "profession" loses its precision when we speak of the "professionalization" of auto-workers in Detroit, so the concept of "career" loses utility when we speak of the "career of a ditch-digger." In dealing with the organization of work, it is better to take a more restricted view of career.

Despite the benefits of the restrictions that Wilensky advocated (which, as we shall see, most modern career scholars adopt in practice, if not theory), it is worth remembering that precision, by definition, requires narrowing and that narrowing entails loss. The critical question is whether the loss involves anything of value. To appreciate exactly what was scuttled by the gradual tightening of the Chicago sociologists' notion of career and to determine whether one or more babies were unwittingly discarded, we must scrutinize more closely the use to which Hughes and his students put the notion of career.

CAREER IN THE CHICAGO TRADITION

What careers were not

Chicago sociologists and their intellectual heirs, the symbolic interactionists, are frequently faulted for vagueness. Wilensky's was, therefore, simply one voice among many that have attempted to bring greater precision to topics initially studied by sociologists working in the Chicago tradition. Although the charge of theoretical wooly-headedness has a certain degree of face value, as Rock (1979:83) astutely noted, the theoretical imprecision that haunts the Chicago tradition is less the upshot of muddled minds than the result of a practiced guard against premature generalization.[6] Schooled in the hybrid epistemology formed by mingling formalist and pragmatist philosophies, those who worked in the Chicago tradition typically aimed their investigations at bounded social worlds. The guiding notion, best articulated by Glaser and Strauss (1967), was that valid theoretical assertions can only emerge from, and must therefore remain grounded in, an understanding of the particulars of a variety of settings. If a theoretical construct is to be relevant for a range of cases, its reach must be demonstrated by its ability to subsume faithfully the details of numerous social worlds. Thus, for Chicago sociologists, generalizability was initially a substantive rather than a statistical issue.

For this reason, Hughes and his students formulated concepts tentatively, employed them as heuristics, and welcomed extension of their scope as a sign that the idea was situationally robust. Consequently, as their data warranted, different researchers elaborated on different connotations of the same heuristic. It would therefore be unrealistic for modern scholars to anoint any one definition as key to the Chicago sociologists' notion of career. Instead, to understand how career was used by members of this speech community, one must examine a number of representative formulations:

A career consists, objectively, of a series of statuses and clearly defined offices . . . subjectively, a career is the moving perspective in which the person sees his life as a whole and interprets the meaning of his various attributes, actions, and the things that happen to him . . . Careers in our society are thought very much in terms of jobs, for these are the characteristic and crucial connections of the individual with the institutional structure . . . But the career is by no means exhausted in a series of business and professional achievements. There are other points at which one's life touches the social order . . . it is possible to have a career in an avocation as well as in a vocation. (Hughes 1937:413)

Medicine, like other professions, is practiced in a network of institutions, formal organizations and informal relationships. The medical career may be conceived as a set of more or less successful adjustments to these institutions and to the formal and informal organizations. (Hall 1948:327)

Traditionally the term career has been reserved for those who expect to enjoy rises laid out within a respectable profession. The term is coming to be used, however, in a broadened sense to refer to any social strand of any person's course through life. The perspective of natural history is taken: unique outcomes are neglected in favor of such changes over time as are basic and common to the members of a social category, although occurring independently of each of them. Such a career is not a thing that can be brilliant or disappointing; it can no more be a success than a failure . . . One value of the concept is its two-sidedness. One side is linked to the internal matters held dearly and closely, such as image of self and felt identity; the other side concerns official position, jural relations, and style of life and is part of a publicly accessible institutional complex. The concept of career, then, allows one to move back and forth between the personal and the public, between self and its significant society. (Goffman 1961:127)

The series of events or conditions under scrutiny must be thought of in terms of a career – a series of related and definable stages or phases of a given sphere of activity that a group of people goes through in a progressive fashion (that is, one step leads to another) in a given direction or on the way to a more or less definite and recognizable end-point or goal or series of goals. This means that there must be a group definition of success or attainment of a goal . . . There must be an interacting (not necessarily face-to-face) group of people with access to the same body of clues for constructing the norms of a timetable. (Roth 1963:94)

A career always consists of a sequence of roles. (Solomon 1968:5)

As a first pass at analyzing these remarks with the eventual aim of reassembling their constituent parts into something resembling a synthetic statement of the Chicago school's notion of career, it is perhaps best to begin with a ploy borrowed from linguistic anthropology (Frake 1964; Goodenough 1981; Levi-Strauss 1963). Central to all structuralist theories of language is the notion that words take on part of their meaning through the process of opposition (de Saussure 1966; Eco 1979; Hawkes 1977). In practical terms, this process dictates that if one is to comprehend fully what a word signifies, one must discover that to which the term does not refer. Thus, linguistic anthropologists do more than simply inquire of informants what a term denotes; they also take pains to discover the contrasts by which insiders bound the term's competent use. The necessity of identifying the boundaries of a word's usage seems especially critical in a case like career where the same term may denote something quite different to members of different theoretical communities who appear, at first glance, to speak much the same language.

Common parlance treats a career as a series of jobs. Wilensky's admonition to restrict the concept's reference was largely a call to confine academic definitions to the term's colloquial scope: "Let us define career in structural terms. A career is a succession of related jobs, arranged in a hierarchy of prestige, through which persons move in an ordered (more-or-less predictable) sequence" (Wilensky 1961:523). The majority of modern sociologists have consciously or unconsciously followed Wilensky's recommendation (Rosenbaum 1984:38; Spilerman 1977; Thompson, Avery, and Carlson 1968:5). Even those who assert that a series of jobs or formal organizational positions are unnecessary for a career (Driver 1980; Hall 1976) nevertheless focus on work-related positions and, hence, unwittingly reinforce the linkage between jobs and careers.

But from the vantage point adopted by Hughes and his students, a career was decidedly not coextensive with a series of jobs. None of the statements cited in the preceding text employ even a synonym for a succession of jobs as a predicate nominative. In fact, Hughes and Goffman explicitly attempted to disabuse their readers of any simple correspondence between a career and a set of work-related positions. To be sure, job chains were held to be the most important instantiation of the concept; but work careers were viewed as only a subset of the term's proper domain. One could also use career appropriately when analyzing phenomena that no competent speaker of English would consider a form of work: for instance, the staged logic of a tubercular patient's hospitalization and recovery (Roth 1963), the plight of a polio victim (Davis 1963), or the process by which inmates of mental hospitals are gradually labeled insane (Goffman 1961).

Moreover, career's sociological utility was not thought to be limited to describing a sequence of roles enacted within the bounds of a formal organization. Following the lead of those early Chicago sociologists who had studied deviance, Becker (1953a, 1963b, c) made the notion of career integral to his analysis of the social process by which individuals became committed marijuana users. Farber (1961) wrote of family life as a set of "mutually contingent careers." And Riesman and Roseborough (1955) even suggested that consumption patterns could be usefully analyzed in terms of a consumer's career. Although the attribution of a career clearly required a social backdrop against which movement could be gauged – for instance, a subculture, a family, or a market basket of goods – neither Hughes nor his students considered formal organizations, or for that matter even work, to be a necessary context for the term's application.

Modern career theory and common parlance also tend to frame careers in terms of advancement along a hierarchy of power or prestige. The notion of vertical mobility is so well entrenched in career research that many of the terms we frequently use to discuss careers make no sense unless hierarchical structures are presumed. Consider, for instance, whether one can comprehend "up and out," "career ladder," "plateauing," "promotion," "demotion," or even "lateral transfer" without at least tacitly referring to the notion of verticality. In fact, a number of more recent theorists and researchers have explicitly made the notion of vertical movement a necessary condition for their research (Sofer 1970:5; Stewman and Konda 1983:643; White 1970; Wilensky 1961:523).

In sharp contrast, Chicago sociologists viewed vertical mobility as but one type of career movement. Hughes and his students clearly recognized that vertical mobility was of overwhelming importance for the careers of certain occupational groups (Dalton 1950; Goldner 1965; Martin and Strauss 1956, 1959). Indeed, Hughes even commented that in an industrial society an ever-increasing number of careers might be played out in hierarchically organized settings (Hughes 1937). But "up" and "down" were thought to be neither the only nor necessarily the most important signposts for constructing a career. As can be ascertained from preceding statements, terms of "vertical classification" (Schwartz 1981) were conspicuously absent from most definitions of career penned by Hughes and his students. In fact, several of Hughes's students actively sought to dispel the notion that vertical movement was necessary for an individual's ability to formulate a meaningful career (Becker 1952:470; Roth 1963:81).

Vertical movement's primacy was dismissed for several reasons. First, by restricting careers to hierarchical advancement, researchers might limit on a priori grounds, without empirical warrant, the type of work to which the concept can be meaningfully applied (Becker 1961; Roth 1963). For example, Van Maanen and Barley (1984:322) have suggested that by taking administrative and professional careers as exemplars, theorists in effect deny more than 80% of the American work force the possibility of a career. Second, by treating vertical movement as a necessary condition, researchers overlook the empirical fact that numerous occupations recognize meaningful careers that involve no movement through a hierarchy of power or control. In the absence of stratification, members of occupations have been shown to construct meaningful careers in terms of movement between work settings (Becker 1952; Gold 1964), mobility across geographical space (Pape 1964; Peterson and Wiegand 1985), movement within the confines of a social network (Crane 1972; Faulkner 1983; Weiss and Faulkner 1983), and even the sort of strong identity that comes from staying in one place but demonstrating an increasingly superior command of the work itself (Bailyn 1985; Reimer 1977; Schein 1971; Van Maanen and Barley 1984). Finally, an emphasis on vertical movement subtly shades into the moral notion that success is equivalent to upward mobility. However, as Becker (1953b:22, 1961:240), Roth (1963), and others repeatedly emphasized, success in a career can only be defined in terms of a subculture's criteria. Those who make the most money, who achieve the most acclaim, or who wield the most power are not always the most successful in the eyes of their peers. Witness both the jazz musician who forgoes commercial success to follow the dictates of aesthetics (Becker 1953b, 1963a) as well as those industrial scientists who turn deaf ears to the lure of management (Marcson 1960).

What careers were

By examining what Chicago sociologists of work did not mean by the term "career," it becomes obvious that specifying their usage requires jettisoning vestiges of colloquial understanding. When sequences of jobs, formally organized contexts, and movement up and down a hierarchy are treated as incidentals, what is left is a construct that, whatever else it might be, seems somewhat foreign in light of career's current usage. Yet, it was precisely the analytic utility of the remainder that made career so central to the Chicago sociologist's notion of what the sociological eye should see. As one might guess, the focus of that eye was not on careers themselves. Rather, in the hands of the Chicago sociologists, career became a lens for peering at larger social processes known as institutions. Thus it was that Hughes and his students composed their fugue-like renditions of career by weaving together four related themes: (a) careers fuse the objective and the subjective; (b) careers entail status passages; (c) careers are rightfully properties of collectives; and perhaps most importantly (d) careers link individuals to the social structure.

Fusing the objective and the subjective. For Hughes and his students, the critical property of a career was its ontological duality. Career was a Janus-like concept that oriented attention simultaneously in two directions (Becker 1963b:24; Becker and Carper 1956a:289; Braude 1975:141; Faulkner 1974:132; Goffman 1961:127; Hughes 1937:403). On one hand, careers pointed to those institutional forms of participation characteristic of some social world: a stream of more or less identifiable positions, offices, statuses, and situations that served as landmarks for gauging a person's movement through the social milieu. These constituted the "objective" face of the career, its structural or public aspect, which could be studied in terms of career lines whose branchings hinged on the turning points and contingencies that members of the social world routinely confronted.

On the other hand, the notion pointed away from the career's structure toward the individual's experience of the career's unfolding. This, the so-called subjective face of the career, consisted of the meanings individuals attributed to their careers, the sense they made of their becoming (Stebbins 1970). Subjective careers involved accounts (Scott and Lyman 1968) or definitions of the situation (McHugh 1968) that enabled individuals to align themselves with the events of their biographies. Subjective careers evidenced themselves in the tales people told to lend coherence to the strands of their life. But most importantly, subjective careers changed with time as individuals shifted their social footing and reconstrued their past and future in order to come to terms with their present (Faulkner 1974:168–169; Strauss 1959:92).

The notion that careers have both objective and subjective elements survives in most modern texts. However, with notable exceptions (Bailyn 1980, 1982; Schein 1971, 1978, 1984; Van Maanen 1977, 1980; Van Maanen and Schein, 1979) recent streams of research focus more or less exclusively on one aspect or the other. In general, psychologically oriented researchers have shown greater interest in subjective interpretations whereas contemporary sociologists have made the objective career their central concern.[7] To be sure, much of value has been learned by attending to a single face of career's duality. However, it is important to recognize that pursuing either aspect in isolation from the other violates the integrity of Hughes's original conception. Hughes insisted that career's two faces were inseparable and that only by attending to both could one fully grasp the social processes to which careers gave analysts access. As if to underscore the inseparability, Chicago sociologists spoke of careers as a series of "status passages" (Glaser and Strauss 1971).

Status passages. "Status passage" was a term borrowed from anthropology where it denoted those ritual occasions when an individual's being was publicly transformed in the eyes of the culture: occasions such as birth, puberty, marriage, and death (Van Gennep 1960; see also Chapter 19). Such ritualized passages typically occurred in a fixed sequence at times ordained by tradition. In appropriating the term, the Chicago sociologists loosened the connotation of temporal regularity. Career transitions in some contexts might indeed unfold according to a rigid timetable. In fact, such regularity was said to be the aim of career planning in formal organizations (Strauss 1959). But status passages in other contexts need be neither formally mandated nor socially celebrated (Strauss 1968). Transitions from one status to another might even occur imperceptibly, as when a physician suddenly realizes that for years he has been functioning as more of an administrator than a doctor (Hughes 1955; Strauss 1968). In fact, some turning points may be completely unpredictable, as when a person's career trajectory is suddenly altered by war or recession (Hughes 1958b).

Thus, from the concept of status passage, Hughes and his students retained the idea that careers unfold in stages while discarding any claim that stages were temporally fixed. However, the Chicago sociologists did not gravitate to the notion of status passage primarily for its imagery of stages. After all, stage thinking had been present in the work of Cressey (1932) and other early analysts of life histories. Instead, it appears that Hughes's students adopted the language of status passages to underscore career's duality.

A status passage connotes not only a temporally staged shift from one social role to another but also a fundamental change in an individual's identity, an alteration in the person's conception of self (Glaser and Strauss 1971; Strauss 1959). As a role shift, a status passage invokes a change in how one presents oneself to others, a change in how one is treated by others, and in many instances, a change in one's interactional partners. But unlike Linton (1936), Parsons (1951), and other functionalists, the Chicago sociologists did not conceive of roles as predefined sets of rights and duties that could be donned and doffed as easily as a well-tailored suit of clothes.[8] Instead, they subscribed to Mead's (1934) notion that roles emerge in an ongoing process of negotiation, a "conversation of gestures" during which individuals develop a repertoire of behaviors and attitudes tailored to specific interactional partners. Role shifts therefore involved "role making" as well as "role taking" and, hence, allowed for variation in the playing of roles (McCall and Simmons 1978; Turner 1962).[9]

Whereas roles referenced the setting's interaction structure, identities referred to the stable definitions of self that enabled persons to enact their roles. Role looked outward toward a pattern of situated activity, whereas identity looked inward toward the actor's subjective experience of that situated being. Role and identity were therefore opposite sides of the same social coin (McCall and Simmons 1978).[10] In Mead's social psychology, identity formation pivoted on the process of naming, the attribution by others and the incorporation by self of a social label to which others orient in interaction and by which actors announce themselves to the world (Gross and Stone 1964; Stone 1962; Strauss 1959). Identities enable people to ascribe meaning and purpose to their actions and, by retrospective construction, to the flow of their lives. As such, identities encapsulate the experience of a role and constitute the basis for developing commitment to a situated self, a sense of the particular me I am here (Stryker and Serpe 1982). The mirror-like relation between role and identity enabled the Chicago sociologists to ground their claim for career's diachronic duality in the synchronic duality of its constituent parts. As Rock (1979:135) put it, the upshot was that Hughes and his students portrayed careers as joint matters of "phasing" and "phrasing."

Careers as properties of collectives. The framing of careers in terms of status passages, roles, and identities shifted attention from the individual as a psychological being to the individual as a social being. As social beings, persons are defined less by their uniqueness than by their membership in a category of actors that populate some setting (Goffman 1961:127). To be sure, careers remained something that only individuals could experience, but they were not solely of the individuals' making. Persons might willfully choose between different courses of action as they progressed through a career. They might even dare to hope and plan. But the options they foresaw and the choices they made were always limited by contextually defined possibilities. Careers, then, were pieced together from the string of alternatives and the set of interpretive resources offered individuals at any point in time by the collectives to which they belonged. As Van Maanen quipped (1977), people don't make careers, careers make people.

Consistent with this line of thinking was the Chicago sociologists' claim that career lines can exist only when a number of individuals have followed the same path. For only when the path is socially recognized can the individual draw from the career a ratified identity (Goffman 1961; Roth 1963). Moreover, to have a "phrased" or socially meaningful career requires individuals to orient themselves to some reference group (Shibutani 1962), which, as Roth (1963:94) noted, need not imply face-to-face contact. Reference groups provide actors with models of the career paths available, with cues for judging career progress, and with a terminology for staking down one's identity and making sense of one's role (Van Maanen 1980). Careers were therefore seen as enacted attributes of the collectives to which individuals belonged. But at the same time that the career made the individual, the individual instantiated the social reality of the career and, by extension, the collective that underwrote its terms (Goffman 1961).

Link between individual and social structure. This latter strand of thought heralds back to Thomas's claim that institutions must be understood in terms of how they influence people's lives. In comparison to Thomas, however, Hughes's students envisioned careers to have a more recursive role in the linking of persons to institutions. Careers were not merely an avenue by which established institutions shaped people's lives; they simultaneously ensured the institution's very existence. For although a person's life might have little meaning outside the context of institutional patterns, institutions could have no reality independent of the lives they shaped:

A study of careers...may be expected to reveal the nature and "working constitution" of a society. Institutions are but the forms in which the collective behavior and collective action of people go on. (Hughes 1937:67)

The study of careers was therefore said to provide access to the empirical relation between social action and social structure. This aim was explicit in Becker and Strauss's (1956:253) claim that the agenda of a sociological theory of career should be "a fairly comprehensive statement about careers as related to both institutions and to persons."

That the Chicago sociologists ultimately failed to synthesize such a comprehensive statement was due, in part, to their cultured proclivity to relegate formal theory to secondary status in favor of ethnographic immersion in the patterned particulars of social settings (Rock 1979). This is not to say, however, that the Chicago sociologists did not pursue the agenda they set for themselves but only that the pieces of their fledgling theory lie scattered among the findings of a variety of studies that were never systematically ordered under a theoretical umbrella. It has therefore been relatively easy for later researchers to pick up the pieces of the unconnected puzzle that Hughes and his students were collecting without fully realizing that the picture under construction was a panorama of the constitution of society rather than a portrait of careers themselves.

CAREERS, INSTITUTIONS, AND THE SOCIAL ORDER

In retrospect, Hughes and his students appear to have glimpsed a vision of social order and change similar to that explicated by Anthony Giddens in his recent work on "structuration theory" (Giddens 1976, 1979, 1984). Like Giddens (1979:69), the Chicago sociologists were interested in the recursion by which institutions jointly "constitute" and are "constituted by" the actions of individuals living their daily lives. Indeed, the conjunction between Giddens's theory and the Chicago school's conception of career may prove fortuitous, not only for structuration theory's maturation but also for career research's future. The Chicago sociologists' notion of career offers structuration theory a much needed point of contact with the empirical world and might even serve as a means by which the theory's practicality can finally be shown. On the other hand, Giddens's theory offers career research a developed conceptual structure consistent with the vision under which the Chicago sociologists labored but were neither able to articulate fully nor achieve. Cross-fertilization might therefore rekindle among career theorists the broad sense of sociological purpose that first drove Chicago sociologists to begin research on careers. To see how career studies could address the question of how social order is possible, consider briefly how careers might be construed within Giddens's framework.

Giddens postulates two realms of social organization: the institutional and the interactional (see Figure 3.1).[11] The *institutional realm* represents a social system's logic: an abstract framework of relations derived from a cumulative history of action and interaction. According to Giddens, institutional orders consist of what Simmel would have called "forms" of signification, domination, and legitimation. One might think of these, respectively, as a system of symbolic codes, a power structure, and a corpus of moral mandates, all of which entwine and reinforce each other. In contrast, the *interactional realm* refers to arrangements of people, objects, and events in the minute-by-minute flow of social life's unfold-

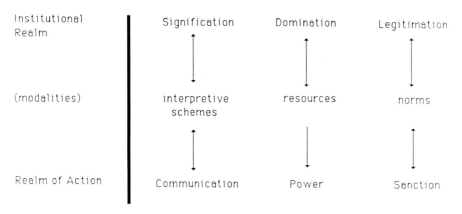

Figure 3.1. Giddens' model of structuration

ing. At the level of interaction the three institutional forms "inform" specific acts of communication, power, and sanction. Institutions are able to inform ongoing action to the degree their systems of signification, domination, and legitimation become part of an actor's stock of practical knowledge, which consists, in turn, of interpretive schemes, resources, and norms. These elements of practical knowledge, which Giddens calls *modalities*, can profitably be construed as a set of *scripts* that encode contextually appropriate behaviors and perceptions (Barley 1986; Schank and Abelson 1977). Scripts may be thought of as plans for recurrent patterns of action that define, in observable terms, the essence of actors' roles. To the degree that institutional forms influence ongoing action via the enactment of scripts that encode the institution's logic, the institution can be said to be reproduced, for institutions can have no existence independent of their instantiation in daily life.

If, as the Chicago sociologists suggested, careers are abstracts of an individual's history of participation in a social collective, if career paths can be construed as plans for participating in a collective, and if careers entail dynamics that link individuals to institutions, then their role in the structuration process can be readily conceived.[12] As portrayed in Figure 3.2, careers can be thought of as temporally extended scripts that mediate between institutions and interactions. Like all scripts, careers should therefore offer actors interpretive schemes, resources, and norms for fashioning a course through some social world. Even though this view of career's role in the structuring process may at first appear daunting, if not grandiose, it is important to note that Hughes's students have already written of careers in surprisingly similar terms. The reader will recall that interpretive schemes and subcultural norms represented a large portion of what Hughes and his students discussed under the heading of the subjective career (Becker and Carper 1956a, b; Faulkner 1973, 1974; Goldner 1965; Marcson 1960; Roth 1963; Van Maanen 1977). Similarly, Chicago sociologists repeatedly depicted the "objective" career's stream of roles as a device for allocating resources and authority (Becker 1963a; Dalton 1951; Hall 1948, 1949; Riesman and Roseborough 1955). Thus, in adopting the perspective of structuration theory, career researchers would be following Hughes's lead in attempting to show how specific insti-

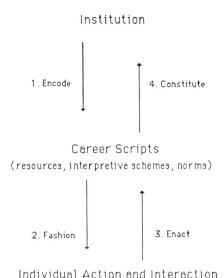

Figure 3.2. Career's role in the structuring process

tutions are maintained or altered by careers' capacities to organize the sequence and meaning of people's lives.

To fully investigate career's role in the structuring process requires attending to both interfaces diagrammed in Figure 3.2. Studies would need to examine the link between career scripts and patterns of interaction as well as the relation between such scripts and the institutions they encode. In the first case, the aim would be to show how career scripts provide resources, interpretive schemes, and norms that shape people's actions and how their actions, in turn, modify career scripts. Exploring the second interface would entail identifying the scripted alternatives that specific institutions provide and then showing how changes in career scripts eventually alter institutions. In practice, this dual focus would require longitudinal studies of social systems that would allow one to explicate the four analytically distinct dynamics that are depicted as arrows in Figure 3.2.

First, researchers would need to examine how career scripts encode forms of signification, domination, and legitimation (arrow 1). Second, researchers would need to show how actors draw on these scripts to fashion meaningful biographies whose patterns are consistent with institutional forms (arrow 2). Third, analysts would need to scrutinize both the subjective and the objective aspects of actual careers to determine the degree to which they follow the scripts that the collective has traditionally offered (arrow 3). Finally, researchers would need to address the issue of how the scripted attributes of actual careers reproduce or alter institutional forms (arrow 4). Each of these four dynamics could be traced in terms of either the resources, the interpretive schemes, or the norms associated with a career's script.

Although structuration theory suggests a general analytic strategy for studying links between careers and institutions, it is essentially a theory of process that offers few specific suggestions for empirical content. If career theorists are to seriously investigate career's role in the structuring process, they will therefore need to determine for themselves the specific referents to which they should attend. At this point, the studies conducted by Hughes and his students prove especially useful. For although the Chicago-trained sociologists undertook no investigations that might serve as fully articulated exemplars, scattered among their reports are clues to the dynamics that compose the structuring process. Consider but two topics that might prove useful to researchers interested in careers and the structuring process: (a) the role of interpretations in the structuring of action and (b) the compatibility between a career's topography and the institution's system of domination. These two topics are sufficient for illustrating how researchers might make more concrete the script–interaction and the script–institution interfaces depicted in Figure 3.2.

Careers, interpretive schemes, and the structuring of power

Most Chicago-inspired career research consisted of detailed descriptions of how members of groups acquire and utilize occupationally specific perspectives for interpreting the events, objects, and people that populate their work (Becker et al. 1961; Davis 1968; Roth 1963; Schein 1971; Van Maanen 1973, 1975). For this reason, Chicago sociologists regularly equated a career's unfolding with the process of adult socialization (Becker and Strauss 1956). In their view, adult socialization consisted largely of learning sanctioned accounts for justifying one's position in the social order in which one was embedded. Thus, in sharp contrast to those who argued that motives and needs prefigured an individual's career (Holland 1973; Roe 1956; Super 1957), the Chicago sociologists claimed that careers actually prefigured motives. Career-specific motives, in turn, served the institution at least as well as they served the individual:

Passage from one [status] to another involves not only changes of action and demeanor, but of the verbalized reasons that are associated with them. Indeed the stability of a given social structure rests largely upon a proper preparation of these sequential steps. Motivations appropriate to earlier – and usually lower – status must be sloughed off and transmuted, and new ones added or substituted ... At any step of this complicated drama of progression, things will go awry if the actors lag behind or speed up unduly in their action or rationale. (Strauss 1959:73)

Career transitions were said to trigger new encounters through which one learns to construe one's actions and the actions of others in terms appropriate for a person of one's new standing. The interpretive shifts that attend career transitions involve more than simply "learning the ropes"; they also entail appropriation of what C. Wright Mills (1940) called a "vocabulary of motive." A vocabulary of motive is a rhetoric typical of the occupants of a specific status. Such rhetorics provide an idiom for justifying one's action, for signaling one's status, and for convincing oneself of the justice of one's fate and the fate of others. Because such idioms characterize specific groups, reference groups should function as distinct speech communities. Hence, mid-level managers and foremen, for instance, should justify identical events differently. Similarly, researchers should view academic policy in a somewhat different light than their colleagues who see themselves primarily as teachers. For as Foote (1951:17) argued, the vocabularies that accompany career transitions act as seed crystals for the formation of an occupational identity: "A rose by any other name may smell as sweet, but a person by another name will act according to that name." Motives, then, are collectively shared social constructions employed in the service of accounts that enable persons to orient to what might otherwise be mistaken for the purely objective circumstances of their careers.

Faulkner's (1973, 1974) comparative study of professional hockey players and classical musicians provides an example of the role rhetorics may play in bringing individual actions in line with institutional requirements. The viability of the system by which major leagues use minor leagues as breeding grounds for personnel depends on the continued motivation of those with objectively slim chances of making the majors. Faulkner argues that hockey players and musicians implicitly support the farming system by learning from each other how to appropriately resign themselves to a career played more or less completely in the minors. As the probability of moving beyond the minors declines, players systematically alter their interpretations of their career to emphasize the benefits of continued participation in the minor leagues. Faulkner notes that only by such modifications could the institution continue to generate individual commitment in the face of what would otherwise be disappointment.

The Chicago sociologists were frequently faulted for overemphasizing subjectivity. Critics have charged that people's perceptions of their careers inaccurately reflect objective reality and that their interpretations are bound to specific contexts (Rosenbaum 1984:3–13). From the vantage point of understanding a career's role in the structuring process, both charges miss the mark. Whether or not subjective interpretations accurately describe a person's objective career is irrelevant. What counts is whether such interpretations spur individuals to accept or reject the institutions their careers encode. For instance, to the degree that perceptions enable individuals to discount inequities, their very inaccuracy supports the inequities' continuation. The adequacy of the details of career accounts are therefore not nearly as important as the way their themes articulate with the surrounding social order (Schein 1984).

In fact, to explore adequately the role careers play in the structuring process may require more, rather than less, attention to how individuals account for their careers. What are needed are longitudinal studies of how career accounts shift with each status passage of a career. If career scripts provide vocabularies keyed to status changes, then we would expect people of similar status to offer similar interpretations. Moreover, we would expect individuals to modify their interpretations of objects, events, and people in systematic ways as they move from one position to another. Although focused on only one such transition, Davis's (1968) investigation of student nurses, Becker et al.'s (1961) work on medical students, and Van Maanen's (1973, 1975) research on rookie police were all studies of how newcomers learn vocabularies of motive that sustain ingrained institutions. To treat these and other such studies as simple ethnographies of adult socialization is thus to oversimplify their message.

If the Chicago school's emphasis on subjective careers is to be faulted, the fault lies, then, not with its interest in bounded interpretive schemes, but with its tendency to focus on institutional stability. Although the Chicago sociologists frequently wrote of how changing interpretations could shift the footing of interaction, they rarely linked such changes to alterations in an institution's structure. In part, the emphasis on stability followed from the tradition's tendency to focus on people's membership in one specific social system. In reality, however, individuals are generally embedded in several institutions simultaneously (Schein 1978). When people belong to multiple social systems that offer competing interpretations of one's fate, it is quite likely that subcultural forces for institutional change will arise. For instance, when employees are simultaneously members of organizational and occupational cultures, competing schemes for understanding one's work and one's career are generally available. Resolution in favor of one institution or the other is rarely a foregone conclusion (Van Maanen and Barley 1984). To understand the role career scripts play in modifying institutional forms will require career researchers to pay attention to the dynamics by which potentially conflicting interpretations arise, how their clash influences an individual's actions, and how new forms of action eventually modify the institution's traditions.

Career topography and systems of domination

To completely articulate career's role in the structuring process will also require investigators to step beyond the question of how individuals are led to accept or reject a collective's career scripts. In addition, researchers need to verify that differently structured careers, in fact, sustain differently ordered institutions. The crucial question is whether certain types of careers are more frequently associated with different institutional forms. If differential association cannot be shown, then the model of career's role in the structuration process breaks down.

A particularly fruitful line of research in this direction would be to investigate the association between specific institutional forms and the syntagmatic structures of career scripts. To pursue such studies would require a taxonomy of career topographies. Although Chicago sociologists usually concerned themselves with subjective careers, several have suggested that an objective career's pattern may in and of itself contribute to the maintenance of social systems. Like the juxtaposition of words in a sentence, a series of statuses can be said to have syntactical properties that influence how people interpret their biographies. This notion was most fully developed by researchers who studied how organizations manage to "cool out" those who fail to advance in a hierarchy of authority or prestige. A career composed of constant lateral movements, of alternating movements up and down the levels of a hierarchy, or of a sequence of positions lacking clear distinction in prestige apparently mitigates perceptions of demotion or stagnation and thereby sustains an individual's commitment to the collective (Clark 1960; Faulkner 1973, 1974; Goldner 1965; Martin and Strauss 1959). If so, the syntactical structures of such scripts should be particularly important for reproducing stratified systems whose stability may depend more on having complacent losers than on having eager winners.

Although career theorists have done little work on the classification of career structures, the literature does contain several potentially useful dichotomies. For instance, Wilensky (1961) distinguished between "orderly" and "disorderly" careers: a dichotomy that rests on the extent to which succeeding positions require incumbency in the immediately preceding position. The syntax of an orderly career can be specified as a chain of statuses in which earlier roles are necessary but insufficient conditions for assuming later roles. In contrast, the linking of positions in a disorderly career would entail neither necessity nor sufficiency.

A second scheme, more widely discussed but rarely investigated, contrasts "vertical" to "horizontal" careers. A vertical career's syntax may be thought to encode movements to successively higher levels of a stratification system and hence entry into successively more elite social networks. A horizontal career's syntax could be specified as movement toward a more central position in a social network located at a specific level of a stratification system. Vertical careers are therefore more likely to trace increments in formal authority, whereas horizontal careers are more likely to encode increments in prestige or expertise. Spatial and temporal properties might also be used to distinguish the syntax of different career scripts. For example, one might depict a career's structure in terms of the identity of the collective in which each status occurred or by the geographic distance the individual traveled in order to assume each successive role. Similarly, researchers could compile a taxonomy of career scripts in terms of temporal profiles that measure the lag between successive status transitions.

Although researchers have produced few studies that systematically link the syntax of career scripts to specific institutional arrangements, hints that such links exist can be found in several sociological studies of career structure. Wilensky's (1961) data suggested that in comparison to individuals with disorderly careers, those with orderly careers were more likely to be involved in the maintenance of a community's infrastructure: its churches, schools, and civic organizations. Orderly careers also appeared to be more conducive to stable kinship patterns. On the other hand, Peterson and Wiegand (1985) have argued that disorderly and geographically transient careers may be crucial for the survival of certain organizational populations that rely on the low wages of the shadow economy.

Baron and Bielby's (1984) recent study showed that finely graded vertical career scripts are more prevalent in firms at an industry's center than in firms on the industry's periphery. One might hypothesize that vertical and horizontal scripts might also be associated with different forms of social integration. Specifically, horizontal scripts may be more closely tied to mechanical forms of solidarity (Van Maanen and Barley 1984). Data consistent with such a hypothesis are to be found in Wilensky's (1961) paper on disorderly careers. Although Wilensky did not perform the calculations himself, his data (Table 1, p. 526) suggests that 71% of his respondents who had horizontal careers also had orderly careers (Wilensky 1961, Table 1). In contrast, only 22% of those with vertical careers had orderly careers. Because Wilensky's research showed that having an orderly career contributes to involvement in institutions associated with mechanical forms of solidarity, one might argue that the tendency toward *Gemeinshaft* forms of organizing should be even stronger among those whose careers have horizontal syntax. One might extend the argument further by hypothesizing that vertical careers are likely to be associated with the breakdown of traditional communal institutions. If so, the finding would cast a very different light on our society's tendency to promulgate the myth of the vertical career's superiority.[13]

Finally, Rosenbaum's (1979, 1984) work on career paths in a large organization implies that different temporal profiles may assist in the replication of a society's stratification system within the confines of an industrial organization. Holding initial positions constant, Rosenbaum found that rapid rates of advancement early in a vertical career were enjoyed more frequently by those with greater formal education. One might hypothesize that differential rates of career transition may also characterize individuals of different race, gender, and age. If so, the temporal structure of vertical careers might operate as a subtle mechanism for reproducing a multiplex stratification system while otherwise appearing to satisfy a philosophy of equal opportunity. Representatives of underprivileged groups would still advance, but at slower rates. Because advancement opportunities appear to decline with age (Lawrence 1984; Rosenbaum 1984), a progressively smaller proportion of the minority group would arrive at successively higher strata before their age prohibited further advancement. The upshot would be to ensure that the top positions in a hierarchy remain heavily populated by majority group members but that there are enough minorities in mid-level positions to diffuse charges of blatant discrimination.

CONCLUSION

As the preceding examples suggest, from the vantage point of structuration theory the term "institution" connotes far more than the formal properties of organizations and occupations. Although systematic relations between organizations, occupations, and the attributes of careers are surely important matters of investigation, structuration extends career theory's scope beyond the contours of occupations and organizations to the structure of industrial employment itself. In fact, to fully chart the articulation of careers and social institutions, analysts must eventually look beyond even relations of production to the family, to religion, and to the structure of communities. The structuration perspective would therefore admonish career theorists to extend their purview to the very fortunes of society itself (Glaser 1968:15).

With declining opportunities for employment in manufacturing, a steadily increasing proportion of the labor force is to be found in the service and information sectors of the economy (Porat 1976). Careers in these sectors are likely to have structures quite different from those associated with employment in the industrial sector. For instance, technical occupations are typically associated with labor markets that span organizational boundaries and geographical distances (Kling and Gerson 1978; Pape 1964; Whalley 1986). If an increasing proportion of the population enters technically oriented careers, then one might expect a number of long-term social changes. Enhanced mobility, for example, may lead to further breakdown in the already atomized structure of the Western family. Greater mobility may also accelerate the demise of closely knit communities and the stability of infrastructural organizations such as churches, schools, and civic leagues. Although at first glance such changes seem to forbode increasing anomie, it is important to recognize that the rise of technical careers may also foster other institutional forms that may act as a countervailing force. For instance, technical specialties typically offer career scripts and social identities propitious for the development of occupational communities and the loosening of organizational control (Van Maanen and Barley 1984). Occupational communities are work-specific collectives that may substitute for certain of the benefits traditionally associated with stable kinship structures and community ties. Nevertheless, such a world would surely consist of institutions whose forms are radically different from those that have populated our society's past, and it is unclear whether more than a small minority of the population would be in a position to take advantage of their benefits.

Ultimately, it is to the rise and fall of such social forms and their implications for the quality of people's lives that career theorists interested in structuration theory would seek to speak. In fact, if researchers were to once again turn concerted attention to how careers function as mechanisms for linking persons to institutions, career theory might find itself at the very vanguard of organization studies. The puzzle of how action and structure are bound lies at the core of the all-too-artificial division of labor that currently separates micro-organizational from macro-organizational behavior. In positioning itself to bridge this gap by recovering the baton Hughes once carried, career theory might take a small step toward the illusive dream of a unified science of social organization.

NOTES

1 For instance, a comprehensive intellectual history of career theory not only would require a careful investigation of those sociological traditions that are glossed in the present text, but would also necessitate attending to lines of inquiry that have their roots planted more firmly in psychological theory. One key issue in such a study would be to account for the process by which various sociological and psychological concerns fused to form a hybrid specialty. As the text makes amply clear, the present essay focuses exclusively on sociologically informed career research conducted by American sociologists whose roots can be traced to the University of Chicago in the first half of the twentieth century. As such, I am concerned only with one branch of modern career theory's genealogical tree.

2 The following account of the Chicago school's early years draws broadly on Faris's (1967) history of the department's development and on Rock's (1979) and Lewis and Smith's (1980) informative discussions of the school's intellectual roots.

3 Rock's (1979) exegesis provides a thorough and convincing account of the centrality of Simmel's thought in the development of early Chicago sociology. Braude (1970) offered a clever indicator of Simmel's importance relative to that of Durkheim and Weber: In Park and Burgess's (1921) classic text Introduction to the Science of Sociology, Simmel received 43 citations, Durkheim 25, and Weber 3.

4 The life history data in Anderson's (1923) account were, in fact, autobiographical, for Anderson had been a hobo before entering the doctoral program at Chicago.

5 However, Shaw and others did edit their informant's grammar, at least in those life histories that were actually published.

6 Explicit testimony to the Chicago sociologist's studied stance toward conceptual heuristics can be found in Strauss's (1959:9–10) justification for using the concept of identity as an analytic tool: "Identity is not a new word, any more than is ego or self; and like these latter terms its referents are ... admittedly vague. But the notion of identity has served me ... as an agent for organizing materials and thoughts about certain aspects of problems traditionally intriguing to social psychologists. In thinking about those problems I experienced ... a kind of partial paralysis that seizes one when he operates with conventional concepts. By deliberately choosing an ambiguous, diffuse term like identity I sensed that I could better look around the corners of my problems, and be less likely to slide down the well worn grooves of other men's thought."

7 In fact, under the umbrella of dual and internal labor market theory, sociological studies of career structures have enjoyed something of a resurgence (Baron and Bielby 1980; Rosenbaum 1979, 1984; Spilerman 1977; White 1970).

8 For further elaboration on an interactionist notion of role and how it differs from role as portrayed by Parsons and Linton, consult Turner (1956, 1962, 1968, 1978), McCall and Simmons (1978), Stryker and Serpe (1982), Colomy and Rhoades (1983), and Zurcher (1983).

9 Because role taking and making generally require interacting with others who have already defined their roles and their expectations of others, status passages were thought to trigger a process of acculturation that assured some measure of continuity with the past. Moreover, by definition, role-related behaviors, no matter how innovative, eventually become routinized and serve as the warrant by which individuals treat themselves

and each other as predictable social objects. To the degree that the making and taking of roles result in patterned continuity, they ensure the preservation of social relations in the face of turnover among players. For the Chicago sociologists, roles constituted the elementary units of a setting's social structure. Role taking and making, in turn, were the dynamics by which the structure was replicated or changed.

10 McCall and Simmons (1978) coined the term "role-identity" to underscore the inseparability of the two notions.

11 Giddens (1984) uses the term "structure" instead of "institution." I have chosen to depart from his usage to keep the language more consistent with the language used by Hughes. Both usages are in fact quite consistent with Gidden's own discussions.

12 One should not conclude from the diagrams or the discussion that careers are the only phenomena that mediate the connection between the institutional and the interactional realms. Structuring takes place through a variety of modalities. For instance, one could study family, political, and other work practices from the perspective of structuration theory. For an example of structuration research that deals with technology rather than careers, consult Barley (1986).

13 Ed Schein (personal communication) has noted that vertical careers foster and are consistent with a cultural assumption of individualism. One might therefore find a rather different orientation toward vertical careers if one were to compare the meaning of careers in America and Japan.

REFERENCES

Anderson, N. (1923). *The Hobo: The Sociology of the Homeless Man.* Chicago: University of Chicago Press.

Bailyn, L. (1980). *Living with Technology: Issues at Mid-Career.* Cambridge, MA: MIT Press.

Bailyn, L. (1982). Resolving contradictions in technical careers. *Technology Review,* October, pp. 40–47.

Bailyn, L. (1985). Autonomy in the industrial R&D lab. *Human Resource Management, 24,* 129–146.

Barley, S. R. (1986). Technology as an occasion for structuring: evidence from observations of CT scanners and the social order of radiology departments. *Administrative Science Quarterly, 31,* 78–108.

Baron, J. N., and Bielby, W. T. (1980). Bringing the firm back in: stratification, segmentation, and the organization of work. *American Sociological Review, 45,* 737–765.

Baron, J. N., and Bielby, W. T. (1984). The organization of work in a segmented economy. *American Sociological Review, 49,* 454–473.

Becker, H. S. (1951). Role and career problems of the Chicago public school teacher. Ph.D. dissertation. University of Chicago.

Becker, H. S. (1952). The career of the Chicago public schoolteacher. *American Journal of Sociology, 57,* 470–477.

Becker, H. S. (1953a). Becoming a marihuana user. *American Journal of Sociology, 59,* 235–242.

Becker, H. S. (1953b). Some contingencies of the professional dance musician's career. *Human Organization, 12,* 22–26.

Becker, H. S. (1961). The implications of research on occupational careers for a model of household decision-making. In N. Foote (ed.), *Household Decision Making.* New York: New York University Press, pp. 239–254.

Becker, H. S. (1963a). Careers in a deviant occupational group. In *Outsiders.* Glencoe, IL: Free Press, pp. 101–119.

Becker, H. S. (1963b). Kinds of deviance. In *Outsiders.* Glencoe, IL: Free Press, pp. 19–40.

Becker, H. S. (1963c). Marihuana use and social control. In *Outsiders.* Glencoe, IL: Free Press, pp. 59–78.

Becker, H. S., and Carper, J. W. (1956a). The development of identification with an occupation. *American Journal of Sociology, 61,* 289–298.

Becker, H. S., and Carper, J. (1956b). The elements of identification with an occupation. *American Sociological Review, 21,* 341–348.

Becker, H. S., Geer, B., Hughes, E. C., and Strauss, A. L. (1961). *Boys in White.* Chicago: University of Chicago Press.

Becker, H. S., and Strauss, A. L. (1956). Careers, personality, and adult socialization. *American Journal of Sociology, 62,* 253–263.

Braude, L. (1970). "Park and Burgess": an appreciation. *American Journal of Sociology, 76,* 1–10.

Braude, L. (1975). *Work and Workers: A Sociological Analysis.* New York: Praeger.

Clark, B. R. (1960). The "cooling out" function in higher education. *American Journal of Sociology, 65,* 569–576.

Colomy, P., and Rhoades, G. (1983). Role performance and person perception: toward an interactionist approach. *Symbolic Interaction, 6,* 207–227.

Crane, D. (1972). *Invisible Colleges: Diffusion of Knowledge in Scientific Communities.* Chicago: University of Chicago Press.

Cressey, P. G. (1932). *The Taxi-Dance Hall: A Sociological Study in Commercialized Recreation and City Life.* Chicago: University of Chicago Press.

Dalton, M. (1950). *Men Who Manage.* New York: Wiley.

Dalton, M. (1951). Informal factors in career achievement. *American Journal of Sociology, 61,* 407–415.

Davis, F. (1963). *Passage Through Crisis.* Indianapolis, IN: Bobbs-Merrill.

Davis, F. (1968). Professional socialization as subjective experience: the process of doctrinal conversion among student nurses. In H. S. Becker, B. Geer, D. Riesman, and R. S. Weiss (eds.), *Institutions and the Person.* Chicago: Aldine, pp. 35–48.

de Saussure, F. (1966). *Course in General Linguistics* (translated and edited by W. Baskin). New York: McGraw-Hill.

Driver, M. J. (1980). Career concepts and organizational change. In C. B. Derr (ed.), *Work, Family and Career: New Frontiers in Theory and Research.* New York: Praeger, pp. 5–17.

Eco, U. (1979). *A Theory of Semiotics.* Bloomington, IN: University of Indiana Press.

Farber, B. (1961). The family as a set of mutually contingent careers. In N. Foote (ed.), *Household Decision-Making.* New York: New York University Press, pp. 276–298.

Faris, R. E. L. (1967). *Chicago Sociology, 1920–1932.* Chicago: University of Chicago Press.

Faulkner, R. R. (1973). Career concerns and mobility motivations of orchestra musicians. *The Sociological Quarterly, 14,* 334–349.

Faulkner, R. R. (1974). Coming of age in organizations: a comparative study of career contingencies and adult socialization. *Sociology of Work and Occupations, 1,* 131–173.

Faulkner, R. R. (1983). *Music on Demand: Composers and Careers in the Hollywood Film Industry.* New Brunswick, NJ: Transaction.

Foote, N. N. (1951). Identification as the basis of a theory of motivation. *American Sociological Review, 16,* 14–21.

Frake, C. O. (1964). Notes on queries in ethnography. *American Anthropologist, 66,* 132–145.

Giddens, A. (1976). *New Rules of Sociological Method.* London: Hutchinson.

Giddens. A. (1979). *Central Problems in Social Theory.* Berkeley, CA: University of California Press.

Giddens, A. (1984). *The Constitution of Society.* Berkeley, CA: University of California Press.

Glaser, B. G. (1968). Introduction. In B. G. Glaser (ed.), *Organizational Careers: A Source Book of Theory.* Chicago: Aldine, pp. 1–123.

Glaser, B., and Strauss, A. (1967). *The Discovery of Grounded Theory: Strategies for Qualitative Research.* Chicago: Aldine.

Glaser, B., and Strauss, A. (1971). *Status Passage.* Chicago: Aldine.

Goffman, E. (1961). The moral career of the mental patient. In *Asylums.* New York: Anchor, pp. 125–170.

Gold, R. L. (1964). In the basement: the apartment building janitor. In P. Berger (ed.), *The Human Shape of Work.* South Bend, IN: Gateway, pp. 1–50.

Goldner, F. H. (1965). Demotion in industrial management. *American Sociological Review, 30,* 714–724.

Goodenough, W. H. (1981). *Culture, Language, and Society.* Menlo Park, CA: Benjamin/Cummings.

Gross, E., and Stone, G. P. (1964). Embarrassment and the analysis of role requirements. *American Journal of Sociology, 70,* 1–15.

Habenstein, R. (1954). *The career of the funeral director.* Ph.D. dissertation. University of Chicago.

Hall, D. T. (1976). *Careers in Organizations.* Pacific Palisades, CA: Goodyear.

Hall, O. (1944). The informal organization of medical practice in an American city. Ph.D. dissertation. University of Chicago.

Hall, O. (1948). The stages of a medical career. *American Journal of Sociology, 53,* 327–336.

Hall, O. (1949). Types of medical careers. *American Journal of Sociology, 60,* 243–253.

Hawkes, T. (1977). *Structuralism and Semiotics.* Berkeley, CA: University of California.

Holland, J. L. (1973) *Making Vocational Choices: A Theory of Careers.* Englewood Cliffs, NJ: Prentice-Hall.

Hughes, E. C. (1928). A study of a secular institution: the Chicago real estate board. Ph.D. dissertation. University of Chicago.

Hughes, E. C. (1937). Institutional office and the person. *American Journal of Sociology, 43,* 404–143.

Hughes, E. C. (1955). The making of a physician. *Human Organization, 17,* 21–25.

Hughes, E. C. (1958a). *Men and Their Work.* Glencoe, IL: Free Press.

Hughes, E. C. (1958b). Cycles, turning points, and careers. In *Men and Their Work.* Glencoe, IL: Free Press, pp. 11–22.

Hughes, E. C. (1971). *The Sociological Eye: Selected Papers on Work, Self and The Study of Society.* Chicago: Aldine.

James, W. (1949). *Pragmatism.* New York: Longmans.

Kling, R., and Gerson, E. (1978). Patterns of segmentation and intersection in the computing world. *Symbolic Interaction, 1,* 24–43.

Lawrence, B. S. (1984). Age grading: the implicit organizational timetable. *Journal of Occupational Behaviour, 5,* 23–35.

Levi-Strauss, C. (1963). *Structural Anthropology,* Vol 1. New York: Basic Books.

Lewis, J. D., and Smith, R. L. (1980). *American Sociology and Pragmatism: Mead, Chicago Sociology, and Symbolic Interaction.* Chicago: University of Chicago Press.

Linton, R. (1936). *The Study of Man.* New York: Appleton-Century-Crofts.

McCall, G. J., and Simmons, J. L. (1978). *Identities and Interactions: An Examination of Human Association in Everyday Life.* New York: Free Press.

McHugh, P. (1968). *Defining the Situation: The Organization of Meaning in Social Interaction.* Indianapolis, IN: Bobbs-Merrill.

Marcson, S. (1960). *The Scientist in American Industry.* New York: Harper & Row.

Martin, N. H., and Strauss, A. L. (1956). Patterns of mobility within industrial organizations. *Journal of Business, 29,* 101–110.

Martin, N. H., and Strauss, A. L. (1959). Consequences of failure in organizations. In W. L. Warner and N. H. Martin (eds.), *Industrial Man.* New York: Harper & Row.

Mead, G. H. (1934). *Mind, Self, and Society.* Chicago: University of Chicago Press.

Mills, C. W. (1940). Situated actions and vocabularies of motive. *American Sociological Review, 5,* 904–913.

Pape, R. H. (1964). Touristry: a type of occupational mobility. *Social Problems, 11,* 336–344.

Park, R. E., and Burgess, E. W. (1921). *Introduction to the Science of Sociology.* Chicago: University of Chicago Press.

Parsons, T. (1951). *The Social System.* New York: Free Press.

Peterson, R. A., and Wiegand, B. (1985). Ordering disorderly work careers on skid row. In R. L. Simpson and I. H. Simpson (eds.), *Research in the Sociology of Work,* Vol. 3. Greenwich, CT: JAI, pp. 215–230.

Porat, M. (1976). The information economy. Ph.D. dissertation. Stanford University.

Reimer, J. (1977). Becoming a journeyman electrician. *Sociology of Work and Occupations, 4,* 87–98.

Riesman, D., and Roseborough, H. (1955). Careers and consumer behavior. In L. H. Clark (ed.), *Consumer Behavior: The Life Cycle and Consumer Behavior,* Vol 2. New York: New York University Press, pp. 1–18.

Rock, P. (1979). *The Making of Symbolic Interactionism.* Totowa, NJ: Rowman and Littlefield.

Roe, A. (1956). *The Psychology of Occupations.* New York: Wiley.

Rosenbaum, J. E. (1979). Organizational career mobility: promotion chances in a corporation during periods of growth and contraction. *American Journal of Sociology, 85,* 21–48.

Rosenbaum, J. E. (1984). *Career Mobility in a Corporate Hierarchy.* Orlando, FL: Academic.

Roth, J.A. (1963). *Timetables: Structuring the Passage of Time in Hospital Treatment and Other Careers.* Indianapolis, IN: Bobbs-Merrill.

Schank, R. C., and Abelson, R. P. (1977). *Scripts, Plans, Goals, and Understanding.* Hillsdale, NJ: Erlbaum.

Schein, E. H. (1971). The individual, the organization, and the career: a conceptual scheme. *Journal of Applied Behavioral Science, 7,* 401–426.

Schein, E. H. (1978). *Career Dynamics: Matching Individual and Organizational Needs.* Reading, MA: Addison-Wesley.

Schein, E. H. (1984). Culture as an environmental context for careers. *Journal of Occupational Behaviour, 5,* 71–81.

Schwartz, B. (1981). *Vertical Classification: A Study in Structuralism and the Sociology of Knowledge.* Chicago: University of Chicago Press.

Scott, M., and Lyman, S. (1968). Accounts. *American Journal of Sociology, 33,* 46–62.

Shaw, C. R. (1930). *The Jack-Roller: A Delinquent Boy's Own Story.* Chicago: University of Chicago Press.

Shaw, C. R. (1931). *The Natural History of a Delinquent Career.* Chicago: University of Chicago Press.

Shaw, C. R. (1938). *Brothers in Crime.* Chicago: University of Chicago Press.

Shaw, C. R., Zorbaugh, F. M., McKay, H. D., and Cottrell, L. S. (1929). *Delinquency Areas: A Study of the Geographic Distribution of School Truants, Juvenile Delinquents and Adult Offenders in Chicago.* Chicago: University of Chicago Press.

Shibutani, T. (1962). Reference groups and social control. In A. M. Rose (ed.), *Human Behavior and Social Processes: An Interactionist Approach.* Boston: Houghton Mifflin, pp. 128–147.

Sofer, C. (1970). *Men at Mid-Career.* Cambridge: Cambridge University Press.

Solomon, D. (1952). *Career contingencies of Chicago physicians.* Ph.D. dissertation. University of Chicago.

Solomon, D. (1968). Sociological perspectives on occupations. In H. S. Becker, B. Geer, D. Riesman, and R. S. Weiss (eds.), *Institutions and the Person.* Chicago: Aldine, pp. 3–13.

Spilerman. S. (1977). Careers, labor market structure, and socioeconomic achievement. *American Journal of Sociology, 83,* 551–593.

Stebbins, R. A. (1970). Career: the subjective approach. *Sociological Quarterly, 11,* 32–49.

Stewman, S., and Konda, S. L. (1983). Careers and organizational labor markets: demographic models of organizational behavior. *American Journal of Sociology, 88,* 637–685.

Stone, G. P. (1962). Appearance and the self. In A. M. Rose (ed.), *Human Behavior and Social Processes.* Boston: Houghton Mifflin, pp. 3–19.

Strauss, A. L. (1959). *Mirrors and Masks.* New York: Free Press.

Strauss, A. L. (1968). Some neglected properties of status passage. In H. S. Becker, B. Geer, D. Riesman, and R. S. Weiss (eds.), *Institutions and the Person.* Chicago: Aldine, pp. 235–251.

Stryker, S., and Serpe, R. T. (1982). Commitment, identity salience, and role behavior: theory and research example. In W. Ickes and E. S. Knowles (eds.), *Personality, Roles, and Social Behavior.* New York: Springer-Verlag, pp. 199–218.

Super, D. E. (1957). *The Psychology of Careers.* New York: Harper & Row.

Sutherland, E. H. (1937). *The Professional Thief: By a Professional Thief.* Chicago: University of Chicago Press.

Thomas, W. I. (1923). *The Unadjusted Girl: With Cases and Standpoint for Behavior Analysis.* Boston: Little, Brown.

Thomas, W. I. (1931). The relation of research to the social process. In W. Swann et al. (eds.), *Essays on Research in the Social Sciences.* Washington, DC: Brookings.

Thomas, W. I., and Thomas, D. S. (1928). *The Child in America: Behavior Problems and Programs.* New York: Knopf.

Thomas, W. I., and Znaniecki, F. (1918). *The Polish Peasant in Europe and America.* Chicago: University of Chicago Press.

Thompson, J. D., Avery, R. W., and Carlson, R. O. (1968). Occupations, personnel, and careers. *Educational Administration Quarterly, 4,* 6–31.

Turner, R. H. (1956). Role taking, role standpoint, and reference group behavior. *American Journal of Sociology, 61,* 316–328.

Turner, R. H. (1962). Role taking: process versus conformity. In A. M. Rose (ed.), *Human Behavior and Social Processes.* Boston: Houghton Mifflin, pp. 20–40.

Turner, R. H. (1968). Role: sociological aspects. In D. L. Sills (ed.), *International Encyclopedia of the Social Sciences.* New York: Macmillan, pp. 552–557.

Turner, R. H. (1978). Role and the person. *American Journal of Sociology, 84,* 1–23.

Van Gennep, A. (1960). *Rites of Passage.* Chicago: University of Chicago Press.

Van Maanen, J. (1973). Observations on the making of policemen. *Human Organization, 32,* 407–418.

Van Maanen, J. (1975). Breaking in: a consideration of organizational socialization. In R. Dubin (ed.), *Handbook of Work, Organization, and Society.* Chicago: Rand-McNally.

Van Maanen, J. (1977). Experiencing organization: notes on the meaning of careers and socialization. In J. Van Maanen (ed.), *Organizational Careers: Some New Perspectives.* New York: Wiley, pp. 15–48.

Van Maanen, J. (1980) Career games. In C. B. Derr (ed.), *Work, Family, and the Career.* New York: Prager.

Van Maanen, J., and Barley, S. R. (1984). Occupational communities: culture and control in organizations. In B. Staw and L. Cummings (eds.), *Research in Organizational Behavior,* Vol 6. Greenwich, CT: JAI, pp. 287–365.

Van Maanen, J., and Schein, E. (1979) Toward a theory of organizational socialization. In B. Staw (ed.), *Research in Organizational Behavior,* Vol 6. Greenwich, CT: JAI, pp. 287–365.

Wager, L. W. (1959). Career patterns and role problems of airline pilots. Ph.D. dissertation, University of Chicago.

Weiss, P. R., and Faulkner, R. R. (1983). Credits and draft production: freelance social organization in the Hollywood film industry. *Symbolic Interaction, 6,* 111–123.

Whalley, P. (1986). *The Social Production of Technical Work.* Albany, NY: State University of New York Press.

White, H. C. (1970). *Chains of Opportunity.* Cambridge, MA: Harvard University Press.

Wilensky, H. L. (1960). Careers, life-styles, and social integration. *International Social Science Journal, 12,* 553–558.

Wilensky, H. L. (1961). Orderly careers and social participation: the impact of work history on social integration in the middle mass. *American Sociological Review, 26,* 521–539.

Zurcher, L. A. (1983). *Social Roles: Conformity, Conflict, and Creativity.* Beverly Hills, CA: Sage.

4 The utility of adult development theory in understanding career adjustment process

SOLOMON CYTRYNBAUM AND JOHN O. CRITES

This chapter examines contemporary adult development theory, particularly as it relates to the theory of careers. It presents a case that to more fully understand the processes of career development, one must attend to the dynamics of life course development and adjustment. Thus, we intend to show the benefit of adding the adult development approach to career theory to help reconcile otherwise contradictory findings in the career literature. To illustrate this point, we start with a comprehensive model of career adjustment that integrates adult development concepts with career dynamics. We then move to a review and critical analysis of the current adult development literature.

A MODEL OF CAREER ADJUSTMENT

In a previous paper, Crites (1976) formulated a comprehensive model of career adjustment in which the dynamics of how workers cope with frustrating conditions on the job were delineated. Briefly, Crites viewed the process of career adjustment as one that includes (1) work motives, (2) conflict and frustration, (3) adjustment mechanisms, and (4) job satisfaction and success. Career adjustment was described against a contextual background of such factors as the general cultural and society *milieu*, organizational climate, psychological dispositions and characteristics, and personal and demographic attributes. Crites assumed that the career adjustment process is developmental but did not articulate how it is projected over time. He developed the model only for early adulthood and did not consider middle and later life stages in the work life. Moreover, a fundamental problem concerning the outcomes of the career adjustment process was not examined: Why is it that two of the most critical and apparently complementary components of career adjustment – job success and job satisfaction – have such a low empirical inter-relationship (Crites, 1969)? This section of the chapter addresses this issue by tracing the career adjustment process across the total span of the adult life course.

The elements in the Crites model are depicted in Figure 4.1. According to this model, a worker is motivated by certain needs or drives to attain a desired degree of career satisfaction and success (Astin, 1968; Crites, 1961). Given that there are no obstacles to the achievement of these goals, no adjustments are necessary. But if there are thwarting conditions, either external frustration or internal conflict (Crites, 1969), which intervene between goal attainment and motivation, then the worker must respond to the anxiety and/or tension this "blocking" generates. How effectively the worker responds ultimately determines the quality of

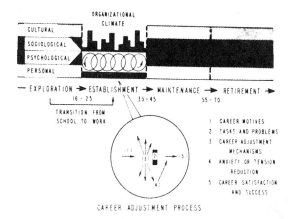

Figure 4.1. Comprehensive model of career adjustment in early adulthood (Crites, 1976)

his or her adjustment. These responses (coping mechanisms) may be more or less integrative, depending upon the extent to which they resolve (eliminate) the thwarting conditions. Projected over time, the criteria (outcomes) of how well the worker has adjusted are the worker's career satisfaction and success. These are considered to be the two principal components of career adjustment, and they are assumed to be complementary (Gellman, 1953; Heron, 1952, 1954; Lofquist and Dawis, 1968; Luria and Weiss, 1942). That is, the satisfied worker should be successful, and the successful worker should be satisfied.

The accumulated empirical research on the interrelationship of career satisfaction and success indicates, however, that they are only negligibly correlated. In their classic review of the literature on this relationship, Brayfield and Crockett (1955) concluded that whatever the definitions, career satisfaction and success were essentially unrelated. Similarly, from studies conducted by the Survey Research Center at the University of Michigan, Kahn (1960, pp. 275, 285–286) observed that "productivity [success] and job satisfaction do not necessarily go together" and that "we should abandon, in our future research, the use of satisfaction or morale indexes as variables intervening between supervisory and organizational characteristics on the one hand, and productivity on the other." Finally, Vroom's review of 120 studies concludes that "there is no simple relationship between job satisfaction and job performance" (1964, p. 186).

This last conclusion has prompted several attempts to explain *why* there is little or no empirical relationship between career satisfaction and success. Most of these explanations have posited some third variable as a *moderator* that accounts for the low (nonsignificant) correlation of career satisfaction with success. For example, Brayfield and Crocket (1955) have proposed that the most salient conditions that may affect the interaction of satisfaction and success are those found in the worker's social environment (1) outside the plant, (2) in relation with co-workers on the job, (3) within the union structure, and (4) in the company (organizational) structure. Morse (1953) has suggested that "strength of needs"

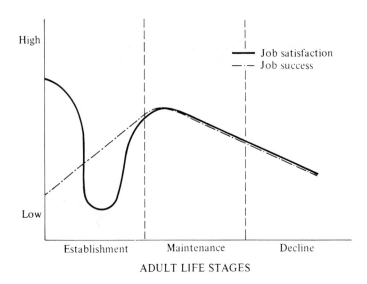

Figure 4.2. Adult life stages and developmental trends in job satisfaction and success

is a third variable that may affect both career satisfaction and success. She hypothesizes that "if a worker's job is rewarding, and if he [sic] has strong needs, then he will be satisfied. If his job is not rewarding, however, his strong needs will make him productive, but he will be dissatisfied" (Crites, 1969, pp. 521–522). Probably the most systematic explanation of this relationship has been that of Triandis (1959), who has hypothesized a "pressure for high production" factor, which has differential effect upon the correlation between career satisfaction and success across the time dimension (Crites, 1969).

A new perspective. None of these "third-variable" explanations of the low relationship between career satisfaction and success has posited adult life stages as a factor that may affect these two supposedly complementary components of career adjustment. Consider, however, first, the development trends in career satisfaction and career success and, second, the longitudinal interface between them as the process of career adjustment unfolds over three of Super's life career strategy (establishment, maintenance, and decline) (see Figure 4.2). There is considerable documentation that career satisfaction follows a cyclical curve. It starts at a high level (upon occupational entry), dips to its nadir during the middle of the establishment stage, when initial expectations of rapid advancement are delayed or thwarted, and then recovers, although not to the previous high level, to an asymptote at about age 40 (Benge and Copwell, 1957; Crites, 1969). In contrast, career success begins at a low ebb and increases linearly from occupational entry to midlife, when an incipient decline sets in. Thus, developmental trends in career satisfaction and success are different across the adult life stages, with the possible exception of their coincidence during midcareer (approximately age 40).

It is their intersect in midlife that suggests a hypothesis to explain the lack of a relationship between career satisfaction and success. During the period between 35 and 40 the development trends in career satisfaction and success have their highest correlation. In contrast, a negative correlation would be expected to occur at the beginning of the work life, at the outset of the establishment stage, when career satisfaction is high and career success is low. Intermediate correlations would be expected between the early establishment and midmaintenance stages. Thus, it is reasonable to assume that past studies have observed little empirical relationship between career satisfaction and success because they collapsed cross-sectional data across different age groups during the adult work life stages, which *canceled out* the effects of career development and adjustment upon the relationship between career satisfaction and success.

Implications for research and intervention

Following the functional mode of hypothesis formulation from the data language level to the theory language level and then back again (Marx, 1951, 1963), the next step in the model-testing process is to design appropriate research from a developmental perspective (Baltes, Reese, and Nesselroade, 1977). The gathering of longitudinal data is necessarily time consuming, but some of the new research designs from life-span developmental psychology shorten this process (e.g., cross-sequential with overlapping cohorts). If empirical evidence confirms the model, there are far-reaching ramifications for both theory and practice. Theoretically, the perplexing problem of why the supposedly complementary outcomes of the career adjustment process, career satisfaction, and career success are not related would be resolved. Projected across the panorama of the adult life course, being viewed longitudinally rather than cross-sectionally, the trends in career satisfaction and success vary from one time frame to another and become highly related only when midcareer is reached. Note that this phenomenon occurs at the beginning of the maintenance stage, *not* at a particular age. A returning woman, for example, who does not reach this stage until 55 or 60 would nevertheless follow the same trends in satisfaction and success (on the average) as a woman who enters the maintenance stage at 35–40.

The implication for practice is that career counseling services and employee development workshops would be oriented toward assisting workers with that facet of career development adjustment, which happens to vary (or deviate) in a given adult life stage. Those who have just entered the world of work typically experience a high level of job satisfaction but are frustrated by slow advancement. From the viewpoint of the career developmental model, their problems will most likely center upon job success. For those later in the establishment stage, when satisfaction lags behind success, their problem may be how to sustain satisfaction until it "catches up" with success. And, paradoxically, workers at the height of the career development adjustment curve, at the beginning of the maintenance stage, may have difficulty with the midcareer crisis of whether to change jobs, because they have attained maximal satisfaction and success, or to continue on with revised aspirations and expectations.

Conclusion: the need to include adult development theory in understanding careers

Whether for theory or practice, then, the adult life stage acts as an important moderator variable in the relationship between career satisfaction and the career development adjustment process. *We would argue further that this satisfaction–success relationship is but one example of the many ways in which career dynamics are affected by life stage development processes.* Although career stages and adult life stages are often used interchangeably (or at least simultaneously), we would argue for a clear separation of the two, so that each one can inform the other.

With the value and the need for an explicit incorporation of adult development concepts into the career literature, we turn to a more detailed examination of the current "state of the art" of adult development theory. We start with a critical review of contemporary adult development research and theory. The implications of gender differences in adult and career development are highlighted. The section concludes with an assessment of persistent dilemmas, including the aforementioned need for better incorporation of adult development theory into theories of career development and adjustment.

THEORIES OF ADULT DEVELOPMENT

Pioneers in the study of adult development

The study of adult development owes much to the pioneering work of Freud (1905), who stressed the importance of developmental processes in early childhood; Van Gennep (1960), who focused on the social implications of major life events such as birth, death, marriage, and divorce for life course development; Jung (1933, 1966); Buehler (1933); and Erikson (1958, 1959, 1963, 1969). Of these, the works of Jung and Erikson have had the most impact.

Jung's interest in adult development pervades his writings. In contrast to his contemporary orthodox Freudian colleagues, Jung saw adulthood, and especially the forties, as a major period of potential psychological individuation, change, and growth. Among other themes, he described how midlife men struggle with the contrasexual opposite or the awareness and integration into personality of the sterotypically "feminine" side of themselves. Midlife women similarly struggle with integrating the more "masculine" aspects of their personalities. Neumann (1959), also writing from a Jungian perspective, offered one of the first systematic descriptions of the psychological development of adult women.

Erikson's psychological theory has greatly influenced subsequent work in adult development. His emphasis on the social context of development, preliminary exploration of gender differences, and identification of the life course developmental tasks and crises can be seen repeatedly in contemporary theory and research. Erikson traces the ego's integration of the social world and infantile psychosexual development through a series of hierarchical ordered stages of personality development from birth to old age. Erikson's eight stages attempt to bridge Freud's theory of infantile sexuality with the child's physical and social growth within the context of family and the larger social structure. Each of Erikson's stages represents a developmental crisis with potential adaptive and pathological outcomes.

Erikson's stages, which have been repeatedly described in detail elsewhere (Erikson, 1963; Hall, 1976), are

trust versus mistrust (ages birth to 2),
autonomy versus shame (ages 2–4),
initiative versus guilt (ages 4–5),
industry versus inferiority (ages 6–12),
identity versus role-diffusion (ages 12–18),
intimacy versus isolation (young adulthood),
generativity versus stagnation (adulthood), and
integrity versus despair (late adulthood).

Erikson hypothesizes an "epigenetic" principle of development. This principle states that development is influenced by the resolution in the proper sequence of each developmental crisis and that each task exists in a predevelopmental form before its critical developmental period arises. The last three stages, intimacy versus isolation, generativity versus stagnation, and ego integrity versus despair encompass adulthood. Contemporary work in adult development has been devoted to elaborating these last three stages.

The influence of Jung and Erikson is evident in the work of several prominent contemporary theorists, including Levinson, Vaillant, Gould, Gutmann, and Neugarten, as the following discussion explicates.

Contemporary theories of adult development

Adult development theories fall into two distinct groups. One group, in the spirit of Erikson, focuses on developmental phases and tasks as they relate to the life course.[1] The other group focuses on psychological and cognitive developments within the person.[2] It is the first group we shall focus on here because of their relative emphasis on the time frames and social contexts in which the person and careers unfold.[3]

The adult development theories that concern us here can be organized along two additional dimensions. The first involves the generalizability of the theory to men, women, or both (as determined by the sample upon which the work was based). The second concerns the extent to which the theory integrates career parameters into the developmental process. Developmental theories can ignore work and career development, incorporate career parameters selectively as part of a particular phase, or fully integrate work and career developmental requirements as integral to the major concepts or as a significant line of development. These parameters were used to generate Table 4.1, which lists relevant adult development theories. The brief review that follows begins with the male-centered theories of Gould and Vaillant. Then, theories that apply to females are presented. And finally, theory and research applicable to both male and female adult development are surveyed.

Gould. From a psychoanalytic perspective, Gould (1975, 1978, 1981) examined the impact of the persistence of deep emotionally based childhood self-protective assumptions concerning the illusion of absolute safety on adult male development. He divided male adult development into four areas, similar to Erikson and Levinson, each with its own self-protective false assumptions, developmental tasks,

Table 4.1. *Classification of contemporary adult development theories by gender generalizability and extent of integration of work and career parameters*

Extent of integration of work and career	Generalizability: theory applies to		
	Males only	Females only	Both
Work and career ignored by theory	Gould, 1978, 1981	—	Pollock, 1981, 1987
Work and career incorporated in one or more phases	Vaillant, 1977	Sales, 1978	Lowenthal et al., 1975
Work and career major component of developmental process	Levinson et al., 1978	Bardwick, 1980; Giele, 1980, 1982; Gilligan, 1980, 1982	Levinson, 1986, in press; Neugarten, 1975, 1979

and conflicts. Adult maturity emerges from challenging and mastering these false assumptions. These assumptions are usually given up intellectually by adolescence, but if they are not given up emotionally at the designated points in the life course, their defensive nature impedes adult development, resulting in stagnation. Gould's phases and false assumptions are summarized from his 1978 book as follows:

> *Leaving our parents' world*, ages 16–22
> Major false assumption: "I'll always belong to my parents and believe in their world." (pp. 47–48)
> *I'm nobody's baby now*, ages 22–28
> Major false assumption: "Doing things my parents' way, with will-power and perseverance, will bring results. But if I become too frustrated, confused, or tired or am simply unable to cope, they will step in and show me the right way." (pp. 75–76)
> *Opening up to what's inside*, ages 28–34
> Major false assumption: "Life is simple and controllable. There are no significant coexisting contradictory forces within me." (p. 153)
> *Midlife decade*, ages 35–45
> Major false assumption: "There is not evil or death in the world. The sinister has been destroyed." (p. 217)

Vaillant. Another male-centered approach is exemplified by Vaillant (1977), who studied a longitudinal subsample of the Harvard Grant Study in order to examine mechanisms of defense and what constituted adaptation and successful intrapsychic development over the male's life course. Vaillant reported that healthier members of the sample used more mature defenses in midlife than in adolescence or young adulthood and that conflict was an inevitable and integral part of development across the life course. He emphasized the importance of career development in this process and identified "career consolidation" as a specific and significant stage of development in the 29–30-year period.

Bardwick and Gilligan. Bardwick (1980) and Gilligan (1980, 1982), among others, have argued strongly for a distinctly separate theory of female adult development. Gilligan's view of the life course development of women emphasizes the importance of relationships and attachments. Bardwick emphasizes that in the early adult transition years during the twenties, even for accomplished professional and career women, traditional roles and interpersonal commitments remain a core part of female identity.

Furthermore, Bardwick believes that the next phase – the settling down period of the second adult life phase (approximately 30–40) – is distinctly different for men and women. For men, she argues that this is a period of enhanced investment in career and, according to Levinson et al. (1978), becoming one's own man. Women, on the other hand, require much more than career and professional success. According to Bardwick, for many women during midlife, careers become unsatisfactory, managing multiple professional and familial roles become too costly, and concerns about femininity and intimate relationships may become paramount, resulting in a major reassessment of career and life patterns.[4]

Pollock. Pollock (1981, 1987) has argued for the possibilities of change throughout the life course, especially during the second half of life. He has also studied different facets of the mourning process in the analytic situation and in the biographies of over 1,500 creative individuals. A striking finding was the high incidence of losses and/or major separations from parents and/or significant others in the early lives of these creative individuals. One of Pollock's major contributions has been to describe the creative potentialities of adaptations to losses throughout the life course.

Neugarten. Neugarten (1968, 1975, 1976, 1983) has written extensively on middle and later life development. She and her colleagues (Neugarten et al., 1964; Neugarten and Brown-Rezanka, 1978) have contributed significantly to the literature on aging and adaptation patterns as well as career implications, ageism and socially defined norms and expectations, attitudes and values in older adults, and policy implications of an aging society. Typical of the earlier findings reported by Neugarten and her colleagues concerning changes in personality during the second half of life are:

1. Time is increasingly viewed in terms of years left to live rather than time from birth.
2. With age there is an increased sense of interiority, self-reflection, and introspection.
3. Death becomes more personalized as applied to self and loved ones.
4. Changes in sex role perception occur, with older men relative to younger men feeling more submissive to women and developing greater acceptance of the nurturing and affiliative impulses and older women tending to become more comfortable with their assertive and aggressive needs.
5. Because of realized expertise, older individuals expect to be able to continue accomplishing as long as they are able.

Most recently, Neugarten has been focusing on the social and policy implications of an "aging society" (Neugarten, 1983).

Lowenthal. Lowenthal et al. (1975) did not propose adult stages of development but studied cross-sectionally four specific samples representing different age-determined phases in the life course. This study was intended to identify concepts useful in understanding adaptation to change across the adult life course. The sample included middle- and lower-middle-class subjects and both women and men. The four groups included preworking senior high school students, first-marriage newlyweds between the ages of 20 and 38, parents of high school students facing empty nests who average 50 years of age, and a preretiree group. The sample intentionally included subjects facing incremental transitions, including role gains, and those experiencing decremental transitions with imminent losses or changes in familial or work roles.

Levinson. Levinson's conception of male adult development and his evolving views on female development have been presented in full (Levinson et al., 1978; Levinson, in press) and in several recent applications and extensive summaries (Levinson, 1980, 1984, 1986; Levinson and Gooden, 1985; Newton, 1983, 1984; Roberts and Newton, 1987). The Levinsonian conception of adult development is well known, controversial, and influential. Work and career also occupy a more central role in Levinson's theory than any other contemporary viewpoint. Since Levinson's work is so important and central to our topic, it will be given detailed examination here.

Levinson et al. (1978), in their first study, used intensive biographical interview to generate in-depth data. Each of the 40 male subjects were interviewed for 10–20 hours over a three month span. The subjects ranged in age from 35 to 45. Because work and career played an important role in conceptualizing the study and in the lives of men, Levinson selected four diverse occupational subgroups: executives, laborers, novelists, and biologists. The four occupational groups (10 people per group) were diverse in social class origins: 15% lower class, 42% working and lower middle class, 32% middle class, 10% upper middle and upper class. Twelve percent of the sample were black, 50% Protestants, 20% Catholic, and 19% Jewish. Seventy percent of the subjects completed college; the biologists and some of the novelists had graduate education. All of these male subjects were or had been married.

Levinson's forthcoming study (Levinson, in press) of female adult development involved a sample of 45 women. The basic sample contained a range of occupations and classes as in the male study. These data were augmented by reviews of the lives of over 100 men and women from different countries and periods of history in biographies, autobiographies, novels, and plays (Levinson, 1986); in-depth data on 40 additional female subjects in four dissertations (Roberts and Newton, 1987); and various biographical studies.

Levinson conceives of the life cycle in terms of a sequence of age-linked development eras of approximately 20 years and alternating relatively stable structure-building and unstable structure-changing or transitional periods of approximately 5–7 years. The tasks of the stable periods include making key choices, forming a structure to implement those decisions and goals, as well as working on particular psychosocial issues emerging at each period. The tasks of transition periods are to commit to critical choices that are the basis for developing a new life structure. Transition periods can reach crisis proportions characterized by inner upheaval and conflict.

Three general concepts are central to Levinson's conception of adult development: the dream, life structure, and mentoring.

- The dream is a deeply personal understanding of self in the world that is projected into the future. It is composed of an array of conscious and unconscious components and is the primary source of direction and energy in the adult life course. Clarifying and expressing this dream through the ever-changing exigencies of external circumstances and internal forces is an overriding purpose and challenge in adult development.

- The life structure is the vehicle used to accomplish this task. Levinson defines life structure as "the underlying pattern or design of a person's life at a given time" (Levinson and Gooden, 1985, p. 5). There are three components to the life structure: the sociocultural world that impinges on a particular individual, the complex aspects and patterns of the self, and the nature of the person's participation in the world through relationships, roles, and transactions between self and world. The life structure is malleable and subject to change. Levinson analyzes it by identifying the person's decisions, how he or she implements them, and how he or she responds to their consequences.

- Levinson also emphasizes the process of mentoring. Its significance for both participants and the dynamics and phases within mentoring relationships have important implications for career adjustment and development.

Levinson views the life structure of an individual as evolving through the life course in orderly, time-bounded periods of stability and change. At each transitional juncture the individual reviews his or her life structure in terms of how "satisfactorily" it is expressing the dream. The life structure for achieving the dream is modified by both external sociological realities and internal psychological processes. The dream is subsequently modified during each major transition.

The macrostructure of the life course, equally applicable to men and women, has been described as follows by Levinson and his associates (Levinson, 1986; Levinson and Gooden, 1985; Roberts and Newton, 1987). The macrostructure begins with eras that include preadulthood (birth to about 22), early adulthood (approximately 17–45; middle adulthood (40–65), late adulthood (60–80), and late late adulthood (80 plus). Figure 4.3, taken from Levinson(1986), presents the eras and period of adult development of men and women.

The first era, preadulthood, covers birth to about 22 and sets the stage for responsible adulthood. The early adult transition, from about 17 to 22, signals the end of preadulthood and the beginning of the early adult era. The second era, early adulthood, spans late adolescence to about 45 and includes the periods of early adulthood (22–28), the age 30 transition (28–33), and building a culminating life structure for early adulthood (33–45).

The early adult era is characterized by crucial decisions in marriage, occupation, and lifestyle. It is a time of activity and drive toward accomplishment, usually in terms of occupational goals. The early adult transition is a time between adolescence and young adulthood. The major tasks include separating both physically and psychologically from the preadult family of origin or the equivalent social structure and transforming earlier dreams into specific aspirations and

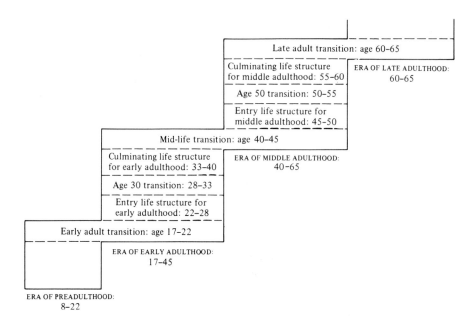

Figure 4.3. Developmental periods in eras of early and middle adulthood (From D. J. Levinson with C. N. Darrow, E. B. Klein, M. H. Levinson, and B. McKee, 1978, *The Seasons of a Man's Life*, p. 57. New York: Knopf; coyright 1978 by Alfred A. Knopf, Inc. Adapted, by permission, in D. J. Levinson, 1986, "A conception of adult development," *American Psychologist, 41*(1), 8; copyright 1986 by the American Psychological Association. Reprinted by permission of the author)

adult relationships to realize these dreams. This psychological work culminates in the establishment of an initial life structure and identification of self in the adult world. The individual who has transcended the preadult family as the pivotal point of his or her life and has exchanged for it a new home based with temporary commitments to the adult world has entered the period of building an entry life structure for early adulthood.

During the building of an entry life structure for the early adulthood period from the early to late twenties, the individual pursues three developmental tasks: (1) the exploration of occupation and marriage or other relationship possibilities offered by the adult world; (2) the establishment of a preliminary self-definition as "adult"; and (3) the creation of an initial or entry life structure that bridges the gap between the identified self and the more global adult world. For men, and increasingly women, career and occupational issues become central components of the life structure during this period. Two patterns for women were identified. For some women, career concerns are a primary focus of the dream, with family considerations secondary. Where marriage and family considerations are primary, there is less commitment to pursuing a career. Two other tasks characterize this period: to form and live out one's dream and to form mentee–mentor relationships.

The end of the twenties signals the arrival of the age 30 transition, which marks the end of the provisional quality of the first life structure. This is a time for working on the flaws of the first life structure. Levinson has termed the phase of early adulthood from approximately 17 to 33 the "novice phase." This phase embraces the early adult transition, building an entry life structure, and the age 30 transition. Generally, the tasks of this novice phase and its associated periods include (1) forming a dream and giving it a place in one's life structure; (2) forming mentor relationships; (3) forming an occupation; and (4) forming love relationships.

Toward the end of building a culminating life structure for the early adulthood stable period, at about 32–40, there is a distinctive period for men that Levinson has entitled "boom," or becoming one's own man. A similar yet unnamed period exists for women. During this period, a man must complete the goals of settling down, becoming a senior member of the world, and being able to speak with authority in his own voice, for which he needs affirmation and respect from the world.

The middle adulthood era, which lasts from about 40 to 65, begins with the midlife transition (40–45) and ends with the late adult transition. The period of midlife transition begins roughly at age 40 and represents the transitional period between young and middle adulthood. Motivated by a shift in time perspective to years left to live, the critical issue is the felt disparity in the gap between that which one has accomplished in life and what one really wants. The major midlife transitional tasks are (1) to evaluate one's late-thirties life structure and terminate the era of early adulthood; (2) to redefine one's sense of self and to become more individuated by integrating the polarities of life with new self-discoveries; and (3) to initiate a new era and form a new and stable life structure. Thus, the midlife transition is a period of major reappraisal and disillusionment with respect to the sense of self in the world; moreover, it involves a major modification of life structure that integrates the personality changes of this period. Levinson depicts increased interiority at midlife as part of the process of achieving an equilibration of the polarities of young–old, destruction–reaction, masculine–feminine, and attachment–separateness. Successful individuation and integration during midlife is characterized by greater self-awareness and wisdom accompanied by energy and imagination, the acceptance of mortality and destructiveness, the emergence of a comfortable sexual bimodality (i.e., integration of the stereotypical masculine and feminine), greater attention to inner experience, and an increased commitment to mentoring the next generation. While acknowledging that there is disagreement (for methodological, sampling, data-gathering, and other reasons) in the literature (e.g., Wrightsman, 1981) on the extent to which midlife is a particularly stressful period, Levinson indicates that the turmoil of the midlife transition abates around age 45 with the initial outcome of reaching a period of restabilization and building an entry life structure to middle adulthood. The task is to shape a life structure that will prove operational for life during the middle adulthood era.

The midlife transition is followed first by building an entry life structure for middle adulthood (45–50). Career concerns are especially salient during this period, and they differ for men and women. In traditional marriages, men may have achieved their highest level of advancement and may be ready to reduce their investment in their careers. Many women, in contrast, in response to children having left home and other considerations, may begin to explore the world of work more seriously. Next, the age 50 transition offers another opportunity to reappraise and attempt to change the existing life structure. Those who may have succeeded in defensively evading some of the psychological work of the midlife transition may experience this transition as particularly stressful.

Following the midlife transition is the developmental task of building a culminating life structure for the middle adulthood period (55–60), where the focus is on enriching and enhancing one's life within the constraints and opportunities of the existing life structure. The later adult transition (60–65) marks the shift from the middle to the later adulthood era. Physiological changes, retirement, changes in family roles, confrontations with death, dying, and the evaluation of one's life characterize this period. Levinson has relatively little to say about this latter period.

Levinson's conception of adult development and his methodology have been repeatedly challenged and criticized (e.g., Bardwick, 1986). His early work on male adult development has especially been criticized for the ambiguity of such key concepts as the life structure, the small size and questionable representatives of his sample, the use of intensive biographical interviews as a primary data source, the claim of universality for the age-specified periods and transitions, the generalizability of his male-based conception of development to female adult development, and the relative failure to explore implications for psychopathology. Levinson and his associates, as will be discussed in the next section, have repeatedly addressed the generalizability question (Levinson, 1986, in press; Levinson and Gooden, 1985; Roberts and Newton, 1987). Similarly, Levinson (1986) has attempted to respond to the other questions and criticisms. Despite these criticisms, Levinson's contemporary conception of adult development and his forthcoming study, tentatively entitled *Seasons of a Woman's Life*, is one of the few efforts to systematically study female adult development based on original data.

Persistent dilemma in the study of adult and career development

Having now reviewed some of the major theories of adult development, we examine several important conceptual and methodological dilemmas that persist despite continuous research and debate. These dilemmas focus on (1) the appropriateness of generalizing from models of adult development based on male subjects to the adult development of women; (2) the relative contribution of individual personality and social systems or organizational parameters to the adult developmental process; and (3) the extent to which adult development theory and career adjustment and development theory have been integrated.

Generalization from male models of adult development to the adult development of women. There has been and continues to be much disagreement with the view that women basically go through similar phases of adult development as men (Betz and Fitzgerald, 1987). Bardwick (1980), Gilligan (1980, 1982), and Giele (1980, 1982), among others, have argued strongly against this point of view. They have emphasized the significance of attachment and relationships and the struggle to combine attachment and achievement in female adult development relative to the importance of separation, autonomy, and work/career accomplishments for men. (See Gallos, Chapter 6; Sekaran & Hall, Chapter 8, for a detailed discussion of this issue.) This dilemma persists despite the fact that recently women's adult development has been studied separately from that of men and that several of the early male-centered theories have been modified to incorporate the unique experiences of women. Erikson's theory is a case in point.

Erikson assumed that developmental crises and the ego development associated with each stage follow the same sequence for males and females. Although he notes that male and female development is similar in many ways, he does indicate that the unique experience associated with gender must be taken into consideration. Because Erikson's developmental stages remain embedded in a Freudian framework, it is assumed that his model of psychosocial development is still that of the male (Chodorow, 1978; Franz and White, 1985; Gilligan, 1982). Franz and White (1985) have questioned each of Erikson's eight stages, including the adulthood stages.

With respect to intimacy versus isolation in young adulthood, Franz and White argue that gender needs to be considered in at least four different ways: "(a) the possibility of a premature step into intimacy (without adequate identity resolution) by women because of cultural norms for the timing of marriage and motherhood; (b) the importance of the recognition of sex differences in order for heterosexual relationships to occur; (c) an emphasis of heterosexuality; [and] (d) the division of sexual activity by sex" (p. 237).

In conceptualizing generativity versus stagnation in adulthood, Erikson asserts that a unique component of women's identity struggle involves the integration of the ability to bear children. Erikson (1963) suggested that women were more likely to express generativity procreatively and men productively and creatively. Franz and White grant that "Erikson has had some success in liberating his theory from some of the anatomy is destiny shackles of... psychoanalytic theory" (p. 238). However, they argue that Erikson's theory remains incomplete "not so much because it is a male theory as because it fails to explain adequately how an individual can become truly intimate and generative through the identity pathway of development" (p. 239).

Franz and White attempted to integrate *attachment* concerns into Erikson's theory as a line of development from infancy to generativity. Such an expanded developmental line can account for the development of the individuated, socially connected personality as well as the attached, interpersonally oriented personality. This expansion of Erikson's theory leads Franz and White to speculate that "if, with changing times and mores, attachment processes were to undergo fuller development in men and individuation process were to undergo fuller development in women, sex differences might become more elusive than ever" (1985, p. 254).

Like Erikson, Levinson has been criticized, primarily by Gilligan (1980, 1982), for applying his theory to women. She questioned whether women have the opportunities to change their life structures the way males seem to in Levinson's schema. Gilligan also criticized Levinson's emphasis on individual achievement in males as inappropriate in studying the lives of women. She argued that "the elusive mystery of women's development lies in the recognition of the continuing importance of attachment in the human life cycle" (p. 23). She related this essential gender difference to the notion that the development of masculinity is linked to separation from the female mother, while the female's gender identity is developed more through the struggle with attachment to the mother. Given these assumptions, Gilligan proposed a three-stage model of female development.

The first stage is self-oriented – "caring for the self in order to ensure survival" (p. 74). The second stage involves a shift to caring for others, the more traditional conception of the woman's role. Her third stage involves a reconciliation of the new recognition of one's own powers as well as realization that "others have a responsibility to their own destiny" (p. 21).

As discussed, Levinson (in press) has studied the adult development of women based on in-depth biographical interviews with 45 women using the same in-depth clinical methods employed in his study of men. Levinson (1986) and his colleagues (Levinson and Gooden, 1985; Roberts and Newton, 1987) concluded, on the basis of preliminary findings, that female development parallels that of men, although the specifics differ. Roberts and Newton (1987), in a recent secondary analysis, focused on the age 30 transition for women. They studied women's adult development from a Levinsonian perspective by carefully reviewing biographies of 39 adult women in four unpublished dissertations. They reported that the women progressed through the same age-linked sequence of stable structure-building and transitional periods as Levinson's male subjects. The timing and nature of the developmental tasks were similar for men and women, but the manner of working through these tasks differed for women. Of particular significance was the age 30 transition. Several patterns emerged. For example, for a large number of women who emphasized career goals in their twenties, marriage, family, and friends became a priority in their thirties. For about half of those who opted for marriage and the relational dream in their twenties, individual career and individuation–separation themes in relation to their husbands became a priority in their thirties. The age 30 transition was particularly stressful for those women with limited relational and career accomplishments. Generally, women's dreams were found to be more complex than men's. Also, consistent with Miller's (1976) and Gilligan's (1980, 1982) findings, attachments and relationships were more important for women and autonomy and occupational achievement more salient for men.

Reinke et al. (1985) offer one potential explanation for this difference. They suggest that the life course of women may be more closely tied to the family life cycle than to chronological age. Others (e.g., Neugarten, 1976; Schwartz, 1980) have also emphasized the importance of the family life cycle in the adult development of women. Therefore, it is reasonable to conclude that efforts to transfer directly findings based on the study of men to the life course of women may lead to oversimplified or erroneous conclusions. In studying the adult development of women, such parameters as stage of development, investment in family role, and the life cycle stage of the family among other parameters must be taken into account.

The relative contribution of individual and social systems parameters to adult and career development. The dilemma here focuses on the extent to which the unfolding of the developmental process for adults is driven by internal forces relative to the contribution of social system or organizational parameters. Much psychological theory and research suggests that the developmental process for adult individuals is propelled by internal biological and psychological needs and that most individuals have considerable control over work, family, and other important settings in which they are embedded, particularly when struggling through a transition. Vaillant's (1977) example of a physician who followed a traditional work route until age 40, then as part of a mid-life transition, left his place of employment and established a private practice is probably unrepresentative. Many midlife adults encounter powerful situational constraints. The question arises as to how individual internal developmental processes are affected by family, work, and organization structural constraints. Lawrence (1980) was one of the first to examine this issue. She found that the midlife "crisis" was not as prevalent as one might expect and that its existence was dependent on social environments. Rosenbaum (1984) addressed the question conceptually as follows: "A psychological perspective ... tends to view life cycle changes in isolation and to give the impression that life cycle changes are inevitable and immutable aspects of people's biological and psychological makeup." He argues that this prevents us "from determining where biology and psychology end and social forces begin" (p. 237). (See Rosenbaum, Chapter 16, for a more detailed discussion of this issue.)

Other research similarly suggests that individual developmental processes may be significantly influenced and/or shaped by social and situational parameters. For example, Erdwins et al. (1983) found a significant difference in personality dimensions among women who have assumed different life roles. There is also some recent evidence to suggest that the contrasexual shift presumed to represent a major midlife task by Gutmann (1975, 1985), Levinson et al. (1978), Cytrynbaum et al. (1980), and others may also be strongly influenced by structural factors. For example, Rice-Erso (1985) found that the career women he surveyed (nurses and lawyers) shifted post-midlife toward manifesting more stereotypically feminine traits and fewer masculine traits, rather than the reverse, which would be predicted from the original contrasexual shift theories.

One of the most systematic examples of this sort of person–environment interactional approach to development is found in the recent work of Lawrence (1987), an examination of organizational norms, and age effects. Lawrence points out that this interactionist perspective is often "lost between the cracks," as demographers tend to exclude the effect of *norms* about age, psychologists often overlook *organizational* effects, and sociologists frequently bypass the effects of *individual* characteristics. Her paper presents an interdisciplinary theory of age effects in organizational settings and tests several propositions derived from the theory.

Accumulating findings suggest that career-minded young adults (both males and females) may be subtly coerced by the organizational structure to move up as far and as fast as they can by age 35–40. If there were recall opportunities for career change and advancement available in late middle or older adulthood, one might expect a delay in the contrasexual shift. If this were confirmed, it would certainly suggest that a major component of the midlife transition is significantly influenced by structural factors.

Veiga (1983) has noted, for example, that at the corporate maturity stage, mobility is associated with career impatience and suggested that frequent mobility at this stage may be one of the ways in which the more anxious managers cope with midlife and midcareer transition issues. In contrast to Levinson, he found that most managers begin to reconcile the plateauing of their careers during their mid-forties and that mobile managers are still unwilling to accept career plateauing even during the preretirement stage. These and similar findings strongly suggest that individual and social system–social structural parameters must be taken into consideration in accounting for significant aspects of life course and career development.

Integration of adult development and career development theories. None of the major adult development theorists cite the literature in career–vocational psychology, and conversely, few references to Levinson, Gould, Vaillant, and so on, are made by the major career development theorists (Super, Holland, Crites, etc.). Clearly, there is a need to extrapolate and apply the central concepts from adult developmental theory to career developmental theory and, reciprocally, for adult development theory to incorporate the subject matter of career development theory. Adult development theories often simultaneously encompass several different levels of development and lines of development within each phase, such as ego development, physical and sexual development, separation–individuation, and emotional development. Although there are some exceptions (Vrondracek, Lerner, and Schulenberg, 1986), few adult development theorists have incorporated work–career parameters as markers of adult life course phases along with family or procreative development and biological development. Vaillant (1977) does include career consolidation as a separate phase, covering ages 25–35. Levinson (1986) does not focus on career development as a separate line of development, but he does incorporate career and work development as a major component of the life structure during the young adulthood and middle adulthood eras. Similarly, Bardwick (1980) incorporates relational and career themes within young and midlife phases of women's adult development. (See Gallos, Chapter 6, for a more detailed summary of Bardwick's theory.) Relatively speaking, however, little integrative work has been done. Levinson (1986; Levinson et al., 1978) is more explicit about the role of career in adult development.

Career development theorists, such as Super (1957, 1980), Hall (1976), Rosenbaum (1984), and Sekaran (1986), have attempted to incorporate aspects of individual adult and family life course development into their career development theories. For example, Hall (1976) proposed a model of the family life course development and explored how the family life cycle intersects with the work cycle. Hall explores the interaction between work and a traditional family developmental model that includes the following phases:

1. Becoming a spouse – begins at marriage and ends with the birth of the first child.
2. Expanding circle – begins with the birth of the first child and ends with the birth of the second child.
3. Peak stage – period in which the family has two or more preschool age children.
4. Full-house plateau – starts when the youngest child enters school and the first child leaves home.
5. Shrinking circle – starts when the first child leaves home and ends when the last child leaves home.
6. Minimal plateau – when all children have left home.

However, Hall fails to examine in detail how alterations in the traditional family model (e.g., divorces, late-life children, second families), which characterize a large segment of the population, fit into his model. (Sekaran and Hall, Chapter 8, address this issue to some extent.)

Few direct applications of adult development theory to the work setting have, in fact, been reported. Such applications are needed to better link career and adult development concepts. Newton (1983), for example, applied Levinson's male model to faculty development in higher education. Similarly, Cytrynbaum et al. (1982) applied contemporary adult developmental theory and research to the career adjustment of five selected faculty groups within the university setting: age 30 transition faculty, dual-career couple faculty, midlife faculty, late-entry faculty, and senior retiring faculty. For example, in discussing midlife faculty, Cytrynbaum et al. (1982) point out that "professionally, midlife faculty may demonstrate an 'intellectually fallow' period . . . Energy is low and used almost exclusively for defense, ego review, or introspective work" (p. 16). This temporary fallow midlife period is examined in terms of the developmental tasks of midlife transition. Ways in which changes in the structure and practices of universities can help alleviate or at least minimize the disruption asssociated with this transition period are suggested. Cytrynbaum et al. (1982) clearly emphasize the importance of organizational and career structure pressures in regulating the intensity of adult development crises.

Probably the most articulate attempt to "bridge the gap" between general adult developmental theory and career–vocational psychology is the recent book by Vrondracek et al. (1986). They acknowledge the contributions of the theories reviewed in this section, but they emphasize that their conceptualizations with regard to career are inarticulate and primitive at best. Vrondracek et al. (1986) make a considerable contribution to this desired rapprochement.

They approach their synthesis of general adult and career development theory, however, from a different frame of reference than Levinson and the others. Vrondracek et al. (1986) formulate a conceptual schema they call *developmental contextualism* (or alternatively, probabilistic epigenesis). They contrast it with Levinson's basically organismic model as well as with the mechanistic models of stimulus–response psychology. They state (Vrondracek et al., 1986, p. 30) that in developmental contextualism, "there is a stress on the active organism in an active world and on the relation between the development organism and its changing context." The parameters of context come primarily from Bronfenbrenner (1979), who delineated four distinct settings within which the individual participates, has an effect upon, and is affected by: (1) microsystem, (2) mesosystem, (3) exosystem, and (4) macrosystem. In vocational psychology, these closely correspond to the four cultural and social systems delineated by Crites (1969). Developmental contextualism proposes that within these four nested settings, through "behavioral agency" and "ecological transitions," the developing individual changes the environment and is changed by it.

Vondracek et al. (1986) apply development contextualism to adolescence to provide an example of how theory and research on career choice can be integrated within their conceptual framework. They do not, however, treat subsequent phases or stages of life-span development.

The model presented at the beginning of this chapter, although formulated 10 years (Crites, 1976) before the work of Vrondracek et al. (1986), is quite consistent with developmental contextualism as well as the contributions of Levinson and other adult development theorists. Like these formulations, the Crites model takes as the basic unit of analysis the *relationship* between the individual adult worker and the organizational environment and ethos rather than focusing on one or the other, as has been true in the past, but it also goes beyond general developmental theory to address phenomena of central concern and interest to career–organizational psychology. These are the developmental trends in career success and satisfaction and, more importantly, the relationship *between* these variables projected over the adult years.

CONCLUSION

We have attempted in this chapter to demonstrate the utility of "adult development" theory for understanding the process of "career adjustment." Although some writers have used the two terms virtually interchangeably, we find that each concept is distinct and, furthermore, has much to offer the other. As the Crites model indicates, occupational phenomena, such as the conflicting results from different studies of the relationship between success and satisfaction, can be shown to make sense when viewed in the context of adult life stage.

To facilitate this integration of adult development theory and career theory, this chapter provided a review of the major models of adult development, examining the state of the art. It seems clear that important gender issues exist in this work, and these are beginning to be addressed. Also, there is a strong need to examine the relative contributions of individual personality and organizational or institutional influences to the adult development process. (Gallos, Chapter 6, and Kanter, Chapter 25, consider each of these influences, respectively).

We conclude with a call for more work in the direction of what Vrondracek et al. (1986) have called developmental contextualism, the analysis of the changing individual in the changing career context. As a contribution to this approach, the present volume extends developmental contextualism to other aspects of adult career development. Betz et al. (Chapter 2) and Barley (Chapter 3), respectively, review work at the individual and the institutional level and develop the need to work from an interactionist perspective. For example, the interaction between individual identity and social role, which Barley describes as a cornerstone of the work of the Chicago school, provides one powerful analytic approach. Arthur and Kram (Chapter 14) on developmental relationships take perhaps the most explicitly interactionist view of the career growth process. Dalton (Chapter 5) and Thomas and Alderfer (Chapter 7) demonstrate how individual–environment interactions affect career processes in the context of organizational career programs and race relationships, respectively. And, finally, Bell and Staw (Chapter 11) and Weick and Berlinger (Chapter 15) show how the individual's exchanges with the general social environment can lead to individual and organizational adaptation. All of these chapters help illustrate how individual developmental processes contribute to career development and how career dynamics can influence the individual's passage through adult life stages.

NOTES

1 Theories in the second group chart progressive age-related sequences of internal structure reorganizations in personality, character, emotion, or intellect within stages that are irreversible, sequential, and hierarchical. Well-known theorists include Piaget (cognitive

development), Kohlberg (moral development), Leovinger (ego development) (meaning system development), and Kegan. These theorists thus posit trends of growth or development from a more immature internal state to more sophisticated, mature, higher order levels of functioning. This work is relevant to the study of careers, although its impact is being most felt through related studies of leadership and organization development (e.g., Kegan and Lahey, 1984; Tobert, 1985).

2 These theories build on the work of Anna Freud (1963) on the notion of developmental lines. For example, Nemiroff and Colarusso (1985) have suggested studying lines of adult development in relation to (1) intimacy, love, and sex; (2) the adult body; (3) time and death; (4) relationships to children; (5) relationships to parents; (6) mentor relationships; (7) relationships with society; (8) work; (9) play; and (10) financial behavior. Winestine (1973), Marcus (1973), Steinschein (1973), and Miller (1987) have similarly described aspects of the developmental line of individuation–separation from childhood to old age.

3 Space limitations prevent a review of psychodynamic theories that identify developmental lines during childhood, adolescent, as well as adult development since our emphasis is on the latter.

4 The contribution of Gilligan and Bardwick to the development of a distinct theory of female adult development and the implications of their work for career development are discussed in considerable detail in Gallos (Chapter 6) and Sekaran and Hall (Chapter 8).

REFERENCES

Astin, A. W. (1958). Dimensions of work satisfaction in the occupational choices of college freshmen. *Journal of Applied Psychology, 42*, 178–190.
Baltes, P. B., Reese, H. W., and Nesselroade, J. R. (1977). *Life-span Developmental Psychology: Introduction to Research Methods.* Monterey, CA: Brooks/Cole.
Bardwick, J. (1980). The seasons of a woman's life. In D. McGuigan (ed.), *Women's Lives: New Theory, Research, and Policy.* Ann Arbor: University of Michigan Center for Continuing Education of Women.
Bardwick, J. (1986). *The Plateauing Trap: How To Avoid It in Your Career and in Your Life.* New York: Amacom.
Benge, E. J., and Copwell, D. F. (1957). Employee morale survey. *Modern Management, 12*, 19–22.
Betz, N. E., and Fitzgerald, L. F. (1987). *Career Psychology of Women.* San Diego: Academic.
Brayfield, A. H., and Crockett, W. H. (1955). Employee attitudes and employee performance. *Psychological Bulletin, 52*, 396–424.
Bronfenbrenner, U. (1979). *The Ecology of Human Development: Experiments by Nature and Design.* Cambridge, MA: Harvard University Press.
Buehler, C. (1933). *Der Menschliche Lebenslauf als Psychologisches Problem.* Leipzig: Hirzel.
Chodorow, N. (1978). *The Reproduction of Mothering.* Berkeley: University of California Press.
Crites, J. O. (1961). Factor analytic definitions of vocational motivation. *Journal of Applied Psychology, 45*, 330–337.
Crites, J. O. (1969). *Vocational Psychology.* New York: McGraw-Hill.
Crites, J. O. (1976). A comprehensive model of career adjustment in early adulthood. *Journal of Vocational Behavior, 9*, 105–118.
Cytrynbaum, S., et al. (1980). Midlife development: a personality and social systems perspective. In L. Poon (ed.), *Aging in the 80s: psychological issues.* Washington, DC: American Psychological Association.
Cytrynbaum, S., Lee, S., and Wadner, D. (1982). Faculty development through the life course. *Journal of Instructional Development, 5*,(3).
Erdwins, C. J., Tyer, Z. E., and Mellinger, J. C. (1983). A comparison of sex-role and related personality traits in young, middle-aged and older women. *International Journal of Aging and Human Development, 17*, 141–152.
Erikson, E. H. (1958). *Young Man Luther.* New York: Norton.
Erikson, E. H. (1959). Identity and the life cycle. *Psychological Issues, 1*, 509–100.
Erikson, E. H. (1963). *Childhood and Society*, 2nd ed. New York: Norton.
Erikson, E. H. (1969). *Ghandi's Truth.* New York: Norton.

Farrell, M., and Rosenberg, S. (1981). *Men in Midlife*. Dover, MA: Auburn House.

Franz, E. D., and White, K. M. (1985). Individuation and attachment in personality development: extending Erikson theory. *Journal of Personality, 53*,(2), 224–256.

Freud, A. (1963). The concept of developmental lines. *Psychoanalytic Study of the Child, 18*, 245–265.

Freud, S. (1905). *Three Essays on the Theory of Sexuality*, standard ed., Vol. 7. London: Hogarth, p. 125.

Gellman, W. (1953), Components of vocational adjustment. *Personnel and Guidance Journal, 31*, 536–539.

Giele, J. (1980). Crossovers: new themes in adult roles and the life cycle. In D. McGuigan (ed.), *Women's Lives: New Theory, Research, and Policy*. Ann Arbor: University of Michigan Center for Continuing Education of Women.

Giele, J. (1982). Women's work and family roles. In J. Giele (ed.), *Women in the Middle Years*. New York: Wiley.

Gilligan, C. (1980). Restoring the missing text of women's development to life cycle theories. In D. McGuigan (ed.), *Women's Lives: New Theory, Research, and Policy*. Ann Arbor: University of Michigan Center for Continuing Education of Women.

Gilligan, C. (1982). *In a Different Voice: Psychological Theory and Women's Development*. Cambridge: Harvard University Press.

Gould, R. (1975). Adult life stages: growth toward self-tolerance. *Psychology Today*, 35–38.

Gould, R. (1978). *Transformations: Growth and Change in Adult Life*. New York: Simon & Schuster.

Gould, R. L. (1981). Transformational tasks in adulthood. In S. Greenspan and D. Pollock (eds.), *The Course of Life: Psychoanalytic Contributions toward Understanding Personality Development*, Vol. III, *Adulthood and the Aging Process*. Washington, DC: U.S. Department of Health.

Gutmann, D. (1975). Parenthood: a key to the comparative study of the life cycle. In N. Datan and L. Ginsberg (eds.), *Life Span Developmental Psychology: Normative Life Crises*. New York: Academic.

Gutmann, D. (1985). The parental imperative revisited: towards a developmental psychology of adulthood and later life. In J. A. Meachen (ed.), *Contributions to Human Development*, Vol. 14. Basil: Karger.

Hall, D. T. (1976). *Careers in Organizations*. Glenview, IL: Scott, Foresman.

Heron, A. (1954). Satisfaction and satisfactoriness: complementary aspects of occupational adjustment. *Occupational Psychology, 28*, 140–153.

Heron, A. (1952). The establishment for research purposes of two criteria of occupational adjustment. *Occupational Psychology, 28*, 140–153.

Jung, C. G. (1933). *Modern Man in Search of a Soul*. New York: Harcourt, Brace, and World.

Jung, C. G. (1966). *Collected Works*. Princeton, NJ: Princeton University Press.

Kahn, R. L. (1960). Productivity and job satisfaction. *Personnel Psychology, 13*, 275–287.

Kegan, R. (1982). *The Evolving Self: Problem and Process in Human Development*. Cambridge, MA: Harvard University.

Kegan, R., and Lahey, L. L. (1984). Adult leadership and adult development: a constructivist view. In B. Kellerman (ed.), *Leadership: Multidisciplinary Perspectives*. Englewood Cliffs, NJ: Prentice-Hall.

Lawrence, B. S. (1980). The myth of the midlife crisis. *Sloan Management Review, 21*, 35–49.

Lawrence, B. S. (1987). An organizational theory of age effects. *Research in the Sociology of Organizations, 5*, 37–71.

Levinson, D. J. (1980). Toward a conception of the adult life course. In N. Smelser and E. H. Erikson (eds.), *Themes of Love and Work in Adulthood*. Cambridge, MA: Harvard University Press.

Levinson, D. J. (1984). The career is in the life structure, the life structure is in the career: an adult development perspective. In M. B. Arthur, L. Ballyn, D. J. Levinson, and H. A. Shepard, *Working with Careers*. New York: Columbia University School of Business.

Levinson, D. J. (1986). A conception of adult development. *American Psychologist, 41*(1), 3–13.

Levinson, D. J. (in press). *The Seasons of a Woman's Life*. New York: Knopf.

Levinson, D. J., et al. (1978). *The Seasons of a Man's Life*. New York: Knopf.

Levinson, D. J., and Gooden, W. E. (1985). The life cycle. In H. I. Kaplan and B. J. Sadock (eds.), *Comprehensive Textbook of Psychiatry*, 4th ed. Baltimore, MD: Williams and Williams.

Lofquist, L. H., and Dawis, R. V. (1968). *Adjustment to Work*. New York: Appleton-Century-Crofts.

Lowenthal, M. F., Thurnher, M., and Chiriboga, D. (1975). *Four Stages of Life: A Comparative Study of Women and Men Facing Transitions*. San Francisco: Jossey-Bass.

Luria, W. A., and Weiss, A. (1942). Analyzing vocational adjustment. *Occupations, 21*, 138–142.

Marcus, T. (1973). The experience of separation–individuation in infancy and its reverberations through the course of life: adolescence and maturity (panel report). *Journal of the American Psychoanalytic Association, 21*, 155–167.

Marx, M. H. (ed.) (1951). *Psychology Theory*. New York: Macmillan.

Marx, M. H. (ed.) (1963). *Theories in Contemporary Psychology*. New York: Macmillan.

Miller, A. G. (1987). Attachment and autonomy: individuation themes in the relationships of 20–40 year old women and their mothers. Ph.D. dissertation. Northwestern University, Evanston, IL.

Miller, J. B. (1976). *Toward a New Psychology of Women*. Boston: Beacon.

Morse, N. C. (1953). *Satisfaction in the White-Collar Job*. Ann Arbor, MI: University of Michigan.

Nemiroff, R., and Colarusso, C. (1985). *The Race against Time*. New York: Plenum.

Neugarten, B. L. (1968). *Middle Age and Aging: A Reader in Social Psychology*. Chicago: University of Chicago Press.

Neugarten, B. L. (1975). Adult personality: towards a psychology of the life cycle. In W. C. Sze (ed.), *The Human Life Cycle*. New York: Jason Aronso.

Neugarten, B. L. (1976). Adaptation and the life cycle. *Counseling Psychologist, 6*(1), 16–20.

Neugarten, B. L. (1979). Time, age and the life cycle. *American Journal of Psychiatry, 136*(7), 887–894.

Neugarten, B. L. (1983). Policy for the 1980s: age or need entitlement. In B. L. Neugarten (ed.), *Age or Need: Public Policies for Older People*. Beverly Hills, CA: Sage.

Neugarten, B. L., and Brown-Rezanka, L. (1978, December). Midlife women in the 1980s. In *Women in Midlife – Security and Fulfillment (Part 1)*. A compendium of papers submitted to the Select Committee on Aging and the Subcommittee on Retirement Income and Employment. U.S. House of Representatives, 95th Congress. Committee Publication 95-100, U.S. Government Printing Office, Washington, DC.

Neugarten, B. L., et al. (eds.) (1964). *Personality in Middle and Later Life*. New York: Atherton.

Neumann, E. (1959). *Psychological Stages of Feminine Development*. New York: Spring.

Newton, P. (1983). Periods in the adult development of the faculty member. *Human Relations, 36*, 441–458.

Newton, P. (1984). Samuel Johnson's breakdown and recovery in middle-age: a life span developmental approach to mental illness and its cure. *International Review of Psychoanalysis, 11*, 93–118.

Pollock, G. H. (1981). Aging or aged: development or pathology. In S. I. Greenspan and G. H. Pollock (eds.), *The Course of Life: Psychoanalytic Contributions toward Understanding Personality Development*, Vol. III, *Adulthood and the Aging Process*. Washington, DC: National Institute of Mental Health.

Pollock, G. H. (1987). The mourning-liberation process: ideas on the inner life of the older adult. In J. Sadavoy and M. Leszcz (eds.), *Treating the Elderly with Psychotherapy*. Madison, CT: International Universities.

Reinke, B. J., Holmes, D. S., and Harris, R. L. (1985). The timing of psychosocial changes in women's lives: The years 25–45. *Journal of Personality and Social Psychology, 48*(5), 1353–1364.

Rice-Erso, H. M. (1985). The impact of midlife on the stereotypically gender-linked personality traits for female lawyers and female nurses. Ph.D. dissertation. Northwestern University, Evanston, IL.

Roberts, P., and Newton, P. (1987). Levinsonian studies of women's adult development. *Psychology and Aging, 2*(2), 154–163.

Rosenbaum, J. E. (1984). *Career Mobility in a Corporate Hierarchy*. New York: Academic.

Sales, E. (1978). Women's adult development. In I. H. Frieze et al. (eds.), *Women and Sex Roles: A Sociological Perspective.* New York: Norton.

Schwartz, P. M. (1980). Working mothers of infants: conflicts and coping strategies. In D. G. McGuigan (ed.), *Women's Lives: New Theory, Research and Policy.* Ann Arbor, University of Michigan.

Sekaran, U. (1986). *Dual Career Families: Contemporary Organizational and Counseling Issues.* San Francisco: Jossey-Bass.

Steinschein, I. (1973). The experience of separation–individuation in infancy and its reverberations through the course of life: maturity, senescence, and sociological implications (panel report). *Journal of the American Psychoanalytic Association, 21,* 633–645.

Super, D. E. (1957). *The Psychology of Careers.* New York: Harper & Row.

Super, D. E. (1980). A life-span life-space approach to career development. *Journal of Vocational Behavior, 26,* 182–296.

Tobert, W. R. (1985). On-line reframing: an integrative approach to organizational management. *Organizational Dynamics, 14,* 60–79.

Triandis, H. C. (1959). A critique and experimental design for the study of relationships between productivity and job satisfaction. *Psychological Bulletin, 56,* 309–312.

Vaillant, G. (1977). *Adaptation to Life.* Boston: Little, Brown.

Van Gennep, A. (1960). *The Rites of Passage.* Chicago: University of Chicago Press. (Original work published 1908).

Veiga, J. F. (1983). Mobility influences during managerial career stages. *Academy of Management Journal, 26*(1), 64–85.

Vrondracek, F. W., Lerner, R. M., and Schulenberg, J. E. (1986). *Career Development: A Life-span Development Approach.* Hillside, NJ: Erlbaum.

Vroom, V. H. (1964). *Work and Motivation.* New York: Wiley.

Winestine, M. (1973). The experience of separation–individuation in infancy and its reverberations through the course of life: infancy and childhood (panel report). *Journal of American Psychoanalytic Association, 21,* 135–154.

Wrightsman, L. S. (1981). Personal documents as data in conceptualizing adult personality development. *Personality and Social Psychology Bulletin, 7,* 367–385.

5 Developmental views of careers in organizations

GENE W. DALTON

As a society, we have a pervasive ambivalence toward organizations. It is not a love–hate relationship. The emotions expressed about organizations tend to be on the dark side: deep suspicion, fear, anger, and even hatred. The other side of the ambivalence is shown, not in the emotions we express about organizations, but in the fact that we seem irresistibly drawn to form, utilize, and join organizations. Along with science and technology, modern organizations have been the most powerful force for change in this century. We feed, clothe, govern, and transport ourselves through organizations.

We have also been moving into organizations in increasing numbers. The first half of this century largely saw the completion of a mass migration of men from individual family farms into complex organizations. The last half of this century has brought a large proportion of adult women into the organizational work place as well as an increasing proportion of what were once considered independent professionals: physicians and lawyers.

The increasing part of our lives that is spent in organizations has raised the question: What happens to us in organizations? Attempts to answer that question have brought with them the increasing use of the term "career" to describe the individual's sequence of experiences, roles, and relationships in work-related organizations. The history of this word in the English language brings with it an interesting connotation. The word came to us from the French word *carriere*, meaning a road or racecourse. Thus the original use of the term in English was to designate a racing course. Usage of the word then expanded to mean "a swift course, as of the sun through the sky" and "one's progress through life or in a particular vocation (Guralnik, 1978)." Thus the word "career" brings with it a connotation of progression or development along some course. Indeed, when the word is used in organizations, it is often linked with the word "development." For example, in recent years, as many as one-third of all the members of the American Society of Training Directors listed career development as one of their major areas of focus and interest.

We shall examine the writings of those theorists who have attempted to conceptualize careers from a developmental point of view – developmental in the sense that they see the individual's experiences, roles, and relationships in work-related organizations as developing, or having the possibility of developing, along some course. These students of career development will not include writers such as Buehler, Erikson, Maslow, or White, whose focus is on individual or human development. Nor will they include writers such as Levinson or Vaillant, who have focused on adult development. The focus of the career development theorist

89

is different, not only because it limits itself to the work setting, but also because the career theorist must not only look at the individual but also take into account the nature and properties of organizations, which usually constitute the work setting. It is this very interplay between the individual and the organization that makes career theory unique – and also gives it power. As Goffman has pointed out, "One value of the concept of career is its two-sidedness. One side is linked to internal matters held dearly and closely, such as an image of self or felt identity: the other side concerns official position, jural relations, and style of life, and is part of a publicly accessible institutional complex" (Goffman 1961:127).

But if we are to fully address the subject of developmental views of organizations, we cannot stop with models of career development, with only an examination of the way careers develop in organizations. The ambivalence toward organizations comes from the question of what happens to individuals in them. How does membership and participation in organizations shape or influence individual development? How do organizational processes inhibit our development as human beings? Conversely, in what ways do organizational processes and career opportunities foster individual growth and development? After we have reviewed the developmental models of careers, we shall turn to this question of the effects of organizations on individual development.

DEVELOPMENTAL MODELS OF CAREERS

Developmental models of careers differ on a number of different dimensions. Some models focus initially on properties of individuals, such as life span or individual differences; others start with properties of organizations. Some models postulate stages and transitions, while others assume development occurs in a much more continuous fashion. We shall begin with those models focusing on properties of the individual.

Life-span models

Interestingly, the two life-span models we shall examine came from quite different disciplines: sociology (Miller and Form 1951) and vocational development (Super 1957). The creators of both models were looking at quite different variables and attributed shifts and transitions during the life span to different causes, but it is the similarities in the models rather than the differences that strike the reader.

Miller and Form (1951) were among the first to formulate a developmental model for careers. They viewed careers as a series of social adjustments the culture imposes on the worker. According to Miller and Form, these social adjustments "begin with birth and end only with death." They fall into a lifework pattern of five periods:

1. preparatory work period, characterized by socialization of the child at home and at school into the work patterns of society;
2. initial period, when the young worker is initiated into the work world through part-time employment;
3. trial period, beginning with the first full-time job and continuing to a more or less permanent work position;

4. stable work period, the period of job permanence; and
5. retirement period.

Miller and Form make it clear, however, that not everyone goes through these stages successfully and achieves stability and security. Those who do experience these stages successfully might follow what Miller and Form call a stable career pattern, in which individuals go directly from their schooling into work with which they stay, or they may follow a conventional career pattern where they move from initial job, to trial job, to stable employment, But there are other patterns where individuals do not make it successfully through these stages. Some individuals develop an unstable career pattern, where they never become established in one area, going from trial jobs to a stable situation but then back to trial jobs again. Other individuals follow a multiple-trial pattern, never staying in one field long enough to achieve stability, moving from one trial job to another.

In their explanation of why different individuals have different experiences within and between these periods, Miller and Form emphasize the importance of social class. Membership in a given social class is their primary predictor of occupational attainment. They cite research that demonstrates a relationship between occupational attainment and five factors:

1. father's occupation;
2. worker's intelligence;
3. father's income and education;
4. accessible financial aid and influential contacts; and
5. social and economic conditions in the general society.

Because four of these five factors demonstrate a relationship between the individual's environment and occupational level attained, Miller and Form are more impressed by the importance of the accident of birth into a certain social class in determining an individual's attainments than by anything the individual does. So while Miller and Form's model is developmental in the sense that it defines a course in which the career is played out, they picture a developmental pattern that is largely determined before it begins. [A rich body of sociological literature continues to substantiate the importance of family social class on subsequent work outcomes (e.g., Blau and Duncan 1967, whose work was replicated and extended by Featherman and Hauser 1978; Raelin 1980); however, the amount of variance in occupational attainment that is unexplained by these social predictors leaves a great deal to be accounted for by other explanatory schemas.]

Super (1957), an authority in vocational counseling, used the self-concept as the construct for examining career development. Career development for him involved "implementing a self-concept and testing this self-concept against reality." Yet, Super's descriptive and explanatory model of career development utilizes a life-span model surprisingly similar to Miller and Form's. He pictures career development as proceeding through five life stages taken from Buehler (1933):

1. The *growth stage*, extending from conception to approximately age 14: During this period the self-concept begins to form through identification with key figures in the family and school. Interests and capacities become more important with increasing social participation.

2.   The *exploratory stage*, ordinarily including the period from ages 15 to 25:

This period, according to Super, is characterized by the emergence of the self-concept through the process of experimentation and testing. The self-concept emerges from what Super calls "reality-testing" – a process by which the young individual tries out ideas of self on the environment, retaining those aspects of the self-concept that bring satisfaction and rejecting those that do not.

3.   The *establishment stage*, spanning the years from 25 to about 45:

Having found an appropriate field, the individual puts forth effort to make a permanent place in it. There may be some further experimentation early in this period, resulting in one or two changes before the life work is found or before it becomes clear that the life work will be a succession of unrelated jobs.

4.   The *maintenance stage*, stretching from 45 to retirement:

The concern here is to hold on to a place already made in the world of work. Usually little new ground is broken, but there is a continuation along existing lines.

5.   The *decline stage*, including the years from retirement to death:

At the time Super formulated this model, he had little to say about this period, but since he has entered this stage himself, Super (1986) has much more to say about the intertwining of work and leisure and the part both play in self-realization.

These two life-span models, because they are built around the biological life cycle, have a great deal of similarity. They each postulate developmental stages, and they each focus on the interaction between the individual and the environment, whether the focus is on the society forcing the individual to adapt to its needs or on the individual forming an identity based on the choices and responses received from the environment. Life-span models also provide such a broad framework that they accommodate a great diversity of empirical findings and points of view. Hall (1976) noted this when he attempted to integrate a number of studies of managers at AT&T and elsewhere. Each of these life-span models also make clear that work-related organizations provide the possibility for an individual to find a role or establish an identity as a competent productive member of society. But both models also make it clear that some individuals are unable to take advantage of this possibility. These models also point out the difficulty that some individuals, and especially those that have reached the midpoint in their careers, have in maintaining a viable place for themselves in organizations.

An individual differences model

Although individual differences are central to the occupational choice literature, they have seldom been the basis for anyone trying to formulate a developmental model of career development. Schein's (1978) work on career anchors is an exception. Schein did not begin to examine individual differences as a basis for a theory of career development. As we shall see later, he had formulated a model of an organization and was looking at the intersect between individual needs and organizational demands by studying the socialization process and the formation of the psychological contract. Schein's career anchors model evolved out of a 10-to 12-year longitudinal study of 44 MBA graduates from the Sloan School at the Massachusetts Institute of Technology. Part of the study included interviews focusing on detailed job histories of each person and reasons given for making career decisions. Schein found little consistency in the job histories but a great deal of consistency in the reasons individuals gave for making the decisions they had made. Moreover, the reasons became more clear-cut, articulate, and consistent as the individuals in the study accumulated greater work experience. The concept of career anchors emerged as a way of explaining the pattern of reasons given by the panelists – patterns of self-perceived talents, motives, and values that served to guide, constrain, stabilize, and integrate individual careers.

Schein defined five career anchors that characterized the lives of his subjects over the period studied:

1. *Technical–functional competence* – Individuals in this group organized their careers around specific areas of technical or functional competence and made job moves essentially by the criterion of maximizing their opportunity to remain challenged in their specific content area. They were not interested in management per se and resisted the idea of going into general management.
2. *Managerial competence* – Individuals with this career anchor were concerned with climbing the corporate ladder to positions of general management, where they could exercise large amounts of responsibility and link organizational achievement to their own efforts. They identified their competence as lying in a combination of three sub-competences critical for a general manager: (a) analytical competence, the ability to solve problems under conditions of uncertainty; (b) interpersonal competence, the ability to influence and lead people to achieve organizational goals; and (c) emotional competence, the capacity to be stimulated by crises rather than exhausted or debilitated by them.
3. *Security and stability* – Individuals with this anchor were preoccupied with stability, either in the continued employment of a particular company or in geographical stability, settling down, stabilizing the family, and integrating oneself into the community.
4. *Creativity* – Members of this group organized all their career decisions around the need to create something: a product, a company, or a service of their own. Schein referred to the members of this group as entrepreneurs.
5. *Autonomy and independence* – Individuals with this anchor found themselves increasingly unable and unwilling to work in large organizations and found for themselves essentially "autonomous" careers in such roles as professor, free-lance writer, or consultant.

Schein's subjects were a relatively highly educated group, who, because of the number of work options available to them, were able to develop careers consistent with their needs and values. Some found in organizations opportunities to grow, sharpen their skills, and increase their abilities. Others found organizations undesirable and fled them. Others were willing to trade time and/or loyalty to the organization in exchange for other things they wanted. Still others created organizations to achieve other goals central to their development. This same wide variation in the orientation toward organizations has been found by other students of careers. Derr (1986) has built a model that is not developmental and will not be discussed here, which focuses on the differences in orientation individuals bring to the organization and managers ignore at their own peril.

A *directional pattern model*

We now move to a model of career development that falls between those we have already examined, which focus primarily on properties of the individual, and those we shall examine later, which focus on organizational properties. Driver's model is essentially a typology of career patterns. Driver describes four "career concepts" that he describes as underlying a person's thinking about his or her career but also seem to be built into certain occupations or organizations:

1.   The *transitory* career concept is one in which no set job or field is ever permanently chosen. The individual moves from job to job with no particular pattern. This concept is found frequently among semi-skilled workers or actors.

2.   The *steady-state* carrer concept is one in which the individual selects a job or field early in life and stays in essentially one work role for life. This has been common among established professions (such as dentists and doctors) or skilled trades (such as barbers and plumbers). But with the recent changes in our society, even people in these professions and trades have been forced to consider other career concepts.

3.   The *linear* career concept is one in which a field is chosen early in life and a plan for upward movement is developed and executed. The linear concept is most commonly found among corporate managers.

4.   The *spiral* career concept involves a view that one develops in a given field for a period of time; then one moves on to a related or perhaps a totally new area on a cyclic basis. This concept, according to Driver (1982) is most frequently found among consultants and writers.

Organizationally based models of career development

Career models in this category also look at the interface between the organization and the individual. However, these career models begin with certain properties of organizations, such as structures and needed functions, and define career development in terms of individuals adapting to and moving through those structures or learning to perform these functions.

One of the earliest and most useful of these models is the adult socialization model of Becker and Strauss (1956). While most sociologists view individuals as members of a social structure, filling certain roles and achieving a certain level of status, Becker and Strauss use the concept of career to focus on movement through structures. They point out that in a given occupation or organization, there is a wide range of specializations and career lines. They note that first choices in a career are important but that a long series of subsequent decisions is required to follow a certain career line. But they also note that, at times, the greatest amount of "success" requires the abandonment of those activities and skills most closely associated with their original training (e.g., a move from research into marketing and then into marketing management). Becker and Strauss focused on the concept of career flow, viewing the flow of individuals through an organization as a number of streams that constitute routes to greater responsibility and higher status. Although greater age and experience may often help a person achieve a certain goal, an excess of training or experience in one area may make it difficult for an individual to change streams. Each type of career has its crisis periods during which decisions to move or stay are particularly crucial.

Becker and Strauss (1956) also emphasize the interdependence of careers: The ability of an individual at one level to obtain a desired assignment or to champion a new product is dependent on the sponsorship of key persons at higher levels in the organization. Further, Becker and Strauss emphasize the relationship between changes in the social structure and changes in adult behavior and self-esteem. Personality change and development result from the patterned trans-actions accompanying career movement. (For example, a new vice-president of marketing may become interested in the proposal of a sales supervisor for pen-etrating a new market. The attention and sponsorship of the vice-president gives the sales supervisor new confidence and visibility in the company. The successful implementation of the proposal results in a promotion for the supervisor, enhances the reputation of both parties, and builds close ties between the two men and strong identification with each other.) Becker and Strauss argue that Freudian and other psychodynamic theories of personality development overstress child-hood experiences and claim that the position of the individual in the social struc-ture is central in accounting for adult identity, that is, a change in social position finds a related change in identity. Adult life characteristically affords and forces frequent and momentous movement from status to status. Consequently, members of those structures who undergo dramatic shifts in their environmental surround-ings must similarly change internally to maintain or regain a sense of personal identity. The process of adult socialization could thus be defined as a moving synthesis of occupational identifications.

Dill, Hilton, and Reitman (1962) also present a model of career development in which individuals develop through a series of interactions between themselves and the organizational environment. Development occurs through the feedback and information individuals receive in response to their decisions and actions. In some respects, this model is similar to those of Super and of Becker and Strauss in the emphasis placed on the developmental impact of the interaction between the individual and the environment. The Dill et al. model, however, places more emphasis on cognition and learning rather than on a concept of oneself or a sense of one's identity.

The first critical element to the Dill et al. model is the decision maker, who accepts uncertainty while trying to reduce it as much as possible. The second critical element is the organizational environment, which provides individuals with opportunities to act and to learn, feedback on performance and knowledge of results, and the criteria by which individuals are judged by others in the organization. In organizational life, an individual's effectiveness is primarily a social rather than a physical reality and can be found only in the generally accepted standards and values that reside in the perceptions of other's in the work environment. The final and the most critical element in the model is the individual's ability to interpret the masses of data, the obscure cues, and the signals indicating changes in the environment. In the Dill et al. model, the organization and its environment is the complex shifting reality, and career development follows the course of learning to interact more and more effectively with that reality. Inability to learn and interpret information effectively blocks an individual's development.

The third organizationally based model of career development we shall examine is a structural model by Schein (1971, 1978) designed to elucidate those aspects of an organization that involve the movement of people through it. Schein's basic proposition is that the organization should be conceived of as a three-dimensional space in the shape of a cone. Movement within the organizations can occur along three conceptually distinguishable dimensions, with movement along any of these three dimensions controlled by boundaries or filters. The three types of movement are:

1. *Vertical* – corresponding roughly to the notion of increasing or decreasing one's rank or level in the organizational hierarchy. Some organizations have a great many levels and some a very few (although the tendency is for organizations to reduce the number of levels in recent years). Vertical boundaries are fairly public, but the filters monitoring vertical movement are usually much less so. Upward movement is usually seen as a positive move, although an individual can be "kicked up stairs" and actually lose influence, informal status, and some of the other rewards that usually accompany upward vertical movement.

2. *Radial* – corresponding roughly to the notion of increasing or decreasing one's centrality in the organization, one's degree of being more or less on the "inside." For many who are dead-ended on the vertical dimension, radial movement toward the center is still possible and potentially meaningful. Movement toward or away from the inner circle is the least public of the three types of movement and the boundaries are the least specific, but movement is most clearly signaled by being given access to special privileges and to the "secrets" of the organization. Such secrets might include being told more about the politics of how things are really done or how the organization views certain people.

3. *Circumferential* – corresponding roughly to the notion of moving from one function or division of the organization to another. Some "specialists" seldom make moves of this kind, while others switch frequently, perhaps moving from engineering to manufacturing to marketing, for example.

Schein built the model to help him look at the reciprocal influence of the organization on the individual (socialization) and the impact of the individual on the organization (innovation). He hypothesized that the influence of the organization on the individual would be greatest just prior to and during boundary passages and that an individual's influence on the organization would be greatest when no boundary changes are anticipated. These are intriguing hypotheses and need to be tested. We all know that individuals shape organizations, but we know little about how that process takes place.

The last of the organizationally based models of career development we shall examine was proposed by Dalton and Thompson (1986), who studied the careers of hundreds of engineers and scientists, first trying to understand the curvilinear relationship they found between age and performance rankings (Dalton and Thompson 1971; Thompson, Dalton, and Kopelman 1974) but with little success. They finally moved to what they considered a more fruitful question, asking why a significant portion of the engineers and scientists continued to be highly valued by the organization while most did not. Their efforts, along with those of Price, resulted in the postulation of what they called a career stages model of careers (Dalton, Thompson, and Price 1977; Dalton and Thompson 1986). In this model, some professionals in organizations, but not all, move through four distinct stages in their careers. Movement from one stage to the next entails changes in activities, changes in their relationships with others in the organization, and new psychological issues with which they have to cope. The characteristic activities and relationships of the individuals in each of the four stages described by the investigators were:

Stage I
Usually works under the direction of another professional.
Work is never entirely his or her own, but assignments are sub-parts of larger projects supervised by another professional.
Is expected to do most of the detailed and routine work.
Stage II
Goes into depth on one problem or technical area.
Assumes responsibility for a project or a definable part of a larger project, process, or client relationship.
Works independently and produces significant results.
Develops credibility and a reputation.
Stage III
Develops greater breadth of technical skills and understands the application of those skills in broader areas.
Stimulates others through ideas and information.
Involved in the development of other people in one or more of the following ways:
　　acts as an idea leader for a small group,
　　serves as a mentor to younger professionals, and
　　assumes a formal supervisory position.
Deals with those outside his or her group for the benefit of others in the group, for example, getting funding, working with clients, and working with higher management.
Stage IV
Provides direction for a significant part of the organization.
Exercises significant formal and informal power.
Represents the organizations to individuals and groups inside the organization as well as to key institutions and individuals outside the organization.
Sponsors promising individuals to test them and prepare them for key roles in the organization in the future.

Significantly, the stages were not age related, as were the life-span models of Miller and Form (1951) and of Super (1957); the average age of professionals in each of the four stages varies within a range of only three years (38–41 years of age). Nor did formal positions account for the stages; in several of the organizations studied, more than half of those described as being in Stage III held no formal supervisory or management positions. In a number of high-technology organizations, the investigators even found a number of individuals who were described as being in Stage IV who had no management or supervisory positions.

Dalton and Thompson (1986) have shown empirically that there is a strong relationship between the stage that an individual is described as performing and that person's performance ratings. Dalton and Thompson maintain that the strong relationship derives from the fact that individuals are evaluated in organizations on the basis of the value of their contribution to the organization. The value of an individual's contribution to an organization is determined, in large part, by the criticality of the functions an individual performs to the viability and growth of the organization. The functions performed by individuals in Stage IV are critical to the present and future performance of the organization as an entity; the functions performed by individuals in Stage I are far less critical. If the Stage IV functions are performed well or poorly, the impact on the organization can be considerable. If the Stage I functions are performed well or poorly, the impact on the organization will usually be negligible. The four stages represent clusters of functions that are progressively more highly valued by those whose job it is to evaluate and reward others on behalf of the organization.

There are some interesting parallels and differences between the four organizationally based models. Both the Becker and Strauss (1956) model and the Dalton and Thompson (1986) model recognize the importance of the social system of sponsors and mentors to the flow of individuals through the organization. Both the Dill et al. (1962) model and the Dalton and Thompson (1986) model focus on the consequences for individuals who are able, or unable, to learn from the organizational environment which activities are valued most and how to perform those activities. The Schein (1971; 1978) model is unique in its balance between the influence of the individual on the organization as well as the influence the organization exerts on the individual.

THE IMPACT OF ORGANIZATIONS ON
INDIVIDUAL DEVELOPMENT

This brief overview of models of career development gives us a starting place to address the larger question of how organizations affect individual development and why we have such ambivalent feelings toward organizations. The very existence of the life-span models formulated by Miller and Form (1951) and Super (1957) point up the pervasiveness and centrality that work-related organizations play in our lives and our development. As Miller and Form point out, organizations play a part in our lives and our development from birth to death. A large part of the training in homes and in schools is designed to prepare us for careers in organizations. Given this training, we are led to expect that we will be able to fulfill many of our needs, including many of our developmental needs, in those organizations. Yet both life-span models also point out that some significant part of the work force is made up of individuals who are unable to establish themselves in the work world and whose "career" is a succession of unrelated jobs. They enter and reenter organizations hoping to meet some of their needs, only to have those hopes frustrated time after time. Certainly individuals in this part of the work force find organizations bewildering and often hated places. Can the word "ambivalent" be used to describe this group? We believe it can. While these individuals keep leaving jobs and usually organizations, they keep taking other jobs and usually entering other organizations. While reentry may be forced by external economic or social pressures, the individuals taking the new jobs must have enough hope that "things might be different this time" that their feeling toward organizations could at least be called ambivalent.

The group of individuals highlighted in these models who are apparently most suspicious that organization life will not provide them with an environment where they can meet their most important needs are the individuals pointed out by Schein's model (1978) as having an "autonomy or independence anchor." As we have seen, Schein reported that over time, individuals with this anchor found themselves increasingly unable and unwilling to work in large organizations. But even among this group, two of the three roles that Schein reported that people with this anchor had found for themselves were those of professor and organizational consultant. Professors and organizational consultants are members of organizations and are teaching or counseling others who will be or are members of work-related organizations. If we could describe those who could not establish themselves in the work world but kept trying as moths who are alternately attracted to and burned by the flame, Schein's individuals with an autonomy career anchor could be described as circling the flame but staying at as safe a distance as possible.

But these are the two groups identified by the model as being least able or least willing to develop careers for themselves in organizations. What about those who were willing and able to develop careers for themselves in organizations? What did we find about the impact of organizations on these individuals? Schein's description of the individuals he studied who had the other four "anchors" were able to find in organizations places where they could learn and grow. All had "developed" as individuals in the sense that, over the decade following graduation from school, they had increasingly begun to make reasoned choices that moved them toward environments that utilized and enhanced their competencies or had at least moved them toward realizing the achievement of things they valued.

Interestingly, however, it is the organizationally based models that place the greatest emphasis on the possibility and necessity for individuals to learn and develop. This is not surprising in one sense: these models take the needs and properties of organizations as a given and examine the adaptation of the individual to those needs and properties as the developmental course. Still, the Dill et al. model (1962) has a surprisingly clear focus on individual learning. Dill and his associates studied individuals who would fall into Driver's (1982) linear orientation and Schein's (1978) managerial competence anchor category and therefore seemed most likely and most able to find organizations compatible to their needs. But the evidence seems clear that for certain individuals, at least, work organizations provide a climate for learning and development.

Of all the career development models we have discussed thus far, however, the one we found most explicit about the possibilities for individual development in organizations as well as the organizational limitations that are placed on individuals who fail to develop in certain directions is Dalton and Thompson's career stages model (1986). No doubt, our greater familiarity with this model allows us to see these possibilities and limitations better than in the other models, but even whatever bias comes from our greater familiarity with this model is an argument for its use. It is therefore along the dimensions of individual development highlighted by each of Dalton and Thompson's career stages – identity, competence, interdependence, and leadership – that we propose to organize our examination of the possibilities and impediments for individual development in organizations. Our examination of each of these possibilities and impediments will also help us explore some of the roots of our ambivalence toward organizations.

Developing a sense of identity

The major personal achievement of the individual who successfully enters into Stage I in Dalton and Thompson's (1986) career stages model is that he or she has "gotten a job" and entered into a work role. Getting a job is a critical step in the establishment of a sense of self or personal identity. It helps the individual, at least temporarily, to answer the terrifying question: Who am I? It also provides a setting where individuals can receive feedback from the environment, enhancing or modifying their sense of identity. We have already seen that Super (1957) used the self-concept as a central organizing construct in examining career development. In fact, most students of individual development include the establishment and stabilization of a sense of self or identity as a crucial dimension of personal development. White (1952:333) identifies as one of his four processes of natural growth the stabilizing of ego identity. "When one takes a long enough span of time," says White, "ego identity can be seen to become not only more sharp and clear, but also more consistent and free from transient influences. It becomes increasingly determined by accumulated personal experience . . . Even praise is not accepted . . . when inner judgement cannot agree that it is deserved." Maslow (1954) concurs that "the most stable and healthy self-esteem is based on deserved respect from others rather than from external fame." But as Strauss (1959) has pointed out, we need to have our identities "upheld in open court." For most men and for an increasing number of women, that open court is in a work role in an organization. When we ask "who someone is," the most expected answer has both a role and an organization in the response: "She is an engineer at Boeing", "He is an IBM salesman", and "He is a welder at the General Dynamics plant." Levinson (1978) found that there was no way to consider adult development apart from occupational life:

A man's occupation places him within a particular socio-economic level and work world. It exerts a powerful influence upon the options available to him, the choices he makes among them, and his possibilities for advancement and satisfaction. . . . Occupation has important sources within the self and important consequences for the self. It is the primary medium in which a young man's dreams for the future are defined, and the vehicle he uses to produce those dreams. At best, his occupation permits the fulfillment of basic values and life goals. At worst, a man's work life over the years is oppressive and corrupting, and contributes to a growing alienation from self, work and society. (1978:102–103)

It is this last point of Levinson's that an individual's work life may not enhance the self but lead to an alienation from oneself that contributes so heavily to the ambivalence we feel toward the organizations in which we work. The criticisms that work life in organizations fail to help the individual establish a sense of identity have a long history. Mayo (1946) was concerned about the "seamy side of progress" and the human problems of an industrial civilization dominated by modern organizations. According to Mayo, we faced a condition that Durkheim described as "anomie," a planlessness in living. Individuals were less and less able to assign meaning to their work. Mayo complained that managers and planners assumed that people were a "dustheap of individuals" and that spontaneous cooperation was not fostered but was channeled into practices such as rate restriction.

The importance of a job or a work role to an individual's sense of identity and the relationship between that sense of identity and the individual's overall well-being is most dramatically shown when individuals are deprived of their work role. Studies of unemployment have revealed serious effects. Eisenberg and Lazersfeld (1938) reported that unemployed workers lost a sense of time and that the release from the discipline of regular work was accompanied by family tension, loss of self-respect, and emotional disturbance.

Thus we see that organizational processes and work roles can play a vital part for some individuals in the development of a sense of identity or self. But the importance of a stable and significant work role to the development and stabilization of one's sense of identity also points out the dependence of the individual on the organizations that provide those work roles. That dependence, along with the fear that organizations cannot be fully depended upon to provide the work roles, is near the root of the ambivalence we feel toward organizations. For individuals such as Miller and Form's (1951) workers who are unable to establish a stable career pattern and for the unemployed, the lack of a stable work role and its effect on individual identity are realized. For others, such as Dalton and Thompson's (1986) professional workers who never move beyond Stage I and who do not feel valued by the organization, the ever-present possibility that they may lose their work role seriously stunts the development of their sense of identity and keeps it constantly under the threat of disintegration.

Developing competence

Those professionals who move into Dalton and Thompson's Stage II do so by developing the capacity to "work independently and produce significant results." This is a second dimension of development that organizations provide for some individuals – the enhancement and exercise of one's capabilities. The development of competence can cover a wide spectrum in capacity. At one end of the spectrum, White (1959) has established that a drive for competence or effectance is one of the most elementary and fundamental tendencies in humans. At a more intermediate level, we see individuals coping more effectively with their environment, developing skills, becoming less dependent, and increasing their capacity to control outcomes important to them. Maslow (1954) has even argued that, for some individuals, there is, at the other end of the spectrum, a tendency toward self-actualization, "to become everything that one is capable of becoming."

For many individuals, organizational work life not only permits individuals to exercise and expand their capabilities and skills, but also facilitates and rewards such activity and growth. Working in organizations often involves learning to deal more effectively with materials, information, customers, colleagues, and organizational processes. It involves the management of oneself and one's time capably enough that others entrust you to work independently to carry off a project, operate sophisticated equipment, handle a territory, or make a loan. Successful work experience engenders self-respect and the respect of others.

We might suspect that, again, those individuals in Miller and Form's (1951) unstable career pattern group and those with Driver's (1982) transitory career concept would find it difficult to develop an increasing sense of competence. But a number of organizational critics fault organizations for blocking growth on this dimension even among steadily employed members. Argyris (1964), an early critic, claimed that organizations retard the development of most of their members by preventing them from experiencing psychological success. "Psychological success," according to Argyris, comes when (a) organizational members aspire to experience an increasing sense of competence through finding opportunities to accomplish tasks that will allow them to accept themselves as well as others and (b) organizations allow their members to determine goals, the means to achieve them, and opportunities for continually challenging work. Argyris argued that modern organizational structures break tasks down into simple acts, requiring employees to use relatively little of their capacity to think. As individuals seek psychological success in such settings, they become disillusioned, frustrated, and discouraged. To avoid those feelings, workers engage in activities such as absenteeism, quota restrictions, "gold-bricking," slow-downs, and so on. They avoid openness and risk-taking and become conforming and dependent.

Dalton (1959) implicitly criticized organizations for undermining the development of work-related competence by rewarding, instead, "unofficial requirements for success." In the one organization he studied intensively, four of the most prominent of these unofficial requirements were membership in the Masons, ethnic background, membership in the local yacht club, and political affiliation. But implicit in Dalton's report of his study is the message that any criteria for advancement that are extraneous to the performance of the organization's work not only diminish the organization's capacity but also discourage the individual development of work-related competence.

One of the newer concerns of students, managers, and employees of organizations is that technical competence alone can become "obsolete" over time. Individuals who spend years of effort and study to become competent to perform work in a certain area can often find their value to the organization decreasing in spite of their efforts to remain technically up to date. This concern came into being and grew as organizations hired more and more university graduates who have spent years learning a professional or technical field. Pelz and Andrews (1966), who studied a number of research and development laboratories in the 1960s, found a strong correlation between age and rated performance among scientists and particularly among engineers. Pelz and Andrews investigated several other measures of competence but used rated performance as the best available measure of competence. Rated performance peaked, depending on the type of scientist or engineer, in the late thirties or middle forties and then declined until the middle fifties when another, less pronounced peak in performance appeared. Pelz and Andrews began to talk about technical obsolescence. By 1971, Dalton and Thompson were reporting that, among design engineers, the highest ratings went to engineers in their early thirties, and that rating declined steadily for each subsequent age group until retirement. Thompson and Dalton (1976) later reported that organizational processes contributed to the fact that many engineers were unable to keep up with the most current technology through such practices as keeping an engineer assigned full time to a product long after the technology on that product ceased to be near the forefront of the engineer's technical field. Kaufman (1974:24–25) reported that managers from 89% of the firms he surveyed considered obsolescence of their technical professionals to be an organizational problem, while 95% of the engineers and 86% of the engineering managers reported it to be a personal concern of their own. By 1980, Bailyn (1980a:70) had concluded that her research on the careers of MIT graduates raised the possibility that engineering as a life-long occupation "either does not exist or is viable only if one withdraws one's 'life investment' from one's work." Dalton and Thompson's findings (1986) corroborated Bailyn's conclusion for engineers who stayed solely in technical work. Indeed, they found that professionally trained employees in general, unless the professionals moved beyond technical work alone and began to develop organizational and people skills and interests, were less likely to be valued by the organizations in which they worked and therefore found it harder to maintain a sense of competence.

Thus we find that organizations are important but often unreliable settings in which to develop and maintain a sense of competence. Increasingly, organizations are the almost exclusive source of occupational employment. Thus organizations are the best available setting for most individuals to develop a sense of competence. The fact that this is the case and that so often employees of these organizations are not given real opportunities to develop along this dimension is another source of the ambivalence we feel toward organizations. The unemployed and those with unstable employment patterns again find it difficult to develop a sense of competence. But even among those steadily employed, many have jobs (although hopefully a decreasing portion of them) designed so that performance in those jobs requires little real skill or genuine competence. Finally, and most ironically, even those in jobs where considerable technical skill and utilization of knowledge are required – engineers and scientists – are now finding it difficult to maintain a sense of competence over time unless they combine their technical skills with the interpersonal skills and broad perspective necessary to get things done in a complex organization setting.

Building mutually developmental relationships

The individuals identified by Dalton and Thompson (1986) as being in Stage III were distinguishable from those in Stages I and II in large part by their capability and interest in establishing interdependent and developmental relationships. Importantly, over half of the individuals in Stage III did not hold management or supervisory positions. In our view, growth in one's ability to form such relationships represents a third important dimension of individual development. As Bellah et al. (1985) have reminded us, we have allowed ourselves in the United States to be so unduly restricted by our vocabulary of individualism that we have slighted those elements of mutual commitment and reciprocal benefit that are central to the relationships that nurture our development. Interdependent relationships have their basis in reciprocity and trust. Each party brings something to the relationship and derives something from it. It is through such relationships that much of the work is done in the world and a large part of the values are transmitted.

A part of this developmental dimension is akin to Erikson's concept of generativity. Erikson (1959:97) defines generativity as "primarily the interest in establishing and guiding the next generation." He suggests that much of this development will be expressed in rearing one's offspring but that it is also expressed in other forms of altruistic concern. The relationships we have in mind may have some altruism in them, but they clearly benefit both parties.

Levinson (1978), in his description of adult development, noted that interdependent mentoring relationships between young men (his subjects were all male) and their more experienced teachers, bosses, editors, and senior colleagues played a critical role in the development of young adults. The mentor provided counsel, support, and influence to facilitate the young man's entry and advancement in the organization or profession: "He (the mentor) fosters the young adult's development by believing in him, sharing the youthful Dream and giving it his blessing, helping him to define the newly emerging self in its newly discovered world and creating a space in which the young man can work on a reasonably satisfactory life structure" (1978:98–99). Levinson was describing the young man's development, but we contend that the relationship is developmental for the mentor as well.

Kram (1985) found in the organizations she studied a wealth of mentoring relationships that were deeply embedded in work performance and clearly interdependent and reciprocal. But because mentoring relationships are not always available, positive, or appropriate, she advocated a closer look at the developmental aspects of peer relationships.

Clawson (1980) contrasted mentor–protégée relationships with superior–subordinate relationships and concluded that the more the latter resembled the former, the more likely it was that "subordinates would learn the things they needed to know to grow and advance" (1980:162).

But such relationships are not the norm in all parts of organizations, as a number of small-group studies in factories and offices have shown. One such study (Zaleznik et al. 1958) reported that the processes on a factory floor resulted in "frozen groups." The researchers defined frozen groups as a form of social pathology that limits their members to incomplete individual development. The researchers concluded: "These groups have few, if any, ways of relating themselves in a positive fashion to the organizational settings in which they live...Their regular members and leaders have little opportunity to exercise their influence, leadership and responsibilities except in the direction of maintaining the group's social life," which consisted of endless one-level elaborations of routine activities, conversations and "gripes": "Opportunities for doing new things, for developing new ways of doing them, for assuming personal responsibility, and for personal self-development are seriously limited" (Zaleznik et al. 1958:390).

More recently, Kanter (1977) was struck by the amount of employee disengagement from work-related relationships she found in a large corporation. With limited advancement opportunities and feeling plateaued, employees became frustrated and began to disengage themselves from the organization and their work in order to cope with their negative feelings. They lowered their aspirations, their commitment to the organization, and their willingness to accept responsibility. They sought social recognition outside the organization and recognition inside the organization in areas not related to job performance.

Clearly, there is evidence that many individuals can and do establish relationships embedded in the central activities of the organization that contribute to their own and to other's development. But again our ambivalence toward organizations is reinforced by the substantial constraints in many organizations that limit growth on this dimension. Work is often designed and/or managed in such a way that building developmental relationships around the accomplishment of work is difficult, if not impossible. For those disengaged from the vital work of the organization, relationships can deteriorate into a set of trivial and meaningless routine joint activities. This is an area where further experimentation and research is needed.

Developing the capacity to lead

Dalton and Thompson (1986) found a number of people in organizations who had moved into a fourth career stage. It was the individuals in Stage IV who provided strategic direction, who were entrusted to exercise power on behalf of the organization, who represented the organization to others, and who trained and selected others to perform these functions in the future. Most of the individuals in this stage occupied senior management positions, although in high-technology organizations there were some non-managers who provided strategic direction for a substantial part of the organization through their technical knowledge and creativity. These Stage IV individuals constituted 11% of the professionally trained employees in the R&D organizations Dalton and Thompson studied and a smaller percentage of the total work force in those organizations. The leadership functions that these Stage IV individuals performed for the organization were similar to the functions Schein's (1978) managerial anchor people were performing or striving to perform. Likewise, the young managers studied by Dill et al. (1962) were working diligently and carefully to earn the right to be entrusted with the performance of these functions.

We often talk about the upgrade in status and rewards that people entrusted to lead organizations are given. But we speak less about the individual development that is both possible and necessary for those who earn the right to be entrusted with the responsibility of providing leadership for organizations. We shall not try to explore all the areas of individual development necessary to earn this entrustment and to carry out these functions. The one area we should like to explore is the capacity to exercise organizational power effectively and responsibly.

Dalton and Thompson (1986) found that the most difficult developmental task for those making the transition into Stage IV was learning to exercise power on behalf of the organization. Schein (1978) made a similar observation about the individuals whom he identified as having a managerial anchor. Schein identified three types of competence, in combination, that were needed to do the work of the general manager: analytical, interpersonal, and emotional. He noted that all three are important but that what differentiated the managerially oriented group most from those with different anchors was the fact that "they explicitly drew attention to the emotional aspects of their job and saw as part of their own development the evolution of the insight that they could deal with emotionally tough situations." This emotional competence included "the capacity to bear high levels of responsibility without becoming paralyzed, and the ability to exercise power without guilt or shame" (Schein 1978:136).

McClelland (1975), who studied power orientations for over two decades, also came to see power as a developmental issue. Individuals, he claims, have the inherent capacity to move through four stages of power orientation. He particularly noted that there are important developmental issues involved in moving away from an orientation toward personal power – the need to dominate or win out over someone else – toward socialized or organizational power – the need to exercise entrusted power for the benefit of the organization or institution that has entrusted him or her with that power.

The reason why the responsible exercise of organizational power requires and facilitates individual development is that organizational power is, indeed, an entrustment. The various stakeholders in an organization rightfully feel that they are entitled to expect that those empowered by the organization will use the power given them in the best interest of the organization. Stakeholders expect that those entrusted with organizational power will place the interests of the organization above their own personal interests or the interests of their friends or family. If those so entrusted use the power given them for personal rather than organizational ends, there has been a violation of trust. If they fail to use the power entrusted to them wisely, judiciously, even c urageously, they have failed in their stewardship.

Much of our ambivalence toward organizations centers around the use of power. On the one hand, many members of the organization fear that they will not be permitted to share in this power. On the other hand, many of us fear that those who are entrusted with this power will not have developed the self-discipline or the judgment to use this power responsibly. We fear that it will be abused. We say to one another that power corrupts. We see few checks and balances in most organizations. We believe that individuals can develop the capacity to exercise organizational power wisely and trustworthily, but we fear that many do not.

SUMMARY AND IMPLICATIONS

We began this chapter by noting that we have ambivalent feelings toward organizations. We depend on them so much and spend so much time in them that we want them to be simple and benign. Organizations are neither simple nor benign; they are complex and dangerous.

Their complexity is demonstrated by the models that have been created to try to conceptualize careers in organizations from a developmental view. Each of the models has been useful, but the combined picture that emerges when we look at them together seems to the author to be more of a patchwork than a complete map of a well-known terrain. The fact that it seems like a patchwork to us does not derive primarily from the fact that the models have been created by scholars from different disciplines, starting from different perspectives, although this is the case. It derives more from the fact that the creators of the models we have examined have studied quite different populations. Some have looked only at management trainees, some have looked only at professionals, and some have tried to look at all classes of employees but have tried to look at the entire life span at the same time. Hopefully, one of the contributions of this handbook will be to help weave the various strands of our knowledge about careers into a rich mosaic.

But even the patchwork we have put together in this chapter is sufficient to see that the terrain of careers in organizations is both complex and shifting. It is complex because the individuals who come to the work place are so different from one another in their expectations and skills and because organizations themselves have so many different needs. It is shifting because the nature and training of the work force is changing rapidly at the same time that organizations themselves are changing in response to environmental pressures and new ideas.

Our attempt to look at the effects that organizations exert on individual development certainly should warn anyone that while the possibilities for individual growth in organizations are great, organizations can be dangerous. They are particularly dangerous if we expect things from organizations they cannot deliver. Too many individuals enter organizations expecting that if they work hard, the organization will take care of them. They do not realize that organizations actually exist only in our own minds and that they are made up of individuals who may not be around to fulfill implied promises at some time in the future. Organizations are dangerous because too often we have organized the jobs in them according to old models of efficiency without taking into account human needs. They are dangerous when we allow ourselves to think that some specialized knowledge or past achievement will make us secure; technology and organizational needs shift so rapidly that it is only our ability to learn and adapt that prepares us for the future.

What are the implications of what we have discussed for individuals, for organizations, and for further study? Certainly one of the implications is that "career development specialists" should not try to promise recruits that they will do "career pathing" for them; they should not because they cannot. Any promised path could disappear tomorrow. Specialists cannot do career development for individuals, only individuals can do the hard work, make the choices, develop the relationships, and take the chances that will make the biggest differences in the way their careers develop.

Hall's conclusion (1976:179–189) that each individual must take responsibility for managing his or her career should be shared with everyone in organization life. Hall recommends that individuals try to clarify for themselves as much as they can about their strengths and interests as well as the opportunities that are currently available. Schein (1978:191–201) agrees and also recommends that managers and planners have regular discussions with individuals about job rotation and assignments. There are organizations now attempting to follow both recommendations. These efforts should be studied.

We noted that work has often been designed and managed so that factory and office workers are neither expected nor even allowed to use their problem-solving skills and to work with others to improve output. Partly in response to foreign competition, a number of companies are experimenting with socio-technical work designs to encourage "autonomous work teams" to work together to improve output and quality. Competition demands that designers, marketers, manufacturing people, suppliers, and even customers work together to get a new product into the market in such short periods of time that old ways of organizing and dividing up duties are no longer feasible. What impact are these changes having on the career development and individual development of factory and office workers, on professionals, on supervisors, and on managers?

Also in response to competition, large organizations have been eliminating levels of middle management and "flattening" their organizations at the same time they have been "down sizing." In the meantime, enough new jobs have been created by smaller organizations to increase the number of total jobs. What impact has this change had on the careers of those whose primary career goals were moving up the hierarchy? Will there be more decision making and problem solving done by non-managers and less emphasis on hierarchical moves? What effect has the turbulence had on the careers of those affected? Are they finding more challenge but less security in smaller organizations?

The life-span models of careers were constructed at a time when employees, mostly men, entered the work force early and stayed in the work force until retirement. With large numbers of women entering and leaving the work force at different ages, what are the new patterns that are emerging? Is it possible that these women may create in organizations what Bailyn and others (Bailyn 1980) have been advocating, genuine alternative ("slow-burn" or even interrupted burn) routes to where one wants to go?

Most fundamentally, if organizations are going to have to adapt to changes in the environment as rapidly as current trends seem to project, what are the processes that members of those organizations will use to form and reform themselves to perform these ever-changing tasks? If organizations actually need the high commitment from individuals that managers and writers seem to think will be necessary for organizations to compete in worldwide markets, how are those organizations going to have to change to allow the kind of individual development that will maintain that commitment?

NOTE

I am deeply indebted to Brent Thomas for his contribution to this chapter.

REFERENCES

Argyris, C. (1964). *Integrating the Individual and the Organization*. New York: Wiley.
Bailyn, L. (1980a) *Living With Technology: Issues at Mid-Career*. Cambridge, MA: MIT Press.
Bailyn, L. (1980b) The slow burn way to the top: some thoughts of the early years of organizational careers. In C. B. Derr (ed.), *Work, Family and the Career: New Frontiers in Theory and Research*. New York: Praeger.
Becker, H. S., and Strauss, A. (1956) Careers, personality, and adult socialization. *American Journal of Sociology*, 62, 253–263.
Bellah, R., Madsen, R., Sullivan, W. M., Swidler, A., and Tipton, S. M. (1985). *Habits of the Heart: Individualism and Commitment in American Life*. New York: Harper & Row.
Blau, P. M., and Duncan, O. D. (1967). *The American Occupational Structure*. New York: Wiley.
Buehler, C. (1933). *Der Menschliche Lebershauf als Psychologisches Problem*. Leipzig: Hirzel.
Clawson, J. (1980). Mentoring in managerial careers. In C. B. Derr (ed.), *Work, Family and the Career: New Frontiers in Theory and Research*. New York: Praeger.
Dalton, G., and Thompson, P. (1971). Accelerating obsolescence of older engineers. *Harvard Business Review*, September/October, pp. 57–67.
Dalton, G., and Thompson, P. (1986). *Novations: Strategies for Career Development*. Glenview, IL: Scott Foresman.
Dalton, G., Thompson, P., and Price, R. (1977). The four stages of professional careers. *Organizational Dynamics*, Summer, pp. 19–42.
Dalton, M. (1959). *Men Who Manage*. New York: Wiley.
Derr, C. B. (1986). *Managing the New Careerists*. San Francisco: Jossey-Bass.
Dill, W. R., Hilton, T. L, and Reitman, W. R. (1962). *The New Managers*. Englewood Cliffs, NJ: Prentice-Hall.

Driver, M. J. (1982). Career concepts – a new approach to career research. In R. Katz (ed.), *Career Issues in Human Resource Management*. Englewood Cliffs, NJ: Prentice-Hall.

Eisenberg, P., and Lazersfeld, P. (1938). The psychological effects of unemployment. *Psychological Bulletin*, 35, 358–390.

Erikson, E. (1959). Growth and the crisis of the healthy personality, identity and the life cycle. *Psychological Issues*, 1, 50–100.

Featherman, D. L., and Hauser, R. M. (1978). *Opportunity and Change*. New York: Academic.

Goffman, E. (1961). The Moral Career of the Mental Patient. In E. Goffman (ed.) *Asylums*. New York: Anchor Books.

Guralnik, D. B. (ed.) (1978). *Webster's New World Dictionary of the American Language*, 2nd College Ed. New York: William Collins + World. p. 214.

Hall, D. T. (1976). *Careers in Organizations*. Pacific Palisades, CA: Goodyear.

Kanter, R. (1977). *Men and Women of the Corporation*. New York: Basic Books.

Kaufman, H. (1974). *Obsolescence and Professional Career Development*. New York: Amacom.

Kram, K. (1985). *Mentoring at Work: Developmental Relationships in Organization Life*. Glenview, IL: Scott Foresman.

Levinson, D. (1978). *The Seasons of a Man's Life*. New York: Knopf.

McClelland, D. (1975). *Power: The Inner Experience*. New York, Irvington.

Maslow, A. (1954). *Motivation and Personality*. New York: Harper and Brothers.

Mayo, E. (1946). *The Human Problems of An Industrial Civilization*. Boston: Division of Research, Harvard Graduate School of Business Administration.

Miller, D. C., and Form, W. H. (1951). *Industrial Sociology*. New York: Harper.

Pelz, D., and Andrews, F. (1966). *Scientists in Organizations*. New York: Wiley.

Raelin, J. A. (1980). *Building a Career*. Kalamazoo, MI: Upjohn Institute for Employee Research.

Schein, E. H. (1971). The individual, the organization and the career: a conceptual scheme. *Journal of Applied Behavioral Science*, 7, 401–426.

Schein, E. H. (1978). *Career Dynamics: Matching Individual and Organization Needs*. Reading, MA: Addison-Wesley.

Strauss, A. L. (1959). *Mirrors and Masks: The Search for Identity*. Glenview, IL: Free Press.

Super, D. E. (1957). *The Psychology of Careers*. New York: Harper & Row.

Super, D. E. (1986). Life career roles: self-realization in work and leisure. In D. T. Hall (ed.), *Career Development in Organizations*. San Francisco: Jossey-Bass.

Thompson, P., and Dalton, G. (1976). Are R & D organizations obsolete? *Harvard Business Review*, November/December, pp. 105–116.

Thompson, P., Dalton, G., and Kopelman, R. (1974). But what have you done for me lately, the boss. *IEEE Spectrum*, October, pp. 85–89.

White, R. (1952). *Lives in Progress*. New York: Holt-Dryden.

White, R. (1959). Motivation reconsidered: the concept of competence. *Psychological Review*, 66, 297–333.

Zaleznik, A., Christensen, R., and Roethlisberger, F. (1958). *The Motivation, Productivity and Satisfaction of Workers: A Prediction Study*. Boston: Division of Research, Harvard Business School.

6 Exploring women's development: implications for career theory, practice, and research

JOAN V. GALLOS

Developmentally, women are different from men. The claim has surfaced so often, it can no longer be denied. Whether the charted gender differences have been framed as inherent female defects in biology (Freud, 1925), feminine deficiencies in reasoning (Kohlberg, 1976), learned responses to a political reality (French, 1985; Schaef, 1981), the recognition of a distinct developmental voice for men and women (Belenky, Clinchy, Goldberger, and Tarule, 1986; Gilligan, 1977), or cause for celebrating a new psychology of women (Miller, 1976), the theme is the same. Women construct their conceptions of themselves, their lives, and the world around them differently from men.

During the fragile early years of the Women's Movement, it was taboo to acknowledge any basic differences between men and women other than the most obvious biological ones. Equality between the sexes required a lock-step belief in what now seems a simplistic definition of equity as sameness. While we spoke of increasing human freedom by challenging stereotypic conceptions of men and women, we implicitly sold the male model of life and work as women's salvation from their second-class citizenship.

But the time has come to move beyond the debate of whether women and men are developmentally different and to focus more clearly on understanding the differences and their implications. Masking these developmental differences serves neither gender. We have begun to admit (Friedan, 1981; Marshall, Chapter 13) that the male model of work and success may be a dead end (and health statistics say that literally may be true). Implicit in women's different vision of reality is the potential for questioning present beliefs about what is essential for a creative and productive society, and how to chart a successful course to manage life's critical adult challenge – the balance between love and work.

The purpose of this chapter is to explore the different vision of reality that women can bring to work, love, and career. More specifically, I will review literature on women's development, as a way of both broadening understanding of women's lives and conceptions of career and beginning to speculate about the implications of women's distinctive development for career theory.

Like early beliefs about equality between the sexes, career theories have been largely built on male models of success and work. Those models are supported by psychoanalytic conceptions of the centrality of work to identity and developmental beliefs that maturity and personal empowerment require separation from others (Erikson, 1968; Levinson, 1978).

110

Women's voices have typically spoken of different truths. The ongoing process of attachment to significant others is an important source of identity, maturity, and personal power for women (Bardwick, 1980; Eichenbaum and Orbach, 1988; Gilligan, 1982; Josselson, 1987; McClelland, 1975). Women's career gains and professional accomplishments are complements, not substitutes, for strong inter-dependent relationships (Abramson and Franklin, 1986; Baruch, Barnett, and Rivers, 1983; Gallese, 1985; Hardesty and Jacobs, 1986; Roberts and Newton, 1986). What do we know about development for women in the adult years? What does women's distinctive developmental voice mean for understanding women's lives and careers? What does a reflection of women's voices mean for conceptions of career and for career theory?

THE STUDY OF WOMEN'S DEVELOPMENT:
THREE POSSIBLE APPROACHES

Three different sets of issues affect women's adult development and provide distinct disciplinary paths for approaching its study. Sociologically based, structural concerns explore how our institutions and social practices contribute to observed differences between men and women (e.g., Berheide and Segal, 1985; Epstein, 1988; Kanter, 1977; Scanzoni, 1983). These institutional or structural perspectives, for the most part, attribute causality for observed gender differences in life choices to socially constructed roles, policies, and conditions. How does, for example, the reality of the "glass ceiling" in organizations affect women's interests, life choices, and commitments (Adams, 1986; Hymowitz and Schellhardt, 1986)? How do institutional practices limit women's opportunities, keep childcare a personal problem, and channel women into low-level jobs (Giele and Kahne, 1978; Sandell, 1977; Strober, 1977)?

Culture too plays a critical role in influencing women's adult development. Here anthropological and social psychologically based research and theories contribute to our understanding of how cultural images of men and women shape roles and life choices at home, in marriage, and in the workplace (e.g., Bamberger, 1974; Hewlett, 1986; Sanday, 1974; Yankelovich, 1981). How do shifting definitions of masculinity and femininity, for example, affect life paths for women (Douglas, 1977; Gerzon, 1982)? What impact does a pan-universal asymmetry in cultural evaluations of the sexes have on women's views of self, other, and the external world (Ortner, 1974; Rosaldo, 1974)?

A third approach to an exploration of women's development is more psychologically oriented: a micro-focus on the individual and the gender-specific ways in which she sees and makes sense out of her world. What, for example, is a woman's way of knowing (Belenky et al., 1986)? What does cognitive–moral–social maturity look like for women (Gilligan, 1982)? What age-specific developmental tasks, achievements, and transitions do women face over the course of a healthy lifetime (Bardwick, 1980; Giele, 1980)?

This chapter explores women's development from this psychological/developmental perspective. My intention is to review the literature as it exists, without opening the potential "can-of-worms" debate as to whether the gender differences that I and others report are the result of innate biological differences, a learned social reality, or a socio-biological process that stands somewhere between the two. From my perspective, understanding the causality is less critical than acknowledging the existence, power, and implications of these gender-based developmental differences for individual lives and for career theory.

ADULT DEVELOPMENT AND WOMEN: A NEW FOCUS

Theories of adult development are relatively new. Historically, psychological development was viewed primarily as a childhood task. Freud and his well-known beliefs about the critical turning points in early childhood and adolescence dominated our understandings of human development for over half a century and fostered implicit assumptions about adulthood as the static legacy of infantile experiences.

Erikson (1968), Gould (1978), Levinson (1978), Kohlberg (1976), Perry (1968), and Vaillant (1977) all challenged Freud's conception of the static nature of adulthood. Each proposed a model of development that charts a predictable sequence of disorganization, transition, and balance in adult life. These theories countered Freudian notions of intrapsychic conflict as a pathological interference with adult stability, ushered in a new era for exploring development in the adult years, and firmly established a male standard for adulthood. These important early works were largely written by and about men.

Levinson, Kohlberg, Perry, and Vaillant all built their theories of development on observations of men's lives. Their findings, however, have been presented and widely accepted as insights into human development. For example, to answer the question "What does it mean to be an adult?" (p. ix), Levinson (1978) studied forty men at mid-life.[1] Levinson is quick to acknowledge the limitations of a study that ignores women's lives (pp. 8–9); however, he then goes on to discuss his work in terms of adult, not just male, development.

This androcentric focus has affected the study of women's development in a number of important ways. It has distorted our views of women and their lives, narrowly influenced our research agendas, and left us falsely confident that women's development could be understood as merely a logical derivative from explorations of the male experience. Such speculations and untested assumptions formed the foundation for our early theories of women's development – mature and healthy women are just like men.

When women's actual lives did not fit these male-based theories, women (not the theories) were typically seen as deficient. Accepting yet another Freudian legacy, developmental theorists have often concluded that women are "less mature" than their male counterparts. Lists of masculine stereotypes read like the definitions of maturity that underpin these male-based theories of development, while the female stereotypes have been equated with childhood and immaturity. Kohlberg repeatedly has found that women remain stages below men in their moral reasoning according to his schema, compromised in their development by their intense attachments, concern for relationships, and context-based decisions (Kohlberg, 1981; Kohlberg and Kramer, 1969). Erikson (1968) sees women's focus on intimacy as a developmental impediment to identity formation. Vaillant, like Levinson (1978), focuses on work and achievement, defining a "healthy life" as one that emphasizes the relationship between self and society, not one "just raising crops or children" (Vaillant, 1977, p. 202).

As theorists have struggled to explain women's "developmental deficiencies" and deviations from male standards, they have often returned to an age-old emphasis on basic biology and biological turning points for women. Childbirth, menstruation, the loss of reproductive functioning, and female hormones have been the cornerstones for theorizing about women's development for centuries, often implying that women are more limited by biology in both their cognitive and social development than men (Ehrenreich and English, 1979; Hancock, 1979; Reeves, 1982). Even today, primitive beliefs that menstruation weakens the supply of blood to the brain (Griffin, 1978) and Victorian images of the womb as the dominant aspect of female emotion and physiology (Douglas, 1977) linger in cocktail-party-expressed theories that women by nature are too emotional to be good leaders and that menstrual cycles might affect their decision-making abilities in organizations. While biology, as Rossi (1977) reminds us, is important in understanding human potential and limitations, it is easily argued that what has become uniquely female is rooted as much in our cultural, political, and social situation as in biological differences between the sexes.

Finally, in addition to providing the measures for assessing development, developmental theories based on male experiences continue to color our perspectives on how to study the adult years. Theories provide lenses that focus our perceptions and understandings of the world around us, and frame the things we see and choose not to see. Male-based developmental theories give us language and terms that then become the basis for looking at women's lives. Studies of women's mentors and mid-life crises, for example, flow directly from Levinson's (1978) observation of men. Although these issues may be critical to understanding women's development, they may also blind us to other distinctive issues for women, like the importance of developing multiple "weak ties" (Keele, 1986) in lieu of a significant sponsor or the implications of stressing both relationships and personal achievement over the course of a lifetime (Barnett and Baruch, 1980).

Since it took years to anchor a feminist challenge to the newly evolving, androcentric theories of adult development, explicit explorations of women's lives have just begun, making it too early in our theorizing about women's development to determine with certainty the causality for observed gender differences or to present our findings as conclusive descriptions of the way women "really" are. Giele (1982) reminds us that theorists studying women's development face many of the same methodological problems in studying aging.[2] How much of a woman's development is due to growth and aging? How much to the times in which she is born and raised? How much to basic biology? How much to political issues between men and women that have existed over the decades? How much to the historical conditions under which she lives at the moment?

As Riley, Foner, Moore, Hess, and Roth (1972), Giele (1982), Lawrence (1980; 1984), Rossi (1980), and others have cautioned, characteristics defined as endemic to women may be caused by historical accident or a particular age and time. Do, for example, Gilligan's milestone findings represent a new understanding of a different developmental voice for women or reflect the concerns of a particular birth cohort raised in the United States during the late 1960s?

It is not yet possible to provide definitive answers to such questions. We have no longitudinal data about women's lives comparable to Vaillant's and Kohlberg's twenty-plus year efforts, although Josselson's (1987) exploration of women's identity development begins to fill that gap. We have just begun to collect cross-cultural data on women's development (e.g., Ecklein, 1982). In that sense, we are limited to speculating about what today's observations mean over the course of a woman's lifespan and for our understandings of women's development.

On the other hand, it is foolish to ignore the distinct themes and patterns that characterize our understandings of women's lives today. Forewarned of the limitations of our knowledge, let us embark on a journey to understand women's development in the adult years and its implications for career theory.

WOMEN'S DEVELOPMENT: DIFFERENT APPROACHES,
WIDESPREAD AGREEMENT

Development in adulthood is explored in two different ways.[3] Phase theories attempt to define a specific sequence of age-related developmental tasks, achievements, transitions, and critical incidents faced over the course of a lifetime. What typically happens to people as they navigate through their twenties? thirties? forties? and so on. Phase theories emphasize what individuals typically do at different chronological ages – how they establish themselves in the adult world during their twenties, settle down in their thirties, reevaluate priorities at mid-life, and so on – providing a portrait of what life is commonly like for all adults.

Erikson (1968), Gould (1978), Levinson (1978), Sheehy (1974), and Vaillant (1977) are well-known examples of a phase approach to the study of development – theories that ignore or subsume women's experiences under "generic" male categories. Bardwick (1980), Giele (1982), and Scarf (1980) redress this male focus with phase theories that specifically explore the age-related patterns in women's lives.

Stage theories, on the other hand, chart a progressive sequence of developmental stages that are only *indirectly* related to chronological age. Stages are abstract concepts – labels for a typical pattern of psychological organization at different points in an individual's development. The term *developmental stage*, then, refers to the frame of reference that one uses to structure one's world and from within which one perceives the world. Different capabilities for self-reflection, relative thinking, acceptance of personal causality, and tolerance for ambiguity are critical dimensions for assessing development in stage theories, with age alone no guarantee of movement to higher or more sophisticated ways of understanding oneself or others.

Kohlberg (1976), Perry (1968), and Loevinger (1976) propose stage theories, with Loevinger's work the only one of the three based on empirical study of an equal number of men and women. Loevinger's stages are congruent with Gilligan's (1977; 1982) important insights into women's perspective on self, other, and morality, and consistent with Miller's (1976), Schaef's (1981), and Josselson's (1987) beliefs about the role of others in the formation of woman's psyche. Unlike Kohlberg (1976) who views development as separation, individuation, and the ability to move beyond the specific to abstract principles of right and wrong, Loevinger's assessment of developmental maturity is based on the self defining and redefining itself in relation to others. For Loevinger, development advances toward a clear differentiation of self and other, but that differentiation is combined with an increasing sense of responsibility, relatedness, and interconnectedness with others.

A dual focus on stages and life phases in exploring women's lives is complementary. Giele (1982) argues that both are essential parts of charting a life-course perspective for women, looking at the connection between female characteristics and chronological age over the lifespan. While a life-course perspective can potentially yield a rich understanding of men's lives as well, it may be particularly useful when studying women's development given the wide variety of life patterns that women actually experience today. But what is even more important to the arguments in this chapter is that both phase and stage theories of women's development yield a consistent finding. Both sets of theories emphasize the centrality of relationships, attachments, and caring for women, affecting how women view the world around them and how they choose to live their lives.

STAGES OF WOMEN'S DEVELOPMENT: SELF
VERSUS OTHERS REDEFINED

Attachment and separation are basic tensions in the process of human development. Each individual must successfully define the self in relationship to others, balancing human needs for both independence and community over the course of a lifetime. The infant's struggle to gain autonomy without sacrificing the necessary care, love, and protection of caretakers resurfaces in adolescence as the conflict between identity and intimacy (Erikson, 1968) and in adulthood as the classic Freudian tension between love and work (Rohrlich, 1980).

The resolution of this basic developmental tension, however, has typically meant something very different for men and for women. In essence, development for men has meant increased autonomy and separation from others as a means of strengthening identity, empowering the self, and charting a satisfactory life course. Concern for specific others compromises high-level functioning and decision making according to Kohlberg (1981), while continued attention to context and situation threatens the loss of identity for both Erikson (1968) and Perry (1968).

The picture for women is different. Development is tied to understanding and strengthening the self in relation to others. For women, attachments and relationships play a central role in both identity formation and conceptions of developmental maturity (Bettelheim, 1965; Block, 1977; Chodorow, 1974; Douvan and Adelson, 1966; McClelland, 1975), coloring how women see themselves, their lives, their careers, and their ongoing responsibility to those around them.

Gilligan (1980) lays out stages of development for women – a schema based on repeated observations of women's lives and one that describes a unique developmental voice. A close look at Gilligan's work shows a developmental process for women that is a mirror image of the developmental process for men. Men and women face the same dilemma of reconciling the conflict between separation and attachment, but they approach the conflict from different directions and with a recognition of opposite truths. For men, development begins with the premise of separation and the importance of increasing individual autonomy. Male developmental patterns revolve around the acceptance of universal principles to define justice and fairness, and chart a developmental sequence that begins with acknowledging the importance of individuality, emphasizes workplace accomplishments, eventually explores intimacy and connections with others, and finally sees others as equally important to oneself.

For women, the developmental process is reversed. Women start from an assumption of connection to significant others, gradually explore ways of managing and tolerating separation, and finally move along a developmental path that allows women to see the self as equal to others. Unlike the men in Vaillant's (1977) and Levinson's (1978) research who saw relationships as something freely contracted if they served utilitarian functions or supported a life's dream, the women in Gilligan's studies (1977; 1980; 1982) saw interpersonal connections as given. Relationships are grist for women's ongoing developmental mill, not a developmental limitation (Kohlberg, 1981) or something relegated to old age when concerns for immortality lead to a new interest in generativity (Erikson, 1968).

Self versus others redefined: political implications

It is important to explore the political implications of these two views of male and female stage development in order to avoid confusing women's developmental concerns for attachment and relationships with stereotypic conceptions of female dependency and powerlessness – the two are not synonymous.

There are clear, contrasting images of power and helplessness in the two views of male and female development. Phrases like "standing on your own two feet," and "learning to go it alone" stress individuality and are consistent with traditional definitions of power as agency – self-assertion, self-expansion, and self-protection as means of accomplishing one's goal (Bakan, 1966; Marshall, Chapter 13). Attachment and a primary concern for others can mean feeling helpless since choices are often dictated by the demands of significant others. Goodness and accomplishment become equated with self-sacrifice: separation and individuation might require decisions that deprive or hurt another. From the perspective of male-based developmental schemes, women seem to avoid power, lack decisiveness, and shy away from empowering themselves. In Gilligan's (1980) terms, women's attachments to others seem like paralyzing entrapments and inevitable preludes to compromise.

McClelland (1975) agrees that women perceive power issues very differently because of their concern for relationships, but he is unconvinced that this gender difference necessarily means that women are developmentally incapable of wanting or using power. For McClelland, the problems lie more with prevailing beliefs about power than with women's innate needs or abilities.

McClelland sees definitions of power as culturally biased. Western cultures look at power as self-reliance and at the individual as the source of power. According to McClelland's own research and his review of the psychological literature, this definition fits male developmental patterns and experiences more than women's. Men approach power as action: competing, dominating, pushing ahead, and taking an aggressive stance toward work and others. Women have traditionally shown more interest in *being* powerful than in acting aggressively – quickly recognizing their interdependence and choosing to strengthen themselves in order to protect and care for others, serve as a resource, or infuse a relationship with emotional intimacy. Power for women combines having and sharing. Nurturance is an act of strength, a reflection of power, and an expression of a morality based on caring (Noddings, 1984).

McClelland's assertions about women and power are consistent with my own research on power issues in dual-career marriages (Gallos, 1985). I have found high-powered, professional women capable of aggressively competing and succeeding in the male corporate world, comfortably assuming what might be defined as a "powerless" position in their marriage – deferring to their husbands for major family decisions, sacrificing their own career and personal needs in order to support their spouse without expecting commensurate support in return, assuming an accommodative stance in order to avoid confrontations, and so on.

Describing these women as power averse or as clinging to traditional stereotypes of femininity at home is too simple. For these dual-career wives, exercising power at home is different from wielding power in the male corporate world. Marital power is an internal strength that the women bring to maintain and nurture their marriages. A deep-seated concern for others allows these professionally successful women paradoxically to view marital accommodation and acquiescence as a way of being powerful at home. Competing, dominating, and acting aggressively are much less important than using their own resources and abilities to support, empower, and strengthen a vulnerable spouse.

Finally, it is wrong to equate women's concern for relationships with dependency as a unique feature of women's development. While women may be more dependent on significant others for their identity and self-satisfaction than men, dependency is very much a part of all human development. Independence in male developmental schemes has meant a separation from people, not lack of dependency. Since men have been socialized to achieve their identity primarily through work and professional accomplishments, in that sense, men are heavily dependent on their work. Beliefs in autonomy as the keys to men's development are distorted – mythic conceptions of the separate individual based more on the lack of friendships that Vaillant (1977) and Levinson (1978) note in their research than any lack of dependency. It is not that women are dependent and men are not, but that the source of the dependency may be different (Bardwick, 1980).

Attachments for women: rational explanations

Chodorow (1974; 1978) provides a simple explanation for this strong sense of interdependence, attachment, and caring that underpins women's development. The fact that women universally are largely responsible for childcare means that critical, early-life interpersonal dynamics between child and care-giving parent are very different for men and women, and that gender significantly affects a child's capacity for independence and for attachment.

Identity formation for boys requires a clear differentiation and separation from mother early in life, resulting in what Chodorow (1978) calls "a more defensive firming of experienced ego boundaries" for boys and a forced curtailment of "empathic tie with their mother" (pp. 166–167). Gender identity for girls is more continuous, requiring a strong identification and ongoing attachment to the mother. For Chodorow, this means that girls emerge from the preoedipal/oedipal period experiencing themselves as "less differentiated than boys, as more continuous with and related to the external object-world, and as differently oriented to their inner object-world as well" (p. 167). Girls have the basis for empathy and caring in their primary definitions of self.

Rossi (1977), Giele (1982), and Hewlett (1986) provide additional explanations for the central role of caring and attachment in women's development. The authors believe that there are obvious and logical reasons to expect that women would be psychologically different from men, given their capacities for childbirth, early-life socialization differences, and social/political pressures for maintaining the traditional feminine role.

Since women alone have the biological capacity for pregnancy and lactation, Rossi (1977) sees 40,000 years of human evolution as possibly providing hormonal and instinctive responses toward caring for newborns, infants, and children. Giele (1982) agrees and adds that women's work and family roles have been substantially different from men's over the years, reinforcing women's capacities for nurturing both at home and in the workplace. Women have been traditionally relegated to service and care-giving positions (e.g., teacher, social worker, nurse, secretary) when socially sanctioned to work outside the home. Although some of that may be changing as women enter the work force in record numbers, all indications show that women still enter a much narrower range of occupations than men (Catalyst, 1982; Cosmopolitan, 1986), still hold primary responsibility for home and family life (Skinner, 1980; Yogev, 1981), and often feel forced to make major career sacrifices for the welfare of their children (Hewlett, 1986).

PHASES OF DEVELOPMENT: OLD THEMES, NEW PATTERNS

Like men, women's development can also be explored by examining life phases – the age-specific marker events and transition periods that occur throughout the life cycle. In developmental phase theories, attachments, caring, and relationships return to the developmental arena for women. There they interact with women's needs for achievement and play a central role in influencing both the critical developmental events that women face over the course of a lifetime and the ease of their developmental struggle.

While independence, self-sufficiency, and an emphasis on work/career underpin life phases for men, interdependence and a struggle to combine attachment and accomplishment are key to explaining the content, non-predictability, and sequencing of women's life phases. Phases of development for women do not have the linear and predictable quality that male life patterns suggest, nor is the process of evaluating life choices as straightforward or singularly focused on work and career. Historical, social, political, and intrapsychic forces contribute to some very different life patterns for women and challenge implicit contentions that women go through the same phases and pace of development as men.

Subtle pressures, hard choices

Gould (1978), Levinson (1978), and Sheehy (1974) have proposed a consistent sequence of life phases: predictable periods of relative stability alternating with periods of evaluation–transition throughout the adult years. Implicit in these phase theories is an assumption that evaluating one's life course and choices is a taken-for-granted, essential means of achieving developmental maturity. While there are differences in people's willingness or ability to evaluate their lives consciously, Levinson (1978) and the others see psychological forces, the reality of everyday life, and social expectations at different ages pushing individuals to look at particular accomplishments and issues and to assess what they are doing with their lives.

Bardwick (1980), however, sees the process of evaluating life choices as more difficult and complex for women. Rather than a taken-for-granted means of increasing self-satisfaction and mastery, evaluating life choices often raises internal contradictions for women and leaves them stuck between seemingly irreconcilable options. For women who live traditional lives as wives and mothers, evaluating life choices can be painful, resulting in feelings of failure in comparison to women with careers, and powerlessness in recognizing that life is fashioned largely by responding to the needs of others. Growing up female has often meant relinquishing freedom of expression and choice in order to sustain relationships (Eichenbaum and Orbach, 1988; Miller, 1976; Schaef, 1981).

Even for women choosing a more non-traditional life course, the pain of feeling that personal life choices mean competition with or rejection of significant others can keep women avoiding a specific answer to the basic developmental questions of "who am I?" and "what do *I* want to do?" Abramson and Franklin (1986), for example, noted an unexpected fluidity in the career and personal plans of the 1974 Harvard Law School alumnae that they studied. Relatively few of these women could say with real confidence that what they were doing at the time of the research is what they would be doing ten years from now.

External pressures also make evaluating life choices complicated for women. The Women's Movement and major social changes over the past two decades have clearly opened life possibilities for women: education, employment, career, and lifestyle options have expanded dramatically. At the same time, however, traditional societal expectations for women are changing slowly. Socialization pressures are contradictory. Many women still feel themselves in the awkward position of needing to defend or reject the family in order to have work on equal footing with men (Kessler-Harris, 1985). Societal acknowledgments that women "have come a long way" are mixed with lingering definitions of traditional femininity that still push women toward an interdependent or dependent sense of self. For Miller (1976), Bardwick (1980), Roberts and Newton (1986), Hewlett (1986), and others, this translates into relatively little change in the importance of a committed relationship for women. What has changed is its expression: Concerns for relationships and attachment, now synonymous with lack of career commitment, have been pushed underground or dealt with through the "superwoman" syndrome.

Seasons of a woman's life: a tentative portrait

Bardwick (1980) speculates about what all this means for a portrait of women's life phases by examining the developmental tasks that women in different age cohorts seem to be facing today. Bardwick emphasizes, as Levinson (1978) does, that the same event at a different age is in many ways not the same developmental task because we are psychologically so changed. But Bardwick adds a different twist. She shows women returning to the same central life question – how do I deal with the importance of relationships? – and finding different answers and emphases over time.

In the *early adult transition years* (age 17 to 28), Bardwick (1980) sees women pushed in the direction of marriage – the undisputed crucial achievement of an adult woman. This is particularly true if one's peers are marrying early since friendship and peer groups have replaced family as significant reference points at this phase of life.

Statistics that show a decline in the annual marriage rate (National Center for Health Statistics, 1986) and a steady increase in the age when women marry (*Cosmopolitan*, 1986) lead to questions about Bardwick's marital assertions. However, replace the term *marriage* with a concern for a committed relationship, and her beliefs about the traditional pressures for the majority of women, at least in early adulthood, seem sound. Research has shown that even with career and professional achievements, traditional roles remain a central part of women's identity, and their occupational commitments are based on a different psychological stance from men. Work is something important to do rather than something to be.

Hennig and Jardim (1978), Gilligan (1977; 1980), and Josselson (1987) found that the women in their studies, despite career interests, commitment, and achievements, continued to define themselves interpersonally. In their review of four unpublished doctoral dissertations that used Levinson's (1978) phase theory to investigate women's adult development, Roberts and Newton (1986) found that marriage and relationships, not careers, were primary in the dreams of all thirty-nine women studied – a finding consistent with Josselson's (1987) longitudinal study of women's identity development. And alumnae of the Harvard Business School class of 1975 (Gallese, 1985) match their alumnae sisters at the Harvard Law School (Abramson and Franklin, 1986) in having less career investment or single-mindedness than their male counterparts.

Defining a central part of the self interpersonally also helps women to maintain more of a psychological fluidity than their male counterparts during these early adult years. While this psychological fluidity has often been confused with weak ego boundaries (Chodorow, 1974; Hancock, 1979), it is more a willingness to remain open to life choices and retain a capacity for caring – a stance Bardwick and Douvan (1972) argue is highly adaptive for career-interested women who wish to marry. Because a partner has not yet been found or because of the difficulties in predicting the implications of a long-term relationship for life and career, women loosely form their dream, in Levinson's terms (1978), and remain more tentative in defining themselves.

Finally, multiple forces during this early adult life phase can make it challenging for women to deal with the realistic problems of balancing work, family and dual-careers issues. It is not surprising, then, that women studied by Baruch et al. (1983) saw the young adult years as the most difficult and stressful. Relationships may ask for career sacrifices and vice versa. Decisions that favor the woman over her husband or child can easily bring guilt and fears of selfishness. The psychological fluidity that characterizes this period for women can make them seem less secure or less professionally oriented than their mates and weaker negotiators on the home front – all this at a time when sophisticated interpersonal skills are still developing and when the pressures of the early career years weigh most heavily on both spouses (Hall and Hall, 1978).

The *settling down period of the second adult life phase* (age 30 to 40) is a time of investing more heavily in work for men. Levinson (1978) describes this process as climbing a ladder to "become one's own man."

Bardwick (1980) is clear that this life phase is very different for women, and Hennig and Jardim's (1978) classic study of women executives, the two major Harvard alumnae studies (Abramson and Franklin, 1986; Gallese, 1985), and a recent exploration of women in corporate America (Hardesty and Jacobs, 1986) all support her assertion. "Becoming one's own woman" requires more than achieving professional success. The biological clock is ticking loudly for women who have not had children. For those who have, the exhaustion of balancing multiple roles may have resulted in cutting back on either professional work or parenting, leading to a sense of unsettledness and personal inadequacy. Few women feel reassured of their womanhood by occupational and professional success alone. On the contrary, those achieving professional success alone can feel anxious about their femininity or wonder what they have sacrificed.

Hennig and Jardim (1978), for example, found that all the women managers in their study who had achieved professional success devised a new strategy at mid-life that put their careers on hold. The women turned their efforts to reassessing their personal lives and became "preoccupied" with femininity and the prospects of an intimate relationship for the first time. Professional success that generates a sense of independence in men had the exact opposite effect for these women. It seemed to increase their dependent needs at mid-life.

Ten years later, Hardesty and Jacobs (1986) found consistent results: Feeling successful was more complicated for women than amassing professional achievements alone. The researchers found scores of professionally successful women in the corporate ranks who reported frustration, emptiness, exhaustion, disillusionment, and a sense of personal failure when they realized the personal and interpersonal costs of their professional success. For these women, power, title, money, and status were not enough. The women wanted fair treatment and compensation, but almost more importantly, they wanted opportunities to be themselves at work and to be connected with the people around them. Not finding this, the women made career shifts or turned to self-employment, and reassessed their career and life priorities – increasingly common choices for professional women as reported in the popular and business press (e.g., *Wall Street Journal*, 1986; *Boston Globe*, September 1986; *Working Woman*, 1986).

Middle adulthood (age 40 to 50) has traditionally been a time of increased assertiveness and professional accomplishment for women. Women now have social permission to work. Their full-time job of mothering is, for the most part, done, and second incomes have always been welcomed for pin-money or to assist in paying for children's college expenses.

Bardwick (1980) sees middle adulthood as a time of great promise for women, despite the increased threat of loneliness from children leaving home, divorce, or widowhood. Women who have sacrificed and succeeded in relationships typically become more autonomous and independent. Those who ambivalently gave up careers for full-time motherhood can return to work with increased options and traditional social acceptance. The empty nest syndrome seems less likely with the changing expectations for women's careers and professional advancement. Societal norms about aging no longer cast women in their forties as past their prime. Realistically and psychodynamically women in their forties are less confined than in previous life phases and, according to Baruch et al. (1983), have a distinct edge over their male counterparts in terms of physical health, well-being, and prospects for the future. If the study of the middle adult years had begun with women's lives, the authors conclude, the mid-life crisis and stress associated with the middle adult years would not have become part of our vocabulary.

Age 50 and older has traditionally been a time for acknowledging one's mortality, learning to enjoy the time left, and accomplishing the single most important developmental task in this life phase – preparing for death. There are symbolic forms of dying during these years like retirement and menopause. There are actual encounters like the death of parents, siblings, or a spouse.

For women, however, these later years may also be a time for significant career accomplishment. Husbands, who are often older than their wives, retire from their jobs, freeing women from the fear or reality that their own career needs might prevent them from adequately supporting their spouse. A husband's retirement also gives the later-life career women the opportunity finally to claim commensurate career support from her now, at-home spouse.

Women whose husbands die are forced to face the reality/opportunity of creating and supporting their own later-year lives. This may mean the freedom to build on earlier career plans and dreams or the economic necessity to test the career/professional accomplishment waters. Assisted by the female hormonal edge that helps women escape the male later-life heart attack and maintain their health and vigor long into the adult years, today's later-life women have the potential to come into their own career-wise.

Despite potential career gains, however, women cannot avoid the traditional, later-life developmental task of preparing for death, which may have different meanings for them. The issues that Baruch et al. (1983) found centered not on male concerns for accepting mortality and having too little time left to accomplish youthful dreams, but on having too much. The women in the study knew that statistics guaranteed them a life well past seventy. They feared being dependent on others and losing the ability to function as vital, active adults. They recognized the reality of being without the enjoyed companionship of spouses or significant others.

Traditionally, aging parents have become the responsibility of their children, with daughters and daughters-in-law often taking on the role of caretaker. It is difficult to predict how this will change when today's career women reach their later life years, although popular press reports show a growing acceptance of this traditional caretaking role (e.g., Stroud, 1986). In 1970, for example, for every aged parent in a nursing home or institution, three were living with one of their children, usually a daughter (Neugarten and Brown-Rezanka, 1978). It would not be surprising, given women's ethic of caring and concern for relationships, to find the superwomen surfacing again – this time balancing career, marriage, and "parenting" of a different kind.

It is important to remember that Bardwick (1980) is attempting to describe a woman's life cycle based on her assessment of women's lives today and in the absence of longitudinal data about life phases for women. The repeated themes of managing attachments, relationships, and accomplishment that weave through her tentative portrait of women's life phases, nonetheless, are consistent with others studying women's development.

Giele (1982), however, argues that linear models of development are too narrow to encompass women's experiences. She reviewed recent historical change in women's roles, the research on women's health and status attainments, and developments in family roles and the workplace over the last thirty years in hopes of discovering what life events and chronological life phases lead to a satisfying and healthy life for women.

From her reviews of the literature and research data, Giele (1982) could cull no specific formula for women's happiness and health. Modern women live longer, have fewer children, and have more time for employment in the workplace. Traditional or dual-career marriage, at-home or at-the-office motherhood, childbirth in the early twenties or forties, single parenting, career focus, family focus, or something in between are all equally viable choices for women. Although the paths are quite different, Giele found research to support all of the various lifestyle options available to women today.

For this reason, Giele (1982) argues for a crossover model of development that acknowledges the relativity of specific life paths and places a positive value on the number and variety of life experiences rather than any particular sequence, event, or activity. A good education, work, and family experience, in any order, serve a woman better than a life where decisions have cut off life options too early or prevent flexible adaptation later in life. For Giele, the more and diverse experiences that one has, the better chances of adapting prior knowledge in new, later-life situations.

Implicit in Giele's crossover model is a reiteration of the importance of combining nurturant and productive roles over the course of a woman's lifetime. Baruch et al. (1983) agree. Their study of 300 women at mid-life found that combining "mastery" and "pleasure" is critical for leading a satisfying life. Traditional views of women have slighted the role that "mastery" (i.e., achievement and accomplishment) plays in a woman's sense of well-being, while more "liberated" views of women have down-played the importance of relationships. In their research, the authors found, however, that talk of achievement and work – jobs, career goals, education – dominated their interviews. For example, when women were asked "If you could live your whole life over, what one thing would you most like to change?" the most frequent response was that they would seek more education or career preparation. At the same time, "pleasure" for the women still centered on the quality of relationships with others.

UNDERSTANDING WOMEN'S DEVELOPMENT: CAREER
IMPLICATIONS FOR THEORY, RESEARCH, AND PRACTICE

Theories of women's development raise critical questions about our understandings of careers and the adequacy of present career theory to capture the experiences of women and men in the 1980s. What do we mean by the terms *career* and *career success*? How much are these definitions influenced by male experiences or gender-specific assumptions about the centrality of work alone to identity? How adequately can women's experiences and career choices be explored in conjunction with theories and research into men's lives, or is there need for advancing a separate theory of women's career development? How can our understandings of women's development and life experiences provide new directions for career theory and offer productive paths for men and women seeking alternatives to traditional models of career management?

Meaning of career: needs for expanded definitions

There are repeating themes in all of the major studies of professional women and their development (e.g., Abramson and Franklin, 1986; Baruch et al., 1983; Gallese, 1985; Hardesty and Jacobs, 1986; Josselson, 1987; Roberts and Newton, 1986) that imply we have yet to shed our commonsense definitions of career as synonymous with "a person's progress in his chosen occupation" (*Merriam-Webster Dictionary*, 1974) and that linear occupational advancement is too limiting a perspective for understanding women's careers.

When women have managed their professional selves over a course of a lifetime in ways that allow for both professional accomplishment and expression of their relationship/family needs, this has not been seen as a unique, women's perspective toward managing a career. Rather these choices are still framed as women "cutting back on career," "dropping off the career path during child-bearing years," "choosing motherhood vs. career," "taking a step down on the career ladder," "accepting less challenging career options," and so on. The implications are clear. Career means work outside the home, but more importantly, career means a specific path toward approaching work that more often fits men's rather than women's options and experiences.

On the career theory side, it is fair to say that there are ongoing efforts to broaden our definitions of career. Schein's (1982) lifestyle anchor and Derr's (1986) getting-balanced careerist are steps in acknowledging that career can no longer be limited to occupational choice and ignore lifestyle issues. On the other hand, we need more ways of describing, without the negative connotations, careers and career choices that reflect the experiences of today's women (and an increasing number of men) who acknowledge the importance of professional work but choose to fashion lives that combine both productive and nurturing roles over time. We have neither adequate language, models, nor illustrative teaching cases to talk about what does a career look like that is simultaneously high on achievement and high on relationship. What does the process of identity formation, individuation, and occupational choice look like in the context of attachment? In what ways do the psychological constructs and powerful relationship lenses that guide women's development influence career preparation, aspirations, choices, and opportunities? How do the career implications of women's developmental needs for attachment and relationships differ from those of men highly involved in home, family, and childrearing?

To the extent that definitions and understandings of career and career success are still heavily based on men's traditional work experiences and assumptions about the primacy of work to identity, then our theories of careers do women an injustice. Just as developmental theories based on male experiences left women looking deficient, deviant, and immature, and blinded researchers to the limitations of their conceptualizations of human development, so it may be with career theories.

Using male-based standards of career and career success, it is easy to assess women, who chose to forge a career that combines achievement and nurturance, as failing professionally. Women who limit work time to parent children or refuse to prove themselves during early career years by assuming the standard workaholic stance easily look less committed to careers. Women who find it hard to define clearly their professional goals or plan a long-term career strategy because of unsureness of what relationships and home demands may bring certainly can look unfocused. Women without an inner drive to aim singularly for the top at all costs can seem unmotivated as their male counterparts zoom ahead, traditional blinders in place. Women who leave successful organizational positions and clearly defined career tracks to gain more control over their lives can look foolish and misdirected. But do these choices necessarily mean that a career is less important to these women or that women are any less committed to careers?

Many of our present theories would say "Yes." For example, in a recent assessment of career development in changing times, London and Stumpf (1986) see the reality of sex discrimination in the workplace, the difficulty of managing multiple roles, and the challenge of making role transitions leading women to feel less career motivation. While all of those conditions certainly affect women's career experiences, the research on women's development cautions against an assessment of women as *less* motivated and suggests that the issue is more complex.

If the women studied by Hennig and Jardim (1978), Gilligan (1977; 1982), Baruch et al. (1983), Nero (1984), Gallese (1985), Abramson and Franklin (1986), Roberts and Newton (1986), and Josselson (1987) represent the experiences of other women, women do not have *less* career motivation as much as a different perspective toward what career means to them. Even in the infant stages of our exploration of women's development and lives, consistent messages about women and careers surface again and again. Women's dreams, in the Levinson (1978) sense, are more complex and compounded than the traditionally work-focused dreams of men – a realistic and adaptive response to women's developmental needs, shifting societal expectations, changing job opportunities, and the realities of pregnancy and children. Women have "split dreams" (Josselson, 1987; Roberts and Newton, 1986) – images of work and relationships that create a preferred lifestyle rather than the concrete plans to play out a particular occupational role that Levinson (1978), Vaillant (1977) and others report about the men in their studies.

But does a split dream necessarily "defuse" the focus of women's lives? The experiences of today's professional women who are charting non-traditional career courses say "No." Must a split dream "use up" women's career motivation, as Roberts and Newton (1986) conclude, leaving women stalled in the internal struggle to reconcile needs for both accomplishment and relationships? Only if we continue to foster beliefs that careers require a singular and unwavering devotion to work alone, and that relationships and family are unnecessary diversions from professional accomplishment – interferences with productivity – rather than part of the baggage that *all* workers bring to enrich their contributions to work and organizations. What is this new perspective toward careers that comes from exploring women's lives and psychological development? What future research does it suggest? How can it enrich our understandings of careers and career theory for both men and women?

Toward a new perspective on careers

A review of the literature on women and their development leaves me intrigued yet struggling to define the particular perspective toward careers that women can bring to the workplace. As Gallese (1985) and others admit, a clear definition is difficult. It is easier to discuss what a woman's conception of career is not – not a lock-step, linear progression of attainments directed by a focus on "the top"; not a job sequence aimed at upward mobility and success at all costs; not job complacency, fear of professional success, or low needs for achievement; not simply a mechanical issue of learning how to juggle marriage, children, and work.

But stopping with this list of "nots" is deceptive. It casts women's perspective toward career in a negative light – a rejection of the male career model that has become synonymous with productivity in our society without articulating productive alternatives. How have women responded when they have found the interpersonal costs of traditional male career patterns too high, the developmental costs too great in their own lives?

As an alternative, many women have tried to forge careers that provide opportunities for meeting personal, professional, and interpersonal goals. In the everyday language of the popular press (e.g., *Newsweek*, 1986; *Working Woman*, 1987), they have sought balance and control in their lives.

Many women have achieved that balance and control by working the organizational system in which they find themselves: Rather than accepting without question traditional expectations for success, they have negotiated for work hours, specific projects, and/or benefits that meet their own needs. While requests for part-time arrangements or reduced work loads might look like expectations for an easy ride, the women in return have offered their organizations someone who makes decisions based on merit (not the politics and games necessary to "climb to the top of the ladder"), is willing to take risks and bring a creative perspective to her work (something that an unwavering focus on promotions and looking good to a boss might block), and brings an ethic of caring (which develops productive and loyal subordinates – the mainstay of any organization). Women have something distinctive to offer organizations (Grant, 1988; Loden, 1985). When such negotiations have failed, many women have been willing to switch jobs or even career fields, in hopes of finding satisfying work that meets their lifestyle and personal needs.

Women have also quickly learned, as Hardesty and Jacobs (1986) illustrate, the hard lesson that identity and self-esteem do not necessarily come from attaching oneself to a prestigious corporation. For more and more women, this has meant starting their own entrepreneurial ventures – ventures whose growth the women can coordinate with their shifting family/relationship responsibilities and whose focus can dovetail with the women's present family demands and interests. A large percentage of the new services for older and working mothers, for example, are companies started by women with significant professional experiences who wanted more control over their work lives and time to devote to new families (*Newsweek*, 1986).

Women also seem to be saying that career is not as distinct an entity for them as it is for men. A career is not something you do for eight plus hours every day until retirement. The boundaries between professional work and everything else in life are more permeable, allowing women to see relationships and family as critical work and reasons to pace their professional lives differently from men. Career for women means expressing their professional selves over a lifetime with commitment to accomplishment and desires for fair treatment and rewards for their efforts – something very different from needing an ongoing organizational affiliation or making life choices that put occupational progress first. Women need to take long-term time perspectives toward careers and to have the patience and confidence to design a satisfying personal/professional life for themselves.

Toward a theory of women's career development

Can women's experiences be adequately explored in the context of our present, mostly male-based theories of careers? Are the major career theories inclusive enough to provide useful concepts for studying men's and women's careers and surfacing gender differences? Is there a need for a separate theory of women's career development?

While expert opinion is divided (Astin, 1984; Brooks, 1984; Diamond, 1987; Fitzgerald and Crites, 1980; Gilbert, 1984; Osipow, 1983), this review of literature on women's development suggests "Yes." Women's distinctive developmental voice and needs point to fundamentally different career perspectives, choices, priorities, and patterns for women that need to be understood and appreciated – differences that are only further expanded when cultural expectations, shifting social norms, employment opportunities, marital practices, childbirth and rearing, organizational policies, and institutional practices are added to the picture.

Advocating a separate theory of women's career development, as Larwood and Gutek (1987) caution, does not imply that women's career achievements are any less likely or important than those of men or that some women do not fit the male model of work and careers. Rather it is time to admit that, on the whole, women face a different set of opportunities and a more compounded set of problems than those seen by most men. Theories of men's careers do not fit women's lives and developmental concerns, and women's careers are no longer novelties that can be ignored.

Working women constitute more than 43% of the work force (Larwood and Gutek, 1987). They no longer work for diversion or pin-money. They are the sole bread winners in a surprisingly large number of families (Nieva, 1985) and significant financial contributors in the increasing number of two-earner families (Hayghe, 1982). The working mother is a national norm: The U.S. Census Bureau reports that more than half of all new mothers now remain in the job market (*Boston Globe*, 1988). Women's career are important to them, their families, and to the national economy. They need to be recognized, understood, and taken seriously.

If a theory of women's careers development is important, do we presently have one? Diamond (1987), Larwood and Gattiker (1987), Larwood and Gutek (1987), and others conclude "No." Much of our research on women's careers is fragmented, inter-disciplinary, and exploratory, lacking a coherent framework into which the developing pieces can be fit.

Larwood and Gutek (1987) propose a "bare bones" outline for what such a comprehensive theory might look like, identifying five concerns that need to be considered when exploring women's experiences: career preparation; societal opportunities; the influence of marriage, pregnancy, and children; timing; and age. Missing from the list, although implied in the influences of marriage and children, is a consideration of women's distinctive developmental needs and voices. Although less easy to observe, study, and distinguish from many cultural and institutional forces, their implicit power in defining how women see the world, their choices, and their opportunities makes developmental concerns a critical part of any attempt to build a comprehensive theory of women's careers.

In the same way that women's lives and development can only be more fully understood by combining our knowledge about psychological and developmental issues, structural and institutional concerns, and cultural beliefs about the genders, so too with our explorations of women's careers. We need to continue to address the hard questions. What really affects women's career and life choices? In what ways are women's careers informed by different approaches to the issue of relationships, career, and career success? How much is this the result of a generation of women caught between the feminine mystique of their mothers and the feminist mystique of the past thirty years, and how much reflects basic innate developmental differences between men and women? What does a long-term career path, underpinned by an ethic of caring, look like? How well does such a career path fit organizational needs? How well does it fit the experiences of women and men in the workplace today? How can we assess and evaluate such careers that deviate from traditional standards of success and definitions of career development?

There is much work to be done in studying and understanding women's careers. We face the large descriptive task of learning more about what career means for successful women, and how these insights can broaden our understandings about career success for both men and women. We need studies that record the new career strides women are taking, and examine the importance of a balanced life for women's self-esteem and feelings of well-being. We need longitudinal data about women's lives and careers. Women's career development, like women's psychological development, is a lifelong process. We, therefore, need long-term studies that look at both areas of development separately, and at the interactive effect between the two.

The findings are important in a number of arenas. They can provide managers with insights useful for managing the diverse work force of the 1990s, which will include large numbers of women. As Schein (1982) and Derr (1986) have shown, implicit in an understanding of individual career motivation are strategies for effectively supervising and maximizing productivity.

But perhaps even more importantly, our findings and theories about women's career development bring us closer to devising new career directions for both men and women. These new directions can provide men with viable alternatives to traditional male approaches to careers that have asked men to forgo nurturing roles and that have literally been dead ends for so many. They can provide women with the support and social sanctions to forge individual careers without risking the negative evaluations that erode confidence and truncate future advancements or keep women swinging between instrumental and nurturing roles and helplessly caught in a no-win situation.

NOTES

1 Since the publication of his original study, Levinson has done research on women's lives. His life phase data on women's lives is due to be published shortly in a book entitled *The Seasons of a Woman's Life*.
2 Much has been written about age, period, and cohort analysis problems. A good starting point for readers who wish to explore these methodological issues in more detail is James E. Birren and K. Warner Schaie (eds.), *The Handbook of the Psychology of Aging*. New York: Van Nostrand Reinhold, 1977.
3 Readers are referred to Crites and Cytrynbaum (Chapter 4) for a more detailed review and discussion of the major theories of adult development.

REFERENCES

Abramson, J., and Franklin, B. (1986). *Where Are They Now*. New York: Doubleday.
Adams, J. M. (1986). Giving up the dream. *Boston Globe*, March 25, pp. 53–54.
Astin, H. S. (1984). The meaning of work in women's lives: a socio-psychological model of career choice and work behavior. *The Counseling Psychologist, 12*, 117–126.

Bakan, D. (1966). *The Duality of Human Existence*. Chicago: Rand McNally.

Bamberger, J. (1974). The myth of patriarchy: why men rule in primitive society. In Lamphere, L., and Rosaldo, M. (eds.), *Women, Culture, and Society*. Palo Alto, CA: Stanford University Press.

Bardwick, J. (1980). The seasons of a woman's life. In D. McGuigan (ed.), *Women's Lives: New Theory, Research, and Policy*. Ann Arbor: University of Michigan Center for Continuing Education of Women.

Bardwick, J., and Douvan, E. (1972). Ambivalence: the socialization of women. In J. Bardwick (ed.), *Readings on the Psychology of Women*. New York: Harper and Row.

Barnett, R., and Baruch, G. (1980). On being an economic provider: women's involvement in multiple roles. In D. McGuigan (ed.), *Women's Lives: New Theory, Research, and Policy*. Ann Arbor: University of Michigan Center for Continuing Education of Women.

Baruch, G., Barnett, R., and Rivers, C. (1983). *Life Prints: New Patterns of Love and Work for Today's Women*. New York: New American Library.

Belenky, M., Clinchy, B., Goldberger, N., and Tarule, J. (1986). *Women's Ways of Knowing*. New York: Basic Books.

Berheide, C. W., and Segal, M. T. (1985). Teaching sex and gender: a decade of experience. *Teaching Sociology*, *12*(3), 267–284.

Bettelheim, B. (1965). The problem of generations. In E. Erikson (ed.), *The Challenge of Youth*. New York: Doubleday.

Block, J. H. (1977). Sex differences in cognitive functioning, personality characteristics, and socialization experiences: implications for education policy. Report to the Presidents of Smith, Wellesley and Mt. Holyoke College.

Boston Globe (1986). Two women who became their own boss. September 15, pp. 49–50.

Boston Globe (1988). 'Working mom' is now the norm. June 16, p. 26.

Brooks, L. (1984). Counseling special groups: women and ethnic minorities. In D. Brown, L. Brooks, and Associates (eds.), *Career Choice and Development*. San Francisco: Jossey-Bass.

Catalyst Career and Family Center Staff (1982). Corporations and two-career families: directions for the future – A report on the findings of two national surveys. New York: Catalyst.

Chodorow, N. (1974). Family structure and feminine personality. In M. Rosaldo and L. Lamphere (eds.), *Woman, Culture and Society*. Palo Alto, CA: Stanford University Press.

Chodorow, N. (1978). *The Reproduction of Mothering*. Berkeley: University of California Press.

The Cosmopolitan Report on Women's Lifestyles in the 1980's (1986). New York: Cosmopolitan Magazine, The Hearst Corporation.

Derr, C. B. (1986). *Managing the New Careerists: The Diverse Career Success Orientations of Today's Workers*. San Francisco: Jossey-Bass.

Diamond, E. E. (1987). Theories of career development and the reality of women at work. In B. A. Gutek and L. Larwood (eds.), *Women's Career Development*. Beverly Hills, CA: Sage.

Douglas, A. (1977). *The Feminization of American Culture*. New York: Avon Books.

Douvan, E., and Adelson, J. (1966). *The Adolescent Experience*. New York: Wiley.

Ecklein, J. (1982). Women in the German Democratic Republic: impact of culture and social policy. In J. Giele (ed.), *Women in the Middle Years*. New York: Wiley.

Ehrenreich, B., and English, D. (1979). *For Her Own Good: 150 Years of the Experts' Advice to Women*. New York: Anchor Books.

Eichenbaum, L., and Orbach, S. (1988). *Between Women*. New York: Viking.

Epstein, C. F. (1988). *Sex, Gender, and the Social Order*. New Haven: Yale University Press.

Erikson, E. (1968). *Identity: Youth and Crisis*. New York: Norton.

Fitzgerald, L. F., and Crites, J. O. (1980). Toward a career psychology of women: what do we know? what do we need to know? *Journal of Counseling Psychology*, *27*, 44–62.

French, M. (1985). *Beyond Power: On Women, Men and Morals*. New York: Ballantine.

Freud, S. (1925). Some psychical consequences of the anatomical distinction between the sexes. In J. Strachey (ed.) (1961), *The Standard Edition of the Complete Works of Sigmund Freud*, Vol. XIX. London: Hogarth.

Friedan, B. (1981). *The Second Stage*. New York: Summit.

Gallese, L. (1985). *Women Like Us.* New York: Signet.

Gallos, J. (1985). Power and competition in dual career marriage: an exploration. Ed.D. dissertation. Harvard Graduate School of Education.

Gerzon, M. (1982). *A Choice of Heroes: The Changing Faces of American Manhood.* Boston: Houghton Mifflin.

Giele, J. (1980). Crossovers: new themes in adult roles and the life cycle. In D. McGuigan (ed.), *Women's Lives: New Theory, Research, and Policy.* Ann Arbor: University of Michigan Center for Continuing Education of Women.

Giele, J. (1982). Women's work and family roles. In J. Giele (ed.), *Women in the Middle Years.* New York: Wiley.

Giele, J., and Kahne, H. (1978). Meeting work and family responsibilities: proposals for flexibility. In *Women in Midlife – Security and Fulfillment (I)*, U.S. House of Representatives, Select Committee on Aging. Washington, DC: U.S. Government Printing Office.

Gilbert, L. A. (1984). Comments on the meaning of work in women's lives. *The Counseling Psychologist, 12,* 129–130.

Gilligan, C. (1977). In a different voice: women's conception of self and of morality. *Harvard Education Review, 47,* 4.

Gilligan, C. (1980). Restoring the missing text of women's development to life cycle theories. In D. McGuigan (ed.), *Women's Lives: New Theory, Research, and Policy.* Ann Arbor: University of Michigan Center for Continuing Education of Women.

Gilligan, C. (1982). *In a Different Voice: Psychological Theory and Women's Development.* Cambridge: Harvard University Press.

Gould, R. (1978). *Transformations: Growth and Change in Adult Life.* New York: Simon & Schuster.

Grant, J. (1988). Women as managers: what they can offer to organizations. *Organizational Dynamics, 16*(3), 56–63.

Griffin, S. (1978). *Woman and Nature.* New York: Harper Colopon.

Hall, D., and Associates. (1986). *Career Development in Organizations.* San Francisco: Jossey-Bass.

Hall, F., and Hall, D. (1978). Dual careers – How do couples and companies cope with the problems? *Organizational Dynamics, 6*(4), 55–77.

Hancock, E. (1979). Women's development in adult life. Qualifying paper. Harvard Graduate School of Education.

Hardesty, S., and Jacobs, N. (1986). *Success and Betrayal: The Crisis of Women in Corporate America.* New York: Franklin Watts.

Hayghe, H. (1982). Marital and family patterns of workers: an update. *Monthly Labor Review, 105,* 53–61.

Hennig, M., and Jardim, A. (1978). *The Managerial Woman.* New York: Pocket.

Hewlett, S. (1986). *A Lesser Life: The Myth of Women's Liberation in America.* New York: Morrow.

Hymowitz, C., and Schellhardt, T. (1986). The glass ceiling: why women can't seem to break the invisible barrier that blocks them from the top jobs. *Wall Street Journal,* March 24, pp. 1D–5D.

Josselson, R. (1987). *Finding Herself: Pathways to Identity Development in Women.* San Francisco: Jossey-Bass.

Kanter, R. M. (1977). *Women and Women of the Corporation.* New York: Basic.

Keele, R. (1986). Mentoring or networking? Strong and weak ties in career development. In L. Moore (ed.), *Not as Far as You Think: The Realities of Working Women.* Lexington, MA: Lexington.

Kessler-Harris, A. (1985). The debate over equality for women in the work place: recognizing differences. In L. Larwood, A. Stromberg, and B. Gutek, (eds.), *Women and Work: An Annual Review,* Vol. 1. Beverly Hills, CA: Sage.

Kohlberg, L. (1976). Moral stages and moralization: the cognitive-developmental approach. In T. Lickona (ed.), *Moral Development and Behavior: Theory, Research and Social Issues.* New York: Holt, Rinehart and Winston.

Kohlberg, L. (1981). *The Philosophy of Moral Development.* San Francisco: Harper & Row.

Kohlberg, L., and Kramer, R. (1969). Continuities and discontinuities in child and adult moral development. *Human Development, 12,* 93–120.

Larwood, L., and Gattiker, U. E. (1987). A comparison of the career paths used by successful women and men. In B. A. Gutek and L. Larwood (eds.), *Women's Career Development.* Beverly Hills, CA: Sage.

Larwood, L., and Gutek, B. A. (1987). Working toward a theory of women's career development. In B. A. Gutek and L. Larwood (eds.), *Women's Career Development.* Beverly Hills, CA: Sage.

Lawrence, B. (1980). The myth of the midlife crisis. *Sloan Management Review, 21*(3), 35–49.

Lawrence, B. (1984). Historical perspective: using the past to study the present. *Academy of Management Review, 9,* 307–312.

Levinson, D. (1978). *The Seasons of a Man's Life.* New York: Knopf.

Loden, M. (1985). *Feminine Leadership or How to Succeed in Business Without Being One of the Boys.* New York: Times.

Loevinger, J. (1976). *Ego Development.* San Francisco: Jossey-Bass.

London, M., and Stumpf, S. (1986). Individual and organizational career development in changing times. In D. Hall and Associates, *Career Development in Organizations.* San Francisco: Jossey-Bass.

McClelland, D. (1975). *Power: The Inner Experience.* New York: Irvington.

Merriam-Webster Dictionary (1974). New York: Pocket, p. 117.

Miller, J. B. (1976). *Toward a New Psychology of Women.* Boston: Beacon.

National Center for Health Statistics (1986). *The Boston Globe,* March 27, p. 5.

Nero, S. (1984). How female MBA's align their needs for career progress and family life. Doctoral dissertation. University of California at Los Angeles.

Neugarten, B., and Brown-Rezanka, L. (1978). Midlife women in the 1980's. In *Women in Midlife – Security and Fulfillment (Part 1).* Select Committee on Aging, and the Subcommittee on Retirement Income and Employment, U.S. House of Representatives, Comm. Pub. 95–170. Washington, DC: U.S. Government Printing Office.

Newsweek (1986). Making it work: how women balance the demands of jobs and children. *Newsweek,* March 31, pp. 46–59.

Nieva, V. F. (1985). Work and family linkages. In L. Larwood, A. H. Stromberg, and B. A. Gutek, (eds.), *Women and Work.* Beverly Hills, CA: Sage.

Noddings, N. (1984). *Caring: A Feminine Approach to Ethics and Moral Education.* Berkeley: University of California Press.

Ortner, S. (1974). Is female to male as nature is to culture? In M. Rosaldo and L. Lamphere, (eds.), *Women, Culture, and Society.* Palo Alto, CA: Stanford University Press.

Osipow, S. H. (1983). *Theories of Career Development.* Englewood Cliffs, NJ: Prentice-Hall.

Perry, W. (1968). *Forms of Intellectual and Ethical Development in the College Years.* New York: Holt, Rinehart and Winston.

Reeves, D. (1982). *Womankind: Beyond the Stereotypes,* 2nd ed. New York: Albine.

Riley, M., Foner, A., Moore, M., Hess, B., and Roth, B. K. (1972). *Aging and Society.* New York: Russell Sage Foundation.

Roberts, P., and Newton, P. (1986). Levinsonian studies of women's adult development. Working paper. Wright Institute, Berkeley, CA.

Rohrlich, J. (1980). *Work and Love: The Crucial Balance.* New York: Harmony.

Rosaldo, M. (1974). Woman, culture, and society: theoretical overview. In M. Rosaldo and L. Lamphere (eds.), *Women, Culture, and Society.* Palo Alto, CA: Stanford University Press.

Rossi, A. (1977). A biosocial perspective on parenting. *Daedalus, 106*(2), 1–31.

Rossi, A. (1980). Life span theories and women's lives. *Signs: Journal of Women in Culture and Society, 6*(1), 4–32.

Sanday, P. (1974). Female status in the public domain. In M. Rosaldo and L. Lamphere (eds.), *Women, Culture, and Society.* Palo Alto, CA: Stanford University Press.

Sandell, S. H. (1977). Life-time participation in the labor force and unemployment among mature women. In *American Women Workers in a Full Employment Economy,* U.S. Congress, Joint Economic Committee. Washington, DC: U.S. Government Printing Office.

Scanzoni, J. (1983). *Shaping Tomorrow's Family: Theory and Policy for the 21st Century.* Beverly Hills, CA: Sage.

Scarf, M. (1980). *Unfinished Business: Pressure Points in the Lives of Women.* New York: Ballantine.

Schaef, A. (1981). *Women's Reality: An Emerging Female System in a White Male Society.* Minneapolis, MN: Winston.

Schein, E. (1982). Individuals and careers. Technical report 19. Office of Naval Research.

Sheehy, G. (1974). *Passages: Predictable Crises of the Adult Life.* New York: Dutton.

Skinner, D. (1980). Dual career family stress: a literature review. *Family Relations, 29*(4), 473–481.

Strober, M. H. (1977). Economic aspects of child care. In *American Working Women in a Full Employment Economy,* U.S. Congress, Joint Economic Committee. Washington, DC: U.S. Government Printing Office.

Stroud, K. (1986). I am mother to my mother. *Newsweek,* August 4, p. 7.

Vaillant, G. (1977). *Adaptation to Life.* Boston: Little, Brown.

Wall Street Journal (1986). A special report: the corporate woman. March 24, section 4, pp. 1D–32D.

Working Woman (1986). How working women have changed America. November, cover story, tenth anniversary ed., pp. 129–156.

Working Woman (1987). A case for the unconventional. February, pp. 80–83.

Yankelovich, D. (1981). *New Rules: Searching for Self-fulfillment in a World Turned Upside Down.* New York: Random House.

Yogev, S. (1981). Do professional women have egalitarian marital relationships? *Journal of Marriage and the Family, 43,* 865–872.

7 The influence of race on career dynamics: theory and research on minority career experiences

DAVID A. THOMAS AND CLAYTON P. ALDERFER

This chapter is concerned with understanding how race and race relations influence career dynamics. Statistics on the occupational status of racial minority groups suggest that race is a strong predictor of position in the labor market and career patterns. According to U.S. 1983 Census Bureau statistics, blacks made up 4.7% of U.S. executives, administrators and managers, and Hispanics constituted 2.8% of this group. The majority of people from both ethnic groups in this job category are located in the public sector. In 1980, the unemployment rate for racial minorities was twice that of whites. The median family income of blacks in 1980 was 57% that of whites. Studies of upward mobility show that white males in low-paying positions are significantly more likely than minority males to advance to positions that pay a middle-class wage (Pomer, 1986). According to a U.S. Commission on Civil Rights report (1980), Asian Americans are underrepresented in managerial and administrative occupations, while they are represented in professional positions at a higher rate than in the population at large.

Since the passage of the U.S. Civil Rights Act in 1964, behavioral science has looked at the relationships between race and work through a number of disciplinary lenses, especially those of economics, sociology and psychology. Economics has focused on issues of pay and labor market activity and sociology on the related issues of status attainment and stratification. These literatures constitute a significant and well-developed body of theory about discrimination (Almquist, 1979; Lester, 1980; Lundahl and Wadensjo, 1984; Pascal, 1972). In addition to using data on disparities in stratification among racial groups to study discrimination in employment, sociologists have also attempted to study the dynamics of racial interaction in the society (Blalock, 1967; Blauner, 1972; Bonacich, 1972; Hraba and Hoiberg, 1983; Kinloch, 1982; Park, 1950; Van den Bergher, 1967; Williams, 1985; Wilson, 1973). These theorists have examined the process of assimilation and the dynamics of intergroup competition between ethnic and racial groups.

Psychologists have also been deeply involved in the study of race relations. This work has primarily focused on understanding the origins of prejudice and the links between racial attitudes and personality. [For an extensive review of this literature, see Harding, Proshansky, Kutner and Chein (1969) and more recently Brewer and Kramer (1985).] A small but significant body of literature exploring the psychology of racism and its impact on the self-concept of blacks and whites has also been developed, primarily by psychiatrists (Cross, 1976; Cross 1985; Fanon, 1967; Grier and Cobbs, 1968; Kovel, 1984).

133

Unlike the behavioral science disciplines of economics, sociology and psychology, only minimal research in this area has been conducted by scholars in organizational behavior (Alderfer and Thomas, 1988). This is especially disappointing since organizational behavior is the discipline most directly focused on the individual's experience in the workplace and has the potential to offer suggestions for improved intraorganizational practice with regard to the management of race relations. Also, organizational behavior has given rise to a subfield of career dynamics, expressly concerned with the time-dependent outcomes of employment practice for both individuals and organizations (Schein, 1978). The concept of career holds particular promise for our understanding of individual–organization interaction in general (Chapter 1) and the occupational experience of racial minorities in particular (Bell, Denton, Herbert and Thomas, 1987). Cox and Nkomo (1987) report that of 9,000 articles published between 1964 and 1986, in twenty of the most commonly read refereed journals in organizational behavior, less than 2% examined the influence of race on organization behavior. Three recent reviews of career theory and research have expressed the need for more work in this area (Greenhaus and Parasuraman, 1986; Hall, 1986; Tinsley and Heesacker, 1984).

Despite the paucity of research conducted by scholars in organizational behavior, several recent books and articles aimed at a general audience attempt to chronicle the experiences of minorities in predominantly white organizations and professions (America and Anderson, 1978; Blackwell, 1981; Davis and Watson, 1982; Dickens and Dickens, 1982; Fernandez, 1981; Irons and Moore, 1985; Jones, 1986). These books and articles provide detailed, descriptive accounts of the aspirations, dilemmas and obstacles faced by minority managers and professionals. This work is limited, however, in that it is, for the most part, atheoretical in orientation, focusing primarily on conveying a sense of the difficulties minorities face and the coping strategies they employ to survive in the corporate environment.

There is also beginning to emerge a small body of research by scholars in organizational behavior that is related to understanding the dynamics of race in organizations (Alderfer, 1982, 1986; Alderfer, Alderfer, Tucker, and Tucker, 1980; Alderfer and Thomas, 1988; Alderfer, Tucker, Morgan and Dragson, 1983; Wells and Jennings, 1983) and minority career and adult development processes (Bearden, 1984; Bell, 1986; Ford and Wells, 1985; Herbert, 1986; Thomas, 1986). Taken together, these two bodies of literature inform one another in significant ways and show the emergence of various issues and themes relevant to understanding the influence of race on career dynamics and the building of theory in this area.

In this chapter, our primary aim is to examine those elements of the research that are most likely to increase our understanding of the complex ways in which race relates to career dynamics. A major limitation is imposed on our work by the nature of the research from which we must draw. Current research in this area is almost exclusively concerned with the experiences of black Americans in predominantly white corporations (Alderfer and Thomas, 1988; Lavender and Forsyth, 1976); while we are aware that there are many similarities in the experiences of racial minorities, we also recognize that there are significant differences. The focus of this review, however, is on identifying and interpreting the aspects of this research that have implications for other racial minorities as well as black Americans. The first section examines research themes that address how race relates to the individual career experiences of minorities. Then two theories are presented that help us to understand the influence of group and organizational forces and their differential impact on the career experiences of minorities and whites. Finally, major themes and key tensions represented in extant research in the field are analyzed and implications for future investigations drawn.

THE RELATIONSHIP OF RACE TO INDIVIDUAL CAREER EXPERIENCES

A review of recent research and writings on minority career experiences suggests four areas in which significant advances in understanding the relationship of race to individual career experiences have been made. The first is in framing the minority experience as bicultural. The second is that researchers have begun to examine how, within the career development process of minorities, race influences the internal sense of self in the world. The third is concerned with minorities' experiences of gaining significant social and instrumental support from superiors and peers. The fourth concerns issues of minority women in organizations and the ways in which gender influences cross-racial relationships between men and women.

Biculturalism: life in two worlds

One of the themes that has emerged in recent books and articles chronicling the experience of racial minorities, particularly black Americans, is that they often feel caught in a struggle between two distinct cultural worlds (Davis and Watson, 1982; Dickens and Dickens, 1982; Hopkins, 1987; McClain, 1980). Du Bois (1903) described this tension over eighty years ago, and his description is perhaps even more apt today:

The Negro is a sort of seventh son, born with a veil, and gifted with second-sight in this American world – a world which yields him no true self-consciousness, but only lets him see himself through the revelation of the other world. It is a peculiar sensation, this double-consciousness, this sense of always looking at one's self through the eyes of a world that looks on in amused contempt and pity. One ever feels his twoness – an American, a Negro; two souls, two thoughts, two unreconciled strivings; two warring ideals in one dark body, whose dogged strength alone keeps it from being torn asunder. (p. 45)

Bell (1986), drawing on the work of Valentine (1968) and Blackwell (1981), has attempted to examine this dynamic, focusing on the coping mechanisms that black women use to manage the stresses associated with moving physically, cognitively and emotionally between the dominant culture and the black subculture. According to Bell, black Americans are by necessity, if not by definition, bicultural. Biculturalism is defined as the "sociocultural repertoire of [racial minorities], as they move back and forth between the black community and dominant culture" (Bell, 1986:21). Bicultural stress is that set of emotional and physical upheavals produced by a bicultural existence.

Figure 7.1 depicts a bicultural life structure mapped on to Bronfenbrenner's (1979) ecological system model of human development. At each level of the system, from the extremes of macro to micro, there is a parallel set of culturally identified institutions and social settings. The bicultural perspective focuses attention on

Figure 7.1. A bicultural life structure (Bell, 1986; used by permission)

the interplay between the two cultures and its effect on the lives of racial minority workers. The dynamics inside of organizations located in the dominant cultural context often pull for minorities to suppress their racial identity (Jones, 1986). This can happen at the level of surface symbols such as dress, hair style and acquired taste and at deeper levels of emotional and ideological attachment such as who one associates with, where one lives and one's political and social values (Davis and Watson, 1982). Such pulls are sources of bicultural stress.

Bicultural stress is amplified by the fact that white-dominated institutions are often not consciously aware that their norms and values represent cultural distinctions for members of racial minority groups or that aspects of their culture represent indictments of various aspects of minority culture. Thus minorities frequently find themselves feeling alone and alienated in their struggles to manage these conflicts within the organization. Conflicts also arise when members of the minority culture are unable to understand the strains that certain other individuals feel while attempting to integrate themselves more deeply into the dominant culture.

Bell's (1986) research in this area provides a framework for researchers to understand the fact that minorities make individual choices about the level and extent to which they will become involved in engaging the bicultural tensions associated with moving between the two cultures. She found three patterns of bicultural life structures among the women she studied.

The first group, career-oriented women, organized their lives around professional activities. Their social networks extended into both the black and white communities. Stress for these women was related to their attempts to balance professional and personal lives and the emotional strains of walking a line between two worlds. Of the three patterns, these women were the most obviously ensconced in the white world.

The second group, black community-oriented women, included women who involved themselves deeply in the black community while maintaining social and emotional distance from the dominant culture. Their stress resulted from inadequate resources often found in black communities, a symptom of the black community's subordinate position vis-à-vis the dominant white culture. They also experienced stress resulting from insufficient social support. Women of this orientation who worked in predominantly white organizations saw their jobs as necessities and did not put great stock in socializing with whites or forming cross-racial developmental relationships. Many took positions in black-oriented businesses and organizations, some assuming leadership roles. On the intrapsychic level, they described little of the conflict of marginality or double consciousness of the career-oriented women.

The third group, family-oriented women, centered their lives around family, with work as a secondary component. Their focus on family, while helping them avoid some of the stresses experienced by women of the first two orientations, produced its own form of disturbance. These women often felt unfulfilled in their career aspirations; they thought of themselves as unaccomplished and one-sided in their development. These women's focus on the home allowed them to view bicultural issues in more deracialized and less conflictual terms. They frequently claimed they formed relationships with people based on interest and personality rather than race.

Bell's work in this area is important for research on minority careers for three reasons. First, she has provided a conceptual framework for understanding the experiences of minority workers, especially managers and professionals, as they have been reported anecdotally in the popular press (Hopkins, 1987; McClain, 1980). Second, this perspective moves away from a focus on minorities as the impacted party, passively reacting to the forces of institutional racism. All of the women Bell studied made choices about how to navigate a bicultural existence: This sense of being an active agent occurs despite the fact that their environments, their prior socialization and the forces of racism limit their alternatives. Third, this work offers insight into the much neglected area of black female career experiences, a topic that will be addressed later in more depth.

Racial identity and career development

That individuals go through a definable sequence of life and career development stages is a widely accepted and espoused notion (Baird and Kram, 1983; Dalton, Thompson and Price, 1977; Levinson et al., 1978; Schein, 1978; Super, 1957). Yet none of these theories takes into account the influence of race on the developmental process.

Herbert (1986) and Gooden (1980) found that Levinson's model of the adult life structure did fit the lives of black men from various walks of life – entrepreneurs, academics, professionals and street men. Malone (1981) also found the model useful in her study of black women. Herbert and Gooden, however, note that for black men the element of race limits choices and opportunities to work on important developmental tasks and constitutes a particular set of developmental tasks. Herbert (1986) noted that the men in his study had to expend considerable energy in coming to grips with their racial identity and the implications of their race in their lives as a whole as a result of the U. S. civil rights movement.

The concept of identity has been an important part of much of the research and theory of human development (Erikson, 1963; Jung, 1933; Levinson et al., 1978). Erikson (1963), in particular, has given voice to the importance of social context and one's relative position within it to shaping identity. However, the focus of these developmental theories on age-linked aspects of identity formation has limited attention to the influence of social–historical context and ethnicity. Meanwhile, theory and research on racial identity has shown social context, more than age, to be a primary predictor of racial identity formation (Cross, 1976; Dickens and Dickens, 1982; Sherif and Sherif, 1970; Thomas, 1971).

Jackson (1978) and Cross (1976) have developed theories of black identity development. Jackson's (1978) model delineates four stages of black identity development: passive acceptance, active resistance, redefinition, and integration. Each of these stages represents a dominant stance toward the individual's own racial identity and race relations. The *passive acceptance* stage occurs when the individual internalizes the dominant culture's view of black people and culture, believes that white values and culture are superior to black values and culture and seeks validation primarily from whites. Pride is taken in *not* being "like other black people." In predominantly white organizations, this person is generally unquestioning of the system's treatment of blacks and believes racial problems lie in the inability of blacks to adjust and behave appropriately in the white world. Racism is considered only to the extent that it is manifest in overt, virulent form, and such behaviors are usually attributed to "white ignorance." The individual also avoids association with blacks for fear of being rejected by whites or being negatively labeled as preferring black over white companionship.

Active resistance is the stage in which the individual begins to question and reject white values and norms. All things black are praised and the individual views interactions with whites as something to be avoided. Personal energy is put into rejecting whites and building black institutions or espousing the need to do so. Validation is sought from black persons and organizations. When in predominantly white organizations, persons with this predisposition avoid non-required contact with whites and "white activities." The individual justifies being in the organization by saying that no other choices were available. The individual also chastises blacks who socialize with whites and have close relationships with them. In this stage, like the one before it, white people are the primary reference group, and most of the individual's behaviors are a reaction to whites.

The *redefinition* phase begins when the individual ceases to respond reactively to whites and begins to develop his or her own unique set of values and goals based on a positive sense of black identity. Time is invested in learning about black history and culture. In predominantly white organizations he or she sup-

Table 7.1. *Model of black career development*

Phase	Attitudes and emotions	Behaviors
Entry	Feeling I've got it made (because of securing desired job); little or no direction in terms of goals; naivete about organizational norms and culture and race relations; contained anger: interpersonal and job discomfort ignored	Reserved behavior: don't make waves; try to fit in and make white peers comfortable
Adjustment	Dissatisfaction with lack of mobility; distress as white peers move ahead; anger, rage and frustration felt; low self-confidence; whites not trusted	Much verbal interpersonal fights with whites; withdraws from required activities with white colleagues; seeks support from blacks; declining job effectiveness
Planned growth	Realizes that to get ahead means expending more energy than whites; understands need for black input; feels self-confident; personal goals set	Consciously acts to remove barriers under one's control; develops own personal style; learns to make proper demands on corporation; nurtures sponsorship relations
Success	Making mistakes not an option; aware of blackness and its effects on organization; aware of subtleties of racism; sensitive to the work environment	Uses communications effectively; continues to refine and smooth personal style; produces high-quality results; continues to set and meet goals; confronts whites, but in a way that leaves them their dignity

Source: Adapted from Dickens and Dickens (1982).

ports the development of black groups for social and cultural support and looks for ways his or her skills can be of use to help the black community.

Internalization is marked by the individual feeling secure about his or her black identity and showing the ability to integrate the lessons learned in the previous two stages into a more whole sense of self. Other roles and group identities can be recognized as important and not antithetical to being black. In predominantly white organizations this person seeks to integrate a positive sense of blackness with one's own professional identity and is committed to combating racism and to challenging blacks on their collusion with it. Dickens and Dickens (1982) have gone further than any other researchers in defining the influence of race on the career development of minorities. One of the strengths of this model is that it defines the career development process of black managers independent of models that describe the experiences of white managers, thus avoiding the problem of forcing the black experience into an existing model that was not designed to include it.

Dickens and Dickens (1982) posit that black career development has four stages: entry, adjusting, planned growth, and success. Associated with each phase are a set of critical issues, attitudes and behaviors. Table 7.1 presents the set of attitudes and behaviors.

Entry marks the beginning of the black individual's relationship with the organization. It is characterized by a feeling of false security in which anger is contained and issues of race are ignored in an effort not to make waves. The individual generally operates under the assumption that rewards are allocated based upon merit and is not very aware of institutional politics or the need for sponsorship.

The *adjusting phase* is divided into two parts. The first is a period of dissatisfaction marked by low self-confidence related to an experience of lack of movement and perceiving inequalities in the way white peers are treated and the black individual is treated. The second is a period of frustration in which the individual's anger and rage cannot be contained. The person is unwilling to let incidents and insults go by. This behavior may be viewed as uncooperative and/or militant by whites. Little personal or professional growth is achieved. However, some psychic benefit is derived from letting go of the anger and rage suppressed during the entry phase.

The third stage is *planned growth*. In this phase the individual learns to manage his or her rage and chooses strategically when to be angry. The individual develops a style that is consistent with corporate norms but maintains his or her uniqueness and sense of self. It is in this phase that the black manager is able to develop satisfactory relationships with whites and to work with them appropriately as resources.

The fourth and final stage is *success*. In this stage the individual has integrated the learning of the previous phases. He or she accepts the burdens of being a manager, is aware of his or her own blackness and its impact on an organization and various situations, needs fewer strokes from others, is results oriented and has a high sense of confidence. The individual in this phase continues to refine his or her interpersonal and task-related skills. A style of confronting whites that leaves them their dignity is developed.

Dickens and Dickens (1982) argue that (1) the amount of time an individual spends in each phase varies depending on personality differences and (2) the phases are likely to repeat if the individual changes organizations or is promoted to higher levels.

Thomas (1986) used the Dickens and Dickens (1982) model to examine the influence of race on black managers and mentor–protégé and sponsor–protégé relationships. He found that there were significant differences in the dynamics of these relationships depending upon where the black manager was in his or her development. Blacks in the entry stage were best able to form close mentor–protégé relationships with whites whom they perceived to have little racial consciousness. Blacks who described themselves as spending an extensive amount of time coping with the issues of the adjustment phase had difficulty maintaining cross-racial relationships. Blacks in the planned growth phase showed more ability to discriminate among relationships with whites, seeing the necessity for some relationships with white sponsors while not relying on them extensively for psychosocial support. Their close mentor–protégé relationships with whites were with persons whom they felt had a significant level of racial awareness. These individuals also actively sought and nurtured developmental relationships with blacks and saw the need for support networks composed of blacks and whites. Thomas's results did not differentiate between dynamics associated with the success and planned growth phases.

These models do not preclude that blacks also evolve through the career development stages defined by researchers concerned primarily with white populations (Dalton, Thompson and Price, 1977; Schein, 1978), but they do imply that models developed by white researchers observing white managers are limited. One implication of the Dickens and Dickens model for blacks progressing through the stages defined by these researchers is that they spend more time grappling with the issues of inclusion and professional identity associated with the early career phase. Also, the implicit psychological contract is more complex for the minority employee because it includes issues of race. Additional research is needed to understand the individual differences that may influence how fast individuals progress through the phases and the influence of organizational context on how minorities cope with the issues at each successive phase.

Developmental relationships: mentors and sponsors

One of the notions that has been propagated in the popular press (Karmel, 1984) and hypothesized about by researchers (Dickens and Dickens, 1982; Levinson et al., 1978) is that racial minorities, especially blacks, do not find mentors in organizations. The majority of the work on mentoring and sponsorship in organizations that has examined minority experiences refutes this notion as a gross generalization.

Ford and Wells (1985) found that 65% of the eighty black public administrators and executives they surveyed said they had mentors. Malone (1981) found that 82% of the black female administrators she studied said they had mentors, and Murray (1982), in a study of middle-class black men who worked in predominantly white corporations in the midwest, found that 51% of her sample said they had mentors. Thomas (1986), in a study of black and white managers in one predominantly white corporation, found that 82% of his black respondents had had mentors or sponsors at some point in their career. Only Herbert (1986) and Gooden (1980) reported that the blacks in their studies were undermentored. This difference in findings raises several issues. First is the issue of how the term *mentoring* has been defined in research. The second issue relates to differences in the populations studied. And, finally, we must concern ourselves with method. The term *mentor* has been applied nondiscriminantly in many studies to any relationship between a senior, more experienced person and a junior, less experienced person, that provides some type of career support for the junior (Ford and Wells, 1985; Malone, 1981; Murray, 1984). Thomas (1986) attempted to address this shortcoming by collecting data about the actual functions the relationship provided and giving the respondents a definition of the mentor–protégé relationship, consistent with that of Levinson. Discriminant analysis revealed that mentor–protégé relationships were distinguishable from other types of developmental relationships. Thomas (1986) also conducted interviews and found the distinction held. The mentor–protégé relationship not only provides instrumental career support but also psychosocial support and is characterized by a high degree of identification and mutuality between the parties. Thomas (1986) found that 57% of the relationships blacks reported having were classified as mentor–protégé. The result is still quite inconsistent with the findings of Gooden (1980) and Herbert (1986).

With regard to the populations studied and methods employed, those using survey methods have all studied black professional and managerial populations

(Ford and Wells, 1985; Malone, 1981; Murray, 1982; Thomas, 1986) with sample sizes ranging from 80 to 139. Gooden (1980) and Herbert (1986) were more broadly interested in the adult development of black males and used the biographical interviewing technique of Levinson et al. (1978). Gooden's (1981) sample of 16 men included academics, blue-collar workers, managerial professionals and chronically unemployed men. Herbert (1986) looked at the lives of 10 black entrepreneurs whose backgrounds varied greatly with regard to exposure and success in mainstream white organizations.

Gooden's (1981) and Herbert's (1986) samples were also homogeneous in age and represented a particular generation of black developmental experience. The depth of the method used by Gooden and Herbert as well as their attention to nonmanagerial persons makes it difficult for us to disregard their findings because of small sample size.

To understand the role of mentoring and sponsorship on minority careers, we must look beyond the broad generalization to the complexities associated with these relationships. Important questions in this line of inquiry are with whom do individuals tend to have developmental relationships and how does race affect the relationship?

The majority of the black respondents in Ford and Wells's (1985) and Malone's (1981) studies had black mentors, while the majority of black respondents in the study by Murray (1982) and Thomas (1986) reported having white mentors and sponsors. White respondents in the Thomas study reported that 98% of their relationships were with other whites. Thomas (1986) also found that 30% of the minorities in his sample had relationships with both black and white mentors or sponsors. The differences in the findings of Ford and Wells (1985), Malone (1981), Murray (1982) and Thomas (1986) may be due in part to differences in context. Ford and Wells and Malone studied public administrators, while Murray and Thomas studied individuals who worked in predominantly white corporations. However, these differences do raise the need to consider the influence of context on the type of relationship that forms, cross-race versus same-race, and to be alert to the effects of method on the data collected.

Thomas (1986) also found that blacks tend to have broader support networks than do whites. The general pattern for blacks and whites was to have relationships inside of one's department and with one's boss. White males were the most common mentors. Blacks differed significantly from whites, male and female, by having more extradepartmental and organizational relationships and more relationships with other blacks and white females. The most significant factor accounting for this difference was the location of black employees' black mentors and sponsors, who were most frequently outside of the department. This suggests that blacks may find it organizationally necessary to have white sponsorship but also respond to a psychosocial need to have developmental relationships with persons of their own race.

Results from the work of Bearden (1984) and Thomas (1986) indicate that cross-race relationships evolve through the same four relationship phases as do same-race relationships: initiation, cultivation, separation and redefinition (Kram, 1985). However, cross-race relationships usually have a longer initiation period than do same-race relations and are characterized by more hesitancy, on the part of minority protégés, to assume that the senior party is willing to act as a mentor or sponsor. Also, cross-race relationships are less likely than same-race relationships to end acrimoniously.

Thomas (1986) found that while both same- and cross-race relationships provide career and psychosocial support, same-race relationships provide significantly more psychosocial support than do cross-race relationships. Cross-race and same-race relationships did not differ significantly in the amount of instrumental career support they provided.

This suggests that while blacks and other minorities may find support from white supervisors early in their careers for the more technical and superficial socialization issues, they may not feel a tremendous amount of attachment, trust or acceptance in these relationships. Despite having black support, it may be relationships with white mentors, sponsors and peers that determine one's place in and relationship to the institution. Concomitantly, the low number of blacks in top-level decision-making positions in predominantly white corporations means that same-race developmental relationships for blacks may be limited in their ability to *directly* influence external career development. Furthermore, the lack of trust and attachment in the cross-race relationship is frequently felt by both parties (Thomas, 1986). Given that the risks of sponsoring people for important jobs in any setting are often great, a feeling of something missing in the relationship that is vital to a sense of comfort with a protégé may cause many white mentors to hesitate in pushing minority candidates or to back down in the face of resistance from peers.

White mentors in cross-racial developmental relationships reported having more difficulty influencing white peers and supervisors to support blacks than their white protégés on promotion review committees (Thomas, 1986). Furthermore, those white mentors who had more progressive views on race relations saw the need to market black protégés differently than white ones. They believed they had to increase the exposure of the minority protégé at the next level prior to submitting him or her for promotion in order to break down what they perceived to be race-induced anxiety felt by other whites concerning the minority manager's ability to perform and manage white employees.

This data suggests that obstacles to black mobility are far more complex than a simple lack of mentoring or sponsorship. Race has profound influences on the dynamics of mentoring and sponsorship in organizations. Furthermore, limitations may be placed on the efficacy of minorities' developmental relationships, whether same-race or cross-race, by the nature of intergroup relations in the organization.

Gender and race in the workplace

Research on black managers generally subordinates the issue of gender to race and, in this way, has tended to replicate the male bias found in much of social science research (Gilligan, 1982; Reinharz, 1985). Those studies that have compared or addressed the experiences of both minority men and women suggest that, while they have much in common, they also have unique experiences (Fernandez, 1981; Thomas, 1986).

The career aspirations and life chances of minority women are significantly impacted by many factors. When compared to other race–gender minority groups, women tend to be the poorest segment of our society, disproportionately represented in single-parent households, welfare roles and low-paying occupations. Bell (1986), a black female, found that the black women in her study registered stress levels on standardized measures that were significantly higher than those reported in the general population. Fernandez (1981), a black male, in a study of over 5,000 managers, found black women report more criticism of their work experience than other race–gender groups.

Research on minority women's career experiences has revealed several themes unique to their distinct position as both racial minority and female in the corporate world. The tensions associated with this position have been captured in the debate over whether this combination of race and gender constitutes an advantage or a double negative. Epstein (1973), a white female, has argued that black females are likely to have unique opportunities afforded because no prescribed roles are set for black women in corporate America, as there are for black men and white women. This notion has also led some to see them as a preferred hire for corporations because they constitute a "two-for" in the affirmative action count. Leggon (1980) and Fulbright (1985) argued that the opposite is true and that being a minority and female resulted in black women being doubly taxed. Furthermore, studies of the coping styles and role stresses of black women as well as personal accounts by professional black women show that they feel both racial and gender discrimination (Davis and Watson, 1982; McClain, 1980) and experience strains in their nonwork lives in the black community that are the result of sexism (Bell, 1986; Davis, 1983).

Dumas (1980) calls our attention to the power of stereotyping in shaping the experiences of black females in leadership. According to her view, the black female leader is often caught in the role of nurturing caretaker, which undermines her executive authority. She likens this role to that of the archetypal "mammy" figure. Not to meet these expectations for caretaking and nurturing can draw the attribution of "bitch." Black women can therefore find themselves in almost untenable executive dilemmas as to appropriate and effective behavior. At this point, we know of no research that has attempted to better understand the content of the attributional processes that surround black females in leadership roles.

Gender complicates not only the internal career experience of minority women, but also the external aspects of careers for both males and females. Thomas (1986) found that the taboos associated with cross-racial sexual encounters made it particularly difficult for blacks to engage in cross-gender, cross-race developmental relationships. Black females expressed reticence about being too closely associated with white male executives because it conjured up the images of the black concubines who, without choice, served white slave owners (Davis, 1983). Black men also reported a reticence to become involved with white females in developmental relationships for fear of retribution by white superiors in the organization. Some of these men also reported having white female subordinates discouraged, by other whites, from becoming too closely associated with them.

These studies suggest strongly that gender and race interact in complex ways to influence individuals' career experiences, both in the macrostructural context that shapes and limits options and in the microcontext in which group and interpersonal relations are influenced by intrapsychic and group tensions. There is also an obvious need for more research that attempts to understand the career experiences of minority women and gender dynamics in cross-race relationships.

THEORETICAL PERSPECTIVES ON RACE, ORGANIZATION AND
CAREER DYNAMICS

The research reviewed in the preceding focuses on the individual career experiences of minorities. The influence of race on career dynamics cannot be understood without also taking account of intergroup and organizational dynamics. Organizations appear to have a "dynamic conservatism" that allows for paradoxes in race relations. For example, minorities have experienced some access and upward mobility in organizations; yet statistics show and minorities report that there are still discriminatory barriers to their advancement beyond a particular level. Similarly, minorities have made more progress in some types of organizations (i.e., government) and occupations (i.e., health care, education, and nonmanagerial technical positions) than others (Collins, 1983). How do we go about understanding the institutional dynamics that operate at multiple levels and that interact with race to influence career dynamics?

Two theoretical perspectives that shed some light on these issues and may guide future research will be presented in what follows. Intergroup theory is a tool for understanding racial dynamics embedded in organizations (Alderfer, 1986; Alderfer, Alderfer, Tucker and Tucker, 1980; Alderfer and Smith, 1982). The implications of this theory for understanding the dynamics of various organizational processes are also discussed. The second theoretical frame explains the frequently observed phenomenon of limited black mobility in predominantly white corporations (Wells and Jennings, 1983).

An intergroup perspective on race and career dynamics

Intergroup theory posits that two types of groups exist within organizations – identity groups and organization groups (Alderfer, 1986). Members of identity groups share common biological characteristics, participate in equivalent historical experiences and, as a result, tend to develop similar world views. The most commonly recognized identity groups are those based on race, ethnicity, family, gender and age. Members of organization groups are assigned similar primary tasks, participate in comparable work experiences and, as a result, tend to develop common organizational views. Most often, organizational groupings are based on task, function and hierarchy. While organization group membership can change as people enter and leave organizations, identity group membership remains constant or, as in the case of age, changes as the result of natural development rather than negotiations.

According to this view, individuals and organizations are constantly attempting, consciously and unconsciously, to manage potential conflicts arising from the interface between identity and organization group memberships. How these tensions are managed depends upon several factors. Chief among these is how the groups are embedded within the organization.

Intergroup embeddedness refers to the interpenetration of group-level effects across different units of analysis: It concerns how system and subsystem dynamics are affected by suprasystem dynamics and vice versa (Alderfer, 1986; Alderfer and Smith, 1982). One may observe embeddedness from the perspective of individuals in relation to one another, of subgroups within groups, of whole groups in relation to one another, of intergroup relations within organizations and so on.

Alderfer and Smith (1982) define two types of embeddedness: congruent and incongruent. Congruent embeddedness pertains to situations in which the power relations among groups at the system level are reinforced by power relations at the suprasystem and subsystem levels. Incongruent embeddedness refers to situations in which power relations among groups at the system level differ from those at other levels. Thus, with regard to race, congruent embeddedness is represented in situations in which whites predominate in high-status positions while blacks are found overwhelmingly in low-power, low-status positions. This pattern mirrors the general power relations between blacks and whites in the suprasystem (society). On the other hand, whites found in black-controlled organizations would be incongruently embedded in the organization.

Organizations in which congruent embeddedness generally exists with regard to race are likely to manage the interface between racial identity group and organization group memberships by operating from an implicit set of values around race relations that reflect the group interests and racial perspective of the suprasystem. When this is controlled by white males, we are likely to find evaluations of racial minorities to be inaccurate or to reflect the anxieties of the dominant group in race relations.

Research on the internal labor markets of organizations and on performance appraisal supports this view. Work (1986) examined the position of black managers in the internal labor markets of several predominantly white corporations. He found that the majority of these managers did not have control over budgets, final hiring authority or profit and loss responsibility regardless of their organizational level. Other researchers have noted the clustering of minorities in particular parts of organizations and in jobs with limited mobility prospects (Almquist, 1979; Saunders, 1977; Work, 1986).

When organizational group membership and racial identity group membership become rigidly correlated, we find that many racist assumptions go unexamined and influence decisions that ultimately impact individuals' career opportunities. Intergroup relations also tend to mirror negative aspects of race relations in the broader environment. For example, Powell (1969), in a study of white male executives' views on managerial succession, found that being black or Hispanic was seen as a hindrance in getting promoted because members of these groups lacked the necessary values, social desirability and intelligence to do managerial work. By contrast, persons of German, Swedish and British descent were seen as most promotable. Most likely, few of these executives had ever worked with a significant number of black and Hispanic managers to accurately make such assessments. The existence, therefore, of correlated intergroup relations – white male being totally coincidental with executive-level positions and racial minorities absent from these roles – under conditions of congruent embeddedness probably reinforced the stereotypes and their impact on executive selection decisions.

Studies of the effects of race on performance appraisal represent, perhaps, the largest single body of research in organizational behavior in which race is examined. The results of these studies have been mixed and have generally focused on the issue of proving or disproving bias in these procedures (Cox and Nkomo, 1986). Intergroup theory suggests that we also attempt to discern if differential criteria are used in the assessments of racial minorities and whites. Cox and Nkomo (1986) found that social skills were more important in the overall performance evaluations of blacks than for whites. Beatty (1973) and Huck and Bray

(1976) obtained results that support the general findings of Cox and Nkomo. This approach to understanding appraisal processes facilitates a greater understanding of the complex interplay between race and organizational processes than emphasis on outcome variables alone. Furthermore, these findings are consistent with the experience that minority workers must bear the primary burden for making whites comfortable with them in social interactions if they are to have a chance at being assessed fairly (Davis and Watson, 1982; Dickens and Dickens, 1982). It also follows that these results support the idea that appraisals of minority competence reflect white concerns about the ability of minorities to fit in.

Alderfer and Tucker (1985), as part of a major systemwide intervention, compared the criteria used by a balanced race–gender selection committee and those of departmental personnel committees, which were predominantly white male, to select low-level managers for the organization's high-potential program. The balanced race–gender selection committee represented an attempt to create incongruence with the general pattern of congruent intergroup embeddedness, which the departmental committees represented. Stepwise canonical discriminant analysis revealed that the candidates' ability to manage differences – cope with diversity – was not a significant criterion in the deliberations of the predominantly white male committees but was an important selection criterion in the decisions of the balanced race–gender selection committee.

Thomas (1986) used an embedded intergroup perspective to examine the influence of the organization on the formation and development of cross-racial developmental relationships. He found that the presence of blacks in the hierarchy of a department had a positive influence on the formation of these relationships. Two reasons were cited. The first is that the minority executives are models to white peers that represent the potential of minorities to occupy and function competently at high levels, which allows whites to diminish their doubts about minorities' abilities and the organization's willingness to accept them in particular jobs. Second, minority executives could exert influence on their subordinates' mentoring and hiring decisions. It was also found that minorities' white protégés sometimes acted as mentors to junior-level minorities, thus providing some support to the idea that embeddedness influences behavior and incongruent embeddedness affects the behavior of both blacks and whites.

The implications of intergroup theory for correcting the negative effects of white-dominated systems on racial minority career aspirations are several. First, it is necessary to move the system in directions that attempt to create more conditions of incongruent embeddedness, for example, increasing the number of racial minorities in high-level executive positions and important middle-level decision-making roles. Recognition of the importance of both identity and organization group memberships also dictates that efforts to thwart the negative effects of congruent embeddedness must facilitate the integration and successful management of tensions between the two types of group membership rather than suppression of racial group identity (Thomas, 1986).

This perspective, because of its concern for the influence of group effects across levels of analysis, also recognizes the importance of changes in the organization's external environment, which can alter the nature of internal intergroup embeddedness. Affirmative action, for example, has had some impact on the perception of the relative power of racial minorities and whites in the external environment and has forced some internal changes in organizations. In fact, many whites, as evidenced in claims of reverse discrimination, have come to see themselves at a power disadvantage (Alderfer and Smith, 1982).

Conditions in the external environment can also influence the nature of embeddedness and minority career experiences by making race a more task-relevant variable. Collins's (1983) study of the growth and formation of the black middle class indicates that the vast majority of black mobility can be accounted for by job advancement in the not-for-profit and government sectors and not the private sector. Also, occupations such as health care provider, educator, non–financial services provider and nonmanagerial technical professional are still the occupations in which minorities find easiest access and greatest mobility (Pomer, 1986). Similarly, we have noticed that black MBA students have an easier time getting jobs in public finance than private finance. In the case of both government and public finance, meaningful minority constituencies can be identified that then make race a task-relevant variable offering the *potential* to influence the power relations among groups as well as the career opportunities of racial minorities.

The Wells–Jennings hypothesis: barriers to black mobility

Much of the research on race relations and minority experiences in organizations has had as its overwhelming or underlying concern understanding those factors that explain and prohibit black upward mobility (Fernandez, 1981; Irons and Moore, 1985; Jones, 1986). This has also been the predominant focus of journalist writing on this issue (Davis and Watson, 1982; Karmel, 1984). Consistent with this activity, promotion patterns and statistics on minority hires have figured prominently in law suits against major corporations (Alvarez et al., 1979). Furthermore, a perception based on these studies has emerged that even in the most liberal of corporate environments, the most qualified of racial minorities can only rise to a certain level before reaching the glass ceiling – that invisible point beyond which they may gaze but cannot go (Fernandez, 1981; Irons and Moore, 1985; Jones, 1986).

Theoretically, the modern organization is depicted as operating from a set of distributive justice principles best captured in the concept of meritocracy – a system by which individuals are rewarded based on performance. Upward mobility processes are depicted as contests among individuals starting from equal points and promotion going to the most deserving. This notion has been successfully challenged. Rosenbaum (1979) has shown that upward mobility dynamics are better explained by a tournament model than the presumptions implicit in the meritocracy paradigm of contest mobility. Kanter (1977, 1979) and Alvarez (1979) have proposed a sponsored mobility paradigm in which sponsorship is seen as the key determinant of upward mobility. While these theories challenge the purity of meritocracy as the primary distributive justice paradigm for organizations, they do not suggest how salient nonability factors such as race influence the resource allocation processes of organizations.

Wells and Jennings (1983) maintain that where blacks are concerned, predominantly white organizations do not function as meritocracies. Rather, they are viewed as "neopigmentocracies." The neopigmentocracy is characterized by the existence of laws stating the enfranchisement of all individuals irrespective of race accompanied, however, by a psychological mindset on the part of the dominant race that reinforces a sense of entitlement characteristic of a racially caste society in South Africa (Vickery, 1974). In the neopigmentocracy, access to resources is unlimited for whites as a group while restricted for blacks, with only a few blacks being allowed to reach significant positions of authority and control over economic resources. Blacks may attain "threshold" or acceptable positions but as a group are excluded from the management hegemony. In these organizations, persons are systemically excluded from the general mobility process be it contest, sponsored or tournament, especially as they move further up the corporate ladder.

The most important element of the Wells–Jennings model is their attempt to explain the internal dynamics of organizations that allow for some upward mobility, which creates the illusion of organizational acceptance of minorities. However, as blacks present the possibility of moving beyond threshold points, racist forces are mobilized to stunt black careers. Three concepts are central to their description of these internal dynamics: (1) white entitlement, (2) scandalous paradox and (3) legitimist impulse.

White entitlement refers to whites' insistence that they deserve certain positions and the right to maintain control over resources. Many whites, for example, have found it hard to accept affirmative action programs as a remedy for white bias in hiring and selection. They prefer to see them as mechanisms to bring in otherwise unqualified minorities (Murray, 1984). This leads to a perpetuation of the view of whites as deserving and racial minorities as undeserving. Threshold positions in the core of the organization's business and peripheral executive level positions, such as Vice President for Affirmative Action, are viewed as what the institution is willing to *give* to minorities rather than what minorities have earned or what the organization needs to be effective.

A *scandalous paradox* occurs when a person who possesses neither legal rights nor social status receives preference over someone who possesses both. The paradox of this event exists in the fact that an individual representative of a disenfranchised racial group is able to make some gains in, for example, a predominantly white system. The scandalous aspect of this phenomenon is represented in the implicit relationship of the disenfranchised person or group with those whites who are in control of the system. A parallel relationship occurred when a slave would receive some right or privilege deemed to be exclusive to the children of the slave owner, such as an education. The slave was often assumed to be the illegitimate offspring of the slave owner. The situation was scandalous (illegitimate offspring) as well as paradoxical (i.e., an educated slave). In modern organizations, this can occur when white members believe that a promotion to middle management that has been given to a member of the minority, such as a black person, constitutes a scandalous situation.

The *legitimist impulse*, in reaction to the scandalous paradox, causes "legitimists" to experience status anxiety and fear that their "rightful" resources are being given away to others. The legitimists defend their privileges and see black advancement as an encroachment upon white entitlement. The legitimist impulse has been offered to explain the origin of the concept of reverse discrimination (Wells and Jennings, 1983:44).

These three factors mobilize in a dynamic way to ignite conscious and unconscious resistance to blacks and other minorities' advancement in the representative American organization. This interrelationship can be described as follows. The existence of a sense of white entitlement creates the context in which minority advancement is viewed as an encroachment on white privilege and prevents minority achievement from being viewed meritocratically. Thus, beyond a certain level, minority advancement is viewed as being the result of a scandalous, or illegitimate, relationship between minorities and upper management, often represented in a strong affirmative action commitment. Minority advancement produces status anxiety for whites and thus the emergence of the legitimist impulse, which, if shared widely by whites at a particular level or function of the organization, can act as a strong barrier to black mobility and perhaps explain why systematically many minorities' careers come to a halt as they pose competition for upper- and middle-level management positions.

The Wells–Jennings model is useful in that it provides an explanation for the fact that blacks and other minorities often reach certain threshold positions and then find their careers abruptly stopped. These points of threshold mobility often occur just prior to reaching positions in which their potential control over resources might be significant enough to allow them to influence how the organization responds to its environment and what the complexion, values and tenor of the company will become. Viewed in light of Schein's (1978) model of organizational inclusion, this perspective suggests that minorities will be found on the periphery rather than at the core of institutional life and, infrequently, in positions of significant power and control.

The theory also forms a bridge between the power conflict models used by sociologists and political scientists to explain the struggle between racial groups for influence in the macrosocial environment (Blauner, 1972; Bonacich, 1972). Recently, scholars favoring the view that class is more powerful than race have argued that the increased number of minorities in management and professional positions means that race has diminished as a dynamic force in constraining black mobility (Freeman, 1976; Sowell, 1981; Wilson, 1978, 1981). According to the Wells–Jennings model, blacks and whites are engaged in a struggle over control of organizational resources, just as in the larger society; however, the dynamics of the internal struggle are complex and often consist of unconscious impulses and unexamined basic assumptions about the rights and roles of majority and minority members. It is therefore insufficient to dismiss the importance of race based on some blacks' attainment of middle-class positions.

A major shortcoming of the Wells–Jennings model is that it has not addressed the similarities and differences between managerial and nonmanagerial careers. Much of the data on reverse discrimination suggests that persons in nonmanagerial positions are just as likely (perhaps more) as those at the middle levels of management to file reverse-discrimination charges and to feel the anxiety associated with the advent of minority advancement. In the spirit of searching for universal constants, the effects of proportionality and tokenism, such as those proposed to explain the experiences of women, might be a fruitful direction to examine in the area of race and organizations (Gutek and Cohen, 1987; Kanter, 1977).

FUTURE RESEARCH AND THE DYNAMICS OF INCLUSION

The paucity of systematic empirical research on the subject of race and careers leaves many options for future research. Several major areas in which future research is indicated will be detailed in what follows.

Key tensions and signs of omission

We have tried in our review and critique of the literature to point out some of the shortcomings of the current research and thereby to suggest where others interested in these lines of inquiry might proceed. Our focus here is to identify what we see as potential tensions in this burgeoning field and to use them as a framework for considering future research. These tensions often indicate how the field of career research in organizational behavior relates to the subject of race.

Managers and professionals versus blue-collar workers. As in much of the literature on careers, the emphasis in research on minority careers is decidedly biased toward the needs of professionals and managers. While much remains to be learned about the experiences of minority professionals, research on the experiences of nonprofessional persons is even more desperately needed. It is especially important that qualitative studies be conducted in this area so as to convey the richness of the vocational experiences of these individuals. Furthermore, given that only a small proportion of racial minorities in the United States and Europe occupy professional and managerial positions, the experiences of a major portion of the minority population (nonprofessionals) are being overlooked.

Describing the experiences of various minority groups. One of the major shortcomings of the work reviewed herein is that it focuses primarily on black Americans. While there are similarities of experience across minority groups, there are also important differences, and these need to be understood. Given changes in the demographic composition of the United States, Hispanics are likely to be the largest minority group in the nation by the turn of the century, and little is known about their career experiences. We might also find that cultural differences constitute even more formidable barriers for Asians than for minorities from cultural backgrounds more heavily laced with European influences (Morishima, 1981).

Minority women. There is frequently a tendency in the work on minority and female career experiences to overlook the special position of minority women. Bell (1986), Denton (1987), Leggon (1980) and Malone (1981) attempt to understand the black female experience on its own terms. Undoubtedly, more research in this area is needed. It is also important that researchers looking at mixed-gender populations examine gender as a factor that interacts with race to shape career experiences.

Comparison studies versus within-group studies. Can we learn anything significant about minorities without studying whites? Our answer is an unequivocal yes. Much of the more recent work in this area has adopted the within-group approach and has yielded rich, descriptive accounts about minority career experiences (Bell, 1986; Gooden, 1980; Herbert, 1986). An area wholly unresearched that should be part of the next generation of studies in this area is the intragroup relations of minorities in organizations and under different conditions of perceived opportunity for advancement. We know little about how minorities manage their own competitive dynamics or how they come together to support one another (Denton, 1987; Thomas, 1986).

Comparative studies are also needed, especially when studying minority experiences in a specific organizational setting. More research is needed, for example, to understand how institutional structures interact with race to produce differential outcomes for minorities and whites. It is necessary to have data on both groups to accurately make such assessments.

Research in predominantly white versus minority-dominated systems. The preoccupation of both society and social scientists with issues of "mainstreaming" minorities has led to emphasis on minority experiences in white-dominated systems to the exclusion of studying career experiences in minority-dominated systems. Intergroup theory suggests that the nature of the embeddedness will differentially influence the career experiences of minority and majority members. Research on career dynamics in minority-dominated systems may also be timely because as minorities in white-dominated systems reach early plateaus or become frustrated, they may come to see minority enterprises as viable alternatives. Furthermore, such studies would open up the possibility of studying white experiences under conditions of incongruent embeddedness.

Studying minorities as subordinates and as superiors. Much of the research in this area is concerned with the experience of minorities as subordinates, protégés or members of low-power groups. This appears to represent an underlying theme and concern with upward mobility. However, there is little known about the experiences of minorities in roles exercising authority or serving as mentors. Dumas's (1980) work on black female leaders moves in this direction. What is the experience of black managers who do exercise authority in predominantly white systems?

The issues represented by these six tensions are not meant to be mutually exclusive but rather to form a matrix of choices that intersect with one another and with areas of existing research.

The dynamics of inclusion

It is often hard for a field to reflect on its own relationship to the issues it studies and to take collective responsibility for the choices that seem to gather consensus and momentum as important issues for investigation. We cannot leave a discussion of where future research in this area should go without speaking directly to the dynamics of the field, which explain the lack of attention to issues of race and may constitute potential barriers to their inclusion in the future.

In the middle 1970s, the Academy of Management formed two interest groups, one on women in management and the other on minorities in management. The former group became a division and the latter disbanded within five years of its inception. This suggests that for some reason issues related to racial minority concerns were not of sufficient interest to scholars in the field. Thus one explanation for the absence of race-related issues in the field of organizational behavior is that it is not of interest to a significant number of people. Why might this appear to be the case?

Mannheim (1936), Sullivan (1953), Devereaux (1967) and, more recently, Berg and Smith (1985) have observed that social science knowledge develops in the context of a relationship. At this point, there is not a widely shared consensus that research results and their interpretation are shaped by the relationships investigators have with themselves, with other investigators and with their respondents. Biographies of famous social scientists, however, have often shown the relationship of their work to issues in their own lives (Alderfer, 1986). Three aspects of the field of organizational behavior may relate to this point in explaining the absence of race as topics in the literature.

First is the obvious absence of minorities in the field. This is not to suggest that all minorities are or should be interested in studying race. However, it is true that outside of work in the area of performance appraisal, research on race and careers has been done by minority scholars, many of them students at the time. It seems plausible that increasing the pool of minorities in the field increases the likelihood that these issues will be examined. The presence of minorities in greater numbers in the field is also likely to place white social scientists more in touch with the issues of race as they confront a more heterogeneous work force in their own professional worlds and, thereby, contribute to their becoming more open to this area of study and supportive of its inclusion in the field.

The second dynamic is that academia mirrors the rest of American society in terms of having a "liberal view" of race and its role in the workplace. Race is often treated as a topic not important unless someone has suffered or committed an overt act of discrimination. This pattern is consistent with the silence on race that characterizes most corporate cultures (Jones, 1986).

The third dynamic has to do with the fact that race remains a sensitive issue and race relations in the United States and Europe are fraught with tension. Research in this area, if done thoughtfully, is likely to be controversial and requires not only that researchers conduct their research competently, but also that they have a capacity to engage the personal relevance of the issues. An ability to reflect on one's personal relationship to the topic is important not only to those minorities and whites who choose to do research in this area, but, even more broadly, to those who will be in positions to critique such research.

We have been impressed when presenting our own work in this area, and observing other colleagues doing so, at the frequency with which the racial aspect of our work is negated or generalized to include white women and nineteenth-century white ethnic immigrants. This is not to say there are no parallels, but the persistence and predictability of this response suggests that there may be institutional dynamics that act to suppress race as a topic. This suppression dynamic also shows itself in the reticence we often observe in students, majority and minority, to do work in this area, even when it interests them, for fear of not being salable on the job market.

Whether the field as a whole attempts to address these issues or not, they are especially important for minorities and whites who currently, or prospectively, conduct research in the area of race and careers. It is our belief and experience that much can be learned about race relations in organizations if that work is conducted in a cross-racial team. Our own collaboration as such a team represents that belief. It is important that the members of such teams be able to discuss the ways in which race influences their relationship to one another and to the individuals they study.

Our perspective is also not value neutral at the level of choosing methods and establishing research relationships. Our own work has been guided by a clinical approach to the choice of method and the conduct of research (Alderfer, 1980; Berg and Smith, 1985). This approach emphasizes that the researchers be directly involved with the individuals and systems they study and place a premium on maintaining integrity in the relationship between researchers and study participants. Another crucial aspect of this perspective is a commitment to self-scrutiny as one conducts the research. There must also be a willingness to change theory or method in response to the research experience. This area is so understudied that a dogmatic application of method or theory, especially if it is a method or theory whose development has been exclusively controlled by white men, may produce invalid results and perhaps information hurtful to those whose experiences we are attempting to understand. There are other tenets of the clinical perspective, but those mentioned in the preceding seem most important for researchers in this area, independent of whether they use observation, experiments, surveys or interviews or whether their analysis is qualitative or quantitative.

We believe that those who find this an important area for research should also think carefully about the meaning of doing work about race relations. Efforts that go forward without such consideration can produce data biased toward the status quo without our being aware of the distortions and promote social intervention that is inconsequential or detrimental.

CONCLUSION

In the limited space provided, we have attempted to call the reader's attention to those streams of current research that possess the greatest potential for increasing our understanding of the relationship of race to career dynamics. Undoubtedly, subjective choices have been made about what work constitutes this body of research. Our hope is that this chapter does more than simply give readers a log of research in the field. We hope that it provides a way of thinking into which new research in the area of careers can be placed.

Future research in the area of race and careers may follow on current topics receiving attention or it may address some of those aspects that have been wholly ignored. If, however, issues of race and race relations are to be included in mainstream career research and theory, those who advance this work must grapple with the dynamics of the field that explain, at least in part, their absence from it. We believe future work will be enhanced only if researchers take a self-reflective perspective on the research enterprise.

REFERENCES

Alderfer, C. P. (1980). The methodology of organizational diagnosis. *Professional Psychology*, *11*, 459–468.
Alderfer, C. P. (1982). The problems of changing white males beliefs and behaviors in race relations. In P. Goodman (ed.), *Change in Organizations*. San Francisco: Jossey-Bass, pp.122–165.
Alderfer, C. P. (1986). An intergroup perspective on group dynamics. In J. Lorsch's (ed.), *Handbook of Organizational Behavior*. Englewood Cliffs, NJ: Prentice-Hall, pp.190–222.
Alderfer, C. P., Alderfer, C., Tucker, R. C., and Tucker, L. (1980). Diagnosing race relations in management. *Journal of Applied Behavioral Science*, *16*, 135–166.

Alderfer, C. P., and Smith, K. K. (1982). Studying intergroup relations embedded in organizations. *Administrative Science Quarterly, 27*, 35–65.

Alderfer, C. P., and Thomas, D. A. (1988). The significance of race and ethnicity for understanding organizational behavior. In C. L. Cooper and I. T. Robertson (eds.), *International Review of Industrial and Organizational Psychology*, Vol.3. London: Wiley, Publishing, pp. 1–41.

Alderfer, C. P., and Tucker, R. C. (1985). Measuring managerial potential and intervening to improve the racial equity of upward mobility decisions. Technical report no.6. Yale School of Organization and Management.

Alderfer, C. P., Tucker, R., Morgan, D., and Drasgon, F. (1983). Black and white cognitions of changing race relations for management. *Journal of Occupational Behavior, 4*, 105–136.

Almquist, E. M. (1979). *Minorities, Gender and Work*. Lexington, MA: Lexington Books.

Alvarez, R. (1979). Institutional discrimination in organizations and their environments. *Discrimination in Organizations*. San Francisco: Jossey-Bass.

America, R., and Anderson, B. (1978). *Moving Ahead*. New York: McGraw-Hill.

Baird, L., and Kram, K. E. (1983). Career dynamics: managing the superior–subordinate relationship. *Organizational Dynamics*, Summer, pp. 46–64.

Bearden, K. W. (1984). Women proteges' perception of the mentoring process. Ph.D. dissertation. University of Louisville.

Beatty, R. (1973). Blacks as supervisors, a study of training, job performance and employers' expectation. *Academy of Management Journal, 16* (2), 196–206.

Bell, E. L. (1986). The power within: bicultural life structures and stress among black women. Ph.D. dissertation. Case Western Reserve University.

Bell, E. L., Denton, T., Herbert, J. I., and Thomas, D. A. (1987). No crystal stair: current research on the courses and life processes of black professionals. Presented Symposium, the Academy of Management, New Orleans, LA.

Berg, D. N., and Smith, K. K. (1985). The clinical demands of research methods. In D. N. Berg and K. K. Smith (eds.), *Defining a Clinical Method for Social Research*. Beverly Hills, CA: Sage.

Blackwell, L. E. (1981). *Mainstreaming Outsiders: The Production of Black Professionals*. New York: General Hall.

Blalock, H. M. (1967). *Toward a Theory of Minority-Group Relations*. New York: Wiley.

Blauner, R. (1972). *Racial Oppression in America*. New York: Harper.

Bonacich, E. (1972). A theory of ethnic antagonism: the split labor market. *American Sociological Review, 41*, 34–51.

Brewer, M. B., and Kramer, R. M. (1985). The psychology of intergroup attitudes and behavior. *Annual Review of Psychology, 36*, 219–244.

Bronfenbrenner, N. (1979). *The Ecology of Human Development*. Cambridge: Harvard University Press.

Collins, S. M. (1983). The making of the black middle class. *Social Problems, 30* (4), 364–382.

Cox, T. Jr., and Nkomo, S. (1986). Differential performance appraisal criteria: a field study of black and white managers. *Group and Organization Studies, 11* (2), 101–119.

Cox, T. Jr., and Nkomo, S. (1987). Race as a variable in OB/HRM research: a review and analysis of the literature. Presented at the Symposium on Black Career Research, Drexel University.

Cross, W. (1976). Stereotypic and non-stereotypic images associated with the negro to black conversion experience. Ph.D. dissertation. Princeton University.

Cross, W. (1985). Black identity: rediscovering the link between personal identity and reference group orientation. In M. B. Spencer, G. K. Brookins, and W. R. Allen (eds.), *Beginnings: The Social and Affective Development of Black Children*. Hillside, NJ: Earlbaum.

Dalton, G., Thompson, P., and Price, R. (1977). The four stages of professional careers: a new look at performance appraisal. *Organizational Dynamics*, Summer, pp. 19–42.

Davis, A. (1983). *Women, Race and Class*. New York: Random House.

Davis, G., and Watson, G. (1982). *Black Life in Corporate America*. New York: Doubleday.

Denton, T. (1987). Social support among black professional women: rituals of restoration. Ph.D. dissertation. Case Western Reserve University.

Devereaux, G. (1967). *From Anxiety to Method in the Behavioral Sciences.* Paris: Monton.

Dickens, F., and Dickens, J. B. (1982). *The Black Manager.* New York: Amacom.

DuBois, W. E. B. (1903). *The Souls of Black Folks.* Chicago: Chicago University Press.

Dumas, R. G. (1980). Dilemmas of Black Females in leadership. *Journal of Personality and Social Systems, 2* (1), 3–14.

Epstein, C. (1973). Black and female: the double whammy. *Psychology Today, 3,* 57–61.

Erikson, E. H. (1963). *Childhood and Society,* 2nd ed. New York: Norton.

Fanon, F. (1967). *Black Skin, White Masks.* New York: Grove.

Fernandez, J. P. (1981). *Racism and Sexism in Corporate Life.* Lexington, MA: Heath.

Ford, D., and Wells, L. Jr. (1985). Upward mobility factors among black public administrators. *Centerboard: Journal of the Center for Human Relations, 3* (1), 33–48.

Freeman, R. (1976). Changes in the labor market for black Americans, 1968–1972. *Brookings Papers on Economic Activity, 1,* 67–120.

Fulbright, K. (1985). The myth of the double advantage: black women in management. Ph.D. dissertation. Massachusetts Institute of Technology.

Gilligan, C. (1982). *In a Different Voice.* Cambridge, MA: Harvard University Press.

Gooden, W. (1980). The adult development of black men. Ph.D. dissertation. Yale University.

Greenhaus, J. H., and Parasuraman, S. (1986). Vocational and organizational behavior, 1985: a review. *Journal of Vocational Behavior, 29,* 115–175.

Grier, W., and Cobbs, P. (1968). *Black Rage.* New York: Bantam.

Gutek, B., and Cohen, A. G. (1987). Sex ratios, sex role spillover and sex at work. *Human Relations, 40* (2), 97–115.

Hall, D. T. (1986). Career development for organization: where do we go from here. In D. T. Hall and Associates (eds.), *Career Development in Organizations.* San Francisco: Jossey-Bass, pp. 332–351.

Harding, J., Proshansky, H., Kutner, B., and Chein, I. (1969). Prejudice and ethnic relations. In G. Lindzey and E. Aaronson (eds.), *Handbook of Social Psychology.* Reading, MA: Addison-Wesley.

Herbert, J. I. (1986). The adult development of black male entrepreneurs. Ph.D. dissertation. Yale University.

Hopkins, E. (1987). Blacks at the top. *New York Magazine,* January, p. 19.

Hraba, J., and Hoiberg, E. (1983). Ideational origins of modern theories of ethnicity: individual freedom vs. organizational growth. *Sociological Quarterly, 24,* 381–391.

Huck, J. R., and Bray, D. W. (1976). Management assessment-center evaluations and subsequent job-performance of black and white females. *Personnel Psychology, 29* (1), 13–30.

Irons, E., and Moore, G. (1985). *Black Managers: The Case of the Banking Industry.* New York: Praeger.

Jackson, B. (1978). Stages of black identity development. Unpublished manuscript. University of Massachusetts at Amherst, School of Education.

Jones, E. W. (1986). Black managers: the dream deferred. *Harvard Business Review, 64,* 84–93.

Jung, C. G. (1933). *Modern Man in Search of a Soul.* New York: Harbrace.

Kanter, R. (1977). *Men and Women of the Corporation.* New York: Random House.

Kanter, R. (1979). Differential access to opportunity and power. In R. Alvarez (ed.), *Discrimination in Organizations.* San Francisco: Jossey-Bass.

Karmel, A. (1984). Why blacks still haven't made it on Wall Street. *American Lawyer,* April, p. 1.

Kinloch, G. C. (1982). Institutionalized racism: some theoretical considerations. *Journal of Social and Behavioral Sciences, 28,* 32–38.

Kovel, J. (1984). *White Racism: A Psychohistory.* New York: Columbia University Press.

Kram, K. E. (1985). *Mentoring At Work.* Glenview, IL: Scott Foresman.

Lavender, A. D., and Forsyth, J. M. (1976). The sociological study of minority groups as reflected by leading sociological journals. *Ethnicity, 3,* 388–396.

Leggon, L. (1980). Black female professionals: dilemmas and contradictions of status. In R. Rodgers (ed.), *The Black Woman.* Beverly Hills, CA: Sage.

Lester, R. A. (1980). *Reasoning about Discrimination.* Princeton, NJ: Princeton University Press.

Levinson, D., Darrow, C. N., Klein, E. B., Levinson, M. H., and McKee, B. (1978). *The Seasons of a Man's Life*. New York: Knopf.

Lundahl, M., and Wadensjo, E. (1984)., *Unequal Treatment: A Study of the Neo-Classical Theory of Discrimination*. London and Sydney: New York University Press.

McClain, L. (1980). The middle-class black's burden. *Newsweek*, October 31, p. 21,

Malone, B. (1981). Relationship of black females mentoring experiences and career satisfaction. Ph.D. dissertation. University of Cincinnati.

Mannheim, K. (1936). *Ideology and Utopia*. New York: Harcourt Brace Jovanovich.

Morishima, J. (1981). Special employment issues for Asian Americans. *Public Personnel Management*, 104, 384–392.

Murray, C. (1984). Affirmative racism. *The Nation, 191* (27), 18–24.

Murray, M. M. (1982). The middle years of life of middle class black men: an exploratory study. Ph.D. dissertation. University of Cincinnati.

Park, R. E. (1950). The race relations cycle in Hawaii. In R. E. Park (ed.), *Race and Culture*. New York: Free Press.

Pascal, A. H. (1972). *Racial Discrimination in Economic Life*. Lexington, MA: Lexington Books.

Pomer, M. I. (1986). Labor market structure, intergenerational mobility and discrimination: black male advancement out of low-paying occupations 1962–1973. *American Sociological Review, 51* (3), 650–659.

Powell, R. M. (1969). *Race, Religion and the Promotion of the American Executive*. Ohio State University: College of Administrative Science monograph no. AA-3.

Reinharz, S. (1985). Feminist distrust: problems of context and content in sociological work. In D. Berg and K. K. Smith (eds.), *Exploring Clinical Methods for Social Research*. Beverly Hills, CA: Sage.

Rosenbaum, J. (1979). Tournament mobility: career patterns in organizations. *Administrative Science Quarterly, 24*, 220–241.

Saunders, C. L. (1977). Notes on the black manager in the private corporation. In L. Howard, L. Henderson, and D. Hunt (eds.), *Public Administration and Public Policy: A Minority Perspective*. Pittsburgh, PA: Public Policy, pp. 149–155.

Schein, E. H. (1978). *Career Dynamics: Matching Individual and Organizational Needs*. Reading, MA: Addison-Wesley.

Sherif, M., and Sherif, C. (1970). Black unrest as a social movement toward emerging self identity. *Journal of Social and Behavioral Sciences. 15* (3), 41–52.

Sowell, T. (1981). *Ethnic America*. New York: Basic Books.

Sullivan, H. A. (1953). *The Interpersonal Theory of Psychiatry*. New York: Norton.

Super, D. (1957). *The Psychology of Careers*. New York: Harper & Row.

Thomas, C. W. (1971). *Boys No More*. Beverly Hills, CA: Glencoe.

Thomas, D. (1986). An intra-organizational analysis of black and white patterns of sponsorship and the dynamics of cross-racial mentoring. Ph.D. dissertation. Yale University.

Tinsley, H. E. A., and Heesacker, M. (1984). Vocational behavior and career development, 1983: a review. *Journal of Vocational Behavior, 25*, 139–190.

U.S. Commission on Civil Rights (1980). *Civil Rights Issues of Asian and Pacific Americans: Myths and Realities*. Washington, DC: U.S. Government Printing Office.

Valentine, C. (1968). *Culture and Counterproposals*. Chicago: University of Chicago Press.

Van den Berghe, P. L. (1967). *Race and Ethnicity: Essays in Comparative Sociology*. New York: Basic Books.

Vickery, K. P. (1974). Herrenvolk democracy and equalitarianism in South Africa and the U.S. South. *Comparative Studies In Society and History. 161*, 309–328.

Wells, L., and Jennings, C. L. (1983). Black career advances and white reactions: remnants of Herrenvolk democracy and the scandalous paradox. In D. Vails-Webber and W. N. Potts (eds.), *Sunrise Seminars*. Arlington, VA: NTL Institute, pp. 41–47.

Williams, J. (1985). Redefining institutional racism. *Ethnic and Racial Studies, 8* (3), 323–348.

Wilson, W. J. (1973). *Power, Racism and Privilege: Race Relations in Theoretical Sociohistorical Perspectives*. New York: MacMillan.

Wilson, W. J. (1978). *The Declining Significance of Race*. Chicago: University of Chicago Press.

Wilson, W. J. (1981). The black community in the 1980's: questions of race, class and public policy. *Annals of the American Academy of Political and Social Scientists, 454*, 26–41.
Work, J. (1986). Management, blacks and the internal labor market. *Human Resource Management*, Fall, pp. 27–31.

8 Asynchronism in dual-career and family linkages

UMA SEKARAN AND DOUGLAS T. HALL

INTRODUCTION: FAMILY IMPACT UPON WORK

For some time now, researchers have been taking a holistic approach to examining the career development of individuals, recognizing the fact that the work and nonwork lives of people are inexorably intertwined (see, e.g., Evans and Bartolome, 1984). The work–family linkages are so strong and pervasive that focusing on career development without simultaneously taking into consideration the family's developmental needs will produce an incomplete understanding of career dynamics. For instance, Bailyn (1978) pointed out the necessity for the accommodation of work to family concerns, and Kanter (1977) proposed a critical review and agenda for research and policy regarding work and family. Schein (1978) discussed the work–family–self interactions in exploring career dynamics, while Rapoport and Rapoport (1980) discussed the dynamics of work, family, and leisure. More recently, researchers have started to investigate the implications of dual-career families for social policy (Walker, Rozee-Koher, and Wallston, 1987) and explored the dilemmas experienced by couples during career transitions (O'Neil, Fishman, and Kinsella-Shaw, 1987). Further, Hall and Hall (1979), Mathews (1984), Stringer-Moore (1981), Betz and Fitzgerald (1987), Hertz (1986), Grant (1988), and Sekaran (1986), among others, have proposed action steps for organizations to make the work–nonwork transitions smoother for dual-career couples.

In this chapter we employ a developmental perspective and explore the dynamics of the relationships between individual, the family, and the career. Only then can we begin to understand the life stages in which the spouses have a relatively easy time establishing the work–family–self linkages and the specific stages where they experience problems. We introduce the concept of *synchronism* as a vehicle for analyzing degrees of conflict between career and family stages. Through such an investigation, we shall be able to provide a framework for career development theory to evolve in the future and also enunciate meaningful practices for organizations that will enhance their productivity and provide satisfying life experiences for the couple.

What is missing: theory versus description

One of the limitations of the research on two-career couples is that it has been extremely descriptive and problem focused. Undoubtedly, this has been because the problems are so strong and serious that they demand very focused attention. However, what has been generally lacking has been a more *theoretical analysis*

159

of the underlying causes of these issues. We need more explanation and less description of the patterns of two-career families.

In particular, we argue that the type of theoretical analysis that is needed is an adult developmental one. We attempt to show that many of the strains inherent in the two-career relationship can be traced to the attempts of the two parties to deal successfully with the normal tasks and transitions of adult life.

In particular, we examine the dynamics of the incompatibility of the family–work interfaces for the husband and the wife at various stages in their lives – which we term "asynchronism" – that is highly detrimental not only to the couples, but also to the organization as well. (See, e.g., Sekaran, 1988; Taylor, 1986). The phenomenon of asynchronism is detected when the developmental roles of the two parties get "out of sync" (i.e., experience incompatible demands) and become detrimental to both the couple and the organizations. Recently researchers have started to examine the dynamics of careers by taking a life span–life space approach individually for male and female workers (Miller, 1984; Super, 1980). What is missing is the investigation of the career cycle, the family cycle, and the individual development and growth cycle for *both* partners in dual-career families in order to determine the stages where the partners get out of sync and the implications this has for career development strategies.

In this chapter, we focus on the dynamics of the transitional experiences that husbands and wives in two-career families encounter as they try to balance their needs for personal growth and development, career advancement, and family satisfactions at different stages of their lives. We then identify some of the nuances of the different stages at which personal preferences, career progress, and family interests get asymmetrically aligned for the husband and the wife. Finally, we draw the implications of our framework for career development strategies that organizations can develop and dual-career members can profitably use. Following Hall and Hall (1979), we use the term "dual-career family" to include all two-income couples regardless of the type of occupation the parties are pursuing. Many of the problems and dilemmas faced by working couples are similar, and in the case of professional couples the problems become more acute due to transfers/relocations and set career paths (Markham, 1987).

Defining success

One of the interesting ways in which analysis of the two-career couple contributes to the wider body of career theory is that any comparison of two careers immediately raises the issue of what is success. One career can be studied within that person's own frame of reference, within her or his own definition of success. But when two careers in an intimate relationship are being considered, comparisons are implicit in the multiple-role relationships that impinge upon the two-career couple: that is, each member of the couple vis-à-vis each other, external perceptions (and evaluations) of the two careers, external perceptions of the relationship, external perceptions of the couple's parenting behavior, the couple's perception of their relationship, the couple's perception of their parenting behavior, and so on. Questions of frame of reference, of criteria of success, become extremely complex.

For the two-career couple, then, the issue of defining success must be raised in a serious way. Progress against an organizational or a cultural timetable for upward mobility (Lawrence, 1987; Rosenbaum, Chapter 16) is only one of the multiple criteria that are relevant here, either for the couple or for an external observer. As Gallos (Chapter 6) and Marshall (Chapter 13) note in relation to women, more internal, less linear models of success must be given greater weight. Since so few models of satisfactory two-career couples are available, even today, in striving for psychological success, the couple will often engage in what Weick and Berlinger (Chapter 15) call self-designing careers or what Hall (1976, 1986) has called the protean career.

Thus, a critical feature of the two-career relationship is the complexity of the outcomes being sought. And, we would argue, this same reality exists increasingly for other individuals in contemporary society as well. This point has been made persuasively in the context of organizations by Kaye (1982) in her descriptively titled book, *Up is Not the Only Way*, as well as by Derr (1986). *Everyone* is concerned about juggling a work life, a personal life, a family life, a leisure life, a home, and other facets of living, not just members of two-career couples. This fact needs greater "play" in our theories of careers.

The ubiquitous two-career couple

The following significant trends in the demographics of the labor force speak eloquently for the need for career theory to incorporate work–family linkages. About forty-seven million persons in the work force are spouses in working-couple households (Conference Board, 1985); the proportion of women in the labor force has increased from one-third in 1950 to one-half now (U.S. Department of Labor, 1987). The percentage of managerial and professional women in the work force has increased from 33.9% in 1970 to 40.6% in 1980, while that of managerial and professional men declined from 66.11 to 59.4% during the same period. Since 1970, nearly half of the increase in the women in the labor force has been among women aged twenty-five to thirty-four, and the percentage of working women with children under six has increased from twelve in 1950 to fifty-two in 1984 (U.S. Department of Labor, 1987); the expected work life span of an average twenty-year-old woman increased from fourteen years in 1950 to twenty-six years in 1977, and the average working woman is expected to have at least thirty to thirty-five active years of life starting from a mid-career point in the future (Vriend, 1977); and by 1990, 70–80% of women are expected to be in the labor force.

Not only are more women entering the labor force with intentions of staying there longer, but young women planning careers still contemplate marriage as a significant event in their lives. The majority of these women plan on having children, though they may consider postponing both their marriages and motherhood beyond their early adult years (Miller, 1984). This implies that there will be a continued increase in the number of dual-career families. It follows, then, that the currently experienced stresses from role overload (stresses from taking on multiple roles), identity diffusion (brought about by cultural expectations of sex role conformities), and role cycling dilemmas (the conflict of wanting to start a family but not wanting to compromise career advancement) will continue to be experienced by the dual-career couple until such time as new structures are evolved by society and organizations to alleviate the tensions presently experienced by the couples. The current stresses bring in their wake frustrations, feelings of competition between the spouses, and other dysfunctional consequences for the partners. As a result, productivity for the organization is compromised. For detailed discussions on these issues, see Sekaran (1986, 1988).

DEVELOPMENTAL PERSPECTIVE: A MISSING ELEMENT IN THE TWO-CAREER LITERATURE

Past research on dual-career families has focused on several aspects related to work–family interfaces. However, what is missing is a developmental perspective considering both the family life cycle and the career stages of the partners. In this section we briefly summarize trends in the current literature and indicate new directions which are needed.

Spouses' attitudes and behavior

Much of the research on two-career couples has centered on the attitudes and behaviors of the two parties in the relationship. A major issue for the couple is the large number of roles to be managed: wife or husband, parent, careerist, self, friend, son or daughter, home manager, and so on. With both spouses working outside the home for the major part of the day, the couple often experiences the home as lacking a homemaker (i.e., a person whose primary responsibility is managing the home). Thus, the critical question is, who does the various home tasks, and what attitude does each partner have toward the two careers, the home, the children, and their other role senders.

Earlier research tended to focus more on attitudes than on behaviors (Andrisani and Shapiro, 1978; Arnott, 1972; Bailyn, 1970; Sekaran, in press). The findings often indicated that, while there might be high commitment to both careers, at decision times when the two came into direct conflict (e.g., when offered a promotion requiring relocation) the husband's career usually took priority (Hall and Hall, 1979). The degree of mutual commitment to both careers and to family was found to be a strong correlate of marital happiness, and often family was required to make accommodations to career (Bailyn, 1970).

Hall and Hall (1980) identified four different types of couples based upon the parties' involvement in home and career: *accommodators* (each party highly involved in a different sphere), *allies* (both involved in the same sphere and not concerned with perfection in the other), *adversaries* (each highly involved in work but wanting the other to do home tasks), and *acrobats* (each highly involved in both home and work). The authors hypothesized that the highest levels of stress would be felt by the acrobats in the process of trying to "have it all." Next would come the competitive adversaries. Because of their more compatible expectations, allies and accommodators were hypothesized to have lower levels of stress.

When behavior, as opposed to attitude, has been studied, it has been clear from the earliest research (Rapoport and Rapoport, 1969) to more recent work (Bird, Bird, and Scruggs, 1984; Yogev, 1982) that women put in more time than men on home and parenting activities. However, Yogev (1982) and Rice (1979) also report that only a few women felt that their husbands were not doing enough in the home; the data indicate that the women did not expect a completely equal sharing of home tasks. Also, Yogev and Brett (1985) found that husbands performed more family activities when the wife's job required long hours at work, travel, and overtime. A later study by Yogev and Brett

(1987) reports that both men and women restructure their jobs in relation to their own work and family conditions as well as in relation to their spouses' work and family conditions.

Boundary differences between spouses

A more recent area of work has been how the two spouses perceive the psychological, temporal, and physical overlaps between the work and family domains (Bailyn, 1978; Crouter, 1984; Hall and Richter, 1988; Pleck, 1977; Richter, 1985). One important issue here is behavioral and attitudinal spillover, as identified by Evans and Bartolome (1984), from work into home life. A recurring theme in this area of research has been that work usually takes priority over home.

Much of this boundary research has examined sources of conflict between roles in the work and home domains. In an analysis of the 1977 Quality of Employment Survey data, Pleck, Staines, and Lang (1980) found that 34% of the men studied felt that work and family interfered with each other. In a study of 229 male engineering graduates, Greenhaus and Kopelman (1981) reported that roughly half of this male sample experienced this inter-role conflict; this conflict was heightened when the wife was employed in a managerial or professional role, when they had children who were all pre-schoolers, and when the men placed great importance on work. Theoretical models that spell out conditions under which career–home role conflict might lead to experienced stress have been proposed by Hall and Hall (1980) and Greenhaus and Beutell (1985). Both make the important distinction between time pressures (role overload) and intrinsic conflict or spillover between roles (role conflict).

A promising new approach to understanding the work–home interface was proposed by Richter (1985). She made a compelling argument that a useful way to capture the dynamics of the interaction between the two domains is to study in depth the way people make the transition back and forth between the two. She proposed the concept of *daily transitions* and presented research using a diary-type interview method to track the hour-by-hour physical and emotional movements of people between work and home. She found strong gender differences that fit with the division-of-labor differences reported earlier; women stayed involved in home activities before leaving the office, whereas men remained involved in work even after they entered the home. Richter also found that women were more likely than men to spend time on work at home in the evening. She identified a typology of transition styles and established a methodology that should be quite useful to future researchers.

Organizational accommodation to family

More recent concerns have centered on the role that employing organizations can play to facilitate dual-career members' attempts to manage the work–home interface. This increased interest by organizations is related to a high rate of attrition among established women managers and professionals caused largely by family pressures. For example, one-fourth of women MBAs from the top business schools in the class of 1976 have quit the managerial work force (Taylor, 1986). Many women in the Harvard MBA class of 1975 have made career trade-offs for two-career considerations (Gallese, 1985).

Hall and Hall (1979) and Stringer-Moore (1981) were among the first to identify a broad range of problems caused by organizational practices and to propose a variety of actions organizations might take. Action areas included revising transfer and relocation policies, re-examining nepotism policies, spouse relocation assistance, childcare assistance, flexible work scheduling, two-career recruiting, assisting couples in career management, revising travel policies, and career and couple counseling services or referrals. Many of these actions are currently being taken by a select set of companies, such as Procter & Gamble, General Foods, IBM, Mellon Bank, and General Motors (Taylor, 1986). More complete and recent discussions of corporate practices in this area, with many specific company examples, are reported in Sekaran (1986) and Hall and Richter (1988).

TAKING A DEVELOPMENTAL PERSPECTIVE:
THE PHENOMENON OF ASYNCHRONISM

We propose that when the chronological age, the career stages, and the family life cycle stages are examined individually as well as jointly for the couple, it becomes very clear that couples get asynchronous (or out of sync) at various stages in their life. In other words, though both spouses might start their careers at the same point, as they progress through their life stages their career focus may progress at different rates, because of organizational policies that make it difficult for couples to intertwine their family and work interests and goals in a smooth way. By fully comprehending the nature of this asynchronism at different points in time and why it occurs, the issues for consideration in career development can be clarified.

Quite apart from its implications for career development, the simultaneous examination of both spouses' transitional phases, which we discuss later in the chapter, offers some ideas for the couples themselves to mesh the transitions in a meaningful way to maintain the family and the career as integral and satisfying parts of their lives. In other words, the interactions among the career transitions, family transitions, and personal transitions and the shifts in career, family, and personal agendas, especially during the mid-life of the spouses, will be the main focus of this chapter. In sum, the strategy of investigating the life space dynamics of both spouses simultaneously, taking a developmental perspective of the personal, family, and career spheres of the couple's life, enables us to very clearly identify the tension points in the family unit's work and family experiences over time.

Let us first discuss the concept of asynchronism, then examine the current career patterns followed by dual-career family members, and finally use the adult development theories to trace the sources of asynchronism in the current patterns. This will enable us to conceptualize and formulate robust, viable career development theories that will pave the way to fully tap the potential of the dual-career partners.

What is "asynchronism"?

Asynchronism is a condition under which the person's or the couple's experience is off schedule in relation to some sort of "timetable" of development. By timetable, we mean a generally accepted understanding about when a person should have attained particular statuses in his or her life or career (Lawrence, 1984). Such timetables are defined by the norms of a particular system, such as a family, an organization, or a society. If, for instance, a society's norms indicate that a man should be married by the age of eighteen, a man who was married at seventeen would feel in sync and a man who was married at thirty-five would feel out of sync. For example, Lawrence (1980), in a study of people making mid-life changes, found that people who are out of sync with societal norms (e.g., people who married late, had children late) experienced considerably more stress when living through another out-of-sync decision: changing a career. Lawrence concluded that there is more social support for people who are on schedule, and this support reduces stress. And since men and women experience life stresses in different ways (Barnett, Biener, and Baruch, 1987), the effects of asynchronism are compounded.

Each role in a society has a different timetable that suggests appropriate scheduling. There is one timetable for being married and raising a family, and there is a different one for the work career and the various career milestones to be reached (Hall, 1976). Furthermore, the career timetables for a society and for a particular organization or profession may diverge under certain conditions as well (Lawrence, 1987). For example, a high school graduate who was not self-supporting by the age of twenty-five would be considered "behind schedule," while a medical student who was not self-supporting at that age would still be "on schedule."

Facets of asynchronism

There are several facets of asynchronism that are relevant here. One issue deals with the *subject* of the asynchronism: Is it the career or the family that is being considered? The other facet is the *referent* for determining synchronism: To what is an entity being compared?

In the case of careers, one referent would be the norms of a particular organization or society regarding appropriate career timetables. Lawrence (1984) and Rosenbaum (1984) have demonstrated that social systems contain occupational age norms that mark career progress. For example, in many organizations, if a person is not promoted to a managerial level by the age of forty, that person is seen as behind schedule and may never attain that rank. We would call this situation *organizational asynchronism.*

In the case of each individual in the couple, another referent could be the partner as well as the norms of an organization or society. For example, if one partner's career started later than the other's, or if the progress of one was slower than the other's, then their careers would be asynchronous (or out of sync) in relation to each other. We would call this situation *couple asynchronism.* An example is illustrated in Figure 8.1.

In the case of couples and families, societies and subcultures also contain norms about ages that represent "early" and "late" timing for the starting of a family (Daniels and Weingarten, 1982). For example, in contemporary American society, when fourteen-year-olds have children, that is considered early, whereas when forty-year-olds first give birth, that is viewed as late. When the couple is either very early or very late in starting a family in relation to societal or subculture norms, we would call this *family asynchronism.*

We shall examine these three facets of asynchronism: careers in relation to organizational norms and social expectations, each partner's career in relation

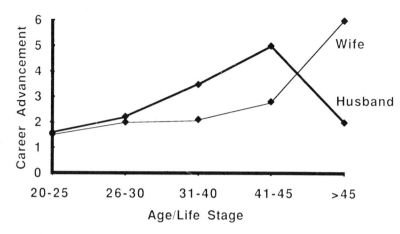

Figure 8.1. Illustration of couple career asynchronism: career swings of two-career partners

to the other partner's career, and the family in relation to society. To comprehend the underlying basis for asynchronisms, especially in the mid-life of the partners, we first take a brief look at the male and female adult development patterns.

A COMPARATIVE ANALYSIS OF MALE AND FEMALE ADULT DEVELOPMENT

Theories of male and female adult development offer us some insights on how careers have a differential impact on husbands and wives in dual-career families. We employ Levinson's (1986; Levinson et al., 1978) theory of male adult development [described in detail by Cytrynbaum and Crites (Chapter 4)] and then contrast it with Bardwick's (1980) theory of female adult development [described by Gallos (Chapter 6)]. We draw upon these two theories to develop the framework for identifying the stress points at certain stages of the life cycle of dual-career spouses. Thereafter, we consider how spouses combine parenting with various career stages.

Let us point out that all three of these topics – male development, female development, and family-career integration – represent literatures that reflect contemporary life-style patterns in which parenting roles are not necessarily equal. That is, they are not gender free. But they are descriptive of current patterns. Later in the chapter we present a more gender-neutral model of the couple vis-à-vis careers.

Male adult development

The most complete model of the stages in male adult development has been proposed by Levinson (1978, 1986). Levinson conceives of the adult life course as containing a series of structure-building periods and structure-changing periods (or transitions) driven in large part by the pursuit of one's life dream. In a structure-building period, the task is to create a life structure (an underlying pattern or design in one's life based primarily on relationships). These periods usually last six to seven years and no more than ten.

In a transitional period, much of the structure of the previous phase is undone, views of self and world are re-examined, and choices are made that will lead to a new life structure. Transitions usually last about five years. No one life structure is permanent, and Levinson (1986) reports that almost half of one's adult life is spent in transitions.

The constancy of change seems apparent in this model. Each transition is both the ending of a previous phase and the beginning of the next. The person is constantly giving up elements of the younger age period and acquiring new elements for the next one.

A major issue for men in early adulthood is building a career and family, with the career often taking precedence. The age-thirty transition is often directed at improving one's lot in the career realm. For men, it is often not until the mid-life transition that they begin to deal in a deep way with family issues and with the conflicts between career and family.

Female adult development

A different cycle of development as well as different correlates of development appear to operate for women. [See Marshall (Chapter 13) and Gallos (Chapter 6) for more detailed analysis of adult and career development for women.] Much of the energy for growth in Levinson's model of male development derives from a quest for one's "dream," with the identity based upon autonomy and task achievement or mastery (e.g., becoming one's own man is the result of career success and disengagement from one's mentor). For women, however, growth, identity, and the dream are based primarily upon interdependence and relationships (Douvan and Adelson, 1966; Gilligan, 1980), that is, from linking as opposed to detaching.

A major issue that confronted the authors in writing this section of the chapter was the choice of whose model of female adult development to use. A problem here is that there has been less empirical work on women's adult development than men's. Levinson is preparing a book tentatively titled *Seasons of a Woman's Life*, but no material from this work was available at the time this chapter was written. Several dissertations on women, conducted at Yale under Levinson, have been completed, and Roberts and Newton (1987) have done some work to analyze these as a whole. However, this approach seems to take the Levinson model as a given and then discuss ways in which the model either does or does not apply to women. It does not seem to be drawn so much from the experiences of women as from the male-based Levinson theoretical model.

Gilligan's (1980) work is a major statement on female adult development, but it has more to do with basic values and moral development than with life stage and career-relevant issues. Gilligan makes a clear case for the greater role of relationships and connectedness in the development of women than in that of men. Her work makes a strong argument that Levinson's model is not adequate to describe the developmental experiences of women. Bardwick (1980) has developed the relational theme identified by Gilligan (1980) and Douvan and Adelson (1966) into a more comprehensive, albeit tentative, view of adult development in women. We have found the Bardwick model to be the most useful for the purposes of this chapter.

Bardwick (1980) refers to the male sense of self as egocentric and the female sense as interdependent. By "egocentric" she means an orientation of autonomy and concern for task achievement, an internal focus on one's own work. By "interdependent" she means being oriented toward relationships, working with and helping others, and defining oneself in terms of the other people in one's life. Bardwick describes this as *the* major gender difference and discusses how this makes the dream in life different for men and women.

The major differences Bardwick sees in male and female developmental stages occur in the thirties and forties. These two decades reflect the following concerns for women.

Age 28–39: the age-thirty transition and the settling-down period of the second adult life structure. This period represents a major gender difference. First, women now in their thirties have probably experienced a more profound and prolonged transition than men at the same age (and are thus out of sync with men) because of the effects of factors such as the "biological time clock," the effects of growing families, the values of the women's movement, and the continuing effects of traditional values. This cohort is a *transitional* one in many ways, pulled between two quite different generations. (This is a period of potentially great asynchronism, as we shall see later.) Women at this age experience strong career changes, whether they are just establishing a career or are in mid-career, as well as strong life and family changes.

Age 40–50: the mid-life transition and middle adulthood. At this point women are feeling more secure and settled in their relationships and are moving toward more autonomy. Men are moving in just the opposite direction; as career and task demands diminish, they are able to become more sensitive to interpersonal relationships and to their internal psychological needs. Each gender is moving toward greater balance of autonomy and interdependence, but from different directions.

SUPERIMPOSING ADULT AND FAMILY DEVELOPMENT OF
DUAL-CAREER SPOUSES

When we superimpose these developmental states for men and women in dual-career families, the resulting dynamics become interesting and offer some vital clues for career development models. The dynamics may vary somewhat depending on the type of dual-career family examined.

For example, Daniels and Weingarten (1982) identified a choice between either *sequential* or *simultaneous* types of family adjustment for mothers in dual-career couples. Fifty-two of the seventy-two mothers in their sample (i.e., more than 70%) used one of the three following subpatterns within the sequential pattern as described in what follows. As can readily be seen, varying degrees of asynchronism occur in each of these subpatterns.

The sequential pattern

Daniels and Weingarten (1982) describe the *motherhood-follows-employment* sequence, where the mother starts the career and then stops the career with the birth of the first child. The dual-career family, as a concept, ceases to exist at this stage. Also, by the time the late-parenting couple start their family, they may both be out of sync with their age peers, many of whose children might be teenagers or older. Second is the *employment-brackets-motherhood* sequence, where the mother interrupts her career, spends full time at home with the children, and resumes her career after the children are older. Third, is the *employment-follows-motherhood* sequence, where the mother completes her parenting responsibilities before she takes up a career. As is readily apparent, the careers of the husband and the wife are out of sync at various times and stages irrespective of the sequence chosen. Both in the employment-brackets-motherhood and in the employment-follows-motherhood sequences, the wife's career is clearly out of sync with organization norms. However, the family is in sync with society in all but the motherhood-follows-employment sequence.

The simultaneous model

This model is based on the traditional pattern of early marriage and what Daniels and Weingarten (1982), again focusing principally on the mother, call *simultaneous enactment of work and family roles*. This imposes several types of asynchronism on the couple during the various life cycle stages. Based upon her descriptive research, Sekaran (1986) defined five relevant family life cycle stages for dual-career couples who follow the simultaneous model, corresponding to various age periods in their lives – the pre-launching stage, young married stage, young parenthood, mature parenthood, and empty nest or pre-retirement stage. Again, this research has described the realities of how many couples have tended to combine career and parenting given contemporary environmental norms and socialization processes. Thus these couple choices do not always represent the ideal in terms of role sharing and equality. Let us examine how dual-career dynamics interact with these family stages.

The pre-launching stage. This is the time when the young prospective partners are contemplating a dual-career life-style in the near future and are discussing their goals and aspirations in relation to their personal needs, career progress, and family desires. Both are probably in their twenties, and the overriding personal concern for the partners is to find two suitable jobs in the same place with neither making excessive compromises. At this stage the partners are likely to be in couple synchronism since they can both be primarily career oriented rather than family oriented.

The young married childless couple stage. In a survey of women with a variety of life structures (such as married, employed, no children; married, at home, children), Baruch, Barnett, and Rivers (1983) found women in this group (married, employed, no children) scored the highest in feelings of mastery (high self-esteem, in control, and valued). They also rated very high on pleasure and enjoyment in life.

The concept of synchronism (see Table 8.1) would explain this high level of mastery and pleasure at this family stage: All three types of synchronism exist here. The organizational careers are in sync for each partner; they are still "on time" in terms of their organizational career timetables (Lawrence, 1980). The couple is in sync in relation to each other's career; neither has started ahead or moved ahead of the other for family reasons. And the couple experience family synchronism – in that being a childless couple is perfectly in sync – and are happy because of it.

Couples who are in the age-thirty transition feel pressures to establish their identities as parents or career persons. Couples who decide not to have children have smoother career development patterns that can be planned and can proceed with fewer family constraints. But for couples who do decide to have a family – and the numbers of such will continue to increase in the future (Jong, 1986) – the personal–career–family goals get out of sync at the next stage. Something has to give.

The young parenthood stage. At this stage the couple have children who are under six years of age (i.e., pre-school) at home. This is perhaps the most tension-ridden period in the lives of the dual-career couple (Sekaran, 1986). For couples in their late twenties and early thirties, this is the stage of settling down, where both spouses are expected to make substantial investments in their careers (Hall, 1976). This is also the most demanding time for the couple in the family sphere, with exacting child-bearing and child-rearing responsibilities.

Being under extreme physical and psychological stress, many couples revert to the culturally prevalent sex role patterns of behavior today. The husband often focuses mainly on the career, and the wife shifts her attention more to the family needs. Such behaviors are also currently reinforced by organizational cues and norms that are basically out of sync for men and women. For instance, when women take time off for child bearing and child rearing, organizations more readily accept the reality of the situation, in contrast to their indirect and un-obtrusive censure of men who want to avail themselves of paternity leave.

For other couples the decision about who cuts back on the career may be made on the basis of factors other than gender. It may be the person whose career or employer is more flexible. It could be the partner who feels less psychologically involved in his or her career. Or, it could be the person who earns less money. These are just a few possible ways the decision could be made.

How this decision is made is a critical topic for future research. For example, Krett (1985) and Norman and Tedeschi (1984) found that companies consider fathers who take paternity leave to be *eccentrics* who cannot possibly be serious about their careers. Such an attitude on the part of the companies, no doubt, has discouraged men from primary involvement in child care activities.

For many reasons, then, for couples having children in their twenties, the career development of one partner, usually that of the wife, is slowed, and the slower career becomes out of sync with the organization's timetable and with the spouse's career (i.e., that partner begins to experience organizational and couple asynchronism).

Mature parenthood. During this fourth stage, when all the children are in school, the career-involved partner (partner A) has reached mid-life and mid-career, but for the home-based partner (partner B) the same is only apparently true. Partner A's career is in sync with organizational norms, and B's is now late. Having thus far invested heavily in the family, B at this stage starts to pay more attention to and increasingly gets involved in the career. Unfortunately, this is the time that A may feel the need to turn attention to the family. Now the couple's family roles are out of sync with each other.

As Evans and Bartolome (1984) discuss, in many cases A is the husband and B is the wife. Men tend to be highly involved in their work up to the mature parenthood stage, and toward the end of this stage they begin to shift gears and try to get more involved in the family. Such a transition is perceived by them to be a functional strategy but, unfortunately, is ill-timed since the children are growing and moving away from the home and the wives have started to shift gears to reinvest themselves in their careers.

The empty nest stage. In this stage the children have left the home to enter their own adult worlds (Levinson, 1986). At this stage the focus shifts from each partner's self as parent to the self in relation to society. This fifth stage in the life of the couple is more smooth sailing for B than for A. Partner B, at this stage, is truly in mid-career. Freed from all heavy family obligations, B feels energetic and enthusiastic about turning undivided attention to the career at this stage. Partner B is in greater organizational synchronism now. Partner B's career may still be late, but it is no longer slow. This is in contrast to A, who, after a lengthy period of competition and stressful striving to succeed in the career, may be experiencing career maintenance or decline (Hall, 1976). As a result, A may become more sensitive to family issues, more affiliative, less aggressive, and more people oriented, and vice versa for B. Again, if A is often the man and B the woman, these changes are consistent with research on men and women in mid-life. Women become more independent, more aggressive, less sentimental, and more career oriented at this life stage (Brim, 1976). According to Bardwick (1986), in present society, men and women in mid-life tend to acquire more of the qualities that had previously been associated more with the opposite sex. Thus, their selves may be out of sync with societal expectations.

The asynchronisms for the various opted lifestyles are depicted in Table 8.1.

OVERVIEW OF DIFFERENT TIMING PATTERNS

What the preceding tells us is that after the first two of the five stages, the fit among personal needs, family desires, and career development get out of sync for the family unit (as depicted in Table 8.1), which results in severe problems for most families.

How do the various sequential and simultaneous timing patterns compare in terms of synchronism and stress? Examination of Table 8.1 helps explain theoretically why the late parenthood (parenthood follows employment) pattern may be seen as the "best solution" for couples in which both parties are highly career involved, according to Daniels and Weingarten (1982). In this pattern, both ca-

Table 8.1. *Career and family timing and synchronism for two-career couples*

Facets of asynchronisms (comparisons)	Simultaneous career–family timing, parenthood parallels employment	Sequential career–family timing		
		Parenthood follows employment	Employment brackets parenthood	Employment follows parenthood
Organizational asynchronism Careers in relation to organizational and societal norms	Start in sync; one becomes out of sync later	In sync	Start in sync; one becomes out of sync later	One in sync; one out of sync
Couple asynchronism Each partner's career in relation to other partner's career	Start in sync; become out of sync later	In sync	Start in sync; become out of sync later	Out of sync
Family asynchronism Family in relation to society	In sync	Out of sync	In sync	In sync

reers start out in sync with organizational norms and with each other. There is career equity for both partners.

However, as Table 8.1 indicates, every timing pattern is asynchronous in one way or another. What is out of sync in the late parenthood option is the family (vis-à-vis societal norms). The violation of these societal norms occurs primarily *before* the arrival of children, usually in the form of unmet expectations of the couple's parents and social comparison with peers. These experiences may be irritating but are not major life stressors. And then when the family is started, even though the couple is "late" in having children, there is great support from parents, friends, and co-workers. Thus, even though the family is asynchronous, in this particular case, asynchronism does not appear to create much stress.

In contrast to this family asynchronism, the career and couple asynchronisms created by the other timing patterns in Table 8.1 causes continuing and growing stress for both the late (or "slow") partner versus the organizational timetable and between the two partners because of the career inequity. These career sacrifices are never fully made up, in contrast to a delayed family.

These manifest asynchronisms, as we see, are basically a function of environmental factors such as socialization patterns and current organizational practices that have not yet adjusted to the changing composition of the work force.

A ROBUST CAREER THEORY

Theories of the actual versus the possible

One of the issues faced by the authors in discussing the possible ways of integrating career and family, either simultaneously or over time, was that of focus:

whether to be *descriptive* and to focus on the dynamics of contemporary couples or to pursue *critical theory*, which would question current arrangements and develop alternative models. The problem with a descriptive focus on contemporary dual-career couples is that the modal patterns tend to favor the man; it is often the wife whose career is slowed, stopped, or interrupted. An example here would be the Daniels and Weingarten (1982) study, which focused primarily on the mother with regard to the parent role. In describing these patterns, there is the risk of implying what is the "norm" is also "normative."

On the other hand, the potential problem with critical theory is that it can be seen as so normative in support of alternative arrangements that exist only in theory that it may be dismissed as idealistic. It is our opinion that the problems of two-career couples are too important to run this risk. The realities of contemporary two-career dynamics deserve just as much conceptual examination as do possible future arrangements.

Our recommendation, then, would be to attempt to combine elements of the two approaches. It appears useful to use the two main contemporary methods of juggling career and family, the sequential approach and the simultaneous approach, but to make no assumptions about which member of the couple performs which role activities. [This is in contrast, then, to Daniels and Weingarten's (1982) approach, which examined parenthood primarily from the mother's perspective.] We would still argue for the *ideal* of an equal sharing of career and family roles by men and women. Thus, when we discuss issues such as parenthood following employment, our position is that either member of the couple could be the one whose career would be delayed to accommodate a period of primary parenting responsibilities.

Reconceptualization of the sequential patterns:
focus on the couple

In the context of the increasing number of dual-career spouses in the work force and their changing values based on the psychology of entitlement of *equality*, the current dynamics within the dual-career family setting and the organizational practices can be soon expected to change. What is required is the conceptualization and development of theoretical models that focus on the *couple* as the constant unit of analysis rather than emphasizing the culturally determined role of only one or the other partner at various critical phases of the family life cycle. Founded on the principle of equality and aiming at minimizing the asynchronisms, we can develop viable career development models both from the perspective of the sequential and the simultaneous patterns discussed earlier.

If we combine the couple as the unit of analysis notion with equality as a prime value, we ought to substitute the term "parenthood" for Daniels and Weingarten's (1982) "motherhood" in the three subpatterns of their sequential model. If we do so, then, in the *parenthood-follows-employment* sequence, both partners will achieve their career aspirations in the early part of their married life and be in sync with each other and their careers. When *either* of the two spouses gives up the career to raise the family, couple asynchronism will be high. The family, of course, will be out of sync with societal norms because of late parenting. The question is, is it really necessary for couples to opt for this life-style if the necessary structural support exists for a continued career for both partners until retirement? We discuss this later.

In the *employment-brackets-parenthood* sequence, both partners alternate the "time-out" periods as the children are being raised, even as the spouse pursuing the career at any particular time consciously shares the domestic responsibilities as equally as possible within the constraints of time available for such duties. The alternating but shared responsibility for child rearing not only bonds both parents equally to the children during their formative years, but also ensures that the couple synchronism is maintained over the long run. Following this pattern, both partners start in high organizational sync but get moderately out of sync at different times. The partners are in sync with each other over the long run, and the family is in sync with societal norms.

In the *employment-follows-parenthood* sequence either of the two partners stays full time at home raising the family and then starts the career. Here, the partner who stays home full time to raise the family experiences organizational and couple asynchronism, but family synchronism is maintained.

The question again is, can organizations design structures that will minimize the asynchronisms? We discuss this more fully later.

Reconceptualization of the simultaneous model: toward balance

Since most of the asynchronisms and tensions in the simultaneous model are currently theorized to be experienced in the young parenthood stage, it makes most sense for both partners to put more emphasis on the family life and somewhat less on the career. Having structural support mechanisms such as household help, proper child care, and a flexible work environment will reduce the stresses considerably for the couple. This will help keep both partners in sync with each other's career and moderately in sync with their organizational careers while keeping family synchronism high. By being able to simultaneously shift gears and concentrate more on the careers during the mature parenthood stage, the couple get aligned with their careers as well. This also facilitates couple synchronism during the empty nest stage, when both parties can continue to focus on their careers and leisure activities and jointly plan for their retirement. They can thus be in sync with all three facets.

IMPLICATIONS FOR CAREER DEVELOPMENT PRACTICES

What is it that can be done to maximize synchronism and minimize asynchronism? We can design career paths that would encourage both partners to shift gears simultaneously from nonwork to work and from work to nonwork spheres as demanded by the exigencies of the work–family–personal preferences at various stages of the couple's life structure. The career development strategy of the organization can at the same time ensure a perennially adequate supply of a full work-focused set of members in the work force. We shall expand upon these ideas.

Later career development: changing organizational timetables

There is no doubt that organizations can enhance their opportunities for both survival and growth through the increased productivity of members by paying attention to the *simultaneous alignment* of career and family interests for both partners in the dual-career household (Hall and Richter, 1988). By introducing flexibility into career timetables, organizations can support couples in slowing down their career progress and shifting their energies to raising a family. In this way, career asynchronism could be reduced.

When the child-rearing responsibilities are reduced and the couples are ready to refocus their attention to career progress again, they should be supported in doing so. *For both women and men, later career development and advancement opportunities should be provided.* This will enable older parents to get back to their careers with renewed vigor. This is also a welcome release to both spouses from the depression of the empty nest syndrome. In effect, both the organization and the employees benefit by such a career development philosophy. This implies that employees will have a bimodal shift in interests (as shown in Figure 8.1) that will be functional for organization productivity and employee satisfaction. By combatting early burnout for men and pent-up frustrations for women, both families and organizations can benefit immensely. This means moving away from exclusive use of the tournament model of early career, one-opportunity, permanent elimination career movement, as described by Rosenbaum (Chapter 16). Companies such as Peat Marwick Mitchell, Gannett, IBM, Lotus, and Procter & Gamble currently permit employees to take extended leaves and/or switch from part-time to full-time work (Taylor, 1986). Such practices are a step in the right direction, but the critical issue is whether the more subtle career timetables have also been changed as well.

Such a later career development philosophy helps organizations in another way as well. It gives organizations flexibility in how they utilize human resources. In a period of high growth for the organization, it can recruit young pre-parenting-stage members as well as older people who have completed their parenting responsibilities, and in periods of stagnation, it can stop hiring younger employees and encourage parenting members to reduce their organizational involvement and focus more on members' nonwork commitments for the desired length of time. Such a philosophy helps organizations in the de-layering, cut-back, and merger and acquisition stages as well. Companies such as Hewlett-Packard have found that parenting employees are eager to reduce their work hours during business downturns, which eliminates the need for layoffs. Thus, the organizational growth cycle can also be meshed with the individual, family, and career cycles. By understanding the dynamics in two-income families as explained in this chapter, individuals can be more effectively utilized in all of their and the company's life stages.

As explained earlier, this new scheme of career development strategy is also healthy inasmuch as men will also be able to enjoy equal parenting opportunities when young children are born and raised in the family. This would prevent men from having regrets in later life because they feel they missed the opportunity for experiencing nurturant fatherhood. The sequential primary involvement in careers and families could be the same for both partners, and the early burnout of the husband and the late career excitement of the wife would become less problematic issues. This also means that organizations need to become serious about paternity as well as maternity leave policies and actively encourage their employees to take advantage of them without stigma.

Are women really "bailing out" in their thirties?

We close this section with one final speculation regarding the current trend in which many women with well-established careers are quitting work in favor of motherhood (Gerson, 1986; Taylor, 1986). Many of these women have successfully mastered the challenges provided by their organizations and professions and are now in their thirties dealing with many of the work versus family concerns identified by Bardwick (1980). The ones who have quit work have decided the rewards of family are greater than work, some because the family is so highly rewarding and some because the rewards from work began to wear off or because the costs of work (commuting, travel, long hours) were becoming too high.

Our hunch is that for many of these women this will be more of a stop-out (a pause) than a bail-out. Even though they might not think so now, in a few years, as the children grow, many of them will resume their careers. The careers may be in different fields than before, and they may be much more protean (Hall, 1976), but their professional socialization and needs for achievement will lead them to an eventual career resumption. Thus, while Daniels and Weingarten (1982) would categorize them in the parenthood-follows-employment sequence, our bet is that they will end up in the employment-brackets-parenthood pattern.

One way of balancing two careers, relationship, and family, then, is to do so over time, which is what the sequential model accomplishes. As organizational career development slows down in the contemporary "downsized" organization, the "slow-burn" career (Bailyn, 1978) will become more the norm in our society. And one form of slow burning is to enact the sequential career pattern. Thus, we would predict that the "normal" organization career timetable in the future will become more in sync with the sequential career of the two-career couple.

Really attacking the definition-of-success problem

At this point, we need to face up to the tough issue. If we are to talk about bimodal careers and second chances in later career, we need to raise the issue of what is success in a serious way.

We would argue that the work force at large (not just two-career couples) has already adopted a more individualized, protean definition of success, which stresses autonomy, flexibility, and balance between work and home (Hall, 1976, 1986). For example, single workers also have work–home tensions, such as the difficulty of being at home when a repair service says they will be there sometime between 1:00 and 5:00 P.M. The traditional fifty-year-old male whose wife does not work outside the home has great difficulty being out of town on business on family birthdays but is often required to do so. As the baby-boom cohort moves solidly into mid-life, more employees of all types are becoming more concerned with balance between work and home, according to adult development theory (Levinson, 1986).

Many writers (e.g., Hall, 1976, 1986) and several chapters in this volume (Gallos, Chapter 6; Marshall, Chapter 13) have called for new definitions of success, to move away from hierarchical advancement as the sole criterion. *We would argue, however, that these new, diverse definitions of success are, in fact, present today in the work force.* Employees, and especially those of the two-career persuasion, as also many others for the reasons stated in the previous paragraph, are not as single mindedly promotion centered as they were ten or twenty years ago. Individualized definitions of success (e.g., psychological success and the slow-burn career) are alive and well in the contemporary work force.

Where these protean definitions of success are not so clearly accepted, however, is in the organization. In a variety of ways, the promotion ethic is perpetuated in the corporate culture. Promotions are written up in the company newsletter, while lateral and downward moves and parental leaves are not. Spouses and families are not involved in the career-planning process. It is time to explicitly raise the issue of what is success for organizational discussion and to use the full resources of the organization to change the idea that advancement is the only indicator of success.

Cross-cultural applicability

Many theories of career development may or may not be applicable to other cultures, but the dual-career issues discussed in this chapter are applicable almost universally. Given today's economic pressures and women's aspirations for advancement in almost all countries around the world – both developed and developing nations – the concerns of two-paycheck families remain largely the same. In some developing countries such as India, the extended families had been a boon for working couples (eliminating the need for external child care) in the past, but the joint family system is now becoming almost extinct in the cities where most of the dual-career families live. Thus, the role conflict and other tensions experienced by couples remain the same in many parts of the world. Also, organizations throughout the world have different expectations about commitment to work for men than for women, differences that trigger conflict in the family system and arrest the organization's progress. Even in Sweden, the most advanced country with regard to liberal parenting policies, the men, who are paid 90% of their regular salaries for paternity leave, are reluctant to take advantage of it because of concerns for their future career success (Norman and Tedeschi, 1984). There seems to be a worldwide stigma attached to men not being dedicated to the organization 24 hours a day throughout their work lives. Thus, the notions, concepts, ideas, and recommendations made here are not culture bound but transferable across several cultures.

CONCLUSION

To assure high productivity, survival, and continued growth, organizations have to keep abreast of the demographic, life-style, and technological shifts that are constantly occurring in society. With the ever-increasing numbers of dual-career families, organizations need to design innovative career development patterns to integrate the preferred career paths of individuals with the organizationally functional career paths. People attach their own meanings to work and family. They punctuate and bracket work and home life with the hope that they will somehow manage to integrate the two into a meaningful life. By helping to facilitate this process for their employees, organizations, more than the employees themselves, will benefit through increased employee motivation, involvement, and productivity. Not only will working partners be in sync, but organizations and the work force will be more in tune as well.

NOTE

The comments of Michael Arthur, Judith Bardwick, Marcy Crary, Barbara Lawrence, Meryl Louis, Thomas Gutteridge, and participants in the 1986 Academy of Management Careers

178 U. SEKARAN AND D. T. HALL

Division Workshops are gratefully acknowledged. Sabbatical support for D. T. Hall from Boston University and its Human Resources Policy Institute was critical to the development of this chapter, as well; special thanks to Dean George McGurn and Fred Foulkes.

REFERENCES

Andrisani, P. J., and Shapiro, W. B. (1978). Women's attitudes toward their jobs: some longitudinal data on a national sample. *Personnel Psychology, 31*, 15–34.

Arnott, C. C. (1972). Husband's attitudes and wives' commitment to employment. *Journal of Marriage and the Family, 34*, 673–684.

Bailyn, L. (1970). Career and family orientations of husbands and wives in relation to marital happiness. *Human Relations, 23*(2), 97–113.

Bailyn, L. (1978). Accommodation of work to family. In R. Rapoport and R. N. Rapoport (eds.), *Working Couples*. New York: Harper & Row.

Bardwick, J. (1980). The seasons of a woman's life. In D. G. McGuigan (ed.), *Women's Lives: New Theory, Research and Policy*. Ann Arbor, MI: The University of Michigan, Center for Continuing Education of Women, pp. 35–55.

Bardwick, J. (1986). *The Plateauing Trap: How to Avoid it in Your Career and Your Life*. New York: Amacom.

Barnett, R. C., Biener, L., and Baruch, G. K. (eds.) (1987). *Gender and Stress*. New York: Free Press.

Baruch, G., Barnett, R., and Rivers, C. (1983). *Life Prints: New Patterns of Love and Work for Today's Women*. New York: McGraw-Hill.

Betz, N. E., and Fitzgerald, L. F. (1987). *The Career Psychology of Women*. New York: Academic.

Bird, G. W., Bird, G. A., and Scruggs, M. (1984). Determinants of family task sharing: a study of husbands and wives. *Journal of Marriage and the Family, 46*(2), 345–355.

Brim, O. G. (1976). Theories of the male mid-life crisis. *The Counseling Psychologist, 6*(1), 2–9.

Conference Board Report No. 868 (1985). *Corporations and Families: Changing Practices and Perspectives*. New York: Conference Board.

Crouter, A. C. (1984). Spillover from family to work: the neglected side of the work–family interface. *Human Relations, 37*(6), 425–442.

Daniels, P., and Weingarten, K. (1982). *Sooner or Later: The Timing of Parenthood in Adult Lives*. New York: Norton.

Derr, C. B. (1986). *Managing the New Careerists*. San Francisco: Jossey-Bass.

Douvan, E., and Adelson, J. (1966). *The Adolescent Experience*. New York: Wiley.

Evans, P., and Bartolome, F. (1984). The changing pictures of the relationship between career and family. *Journal of Occupational Behaviour, 5*, 9–21.

Gallese, L. R. (1985). *Women Like Us: What is Happening to the Women of the Harvard Business School, Class of 75 – The Women Who Had the First Chance to Make It to the Top?* New York: Morrow.

Gerson, K. (1986). Briefcase, baby, or both. *Psychology Today, 20*, 30–36.

Gilligan, C. (1980). Restoring the missing text of women's development to life cycle theories. In D. G. McGuigan (ed.), *Women's Lives: New Theory, Research and Policy*. Ann Arbor, MI: The University of Michigan, Center for Continuing Education for Women, pp. 17–33.

Grant, J. (1988). Women as managers: what they can offer to organizations. *Organizational Dynamics, 16*, (3), 56–63.

Greenhaus, J. H., and Beutell, N. J. (1985). Sources of conflict between work and family roles. *Academy of Management Review, 10*, 76–88.

Greenhaus, J. H., and Kopelman, R. E. (1981). Conflict between work and nonwork roles: implications for the career planning process. *Human Resource Planning, 4*, 1–10.

Hall, D. T. (1976). *Careers in Organizations*. Glenview, IL: Scott Foresman.

Hall, D. T. (1986). Midcareer choice and subidentity development: breaking career routines. In D. T. Hall and Associates (eds.), *Organizational Careers*. San Francisco: Jossey-Bass.

Hall, D. T., and Hall, F. S. (1980). Stress and the two-career couple. In C. Cooper and R. Payne (eds.), *Current Concerns in Occupational Stress*. New York: Wiley, pp. 243–266.

Hall, D. T., and Richter, J. (1988). Balancing work life and home life: what can organizations do to help? *Academy of Management Executive, 2*, 213–223.

Hall, F. S., and Hall, D. T. (1979). *The Two Career Couple.* Reading, MA: Addison-Wesley.

Hertz, R. (1986). *More Equal Than Others: Men and Women in Dual-Career Marriages.* Berkeley, CA: University of California Press.

Jong, E. (1986). The awful truth about women's lib. *Vanity Fair, 49*(4), 92–119.

Kanter, R. M. (1977). *Work and Family in the U.S.: A Critical Review and Agenda for Research and Policy.* New York: Sage.

Kaye, B. (1982). *Up Is Not the Only Way.* Englewood Cliffs, NJ: Prentice-Hall.

Krett, K. (1985). Maternity, paternity, and child-care policies. *Personnel Administrator, 30*(6), 125–136, 218.

Lawrence, B. S. (1980). The myth of the midlife crisis. *Sloan Management Review, 21,* 35–49.

Lawrence, B. S. (1984). Age grading: the implicit organizational timetable. *Journal of Occupational Behaviour, 5,* 23–35.

Lawrence, B. S. (1987). An organizational theory of age effects. In S. Bacharach and N. DiTomaso (eds.), *Research in the Sociology of Organizations.* Greenwich, CT: JAI.

Levinson, D. J. (1986). A conception of adult development. *American Psychologist, 41*(1), 3–13.

Levinson, D. J., with Darrow, C. N., Klein, E. B., Levinson, M. H., and McKee, B. (1978). *The Seasons of a Man's Life.* New York: Knopf.

Markham, W. T. (1987). Sex, relocation, and occupational advancement: the "real cruncher" for women. In A. H. Stramberg, L. Larwood, and B. A. Gutek (eds.), *Women and Work: An Annual Review,* Vol. 2. Newbury Park, CA: Sage, pp. 207–231.

Mathews, P. A. (1984). The changing workforce: dual-career couples and relocation. *Personnel Administrator, 29,* 56–62.

Miller, J. V. (1984). *The Family–Career Connection: A New Framework for Career Development.* Columbus, OH: National Center for Research in Vocational Education.

Norman, N., and Tedeschi, J. T. (1984). Paternity leave: the unpopular benefit option. *Personnel Administrator, 29,* 39–43.

O'Neill, J. M., Fishman, D. M., and Kinsella-Shaw, M. (1987). Dual career couples career transitions and normative dilemmas. *The Counseling Psychologist, 15*(1), 50–96.

Pleck, J. H. (1977). The work–family role system. *Social Problems, 24*(4), 417–425.

Pleck, J. H., Staines, G. H., and Lang, L. (1980). Conflicts between work and family life. *Monthly Labor Review, 103,* 3, 29–32.

Rapoport, R., and Rapoport, R. N. (1969). The dual-career family: a variant pattern and social change. *Human Relations, 22,* 3–30.

Rapoport, R., and Rapoport, R. N. (1980). Balancing work, family, and leisure: a triple helix model. In C. B. Derr (ed.), *Work, Family, and the Career.* New York: Praeger, pp. 318–238.

Rice, G. D. (1979). *Dual Career and Marriage: Conflict and Treatment.* New York: Free Press.

Richter, J. (1985). Switching gears between the office and the living room. Paper presented at the Academy of Management Meetings, San Diego, CA.

Roberts, P., and Newton, P. M. (1987). Levinsonian studies of women's adult development. *Psychology and Aging, 2*(2), 154–163.

Rosenbaum, J. E. (1984). *Career Mobility in a Corporate Hierarchy.* New York: Academic.

Schein, E. H. (1978). *Career Dynamics: Matching Individual and Organizational Needs.* Reading, MA: Addison-Wesley.

Sekaran, U. (1986). *Dual Career Families: Contemporary Organizational and Counseling Issues.* San Francisco: Jossey-Bass.

Sekaran, U. (1988). Organization design for facilitating satisfying work–family linkages through a better understanding of couple dynamics. *Canadian Journal of Administrative Sciences,* December, pp. 12–19.

Sekaran, U. (in press). Understanding the dynamics of self concept of members in dual career families. *Human Relations.*

Stringer-Moore, D. M. (1981). Impact of dual career couples on employers: problems and solutions. *Public Personnel Management, 10*(4), 393–401.

Super, D. E. (1980). A life-span life-space approach to career development. *Journal of Vocational Behavior, 26,* 182–296.

Taylor, A., III (1986). Why women managers are bailing out. *Fortune,* August 18, pp. 16–23.

U.S. Department of Labor (1987). *Employment in Perspective: Women in the Labor Force.* Bureau of Labor Statistics, Report 740.

Vriend, T. J. (1977). The case for women. *Vocational Guidance Quarterly, 25*(4), 329–331.

Walker, L. S., Rozee-Koker, P., and Wallston, B. S. (1987). Social policy and the dual career family: bringing the social context into counseling. *The Counseling Psychologist, 15*(1), 97–121.

Yogev, S. (1982). Are professional women overworked: objective or subjective perception of role loads. *Journal of Occupational Psychology, 55,* 165–169.

Yogev, S., and Brett, J. M. (1985). Patterns of work and family involvement among single and dual earner couples. *Journal of Applied Psychology, 70,* 754–768.

Yogev, S., and Brett, J. M. (1987). Restructuring work for family: how dual-earner couples with children manage. Unpublished manuscript. Center for Urban Affairs, Northwestern University, Evanston, IL.

9   *Transitions, work histories, and careers*

NIGEL NICHOLSON AND MICHAEL WEST

TRANSITIONS AND THE CONCEPT OF CAREERS

As social scientists we often run into difficulties because of the language we use. Try as we might, we have generally failed to create a lexicon of technical usage that is separate and distinct from the discourse of everyday life and thereby achieves the scientific virtues of precision, neutrality and malleability. The language of mathematics has provided a convenient but overused refuge, but still the social scientist must come out from under its cover to speak to the world about what he or she knows.

Here's where the problems start, and often the cause is that the implicit metaphors lurking in the terms we use confound our attempts to operationalize, define and fix their limits. Concepts are still inclined to spread beyond the boundaries we set for them; other meanings creep back in, like stowaways re-embarking after a craft has been inspected and cleared for departure. The notion of "career" is a case in point. The metaphor of journey can be detected at its center and is traceable to its complex etymological origins. The use of the term career to mean "course" is a fairly recent linguistic re-adoption from several Romance languages, where its semantic root denoted a "carriage way" or road (Onions, 1966).

Thinking of careers as journeys is clearly both apt and attractive for many people. Journeys have beginnings and ends, with purposes connecting them – a reassuring image. But the dangers of this epic metaphor are twofold: It encourages reification of the integrity of careers and it inclines one to view the journey as an attribute of the traveler rather than the compulsive shape of the terrain. The consequence is that the careers literature takes individual careers as the main units of analysis and treats these as extensions of individual differences in personality, life-style, marketable skills, cognition and the like. The broad definition of "career" adopted for this volume (see Introduction to Part I) avoids these assumptions but does not rid the term of its metaphorical associations.

We would recommend use of the more neutral term "work histories" to denote sequences of job experiences and reserve the term "career" for the sense people make of them. The latter is important, for how people explain their past work histories is part of the process by which people form the purposes and cognitions that may help shape their futures. So, in a sense, if work histories are lifetime journeys, then careers are the tales that are told about them. It is apparent that scholars are not immune from the same autobiographical compulsion that leads respondents to find connections, themes and stories in their lives (Nicholson and West, 1985). We all like a good story, and the story making of occupational lives is to be found in much of the media we are exposed to in childhood, the tales we are told, the games we play and the answers we seek to the question "what are

181

you going to be when you grow up?" This compulsion serves important psychological and social functions. It keeps at a comforting distance the unsettling thought that in an uncertain world our plans are delusory, or that we may effect little control over our options, opportunities and influences. It also helps to justify the existence and employment of several groups of professionals: school teachers, careers advisors, counsellors, vocational analysts and trainers. Within organizations the myth is perpetuated by recruiters and company agents who try to secure the human resources they require by telling recruits optimistic or imaginative stories about their future lives within the organization.

It is our contention that work histories and careers can and should be studied in three quite different ways. First, the integrity and meaning of work histories should be studied empirically, through a fine-graded analysis of transitions and the periods between them. Only through well-grounded induction can we establish how occupational themes do or do not emerge from these particular interactions of human personality and social structure. Second, careers should be studied as psychological constructs that impart meaning to individual lives and shape their futures. This implies an explicitly biographical and interpretive approach, which, because it may influence future action, also entails some degree of intervention in the subject matter under study. Third, careers can be studied as elements of particular cultures and sub-cultures. If one defines culture in terms of shared belief systems and ways of living, then careers comprise some of the myths, historical themes and action structures that make up their content. Studying careers in particular times and settings is therefore one way of analyzing culture.

It is our thesis here that the first of these three approaches can enlighten the latter two. However we conceive of and study careers, it is essential that we understand their punctuation: the pauses and turning points that shape their course. The study of transitions can help to achieve a reintegration of these three hitherto disparate orientations. In pursuit of this goal we shall outline a simple analytical model of transitions and draw out four linked major themes from the literature on job change.

TRANSITIONS: THEMES AND VARIATIONS

If transitions are to figure as units of analysis in the study of careers, then we need to look closely at what kinds of events they are, so let us start with a definition. Work role transitions are any major change in work role requirements or work context. This definition aims to encompass all the main varieties of inter- and intra-organizational mobility identified by Louis (1980a) as well as times when the job itself changes around the immobile incumbent, such as instances of job redesign or when there is a redefinition of the role through the succession of a new boss or other important co-workers. To explore the significance of such role changes for individuals and organizations, Nicholson (1986, 1987b) has proposed a process model of the transition cycle, comprising the following stages:

I.	Preparation:	Processes of expectation and anticipation before change.
II.	Encounter:	Affect and sense making during the first days or weeks of job tenure.
III.	Adjustment:	Subsequent personal and role development to reduce person–job misfit.

IV.   Stabilization: Settled connection between person and role.
V/I.   Preparation: The renewal of the cycle.

Other writers have suggested similar stage models of work adjustment (Feldman, 1976; Katz, 1980; Van Maanen, 1976), but the transition cycle differs from these models in several respects. In particular, it embodies three important assumptions:

1.   Recursion: the last stage of one cycle is the first of the next, and indeed, if change is rapid, cycles may short-circuit one another; for example, adjustment may be interrupted by the preparation and encounter stages of a new cycle.
2.   Interdependence: the content of experience at one stage will strongly influence the content of experience at subsequent stages; for example, inappropriate preparation heightens the challenge of encounter and adjustment.
3.   Distinctiveness: experiences have distinctive qualities at each stage because they invoke different psychological and social systems.

It is apparent that one large area of careers theory – vocational choice – is almost exclusively concerned with the preparation stage, though often making assumptions (usually without direct test) of future stabilized performance. Early formulations of expectancy-valence theory (Vroom, 1964) were also primarily concerned with occupational choice. Less has been written about the encounter phase largely because few writers have recognized its distinctiveness, but two contrasting descriptive theories stand out. Hopson and Adams (1976) have adapted the Kubler–Ross phase model of coping with bereavement to portray employee stages in reacting to the reality shock of a new job. This has value in alerting us to affective responses to change, but the model is only as adequate as the rather insubstantial empirical origins of its parent theory, and moreover it is questionable whether one should generalize from the trauma of loss to the much more varied meanings of job change. A more cognitive view of encounter is to be found in Louis's (1980b) description of newcomers' early sense making, analyzing how their adjustment to surprises and contrasts is guided by social influence processes and attribution.

Moving on to the adjustment phase, much has been written about how people adjust by adapting themselves to their jobs (e.g., Dawis and Lofquist, 1984), but few have given equal emphasis to how people adjust by molding jobs to fit their personal requirements. Both processes – personal change and role innovation – are theoretically and practically important outcomes of the job change process (Toffler, 1981; Van Maanen and Schein, 1979). The stabilization phase has probably enjoyed the lion's share of theorizing in organizational behavior since it could be said that in such areas as job attitudes and motivation, leadership and group performance most theory and research are concerned to explain established relationships between people and jobs.

However, there is a growing literature on job change and transfers that can begin to fill out our understanding of the dynamics of transitions. To explore the implications of a transitions perspective, we shall examine four interconnected themes that have a bearing on the study of careers. They are all concerned in different ways with the outcomes of transition on the reasoning that if work histories or careers are chains of transition cycles, then we need to understand the meaning of their constituent linkages to explain their lifelong patterning. Our first theme focuses on the experiential content of the immediate antecedents and consequences of the change event, that is, the preparation and encounter phases. Theme 2 extends this analysis by considering how different adjustment strategies originate, contrasting change outcomes for the individual and for the organization. Theme 3 turns to the linkages between transition cycles, considering how discontinuities and continuities in career patterns can be seen to arise from the characteristics of transitions. Last, theme 4 takes up an issue seriously neglected in the careers literature: how forces originating in the person and in the organization interact to create the process and outcomes of job mobility.

Theme 1: the affective content of transition

Most of the running in the literature on the experience of transition has been made by those who would see it as a stressful life event (Brett, 1980), but empirical studies give cause to doubt the generality of this view, and here we shall be exploring its limits. The origins of this emphasis can be traced to the long-standing interest of psychologists in how people cope with the traumas of major life-space transitions such as bereavement, and it is in this tradition that one finds the life-events literature aggregating job changes as stressors along with miscellaneous unrelated experiences (Holmes and Rahe, 1967). Quite apart from a growing body of opinion that stress may emanate more from "daily hassles" than from the cumulative impact of infrequent major events (Kanner et al., 1981), it is an empirically testable question whether work role transitions are stressful, or more specifically, to which kinds of work role transitions does a stress-coping model most helpfully apply.

First, let us consider preparation for change. This is difficult to study directly since the onset of many work role transitions is unpredictable. However, evidence from the retrospective reports of some 2,300 managers in our own recent research suggests that, for the vast majority, anticipation of job change is, at most, only mildly anxiety provoking, with people's greatest worries centering on their competence to fulfil role requirements (Nicholson and West, 1988; see also Marshall and Cooper, 1976). This research indicates, as have our studies of graduate entry and adjustment to corporate life (Arnold, 1985, 1986; Nicholson, 1987a), that anticipatory anxiety before a change is a minor sub-theme to the more general and positive anticipation of future challenge and new experience.

Looking at the settling-in period of "encounter," we find that managers are generally quite prepared to describe the experience as stressful, but further analysis reveals these reports to be highly positively correlated with reports of challenge, freedom, authority, satisfaction and fulfilment (Nicholson and West, 1988). Both this research and our work with graduates do indicate that post-change disillusionment is a common experience, particularly among those in career entry level jobs (see also Arnold, 1985 and 1986; Mansfield, 1975; Richards, 1984a, b; Vroom and Deci, 1971). Disenchantment also appears to focus especially on aspects of the organizational context. But the generally low intensity with which these reactions are expressed and their relatively short-lived duration (Richards, 1984b) leave room for doubt as to whether these reactions might not be better regarded as "problem solving" or "pathfinding" than as "stress coping."

Indeed, neither has the generality and importance of stress reactions been sustained by researchers who have approached the study of job change from a stress-coping theoretical framework. For example, Brett (1982) failed to find the expected negative connection between job change and well-being in a study of 346 transferred employees; indeed, many found the experience made their family lives more interesting and satisfying. Werbel (1983) also set out to look at a smaller sample's relocation as "an acute job stressor," and although he found that low self-esteem and uncertainty about performance did contribute to feelings of stress, effects were inconsistent over time. Werbel interprets this as signifying that negative elements in the experience of encounter rapidly fade as mastery grows. Less equivocal about the positive outcomes of transition are the studies of Burke (1974), who recorded increased job satisfaction among lateral transfers; Keller and Holland (1981), who observed heightened performance, innovation, satisfaction and autonomy in a field experimental study of the job changes of R&D professionals; and Kirjonen and Hanninen (1986), who actually found reductions in stress symptoms when comparing mobile with non-mobile blue-collar workers. This latter study is of particular interest in showing that the benefits of mobility are not restricted to white-collar employees; and this result was also replicated by longitudinal data from a sub-sample of 1,100 in our study of managers that revealed that job changers experienced increases in their psychological adjustment and higher order needs, while immobiles recorded falls on these factors. Latack (1984) reports that her sample of managers and professionals experienced less role overload after major than minor transitions and reaches a similar conclusion to ours: little support for generality of the stress model; people actively seek out the "stress" of desirable moves.

So when are negative affective outcomes of job change most likely? Some studies indicate that extremely radical forms of job change tend to be stressful (Vaitenas and Wiener, 1977; Viney, 1980), and our research confirms this, but only with the important qualification that radical change is a positive and manageable experience where the individual has supports and resources (West, Nicholson and Rees, 1987). Frese (1984) also emphasizes the importance of moderating variables, such as person–environment fit, predictability and personal control (e.g., Karasek, 1979) in making transitions stressful. Among the most important mediating variables must be counted individual differences in psychological dispositions and life circumstances. For example, for upward mobile managers fear of failure and anxiety seem to be particularly critical factors in the quality of job change experience (Brewin, 1980; Marshall and Cooper 1976). Another vulnerable group are managers relocating, though there appear to be wide differences in the problems of life-space adjustment created by people's personal circumstances (Brett and Werbel, 1978; Pinder, 1977).

Finally, mention may be made of two of the ostensibly most radical and undesirable of all work role transitions: downward status moves and job loss. Our research has found the former to be the one kind of job change whose outcomes are consistently negative (Nicholson and West, 1988). Elsewhere, there is plentiful evidence for the deleterious effects of unemployment on mental health (Warr, 1987). However, even here researchers have drawn attention to the fact that a minority are still able to find unexpected and positive outcomes in the experience and the new directions it can presage (Fineman, 1983; Hartley, 1981; Latack and Dozier, 1986).

One can interpret such instances of positive outcomes to what are manifestly negative events as testaments to the indomitability of the human spirit. They epitomize people's capacity to turn crises into opportunities and to undertake challenges with the sense of self-directedness that yields future fulfilment. This brings us to our second theme, for the study of transitions raises the question of how different modes of adjustment to the demands of change are engendered.

Theme 2: modes of adjustment to transition

In his theory of work role transitions Nicholson (1984) derives a number of propositions to predict adjustment strategies on two orthogonal outcome dimensions: personal change, where the individual undergoes minor or major identity transmutations to accommodate the demands of new roles; and role development, where the mover effects changes in work roles or contexts so that they better accommodate him or her. Both of these modes of adjustment provide important linkages in the construction of the life/career course and can help to illustrate how careers intersect with organizational evolution. Personal change through transition helps to explain career and identity development and connects it with the socializing forces that stabilize and replicate organizational systems. Role development supplies the reciprocal dynamic of what Super calls "implementation of the self" (1957); in order to preserve and enact valued aspects of identity, the newcomer adjusts the role, thereby providing a potentially important mechanism for organizational innovation.

Both adjustment processes have figured in empirical research, though in disparate and generally non-cumulative ways. Two of the earliest demonstrations of the transforming power of role transitions were conducted in the late 1950s within the social psychological paradigm of attitude change. In a classic study Lieberman (1956) observed how workers' attitudes to unions and management shifted toward more pro-union positions on assumption of the shop steward role and toward pro-management positions on assumption of the foreman role, reverting to their original values after ceasing to occupy either role. In the important Bennington study, Newcomb (1958) similarly found college women's values shifted progressively toward the ambient norm in their student community and reverted to their prior (parentally socialized) values after leaving college. Both studies are in the tradition of social psychology, which places the causal emphasis of adjustment on situational demands rather than individual differences, though the Newcomb study interestingly did note that the adjustment effects were moderated by the direction and magnitude of the shift from parental values.

The careers literature has tended to emphasize personal continuity rather than change by looking at careers through the lens of occupational choice, where psychologically "reliable" (i.e., structurally stable) measures of individual traits have been mapped on to comparable dimensions of occupational roles. Foremost among such theories are those of Dawis and Lofquist (1984) and Holland (1973/1985), both invoking consistency assumptions to generate predictions about occupational choice, the affective quality of work adjustment and job-quitting behavior. These theories have certainly generated huge numbers of studies, from which they claim substantial support, though surprisingly few attempts have been made to extend their scope through empirical research to post–career entry job changes. They have remained absorbed with the measurement of initial preference and entry. Moreover, the few studies that have examined subsequent job histories have not always been sympathetic to the theory. It seems, for example, that people make anticipatory *pre*-transitional attitude adjustments to achieve congruence with their new settings (Krau, 1983), undergo environmentally consistent post-change shifts in attitude and aspiration (Gottfredson and Becker, 1981; Schein, 1967; Vroom, 1966) and undertake subsequent mid-career job changes that do not conform with the theories' predictions (Gottfredson, 1977; Robbins et al., 1978). An explicitly focused transitions perspective would seem to be needed to reconcile these discrepant findings. One recent careers theory has gone some way toward this by conceiving of career paths in terms of sequential decisions and differential effects from person–role discrepancies (Mihal et al., 1984), though without elaborating the nature of developmental outcomes.

The evolution of identity in response to changing qualities of work experience has recently been the subject of more sophisticated corroboration than previously in the multivariate longitudinal studies of Kohn and Schooler (1983), Mortimer and colleagues (1986) and Brousseau (1983). Specifically, they all demonstrate that self-determination (or equivalent constructs) is heightened by prolonged exposure to complex and challenging job demands (Frese, 1982). However, a limitation of these studies is that their methodologies do not enable them to specify the nature of the transitions people have undergone or the organizations and roles they have passed through.

Organizational scholars have taken a more genuinely interactive view of adjustment to change than have most career theorists. Schein, for example, posits the existence of "career anchors" (occupationally related value systems) as influencing people's response to work, while simultaneously acknowledging that personal change is an outcome of socializing forces that impact on mobile employees (1978). Hall's (1971, 1976) theorizing about the formation of career sub-identity development has a similar dualistic character: Values acquired through work experience can come to direct subsequent career behavior and choice.

Role innovation in response to job change – molding the role to meet one's requirements – has been the subject of little empirical research since Schein introduced the notion (1971a), though Van Maanen and Schein (1979) have developed a series of specific predictions about how different organizational socialization strategies are likely to produce "custodial" (conforming) or innovatory responses. Van Maanen and Schein also briefly acknowledge that individual differences are likely to mediate these reactions. This theme has been taken up by Jones (1986) in the one partial test of their theory published to date. His research confirmed the prediction that the adjustment responses of people with low self-efficacy would be more clearly consistent with the theory than those of people with high self-efficacy.

It is clear that individual differences in reactions to job change are of considerable importance, and their influence can be detected in many studies. They are evidently central to the results of Latack's (1984) study, mentioned earlier, and in Hall and Schneider's (1973) study of priests' adjustment to job change and reactions to disillusionment. They have been directly highlighted in Rychlak's documentation of the changes over time in the life themes of young male managers in a follow-up to the classic AT&T study (Bray et al., 1976; Rychlak, 1982).

It is, of course, important to separate individual differences in psychological characteristics from differences in the character of the job change itself. Feldman and Brett (1983), for example, found more proactive adjustment strategies were enacted by internal transfers than new hires. Our own research confirms the importance of both individual and circumstantial variables. There are, for example, complex differences in the magnitude and nature of personal change as a function of different dimensions of job transitions (e.g., functional vs. status vs. employer change) and as a function of individual differences in higher order needs and psychological adjustment. We found similarly complex interactions when we looked at role innovation as the dependent variable (Nicholson and West, 1988).

We have commented that attention in the literature to these two adjustment dimensions, personal change and role development, has tended to be fragmented, but Schein (1971b) and Katz (1980) have linked them in theoretical analyses of individual adjustment to organizational roles. Both these formulations seem to assume that as strategies they are bipolar alternatives, and both state that they expect personal change to be a feature of early socialization – adjustment and role development to occur later. Our research challenges both assumptions. Consistent with our theoretical premise that they are orthogonal rather than alternative adjustment modes, we have found them to occur more often together than separately: In the terminology of Nicholson's theory (1984) "exploration" is a more common mode of adjustment than either "absorption" or "determination," contrary also to Brett's (1984) prediction that most adjustment will take the form of the two latter modes. Moreover, role development among managers seems to be a strong and fairly continual response to work – similar to Gabarro (1985) we find it common for managers to "hit the ground running" in new jobs (see also West and Savage, 1987) – while personal change is a longer, slower and harder to detect mode of adjustment.

The implications of this review of adjustment outcomes for careers are complex. Certain combinations of individual differences, characteristics of transitions and contextual influences endow individual transitions with different significance to the career course; in other words, for some people particular kinds of job changes will be more likely to be career-redirecting turning points than they are for others. Our third theme explores this issue further.

Theme 3: continuity and change in work histories

Again, to address this theme, we must review ideas and findings from literatures that not only have quite different sets of assumptions and methods but also seem to be unhelpfully oblivious to each other's existence. First, there is typological theory and research of various kinds. Among these are those who would classify individuals according to the formal characteristics of the sequences of move experienced, such as Watts's (1981) discussion of "spiralist," "sequential," "regressive" and other patterns. Then there are those typologies that confound histories of move types with the motives presumed to underlie them, such as Rapoport's (1970) division of a managerial sample into "humanistic," "incremental," "metamorphic" and "tangential" types; Murray et al.'s (1971) division of people into "routine," "self-determined," "situation determined" and "accommodative" types; and the AT&T researchers' division of managers into "enfolders" and "enlargers" (Bray et al., 1974). Another approach is to model move patterns according to circumstantial forces: external influences such as opportunity structures (Miller and Form, 1951) and personal influences such as life-stage variables (Super, 1957).

Combining these are those scholars who have taken a biographical perspective and used case data to illustrate recurrent patterns, exceptional forms and their causes. These writings vary in their intensity and breadth. For example, none in the literature is more detailed than White's remarkable analysis of just three working lives (1952), while Levinson et al.'s (1978) study of 40 men in mid-life attempted a more general modeling of life-span and career development. Sheehy's more journalistic in style, but nonetheless illuminating, case histories (1975, 1981) and Osherson's (1980) reports on 20 men in mid-life radical career change are examples in the same genre. There are abundant riches and insights to be found in these biographical analyses, but their reliance on historical ex post facto reconstruction or temporal inferences from cross-sectional methods raises questions about the generalizability of the normative typologies and stage models that they generate. These are arguably culture bound and in some instances seem arbitrary or deterministic in their causal ascriptions. If we follow the reasoning of life-span theorists such as Riegel (1975), Gergen (1980) and Starr (1983), indeterminacy is the pre-eminent principle of the life course; individuals are agents of their own development through their ideational self-constructions and the dialectic of their involvement with the world. Sarbin (1984) applies similar reasoning to episodes of individual transitions when he describes them as indeterminate "social dramas" in which social identity is reconstructed through interaction. We would not wish to deny that repeated patterns can be discerned, but many of these can perhaps be seen as reflections of the way our culture and social worlds are structured. We should take care in reifying them as psychic structures. At a deeper level, however, they can be seen to correspond to psychic themes that recur because of the similarity within our culture of certain early experiences (Csikszentmihalyi and Beattie, 1979).

Whichever line one follows of the theoretical approaches we have reviewed, the ideas and data they have produced on the theme of continuity and change tell us two things: first, career patterns exhibit many possible forms, varying considerably in their manifestations of continuity and discontinuity; second, it is apparent that research from highly individualistic perspectives has provided too little empirical data to allow us to test the generality of their models or even to establish how common are different career patterns.

The same conclusions can be drawn from research within more occupational and organizational perspectives. We have already seen that the continuity of career development suggested by occupational choice theory is elusive, though some large-scale empirical studies have been successful in predicting the character of first jobs from background and biographical factors (Raelin, 1980) and subsequent mobility rate from the character of early work experience, family ties and current marketability (Veiga, 1983). Veiga's work (1981) also suggests that these and similar variables uncover three empirically distinct career paths for managers: upward mobiles and two types of immobility, "deadwood" and "solid citizens." None of these studies directly addresses the issue of continuity or discontinuity among the moves that people do make, beyond suggesting that status mobility is the simplest and most common type of continuity to be found in the job changes of managerial and professional populations. Organizationally based studies underline this conclusion. Scholl's (1983) research, for example, revealed that "escalator" models of career progression held sway in two large organizations studied; Rosenbaum (1979, 1984) illustrates the impact of "tournament" contests in organizational status climbing; and Kanter (1977, 1984) shows the pervasive-

ness of "vertical" models of career development in many paternalistic and segmented organizations. This is amplified by the recent study of Baron et al. (1986),
which found promotion ladders to be pervasive but highly differentiated within
and between organizations.

Our own research attempted to provide some much needed descriptive data
about how common are different move and career types among managers and to
analyze their causes. First we confirmed and extended analysis of post-war mobility trends, previously documented in both the United States and the United
Kingdom, to the effect that there has been a high and rising rate of inter-
organization job change, unabated by the impact of recession (Alban-Metcalfe
and Nicholson, 1984; Guerrier and Philpot, 1978; Jennings, 1967; Sell, 1983;
Warner and Abegglen, 1955). Second, unlike previous surveys, we were able to
analyze the frequency of different move types, 12 in all, constructed by classifying
transitions on the three dimensions of status, function and employer change.
These data showed that "conventional" or "incremental" move types – those such
as simple promotions or lateral moves, which are stereotypically considered to
be normal in organizational life – are relatively uncommon, accounting for less
than 1 in 10 moves. In contrast, more than half of all job moves are of the radical
"spiralling" kind – simultaneous changes of status and function – and, for around
half of these, also involve mobility between organizations.

These are genuinely radical moves, for further analysis showed that most functional and inter-organizational moves take people out of one family of occupational
roles or organizational types into quite different ones. More subjective data from
managers' descriptions of their career types in standardized measures confirmed
that upward progression is almost the only widely experienced form of continuity;
otherwise, there were frequent reports of careers having been "planless" or punctuated by radical changes in a continuing search for fulfilment and challenge.
Any continuity for these people resides in their selves, not their work histories.
We would concur with Rothstein's (1980) conclusion from his review of the careers
literature that there is less evidence for the existence of orderly patterns of choice
and development toward well-defined goals than there is for a model of careers
as made up of changing responses to unfolding opportunities. However, we see
no need for an "opportunity structure model" to be a mutually exclusive alternative to the choice model – human qualities of self-determination and ingenious
improvisation in the face of uncertainty argue for an interactionist view of personal and situational forces.

One important contingency governing career patterns is organizational size
and structure, and we saw earlier that conventional career patterns are a prominent feature of life in some large corporations. Further analysis of our data has
confirmed that non-radical move types and continuous careers are much more
common in large bureaucratic organizations than in other kinds of organization
(Nicholson and West, 1988). It is, indeed, perhaps because researchers often draw
their data from large corporations rather than from more general managerial
populations that they conclude, as did Brett on the basis of her work with Feldman
(Brett, 1984), that most transitions are non-radical. However, perhaps the most
telling reflection on the issue of continuity emerged from our longitudinal data.
We asked managers at time 1 to predict the likelihood of their experiencing
different types of mobility over the coming year and then tested accuracy of their
predictions at time 2, just over a year later (Nicholson et al., 1985). Fewer than

half the managers who were promoted or changed employer between time 1 and time 2 had predicted either move at time 1, and only around a quarter of those who had predicted either of these moves at time 1 in fact achieved them by time 2. The only reason managers' predictions of their own future mobility were statistically better than chance expectation was because of a large number of "stables": people who correctly predicted that they would *not* change jobs. And, as we have seen, these are people who are mostly in large and conventional institutional structures. The remainder are being blown by winds of change that they clearly have difficulty in forecasting.

This implies that much of the order to be found in career development is a property of the way transitions are environmentally structured. Others are making changes more opportunistically, evidently without good maps of career opportunity structures yet believing that they have sufficient insight and control to be able to make confident, if erroneous, predictions about their immediate futures. Two conflicting interpretations can be put upon this. One is that continuity and control are self-delusions: Careers are autobiographical fictions with which many people try to imbue a sense of agency and self-direction into work histories that were in reality generated by random or capricious forces. The alternative view is that uncertain opportunities and influences are the raw material upon which the self-directed person exercises improvisational skill. The way people construct routes to fulfil their individual purposes could be seen as akin to the way Mintzberg (1973) observed some managers are able to construct planful roles out of fragmented and unpredictable situational demands. Self-report and other data from our managerial sample offer support for both views. For many managers the uncertainty of career trajectories is a sympathetic rather than an antagonistic theme to their continuing search for fulfilment. Others, however, do appear genuinely confused and persist in believing in the goal-directed rationality of their moves, even though, as Kafka's hero in *The Castle*, each step seems to take them in an unpredicted direction. In either event, the conventional paradigm of orderly careers and planful development would seem to have limited applicability.

It is apparent from the foregoing that the relationship between transitions and work histories or careers is mediated by qualities of organizational experience, and yet the careers literature has almost nothing to say on the subject. For example, a recent handbook on careers fails even to have "organization," "role" or equivalent terms in its index (Brown and Brooks, 1984). So let us consider how a transitions perspective can link the individual with the organization in ways that help advance our thinking about careers.

Theme 4: individual–organization interaction in transition

Each stage of the transition cycle described earlier has some reciprocal in organizational structure and process (Nicholson, 1987b). Preparation is a function of recruitment/transfer practices for the new setting and reflects the presence of career development or counselling practices in the old. Encounter experiences are a product of organizations' induction–socialization practices and organizational demography. Adjustment is a function of job design, training and supervision. Stabilization is guided by the information and management systems that regulate and control performance.

The literature on turnover can be seen as attempting to combine individual with organizational and opportunity structure variables in order to predict one possible outcome of the transition cycle, the decision to quit or not to quit (Mobley et al., 1979). It is unfortunate that this literature has been developed in isolation from other fields, for clearly there is unrealized scope for its integration with the careers literature and organization theory (Watson and Garbin, 1981). Argyris's (1964) discussion of the relationship between organizational control and individual response and Hirschman's (1970) exit-voice-loyalty utility theory of organizational behavior and turnover can both be seen as pioneering attempts to generate such theoretical linkage. A promising avenue for future research exploration would seem to be closer attention to the relationship between organizational career systems and how different transitions – principally turnover versus forms of intra-organizational mobility – are perceived and enacted. Scholl's research (1983), for example, showed that individuals develop timetables for promotions, and that as employees approach and pass the expected transit time for their promotions, intent to remain in the organization falls and then increases.

The emerging literature on organizational culture would seem to offer a way forward toward more contingent and contextually embedded constructions of the relationship between organizations and individual career development than is current in the turnover literature. An early example of this kind of thinking was Presthus's (1978) analysis of how the climate of values in corporate bureaucracies is reflected in the content of occupational socialization and mobility patterns. More recently, Sathe (1985), Hedberg (1984) and Schein (1985) have shown how organizational culture is both a cause and an effect of the way the transitions of individual members across its internal and external boundaries are managed. Kanter's empirical research (1977, 1984) has explored this issue in depth, linking critical differences in climate and mobility patterns with organizational structure and performance. The literature on management succession has also focused on the relationship between transitions and performance, generally supporting Grusky's (1963) vicious cycle theory that job change is both a scapegoating response to and a cause of performance problems in organizations (Allen and Panian, 1982; Brown, 1982).

It may be inferred from these researchers that organizations could attempt to change their cultures, reform their structures and improve their performance through strategies that include some conscious manipulation of the transition process: the form and frequency of transitions and the support systems that affect how individuals experience them. Well-designed and practical counselling of job changers through the experience of transition can play an important part in fostering beneficial outcomes for both the individual and the organization (Schlossberg, 1984). Yet it has been suggested that organizations are more likely to see the management of job change purely as an instrument of control rather than consider its potential use as a primary tool in the personal development of employees (Pinder, 1981; Pinder and Walter, 1984). One of the most important recent theoretical approaches to this issue has been Van Maanen and Schein's (1979) theory of organizational socialization, discussed earlier. Nicholson's (1984) theory of work role transitions suggests some modifications to this formulation and adds a number of propositions about how individual differences and role requirements can induce personal development and/or role development as adjustment outcomes. Our research based on these ideas has found, for example, that the experience of innovation in one job predicts innovativeness in the next (Nicholson and West, 1988).

However, as Brett (1984) has noted, work role transitions are generally neglected opportunities in terms of their potentially developmental outcomes for organizations and individuals. It is rare for comparative organizational research to report on the management of transitions, though one notable exception is to be found in the work of Edstrom and Galbraith (1977). Out of the four European multinational companies in their sample they found two used transitions consciously to develop managers for future positions of responsibility, and one of these used them as an organizational development strategy for the creation of "decentralized coordination" among sub-units.

Such companies are probably few and far between. Our own research has painted a bleak picture of organizational involvement (or rather the lack of it) in career development (Nicholson and West, 1988). It seems that most companies act as if their responsibility for managing transitions begins and ends with recruitment procedures. In most organizations there is no management of the joining-up process, haphazard placement, poor initial training, few early supports, scant feedback and supervision as experience develops and no career planning or consultation once performance has stabilized. Medium-sized companies appear to be the most neglectful of these issues: In small companies these activities are more likely to develop spontaneously as a function of their more fluid human resource management systems; in large companies they are more likely to be regulated by standardized human resource management functions. Middle-sized companies seem to lack the spirit to handle such issues organically and the willingness to expend resources to handle them bureaucratically.

In another of our recent investigations we undertook an intensive longitudinal analysis of graduate entry, adjustment and subsequent job changes in a major oil company (Nicholson and Arnold, in press a, b). Even here, where more attention was paid than in most companies to the management of transitions, we found wide variations in company practice, which had complex consequences for individual development (Nicholson, 1987a). Two of the most important and noticeable of these were the setting in motion of what Hall calls success cycles (1976) and failure cycles, the latter occurring where the damaged self-esteem of individuals narrowed their perception of opportunity structures and inhibited their responses to the demands of uncertainty. Critical influences on these outcomes included initial expectations, socialization–induction processes, task factors, feedback, supervisory style and perceptions of career development contingencies. We found the complex interactions of factors could be simply summarized in terms of four distinctive developmental sub-cultures in the four departments studied: task centered, training centered, human-relations oriented, and competitive/achievement oriented. Our case analyses suggested that career developmental outcomes were dependent upon degrees of fit or misfit between the character and dispositions of individuals and these sub-cultures. More generally, it could be inferred from the study that a flexible mix of these cultural orientations would best meet the organization's goal of optimizing the developmental potential of its heterogeneous graduate intake. One implication of this sub-cultural view is that work group dynamics will mediate adjustment processes (Moreland and Levine, 1983), a topic deserving much greater research attention for both theoretical and practical reasons.

Even when organizations make an effort to control the initiation, experience of and outcomes to transition, many do so with little subtlety or skill. The net result of these shortcomings is that organizations play very little part in regulating the career development process, apart from providing an opportunity structure through their organizational hierarchy and design. Even this is a prime source of uncertainty, for our research shows that a great many job changes are occasioned by unexpected upheavals in structural arrangements (Nicholson and West, 1988). We also find that employer changes, some of the most productive career moves made by managers, are often made as a result of dissatisfaction with one's previous setting or because of external pressures. These data carry a message for the turnover literature. The well-documented causes of quitting, such as low job satisfaction and low commitment, far from operating as a form of natural selection to be welcomed because they remove the misfits, should be deprecated because they signify a climate of neglect that is forcing the best people to seek their fortunes elsewhere. All of this reinforces our earlier observations about uncertainty in career trajectories. Yet, here we may be confronting a paradox, for if as our research indicates, radical inter-organizational job change has more beneficial developmental outcomes than conventional in-company mobility, then what the organization loses through the exit gate it could recover later, with "added value," through recruitment. The problem is that most organizations are not equipped to minimize the costs and reap the benefits of this process.

There is much more to be said about the management of transitions than we have space for here, but it may be concluded that it is a matter of great importance for the study of careers how differences in organization design and process govern the form, experience and outcomes of transitions.

THE STUDY OF TRANSITIONS

The four themes we have considered are not the only ones of importance in the study of transitions. Two more in particular stand out, but these cannot be discussed at length here. First is the critical issue of social divisions in relation to transitions, especially those of class, gender and ethnicity. Second, the relationship between work role transitions and other life transitions is also of the utmost practical and social importance. These two issues raise the question of what might be the limiting conditions to the comments we have made here. The ground on which we have debated the nature of transitions is predominantly the field of white-collar professional managerial and technical roles. There is evidence that much of what we have observed holds equally for blue-collar populations, though stress coping, reactivity and continuity may be more characteristic of blue- than white-collar transitions. From our research we also conclude that there are important gender differences in orientations to transitions that result in markedly different work history norms for men and women. Women in managerial occupations seem better adapted to the increasing uncertainty of labor markets and opportunity structures by virtue of their more "existentialist" (value-driven) orientations toward career development, in contrast to the more characteristically "rationalist" (goal-directed) orientation of male managers. A consequence of this is that men undertake most of their radical transitions early in their careers, whereas women maintain a higher rate of divergent mobility throughout their careers (Nicholson and West, 1988). Turning to other life events as an issue, there is no doubt that these do intersect with work role transitions in important ways, but our research indicates that job changes are among the most frequent and most important life-space transitions that people experience.

That being said, let us return to our starting point: how the study of transitions can contribute to careers theory and practice. The four themes we have reviewed carry some clear implications. First, qualities of experience through transitions vary according to individual differences among those who move, the types of change encountered and the contexts in which they occur. Second, these qualities are integral to the adjustment outcomes of the change process for individuals and organizations, that is, whether change begets stability or development in personal and social systems. Third, the complexity and uncertainty of the confluence of forces in the transition process gives work histories indeterminate trajectories, even in the short run for many people. Fourth, a life-span perspective is a necessary but not sufficient method for understanding the widespread differences in the continuities and discontinuities of careers; the management of careers in organizations and occupational processes are major explanatory factors.

In more general terms, our analysis implies that a transitions perspective to careers supplies a way of mapping how the stratification of society and the design of organizations impose constraints upon individual choice. These require but have yet to receive the kind of analysis that social anthropology might bring to bear upon the subject. The time is ripe for this within the emerging study of organizational cultures and their social contexts. The study of transitions and how they link to make up "careers" can be seen as a way of exploring the evolution of social boundaries, the form taken by passages across them and the symbolic values and behaviors that attach to them. Transitions are critical incidents in the nexus between self-consciousness and social structure (Glaser and Strauss, 1971; Strauss, 1959).

If the study of transitions is to offer a new way of contributing to the componential, biographical and cultural analyses of careers, then we need new methods for the purpose. One may be to take the transition cycle described earlier as a basic unit of analysis to explore how their form and patterning characterize environments and persons. This suggests the need to elaborate the language with which we describe them, and toward this goal Nicholson (1987b) has suggested nine dimensions of transition cycles with which one might profile their complex character and identify their critical elements. The dimensions are:

Speed:	How rapid is transit through one or more cycles.
Amplitude:	How novel or how radical are the demands of the transition.
Symmetry:	How much relative time is spent in different stages of the cycle.
Continuity:	How inter-linked are cycles and the extent to which they follow any logical sequence.
Discretion:	How much control the mover has over passage through the stages of the cycle.
Complexity:	How clearly or easily can the tasks of the transition cycle be defined.
Propulsion:	The extent to which the cycle was initiated by the person or by external events and forces.

Facilitation: What supports and resources are available to aid the person's passage through the stages of the cycle.

Significance: How personally or organizationally important are the outcomes of transition.

We shall not attempt here to summarize the outcomes that are predicted from these dimensions in terms of psychological response and organizational effectiveness, and the reader is referred to the original source for this (Nicholson, 1987b). But we can briefly conclude by summarizing how this framework might advance the theory and practice of careers.

First, it may be established empirically which forms of the transition cycle yield effects of particular social or personal significance, such as innovation, conformity, psychological strain and future change. Second, using the language of the nine dimensions we may be able to describe careers in terms of sequences of particular types of transition cycles and so generate new and more flexible accounts of careers as well as the different forms career "stages" may exhibit. Third, we may be able to use this same language to characterize organizational environments, sub-cultures and occupations, that is, as aggregates of cycles of certain types. Fourth, the nine dimensions may be useful as a simple diagnostic inventory for careers counselling, self-appraisal and life planning or for action-oriented evaluation of organizational career structures.

CONCLUSION

In Martin Amis's (1984) novel *Money*, a savagely satirical depiction of solipsist and materialistic excess in the fast lane of the urban 1980s, anti-hero John Self, ruminating sourly on his past "time travel," reflects: "Points of a journey do not matter when the journey has no destination, only an end." Careers and work histories, as we have been considering them, seem to be journeys with ends rather than destinations; so does the conclusion follow that transitions do not matter? They might be of no interest to the more psychopathic traveler, who, as John Self, is locked into their current stream of consciousness, but they would not be without import. Indeed, we would argue quite the contrary: Transitions are of least significance in the most "conventional" career development, where the destination is a foregone conclusion from the outset, for then it is only the timing, not the content, of transitions that has high uncertainty. For others – evidently the majority – the "end" of the journey lies in the developing occupational and personal identity of the individual. In this sense the journey's end is as much where one is now as where one will be at any future point. Predicting future points (i.e., "ends") in work histories is akin to the medium- or long-range forecasting of any complex indeterminate system, such as the weather or the economy: Projections require successive revisions in the light of intermediate changes. These changes – transitions – make our ends; we can understand where we are now by reviewing our past experiences of change, and find auguries of the future by divining their patterns of occurrence, experience and outcome whether or not, as John Self, we care.

To conclude, our view of the concept of transition is that it has a unique capacity to traverse boundaries between areas of research and theory that bear in important ways upon the study of careers but have too long been provinces of splendid isolation for many scholars. In particular, organization theory (the study of labor turnover, careers and vocational psychology), life-span development (the study of social identity) and organizational socialization (the study of work attitudes and job characteristics) are all concerned in one way or another with transitions. Here we have tried to make explicit some of the implicit links between these areas and show how a transitions perspective, by exploring the nature and outcomes of change events, can offer a revitalized and reintegrated approach to the study of careers and work histories.

REFERENCES

Alban-Metcalfe, B., and Nicholson, N. (1984). *The Career Development of British Managers.* London: British Institute of Management.
Allen, M. P., and Panian, S. K. (1982). Power, performance, and succession in the large corporation. *Administrative Science Quarterly, 27,* 538–547.
Amis, M. (1984). *Money: A Suicide Note.* London: Jonathan Cape.
Argyris, C. (1964). *Integrating the Individual and the Organization.* New York: Wiley.
Arnold, J. (1985). Tales of the unexpected: surprises experienced by graduates in the early months of employment. *British Journal of Guidance and Counselling, 13,* 308–319.
Arnold, J. (1986). Getting started: how graduates adjust to employment. *Personnel Review, 15*(1), 16–20.
Baron, J. N., Davis-Blak, A., and Bielby, W. T. (1986). The structure of opportunity: how promotion ladders vary within and among organizations. *Administrative Science Quarterly, 31,* 248–273.
Bray, D. W., Campbell, R. J., and Grant, D. L. (1974). *Formative Years in Business.* New York: Wiley.
Brett, J. M. (1980). The effect of job transfer on employees and their families. In C. L. Cooper and R. Payne (eds.), *Current Concerns in Occupational Stress.* London: Wiley.
Brett, J. M. (1982). Job transfer and well-being. *Journal of Applied Psychology, 67,* 450–463.
Brett, J. M. (1984). Job transitions and personal and role development. In K. Rowland and J. Ferris (eds.), *Research in Personnel and Human Resource Management,* Vol. 2. Greenwich, CT: JAI, pp. 155–185.
Brett, J. M., and Werbel, J. D. (1978). The effect of job transfers on employees and their families. Technical report to the Employee Relocation Council, Washington, DC.
Brewin, C. (1980). Work role transitions and stress in managers: illustrations from the clinic. *Personnel Review, 9*(5), 27–30.
Brousseau, K. R. (1983). Toward a dynamic model of job–person relationships: findings, research questions, and implications for work system design. *Academy of Management Review, 8,* 33–45.
Brown, D., and Brooks, L. (eds.) (1984). *Career Choice and Development.* San Francisco: Jossey-Bass.
Brown, M. C. (1982). Administrative succession and organizational performance: the succession effect. *Administrative Science Quarterly, 27,* 1–16.
Burke, R. J. (1974). Personnel job transfers: some data and recommendations. *Studies in Personnel Psychology, 6,* 35–46.
Csikszentmihalyi, M., and Beattie, O. V. (1979). Life themes: a theoretical and empirical exploration of their origins and effects. *Journal of Humanistic Psychology, 19,* 45–63.
Dawis, R. V., and Lofquist, L. H. (1984). *A Psychological Theory of Work Adjustment.* Minneapolis: University of Minnesota Press.
Edstrom, A., and Galbraith, J. R. (1977). Transfer of managers as a coordination and control strategy in multinational reorganizations. *Administrative Science Quarterly, 22,* 248–263.
Feldman, D. C. (1976). A contingency theory of socialization. *Administrative Science Quarterly, 21,* 433–452.
Feldman, D. C., and Brett, J. M. (1983). Coping with new jobs: a comparative study of new hires and job changers. *Academy of Management Journal, 26,* 258–272.

Fineman, S. (1983). *White Collar Unemployment: Impact and Stress.* Chichester: Wiley.

Frese, M. (1982). Occupational socialization and psychological development: an underemphasized research perspective in industrial psychology. *Journal of Occupational Psychology, 55,* 209–224.

Frese, M. (1984). Transitions in jobs, occupational socialization and strain. In V. L. Allen and E. van de Vliert (eds.), *Role Transitions: Explorations and Explanations.* London: Plenum.

Gabarro, J. N. (1985). When a new manager takes charge. *Harvard Business Review, 63*(3), 110–123.

Gergen, K. J. (1980). The emerging crisis in life-span developmental theory. In P. B. Baltes and O. G. Brim (eds.), *Life-Span Development and Behaviour,* Vol. 3. London: Academic.

Glaser, B. G., and Strauss, A. L. (1971). *Status Passage.* Chicago: Aldine.

Gottfredson, L. S. (1977). Circumscription and compromise: a developmental theory of occupational aspirations. *Journal of Counselling Psychology Monograph, 28,* 545–579.

Gottfredson, L. S., and Becker, H. J. (1981). A challenge to vocational psychology: how important are aspirations in determining male career development? *Journal of Vocational Behaviour, 18,* 121–137.

Grusky, O. (1963). Managerial succession and organizational effectiveness. *American Journal of Sociology, 69,* 21–31.

Guerrier, Y., and Philpot, N. (1978). *The British Manager: Careers and Mobility.* London: British Institute of Management.

Hall, D. T. (1971). A theoretical model of career subidentity development in organizational settings. *Organizational Behavior and Human Performance, 6,* 50–76.

Hall, D. T. (1976). *Careers in Organizations.* Pacific Palisades, CA: Goodyear.

Hall, D. T., and Schneider, B. (1973). *Organizational Climates and Careers: The Work Lives of Priests.* New York: Seminar.

Hartley, J. F. (1981). Career transitions among managers over forty. In C. L. Cooper and D. Torrington (eds.), *Over 40: The Time For Achievement.* Chichester: Wiley.

Hedberg, B. (1984). Career dynamics in a steelworks of the future. *Journal of Occupational Behaviour, 5,* 53–59.

Hirschman, A. O. (1970). *Exit, Voice and Loyalty.* Cambridge, MA: Harvard University Press.

Holland, J. L. (1973/1985). *Making Vocational Choices: A Theory of Careers,* 1st and 2nd eds. Englewood Cliffs, NJ: Prentice-Hall.

Holmes, T. H., and Rahe, R. H. (1967). The social readjustment scale. *Journal of Psychosomatic Research, 11,* 213–218.

Hopson, B., and Adams, J. (1976). Towards an understanding of transition: defining some boundaries of transition dynamics. In J. Adams, J. Hayes, and B. Hopson (eds.), *Transition.* London: Robertson.

Jennings, E. E. (1967). *The Mobile Manager: A Study of the New Generation of Top Executives.* New York: Appleton.

Jones, G. R. (1986). Socialization tactics, self-efficacy, and newcomers' adjustments to organizations. *Academy of Management Review, 29,* 262–279.

Kanner, A. D., Coyne, J. C., Schaefer, C., and Lazarus, R. S. (1981). Comparison of two modes of stress measurement: daily hassles and uplifts versus major life events. *Journal of Behavioral Medicine, 4*(1), 1–39.

Kanter, R. M. (1977). *Men and Women of the Corporation.* New York: Basic Books.

Kanter, R. M. (1984). *The Change Masters.* London: Unwin.

Karasek, R. A. (1979). Job demands, job decision latitude, and mental strain: implications for job redesign. *Administrative Science Quarterly, 24,* 285–304.

Katz, R. (1980). Time and work: toward an integrative perspective. In B. M. Staw and L. L. Cummings (eds.), *Research in Organizational Behavior,* Vol. 2. Greenwich, CT: JAI.

Keller, R. T., and Holland, W. E. (1981). Job change: a naturally occurring field experiment. *Human Relations, 34,* 1053–1067.

Kirjonen, J., and Hanninen, V. (1986). Getting a better job: antecedents and effects. *Human Relations, 39,* 503–516.

Kohn, M. L., and Schooler, C. (1983). *Work and Personality.* Norwood, NJ: Ablex.

Krau, E. (1983). The attitudes toward work in career transitions. *Journal of Vocational Behavior, 23,* 270–285.

Latack, J. C. (1984). Career transitions within organizations: an exploratory study of work, nonwork and coping strategies. *Organizational Behavior and Human Performance, 34* 296–322.

Latack, J. C., and Dozier, J. B. (1986). After the axe falls: job loss as a career transition. *Academy of Management Review, 11*, 375–392.

Levinson, D. J., Darrow, C. N., Klein, E. G., Levinson, M. H., and McKee, B. (1978). *The Seasons of a Man's Life.* New York: Knopf.

Lieberman, S. (1956). The effect of changes in roles on the attitudes of role occupants. *Human Relations, 9*, 385–402.

Louis, M. R. (1980a). Career transitions: varieties and commonalities. *Academy of Management Review, 5*, 329–340.

Louis, M. R. (1980b). Surprise and sense-making: what newcomers experience in entering unfamiliar organizational settings. *Administrative Science Quarterly, 25*, 226–251.

Mansfield, R. (1971). Career development in the first year at work. *Occupational Psychology, 45*, 139–149.

Marshall, J., and Cooper, C. L. (1976). The mobile manager and his wife. *Management Decision, 14*(4), 4–48.

Mihal, W. L., Sorce, P. A., and Comte, T. E. (1984). A process model of individual career decision making. *Academy of Management Review, 9*, 95–103.

Miller, D. C., and Form, W. H. (1951). *Industrial Sociology.* New York: Harper & Row.

Mintzberg, H. (1973). *The Nature of Managerial Work.* New York: Harper & Row.

Mobley, W. H., Griffith, R. W., Hand, N. H., and Meglino, B. M. (1979). Review and conceptual analysis of the employee turnover process. *Psychological Bulletin, 86*, 493–522.

Moreland, R. L., and Levine, J. M. (1983). Socialization in small groups: temporal changes in individual–group relations. *Advances in Experimental Social Psychology, 15*, 137–192.

Mortimer, J. T., Lorence, J., and Kumka, D. S. (1986). *Work, Family and Personality.* New York: Ablex.

Murray, J. L., Powers, E. A., and Havinghurst, R. J. (1971). Personal and situational factors producing flexible careers. *The Gerontologist, 11*(4), 4–12.

Newcomb, T. M. (1958). Attitude development as a function of reference groups: the Bennington study. In E. E. Maccoby, T. M. Newcomb, and E. L. Hartley (eds.), *Readings in Social Psychology*, 3rd ed. New York: Holt, Rinehart and Winston, pp. 265–275.

Nicholson, N. (1984). A theory of work role transitions. *Administrative Science Quarterly, 29*, 172–191.

Nicholson, N. (1986). Turning points, traps and tunnels: the significance of work role transitions in the lives of individuals and organisations. In H. W. Schroiff and G. Debus (eds.), *Proceedings of the West European Conference on Work and Organization.* Amsterdam: North-Holland.

Nicholson, N. (1987a). Good and bad practices in graduate development. *Personnel Management*, February, pp. 34–38.

Nicholson, N. (1987b). The transition cycle: a conceptual framework for the analysis of change and human resources management. In K. M. Rowland and G. R. Ferris (eds.), *Research in Personnel and Human Resources Management*, Vol. 5. Greenwich, CT: JAI.

Nicholson, N., and Arnold, J. M. (in press a). Graduate entry and adjustment to corporate life. *Personnel Review.*

Nicholson, N., and Arnold, J. M. (in press b). Graduate early experience in a multinational corporation. *Personnel Review.*

Nicholson, N., and West, M. A. (1985). Life stories. *New Society, 70*, 1146.

Nicholson, N., and West, M. A. (1988). *Managerial Job Change.* London: Cambridge University Press.

Nicholson, N., West, M. A., and Cawsey, T. F. (1985). Future uncertain: expected versus attained job mobility among managers. *Journal of Occupational Psychology, 58*, 313–320.

Onions, C. T. (1966). *The Oxford Dictionary of English Etymology.* London: Oxford University Press.

Osherson, S. (1980). *Holding On or Letting Go: Men and Career Change at Midlife.* New York: Free.

Pinder, C. C. (1977). Multiple predictors of post-transfer satisfaction: the rule of urban factors. *Personnel Psychology, 30*, 543–556.

Pinder, C. C. (1981). Mobility and transfer. In H. Meltzer and W. Nord (eds.), *Making Organizations Humane and Productive*. New York: Wiley.

Pinder, C. C., and Walter, G. A. (1984). Personnel transfers and employee development. In J. Ferris and K. Rowland (eds.), *Research in Personnel and Human Resources Management*, Vol. 2. Greenwich, CT: JAI, pp. 187–218.

Presthus, R. (1978). *The Organizational Society*. New York: St. Martins.

Raelin, J. A. (1980). *Building a Career*. Kalamazoo, MI: Upjohn Institute for Employment Research.

Rapoport, R. (1970). *Mid-Career Development*. London: Tavistock.

Richards, E. W. (1984a). Undergraduate preparation and early career outcomes: a study of recent college graduates. *Journal of Vocational Behavior, 24*, 279–304.

Richards, E. W. (1984b). Early employment situations and work role satisfactions among recent college graduates. *Journal of Vocational Behavior, 24*, 305–318.

Riegel, K. F. (1975). Adult life crises: a dialectical interpretation of development. In N. Datan and L. H. Ginsberg (eds.), *Life-Span Developmental Psychology: Normative Life Crises*. New York: Academic.

Robbins, P. T., Thomas, L. E., Harvey, D. W., and Kandefer, C. (1978). Career change and congruence of personality type: an examination of the DOT-derived work environment designations. *Journal of Vocational Behavior, 13*, 15–25.

Rosenbaum, J. E. (1979). Tournament mobility: career patterns in a corporation. *Administrative Science Quarterly, 24*, 220–241.

Rosenbaum, J. E. (1984). *Career Mobility in a Corporate Hierarchy*. New York: Academic.

Rothstein, W. G. (1980). The significance of occupations in work careers: an empirical and theoretical review. *Journal of Vocational Behavior, 17*, 328–343.

Rychlak, J. F. (1982). *Personality and Life Style of Young Male Managers: A Logical Learning Theory Analysis*. New York: Academic.

Sarbin, T. R. (1984). Role transitions as social drama. In V. L. Allen and E. van de Vliert (eds.), *Role Transitions*. New York: Plenum.

Sathe, V. (1985). How to decipher and change corporate culture. In R. H. Kilman, M. J. Saxton, R. Serpa, and associates (eds.), *Gaining Control of the Corporate Culture*. San Francisco: Jossey-Bass.

Schein, E. H. (1967). Attitude change during management education: a study of organizational influences on student attitudes. *Administrative Science Quarterly, 11*, 601–628.

Schein, E. H. (1971a). Occupational socialization in the professions: the case of the role innovator. *Journal of Psychiatric Research, 8*, 521–530.

Schein, E. H. (1971b). The individual, the organization, and the career: a conceptual scheme. *Journal of Applied Behavioral Science, 7*, 401–426.

Schein, E. H. (1978). *Career Dynamics: Matching Individual and Organizational Needs*. Reading, MA: Addison-Wesley.

Schein, E. H. (1985). *Organizational Culture and Leadership*. San Francisco: Jossey-Bass.

Schlossberg, N. K. (1984). *Counseling Adults in Transition: Linking Practice with Theory*. New York: Springer.

Scholl, R. W. (1983). Career lines and employment stability. *Academy of Management Journal, 26*, 86–103.

Sell, R. R. (1983). Transferred jobs: a neglected aspect of migration and occupational change. *Work and Occupations, 10*, 179–206.

Sheehy, G. (1975). *Passages: Predictable Crises in Adult Life*. New York: Dutton.

Sheehy, G. (1981). *Pathfinders*. New York: Morrow.

Starr, J. M. (1983). Toward a social phenomenology of aging: studying the self process in biographical work. *International Journal of Aging and Human Development, 16*, 255–270.

Strauss, A. L. (1959). *Mirrors and Masks: The Search for Identity*. Glencoe, IL: Free.

Super, D. E. (1957). *The Psychology of Careers*. New York: Harper & Row.

Toffler, B. L. (1981). Occupational role development: the changing determinants of outcomes for the individual. *Administrative Science Quarterly, 26*, 396–418.

Vaitenas, R., and Wiener, Y. (1977). Developmental, emotional, and interest factors in voluntary mid-career change. *Journal of Vocational Behavior, 11*, 291–304.

Van Maanen, J. (1976). Breaking-in: socialization to work. In R. Dubin (ed.), *Handbook of Work, Organization, and Society*. Chicago: Rand McNally.

Van Maanen, J., and Schein, E. H. (1979). Toward a theory of organizational socialization. In B. M. Staw (ed.), *Research in Organizational Behavior*, Volume 1. Greenwich, CT: JAI, pp. 209–264.

Veiga, J. F. (1981). Plateaued versus nonplateaued managers: career patterns, attitudes, and path potential. *Academy of Management Journal, 24*, 566–578.

Veiga, J. F. (1983). Mobility influences during managerial career stages. *Academy of Management Journal, 26*, 64–85.

Viney, L. L. (1980). *Transitions*. New South Wales: Cassell Australia.

Vroom, V., and Deci, E. (1971). The stability of post-decision dissonance: a follow-up study of job attitudes of business school graduates. *Organizational Behavior and Human Performance, 6*, 36–49.

Vroom, V. H. (1964). *Work and Motivation*. New York: Wiley.

Vroom, V. H. (1966). Organizational choice: a study of pre- and post-decision processes. *Organizational Behavior and Human Performance, 1*, 212–225.

Warner, W. L., and Abegglen, J. (1955). *Occupational Mobility in American Business and Industry*. Minneapolos, MN: University of Minnesota Press.

Warr, P. B. (1987). *Work, Unemployment and Mental Health*. Oxford: Oxford University Press.

Watson, C. A., and Garbin, A. P. (1981). The job selection process: a conceptual reapproachment of labor turnover and occupational choice. *Human Relations, 34*(11), 1001–1011.

Watts, A. G. (1981). Career patterns. In A. G. Watts, D. E. Super, and J. M. Kidd (eds.), *Career Development in Britain*. Cambridge: Hobsons, pp. 213–245.

Werbel, J. D. (1983). Job change: a study of an acute job stressor. *Journal of Vocational Behavior, 23*, 242–250.

West, M. A., Nicholson, N., and Rees, A. (1987). Transitions into newly created jobs. *Journal of Occupational Psychology, 60*, 97–113.

West, M. A., and Savage, Y. (1987). Innovation among health care professionals. Paper presented at Third West European Congress on the Psychology of Work and Organization, Antwerp, April 1987.

White, R. W. (1952). *Lives in Progress*. New York: Dryden.

10   Career system profiles and strategic staffing

JEFFREY A. SONNENFELD

INTRODUCTION

A career does not exist in a social vacuum but is in many ways directed by the employer's staffing priorities. Over a quarter of the U.S. work force is thought to hold continuing employment with the same employer for over 20 years (Hall, 1982). Given this pattern of long service with a single employer, it seems logical that emphasis should be placed upon the notion of career systems, paths through which employees progress during their term of employment within an organization. Despite the importance of career systems for the individual and the organization, however, we know very little about the dynamics of employment conditions within which firms define opportunities and equip people for changing assignments. In particular, we often fail to explain the wide variation in career system practices across employers. Differences in human resource management approaches, from firm entry to exit, are not arbitrary company features but rather reflect strategic staffing choices.

In order to more clearly understand these variations in policy, we might find it useful to propose a framework for interpreting the HRM policies of different companies. Such a framework would define the factors that influence career paths and show how they interact to produce a coherent HRM strategy and set of policies (Walton and Lawrence, 1985). These factors include the way in which employees enter and exit a firm as well as the process of development they undergo in the course of their term of employment. In this chapter we look at two critical dimensions of career movements across firms: first, the movement between outside labor supply and the firm, the "supply flow," and second, the movement across job assignments and promotions within the firm, the "assignment flow." The interaction of these two dynamic mechanisms provides for a four-cell typology of career systems. It is hypothesized that this typology is a human resource projection of the different choices firms make in managing their strategic context. Firms have an implicit career system that guides staffing decisions appropriate to the strategy. The career system profiles extracted from the typology both describe and predict a company's work force composition.

DEFINING CAREER SYSTEMS

Career systems refer to the dynamic aspects of human resource management (HRM) policies. The career system focuses on the changing, longitudinal issues regarding the creation and maintenance of the firm's membership. Its activities can be clustered into three functions: (1) entry, which includes human resource planning, recruiting, and selection; (2) development, which involves socialization, training, career planning, succession planning, and promotions; and (3) exit,

202

which includes retirement, layoffs, resignations, and dismissal (Sonnenfeld, 1984, 1985). A well-developed career system coordinates staffing activities into a process that helps the firm adapt its membership to its environment.

However, the HRM-oriented research on company practice rarely takes a systemic approach to careers. This research has generally taught us more about individual employees than firms. The important HRM research on careers has highlighted the approaches for managing a specific activity, but not the coordination of these activities into a total organizational system. In this chapter we consider some of the leading contributors to our understanding of specific career activities. Throughout the review, we see large, unanswered theoretical questions about the total career system. We then call for an expanded view of career systems that embraces a more theoretical approach.

Entry. Studies of strategic human resource management (Tichy, Fombrun, and Devanna, 1982; see also Fombrun, Tichy, and Devanna, 1984) suggest firms can forecast their staffing needs by combining an internal membership audit with a review of the external labor market and the corporate strategic plan. Once gaps are identified, the firm can begin to specify its recruiting needs. The degree of required skill and experience should determine where firms look for talent. Campus recruiting, newspaper advertising, professional networks, employment agencies, and executive search firms yield different pools of candidates (Schwab, 1982). Furthermore, less obvious variables such as company image, recruiter knowledge of the employing firm, candidate appearance (i.e., race, ethnicity, age, attractiveness) must be anticipated to ensure that accurate exchange of information takes place (Beehr and Gilmore, 1982; Dipboye, 1982; Orpen, 1982; Weiner and Schneiderman, 1974). The socialization of newcomers hired is enhanced if, in the recruitment process, realistic job previews are used to convey appropriate employment expectations (Kotter, 1973; Wanous, 1980).

Several unanswered theoretical questions remain despite such rich, prescriptive research. For instance, why do many firms hire to fill particular vacancies while others hire to fill career tracks? Why do some firms rely regularly on outside sources and thus seek to "buy" rather than "make" the skills they need? Finally, how can incumbent members see past their blinders to recognize a need for membership different from themselves?

Development. The next research cluster refers to an even larger set of activities. Most HRM career literature addresses a specific developmental activity such as promotion, assignments, training, succession, and career planning (Sonnenfeld, 1984, 1985). In perhaps the most comprehensive approach, Schein (1978) suggests three fundamental dimensions of career mobility within a firm: (1) increasing centrality and acceptance to the core membership; (2) lateral movement across functions; and (3) hierarchical ascension through promotions. Schein offers a cone-shaped figure to represent these three forms of mobility. Taking a different but equally inclusive approach, Hall (1986b) argues for linking the selection and development of top-level executives to a firm's strategic planning process. Only such an integrated system leads to executive learning that has meaning for both the individual and the firm.

Rather than build on the conceptual view of the total firm, the leading researchers revert to examination of the individual experience. Veiga's (1983) research argues that career stages in an employee's life lead to preferences for different forms of mobility. For example, centrality and acceptance may be especially salient to newcomers. Older members may be less interested in hierarchical advancement that requires relocation. Hence they may prefer growth through lateral movements. Similarly, Driver (1979) proposes that some workers may prefer lateral assignments through their careers while others are interested in lateral movements only if blended with an upward move. Driver calls the first group holders of a "transitory" career concept and the second group holders of a "spiral" career concept. Those interested strictly in upward hierarchical movement are labeled "linears"; those not moving at all are labeled "steady-staters." Research on these steady staters or low-mobility employees has distinguished high-performing "solid citizens" from poor-performing "deadwood" (Ference, Stoner, and Warren, 1977).

Other researchers have looked at outcomes of different functions. The initial successes of early assignments of managers was one of the best predictors of later career success at AT&T (Bray, Campbell, and Grant, 1973). As valuable as this research was, we learned not about AT&T as a career system but about individual differences in a given system. Research on the specific learning for various general management assignments shows that such conditions as start-ups, turnarounds, or project teams develop different sets of leadership skills (McCall, Lombardo, and Morrison, 1988). Research on engineers indicates that different career paths may apply to technical professionals. For example, some may desire to select out of the technical pool into a managerial track, while others may require development that updates professional skills (Bailyn, 1980; Dalton, Thompson, and Price, 1977; Raelin, 1986).

Formal training and education in industry appears in a variety of settings from in-house seminars to campus-based university programs, independent of a coherent concept of the firm as a career system. The selection of the source of training, the identification of which employee groups receive how much training, the timing of the interventions in the course of one's career, and the employees' involvement in the design and the delivery of the training vary greatly (Sonnenfeld and Ingols, 1986). Research suggests that less confidence in the continued value of one's skills, a better understanding of the purpose of one's training, and greater involvement in the learning process enhance receptivity to retraining (Hill and Sonnenfeld, 1986). Asking what are the organizational rather than individual implications of training, Ingols (1987) finds that the selection and participation in training programs carry powerful symbolic messages in a firm. Nonselection can communicate equally significant signals that need to be acknowledged and managed.

In practice, many companies have attempted to coordinate these HRM activities with an employee's personal career concerns through career planning programs. These programs facilitate individual development and encourage employees to be more willing and prepared for change. Shared information regarding job opportunities reduces the likelihood of skill obsolescence, traumatic disappointments, the hoarding of valuable talent by a given boss, and unfair discrimination in personnel decisions. These programs can involve a variety of techniques, focusing either on the employee through such vehicles as workbooks and self-assessment and testing instruments or on the career system through job postings, career paths, employee evaluations, and career counseling (London and Stumpf,

1982; Walker and Gutteridge, 1979). High-potential talent can be monitored, and the lost potential of exhausted laborers may be replenished.

Succession planning programs prepare replacement candidates for key positions. However, rarely do the career planning programs tie into corporate succession planning programs. Hence another disjointed intervention. Furthermore, research shows that even comparably sized *Fortune 500* firms vary along such dimensions as formalization of the succession process, the type of promotion criteria used, and the role of staff in shepherding the process. Neither financial performance nor corporate reputation seem to be enhanced with the greater formalization of these programs (Friedman, 1984, 1986).

Unanswered theoretical questions across these development activities abound. Why do some firms spend great sums of money and allocate sheltered time for training while others routinely spare such expenses? Some firms will build up layers of management preparing to move people into positions as they become vacant while other firms recoil at the thought of an underemployed "bench squad." Why are some firms net producers of talent and others are net consumers? In general, we better understand how individuals vary in their responses to the same opportunities for advancement in a given firm, but why do firms differ in the array of opportunities they offer?

Exit. Like entry and developmental issues, the interpretation of behaviors that lead to exit from firms is complex. For example, turnover rates are sometimes symptomatic of underlying organizational pathologies (Price, 1971), but at other times they reflect a normal flow for that industry. Retirement procedures and the recourse to layoffs vary greatly across firms in periods of crisis (Cappelli, 1985; Sonnenfeld, 1988). Research shows that the firm needs to continue to maintain core HRM functions, redesign work, develop teams, and selectively innovate while simultaneously responding to increasing pressures of scarcity and time. During a layoff strategies for developing and retraining key personnel and inspiring survivors require promptness and imagination (Gilmore and Hirshorn, 1984). Only the individual cost of job loss has been well studied (e.g., Brenner, 1973); however, the ramifications of firm-initiated exit also extend to the firm itself. Such results as lowered morale and aversion to risk taking and innovation among employees have a prolonged impact upon the organization, and by addressing issues of forced exit, the firm can avert the lasting consequences of poor planning.

The missing link in HRM research. There have been insightful recommendations for better linking staffing practices with corporate strategic and organizational priorities. However, these pragmatic writings do not offer overall theoretical perspectives on the firm (Lorange and Murphy, 1984; Miller, 1984). Before suggesting optimal practices for career system management, we must understand why firms make implicit choices that are so different. Variations in career system practices may result from poor management and mistakes, or they may be the result of rational and appropriate choices. In general, HRM research has focused on descriptions of fragments of career systems, leading at times to prescriptions for improved managerial practice. But the overall coordination of these activities into a coherent plan to support the strategy of the firm has not been addressed in the HRM research. This research lacks a theory of the firm as a career system. Schein (1985) gives support to this criticism:

How does better theory come about? . . . we need to build concepts and models around what I call the "realities" of how things really work in organizations. We need more and better descriptive studies of how things work so that concepts and models mirror what really goes on rather than what we normatively wish would go on. Being normative is very comfortable until one starts to take the concept of culture seriously. One then discovers that the career field is shot through with cultural biases . . . Different authors focus on very different aspects, all under the single label of career research and theory. (p. 317)

The HRM research regarding careers presumes common values regarding labor supply and labor assignment. For example, researchers often assume employment security and internal development should be corporate goals for improved internal resource management, regardless of firm or industry. The missing link, then, is that such common assumptions fail to differentiate among differing staffing objectives across firms. These differing objectives can be examined through two systemic dimensions: supply flow (entry and exit) and assignment flow (internal movement) of labor.

Two schools of thought dominate supply flow theory. Rarely do they address each other. One focuses on the external supply of labor and includes the status attainment, neoclassical, and human capital schools of thought. The second school of thought focuses on internal supply of labor and includes institutional economics, transactional costs, internal labor market, and human relations theory. Each school of thought is enlightening, and perhaps accurate, when applied to particular aspects of careers or to specific firms. The problem is, however, that contrasting realities require differing models and concepts. The typology offered in this chapter suggests when each school of thought is relevant to a particular situation. Similarly, the movement within the firm – assignment flow – is explained by such widely different approaches as strategic choice, structure, vacancy chains, and the process of competitive tournaments. Whether scholars examine supply or assignment, they emphasize the external context, internal firm structure, or internal firm process to explain career system dynamics. Depending on their theoretical orientation, they will then study only the relevant career system levers. For example, theoretical emphasis on external context leads to research on recruitment from the outside. By contrast, theory focused on internal firm processes will lead to research on assignments and promotions. In essence, the typology that follows categorizes organizations according to the ways in which they manage careers.

SUPPLY FLOW AND CAREER SYSTEMS

Supply flow: external contexts

In this section, we examine the movement of workers from the external environment into the firm – supply flow. Supply flow denotes the attributes workers acquire before entry to the firm. Three schools of thought look at worker attributes. At the end of this chapter we show how each of these schools is relevant in given firms.

The wider career context has been studied by sociologists and by economists through the long-standing fields of inquiry labeled "status attainment theory," "human capital theory," and "credentials theory." While the status attainment school is decades older than human capital theory and far more attentive to the deterministic role of family background, the two schools share a common emphasis upon the societal factors that overtake the influence of career system activities of the firm.

The status attainment school is a direct outgrowth of the explorations of the pioneers of sociology. Intergenerational occupational mobility has been a key variable in the studies of transitions from traditional societies where occupational roles are ascribed to modern industrial societies where occupations are more freely chosen (Durkheim, 1902; Eisenstadt, 1966; Firth, 1939; Malinowski, 1932; Marx, 1867; Parsons, 1959; Simmel, 1950; Sorokin, 1947; Tönnies, 1935; Weber, 1922).

This concept of intergenerational change, labeled "vertical mobility" (Sorokin, 1947), guided a long stream of research on occupational roles. Such research echoed the findings that while there were no rigidly prescribed occupational roles, social class is an important determinant of occupational attainment and the careers of children closely resemble those of their fathers (Blau, 1956; Blau and Duncan, 1967; Davidson and Anderson, 1937; Hollingshead, 1951; Jencks et al., 1972, 1979; Lipset and Bendix, 1959; Miller and Form, 1951; Mills, 1945; Rogoff, 1955; Sewell, Haller, and Ohlendorf, 1970; Warner and Abegglen, 1955). Social class, as measured through father's occupation and education, was found to predict a person's first job, which in turn could predict one's current job. The status attainment literature suggests that social class affects both the shaping of individual career values as well as the occupational opportunities available to the individual.

This research has been criticized for its inability to explain later status changes of individuals once they begin employment as well as on the measurement of occupational status and the imprecision over the process by which social status actually operates. In essence, social status attainment research has overlooked five critical elements in making structural explanations of career development.

First, social status researchers generally fail to consider that occupational status shifts across occupations over time. The popular Duncan Occupational Status Scale used by Jencks et al. (1979) and many others was based on 1950 data. On the scale, an engineer drops down in status with a promotion up the management ranks. Second, these researchers generally neglect any changes of individual occupational status within one's career. Studies comparing career success of fathers to sons at different points in their lives may be highlighting career stage differences and not intergenerational mobility. Third, status attainment researchers virtually ignore changes in occupational status patterns due to structural transformations in the economy (e.g., the tremendous decline in the agricultural and manufacturing sectors while the service sector work force grows swiftly). Fourth, despite the fact that social structure is inferred by studies of individuals, social status research has largely overlooked the shifts in career values in our society that have led to more heterogeneity in the definition of career success (Weiss, Harwood, and Riesman, 1971; Yankelovich, 1979). Fifth, and most important, regardless of how occupational status is measured, an occupation itself is probably not the proper unit of analysis to study career attainment. Salary grades and cultural attributes may lead to the relative valuation of the same jobs differently across firms and across industries (Rosenbaum, 1984; Schein, 1985). The most relevant occupational status hierarchy for many is that developed within the firm (Kanter, 1977; Vroom and Macrimmon, 1968).

Furthermore, it is more sensible to study career attainment within occupations or organizational hierarchies because this is where most of the advancement occurs, not between occupations (Spilerman, 1977; Spenner, 1981). Even status attainment researcher Jencks (1972, 1979) acknowledged that two-thirds of income variation was within occupational groups. This emphasis on status attainment has been located only on the supply side of labor, that is, worker attributes, but not on the demand for labor by the firm as expressed through job specifications and the decision process that matches workers to jobs (Granovetter, 1981, 1982).

Unlike sociologists, economists have been less enamored of intergenerational occupational mobility. Nonetheless, some parallel problems appear as, once again, the firm is underestimated. Neoclassical economic theories do not deny the existence of the firm, but the theory attributes only a rational, technical relationship between labor's price and its use by the employer. Labor as a factor input is thought to be limited by its productivity and price. Labor is utilized until the marginal contribution of the labor no longer exceeds the marginal costs. This free flow of labor from the external market into the firm has been challenged by a wide variety of institutionists (economists and historians) who have identified external factors such as government, trade unions, and geographical distance, which produce constraints on such hire–fire freedom, as well as by the growth of internal labor markets as an adaptive response to decentralized, multidivisional firms (Caves, 1980; Chandler, 1962, 1977; Doeringer and Piore, 1971; Galbraith, 1967; Gordon, 1972; Piore, 1975; Thurow, 1975; Williamson, 1975). The use of training, job ladders for skills and advancement, and hierarchies of authority minimize costly turnover. The transaction costs of hiring and firing and the subsequent loss of human capital investments and expense of additional recruitment are kept to a minimum. Furthermore, the firm gains more efficient talent allocation and greater firm loyalty than class loyalty. Thus,

only the small periphery establishments, without internal labor markets, would operate along the lines of neoclassical theory. It has been suggested that these firms would have few well-defined promotion lattices, fewer levels of supervision, and relatively low skill requirements. Individual attributes such as "trainability" and long-run commitment to the firm should be less important criteria for selection. (Baron and Bielby, 1980, p. 747)

Human capital theory builds upon such neoclassical frameworks to suggest that a labor market represents open opportunity to all workers. A worker's career attainment is thus largely a function of hard effort, ability, education, and training. Human capital is increased by individuals themselves as they invest in education and training (Becker, 1964; Mincer, 1974; and Wachter, 1974). Individuals are thought to concentrate their investments in costly formal education early in their careers and thus amortize this investment throughout their career. No barriers are thought to exist for individuals with ability and education. This complete opening has been challenged by the work on segmented and dual labor markets where advancement, training, and employment security are thought to be accessible only to upper and middle segments of the work force (Doeringer and Piore, 1971; Piore, 1975, 1979; Piore and Sable, 1984). These theorists propose instead (1) a secondary labor market of transient, low-paying, dead-end jobs; (2) a lower tier of the primary labor market with routine but steady jobs connected to promising job ladders; and (3) an upper tier of the primary labor market with high-status jobs associated with high, voluntary interfirm mobility. Furthermore, research has found that firms will pay seniority premiums to workers that are not cost justified through productivity increases with experience (Lazear, 1981; Medoff and Abraham, 1980).

Recent research on the impact of status attainment of structural variables beyond investments in education show differences by occupation, industry, and firm (Beck, Horan, Tolbert, 1978; Spenner, Otto, and Call, 1982; Stolzenberg, 1978). Thurow's (1975) job competition model suggests that people acquire the enhanced human capital which jobs confer to new incumbents once they obtain the position. The position's wage is determined, and then a candidate is found. The wage is not set based on the human capital of this individual but rather on the utility of the job. Furthermore, human capital theory seems to make no use of the signaling value of educational credentials as an index of employee potential or label of social background rather than merely as an indicator of valued knowledge (Berg, 1971; Bowles and Gintis, 1976; Collins, 1979; Kanter, 1977; Spence, 1974). Rosenbaum's (1984) study of a single firm's career system raises several challenges to the human capital theory. Job training, for example, did not correspond with salary differences. The amount of education only mattered before interviewing for a job in an organization. Furthermore, differences in positional attainment preceded differentials in earnings. Finally, employees who took lower initial earnings in their first years attained lower, not higher, relative job status. No trade-off between earnings and job training was found as predicted by the theory. Rewards were stratified by position throughout the career and acted as a function of training or experience. Granovetter (1974, 1981) has suggested that some people enter firms through networks of personal contacts, tend to stay if they are better integrated in these networks, and advance through better matches with positions given the superior information passed along through personal contacts.

Supply flow: internal structure and processes

In this section, we first consider perspectives on the purposes leading to the creation of internal labor markets. Internal labor markets represent an extreme form of supply where hiring is restricted to lower, entry-level positions and higher status positions are filled through internal development. Next we review the newly accumulated wisdom on these structures. Having argued that the status attainment and human capital schools have failed to account for the role of the firm as a career system, we shall examine the development of internal labor markets more closely. Perhaps the more traditional sociological and economic theories appropriately described the employment relationship before the development of these internal labor markets. Furthermore, neoclassical theorists may yet characterize firms that have not developed sophisticated internal markets. Social theorists dating back to Durkheim (1902) and Weber (1922) articulated the advantages to the employer of lifetime employment and internal development within large organizations of specialized workers. Sophisticated internal markets did not become commonplace until far more recently. The iconoclastic utopian employer, Robert Owen (1929), wrote of his integrated work community New Lanark, "if due care to the state of the inanimate machines can produce such beneficial results, what may not be expected if you devote equal attention to your vital machines?" (p. 8).

There are two prominent theories – one of management efficiency and one of class control – that have been advanced to explain the transition to internal labor markets. This chapter concludes by agreeing with a third implicit theory that combines the two to form an institutional perspective of mutual gain.

The management efficiency argument (Chandler, 1962, 1977; Williamson, 1975) suggests that internal labor markets are an efficient solution to the problems of managing complex environments given the industrial growth that brought about the modern multidivisional firm guided by management capitalism rather than the earlier family (or financial) capitalism. Chandler (1977) states that the modern business enterprise came into being by internalizing and routinizing the transactions between units and lowering the costs of the transactions. Furthermore,

the advantages of internalizing the activities of many business units within a single enterprise could not be realized until a management hierarchy had been created . . . to carry out the functions formerly handled by market mechanisms . . . Thus the existence of a management hierarchy is a defining characteristic of the modern business enterprise . . . selection and promotion became increasingly based on training, experiences, performance, rather than on family relationship. With the coming of modern business enterprise, the businessman, for the first time, could conceive of a life-time career involving a climb up the hierarchical ladder. In such enterprises, management training became increasingly longer and more formalized. (pp. 7–10)

Williamson (1975) has stated this point more broadly in applying the staffing efficiency theory beyond the managerial work force. He argues that promotion hierarchies are favored over perfectly competitive labor markets because (1) neither workers nor their bosses possess sufficient information to foresee future labor supplies and their conditions; (2) employment security promotes on-the-job learning through cooperation between more skilled and less skilled workers; and (3) internal labor markets establish rules and procedures that reduce the need for monitoring and the incentive to engage in destructive, short-term opportunism by both parties.

This perspective has not gone without challenge, however. Osterman (1984) states that

taken as a whole, this approach seems unsatisfying. It is easy to establish efficiency-limiting aspects of internal market procedures. For example, seniority provisions may prevent those most able from attaining jobs in which their talents are best used. More generally, the rules and procedures of internal markets considerably limit management discretion concerning deployment of this labor force. For proponents of the efficiency-based explanation to prevail, they must assume on a matter of faith, since no data are available on costs and benefits of different procedures, that the arrangement that dominates is, by definition, the most efficient. The theory is reduced to a tautology. (p. 9)

Osterman (1984) further argues that while supportive cost data are not offered, the accessible historical record also diminishes the force of the maximizing explanations. First, employers themselves frequently waged fierce, even bloody resistance to the establishment of seniority systems, formalized wage-setting procedures, and other labor market activities. Second, the discontinuous nature of the appearance of internal labor markets around World War I and the Great Depression suggest an important role for union organizations and for government intervention in this new social creation.

Similarly, Jacoby's (1984) study of the development of internal labor markets suggested that pre–World War I employers were content with their reliance upon autocratic foremen to hold down labor costs and allowed the unstable, inequitable work conditions. A survey of firms introducing the then new scientific management principles showed no interest in improved employment practices to better mesh with the new systematization of work (Hoxie, 1915). Jacoby concluded that the erratic growth of the internal labor market reflected the limited emphasis given to employment policy by most manufacturing firms. Line managers, many of whom rose up the ranks from foremen, were hostile to the upstarts in the personnel office and the union agitators: "Often it was the unions, not management, that pushed most strongly for job ladders, wage classifications, allocation rules, and employment stability" (Jacoby, 1984, p. 39).

This worker interest in internal labor markets also presents a challenge to the class-based radical explanations for the growth of internal labor markets. These theorists argue that internal labor markets are a tool for capitalists to control a volatile work force (Edwards, 1979; Gordon et al., 1982; Marglin, 1974; Stone, 1974). They argue that the introduction of job ladders divides the work force because of the relative privileges afforded some and denied others. Furthermore, they argue job ladders legitimize top-down hierarchical control because the system appears deceptively just.

These arguments miss an interesting paradox. First, nonunion firms' managements have led some of the most innovative and progressive internal labor market improvements (Foulkes, 1980), which were greeted eagerly by workers in those firms. Second, workers themselves lobbied in heavily unionized industries (such as iron and steel) and through collective pressure encouraged employment security agreements, rigid internal promotion rules, and wage structures. Foulkes's research is consistent with findings elsewhere that unions frequently introduce workplace stability through internal labor procedures (Freeman and Medoff, 1979; Slichter, Healy, and Livernash, 1960). It is possible to see both workers and management as winners through the creation of internal labor market practices. Thus we can understand why the enthusiasm generally remains high for such policies even as union strength erodes. At the same time, these practices are far from universal, and they have been known to fade in some locations (e.g., some airlines at present). This should inspire some reflection as to where and when internal labor markets may add the greatest value. Before considering this question of applicability, we will review some of the more general lessons of research on internal labor markets.

This review of this research literature on internal labor markets finds a fair number of inconclusive theoretical fragments and often inadequate research methods. Baron (1984) suggests that we encourage comprehensive and comparative research that looks explicitly at the career system and does not revert to the individual-, industry-, or occupational-level data bases with firm inferences projected back to the reader. He cautions that the prevailing analytic approaches

are likely to experience diminishing returns, since the hypotheses of interest primarily concern why certain firms provide greater opportunities than others and why they utilize particular procedures in hiring and promotion. (p. 61)

Overall, scholars study either external markets and structures or internal markets, internal structures, or human resource management. As we turn to assignment flow, we will again see emphasis on context, structure, or process.

ASSIGNMENT FLOW AND CAREER SYSTEMS

Assignment flow: external contexts

In this section, we examine assignment flow – the movement of employees across positions and through the hierarchy once they have become employed by the firm. In any industry there are firms that compete on the basis of size through their economies of scale, while others with a small market share compete on the basis of specialist services or differentiated products (Porter, 1980). Large corporations that sell their products in concentrated markets are often referred to as "core firms" by researchers. These core firms, as career systems, typically offer high rewards for a given quality of labor, more opportunities to acquire transferable skills and more opportunities to advance within the firms' hierarchy of jobs (Oster, 1978; Ryan, 1984; Sadowski, 1982). It has been suggested that core firms create these policies to assist them in recruiting, to allow them to retain the talent they develop, to stay ahead of union pressure, and because they have ample resources to make such provisions. Greater stability on the outside is often reflected internally in the career system.

The polar opposites of these "core firms" in terms of labor market segmentation are called "periphery firms" where products face stiff competition. Advancement in these periphery firms mirrors their market competition. These periphery employers face higher turnover and thus are heavily involved in recruiting. Employees are not groomed within the firm through assignments that develop them for advancement. Training investments are made sparingly with every effort made to keep training directed toward narrow, nontransferable, immediately productive skills. Competition is so fierce job incumbents must perform optimally right away to survive and to advance. There is little time for sheltered learning. Job holders must "hit the ground running." When they fail to meet or surpass the performance of rival candidates for a position, they often leave. Many people advance by leaving for better positions at another firm.

In general, strategic considerations give priority to different career system activities. For example, the availability of appropriately skilled, professional labor can limit the firm's interest in training as well as concern with turnover. If needed skills are portable, whether high or low in the hierarchy, the firm will not risk investing in these people. They will enter with the education they need. More up-to-date expertise is recruited from the outside when needed. If needed skills are sparse in the marketplace, if company-specific knowledge is desired, or if continuity of relationships is important to corporate strategy, the firm will work to develop and retain its work force. Empirical work is needed to demonstrate these hypotheses.

Even within large, stable companies, we can see employees who are denied access to advance into the superior internal labor market. They work within a secondary sphere of more transitory, less skilled work and buffer the firms through times of expansion and contraction (Piore, 1975). At the same time, very senior management and professional ranks tend to be more voluntarily mobile across firms, with the exception of more closed "up or out" internal labor markets in several law firms studied (Doeringer and Piore, 1971; Piore, 1975; Wholey, 1985). Thus, we can find segmentation of opportunities between as well as within firms.

Assignment flow: internal structure and processes

Despite academic confusion over how organization size is studied and how it is defined (Kimberly, 1976), research indicates that higher wages, especially among manufacturers in the same industry, are paid by larger companies (Masters, 1969, Stolzenberg, 1978). Furthermore, these firms make larger investments in education. These conclusions are tentative in that we must resolve whether they are confounded by the urban location of larger companies, the commute, or other such factors.

While growth creates opportunities for all, the beneficiaries do not all share equally. Those less likely to be promoted gain most (Rosenbaum, 1979). Rosenbaum (1984), however, reported that elite college groups do not gain during times of growth, but also do not suffer during times of contraction. Growth has been found to increase the opportunities for disadvantaged workers (Shaeffer and Lynton, 1979).

Long-linked (assembly-type) technologies provide more interchangeability and greater opportunity for lateral mobility. However, mediating, intensive technologies, or more specialized professional and job shop labor arrangements, encourage more specialized credentials and hence lead to either more upward mobility or interfirm mobility (Vardi, 1980; Vardi and Hammer, 1977).

The work of career stage researchers (Dalton, Thompson, and Price, 1977; Hall, 1976; Ornstein, Cron, and Slocum, in press; Schein, 1978; Veiga, 1983) suggests that different opportunities and tasks appear at different life stages as an employee seeks to obtain, renew, and retain a membership role over time in an organization (e.g., gaining entry, becoming established, seeking new opportunities, gaining recognition, preserving reputation, and finally, planning disengagement). Changing responsibilities and personal values bring about many of these challenges.

By contrast, Rosenbaum's (1979) study of tournament mobility suggests a dynamic series of implicit competitions generated by organizational events. One's prior success in earlier trials influences one's ability to participate in later contests. However, some cultures prefer open contests, thus keeping alive opportunity for "late bloomers." Furthermore, elites and "deadwood" are pruned out quickly. Other cultures favor the efficiency of "sponsored mobility," where an elite is groomed for a series of developmental assignments following very early selection (Turner, 1960).

In a compromise position between these two theories, Rosenbaum (1984) argues that each contest progressively differentiates a cohort of employees throughout their career, each time further defining their opportunities for future attainment. Rosenbaum reports different segments enjoyed various degrees of continuity with the harshest earlier competition (pre–age 35) among college-educated men who are sorted out into slower and faster tracks the first few years on the job. Like the tracking systems of secondary school, early winners receive a challenging later socialization while others receive a custodial socialization. The "instant death" impact of loss in a tournament discourages risk taking and innovation. One's performance, after being eliminated from the tournament, is less relevant and largely goes unnoticed. Tests remain open as long as a candidate continues to win. Conformity is seen as a safer strategy for remaining in the competition for later trials in secondary tournaments.

Structural attainment in this system has a rather circular effect on mobility in that winners signal greater presumed ability. To some extent, however, ability is determined by the career system. The career system defines (1) how many winners there will be; (2) how quickly they will be tested for further advancement; and (3) when and if losers will be offered subsequent competitions in which they can participate. "High-potential" status is conferred on the most valued members, but this "ability" is not really a property of individuals alone but is a socially assigned status determined at least as much by the agenda and structure of the career systems as by the qualities of the individual (Rosenbaum, 1979).

The purity of each of these contests may be subject to biased assessments due to an organizational timetable or age grading (Lawrence, 1984), minority discrimination whereby "homosocial reproduction" leads assessors to select those most similar to themselves (Kanter, 1977), or the quality of one's professional network (Granovetter, 1974, 1981). These networks are critical to acquire the necessary information to compete successfully in many professions, company top management, and some crafts characterized by ambiguity, uncertain peer criteria, interfirm ties, and intensive collegial collaboration. They must be current and "in circulation" (Granovetter, 1974; Collins, 1979). Cultural, political, interpersonal, and marketplace issues are often moving targets for "exposed" people who are judged on quality of their information.

Research on the turnover of corporate officers suggests that newly arriving top corporate officers may be driven out by those outside their cohort (Pfeffer, 1979; Wagner et al., 1984). Members of smaller cohorts enjoy greater opportunity for promotion (Stewman and Konda, 1983). The high turnover in semiconductor firms has been attributed in part to blocked pathways due to shared demographics.

In this discussion of assignment flow, as with the prior discussion of supply flow, the firm's strategic context and internal structures and processes have been highlighted as contributing factors in the design of a firm's coherent career system. An accurate rendering of a firm's career system requires us to recombine the fragmented truths that emerge from the focused research studies. Before doing so, we must first combine the two sets of descriptive dynamics – supply and assignment flows. By integrating the sets, four profiles emerge.

A TYPOLOGY OF CAREER SYSTEMS

We do not have a uniform model of career systems because a single model would be either too generic to capture the variations of different career systems or too cumbersome to offer any clarity to a complex structure.[1] How, for example, could we compare an older, *Fortune 500* manufacturing firm in the industrial northeast to a small, western, professional organization such as a law firm (Wholey, 1985) and expect to find common properties regarding entry and competition? The research review of the prior section reminds us that we should expect to find differences based upon market control, size, demographics, growth, and interfirm networks.

We can profile many of these variations by plotting firms along two dimensions. First we must consider the openness of the "supply flow" of the career system to the external labor market (Doeringer and Piore, 1971; Wholey, 1985). For example, IBM has an almost total reliance on its internal labor market, creating a "closed" supply flow except at the entry level. However, most semiconductor,

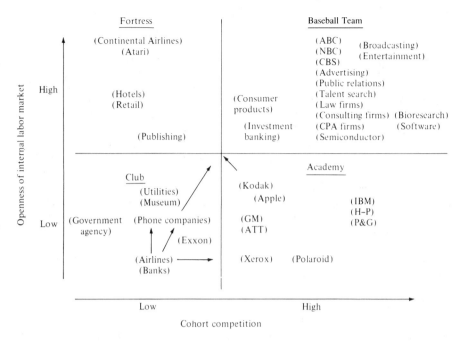

Figure 10.1. Models of career systems

advertising, broadcasting, and entertainment firms rely on extensive midcareer recruitment, and therefore positions other than entry level are more open to outside supply. This dimension deals with community cohesiveness and expresses itself through employment security, loyalty to long-service employees, openness to new members, and turnover.

The second dimension, "assignment flow," describes the mechanism by which assignment and promotion decisions are made (Kanter, 1977; Rosenbaum, 1979, 1984; Thurow, 1975; Turner, 1960). This dimension determines the pace and pressure in the career pipeline. It is affected by the vacancy rate, growth, and demographics (Pfeffer, 1979; Rosenbaum, 1984; Stewman and Konda, 1983; Wagner et al. 1984; and White, 1970).

Figure 10.1 displays these two dimensions with prominent companies in these industries, with likely prevailing career systems plotted in a hypothetical fashion. In combining these two dimensions, four cells are created. A firm is plotted along a range in each dimension rather than being merely assigned to a cell. The cells have been given descriptive labels that conjure up groups with distinctively different methods of maintaining membership. Many sport teams, especially baseball teams, rely upon skilled, individual performers with transferable talents that can be taken to other teams. An elaborate infrastructure of agents and scouts exists to facilitate the exchange of performers. By contrast, an "academy" is thought of as a more stable institution with an objective of developing the knowledge of its highly committed members. A "club" or fraternal order tends to be oriented toward rules of fair treatment of its members with loyalty shown through seniority as an especially valued feature of the system (Kallenberg and Sorenson,

1979). Finally, a "fortress" is an institution under siege, with low commitment to individuals. The larger goal is institutional survival, even at the cost of individual members.

This typology accommodates many of the theoretical disputes captured in this research review. For example, Osterman's (1984) challenge that Williamson (1975) and Chandler (1977) have not allowed for the inefficiencies and complacency of a seniority-bound internal labor market can be better explained. Both sets of scholars are concerned about internal labor markets, but the dispute is along a different dimension. Osterman is concerned with the fraternal clubs that do not have the same degree of competition and rigorous life-long career development of the academy. Kanter (1984) has identified key characteristics of large high-technology firms that distinguish them from the more rigid, "matured corporate bureaucracies." These features she offers – including lateral career paths, rapid early career progress to general management for some, limited functional identification, and dual ladders for management and professional career tracks – help us to visualize how the career systems of "academies" differ from those of the other career system models. Important to these systems are such contextual qualities as task uncertainty, firm-specific knowledge, related job sequences, and competition for scarce skills. These systems seek to develop and retain their own talent.

The academy embraces the assumptions of Williamson, Chandler, and Rosenbaum. In practice, it is the bane of the executive recruiting industry. The club is frequently shielded by regulatory buffers or a monopoly situation. Its stability represents the "pyramidic" or vacancy chains attacked by Rosenbaum (1984) and described by White's (1970) model of a church hierarchy. The academy is often a dominant, or "core," competitor (Oster, 1978; Ryan, 1984) while the club is shielded from the market. Workers in the academy see themselves as members of a modern guild. They see professional growth as a personal goal and a community obligation. Skillful team work rather than solo performances are valued. In the club security and membership are the essence of commitment. Status attainment prior to employment such as schooling is highly valued here (Collins, 1979; Jencks, 1979; Klitgaard, 1985). Here workers often see their employer (e.g., public utilities) as an institution with a mission to serve the public interest, which transcends marketplace concerns.

IBM is a continuing example of the employment security the academy seeks to provide. In 1985, more than 200 major firms announced massive layoffs, closings, unpaid vacations, and so on, while IBM maintained its 50-year tradition of employment security. Cutbacks in particular production programs as well as various cyclical jolts threaten to idle several thousand each year, but the firm retrains and repositions people around the system instead. Between 1971 and 1977, 12,000 IBM employees volunteered for and received retraining, followed by new career lines in the firm (Kinney, 1986). Recently, to avoid layoffs, IBM has severely restricted hiring, cut overtime, asked employees to use leftover vacation time, and pulled back work from subcontractors. The firm continually retrains and redeploys workers. The direct costs of education for 1985, exclusive of salaries, travel, and the like were $550 million. Over 10,000 employees were trained for new jobs. Roughly 7,300 switched locations at a cost of $60,000 each (Bernstein, Ticer, and Levine, 1986). Many other firms ranging from computers and electronics to banking and insurance have tried to keep pace and have succeeded.

Many other firms have had to withdraw from academy-like employment plans (e.g., Kodak, Xerox, Exxon, Intel, Apple) (Kanter, in press; Tomasko, 1987).

Some academy-like firms such as IBM, Du Pont, Proctor & Gamble, Johnson & Johnson, General Motors, Merck, Corning Glass, Digital, and Cargill have been cited by executive search recruiters as notoriously hard-to-crack career systems (Byrne, 1986). These firms prefer to "make" versus "buy" their midcareer talent. By contrast, for the "baseball teams," where innovation is at a premium, the lack of employment security heightens the pressure for creativity. The pool of risk takers is not limited to the internal labor market but can also involve midcareer hires of expert or celebrity status. The spirit in the baseball team is upbeat where employees see themselves as minor celebrities hoping for a shot to be a true star. When complacency sets in at baseball-type firms (such as advertising, broadcasting, or semiconductor), professional networks, trade associations, and intermediary-like recruiters seek new talent (Pfeffer and Leblebici, 1973).

Finally, the fortress is amidst a struggle for survival. This type of firm may have hired and fired reactively to market conditions along the lines of neoclassical economic theories. These may be firms never in control of their strategic environment because of the highly competitive nature of the business or the shortage of key resources (Lawrence and Dyer, 1983). It may also be a firm that was caught in a threatening crisis and now faces turnaround challenges. Workers in these fortress industries may have been attracted to the presumption of glamor in the business (e.g., publishing, hotels, retail). They may also have joined the firms in a healthier period. Or finally, they may have backed in by mistake. Employees here see themselves as soldiers locked in combat.

STRATEGIC CHOICE AND CAREER SYSTEMS

These differing management practices of each career system profile are frequently the product of strategic intentions. To create the needed pool of labor to accomplish distinct missions, firms will vary in their emphasis upon such membership qualities as professional expertise, competitiveness, loyalty, flexibility, and company-specific knowledge. Table 10.1 applies the strategic choice models of Miles and Snow (1978) to explain why each of these firms requires a different means of staffing their organization.

Miles and Snow refer to four strategic types of firms: "prospectors," "defenders," "analyzers," and "reactors." Prospectors are companies that thrive on product innovation and the creation of new markets. This draws upon the research on periphery firms discussed earlier in the chapter. Leaders of these firms pioneer strategies that identify emerging trends in the environment. They sacrifice internal efficiency in their effort to stay innovative. As a career system they must locate creative experts who are both independent producers and on the "cutting edge" of new ideas. The next group, defenders, are firms with narrow product/market domains. They are often what researchers label "core firms." Their leaders seek mastery over a narrowly defined organization. They rarely make fundamental changes and instead focus on continuity and reliability. Therefore, the defenders' career system must produce loyal, long-term members committed to maintaining the institution. Analyzers, the third group, contain properties that fall between the innovativeness of the prospectors in new markets and the reliability of defenders in stable markets. They do not take the risks of prospectors,

Table 10.1. *Career system properties*

	Academies	Clubs	Teams	Fortresses
Strategic mission	analyzer	defender	prospector	reactor
Career system priority	development	retention	recruitment	retrenchment
Openness of supply flow	exclusive entry at career	preferred entry at career	entry throughout career	selected turnaround talent
Assignment flow	tournament sponsored	seniority	tournament contest	seniority sponsored
Size	large	large, medium, small	small to medium	large to medium
Growth	moderate	stable or contracting	moderate or high	contracting
Training	whole career retraining cycles for new jobs	early career emphasis and scattered general usage	on-the-job	little
Exit	retirement	retirement	dismissal resignation	layoffs dismissal

but they do excel in the delivery of newer products and services. The career system must develop those who take moderate risks and strive for freshness but remain loyal to the firm. Finally, reactors are those firms that are buffeted by their environment because either they have little control over vital resources or they lack foresight regarding changes in their environment. Their career system must accommodate retrenchment and other exiting activities as well as the limited recruitment of turnaround experts.

In Table 10.1, we see the presentation of a coherent set of staffing policies to match a selected strategic posture. Any one of these four strategic types corresponds to different career system practices to provide the degree of required skill and continuity in the work force. For example, an "analyzer" strategy requires innovation by a skilled work force and institutional memory of a stable work force to ensure the expedient and reliable delivery of new goods and services. The analyzer strategy of the academies leads them to survey carefully their context and inventory their internal resources before plunging into new activities. They are most skillful at execution and rarely lead in the market with new ideas but rather with better quality products and services. Their career system must be anticipatory so that they have the infrastructure to ensure reliable delivery upon their commitments. The "prospecting" strategic orientation of the more feisty baseball teams attracts innovative talent that often has more cosmopolitan commitment to the occupation or profession than to the firm. The clubs hold a defender's concern with maintaining their strategic domain instead of seeking new expansion. Regulatory protection and general community support are often important. Hence, their employment practices are often managed in ways that promote their identity as benevolent public institutions. Finally, the fortresses' strategic style suggests that as reactors they have lost control over their environment. These firms may be analyzers, defenders, or prospectors that failed at their mission. Many firms may pass through this style while retrenching or turning themselves around.

CONCLUSIONS

The goals of this chapter were to suggest that (1) HRM research must take the perspective of the firm to contribute to career system theory and (2) disagreements across career system theorists reflect insufficient attention to career system properties of strategically diverse firms. This chapter proposes that the strategic orientation of a firm shapes the supply and assignment flows for its work force. The strategic purposes of a firm will lead to different emphasis on various career system activities. Thus distinct career system profiles emerge. This paper offered four labeled systems: the club, academy, baseball team, or fortress. The strategic positioning of a firm predicts its emphasis on various career system practices from recruitment to retirement. As with other organizational practices, career systems are contingent with structural and strategic factors (Thompson, 1967; Lawrence and Lorsch, 1967).

Just as environmental forces change structural and strategic factors of a firm, so too can we predict changes in a company's career system to match strategic transformations. The regulatory buffers that protected industries such as domestic airlines, commercial banks, and telecommunications had allowed many firms to operate as clubs. Now some have become less homogeneous in their career system approach, abrogating employment traditions and moving into the fortress mode to save costs, while others push to become more innovative and to draw upon the expertise of intermediaries who recruit from the outside labor market (Bennett, 1986). Thus, scholars should not expect a single universally applicable model of a career system. Nor should they expect career systems that are unchanging in dynamic business environments. Instead, researchers need to shift their discussion of career systems from an examination of isolated human resource activities to an integrated study of strategic staffing. This requires that we stop searching for a "one-best-way" career system and instead appreciate the complexities of the firm's environment.

NOTE

1 A related discussion of the last two sections of this chapter appears in Sonnenfeld and Peiperl (1988).

REFERENCES

Aronowitz, S. (1973). *False Promises*, New York: McGraw-Hill.
Bailyn, L. (1980). The slow-burn way to the top. In C. B. Derr (ed.). *Work, Family, and the Career*. New York: Praeger.
Baron, J. N. (1984). Organizational perspectives on stratification. *Annual Review of Sociology, 10*, 33–69.
Baron, J. N., and Bielby, W. T. (1980). Bringing the firms back in: stratification, segmentation, and the organization of work. *American Sociological Review, 45*, 737–765.
Beck, E. M., Horan, P. M., and Tolbert, C. M. II (1978). Stratification in a dual economy: a sectoral model of earnings determination. *American Sociological Review, 43*, 764–720.
Becker, G. (1964). *Human Capital*. New York: Columbia University Press.

Beehr, T. A., and Gilmore, D. C. (1982). Applicant attractiveness as a perceived job relevant variable in selection of management trainees. *Academy of Management Journal, 25,* 607–617.

Bennett, A. (1986). Middle managers face job squeeze as cutbacks and caution spread. *Wall Street Journal,* April 25, p. 26.

Berg, I. (1971). *Education and Jobs.* Boston: Beacon.

Bernstein, A., Ticer, S., and Levine, J. B. (1986). IBM's fancy footwork to sidestep layoffs. *Business Week,* July 7, pp. 54–55.

Blau, P. M. (1956). Social mobility and interpersonal relations. *American Sociological Review, 21,* 290–295.

Blau, P. M., and Duncan, O. D. (1967). *The American Occupational Structure.* New York: Wiley.

Bowles, S., and Gintis, H. (1976). *Schooling in Capitalist America.* New York: Basic Books.

Bray, D. W., Campbell, R. J., and Grant, D. L. (1973). *The Management Recruit: Formative Years in Business.* New York: Wiley.

Brenner, M. H. (1973). *Mental Illness and the Economy.* Cambridge: MA: Harvard University Press.

Byrne, J. A. (1986). *The Headhunters.* New York: Macmillan.

Cappelli, P. (1985). Competitive pressures and labor relations in the airline industry. *Industrial Relations, 24,* 316–338.

Caves, R. E. (1980). Industrial organization, corporate strategy and structure. *Journal of Economic Literature, 18,* 64–92.

Chandler, A. D. Jr. (1962). *Strategy and Structure.* Cambridge, MA: MIT Press.

Chandler, A. D. Jr. (1977). *The Visible Hand.* Cambridge, MA: Belknap/Harvard.

Collins, R. (1979). *The Credential Society.* New York: Academic.

Dalton, G. W., Thompson, P. H., and Price, R. L. (1977). The four stages of professional careers – a new look at performance by professionals. *Organizational Dynamics, 6,* 19–42.

Davidson, P. E., and Anderson, H. P. (1937). *Occupational Mobility in American Community.* Palo Alto: Stanford University Press.

Dipboye, R. L. (1982). Self fulfilling prophecies in the selection–recruitment interview. *Academy of Management Review, 7,* 579–586.

Doeringer, P. B., and Piore, M. J. (1971). *Internal Labor Markets and Manpower Analysis.* Lexington, MA: Heath.

Driver, M. (1979). Career concepts and career management in organizations. In C. L. Cooper (ed.), *Behavioral Problems in Organizations.* London: Prentice-Hall, pp. 79–139.

Durkheim, E. (1902). *The Division of Labor and Society,* Glencoe, IL: Free Press.

Edwards, R. C. (1979). *The Contested Terrain.* New York: Basic.

Eisenstadt, S. (1966). *Modernization: Protest and Change.* Englewood Cliffs, NJ: Prentice-Hall.

Ference, T. P., Stoner, J. A. F., and Warren, E. K. (1977). Managing the career plateau. *Academy of Management Review, 2,* 602–612.

Firth, R. (1939). *Primitive Polynesian Economy.* London: Routledge.

Fombrun, C. J., Tichy, N. M., and Devanna, M. A. (1984). *Strategic Human Resource Management.* New York: Wiley.

Foulkes, F. R. (1980). *Personnel Policies in Large Nonunion Companies.* Englewood Cliffs, NJ: Prentice-Hall.

Freeman, R. B., and Medoff, J. L. (1979). The two faces of unionism. *The Public Interest, 57,* 69–93.

Freeman, R. B., and Medoff, J. L. (1985). *What Do Unions Do?* New York: Basic.

Friedman, S. D. (1984). *Succession systems and organizational performance in large corporations.* Ph.D. dissertation. University of Michigan, Ann Arbor, MI.

Friedman, S. D. (1986). Succession systems in large corporations: characteristics and correlates of performance. *Human Resource Management Journal, 25,* 191–213.

Galbraith, J. K. (1967). *The New Industrial State.* New York: Houghton-Mifflin.

Gilmore, T. M., and Hirshorn, J. (1984). Managing human resources in a declining context. In C. J. Fombrun, N. M. Tichy, and M. A. Devanna (eds.), *Strategic Human Resource Management.* New York: Wiley, pp. 297–318.

Gordon, D., Edwards, R., and Reich, M. (1982). *Segmented Work, Divided Workers.* Cambridge: Cambridge University Press.
Gordon, D. M. (1972). *Theories of Poverty and Underemployment.* Lexington, MA: Heath.
Granovetter, M. (1974). *Getting a Job: A Study of Contacts and Careers.* Cambridge, MA: Harvard University Press.
Granovetter, M. (1981). Toward a sociological theory of income differences. In I. Berg (ed.), *Sociological Perspectives on Labor Markets.* New York: Academic, pp. 11–47.
Granovetter, M. (1982). Who gets ahead? A review. *Theory and Society, 11,* 239–262.
Hall, D. T. (1976). *Careers in Organizations.* Pacific Palisades, CA: Goodyear.
Hall, D. T. (ed.) (1986a). *Career Development in Organizations.* San Francisco: Jossey-Bass.
Hall, D. T. (1986b). Dilemmas in linking succession planning to individual executive learning. *Human Resource Management, 25,* 235–265.
Hall, R. E. (1982). The importance of lifetime jobs in the U.S. economy. *American Economic Review, 72,* 716–724.
Hill, L. A. and Sonnenfeld, J. A. (1986). Training in transition: renewal in financial service firms. Paper presented at the 49th Annual Meeting of the Academy of Management, San Diego, CA.
Hollingshead, F. X. (1951) Trends in social stratification: a case study. *American Sociological Review, 17,* 679–686.
Hoxie, J. H. (1915): *Scientific Management and Labor,* as referenced in P. Osterman (ed.), *Internal Labor Markets.* See also C. J. Morrison (1914), Short-sighted methods in dealing with labor, *The Engineering Magazine, 46,* 568, and F. H. Rindge, Jr. (1917), From boss to foreman, *Industrial Management, 53,* 508–509.
Ingols, C. A. (1987). Management education: articulating the unspoken, riding the herd, wasting money, or preparing for tomorrow? In L. May, S. Zammit, and C. A. Moore (eds.), *Evaluating Business and Industry Training.* Norwell, MA: Kluwer.
Jacoby, S. M. (1984). The development of internal labor markets in American manufacturing firms. In P. Osterman (ed.), *Internal Labor Markets.* Cambridge: MA: MIT Press.
Jencks, C., et al. (1972). *Inequality: A Reassessment of the Effect of Family and Schooling in America.* New York: Basic.
Jencks, C., et al. (1979). *Who Gets Ahead?* New York: Basic.
Kallenberg, A. L., and Sorenson, A. B. (1979). The sociology of labor markets. *Annual Review of Sociology, 5,* 351–379.
Kanter, R. M. (1977). *Men and Women of the Corporation.* New York: Basic.
Kanter, R. M. (1984). Variations in managerial career structuring in high-technology firms: the impact of organizational characteristics on internal labor market patterns. In P. Osterman (ed.), *Internal Labor Markets.* Cambridge, MA: MIT Press, pp. 109–131.
Kanter, R. M. (in press). *The Corporate Tightrope* (working title). New York: Simon & Schuster.
Kimberly, J. R. (1976). Organizational size and the structuralist perspective: a review, critique, and proposal. *Administrative Science Quarterly, 21,* 571–597.
Kinney, H. (1986). A matter of balance. *Think, 2,* 2–8.
Klitgaard, R. (1985). *Choosing Elites.* New York: Basic.
Kotter, J. P. (1973). The psychological contract: managing the joining up process. *California Management Review, XV*(3), 91–99.
Kotter, J. P. (1982). *The General Manager.* New York: Free Press.
Lawrence, B. S. (1984). Age grading: the implicit organizational timetable. *Journal of Occupational Behaviour, 5,* 23–36.
Lawrence, P. R. (1985). The history of human resource management in American industry. In R. E. Walton and P. R. Lawrence (eds.), *HRM: Trends and Challenges.* Boston: Harvard Business School Press, pp. 15–34.
Lawrence, P. R., and Dyer, D. (1983). *Renewing American Industry.* New York: Free Press.
Lawrence, P. R., and Lorsch, J. W. (1967). *Organizations and Environments.* Homewood, IL: Irwin.
Lazear, E. P. (1981). Agency, earnings profiles, productivity and hours restrictions. *American Economic Review, 71,* 606–620.
Lipset, S. M., and Bendix, R. (1959). *Social Mobility in Industrial Society.* Berkeley: University of California Press.
London, M., and Stumpf, S. A. (1982). *Managing Careers.* Reading, MA: Addison-Wesley.

Lorange, P., and Murphy, D. (1984). Bringing human resources into strategic planning: systems design considerations. In C. J. Fombrun, N. M. Tichy, and M. A. Devanna (eds), *Strategic Human Resource Management*. New York: Wiley, pp. 275–296.

McCall, M. W., Jr., Lombardo, M. M., and Morrison, A. M. (1988). *The Lessons of Experience: How Successful Executives Develop on the Job*. Lexington, MA: Lexington.

Malinowski, B. (1932). *Argonauts of the Western Pacific*. London: Routledge.

Marglin, S. A. (1974). What do bosses do? The origins and functions of hierarchy and capitalist production. *Review of Radical Political Economics, 6*, 60–112.

Marx, K. (1963, 1867 original). In T. B. Buttomore (ed.), *Early Writings*. New York: McGraw-Hill.

Masters, S. H. (1969). An interindustry analysis of wages and plant size. *Review of Economic Statistics, 51*, 341–345.

Medoff, J. L., and Abraham, K. G. (1980). The role of seniority at U.S. work places: a report on some new evidence. Working paper, Research Division, Harvard Business School.

Miles, R. E., and Snow, C. C. (1978). *Organizational Structure, Strategy, and Process*. New York: McGraw-Hill.

Miller, D. C., and Form, W. H. (1951). *Industrial Sociology*. New York: Harper & Row.

Miller, E. (1984). Strategic staffing. In C. J. Fombrun, N. M. Tichy, and M. A. Devanna (eds.), *Strategic Human Resource Management*. New York: Wiley, pp. 57–68.

Mills, C. W. (1945). The American business elite: a collective portrait. *Journal of Economic History, 5,* 20–44.

Mincer, J. (1974). *Schooling, Experience, and Earnings*. New York: National Bureau of Economic Research.

Ornstein, S., Cron, W. L., and Slocum, J. W., Jr. (in press). Life stage versus career stage: a comparative test of the theories of Levinson and Super. *Journal of Organizational Behavior*.

Orpen, C. (1982). The effects of race of applicant and type of job on hiring decisions. *Journal of Social Psychology, 118*, 279–280.

Oster, G. (1978). A factor analytic test for the theory of the dual economy. *Review of Economics and Statistics, 61*, 33–39.

Osterman, P. (ed.) (1984). The nature and importance of internal labor markets. *Internal Labor Markets*. Cambridge, MA: MIT Press.

Owen, R. (1927). *A New View of Society and Other Writings*. New York: Dutton.

Parsons, T. (1959). *Structure and Process in Modern Societies*. New York: Free Press.

Pfeffer, J. (1979). Some consequences of organizational demography: potential impacts of an aging workforce on formal organizations. Paper presented at the Committee on Aging, National Academy of Sciences, Annapolis, MD.

Pfeffer, J., and Leblebici, H. (1973). Executive recruitment and the development of interfirm organizations. *Administrative Science Quarterly, 18*, 449–461.

Pfeffer, J., and Ross, J. (1981a). Unionization and income inequality. *Industrial Relations, 20*, 271–285.

Pfeffer, J., and Ross, J. (1981b). Unionization and female wage status attainment. *Industrial Relations, 20*, 179–185.

Piore, M. J., (1975). Notes for a theory of labor market stratification. In R. L. Edwards, M. Riech, and D. M. Gordon (eds.), *Labor Market Segmentation*. Lexington, MA: Heath.

Piore, M. J. (1979). *Birds of Passage: Migrant Labor and Industrial Societies*. New York: Cambridge University Press.

Piore, M. J., and Sable, C. F. (1984). *The Second Industrial Divide: Possibilities for Prosperity*. New York: Basic Books.

Porter, M. E. (1980). *Competitive Strategy: Techniques for Analyzing Industries and Competitors*. New York: Free Press.

Price, J. L. (1971). *The Study of Turnover*. Ames, IA: Iowa State University Press.

Raelin, J. (1986). *The Clash of Cultures*. Boston, MA: Harvard Business School Press.

Rogoff, N. (1955). *Recent Trends in Occupational Mobility*. Glencoe, IL: Free Press.

Rosenbaum, J. E. (1979). Tournament mobility: career patterns in a corporation. *Administrative Science Quarterly, 24*, 220–241.

Rosenbaum, J. E. (1984). *Career Mobility in a Corporate Hierarchy*. New York: Academic.

Ryan, P. (1984). Job training, employment practices, and the large enterprise. In P. Osterman (ed.), *Internal Labor Markets*, Cambridge, MA: MIT Press, pp. 191–230.

Sadowski, P. (1982). Corporate training investment decisions. In G. Menseh and R. Nichaus (eds.), *Manpower Planning and Technological Change*. New York: Plenum.

Schein, E. H. (1978). *Career Dynamics: Matching Individual and Organizational Needs*. Reading, MA: Addison-Wesley.

Schein, E. H. (1985). *Organizational Culture and Leadership*. San Francisco: Jossey-Bass.

Schwab, D. P. (1982). Organizational recruiting and the decision to participate. In K. Rowland and G. Ferris (eds.), *Personnel Management: New Perspectives*. Boston, MA: Allyn & Bacon.

Sewell, W. H., Haller, A. O., and Ohlendorf, G. W. (1970). The early education and early occupational attainment process. *American Sociological Review, 35*, 1014–1027.

Shaeffer, R., and Lynton, E. (1979). *Corporate Experience in Improving Women's Job Opportunities*. New York: Conference Board.

Simmel, G. (1950). *The Sociology of George Simmel* (translated by K. H. Wolf). New York: Free Press.

Slichter, S. H., Healy, J. J., and Livernash, E. R. (1960). *The Impact of Collective Bargaining on Management*. Washington, DC: Brookings.

Slocum, J., and Cron, W. L. (1988). Business strategy and career opportunities. In E. Mone (ed.), *Human Resource Professional and Employee Career Development*. London: Quorum Praeger, pp. 135–151.

Sonnenfeld, J. (1984). *Managing Career Systems: Channeling the Flow of Executive Careers*. Homewood, IL: Irwin.

Sonnenfeld, J. (1985). Education at work: demystifying the magic of training. In R. E. Walton and P. R. Lawrence (eds.), *HRM: Trends and Challenges*, Boston: Harvard Business School Press, pp. 285–318.

Sonnenfeld, J. (1988). *The Heroes Farewell: The Retirement and Renewal of Chief Executives*. New York: Oxford University Press.

Sonnenfeld, J., and Ingols, C. (1986). Working knowledge: charting a new course for training. *Organizational Dynamics*, Autumn 1986, pp. 63–79.

Sonnenfeld, J., and Kotter, J. P. (1982). The maturation of career theory. *Human Relations, 35*, 19–43.

Sonnenfeld, J. A., and Peiperl, M. A. (1988). Staffing policy as a strategic response: a typology of career systems. *Academy of Management Review, 13*, 588–600.

Sorokin, P. O. (1947). *Social Mobility*. New York: Harper & Row.

Spence, A. M. (1974). *Market Signaling: Information Transfer in Hiring and Related Processes*. Cambridge, MA: Harvard.

Spenner, K. I. (1981). Some elementary properties of career lines. Unpublished manuscript. Boystown Center for the Study of Youth Development, Boystown, NE.

Spenner, K. I., Otto, L. B., and Call, V. R. A. (1982). *Career Lines and Careers*. Lexington, MA: Lexington.

Spilerman, S. (1977). Careers, labor market structure, and socioeconomic achievement. *American Journal of Sociology, 83*, 551–593.

Stewman, S., and Konda, S. L. (1983). Careers and organizational labor markets: demographic models of organizational behavior. *American Journal of Sociology, 88*, 637–685.

Stolzenberg, R. M. (1978). Bringing the boss back in: employer size, employee schooling, and socioeconomic achievement. *American Sociological Review, 43*, 813–828.

Stone, K. (1974). The origins of job structures in the steel industry. *Review of Radical Political Economics, 6*, 113–173.

Thompson, J. D. (1967). *Organizations in Action*. New York: McGraw-Hill.

Thurow, L. C. (1975). *Generating Inequality*. New York: Basic Books.

Tichy, N. M., Fombrun, C. J., and Devanna, M. A. (1982). Strategic human resource management. *Sloan Management Review, 23*, 47–61.

Tomasko, R. (1987). *Downsizing*. New York: American Management Association.

Tönnies, F. (1935). *Community and Association*. London: Routledge.

Turner, R. (1960). Modes of social ascent through education: sponsored and contest mobility. *American Sociological Review, 25*, 855–867.

Vardi, Y. (1980). Organizational career mobility: an integrative model. *Academic Management Review, 5*, 341–355.

Vardi, Y., and Hammer, T. H. (1977). Intraorganizational mobility and career perspectives among rank and file employees in different technologies. *Academy of Management Journal, 20*, 622–634.

Veiga, J. F. (1983). Mobility influences during managerial career stages. *Academy of Management Journal, 26*, 64–85.

Vroom, V. H., and Macrimmon, K. R. (1968). Toward a stochastic model of managerial careers. *Administrative Science Quarterly, 13*, 26–46.

Wachter, M. L. (1974). Primary and secondary labor markets: a critique of the dual approach. *Brookings Papers on Economic Activity, 3*, 637–693.

Wagner, W. G., Pfeffer, J., and O'Reilly, C. A. (1984). Organizational demography and turnover in top management groups. *Administrative Science Quarterly, 29*, 74–92.

Walker, J. W., and Gutteridge, T. G. (1979). *Career Planning Practices: An AMA Survey Report.* New York: Amacom.

Walton, R. E., and Lawrence, P. R. (eds.) (1985). *HRM: Trends and Challenges.* Boston: Harvard Business School Press.

Wanous, J. P. (1980). *Organizational Entry, Selection and Socialization of Newcomers.* Reading, MA: Addison-Wesley.

Warner, W. L., and Abegglen, J. C. (1955). *Occupational Mobility in American Business and Industry, 1928–1952,* Minneapolis: University of Minnesota Press.

Weber, M. (original 1922, 1947). *The Theory of Social and Economic Organization* (translated by A. D. Henderson and T. Parsons). New York: Free Press.

Weiner, M., and Schneiderman, M. S. (1974). Use of job information in employment decisions of interviewees. *Journal of Applied Psychology, 59*, 699–704.

Weiss, R. S., Harwood, E., and Riesman, D. (1971). Work and automation. In R. K. Merton and R. Nisbet (eds.), *Contemporary Social Problems.* New York: Harcourt Brace Jovanovich.

White, H. C. (1970). *Chains of Opportunity.* Cambridge, MA: Harvard University Press.

Wholey, D. R. (1985). Determinants of firm internal labor markets in large law firms. *Administrative Science Quarterly, 30*, 318–335.

Williamson, O. E. (1975). *Markets and Hierarchies.* New York: Free Press.

Yankelovich, P. (1979). Who gets ahead in America. *Psychology Today, 13*, 28–40.

PART II

New ideas for the study of careers

Introduction to Part II

In Part II we look at careers through a different lens. Whereas in Part I we considered different streams in the career literature, in Part II we examine career theory through the multiple lenses provided by social science disciplines. As we said in the Preface, the concept of Part II was to ask scholars not necessarily associated with the study of careers to look at the domain of their particular fields and to "think careers" while they did so. We asked them to pull out concepts from their area that they thought could be useful in understanding how people's work behaviors and attitudes change over time as a career unfolds.

While it is clear to us why each of the following chapters is important, we have been unable to come up with any obvious sequence in which to present them. If Part I of this handbook showed us the present landscape of career theory, Part II is the garden store of new materials with which the landscape might be changed. And we hope readers will agree the store is full and the materials tempting. To preview the selections, there are ideas drawn principally from psychology (Bell and Staw, Latack, and Marshall, Chapters 11–13, respectively), organizational behavior (Arthur and Kram, Derr and Laurent, Chapters 14 and 22), social psychology (Weick and Berlinger, Chapter 15), sociology (Rosenbaum, Thomas, Chapters 16 and 17), political science (Pfeffer, Chapter 18), anthropology (Trice and Morand, Chapter 19), economics (Barney and Lawrence, Chapter 20), and rhetoric (Gowler and Legge, Chapter 21). Another way to consider the chapters is according to their level of analysis, which moves from individual, to group, to organizational, to societal, and finally to international as the section unfolds. The chapters represent a diverse group of the social sciences, and as you will see, each chapter has something to offer about the way we see careers.

To begin with a perspective from psychology, Bell and Staw (Chapter 11) use personality theory to make a case for the individual quality of personal disposition as a critical career influence. They make the point that the career literature has perhaps overemphasized the impact of social and organizational variables at the expense of individual differences (or person variables). [This argument, then, comes at the issue from the opposite direction of Betz, Fitzgerald, and Hill (Chapter 2) in Part I, who argue that vocational psychology has underestimated the impact of organizational and interaction variables. These two chapters together represent an interesting point and counterpoint.] Bell and Staw review recent longitudinal research findings that show remarkable predictability of individual difference variables on various aspects of psychological well-being; and these personal disposition variables had greater predictive power than did changes in people's work and personal situations. The chapter concludes with a new model of personal control in organizations, tracing a chain of relationships between individual characteristics, personal control activities, and individual outcomes.

Latack (Chapter 12) also deals with the issue of individual control, but in the context of psychological stress and its relationship to career outcomes. The chapter starts by examining recent process models of stress and considers their utility for the development of career theory. She gives particular attention to coping strategies and social support as positive factors that might either prevent or ameliorate stress-induced problems for the individual. She develops a research agenda, built from a number of critical research questions, that take off from a number of studies of stress and careers. The goal of the chapter is to stimulate further integrative conceptual models of careers that make explicit use of underlying assumptions about career stress.

Marshall (Chapter 13) provides a feminist perspective inviting us to *re-vision* the career concepts we hold. The choice of term re-vision is deliberate, for it is her thesis that themes of feminism have been excluded from the way ideas about careers have been formed. Drawing on a basic distinction between "agency" and "communion" as two principles of human functioning, Marshall argues our ideas about careers, and also about the social science that informs them, have relied heavily on the agentic principle. The neglected principle of communion is more inwardly than outwardly oriented and more concerned with relationships than individual achievements over time. The feminist perspective that aligns with communion calls for us to appreciate non-agentic phenomena such as inaction, interdependence, cyclic phases, and whole lives. This appreciation should span both the structure and content of career theory, as well as the methods by which it gets developed.

The next two chapters look at the interface between the individual and the organization and develop ideas about how this interaction affects careers. Arthur and Kram (Chapter 14) take some of the adult development processes described in Part I (e.g., in Chapter 4) and relate them to the development of organizations to raise some novel ideas about organizational career development. The chapter begins by presenting the concept of reciprocity, the extent to which individual and organizational needs are separately and simultaneously satisfied. Arthur and Kram use the notion of reciprocity with a three-stage model for linking the needs and satisfaction of the individual career with the organization's developmental needs. They go on to examine issues of individual–organization fit at the micro and macro levels of analysis. Two separate forms of lack of fit, for both individuals and organizations, are identified. A model and propositions to guide research on individual and organizational needs are proposed; these propositions apply to developmental stages, transitions, and strategic choice and political behavior.

Weick and Berlinger (Chapter 15) start with the recently popularized notion of adaptive, self-designing organizations and spin out the implications for self-designing careers within these systems. The "stability through change" sought in self-designing organizations is illustrated by descriptions of six characteristics – concerned with redesign, impermanence, learning, meta-analyses, information filtering, and commitment – that these organizations usually embody. For further clarification, the subtle distinctions between self-designing organizations and various related (e.g., organic) forms of organization are noted. Career paths in self-designing contexts are described to rely heavily on the notion of the subjective career, placing a series of unique demands on the person. Through such acts as cultivating "spiral" career concepts, decoupling identity from jobs, and preserving discretion, the person can prepare for the lifetime of learning and exploration for which the self-designing organization calls.

Two more chapters take a sociological perspective. Rosenbaum (Chapter 16) examines the perplexing question of why employees misperceive the realities of organizational career systems. He suggests that Americans have long used individualistic career models in which each person exerts control over his or her own career. This, however, ignores the structural features of organizations, such as internal labor markets, vacancy chains, and organization policies, that influence careers regardless of individual choices. Rosenbaum proposes a tournament model of careers that incorporates structural features into an individualistic model. He then compares the career predictions of the tournament model against an individualistic model, human capital theory, using data from several studies. The results suggest that the tournament model better explains employees' career experiences, and further, that employees rarely perceive the structural aspects of tournaments accurately. Rosenbaum concludes by examining how such misperceptions may influence employees and discusses the implications of these effects for organizational policies.

Thomas (Chapter 17) makes a case for the relevance of career theory to the work of blue-collar workers but cautions that many of the normative assumptions about upward career mobility simply do not apply. In contrast to popular psychological and ideological interpretations about freedom of choice, careers for Thomas reflect the social milieu of class, the organizational arrangement of occupations, and labor market segmentation. These, in turn, serve as coordinates of a three-dimensional framework for considering how career responses, particularly blue-collar career responses, come about. People's sense-making, and subsequent coping and political strategies, reflect the way they locate themselves along these coordinates. The shift away from individual-centered analyses has particular relevance for the way we view recent initiatives for flexible and participative production systems. We are warned that failure to understand the structural forces behind workers' career behavior will condemn such initiatives to be short-lived fads.

Power and politics, two factors prominent in the popular writing on career, receive serious treatment from Pfeffer (Chapter 18). In contrast to much of the individually focused work on careers, Pfeffer takes a more political and organizational perspective, using as critical concepts interests, environments, and networks. The core of the political perspective is that there are multiple and distinct interests in organizations, with each pursuing its own objectives. Pfeffer goes on to develop the implications of this notion in relation to the formation of interest groups, coalitions, and networks. He reviews research that shows the impact of these influences on such career-affecting activities as hiring, internal labor markets, wage determination, and succession. The chapter concludes with a call for more work on careers with a political perspective, arguing that this would produce research findings that are at once more realistic and stronger conceptually.

Trice and Morand (Chapter 19) bring an anthropological view proposing that work careers are a series of transitions from one role to another, and thus that the study of rites of passage is central to an understanding of organizational and occupational work careers. Utilizing Van Gennep's conception of such passages as three consecutive stages – separation, transition, and integration – the authors trace numerous examples of how rites of passage serve to socialize people into occupations. They then examine how organizations provide rites of passage through training programs, which, although serving an admittedly technical function, also provide an expressive function as rites of passage. Trice and Morand discuss the implications of this conception of careers for both occupations and organizations. For instance, the disaffection of middle management observed in many organizations may result because the rites of passage associated with this career stage are insufficient in number or too weak to exert a positive commitment experience. The authors conclude by suggesting that while rites of passage are neither inherently good nor bad, they produce powerful social consequences for individuals within work careers and should be recognized as an important aspect of organizational and occupational life.

Barney and Lawrence (Chapter 20) use modern microeconomic theory, and in particular the work on imperfect labor markets, to propose a model of individual career strategy in organizations. Drawing from economic views about job search, employment relations, human capital, market signaling, and implicit contracts they propose a model contrasting the likely perceived value of a human capital investment with the number of employees making the investment. The model allows for consideration of what individuals and organizations should each rationally do to maximize economic outcomes. In turn, the model is proposed to help us highlight differences between employee beliefs and organizational practice about what career investments are valued, and so in turn to help us reconsider the effectiveness of established reward structures.

Gowler and Legge (Chapter 21) take us into the world of language, in which rhetoric both produces and is produced by our ideological approaches to careers. From this perspective, peoples' actions and thoughts are constrained, and to a great extent determined, by the meanings their language conveys. In particular, the authors explore how the language used to describe organizational life has resulted in four bureaucratic ideologies of control: hierarchy, accountability, achievement, and membership. These four ideologies, then, produce the dominant meaning of career in our society. Gowler and Legge next describe an important example of how the association between rhetoric and careers influences behavior. They document the ties between careers and reputation and show that when considered as reputations, careers become commodities in which the employee is the seller and the employer is the buyer. Because bureaucratic ideologies of control enhance some reputations more than others, this results in a socially accepted "aggrandizement" of managerial careers relative to other types of work.

Finally, national culture (versus the organizational culture) is another understudied factor in careers, as Derr and Laurent demonstrate (Chapter 22). This chapter introduces an international perspective, concerned with how national culture affects the interaction between internal and external career components. For these authors, national culture underlies the basic assumptions – or social constructions of reality – both individuals and organizations bring to the career negotiation process. Some preliminary evidence of national differences in both internal and external careers is provided, and a model of how national culture affects the interaction between the internal and external careers is proposed. Derr and Laurent press us to consider how much careers are cultural artifacts, and to what extent our attributions of career outcomes to individual or organizational variables cloud the role of culture from our understanding. In contrast, a better appreciation of cultural effects would influence our views on the possibilities for organizational change and intra-organizational relationships, in both uninational and multinational organizations.

This section, then, with its diverse disciplinary perspectives and creative application of new concepts, is probably unlike most other material on careers that you have seen before. We hope it will change your thinking on the subject.

11 *People as sculptors versus sculpture: the roles of personality and personal control in organizations*

NANCY E. BELL and BARRY M. STAW

The popular literature on careers advises individuals to take charge of their situations – to be active agents in shaping their work environments and career opportunities.

> We believe you will improve your effectiveness and your sense of yourself as a person 300% if you can learn to think (or if you already think) of yourself as *an active agent* helping to mould your own present environment and your own future, rather than a passive agent, waiting for your environment to mould you. (Bolles 1980:74)

> You *have to* take over the management of your own job-hunt or career-change, if it is to be successful. (Bolles 1988:43)

> You can create opportunity for the future by putting yourself in charge of your career. Your initial commitment is to take full control of your actions. (Greco 1975:19)

In contrast, a major school of thought in the academic literature on careers, the socialization literature, views individuals as much more passive and malleable. Often, individuals are portrayed as if they join the organization practically as lumps of clay, ready to be shaped by all those around them, from co-worker to supervisor to mentor. As mainly *receivers* of influence, individuals attempt to "learn the ropes" in the organization, modeling not only their behaviors but also their attitudes on those who appear to be successful participants:

> Like a sculptor's mold, certain forms of socialization can produce remarkably similar outcomes no matter what individual ingredients are used to fill the mold. (Van Maanen and Schein 1979:231)

To be fair, we recognize that the academic literature does not totally ignore the individual in its treatment of careers. Researchers have given careful consideration to personality and other individual difference variables in examining the selection stage of the career process (e.g., Holland 1966, 1976, 1985; Neiner and Owens 1985; Owens 1976). In fact, the focus on organizational participants as sculpture, or as malleable receivers of influence, is a relatively recent phenomenon. Much of the early academic literature on careers took an explicitly psychological approach, emphasizing the fit between specific personality traits and particular careers (see, e.g., Hansen and Campbell 1985; Strong 1943).

Person variables have been given far less consideration in recent work. This may be due to the emphasis in the literature on the early stages of careers, when people are thought to be most open to organizational influence (Hall 1986). Because this literature is strongly rooted in a socialization view of careers, the picture that emerges shows the organization as the dominant entity, much more of an "agent" than the individual. The individual is at best viewed as a diagnostician or planner, reacting to organizational contingencies rather than proactively shaping those contingencies. Sometimes the person is seen as negotiating a "psychological contract" (e.g., Schein 1970) with the organization; yet even in these cases, if such a contract proves difficult to negotiate, the individual's only alternative is to exit the organization.

This emphasis on the individual as a rather passive receiver of influence is not unique to the organizational socialization literature. A great deal of recent organizational literature has stressed the influence of situational variables in shaping behavior, while giving little attention to the role of person variables in forming the behaviors and attitudes of organizational participants. For example, in the past decade researchers studying job satisfaction have focused on the comparative merits of two situational explanations – the job characteristics model (Hackman and Oldham 1976, 1980) and social information processing (Salancik and Pfeffer 1978). Proponents of the job characteristics approach have argued that job attitudes are formed largely in reaction to features of the task being performed, such as its significance and the skill variety required to perform it. Advocates of the social information processing approach, by contrast, have argued that individuals rely largely on social cues in deciding how they feel about their jobs. A number of empirical studies have pitted these two theories against each other (e.g., Griffin 1983; O'Reilly and Caldwell 1979; White and Mitchell 1979). However, in emphasizing forces that are external to the person, both theories provide situational explanations of job attitudes. In this sense, both the job characteristics and social information processing models treat individuals as sculpture rather than as more proactive sculptors of their own behaviors and attitudes.

The emphasis on situational variables in the job attitude literature – to the exclusion of person variables – is a relatively recent phenomenon. Just as the early career literature had more of a person-oriented approach, the early job satisfaction literature traced job attitudes to dispositional sources. For example, as far back as 1913, Munsterberg noted that "the feeling of monotony depends much less on the particular kind of work than upon the special disposition of the individual" (1913:198).

Our recent work, which we discuss later in this chapter, attempts to revitalize the dispositional view of job attitudes. We show how a person variable, affective disposition (a general tendency toward positive or negative evaluation of life stimuli), can predict job attitudes. In this chapter, we will argue for a similar emphasis on the person in the career/socialization literatures – for the individual to be viewed more as sculptor than sculpture. While we do not deny the significant contributions of "situational" approaches that look at how the organization shapes the person, we think that the field has swung too far in the situational direction. In our view, it is now time to pay more attention to the individualization of organizational life (cf. Jones 1983; Schneider 1983; Staw, Bell, and Claussen 1986; Weiss and Adler 1984). This view is compatible with that of more psychologically oriented career theory, such as Hall's (1976) work on the self-directed "protean" career and Tiedeman and Miller-Tiedeman's (1984) notion of personal agency (or

"'I' power") in the career. Thus we will focus on the roles of personality and personal control in organizations, hoping to balance the situational perspective so dominant in the current literature with a fresh perspective that emphasizes people as the shapers of their own organizational fates.

In addressing the roles of personality and personal control, we first review an ongoing debate in psychology over the relative influence of person versus situation in determining behavior and attitudes. We consider some evidence that indicates that people may not be as open to organizational influence as they are often depicted to be. The person versus situation debate also offers some insights into what kinds of situations should promote individualistic, rather than conforming, behavior. After reviewing the evidence for a dispositional and proactive view of individual behavior, we propose a model of personal control in organizations. We contend that personal control is the mechanism by which individual differences get expressed in organizational and career settings. Finally, in order to highlight some explicit testable links in the model, we describe a process whereby power needs affect people's efforts at personal control as well as subsequent perceptions of self-efficacy.

CAREERS AS PERSONALITY OR SITUATION

The question of whether career outcomes are due more to the person or to the organizational context is not a new one. Over the past fifty years, personality theorists as well as social psychologists have been engaged in a very similar debate over the relative influence of person versus situation in determining attitudes and behavior. The debate has roots in the controversy between Watson's extreme environmental determinism views of behavior (Watson 1925) versus the ideographic trait formulations of Allport (1937). For Watson, the situation was paramount. He maintained that, given the proper environment, he could control behavior regardless of a person's individual characteristics. Allport, on the other hand, maintained that knowledge of a person's traits would allow prediction of that person's behavior, even in situations in which the researcher had not previously observed the individual.

A more recent form of this debate began in 1968 with the publication of a seminal book by Walter Mischel in which he took issue with the work of trait theorists. Mischel's argument was essentially that traits had proven to be poor predictors of behavior and showed little cross-situational consistency. Mischel argued that if we wish to predict behavior we should switch our emphasis away from traits and dispositions and instead look at the contingencies posed by the situations in which individuals find themselves.

There have been numerous replies to Mischel's critique of personality research. Bem and Allen (1974) pointed out that individuals differ from one another both in the way traits are related to each other within each person and in whether or not a given trait is even relevant for the person in question. They argued for an idiographic rather than a nomothetic approach to personality. As an example, consider the case in which two people score equally high on a measure of need for achievement, and therefore (using the typical nomothetic approach) receive the same score on the achievement measure. Such a nomothetic measure would then be related to some outcome measure, such as career mobility, with the usual result being a weak relationship between trait and outcome. In contrast, the idiographic approach would emphasize that need for achievement may not be equally *relevant* to all people, even though they might have the same score on this trait measure. The idiographic approach, argued Bem and his colleagues (Bem and Allen 1974; Bem and Funder 1978), will be more predictive of behavioral outcomes because it taps the *relevance* as opposed to simple magnitude of trait variables (for recent evidence supporting this assertion, see Zuckerman et al. 1988).

Another rejoinder of the "personologists" to the "situationists" has to do with the nature of the dependent variables used in personality research. Most often, these dependent variables have been measured by single acts. However, researchers such as Epstein (1979) and Buss and Craik (1983) have argued that we must take multiple measures of our behavioral criteria. Epstein's argument is that while any one act may not show great consistency with personality, an index or aggregate of acts thought to be related to the personality construct in question will show a stronger relationship. Thus, careers should be ideally suited to this method of research since they are, by definition, aggregates of people's experiences. While any one cross-sectional measure may show weak results, an aggregate of a person's work experiences should show a stronger relationship to measures of personality, especially if the personality measures are also based on aggregated data.

Strong versus weak situations

One of the most important concepts to emerge from the person versus situation debate is that of "strong versus weak situations" (Mischel 1977). A strong situation is one that (1) leads everyone to construe the situation in the same way, (2) induces uniform expectancies regarding appropriate response patterns, (3) provides incentives for the performance of certain response patterns, and (4) requires skills that everyone has (Mischel 1977·347). Weak situations, by contrast, are more ambiguous or less structured (Snyder and Ickes 1985). Weak situations exert few pressures for conformity and may not even provide cues as to what would constitute conforming behavior.

When we examine situations according to their relative strength we can begin to see why traits have proved to be such poor predictors of behavior in comparison with contexts. As a number of researchers have pointed out (Bowers 1973; Weiss and Adler 1984), the typical study offering support to the situationist position is a laboratory experiment. In the lab, the conditions for a strong situation are purposely created so as to have a "good" manipulation and "experimental control." In fact, the manipulation checks for an experiment often assess whether subjects heeded the four characteristics of strong situations noted, with variability due to individual differences considered as error variance. Thus, having reduced the possible variation due to people, it should come as no surprise that experimental studies usually show weak results for person variables (Schneider 1987). In a test of this position, Monson, Hesley, and Chernick (1982) investigated the influence of situational strength on the effects of personality variables. They varied the strength of situations and examined the ensuing relationships between a trait, extraversion, and a behavior, talkativeness. Their results showed that in strong situations the correlation between personality and behavior was rather low (average $r = .24$), but in weak situations personality showed a more significant relationship to behavior (r = .56). Further, recent work by Maslach and her colleagues (Maslach, Santee, and Wade 1987; Maslach, Stapp, and Santee 1985) on "individuation" has shown that the link between personality and behavior can be quite strong, even in strong situations. They argued that some strong situations may actually trigger attempts to behave in more self-expressive ways. Thus a strong situation can make traits and self-concept more – rather than less – salient to the individual.

An example of empirical research that also has bearing on the question of strong versus weak situations is the work of Swann and his associates on "self-verification" (e.g., Swann 1987; Swann and Ely 1984; Swann and Read 1981). Self-verification refers to the tendencies of people to "create – both in their actual social environments and in their own minds – a social reality that verifies and confirms their self-conceptions" (Swann 1982:33). In an investigation of such tendencies to preserve existing self-concepts, Swann and Ely (1984) did a study of undergraduate women in which research participants designated as "perceivers" were given false information about the tendencies toward introversion or extraversion of research subjects designated as "target" persons. While the perceivers acted in such a way as to elicit the behavior (either extraverted or introverted) that they had been led (by the experimenters) to expect, the target individuals acted to confirm these expectations only when they themselves were uncertain about their own tendencies. When the target person had a clear idea of herself as either an extravert or an introvert, she behaved in a manner consistent with her view of herself, *regardless* of the situational pressures (being exerted by the perceiver) to act otherwise. In other words, target persons only treated the perceivers' behavior as a strong situation when they themselves were uncertain about their own tendencies. When the target person had a well-defined self-concept, the situation was not strong enough to cause a change in her behavior.

While we can easily imagine situations where the constraints are so strong that people will not act to verify their own self-concepts (if I hold a gun to your head and threaten to shoot you if you do not act like an extravert, you will probably try to oblige me no matter what your self-concept is), most situations in organizations are probably of intermediate situational strength. This suggests that when contextual pressures in an organization conflict with individuals' own views of their personality characteristics, people may choose to act to verify their own sense of self rather than to confirm the expectations of others. Thus, in many situations, even those of moderate strength, we may expect that enduring and salient aspects of individuals' personalities will influence their personal and work outcomes.

Organizations as strong or weak situations

Usually it is argued that organizational socialization provides entrants with a shared set of values and norms, with strong cues for conformity (Van Maanen and Schein 1979). It has also been argued that organizations are themselves mechanisms for behavioral control (Thompson 1967), where individuals receive behavioral instructions and act on these cues to perform their respective roles (Katz and Kahn 1978). Yet, are organizations such powerful situations, capable of homogenizing behavior in the face of individual differences?

To answer this question, first let us note that few situations are so compelling as to force behavior in a prescribed direction. Even in the famous Asch (1956) conformity experiments, those usually cited to illustrate the effects of situational pressure, only a minority – about one-third – of the subjects actually conformed. While one-third of the subjects is significant and provides us with a valuable insight into human nature, the fact that the majority did not conform suggests that people will often behave in ways that they believe to be "right," even at the expense of violating a norm that seems to be shared by everyone else in the situation .

Some scholars have also noted that organizations are not as strong and coherent as they might appear. Thompson (1967), for example, emphasized that although the technology of an organization's production may be relatively known, firms must deal with uncertainties in their interactions with customers, financial institutions, and social/legal institutions. The managers who must cope with such uncertainties rarely have routinized or prescribed roles where correct solutions are fully known. Instead, idiosyncratic styles and behavioral repertoires are used by managers in hopes of placing some structure or algorithmic solutions on the ambiguity (Miner and Estler 1985). Consequently, when a successful manager leaves the organization, the firm often tries to replicate that person as closely as possible since the traits of the role occupant (e.g., aggressive yet friendly) may be better known than the specific skills necessary to solve the organization's problems. Thus, the unique "personal style" of a role occupant is subsequently used as a "pattern" to be followed by later occupants of that role (Turner 1988:3).

Logically, as one proceeds up the hierarchy of a firm, it is expected that organizational roles increase in degrees of uncertainty. This ordering is implicit in Jaques's (1961) notion of "time span of discretion," the time period necessary to obtain feedback on one's performance. It is also implicit in Simon's (1957) notion of administration as the absorption of uncertainty and in the fact that the hiring of managers is frequently based more on commonality of values and personality than on a bundle of requisite skills (Kanter 1977). In addition, many authors have taken pains to note the power and discretionary influence of those at even the lowest levels (e.g., Crozier 1964; Mechanic 1962), with the assumption of organizational roles often being more a product of negotiation and mutual influence than the result of simple role sending and conformity (Graen 1976; Graen, Orris, and Johnson 1973). Thus, while one would expect the personality of the founder or top manager of a firm to be manifested more strongly in his or her role than that of the person on the shop floor, even at the lowest levels of the organization the influence process is not entirely one way, nor is conformity the only explanation of behavior.

The most extreme view of organizations as being characterized by ambiguity rather than by structure is taken by March and his associates (March 1978; March and Olsen 1976). They argue that much of organizational life is imbued with ambiguity and that, often, the workings of an organization more closely resemble a random process than some finely tuned vehicle of production. Alternatively, Pfeffer (1981) has noted that organizational contexts can differ in terms of their degree of uncertainty, and that the most uncertain situations are precisely those contexts where power can be exerted by individuals and organizational subunits. House (1988) has recently extended this argument by noting that personal dispositions for power will be most strongly expressed under conditions of greatest organizational ambiguity, in settings where routines are not in place or are undergoing large-scale change. Such a hypothesis is similar to saying that organizational situations can vary in strength and clarity, and that dispositions will be most strongly expressed in the weakest of these contexts.

Uncovering the person in organizational behavior

Some research has specifically shown that individual dispositions are expressed in organizational settings, rather than being swamped by forces for conformity. Research on need for achievement and power, for example, has shown that people high in these characteristics manage to climb the organizational ladder with more success than do others in the organization (McClelland and Boyatzis 1982). Research has also indicated a relationship between personality and satisfaction with career decisions, with those individuals high in trait anxiety exhibiting relatively low satisfaction with their career choices (Kimes and Troth 1974). Other work has shown that individuals high in internal control [using Rotter's (1966) I/E scale] make more money and assume occupations of higher status than individuals who score higher in external control (Andrisani and Nestel 1976). However, because much of this personality research is based on cross-sectional data, the results can be interpreted as evidence for situational rather than dispositional effects. That is, the association between personality and organization could be due to the power of the organizational situation in shaping the person. Like Pygmalion, individuals' personalities could be products of organizational socialization and the taking of particular roles.

Much stronger evidence for the expression of personal dispositions has recently come from two longitudinal studies on job attitudes. In one study, Staw and Ross (1985) found that individuals' job attitudes were somewhat impervious to objective job changes. They found job satisfaction to be consistent over time, regardless of whether individuals changed employers or occupations. They also found that initial job satisfaction was a far better predictor of subsequent job attitudes than were changes in job status or pay. Staw and Ross's results thus show the individual as rather resistant to organizational influence, with attitudes determined more by personal or dispositional characteristics than by the job situation.

Staw, Bell, and Claussen (1986) provided additional evidence for dispositional as opposed to situational influence. They examined the effects of a personality characteristic, affective disposition, upon job satisfaction in a longitudinal sample that spanned much of their research subjects' working lives. The data for the study were taken from the Intergenerational Studies (IGS) conducted by the Institute of Human Development at the University of California, Berkeley. The IGS data are an aggregation of three separate longitudinal studies that investigated the lives of selected individuals from their childhood in the late 1920s and 1930s up to the present.

Personality data were available from Q-sorts (Block 1971). The IGS Q-sorts contained a set of cards with statements about the person, such as "initiates humor," "irritable," "cheerful," or "seeks reassurance from others." The cards were placed by judges into a forced normal distribution in which lower categories (1–3) represented qualities or traits least characteristic of the person being judged, middle-range scores (4–6) represented moderately characteristic traits, and high scores (7–9) represented those traits that were most characteristic of the person being rated. Thus, the Q-sort methodology provided an ipsative measure of the salience of various dimensions of the individual's personality, rather than a normative rating of the individual against age or sex peers. This methodology therefore avoided the problems (discussed earlier in this chapter) associated with nomothetic measures of personality. Further, each Q-sort was based on multiple observations of the research participants; thus the data fit Buss and Craik's and Epstein's recommendations of multiple measurement in personality research.

Using the Q-sort data, Staw, Bell, and Claussen found that affective disposition, measured from as early as the junior high school years, significantly predicted job satisfaction (measured by questionnaires and interviews) up to forty years later. People who had shown a general tendency toward positive affective states tended to be more satisfied with their jobs than those who scored low on the measure of positive affect. Controlling for a situational variable, the substantive complexity of subjects' jobs (akin to job characteristics), did nothing to diminish the strength of the relationship of people's dispositions to subsequent job attitudes. Likewise, controlling for the socioeconomic status of the job did not alter the relationship between disposition and job attitudes. Thus, across a range of occupations and different organizations (i.e., differing situations), personality appeared to influence individual responses to the job situation.

Parallel to these findings, recent work by personality psychologists has shown that individual differences are predictive of well-being across many areas of people's lives. In a longitudinal study of over 4,900 men and women, Costa, McCrae, and Zonderman (1987) found that both general well-being, and its component parts (positive affect, negative affect, and health concerns), were stable over time. In addition, this stability was as high for people who had experienced major changes in areas of their lives (e.g., changes in marital status, residence, or employment) as for those who had experienced relatively little situational change. In other words, stable individual differences were more predictive of people's well-being than were dramatic alterations in people's situations. In terms of people's careers, these findings imply that career satisfaction may be determined as much (or more) by individuals' stable predispositions as by the "objective" features of the career.

A MODEL OF PERSONAL INFLUENCE IN
ORGANIZATIONAL SETTINGS

So far we have tried to knock organizational influence down a peg or two and to build up the role of the individual. Although we would not argue that conformity is nonexistent, we think its degree and frequency have been overplayed. To say that personality has effects in the organization does not, of course, mean that individuals will dominate the work situation. It simply means that, when properly measured, it is possible to discern individualization rather than homogenization in the work force. It also means that socialization, role taking, and social influence are at best incomplete forces, not capable of smoothing out all the idiosyncracies that people bring to the organization. Especially when traits or predispositions are strong, they will be less likely to be overridden by situational forces (Dweck and Leggett 1988). Organizational roles are far more ambiguous than scholars usually realize, and in the space created by such ambiguity, individuals are able to maneuver and express their own individuality. Thus, from our perspective, individuals are proactive and often significant forces in the way organizational roles are carried out.

The personality literature we have discussed certainly illustrates the potential for people to shape their own organizational outcomes, yet this literature does not address the *process* by which people act as sculptors. In the remainder of this chapter, we outline a model that uses personal control as the means by which individuals' personalities and traits influence work outcomes. By personal control, we refer to individuals' *proactive regulation of their work lives.* This definition is compatible with recent work by Greenberger and Strasser (1986; Greenberger, Strasser, and Lee 1988), who describe personal control as "an individual's beliefs, at a given point in time, in his or her ability to affect a change, in a desired direction" (Greenberger and Strasser 1986:165). They observe that members of organizations are more likely to initiate action when they perceive themselves to have personal control, and our usage of personal control also emphasizes this action component. We believe personal control encompasses not only the expression of individuality in organizational settings but also how individuals manage to change their work situations. Thus, we posit that it is possible to take the arguments of the "personologists" a step further, by indicating how personality, through the process of personal control, can actually affect outcomes that are normally thought to be governed by environmental forces.

In an effort to show how work roles can be individualized, we will first present a general model of personal control in organizations. We will then provide an example of how one specific person variable, need for power, might lead to varying attempts at personal control as well as varying consequences for the individual.

A general model of personal control in organizations

Individual characteristics. The model depicted in Figure 11.1 shows that certain individual characteristics influence whether or not a person attempts to exert control in an organizational context. Several personality characteristics are posited to be related to the person acting as an agent (initiating control attempts), rather than reacting passively to his or her organizational situation. Each of the characteristics discussed here was chosen on the basis of its robustness in related research contexts and is therefore promising for future research. This is not, however, meant to represent an inclusive set of personality characteristics that might influence personal control, and we would hope that future research would expand on this set of traits.

First, whether a person is a high or a low self-monitor will influence the probability of personal control. Self-monitoring refers to an individual's tendency to rely on features of the situation when making behavioral choices (Snyder 1974; Snyder and Ickes 1985). High self-monitors are those individuals whose behavior is largely regulated by situational contingencies. Therefore, their behaviors tend to be situation-specific. Low self-monitors, by contrast, rely on their own inner states in making behavioral choices. Low self-monitors are more resistant to situational pressures or less inclined to view situations as strong or compelling. A closely related finding from the organizational literature is that people who are "field dependent" are more susceptible to social influence at work than are people who are "field independent" (Weiss and Nowicki 1981; Weiss and Shaw

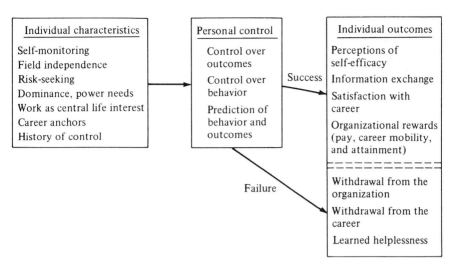

Figure 11.1. General model of personality and personal control in organizations

1979). We can hypothesize that low self-monitors or high field independents will therefore be more likely to initiate attempts at personal control. It should be noted that the model at this point does not assume that these attempts will necessarily be successful. (Both positive and negative outcomes will be considered later in this discussion.) It is conceivable that while low self-monitors (or high field independents) will be less hesitant about acting proactively, they may also attend less to situational cues that might be helpful in suggesting what *form* such influence attempts should take (e.g., rewards, ingratiation, persuasion, manipulation of information given to other organizational actors, and so on). Low self-monitors may therefore make relatively more errors in choosing among influence strategies than would other people.

Whether a person is risk seeking, versus risk averse, has been argued to be a factor in whether the individual will attempt upward political influence in an organization (Porter, Allen, and Angle 1981). We would expand this argument to include any attempt at personal control, whether the attempt is political or not. To the extent that a person is risk seeking, he or she should be more willing to test the environment by exerting attempts to change or control it.

Dominance and the need for power are almost by definition related to attempts at personal control. People with high needs for power are concerned with control over their environment and with influencing others (Porter, Allen, and Angle 1981). Managers who are high in dominance or need for power are thus more likely to engage in influence attempts than are others (for a review, see House 1988). For example, Mowday (1978) found that elementary school principals who were rated high in influence activity had high power motivation as well. Mowday also suggested that need for achievement should be related to influence attempts. While he reasoned that people with a high need for achievement would be more self-confident, and therefore more likely to risk an influence attempt, there is an even more direct reason for expecting need for achievement to be related to attempts at personal control. This is because people who are high in need for achievement are task oriented, and attempts to control contingencies in the environment may be necessary in order to succeed at many work tasks (cf. Kanter 1977; Staw 1986).

Another personality variable related to the likelihood of initiating an influence attempt would be whether or not the person holds work as a central life interest. Dubin and Champoux (1975) found that workers who held work, rather than nonwork activities, as a central life interest perceived themselves as being more decisive and as taking more initiative than did workers with other central life interests (either neutral, or non-work). Insofar as individuals hold work (or work-related activities, such as union activism) as a central part of their identities, they should have a high stake in controlling the course of their careers, as well as the outcomes.

A person's occupational self-concept, or "career anchor" (Schein 1978), should also be related to his or her likelihood of exerting personal control at work. Schein defines a career anchor as being composed of three types of self-perception, each of which is based on the person's actual work experiences. These are the person's self-perceived talents and abilities, the person's self-perceived motives and needs, and the person's self-perceived attitudes and values. Schein outlines five major career anchors. Of these, we would expect those individuals whose career anchor is "stability and security" to make relatively few efforts at personal control. This is similar to our predictions for risk-averse versus risk-seeking people. At the other extreme, those with the career anchor of "creativity" would be expected to engage in a lot of control activity.

Finally, the person's history of control should affect future influence attempts. To the extent that the person has made previous attempts at personal control, he or she should understand what is involved in making these attempts. Such an understanding or feeling of capability may be a prerequisite for many attempts at personal control. To the extent that these attempts have been rewarded in the past, the person will have learned which sorts of attempts have high probabilities of success, and that these attempts can indeed pay off.

Forms of personal control. Though individual characteristics can affect attempts at personal control, it is not clear what form these control attempts will take. Figure 11.1 therefore addresses three types of personal control: control over outcomes, control over behavior, and the ability to predict outcomes and behavior (Staw 1986). It is hypothesized that the most desirable form of influence is control over the distribution of outcomes. If people identify strongly with the organization, and/or occupy managerial roles, they may, for example, want to influence organizational outcomes, such as make-or-buy decisions or decisions to enter new markets. However, for most organizational participants, the primary concern will be influence over matters like pay, promotion, and benefits. Controlling these outcomes immediately affects participants' personal welfare.

Outcome control attempts can take many forms, from outright manipulation, to more subtle persuasion and ingratiation attempts. When the organizational member has legitimate power to specify outcomes, a control attempt could take the form of a direct order or outright manipulation of returns. For example, the supervisor who does the scheduling for shift work often has control over his or her own schedule as well. The outcome over which the individual has control in this case might be having desirable days off, such as the week-end. When individuals do not have the power to manipulate their outcomes directly, they may try persuasion. Again using the example of desirable time off, individuals might try to persuade the supervisor to schedule them according to their preferences, perhaps by suggesting that their preferred schedule will result in higher efficiency. Finally, individuals might try to gain control of outcomes more indirectly, through ingratiation. Here, it may be that individuals never directly state what they want; rather, they hope that by being in the good graces of more powerful others, positive outcomes will be provided (Wortman and Linsenmeier 1977).

Frequently, control over outcomes is impossible. An employee may desire a pay raise, but wages are frozen; more overtime may be wanted, but production is slow; a promotion may be yearned for, but the firm is not growing. In these cases, the next most desirable contingency to control would be control over behavior. Because most people want to feel efficacious, they are likely to attempt some measure of control over their environments. Thus, if control over outcomes is not possible, individuals may attempt a second kind of personal control, control over their own work behavior or inputs to the production process. Examples of behavioral control might include decisions about actual work methods, pace, amount of effort, dress, and even language and demeanor shown at work. These forms of behavioral control will often serve to satisfy desires for self-determination. They may also even affect people's *perceptions* of outcome control. In this vein, research has shown that individuals often cognitively confuse outcome and behavioral control (cf. Langer 1975, 1978, on the "illusion of control"). Thus, people who have some measure of behavioral control may come to believe that they possess outcome control as well.

The third kind of personal control depicted by the model is the ability to make sense of or predict one's environment. If real outcome control is not possible, and if the work is structured in a manner that leaves little room for people to exert control over their own behavior, people may gain a sense of efficacy by learning to *predict* their behavior and outcomes (Staw 1977). Being able to predict one's behavior means knowing what one is going to be asked to do, even though there may be little choice in the compliance with such role demands. Being able to predict outcomes refers to knowledge of rewards and punishments connected to the role, their occurrence and contingencies, even though the individual may have little power over the administration of these outcomes.

By reducing ambiguity and by clarifying the reinforcement contingencies in their environments, people gain some sense of control. As observed by Louis (1980), efforts toward predictive power, or what she calls "sensemaking", are especially prevalent during the early stages of organizational socialization. Extending this idea, we contend that the ability to predict one's environment is vital throughout one's career. Not only is this necessary for a sense of personal efficacy, but it may also increase people's future chances of upgrading their form of personal control to either behavioral or outcome control. For example, people who are in highly structured jobs may, through their knowledge of the job, be able to suggest more efficient ways of performing their tasks. The changes could also involve more discretion on the person's part. If the person is successful in persuading those higher up to approve the changes, then he or she will have successfully upgraded the form of control from predictive to behavioral control. At this point, the individual may be able to lobby successfully for greater pay or benefits, thereby moving from behavioral control to control over outcomes. Thus, the three forms of control shown in Figure 11.1 may be hierarchical in nature. Not only can individuals work their ways up the control ladder, but influence at each level is likely to include the forms of influence at the preceding level.

Results of control. If the person finds that he or she cannot exert any of the three levels of control in Figure 11.1, the model shows two possible outcomes. Depending on the individual characteristics depicted in the first stage of the model, the person will either withdraw from the organization (and perhaps even from an entire career path) or enter a state of learned helplessness. If the person scores highly on the traits discussed earlier, it is predicted that these proactive tendencies will push him or her to change directions, either in terms of the organization or the career. By contrast, if the person is low on the traits depicted in the model, he or she is likely to react with increasing feelings of helplessness. This, in turn, can create a vicious cycle. When people have less motivation or energy for initiating control attempts of any sort (including withdrawing, as a more proactive person might do), they receive less and less opportunity for control, thus leading to even more feelings of helplessness.

What outcomes might we expect from successful attempts at personal control? First, any of the three types of personal control would likely increase people's senses of self-efficacy. In contrast to the learned helplessness that may be engendered by unsuccessful control attempts, people who have successfully exercised personal control should infer that they can be influential or efficacious in the organizational context. Personal control might also lead to greater information exchange with the organization. Through testing their environments, individuals should garner information with which to predict their future behavior and outcomes. In some cases, the individuals may provide the organization with valuable feedback on employee preferences as well as new and better ways to do the work. Of course, successful control attempts may not always result in an *even* exchange of information between the employee and the organization. This is because one way of controlling one's behavior may be to restrict information to others about one's work procedures. Katz (1980), for example, suggests that people in the adaptation stage of the socialization process may surround their work with secrecy and ritual so that others in the organization leave them alone to do their work as they please.

Control over work behavior and inputs should result in greater satisfaction with the career, and perhaps even in greater career involvement. This follows from research on job design, which shows that to the extent that people feel responsible for their work, they should have more positive affective reactions toward it (Hackman and Oldham 1980). Likewise, in the case of control over outcomes, individuals are also expected to feel greater career satisfaction and career involvement due to the self-efficacy that is created by successful personal control. In addition, if people manage to significantly improve their level or mix of organizational rewards, outcome control should have a rather direct effect on job attitudes. As shown in Figure 11.1, increased pay, career mobility, and attainment are just a few of the possible products that control over outcomes may provide.

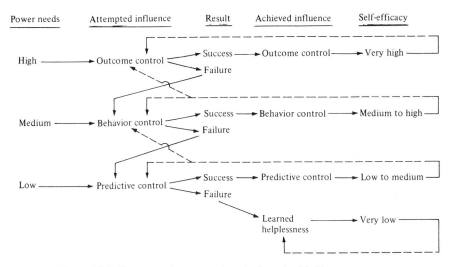

Figure 11.2. Power needs, personal control, and self-efficacy

Example: power needs, personal control, and self-efficacy

Figure 11.2 uses a subset of the variables just discussed in order to provide a more detailed outline of the control process. The figure shows an individual characteristic, power needs, leading to attempts at personal control, which in turn lead to perceptions of self-efficacy. We will discuss this process model of personal control using an example from the careers literature – that of a person in a static mid-career, who may need to take action to regain a sense of career growth (Hall 1986).

Power needs and control attempts. We first hypothesize that the person's level of need for power will influence the form of his or her control attempt. The model shows that high needs for power will be associated with attempts to control *outcomes.* People low in need for power may be content with *predictive* control, while those with intermediate needs may characteristically opt for control over their own *behavior.* Thus, if our hypothetical mid-career individual is high in power needs, he or she might be expected to try to directly control career outcomes. Such direct control might include looking for a more stimulating or prestigious job outside one's current firm, seeking out intra-firm possibilities for new, more stimulating work, or unilaterally enlarging the scope of the existing job. At the extreme, this person might opt for a complete change to a new career or line of work.

If the person has only intermediate power needs, we might expect that he or she would attempt an intermediate form of personal control. Rather than trying to directly manipulate career outcomes, this person may rely more on a strategy of control over behavioral inputs. In the case of breaking out of static career routines, this might involve attending company-sponsored career workshops or reading up on new areas of work related to one's current area. The person who is higher in power needs might also employ these strategies; the difference is that people higher in power needs are likely *additionally* to try some of the more directly proactive moves listed earlier. For example, the person high in need for power might attempt to change major facets of his or her role in the organization. Such role-building attempts can sometimes result in the person actually changing the organization by legitimizing a new role or job title, which persists in the organization even after this person is gone [see, e.g., Miner (1986, 1987) on "idiosyncratic jobs"]. By contrast, people who are lower in need for power may only attempt smaller changes in their jobs, such as changes in the hours worked or the amount of interaction with co-workers.

Finally, a person who is low in need for power may attempt only predictive control. For this person, it may be enough to merely feel that the work environment is relatively known and predictable. With regard to breaking out of midcareer routines, this person might only gather information that would enable him or her to predict what the firm's expectations might be over the next few years. Rather than creating a new job for themselves, people low in power need might be content with knowledge of what others are going to expect from them.

Effects of influence attempts. In Figure 11.2, we posit that if people are unsuccessful in exerting control at one level, they will subsequently try weaker forms of personal control. Thus, a person who is unsuccessful at exerting outcome control may try instead to increase behavioral control, and individuals who do not have control over their behavioral inputs may turn to prediction and sensemaking. Faced with unsuccessful outcomes at any of the three levels of personal control, the tendency to attempt personal control might be extinguished, resulting in a state of learned helplessness. In terms of the individual who had hoped to break out of static career routines, this state of learned helplessness would engender an even more static state, where further attempts at career growth would be unlikely. If people in this predicament do not channel their energies into successful attempts to grow in their non-work lives, then this outcome would be particularly bleak. Again, other variables from Figure 11.1 may be important here. For example, if the person holds non-work activities as his or her central life interest, a state of learned helplessness at work, while not desirable, will not be as crippling as it would be for the person who holds work as a central life interest.

On a more positive note, *successful* outcomes resulting from control attempts provide positive reinforcement of influence tendencies. When personal control attempts are successful, not only may people try the same strategy again in the future, but they may test the organizational environment by trying to upgrade their forms of personal control. People who find that they have a fair amount of predictive control may, for example, experiment with attempts at behavioral control, and people who have success with behavioral control may try to add outcome control to their repertoires.

Effects of personal control on self-efficacy. The model predicts that the level at which personal control is currently successful will affect the person's sense of self-efficacy. This sense of self-efficacy or competence is an important component of adequate adaptation (White 1959) and thus may be crucial to people's continuing growth in their careers.

If outcome control attempts are generally successful, this should result in strong feelings of being a sculptor or agent of one's own fate and thus high perceptions of self-efficacy. The dotted arrow in Figure 11.2, leading from high self-efficacy back to outcome control, indicates that a strong sense of self-efficacy should reinforce attempts at outcome control. For example, the person who has broken out of a career routine by creatively expanding the parameters of his or her current job, and who in turn is feeling highly efficacious, should be less hesitant about further proactive career growth.

Successful behavioral control attempts should also result in feelings of self-efficacy, although these feelings may be somewhat less than those engendered by outcome control. Again we show a dotted arrow in Figure 11.2, leading back to attempts at behavioral control, which indicates that these perceptions of self-efficacy should engender future career growth in the form of behavioral control. We also show a dotted arrow to outcome control, since the moderately strong sense of self-efficacy should also lead to an increased likelihood that the person would venture some outcome control attempts in the future. For example, having exerted behavioral control in the form of attending company career workshops and reading up on career opportunities, the person's resultant sense of self-efficacy may then lead him or her to lobby for rotation within the company to a more stimulating job. This would constitute attempted outcome control.

We posit that predictive control would lead only to low-to-medium perceptions of self-efficacy. Since the person is still in a basically passive state, self-efficacy should not be greatly increased by being able to predict the work environment. On the other hand, success at predictive control may give the person the incremental bit of confidence needed to attempt behavioral control in the future, thus providing a chance to work upward on the control ladder.

Finally, if failed influence attempts result in perceptions of helplessness, this is equivalent to feelings of very low self-efficacy. As shown in Figure 11.2, when self-efficacy is extremely low, people may not have the energy or the motivation to upgrade their forms of personal control. Thus, we show the relationship between low self-efficacy and helplessness as a closed loop. In the case of learned helplessness, the organization (or perhaps people from the person's non-work environment) may need to intervene in order to break the vicious circle.

CONCLUSION

We began this chapter by noting that there is a disparity between the popular and academic views of careers concerning the amount of control individuals can exert over their organizational lives. Drawing on a similar debate in psychology about the relative influence of person versus situation, we noted that people may not be as malleable or open to organizational influence as they are often depicted to be. We attempted to resolve the issue of individual versus organizational influence by discussing the concept of situational strength and by noting that many organizational contexts are weak or ambiguous enough to let personal dispositions shine through. People may shape their environments as much or more than they are shaped by their environments.

To suggest a process by which this individualization or modification of the environment might occur, we outlined a model of personal control in organizations. In our view, personal control is a primary mechanism by which individual dispositions come to be expressed in organizational settings. We also elaborated a more specific process model that could show how power needs affect the means by which personal control is expressed, as well as its likely consequences. Using this model, we examined the case of a plateaued individual who wants to break out of career routines.

Our models of personal influence in organizations provide only a few of the ways in which personality and individual differences are likely to be expressed in career actions and outcomes. We have specified some of the simplest interrelationships, yet even these are, at present, based more on speculation than on concrete research. The effects of personality and personal control are thus prime candidates for future career research.

REFERENCES

Allport, G. W. (1937). *Personality: A Psychological Interpretation*. New York: Holt.
Andrisani, P. J., and Nestel, G. (1976). Internal–external control as contributor to and outcome of work experience. *Journal of Applied Psychology, 61,* 156–165.
Asch, S. E. (1956). Studies of independence and conformity. *Psychological Monographs, 70* (whole no. 416).
Bem, D. J., and Allen, A. (1974). On predicting some of the people some of the time: the search for cross-situational consistencies in behavior. *Psychological Review, 81,* 506–520.
Bem, D. J., and Funder, D. C. (1978). Predicting more of the people more of the time: assessing the personality of situations. *Psychological Review, 85,* 485–501.
Block, J. (in collaboration with N. Haan) (1971). *Lives Through Time*. Berkeley, CA: Bancroft Books.
Bolles, R. N. (1980). *What Color Is Your Parachute?* Berkeley, CA: Ten Speed.
Bolles, R. N. (1988). *What Color Is Your Parachute?* Berkeley, CA: Ten Speed.
Bowers, K. S. (1973). Situationism in psychology: an analysis and critique. *Psychological Bulletin, 80,* 307–336.
Buss, D. M., and Craik, K. H. (1983). The act frequency approach to personality. *Psychological Review, 90,* 105–126.
Costa, P. T., Jr., McCrae, R. R., and Zonderman, A. B. (1987). Environmental and dispositional influences on well-being: longitudinal followup of an American national sample. *British Journal of Psychology, 78,* 299–306.
Crozier, M. (1964). *The Bureaucratic Phenomenon*. Chicago: University of Chicago Press.
Dubin, R., and Champoux, J. E. (1975). Workers' central life interests and personality characteristics. *Journal of Vocational Behavior, 6,* 165–174.
Dweck, C. S., and Leggett, E. L. (1988). A social-cognitive approach to motivation and personality. *Psychological Review, 95,* 256–273.
Epstein, S. (1979). The stability of behavior: I. On predicting most of the people much of the time. *Journal of Personality and Social Psychology, 37,* 1097–1126.
Graen, G. (1976). Role-making processes within complex organizations. In M. D. Dunnette (ed.), *Handbook of Industrial and Organizational Psychology*. Chicago: Rand McNally.
Graen, G., Orris, J. B., and Johnson, T. (1973). Role assimilation processes in a complex organization. *Journal of Vocational Behavior, 3,* 395–420.
Greco, B. (1975). *How To Get the Job That's Right For You*. Homewood, IL: Dow Jones-Irwin.
Greenberger, D. B., and Strasser, S. (1986). The development and application of a model of personal control in organizations. *Academy of Management Review, 11,* 164–177.
Greenberger, D. B., Strasser, S., and Lee, S. (1988). Personal control as a mediator between perceptions of supervisory behaviors and employee reactions. *Academy of Management Journal, 31,* 405–417.
Griffin, R. A. (1983). Objective and social sources of information in task redesign: a field experiment. *Administrative Science Quarterly, 28,* 184–200.
Hackman, J. R., and Oldham, G. R. (1976). Motivation through the design of work: test of a theory. *Organizational Behavior and Human Performance, 16,* 250–279.
Hackman, J. R., and Oldham, G. R. (1980). *Work Redesign*. Reading, MA: Addison-Wesley.

Hall, D. T. (1976). *Careers in Organizations*. Pacific Palisades, CA: Goodyear.
Hall, D. T. (1986). Breaking career routines: midcareer choice and identity development. In D. T. Hall (ed.), *Career Development in Organizations*. San Francisco: Jossey-Bass.
Hansen, J., and Campbell, D. P. (1985). *Manual for the SVIB-SCII*. Palo Alto, CA: Consulting Psychology.
Holland, J. L. (1966). *The Psychology of Vocational Choice*. Waltham, MA: Blaisdell.
Holland, J. L. (1976). Vocational preferences. In M. D. Dunnette (ed.), *Handbook of Industrial and Organizational Psychology*. Chicago: Rand McNally.
Holland, J. L. (1985). *Making Vocational Choices: A Theory of Vocational Personalities and Work Environments*, 2nd ed. Englewood Cliffs, NJ: Prentice-Hall.
House, R. J. (1988). Power and personality in complex organizations. In B. M. Staw and L. L. Cummings (eds.), *Research in Organizational Behavior*, Vol. 10. Greenwich, CT: JAI.
Jaques, E. (1961). *Equitable Payment*. New York: Wiley.
Jones, G. R. (1983). Psychological orientation and the process of organizational socialization: an interactionist perspective. *Academy of Management Review, 8*, 464–474.
Kanter, R. M. (1977). *Men and Women of the Corporation*. New York: Basic Books.
Katz, D., and Kahn, R. L. (1978). *The Social Psychology of Organizations*, 2nd ed. New York: Wiley.
Katz, R. (1980). Time and work: toward an integrative perspective. In B. M. Staw and L. L. Cummings (eds.), *Research in Organizational Behavior*, Vol. 2. Greenwich, CT: JAI.
Kimes, H. G., and Troth, W. A. (1974). Relationship of trait anxiety to career decisiveness. *Journal of Counseling Psychology, 21*, 277–280.
Langer, E. J. (1975). The illusion of control. *Journal of Personality and Social Psychology, 32*, 311–328.
Langer, E. J. (1978). Rethinking the role of thought in social interaction. In J. H. Harvey, W. I. Ickes, and R. F. Kidd (eds.), *New Directions in Attribution Research*, Vol. 2. Hillsdale, NJ: Erlbaum.
Louis, M. R. (1980). Surprise and sense making: what newcomers experience in entering unfamiliar organizational settings. *Administrative Science Quarterly, 25*, 226–251.
McClelland, D. C., and Boyatzis, R. E. (1982). Leadership motive pattern and long term success in management. *Journal of Applied Psychology, 67*, 737–743.
March, J. G. (1978). Bounded rationality, ambiguity, and the engineering of choice. *Bell Journal of Economics, 9*, 587–608.
March, J. G., and Olsen, J. P. (1976). *Ambiguity and Choice in Organizations*. Bergen, Norway: Universitetsforlaget.
Maslach, C., Santee, R. T., and Wade, C. (1987). Individuation, gender role, and dissent: personality mediators of situational forces. *Journal of Personality and Social Psychology, 53*, 1088–1093.
Maslach, C., Stapp, J., and Santee, R. T. (1985). Individuation: conceptual analysis and assessment. *Journal of Personality and Social Psychology, 49*, 729–738.
Mechanic, D. (1962). Sources of power of lower participants in complex organizations. *Administrative Science Quarterly, 7*, 349–364.
Miner, A. S. (1986). Systematic serendipity: ambiguity, uncertainty and idiosyncratic jobs. University of Wisconsin–Madison, Graduate School of Business Working Paper No. 7–86–23.
Miner, A. S. (1987). Idiosyncratic jobs in formalized organizations. *Administrative Science Quarterly, 32*, 327–351.
Miner, A. S., and Estler, S. E. (1985). Accrual mobility: job mobility in higher education through responsibility accrual. *Journal of Higher Education, 56*, 121–143.
Mischel, W. (1968). *Personality and Assessment*. New York: Wiley.
Mischel, W. (1977). The interaction of person and situation. In D. Magnusson and N. S. Endler (eds.), *Personality at the Crossroads: Current Issues in International Psychology*. Hillsdale, NJ: Erlbaum.
Monson, T. C., Hesley, J. W., and Chernick, L. (1982). Specifying when personality traits can and cannot predict behavior: an alternative to abandoning the attempt to predict single act criteria. *Journal of Personality and Social Psychology, 43*, 385–399.
Mowday, R. T. (1978). The exercise of upward influence in organizations. *Administrative Science Quarterly, 23*, 137–156.

Munsterberg, H. (1913). *Psychology and Industrial Efficiency*. Boston: Houghton Mifflin.

Neiner, A. G., and Owens, W. A. (1985). Using biodata to predict job choice among college graduates. *Journal of Applied Psychology, 70,* 127–136.

O'Reilly, C. A., and Caldwell, D. (1979). Informational influence as a determinant of perceived task characteristics and job satisfaction. *Journal of Applied Psychology, 64,* 157–165.

Owens, W. A. (1976). Background data. In M. D. Dunnette (ed.), *Handbook of Industrial and Organizational Psychology*. Chicago: Rand McNally.

Pfeffer, J. (1981). *Power in Organizations*. Marshfield, MA: Pitman.

Porter, L. W., Allen, R. W., and Angle, H. L. (1981). The politics of upward influence in organizations. In B. M. Staw and L. L. Cummings (eds.), *Research in Organizational Behavior,* Vol. 3. Greenwich, CT: JAI.

Rotter, J. B. (1966). Generalized expectancies for internal versus external control of reinforcement. *Psychological Monographs, 80* (whole No. 609).

Salancik, G. R., and Pfeffer, J. (1978). A social information processing approach to job attitudes and task design. *Administrative Science Quarterly, 23,* 224–253.

Schein, E. H. (1970). *Organizational Psychology*. Englewood Cliffs, NJ: Prentice-Hall.

Schein, E. H. (1978). *Career Dynamics: Matching Individual and Organizational Needs*. Reading, MA: Addison-Wesley.

Schneider, B. (1983). Interactional psychology and organizational behavior. In B. M. Staw and L. L. Cummings (eds.), *Research in Organizational Behavior,* Vol. 5. Greenwich, CT: JAI.

Schneider, B. (1987). The people make the place. *Personnel Psychology, 40,* 437–453.

Simon, H. A. (1957). *Administrative Behavior*. New York: Macmillan.

Snyder, M. (1974). The self-monitoring of expressive behavior. *Journal of Personality and Social Psychology, 30,* 526–537.

Snyder, M., and Ickes, W. (1985). Personality and social behavior. In G. Lindzey and E. Aronson (eds.), *Handbook of Social Psychology,* 3rd ed., Vol. 2. New York: Random House.

Staw, B. M. (1977). Motivation in organizations: toward synthesis and redirection. In B. M. Staw and G. R. Salancik (eds.), *New Directions in Organizational Behavior*. Chicago: St. Clair.

Staw, B. M. (1986). Beyond the control graph: steps toward a model of perceived control in organizations. In R. N. Stern and S. McCarthy (eds.), *The Organizational Practice of Democracy*. Chichester: Wiley.

Staw, B. M., Bell, N. E., and Claussen, J. A. (1986). The dispositional approach to job attitudes: a lifetime longitudinal test. *Administrative Science Quarterly, 31,* 56–77.

Staw, B. M., and Ross, J. (1985). Stability in the midst of change: a dispositional approach to job attitudes. *Journal of Applied Psychology, 70,* 469–480.

Strong, E. K., Jr. (1943). *Vocational Interests of Men and Women*. Stanford, CA: Stanford University Press.

Swann, W. B., Jr. (1982). Self-verification: bringing social reality into harmony with the self. In J. Suls and A. G. Greenwald (eds.), *Psychological Perspectives on the Self,* Vol. 2. Hillsdale, NJ: Erlbaum.

Swann, W. B., Jr. (1987). Identity negotiation: where two roads meet. *Journal of Personality and Social Psychology, 53,* 1038–1051.

Swann, W. B., Jr., and Ely, R. J. (1984). A battle of wills: self-verification versus behavioral confirmation. *Journal of Personality and Social Psychology, 47,* 1287–1302.

Swann, W. B., Jr., and Read, S. J. (1981). Acquiring self-knowledge: the search for feedback that fits. *Journal of Personality and Social Psychology, 41,* 1119–1128.

Thompson, J. D. (1967). *Organizations in Action*. New York: McGraw-Hill.

Tiedeman, D. V., and Miller-Tiedeman, A. (1984). Career decision making: an individualistic perspective. In D. Brown and L. Brooks (eds.), *Career Choice and Development*. San Francisco: Jossey-Bass.

Turner, R. H. (1988). Personality in society: social psychology's contribution to sociology. *Social Psychology Quarterly, 51,* 1–10.

Van Maanen, J., and Schein, E. H. (1979). Toward a theory of organizational socialization. In B. M. Staw and L. L. Cummings (eds.), *Research in Organizational Behavior,* Vol. 1. Greenwich, CT: JAI.

Watson, J. B. (1925). *Behaviorism*. New York: Norton.

Weiss, H. M., and Adler, S. (1984). Personality and organizational behavior. In B. Staw and L. Cummings (eds.), *Research in Organizational Behavior*, Vol. 6. Greenwich, CT: JAI.

Weiss, H. M., and Nowicki, C. E. (1981). Social influences on task satisfaction: model competence and observer field dependence. *Organizational Behavior and Human Performance, 27*, 345–366.

Weiss, H. M., and Shaw, J. B. (1979). Social influences on judgements about tasks. *Organizational Behavior and Human Performance, 24*, 126–140.

White, R. W. (1959). Motivation reconsidered: the concept of competence. *Psychological Review, 66*, 297–333.

White, S. E., and Mitchell, T. R. (1979). Job enrichment versus social cues: a comparison and competitive test. *Journal of Applied Psychology, 64*, 1–9.

Wortman, C. B., and Linsenmeier, J. A. W. (1977). Interpersonal attraction and techniques of ingratiation in organizational settings. In B. M. Staw and G. R. Salancik (eds.), *New Directions in Organizational Behavior*. Chicago: St. Clair.

Zuckerman, M., Koestner, R., DeBoy, T., Garcia, T., Maresca, B. C., and Sartoris, J. M. (1988). To predict some of the people some of the time: a reexamination of the moderator variable approach in personality theory. *Journal of Personality and Social Psychology, 54*, 1006–1019.

12 Work, stress, and careers: a preventive approach to maintaining organizational health

JANINA C. LATACK

STRESS IN A CAREERS CONTEXT

The purpose of this chapter is to apply key stress models and concepts to building career theory. There are several reasons why the time is particularly ripe for researchers to consider stress in a careers context: Over time, job stress aggregates to career stress, career events are key sources of stress, and career researchers have not generally tapped the voluminous stress literature in formulating models and empirical research.

First, within stress research, job stress in organizations has emerged as a central focus (Beehr and Bhagat, 1985; Matteson and Ivancevich, 1987; Murphy and Schoenborn, 1987; Sethi and Schuler, 1983; Spector, Dwyer, and Jex, 1988). There are considerable human and organizational costs associated with job stress, including depression and burnout, ulcers, low job satisfaction, absenteeism and turnover, decreased productivity, lawsuits, and health care costs. It has been estimated that job stress costs American industry $150 billion annually in diminished productivity, absenteeism, and medical costs (Landers, 1987). In addition, 15% of worker's compensation claims are now stress related (Dentzer, McCormick, and Tsuruoka, 1986). Job stress as a management problem continues to capture major media attention, as evidenced by a *Wall Street Journal* special report section on medicine and health with a lead article entitled "Is your job making you sick?" (Bennett, 1988). A recent cover story by *Newsweek* (Miller, 1988) headlined stress on the job. Jobs are the building blocks of careers. Therefore, over time, stressful job experiences aggregate to yield stressful careers.

Second, career issues are becoming increasingly salient and common stressors in work organizations. That is, in addition to stress in the immediate job situation that might involve work overload, ambiguity, or other contextual and role-related stressors (Abdel-Halim, 1981; Beehr and Newman, 1978; Parasuraman and Alutto, 1984), individuals face stress around issues that are a direct outgrowth of how careers unfold over time and across life domains – obsolescence, mid-career renewal, job loss or threat of job loss, lack of upward mobility, forced early retirement, dual-career pressures, assimilation of women and minorities into nontraditional careers, and work–nonwork balance (London and Stumpf, 1986; Pines and Aronson, 1988). As organizations pay increasing attention to employee careers and to health problems, focus on stress that originates in career issues will intensify.

Third, careers research assumes that many career events and processes are

252

stressful and, as such, need to be managed more effectively. For example, Van Maanen and Schein (1979) argue that the most important assumption underlying socialization processes is that individuals undergoing any organizational transition are in an anxiety-producing situation. Similarly, Louis (1980) notes that during career transitions, individuals must "cope" with a variety of change dimensions and reactions to them. At present, however, there are few theoretical formulations or empirical studies of careers that draw systematically upon the voluminous stress literature when formulating models and developing variables for examination.

This chapter considers current process models of stress (Beehr and Bhagat, 1985; Lazarus and Folkman, 1984; Schuler, 1985) as a mechanism for building career theory. Particular attention is paid to coping strategies and social support as key preventive influences that may avert or alleviate stress-related health problems. In addition, future research agendas are proposed that build on current integrative studies of stress and careers (e.g., Feldman and Brett, 1983; Latack, 1984; Osipow, Doty, and Spokane, 1985). The goal is to stimulate more integrative models of careers that make explicit use of underlying assumptions about career stress and to address crucial stress-related problems that originate in career dilemmas and challenges.

STRESS AND COPING: DEFINITIONS AND MODELS

It is important to note at the outset that conceptual definitions of stress typically allow for both positive and negative effects of stress. Up to a point, stress can be positive because it motivates and excites. Similarly, the careers literature has acknowledged the importance of deliberately imposing some degree of stress, such as early job challenge (Hall, 1976). This positive aspect has long been recognized in stress research. The goal is not to eliminate stress; as Selye (1956) has pointed out, the only people who have no stress are dead! Nonetheless, current research emphasis and managerial concern is based on problematic aspects of stress – the costs of stress that accrue when stress is too high or continues for a prolonged period of time. Thus, the preventive perspective adopted here recognizes the positive, developmental aspects of stress but focuses on avoiding the negative outcomes. In short, the most pressing issue is that stress *can* do more harm than good – and researchers interested in careers can make an important contribution to solving stress-related problems.

Although stress has been defined in terms of "stressful situations," such as critical life events (Holmes and Rahe, 1967; see Kessler, Price, and Wortman, 1985 for a review), another stream of thought defines stress as the individual's response to a situation. For example, Selye's (1956, 1983) General Adaptation Syndrome (GAS) model, viewed as a seminal influence in stress research, defines stress as the nonspecific response of an organism to any demand. Renowned as the father of stress research, Selye observed three stages of individual stress response: alarm reaction, a stage of resistance, and finally, exhaustion. Subsequent views of stress have specified the characteristics of the "demand," arguing that the stress response occurs when individuals face situations that tax or exceed their resources (McGrath, 1976; Monat and Lazarus, 1977).

More recently, however, relational definitions of stress have been emphasized. Relational definitions portray stress not in terms of the situation or the individual's response but rather in terms of the *relationship* between the individual and the situation. One prominent relational model has emerged from a research program at the University of Michigan Institute for Social Research. In this model, stress is defined as a function of person–environment fit (Van Harrison, 1985). Stress occurs when there is misfit between job rewards and individual needs or between job demands and individual skills.

Current integrative models of stress (Beehr and Bhagat, 1985; Lazarus and Folkman, 1984; Schuler, 1985) view the person–environment relationship as a transactional process that emphasizes the individual's appraisal of that relationship as taxing or exceeding his or her resources (Lazarus and Folkman, 1984:19). A transactional process means that individuals function in continuously unfolding, dynamic relationships with environmental factors. In transactional process models, relationships are not linear but reciprocal; each variable in the model can be both the cause and effect of the other variables [see Lazarus and Folkman (1984) and Schuler (1985) for a discussion of transactional models.]

These process models are complex, but the key variables include a stressor situation, cognitions about the situation and possible ways of dealing with it, stress reactions, coping strategies, duration over time, and a range of environmental factors (e.g., social support) and individual characteristics (e.g., Type A personality, self-esteem) that can influence the stress process.

To pave the way for research on managing career stress in a preventive manner, transactional process models of stress and coping serve as a basis for a model of career stress. The model presented here distills these more complex versions in order to portray the central issues for career theory.

A model of career stress

The key dimensions in the model are shown in Figure 12.1: stressor situation, cognitions, stress reactions, coping, social support, duration, and individual characteristics. The transactional nature of the model is indicated with bidirectional arrows. The model will first be explained, and then the subsequent discussion will focus on the critical linkages for career research.

The *stressor situation* can be a demand, constraint, or opportunity (Schuler, 1980). It is important to note that the stressor situation may be externally generated, such as taking a new job that one has been offered, or it may be internally generated, such as a mid-career adjustment that takes the form of a shift in personal views.

Cognitions are important mechanisms in the process, specifically the individual's perceptions that the situation poses uncertainty about obtaining outcomes, and the perceived importance of those outcomes (Beehr and Bhagat, 1985). Outcomes can be positive or negative and are related to gaining or losing something valuable (e.g., a promotion, esteem of a loved one). The stress literature has tended to emphasize cognitions related to loss, or "disvalued circumstances – those that in reality or fantasy signify great and/or increased distance from desirable (valued) experiential states" (Kaplan, 1983:196). More recently, however, Schuler (1985) has acknowledged the importance of cognitive processes related to positive outcomes. The key question relative to outcomes is: What is at stake? These cognitive processes help to explain why individuals vary greatly in the extent of stress they experience in the same situation.

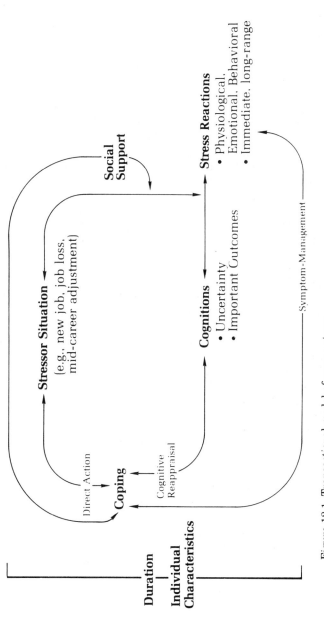

Figure 12.1. Transactional model of career stress

Stressor Situation
(e.g., new job, job loss, mid-career adjustment)

Social Support

Stress Reactions
• Physiological.
  Emotional. Behavioral
• Immediate. long-range

Cognitions
• Uncertainty
• Important Outcomes

Direct Action

Coping

Cognitive Reappraisal

Symptom-Management

Duration

Individual Characteristics

Stress reactions can be physiological (e.g., increased pulse rate), emotional (e.g., feelings of anxiety or tension), or behavioral (fidgeting, loss of sleep). Both immediate reactions (job dissatisfaction) and long-range effects (illness, changing careers) are of interest.

Coping is defined as "constantly changing cognitive and behavioral efforts to manage specific external and/or internal demands that are appraised as taxing or exceeding the resources of the person" (Lazarus and Folkman, 1984:141). Coping strategies may focus on the situation directly (direct action), on the cognitions (cognitive reappraisal), or on the stress reactions (symptom management). In this discussion, coping is viewed broadly as incorporating both individual and organizational efforts to manage stress (Sethi and Schuler, 1983). Coping is an important intervening process that helps to explain the effects of stressful situations on individuals. Specifically, the extent to which deleterious effects of stress are observed is in part dependent upon how and how well people cope with stress.

Along with coping, *social support*, an environmental factor, has emerged as an important preventive mechanism. Various definitions of social support have been offered (Beehr, 1985), but a common theme is that social support provides information that tells people they are loved, esteemed, or valued and part of a network of mutual obligation (Cobb, 1976). Although the manner in which social support may operate is the subject of considerable debate, two prominent suggestions are that social support may protect people from negative stress effects by influencing stress responses to stressor situations (the cognitions–stress reactions linkage) or by generating coping strategies (Cohen and Wills, 1985; Thoits, 1986).

The entire stress process occurs over time, and hence *duration* plays a central role; other things equal, uncertainty about important outcomes that endures over time is more stressful and more likely to engender health problems than uncertainty that is short-lived. The duration of the stressful situation is a critical link in the stress–health chain and has long been considered a major factor in disease and psychopathology. Enduring or chronic stress is thought to wear individuals down emotionally and physically (Lazarus and Folkman, 1984:98), resulting in health problems that may take years to emerge, such as high blood pressure and heart disease. Selye (1956) spurred this line of reasoning with his three-stage GAS model, which points out that adaptability to stress is finite, and exhaustion follows if stress continues unabated (Selye, 1983). Similarly, it has been suggested that relative to long-term well-being, the "daily hassles" one experiences may be more detrimental than critical life events (Lazarus and DeLongis, 1983).

Finally, a variety of *individual characteristics* (e.g., Type A personality, self-esteem) can influence the process at any point, determining aspects of the situation itself, the way it is perceived, individual stress reactions, and coping strategies.

The following discussion highlights four aspects of the model in order to examine the mechanisms through which career stressor situations may generate stress reactions and, ultimately, ill health. A more detailed discussion of cognitions, coping strategies, social support, and individual characteristics will lead us to promising directions for future career theory and research.

Cognitions and career stress

To apply a transactional view to career stress, let us begin by considering what types of cognitions might generate career stress. Perceptions of uncertainty and important outcomes are key determinants of how much career stress people will experience and of how they will cope. For example, the individual who has accepted a new job may experience uncertainty about how to succeed and whether he or she will be accepted by colleagues. The person who has been fired often faces doubts about competency, financial well-being, and the likelihood of finding a job as good as the previous one. The individual facing mid-career adjustment may struggle with uncertainty related to finding new work involvements or, perhaps, decreasing work centrality in favor of personal life.

If succeeding in the new job, finding another job, or finding new work involvements are important outcomes, these individuals experience career stress. These cognitive processes help to explain why the same career stressors affect people differently. For example, we can compare the individual facing the threat of being terminated from a very satisfying job that is the only source of income with the person facing termination from a dissatisfying job who has other sources of income. The first individual will likely experience more career stress than the second because the first individual will likely see more at stake – in this case, bigger potential losses.

Uncertainty about obtaining important outcomes is thus a key dimension of understanding career stress. People experience career stress to the extent they perceive situations as demands, constraints, or opportunities that pose uncertainty related to gaining or losing something important. An individual's cognitions, however, are intertwined with two other key variables that have been identified as preventive mechanisms: coping and social support.

Key preventive mechanisms: coping and social support

At present, we know very little about how to manage stress in a preventive manner that maintains health. On one level, it could be argued that career uncertainty and the importance people attach to career-related outcomes is inherent – a fact of occupational life. After putting a stop to stress management training programs for managers, the president of a rapidly expanding bank put it this way: "Banking is a stressful job. If they can't take the stress, they should get out of the profession."

A longer range view of organizational effectiveness and careers, however, argues for more proactive responses. Current theory and research on job stress has zeroed in on two preventive mechanisms that may avert some of the stress-related health consequences that occur over time: Coping (Folkman, 1982; Lazarus and Folkman, 1984; Schuler, 1985) and social support (Beehr, 1985; Cohen and Wills, 1985; House, 1981). If we are to understand how to maintain health, we must focus not only on stressful life events but on coping strategies and social support that may intervene between stress and health outcomes.

Research evidence on the ameliorating potential of coping and social support on job stress is inconclusive, not only because of the complexity of the processes but also because different conceptual frameworks and measures are used (Cohen and Wills, 1985; Latack, 1986). The following discussion illustrates some of the findings that have implications for career theory and research.

Coping. As illustrated in Figure 12.1, coping can be directed toward the symptoms, toward the stressor situation, or toward cognitions. Symptom management, popularly referred to as the "gelusil, jogging and gin" approach (Switzer, 1979), is included in "emotion-focused" coping (Lazarus and Folkman, 1984). Emotion-focused strategies do not aim to alter the situation; they alter stress reactions. Direct actions that are aimed at resolving or changing the stressful situations are referred to as "problem focused" (Lazarus and Folkman, 1984) because they make direct attempts to change the stressor situation or one's relationship to it. Finally, cognitive reappraisal attempts to reframe cognitions about the situation so that it is interpreted as less stressful. Cognitive strategies can be either problem focused ("Think of the situation as an opportunity to show what I can do") or emotion focused ("Try not to worry about it") (Latack, 1986). These cognitive strategies grow out of rational–emotive psychotherapy (Ellis, 1978) and cognitive behavior modification (Meichenbaum, 1977; Meichenbaum and Cameron, 1983).

On a global level, coping reflects efforts to restore a sense of personal control. Although the connection between personal control and stress is far from clearly formulated at this point, stress is frequently related to a sense of loss of control (see Folkman, 1984; Greenberger and Strasser, 1986; Sutton and Kahn, 1987). As such, coping represents efforts to re-exert control in a stressful situation and may be more efficacious when an individual realistically appraises a situation both as controllable and as a challenge rather than a threat (Folkman, 1984). The model in Figure 12.1 answers the question, "Control over what?" People exert efforts to control the situation or the outcomes of the situation, to control their cognitive processes, and/or to control individual stress reactions.

Studies that examine coping have tended to emphasize determinants of coping [see Kessler, Price, and Wortman (1985) for a review]. Particularly noteworthy for careers research are studies suggesting that job characteristics may enable people to cope effectively with stress. For example, Karasek (1979) found that job demands alone do not explain stress. Rather stress is conditioned by a second factor, decision latitude, defined as how much discretion workers have in deciding how to meet job demands, that is, how they cope. Another recent study hints that job characteristics such as autonomy and feedback may enable people to cope using problem-solving rather than symptom management strategies (Latack, Aldag, and Josephs, 1986). Individuals whose jobs allow autonomy and decision latitude may be able to call upon a range of effective problem-focused strategies. Similarly, feedback may guide an individual as to where to direct coping strategies.

Of those studies that examine coping effects, few studies compare multiple methods of coping, and these are primarily cross-sectional. There is little evidence that one form of coping is superior to others, but these results reflect in part the choice of different outcome measures [e.g., felt stress vs. problems experienced; see Menaghan (1983) for a review]. A number of studies show that direct actions, such as seeking information and engaging in problem-solving efforts, are associated with lower stress levels (e.g., Anderson, 1976; Latack, 1986; Parasuraman and Cleek, 1984). It is clear, however, that a positive role can be played by cognitive and symptom-focused strategies as well (e.g., Matteson and Ivancevich, 1983; Menaghan and Merves, 1984; Rose and Veiga, 1984).

Two longitudinal studies of job stress illustrate the empirical approach needed. Menaghan and Merves (1984) compared four different coping strategies and found that cognitive strategies (optimistic comparison and avoidance of a resigned, impotent stance) were associated with lower distress in the present and over time. Direct actions, however, had no effect on either distress or on resolution of stressful situations (overload, unfair treatment, inadequate rewards, noxious work environment) either concurrently or over time. Orpen (1984) studied managers who used symptom management strategies (relaxation training) and found that three months later, levels of psychological and physical strain were lower and levels of job satisfaction were higher, but no impact on job performance or physiological stress measures (heart rate, blood pressure) was observed. Thus, studies imbedded in a career context can make a substantial contribution by exploring the relative effectiveness of multiple coping strategies on multiple outcomes.

Social support. Social support has been conceptualized in a variety of ways (Cohen and Wills, 1985; Gore, 1981). In some cases, social support is defined structurally, as being imbedded in a social network, and therefore focuses on being married or single, number of friends and family members, and so on (Beehr, 1985; Hammer, 1981). Alternatively, it is argued that the more salient concept is functional social support, which refers to *what* is provided by various members of the individual's support network.

Functional measures of social support tell us more about the "feeling" people have of being supported (Beehr, 1985) rather than the type and number of members in a network. For example, House (1981) defined social support as "emotional concern, instrumental aid, information and/or appraisal" (p. 26). Cobb (1976) defines it as information that communicates the person is loved, esteemed, or valued, part of a group, the members of which share information and mutual obligations. It has been proposed that there are three types of social support (Schaefer, Coyne, and Lazarus, 1982): Emotional support (attachment, reassurance, being able to rely on and confide in a person); tangible support (providing direct aid such as loans, gifts, doing work, or taking care of things); and informational support (providing information, feedback, and advice).

Studies of social support yield contradictory results about the mechanism through which social support may operate (main effect vs. moderating effect) and also about the nature of its impact (protective vs. exacerbating effect). Concerning the mechanism through which social support operates, some studies have found that social support may be beneficial in its own right (main effect), but other studies show it operates to "buffer" people from detrimental impacts of stressful situations (moderating effect) depending on how it is defined [see Cohen and Wills (1985) for a review]. Several studies have found that people in stressful job situations show lower psychological stress and higher job satisfaction if they have social support, usually defined as supervisory support (Beehr, 1985; Etzion, 1984). Recent evidence related to job stress suggested social support may play its moderating role through fostering coping strategies (Newton and Keenan, 1985; Seers et al. 1983; Thoits, 1986).

Concerning whether social support protects people or exacerbates stress, when an effect is observed, it is usually protective (e.g., lower stress) (Beehr, 1985; Cohen and Wills, 1985; Etzion, 1984). Paradoxically, however, social support can also act in a "reverse buffering" fashion; that is, some studies have found a stronger, not weaker, positive relationship between stressors and stress reactions dependent on social support. One possible explanation is that the same individuals who buffer one from stress can also be a source of stress (Beehr, 1985; Kaufman and Beehr, 1986). This finding is consistent with Mechanic's (1962) earlier observations that, as doctoral students prepared for examinations, they sought support from other students but also found that social contact could increase anxiety by possibly exposing areas in which they lacked preparation.

Because career researchers consistently argue for consideration of nonwork life roles (Bailyn and Schein, 1976; Evans and Bartolome, 1981), the construct of social support is particularly applicable to the study of career stress. Specifically, the careers literature has often focused on family and social networks as sources of role conflict (e.g., Greenhaus and Beutell, 1985; Hall, 1972) or as arenas in which the "negative emotional spillover" from work stress gets played out (Evans and Bartolome, 1981). More recently, the stress inherent in maintaining dual careers has been highlighted (Sekaran, 1986). Alternatively, other studies (e.g., Handy, 1978) have focused on the extent to which extra-work social networks can be supportive, usually from the point of view of wives supporting husbands' careers but more recently from the point of view of husbands' supportive attitudes toward wives' work involvements (Beutell and Greenhaus, 1983).

In light of the potential preventive effects of social support, additional explicit attention to the functions of social support related to career stress is appropriate, not only family and friendship relationships but also work-based support. For example, one study of job loss found work-related sources of support were viewed as more beneficial than family support (Schlossberg and Leibowitz, 1980). Other studies confirm the importance of supervisory support in buffering job stress effects (Kasl and Wells, 1985; Kirmeyer and Dougherty, 1988). Similarly, recent work on mentoring (Kram, 1985) has underscored the supportive functions of mentor relationships on career development; these functions could be extended to focus on stress management as well.

Individual characteristics

Individual characteristics have been viewed in the stress literature as influencing the stress process at virtually any juncture. Individual characteristics, such as age and socioeconomic status, can predispose people to different stressor situations or levels of stress reactions [see Kessler, Price, and Wortman (1985) for a review]. Personality traits can modify the impact of the stressor situation on stress reactions (Fleishman, 1984; Kobasa, 1979).

Relative to coping, individual characteristics have been examined primarily as determinants of coping strategies [see Kessler, Price, and Wortman (1985) and Menaghan (1983) for reviews]. Studies related to job stress have emphasized locus of control (e.g., Anderson, 1976; Parkes, 1984) and Type A behavior pattern (e.g., Friedman and Rosenman, 1974; Ivancevich, Matteson, and Preston, 1982; Pittner and Houston, 1980) as well as sex (Fleishman, 1984; Stone and Neale, 1984) and age (e.g., Lazarus and De Longis, 1983; Pearlin and Schooler, 1978).

Studies of personality characteristics and coping strategies, however, assume that coping strategies are rooted in stable personality characteristics (e.g., Fleishman, 1984), but other evidence makes the point that people are more variable than stable in coping behaviors across situations (Folkman and Lazarus, 1980). It has been convincingly argued that rather than focusing on stable, cross-situational coping styles that approach personality traits, researchers should emphasize coping behaviors in specific stressful encounters (Folkman, 1982). From the point of view of preventive stress management as well, cross-situational coping styles are of less importance than situation-specific coping behaviors because the latter are more amenable to managerial intervention and developmental programs.

Concerning sex differences, studies have not found strong evidence that men and women cope with job stress differently. Women tend to be somewhat more likely than men to use more emotion-focused and less problem-focused coping (Folkman and Lazarus, 1980), more avoidance and symptom-focused coping (Fleishman, 1984; Siegler and George, 1983; Stone and Neale, 1984), and more help seeking (Funabiki, Bologna, Pepping, and Fitzgerald, 1980; Ilfeld, 1980; Rippere, 1976).

Studies examining age differences have yielded more contradictory results. For example, Pearlin and Schooler (1978) found that older workers were more likely to use mental avoidance mechanisms and less likely to use positive thinking. Fleishman (1984) noted that older people were less likely to engage in direct action. For people middle-aged or younger, age is positively related to acceptance or resignation and negatively related to help seeking (Burke and Belcourt, 1974; Fleishman, 1984; Ilfeld, 1980). In contrast, Howard et al. (1975) concluded that use of most coping techniques stayed the same with age, and Folkman and Lazarus (1980) observed no effects for age among a sample aged 45–64.

From the standpoint of careers, there is a considerable contribution to be made by overlaying a careers perspective on some of the individual difference findings for two reasons. First, variables that figure prominently in career research, such as career or life stage (Schein, 1978; Veiga, 1983) or career motivation (London and Stumpf, 1986), may explain some of the confusing findings discussed in the preceding paragraphs. Second, it is clear that we need more studies focusing on stress relative to minorities and women, which is a current focus of career researchers. For example, some of the confusion relative to age effects could accrue from sampling different or incomplete age ranges or from grouping across a large age range, which aggregates individuals who are at different career or life stages (Schein, 1978; Veiga, 1983). It is plausible that career stressors as well as coping strategies differ according to career or life stage.

Alternatively, contradictory results relative to age might be the result of failure to control for other career variables, such as London's (London and Stumpf, 1986) concept of career motivation. He argues that people differ along three dimensions: resilience in the face of career disruptions and barriers, accuracy of self-insight, and the extent to which they define their identity by work. It may be that level of career motivation as well as age play a role in explaining stress and coping strategies.

Moreover, career stress experienced by women and minorities in nontraditional careers is a critical career issue (see Gallos, Chapter 6; Thomas and Alderfer, Chapter 7). Although attention to women and job stress has been growing (Baruch, Biener, and Barnett, 1987; Jick and Mitz, 1985), there has been very little attention to minorities in job stress research (Ford, 1985). Some writers have expressed concern that as women move into nontraditional careers, they are destined to experience the same or perhaps a greater degree of stress-related illnesses than men (Jick and Mitz, 1985; Nelson and Quick, 1985). In fact, one recent study of managers justifies that concern. Zappert and Weinstein (1985) found that women demonstrated significantly more psychological and physical manifestations of stress than men. Other studies have found no sex differences in stress levels, however (Baruch et al., 1987). Studies of minority job stress [see Ford (1985) for a review] suggest that black career stress reflects a "Black Tax" – that is, attempting to prove competence through workaholism, mutual feelings of distrust between black executives and peers and superiors, and participating in organizational policies not in the best interest of blacks.

The preceding discussion suggests that job stress research could benefit from attention to individual variables that are receiving attention in careers research. Thus, studying the stress-coping process as it relates to career and life stage, career motivation, race, and sex represents a logical integration point between career theory and job stress research.

FUTURE THEORY AND RESEARCH: PROMISING DIRECTIONS
FOR PREVENTIVE MANAGEMENT OF STRESS AS
CAREERS UNFOLD

The preceding discussion suggests several promising and intriguing directions for career theory. In this closing section, directions for theory building and research are proposed. Because the focus on job stress is relatively new, theoretical views are still emerging and, as noted, empirical studies have yielded a morass of contradictory results. In addition, career researchers have argued for more descriptive research (Schein, 1986). That argument is certainly appropriate to careers and stress. Therefore, rather than offering specific propositions and hypotheses, this section delineates critical research areas and formulates questions that focus on career transitions as a stress process, coping strategies from a careers perspective, and social support in work and nonwork arenas. To conclude, key issues relative to assumptions and research design are identified: value bias, the positive aspects of stress, and the time dimension.

Career transitions as a stress process: a critical focus

The emphasis on career-related change and adjustment over the course of careers is unprecedented. Issues of career resilience and multiple careers are paramount in current career theory (Hall et al., 1986), and these issues highlight the importance of understanding how individuals manage increasingly frequent and stressful career transitions (Hill, Miller, and Lowther, 1981; Hymowitz, 1987). In addition to rapid technological change, mergers and takeovers, downsizing, and shifts in corporate strategic direction, there are value-laden questions related to work–nonwork balance, combining family responsibilities with career at different career/life stages, and access of women and minorities not only to new occupations but also to upper levels within the organization. These forces heighten concern about career stress of a transitional nature such as plateauing at mid-career or earlier, moving downward in the organization, experiencing involuntary job loss, finding new careers at mid-life, adjusting to repeated changes in job responsibilities, interrupting or curtailing careers for family reasons, or early retirement (London and Stumpf, 1986). As careers unfold over time, career transitions emerge as critical stress points that could have substantive impact on maintenance of employee emotional and physical well-being over time.

Therefore, a key departure point for integrating stress theory with careers is the concept of career transitions. A career transition has been defined as "the period during which an individual is either changing roles (taking on a different objective role) or changing orientation to a role already held (altering a subjective state)" (Louis, 1980:330). Nicholson and West (Chapter 9) broaden this definition to include times when the job itself changes around an immobile incumbent, such as job redesign, change of boss, or co-workers. Thus, an inclusive definition of career transitions is consistent with the notion that a stressor situation can be externally or internally generated.

Career transitions are important to stress research for two reasons: First, they represent potentially frequent and recurring career stress for many people in the next decade and, second, they are time periods when people are at risk of establishing chronic stress situations over the course of a career.

The issue of frequent, recurring career stress is problematic in light of the connection between repeated exposure to changes and health problems (Bhagat, 1985; Holmes and Rahe, 1967). The current emphasis in stress research is no longer on change per se, but on intervening and moderating factors that determine who stays healthy and who becomes the victim of stress-related disorders. If frequently occurring transition periods are not effectively managed, people run the risk of exhaustion and burnout over time from the repeated stress.

The second issue, the risk of establishing chronic stress situations, relates to duration of stress as a critical health factor. In this vein, the importance of studying transitions is based not so much on how long they last because the actual duration of each transition may be relatively short. The importance derives from the fact that they are times of risk and uncertainty that expose people to choices (Schlossberg, 1984) and, as such, are "an opportunity for psychological growth and a danger of psychological deterioration" (Moos and Tsu, 1976:13). If stress is extreme, people are less likely to make reasoned, considered career-related choices rooted in accurate self-assessment and problem-solving strategies. The detrimental result could be chronic stress and career dissatisfaction and perhaps an escalating spiral of career stress. For example, research on job loss indicates that people who are not successfully re-employed within a relatively short period of time risk extreme psychological withdrawal and chronic unemployment (Kaufman, 1982; Latack and Dozier, 1986).

Moreover, the job stress literature tends to focus on the immediate, ongoing job situation rather than on how people cope with the transition periods evoked by career-related changes. Thus, career researchers are presented with a unique opportunity not only to draw in stress concepts to understand transitions, but also to make a contribution to the study of job stress in an area that has not been adequately researched.

Recent integrative conceptual work suggests ways of studying transitions from a stress-coping vantage point. For example, work by Nicholson (1984) presents modes of adjustment to transitions involving both personal and role adjustment and explores the individual and organizational processes that affect adjustment to transitions (see also Nicholson and West, Chapter 9). In addition, Latack and Dozier (1986) discuss the stress of job loss from the vantage point of career transitions, noting factors that may turn the experience of involuntary job loss toward future career growth.

There is a growing empirical literature on career transitions and career changes in general (see Hall and Associates, 1986) but there has been little comparative study of various types of career transitions relative to stress. Rather, studies have tended to examine one type of career transition and compare individuals who are making that transition to others who have not made such a change. For example, Brett (1982) looked at job transfer and did not find support for the notion that the well-being of mobile individuals suffered from the move. Although conventional wisdom suggests that certain types of transitions may be more stressful than others (job loss vs. promotion; starting a new job vs. early retirement), there is a need for systematic, comparative studies. Specifically, researchers could compare individual stress reactions related to different types of career transitions across individuals or for the same individual across time.

> *Research question 1*: Are certain types of career transitions more stressful inherently than others?

As the previous discussion suggests, however, there are numerous moderating factors that could make a transition more or less stressful, particularly cognitions about the transition. For example, there is support for the commonsense notion that transitions that are perceived as involuntary and as negative by the individual are more detrimental to mental and physical well-being than those seen as positive and voluntarily chosen (Fontana et al., 1979; Pearlin et al., 1981). Nicholson and West (Chapter 9) conclude that people may actively seek out the stress of desirable moves and therefore the detrimental health effects of these types of transitions may not emerge. This empirical question remains to be tested. A recurring theme in organizational stress research is that situations are more stressful if individuals cannot influence the onset or duration of the stressful situation (Sutton and Kahn, 1987). Since economic and organizational constraints dictate the necessity of exploring career moves that do not involve promotion, such as downward moves (Hall and Isabella, 1985), job loss (Latack and Dozier, 1986), and early retirement (Beehr, 1986), there is some urgency about exploring career moves that are likely to be perceived as unpredictable, negative, or involuntary.

Other factors that contribute to or alleviate stress during transitions bear systematic exploration. For example, Lawrence (1980) suggested that constraints in the social environment in the form of social expectations are a major influence on how career events are experienced. In particular, being "on-time" or "off-time" with an organization's concept of successful career advancement may have a powerful impact whether or not a transition is experienced as a mid-life crisis. Researchers interested in pursuing this line of inquiry could explore the moderating effects of the numerous individual (e.g., cognitions about desirability, career stage, career motivation) and situational (e.g., job characteristics, on-time vs. off-time) factors discussed in this chapter.

> *Research question 2*: What individual and situational factors contribute to a particular type of transition being experienced as more or less stressful?

Coping strategies: incorporating a careers perspective

The issue of determinants and consequences of coping is a prominent one in job stress research. A careers emphasis would suggest incorporating key career variables as both determinants and consequences of coping. For example, career researchers are interested in the career dilemmas of women and minorities so the inclusion of sex and race as potential coping influences would be useful. This is particularly important because of the small number of studies examining minority stress (Ford, 1985) and because some studies comparing men and women suggest that the linkage between stress and health-related problems may be stronger among women (Linsky, Colby, and Strauss, 1986; Zappert and Weinstein, 1985). Other career variables such as career motivation (London and Stumpf, 1986) or career stage (Schein, 1978) could also be important determinants of coping strategy.

Beyond these variables, however, it would be important to focus on individual characteristics upon which the organization could have some impact rather than on stable personality traits or coping styles. Bandura's work on situational-specific self-efficacy perceptions (Bandura, 1982, 1986) offers a promising example of an individual characteristic that has direct implications for preventive measures and for teaching employees how to cope with career stress.

In a related vein, the characteristic referred to as "hardiness" (Kobasa, 1979) has received attention. Hardiness has identified people who withstand stress without becoming ill (Kobasa, 1979; Kobasa, Maddi, and Kahn, 1982; Pines, 1984). Hardy individuals have three traits: (1) involvement and commitment in various aspects of their lives, (2) a sense of control over their lives, and (3) openness to change, welcoming it as a challenge rather than favoring security and familiarity. Although hardiness is learned in early childhood, it is argued that it can be taught later in life as well (Pines, 1984).

Recent examples of empirical studies illustrate a careers perspective on coping. For example, using a career development perspective, Osipow et al. (1985) studied coping across the life span and found support for the notion that coping strategies varied as a function age. Older workers used more physical strategies (self-care) along with recreational and cognitive strategies than did younger workers. Feldman and Brett (1983) found that coping strategies differed according to type of career transition. Their comparison of new hires versus job changers hints at career stage differences in coping as well. They found that job changers try harder to control and change their job situations than do new hires, who seek out more social support and more aid from others. No differences were found, however, in degree of symptom management coping across the two groups. Latack (1984) found that coping with job stress subsequent to career transitions varied as a function of personal life transitions. Those individuals facing more personal life transitions tended to rely more on symptom management for coping with job stress than did those whose personal lives were more tranquil. Therefore, one suggested research strategy is systematic examination of the career variables discussed here as potential determinants of coping strategies.

> *Research question 3*: Do individual coping strategies vary by sex, race, type of transition, career/life stage, career motivation, or nonwork variables?

> *Research question 4*: Do coping strategies vary by type of career transition?

Concerning relative effectiveness of different coping strategies, few studies systematically compare multiple coping strategies. Studies offering comparative data provide little clear support for one form of coping over another (Bruning and Frew, 1987). We need studies that assess the relative effectiveness of various coping strategies on multiple psychological, physical, and behavioral outcomes. In addition, the individual and situational determinants of coping discussed earlier could also operate as moderators relative to coping effectiveness. For example, what "works" to control stress effectively for the mid-career person facing job change may be less effective for the early career person in a similar situation. Thus, career research should be concerned not only with identifying the determinants of different coping strategies but with comparing the relative effects of different coping strategies for various types of career stressors and stress reactions.

> *Research question 5*: What is the relative effectiveness of various coping strategies for different career stressors and stress reactions?

Evidence about the limits of coping ability for resolving stressful situations at work (Menaghan and Merves, 1984; Murphy, 1985) argues for attention to organizational coping strategies (Sethi and Schuler, 1983) as well as individual strategies. If individual coping strategies are not effective on certain outcomes, then our focus turns to organizational career management (Sonnenfeld, 1984) and human resource management (Matteson and Ivancevich, 1987; Schuler and Jackson, 1986) practices as variables to examine for maintaining health. This focus should extend beyond training programs that teach individuals to cope, particularly since there is little evaluative data supporting that these programs are generally effective over time (e.g., Ganster et al., 1982).

Additional organizational variables are suggested by considering the origins of people's uncertainty about their careers. Some sources of uncertainty would be career management policies of the organization, such as lack of information on career opportunities and career paths or inadequate supervisory evaluations and feedback. In many organizations, individuals are not drawn into decisions about career moves and may not even know why they are being moved. This creates career uncertainty, feelings of lack of control resulting in stress.

In light of these arguments, top-management support for employee involvement in career development, well-developed career information systems, and regular career counseling for employees could be conceptualized as stress management interventions that act directly on employee uncertainty about career issues and foster the sense of control and decision latitude that has been shown to moderate the impact of high-demand jobs (Karasek, 1979). These systems also provide data for individual coping efforts that have a situational, problem-focused orientation.

Researchers could capitalize on the current managerial interest in career development systems and construct field experiments in organizations when various components of career development systems are introduced. The resulting impact on postintervention stress-related variables (e.g., uncertainty, coping, stress reactions, turnover) could be assessed in order to determine if career management functions as a stress management intervention. A more feasible approach might be to compare employees across organizations that vary in the amount and type of career development programs offered (see Granrose and Portwood, 1987), but these studies would need to control for the numerous factors discussed earlier that influence stress and coping.

> *Research question 6*: What is the impact of systematic career management efforts (e.g., career path data, career planning sessions with supervisors) on coping and stress?

Social support in work and nonwork

The current state of knowledge relative to social support argues for models that test for both main effects and interaction effects of social support on stress. That is, we need to allow for the possibility that social support is beneficial regardless of career stressor and/or that it operates to buffer or moderate the effects of a stressor situation on employee health.

> *Research question 7*: Does social support have a main effect on career stress or does it moderate the impact of career stressors on stress?

Beyond that, however, the conditions under which social support is associated with lower as opposed to higher stress is an important issue for theorists who wish to integrate stress and career theory. The reverse buffering aspects of social support (Beehr, 1985) are relevant here. That is, there may be times when individual members of a support network function both as a support and a stressor. For example, the spouse who supports your career also creates stress as he or she pursues his or her own career. Managing home demands and role overload by hiring help also creates another relationship in the constellation of relationships to manage. A boss can be supportive while also holding high expectations or modeling workaholic behavior.

Thus, career theorists could specify the career stressor situations in which various sources of social support act as buffers or as sources of stress. A recent study of career transitions (Stout, Slocum, and Cron, 1987) provides an intriguing example. They found that supervisors who had undergone a major career transition gave subordinates lower performance ratings than supervisors who had experienced a career transition of medium magnitude. They reasoned that performance expectations of supervisors may be unrealistically high after a major career transition and that the subordinate could be serving a "scapegoat" role for the supervisor's own stress. In short, the supervisors own career transition might turn a supportive supervisor into a stressor. In a related vein, the extent to which a spouse is experienced as supportive versus stress inducing may depend upon the spouse's career stage. An individual in the early advancement stage of his or her career may not have as much support capacity as someone who is in a more established, stable career stage.

> *Research question 8*: Under what conditions are members of support networks experienced as buffers as opposed to sources of stress?

The foregoing discussion also highlights a need to examine multiple sources of support, both work and nonwork, and to distinguish types of social support (emotional, tangible, informational). Although there is no clear evidence that people with multiple sources of social resources are better off than those who have only one, we do not know whether or how people may use multiple sources of social support in specific career stress situations. If social support can operate as a buffer *and* a stressor, then it stands to reason that people with multiple support persons may turn to one source for support when another source of support is functioning as a stressor. Although there is some indication that people find work-related sources most useful in job stress situations (Dressler, 1985; Schlossberg and Leibowitz, 1980), the distinction between *sources* as well as *types* of social support has not been clearly drawn. Thus, the question of whether or how people draw on or "trade off" alternative sources and types of support to cope with career stress would be a fruitful direction to explore.

Research question 9: Do people who have multiple sources and types of support experience lower stress?

Research question 10: Do people use one source or type of support to compensate when another source of support is missing or being experienced as a stressor?

Finally, the results of some studies suggest a coping hypothesis (Newton and Keenan, 1985; Seers et al., 1983) that has particular relevance for career researchers. This hypothesis suggests that social support moderates stress by spurring effective coping. A recent study supports this hypothesis. Kirmeyer and Dougherty (1988) found that subordinates who experienced high work loads engaged in more coping actions and felt less tension anxiety if they had social support from their supervisors.

Additional studies are needed that assess the role of social support in generating effective coping strategies. For example, if individuals know they are valued and supported, this may bolster confidence and self-efficacy (Bandura, 1982), which may generate problem-solving coping rather than coping directed solely toward emotional or physical release. If they receive tangible, task-focused social support, coping efforts may be more likely to take a problem-focused direction because they may have additional problem-solving resources to bring to bear.

Exploring the link between social support and coping may also shed light on the reverse buffering effect discussed earlier. That is, a given individual in the support network may function as both supportive *and* stress inducing depending on which coping strategy is being addressed. If the support person is helping the person deal with the situation, then support could be stress inducing in the short run but stress reducing in the long run because they are pushing the person to resolve the situation. If support is more focused on emotional comfort, there is a higher likelihood that social support would lower felt stress in the present. The issue then is what kind of support is needed at a particular point in time. When is a swift kick more beneficial than a shoulder to cry on?[1]

Research question 11: How do coping strategies vary as a function of social support?

Research assumptions and design issues

The first issue related to assumptions is one of value bias in the selection of variables for study. The literature on job stress reflects a bias toward individual action and responsibility. Studies cited here have focused on individual coping efforts or on organizational programs designed to train people how to cope. As is reflected in this volume, however, career theory is focusing increased attention on organizational influences and economic constraints on careers (Rosenbaum, Chapter 16) and has long emphasized the organization's shared responsibility with the individual for fostering career development (Gutteridge, 1986; London and Stumpf, 1982). Therefore, as career researchers consider integrating stress concepts with career theory, they will want to focus not only on individual coping strategies or on organizational interventions that teach individuals to cope but also on organizational career management strategies that have stress-alleviating potential.

This organizational focus is particularly important in light of studies suggesting that work role stress is relatively impervious to individual coping efforts, even over time (Menaghan and Merves, 1984; Murphy, 1985; Pearlin and Schooler, 1978). In short, models of career stress should not assume that it is the individual's responsibility to cope but should consider organizational-level interventions as well.

In addition, the stress literature has tended to focus on individual-level effects, such as self-perceived tension, anxiety, and psychosomatic symptoms and illness. The foregoing discussion also suggests that organizational-level outcomes should be considered as relevant outcomes in theorizing about career stress. Thus, in addition to including measures of emotional and physical health, career theorists will also want to attend to measures of organizational adaptation and competitiveness, innovation, health insurance costs, lost work time, turnover rates, commitment, and retention of valued employees.

A second key issue concerns assumptions about positive versus negative effects of stress. Although studies of job stress primarily cast stress as a problem and assume that stress is to be "reduced," a careers focus would argue for identifying ways of preserving the positive, developmental aspects of stress – referred to by some writers as the "power" (Anderson, 1978) of stress. Therefore, careers research from a stress perspective not only would examine how employees perceive stressful situations affecting their careers in the present, but also would explore their futuristic and retrospective views. That is, individuals might experience career transitions as extremely stressful at certain points but in retrospect may view them as positive experiences in the context of resulting career development. A careers approach could complement other research agendas for identifying factors that keep stress at some moderate, growth-producing level or that reduce it when it becomes dysfunctional.

A final note is appropriate concerning research design. In research on career stress, the importance of the time dimension cannot be overstated. The requirement of longitudinal research designs for illuminating some of the questions posed here goes beyond the usual exhortations regarding causal interpretation and understanding processes over time. The concept of duration is inherent *both* to careers and to transactional process models of stress and coping and argues that this process can *only* be studied over time.

The severity of the problem with cross-sectional studies can be illustrated as follows. If we study how people are coping and find, for example, that problem-focused strategies are associated with lower anxiety, we do not know if the results reflect that people experiencing lower levels of anxiety are simply better able to engage in these strategies or if problem-focused strategies are indeed "effective" in lowering anxiety. Furthermore, problem-focused strategies may in fact *increase* felt stress in the short run because they involve direct actions that may involve change and risk taking that ultimately resolve the situation in a satisfactory manner and thus *lead to* lower felt stress. Thus, stress can be both a determinant and consequence of coping, depending on the point in time we enter the process. Therefore, we must study the same person repeatedly over time to tease out the complexities of the transactional process.

In closing, it is exciting to contemplate the potential integration of career theory with stress research. Career theory can contribute to preventing stress-related health problems and to clarifying some of the confusion surrounding the research on job stress. Researchers who study careers from a stress perspective will move us toward a much-needed theoretical integration between the two domains and toward the longer time frame required to foster preventive strategies for employee health.

NOTE

Helpful comments on an earlier draft were provided by Gene Bocialetti. Valuable research assistance was provided by Carol Brody and Steve Havlovic.
1 Appreciation is expressed to Tim Hall for bringing this idea to my attention.

REFERENCES

Abdel-Halim, A. A. (1981). Effects of role stress–job design–technology interaction on employee work satisfaction. *Academy of Management Journal, 24*(2), 260–273.
Anderson, C. R. (1976). Coping behaviors as intervening mechanisms in the inverted-U stress-performance relationship. *Journal of Applied Psychology, 61,* 30–34.
Anderson, R. A. (1978). *Stress Power.* New York: Human Sciences.
Bailyn, L., and Schein, E. H. (1976). Life/career considerations as indicators of quality of employment. In A. D. Biderman and T. F. Drury (eds.), *Measuring Work Quality for Social Reporting.* New York: Wiley.
Bandura, A. (1982). Self-efficacy mechanism in human agency. *American Psychologist, 37,* 122–147.
Bandura, A. (1986). *Social Foundations of Thought and Action: A Social Cognition Theory.* Englewood Cliffs, NJ: Prentice-Hall.
Baruch, G. K., Biener, L., and Barnett, R.C. (1987). Women and gender in research on work and family stress. *American Psychologist, 42,* 130–136.
Beehr, T. A. (1985). The role of social support in coping with organizational stress. In T. A. Beehr and R. S. Bhagat (eds.), *Human Stress and Cognition in Organizations: An Integrated Perspective.* New York: Wiley.
Beehr, T. A. (1986). The process of retirement: a review and recommendations for future investigation. *Personnel Psychology, 39,* 31–55.
Beehr, T. A., and Bhagat, R. S. (1985). *Human Stress and Cognition in Organizations: An Integrated Perspective.* New York: Wiley.
Beehr, T. A., and Newman, J. E. (1978). Job stress, employee health, and organizational effectiveness: a facet analysis, model, and literature review. *Personnel Psychology, 31,* 663–699.
Bennett, A. (1988). Is your job making you sick? *Wall Street Journal,* Special Report on Medicine and Health, April 22.
Beutell, N. J., and Greenhaus, J. H. (1983). Integration of home and non-home roles: women's conflict and coping behavior. *Journal of Applied Psychology, 68,* 43–48.
Bhagat, R. S. (1985). The role of stressful life events in organizational behavior and human performance. In T. A. Beehr and R. S. Bhagat (eds.), *Human Stress and Cognition in Organizations: An Integrated Perspective.* New York: Wiley, pp. 205–212.
Brett, J. M. (1982). Job transfer and well-being. *Journal of Applied Psychology, 67,* 450–463.
Bruning, N. S., and Frew, D. R. (1987). Effects of exercise, relaxation and management skills training on physiological stress indicators: a field experiment. *Journal of Applied Psychology, 72,* 515–521.
Burke, R. J., and Belcourt, M. L. (1974). Managerial role strain and coping responses. *Journal of Business Administration, 5*(2), 55–68.
Cobb, S. (1976). Social support as a moderator of life stress. *Psychosomatic Medicine, 38,* 300–314.
Cohen, S., and Wills, T. A. (1985). Stress, social support and the buffering hypothesis. *Psychological Bulletin, 98,* 310–357.
Dentzer, S., McCormick, J., and Tsuruoka, D. (1986). A cure for job stress. *Newsweek,* June 2, pp. 46–47.

Dressler, W. W. (1985). Extended family relationships, social support and mental health in a southern black community. *Journal of Health and Social Behavior, 26,* 39–48.

Ellis, A. (1978). What people can do for themselves to cope with stress. In C. Cooper and R. Payne (eds.), *Stress at Work.* New York: Wiley, pp. 209–222.

Etzion, D. (1984). Moderating effect of social support on the stress–burnout relationship. *Journal of Applied Psychology, 69,* 615–622.

Evans, P., and Bartolome, F. (1981). *Must success cost so much?* New York: Basic.

Feldman, D. C., and Brett, J. M. (1983). Coping with new jobs: a comparative study of new hires and job changers. *Academy of Management Journal, 26,* 258–272.

Fleishman, J. A. (1984). Personality characteristics and coping patterns. *Journal of Health and Social Behavior, 25,* 229–244.

Folkman, S., and Lazarus, R. S. (1980). An analysis of coping behavior in a middle-aged community sample. *Journal of Health and Social Behavior, 21,* 219–239.

Folkman, S. F. (1982). An approach to the measurement of coping. *Journal of Occupational Behavior, 3,* 95–158.

Folkman, S. F. (1984). Personal control and stress and coping processes: a theoretical analysis. *Journal of Personality and Social Psychology, 46,* 834–852.

Fontana, A., Hughes, L., Marcus, J., and Dowds, B. (1979). Subjective evaluation of life events. *Journal of Consulting and Clinical Psychology, 47,* 906–911.

Ford, D. L. (1985). Job-related stress of the minority professional: an exploratory analysis and suggestions for future research. In T. A. Beehr and R. S. Bhagat (eds.), *Human Stress and Cognition in Organizations.* New York: Wiley, pp. 287–324.

Friedman, M., and Rosenman, R. H. (1974). *Type A Behavior and Your Heart.* Greenwich, CT: Fawcett.

Funabiki, D., Bologna, N., Pepping, M., and Fitzgerald, K. (1980). Revisiting sex differences in the expression of depression. *Journal of Abnormal Psychology, 89,* 198–202.

Ganster, D. C., Mayes, B. T., Sime, W. E., and Tharp, G. D. (1982). Managing organizational stress: a field experiment. *Journal of Applied Psychology, 67,* 533–542.

Gore, S. (1981). Stress-buffering functions of social support: an appraisal and clarification of research models. In B. S. Dohrenwend and B. P. Dohrenwend, *Stressful Life Events and Their Contexts.* New York: Prodist, pp. 202–22.

Granrose, C. S., and Portwood, J. D. (1987). Matching individual career plans and organizational career management. *Academy of Management Journal, 30,* 699–720.

Greenberger, D. B., and Strasser, S. (1986). Development and application of a model of personal control in organizations. *Academy of Management Review, 11,* 164–177.

Greenhaus, J. H., and Beutell, N. J. (1985). Sources of conflict between work and family roles. *Academy of Management Review, 10,* 76–88.

Gutteridge, T. G. (1986). Organizational career development systems: the state of the practice. In D. T. Hall and Associates, *Career Development in Organizations.* San Francisco: Jossey-Bass, pp. 50–94.

Hall, D. T. (1972). A model of coping with role conflict: the role behavior of college educated women. *Administrative Science Quarterly, 17,* 471–486.

Hall, D. T. (1976). *Careers in organizations.* Pacific Palisades, CA: Goodyear.

Hall, D. T. (1986). Career development in organizations: where do we go from here? In D. T. Hall and Associates, *Career Development in Organizations.* San Francisco: Jossey-Bass, pp. 332–351.

Hall, D. T., and Associates (1986). *Career Development in Organizations.* San Francisco: Jossey-Bass.

Hall, D. T., and Isabella, L. (1985). Downward moves and career development. *Organizational Dynamics, 14,* 5–23.

Hammer, M. (1981). "Core" and "extended" social networks in relation to health and illness. *Social Science and Medicine, 17,* 405–411.

Handy, C. (1978). The family: help or hindrance? In C. L. Cooper and R. Payne (eds.), *Stress at Work.* New York: Wiley.

Hill, R. E., Miller, E. L., and Lowther, M. A. (eds.) (1981). *Adult Career Transitions: Current Research Perspectives.* Ann Arbor, MI: Division of Research, Graduate School of Business Administration, University of Michigan.

Holmes, T., and Rahe, R. (1967). The social readjustment rating scale. *The Journal of Psychosomatic Research, 11,* 213–218.

House, J. S. (1981). *Work Stress and Social Support.* Reading, MA: Addison-Wesley.

Howard, J. H., Rechnitzer, P. A., and Cunningham, D. A. (1975). Coping with job tension – effective and ineffective methods. *Public Personnel Management, 4*, 307–326.

Hymowitz, C. (1987). Stable cycles of executive careers shattered by upheaval in business. *Wall Street Journal*, May 26, pp. 35.

Ilfeld, F. W. (1980). Coping styles of Chicago adults: description. *Journal of Human Stress, 6*, 2–10.

Ivancevich, J. M., Matteson, M. T., and Preston, C. (1982). Occupational stress, Type A behavior and physical well-being. *Academy of Management Journal, 25*, 373–391.

Jick, T. D., and Mitz, L. F. (1985). Sex differences in work stress. *Academy of Management Review, 10*, 408–420.

Kaplan, H. B. (1983). Psychological distress in a sociological context: toward a general theory of psychosocial stress. In H. B. Kaplan (ed.), *Psychosocial Stress: Trends in Theory and Research*. New York: Academic.

Karasek, R. A. (1979). Job demands, job decision latitude and mental strain: implications for job redesign. *Administrative Science Quarterly, 24*, 285–308.

Kasl, S. V., and Wells, J. A. (1985). Social support and health in the middle years: work and family. In S. Cohen and S. L. Syme (eds.), *Social Support and Health*, Orlando, FL: Academic, pp. 175–198.

Kaufman, H. G. (1982). *Professionals in Search of Work*. New York: Wiley.

Kaufman, T. A., and Beehr T. A. (1986). Interaction between job stressors and social support: some counterintuitive results. *Journal of Applied Psychology, 71*, 522–526.

Kessler, R. C., Price, R. H., and Wortman, C. B. (1985). Social factors in psychopathology, stress, social support and coping processes. *Annual Review of Psychology, 36*, 531–572.

Kirmeyer, S. L., and Dougherty, T. W. (1988). Workload, tension and coping: moderating effects of supervisor support. *Personnel Psychology, 41*, 125–140.

Kobasa, S. C. (1979). Stressful life events, personality and health: an inquiry into hardiness. *Journal of Personality and Social Psychology, 37*, 1–11.

Kobasa, S. C., Maddi, S. R., and Kahn, S. (1982). Hardiness and health: a prospective study. *Journal of Personality and Social Psychology, 42*, 168–177.

Kram, K. E. (1985). *Mentoring at Work: Developmental Relationships in Organizational Life*. Glenview, IL: Scott, Foresman.

Landers, S. (1987). Rising work stress claims hit employers in the pocket. *APA Monitor*, August, pp. 6–7.

Latack, J. C. (1984). Career transitions within organizations: an exploratory study of work, nonwork and coping strategies. *Organizational Behavior and Human Performance, 34*, 296–322.

Latack, J. C. (1986). Coping with job stress: Measures and future directions for scale development. *Journal of Applied Psychology, 71*, 377–385.

Latack, J. C., Aldag, R. J., and Josephs, B. (1986). Job stress: determinants and consequences of coping behavior. Working paper. Ohio State University.

Latack, J. C., and Dozier, J. B. (1986). After the ax falls: job loss as a career transition. *Academy of Management Review, 11*, 375–392.

Lawrence, B. S. (1980). The myth of the midlife crisis. *Sloan Management Review, 21*, 35–49.

Lazarus, R. S., and DeLongis, A. (1983). Psychological stress and coping in aging. *American Psychologist, 38*, 245–254.

Lazarus, R. S., and Folkman, S. F. (1984). *Stress, Appraisal and Coping*. New York: Springer.

Linsky, A. S., Colby, J. P., and Strauss, M. A. (1986). Social stress, smoking behavior and mortality from cancer of the respiratory system: a macro-social analysis. Paper presented at the Second National Conference on Social Stress Research, June 2–3, University of New Hampshire.

London, M., and Stumpf, S. (1982). *Managing Careers*. Reading, MA: Addison-Wesley.

London, M., and Stumpf, S. A. (1986). Individual and organizational career development in changing times. In D. T. Hall and Associates, *Career Development in Organizations*. San Francisco: Jossey-Bass, pp. 21–49.

Louis, M. R. (1980). Career transitions: Varieties and commonalities. *Academy of Management Review, 5*, 329–340.

McGrath, J. E. (1976). Stress and behavior in organizations. In M. D. Dunnette (ed.), *Handbook of Industrial and Organizational Psychology*. Chicago: Rand McNally.

Matteson, M. T., and Ivancevich, J. M. (1983). Note on tension discharge rate as an employee health status predictor. *Academy of Management Journal, 26*, 540–545.

Matteson, M. T., and Ivancevich, J. M. (1987). *Controlling Work Stress: Effective Human Resource Management Strategies*. San Francisco: Jossey-Bass.

Mechanic, D. (1962). *Students under Stress: A Study in the Social Psychology of Adaptation*. New York: Free Press.

Meichenbaum, D. (1977). *Cognitive-Behavior Modification: An Integrative Approach*. New York: Plenum.

Meichenbaum, D., and Cameron, R. (1983). Stress inoculation training: toward a general paradigm for training coping skills. In D. Meichenbaum and M. E. Jaremko (eds.), *Stress reduction and prevention*. New York: Plenum.

Menaghan, E. G. (1983). Individual coping efforts: moderators of the relationship between life stress and mental health outcomes. In H. B. Kaplan (ed.), *Psychosocial Stress: Trends in Theory and Research*. New York: Academic.

Menaghan, E. G., and Merves, E. S. (1984). Coping with occupational problems: the limits of individual efforts. *Journal of Health and Social Behavior, 25*, 406–423.

Miller, A. (1988). Stress on the job. *Newsweek*, April 22, pp. 40–45.

Monat, A., and Lazarus, R. S. (eds.) (1977). *Stress and Coping: An Anthology*. New York: Columbia University Press.

Moos, R. H., and Tsu, V. (1976). Human competence and coping. In R. H. Moos (ed.), *Human Adaptation: Coping with Life Crises*. Lexington, MA: Heath.

Murphy, L. R. (1985). Individual coping strategies. In C. L. Cooper and M. J. Smith (eds.), *Job Stress and Blue Collar Work*. New York: Wiley.

Murphy, L. R., and Schoenborn, T. F. (1987). *Stress Management in Work Settings*. NIOSH, U.S. Department of Health and Human Services Publication 87-111.

Nelson, D. L., and Quick, J. C. (1985). Professional women: are distress and disease inevitable. *Academy of Management Review, 10*, 206–218.

Newton, T. J., and Keenan, A. (1985). Coping with work related stress. *Human Relations, 38*, 107–126.

Nicholson, N. (1984). A theory of work role transitions. *Administrative Science Quarterly, 29*, 172–191.

Orpen, C. (1984). Managerial stress, relaxation and performance. *Journal of Management Development, 3*, 34–47.

Osipow, S. H., Doty, R. E., and Spokane, A. R. (1985). Occupational stress, strain and coping across the life span. *Journal of Vocational Behavior, 27*, 98–108.

Parasuraman, S., and Alutto, J. A. (1984). Sources and outcomes of stress in organizational settings: toward the development of a structural model. *Academy of Management Journal, 27*, 330–350.

Parasuraman, S., and Cleek, M. A. (1984). Coping behaviors and managers' affective reactions to role stressors. *Journal of Vocational Behavior, 24*, 179–193.

Parkes, K. R. (1984). Locus of control, cognitive appraisal and coping in stressful episodes. *Journal of Personality and Social Psychology, 46*, 655–668.

Pearlin, L. I., Lieberman, M. A., Menaghan, E. G., and Mullan, G. T. (1981). The stress process. *Journal of Health and Social Behavior, 22*, 337–356.

Pearlin, L. I., and Schooler, C. (1978). The structure of coping. *Journal of Health and Social Behavior, 19*, 2–21.

Pines, A., and Aronson, E. (1988). *Career Burnout: Causes and Cures*. New York: Free Press.

Pines, M. (1984). Ma Bell and the Hardy Boys. *Across the Board, 21*, 37–42.

Pittner, M. S., and Houston, B. K. (1980). Response to stress, cognitive coping strategies and the Type A behavior pattern. *Journal of Personality and Social Psychology, 39*, 147–157.

Rippere, V. (1976). Antidepressive behavior: a preliminary report. *Behavior Research and Therapy, 14*, 289–299.

Rose, R. L., and Veiga, J. F. (1984). Assessing the sustained effects of a stress management intervention on anxiety and locus of control. *Academy of Management Journal, 27*, 190–198.

Schaefer, C., Coyne, J. C., and Lazarus, R. S. (1982). The health-related functions of social support. *Journal of Behavioral Medicine, 4,* 381–406.

Schein, E. H. (1978). *Career Dynamics: Matching Individual and Organizational Needs.* Reading, MA: Addison-Wesley.

Schein, E. H. (1986). A critical look at current career development theory and research. In D. T. Hall and Associates, *Career Development in Organizations.* San Francisco: Jossey-Bass.

Schlossberg, N. K. (1984). *Counseling Adults in Transition.* New York: Springer.

Schlossberg, N. K., and Leibowitz, Z. (1980). Organizational support systems as buffers to job loss. *Journal of Vocational Behavior, 17,* 204–217.

Schuler, R. S. (1980). Definition and conceptualization of stress in organizations. *Organizational Behavior and Human Performance, 25,* 184–215.

Schuler, R. S. (1985). An integrative transactional process model of coping with stress in organizations. In T. A. Beehr and R. S. Bhagat (eds.), *Human Stress and Cognition in Organizations: An Integrated Perspective.* New York: Wiley.

Schuler, R. S., and Jackson, S. E. (1986). Managing stress through PHRM practices: an uncertainty interpretation. In K. M. Rowland and G. R. Ferris (eds.), *Research in Personnel and Human Resource Management,* Vol. 4. Greenwich, CT: JAI.

Seers, A., McGee, G. W., Serey, T. T., and Graen, G. G. (1983). The interaction of job stress and social support: a strong inference investigation. *Academy of Management Journal, 26,* 273–284.

Sekaran, U. (1986). *Dual Career Families: Implications for Organizations and Counselors.* San Francisco: Jossey-Bass.

Selye, H. (1956). *The Stress of Life.* New York: McGraw-Hill.

Selye, H. (1983). The stress concept: past, present and future. In C. L. Cooper (ed.), *Stress Research: Issues for the 80's.* New York: Wiley.

Sethi, A. S., and Schuler, R. S. (eds.) (1983). *Handbook of Stress Coping Strategies and Techniques.* Cambridge, MA: Ballinger.

Siegler, I. C., and George L. K. (1983). The normal psychology of the aging male: sex-differences in coping and perceptions of life events. *Journal of Geriatric Psychiatry, 16,* 197–209.

Sonnenfeld, J. A. (1984). *Managing Career Systems.* Homewood, IL: Irwin.

Spector, P. E., Dwyer, D. J., and Jex, S. M. (1988). Relation of job stressors to affective, health and performance outcomes: Comparison of multiple data sources. *Journal of Applied Psychology, 1,* 11–19.

Stone, A. A., and Neale, J. M. (1984). New measure of daily coping: development and preliminary results. *Journal of Personality and Social Psychology, 46,* 892–906.

Stout, S. K., Slocum, J. W., and Cron, W. L. (1987). Career transitions of superiors and subordinates. *Journal of Vocational Behavior, 30,* 124–137.

Sutton, R. I., and Kahn, R. L. (1987). Prediction, understanding and control as antidotes to organizational stress. In J. Lorsch (ed.), *Handbook of Organizational Behavior.* Englewood Cliffs, NJ: Prentice-Hall, pp. 272–285.

Switzer, L. (1979). Gelusil, jogging and gin: how executive educators deal with stress. *Executive Educator, 1,* 27–29.

Thoits, P. A. (1986). Social support as coping assistance. *Journal of Consulting and Clinical Psychology, 54,* 416–423.

Van Harrison, R. (1985). The person–environment fit model and the study of job stress. In T. A. Beehr and R. S. Bhagat (eds.), *Human Stress and Cognition in Organizations.* New York: Wiley.

Van Maanen, J., and Schein, E. H. (1979). Toward a theory of organizational socialization. In B. M. Staw and L. L. Cummings (eds.), *Research in Organizational Behavior,* Vol. 1. Greenwich, CT: JAI.

Veiga, J. F. (1983). Mobility influences during managerial career stages. *Academy of Management Journal, 1,* 64–85.

Zappert, L. T., and Weinstein, H. M. (1985). Sex differences in the impact of work on physical and psychological health. *American Journal of Psychiatry, 142,* 1174–1178.

13 Re-visioning career concepts: a feminist invitation

JUDI MARSHALL

INTRODUCTION

In this chapter I take a feminist perspective on career theory. There is no one feminism; rather this umbrella label covers many diverse perspectives held together by several broad uniting themes. Feminists tend to share a belief that women are oppressed in a society dominated by men (patriarchy) and concerns to change this situation and to honor and voice women's experiences and meanings. Beyond this there is considerable variety. Neither is feminism static: It is lived, in the sense that it arises from and informs being and doing and is continually evolving and changing. I cannot therefore speak for other women, although I draw on and value their work and experiences. This chapter is my current personal perspective, one story from a range of possibilities.

The chapter is in two main parts: The first offers some core strands in feminist thinking, which are then woven together in the second part, which explores their relevance to career theory. The first part is a brief tour of a vast and complex area. It starts with a selective history of the development of feminism. A historical perspective is necessary in order to understand the social context within which theory about women is developing. There have been major changes since 1960 in women's roles in society and in their attitudes toward employment. Feminism's potential contribution to career theory is shaped by these changes.

Within feminism, writers have offered a wide range of approaches to understanding women's experiences and their traditionally subordinate social position; these explanations range from the psychological to the structural, from the biological to the social and so on. Often these explanations seem to be competing as "the truth," and yet each alone is partial. To avoid oversimplification, feminism must understand the complex interplay between individuals and the structures and contexts within which they operate. I shall next, therefore, explore one psychological and one sociological framework for making sense of women's experiences in employment. Twinning these two makes it possible to achieve some sense of a whole picture of individual, organizational and social issues from which to develop career theory.

This chapter has been described by reviewers as sometimes having a "nonlinear style." It does not always proceed by cumulative argument but instead moves between significant debates and issues to give the reader their flavor. Although not originally intentional, this style has some meaning in relation to the topics addressed. It reflects the discontinuities significant in many women's careers, and it resonates with two of the chapter's key proposals, that we move away from linearity in career theory and practice and that we learn to perceive

275

and value diversity. In this sense, style will reflect content, the analogic form of the communication will reflect the digital, symbolic messages (Watzlawick et al., 1967). I hope the reader finds this added dimension interesting rather than obstructive.

DEVELOPING FEMINISM: KNOWLEDGE IN ACTION

My purpose in this section is to show some of the major shifts in emphasis that have occurred within feminism and to provide a context for the more detailed frameworks offered. I shall start my selective history of feminism with its renewed development in the 1960s. [See Eisenstein (1984) and Spender (1985) for extended accounts and appraisals.] Some women began to recognize their disadvantaged social position and to write about it as a way of contacting other women (e.g., Friedan, 1963). They realized that men have dominated society in recent history and created institutions in their own image. With their power they have enforced patriarchal values and have left out and systematically devalued women (Millett, 1972).

At this stage some women became involved in consciousness-raising groups. They shared their experiences of limited opportunities and frustration, coming to realize that these were generally not due to their inadequacies but to structural inequalities in social power. Such processes led to a great deal of anger directed at men and the world they had created, which shocked and frightened many men and other women. Theory making was passionate, voicing and bearing witness to women's oppression (Greer, 1970). From this phase comes the slogan "the personal is political"; the experiences of any individual were seen to be inextricably linked to the workings of social and political power. Although much of this phase of feminism was expressed in writing, the underlying theme was of action rather than academic development. Much of the action was taken by socialist and lesbian separatist feminists and was highly critical of established social structures and norms.

The next phase of feminism sought reform. Major legislation had by then been enacted to achieve the "equal rights" women were now demanding to join in men's prestigious organizations and patterns of life. Women wanted access to whatever men had, particularly employment. In academic accounts, theories of women's experience were added to those developed for men: attempts were made to "complete the record" (Bridenthal and Koonz, 1977; Hennig and Jardim, 1978). In this phase women wanted men as allies to enable their progress. Ironically, asking men for equal rights for women affirmed men's social power.

More recently, many women have become disillusioned with reform. Their participation in the world that men have shaped does little to counteract its basic devaluing of female characteristics. Women were offered opportunities to join men on their terms, men making little accommodation in return. Disillusion about the burden of having multiple roles (Davidson and Cooper, 1983) and adapting to organizational norms hostile to more female ways of being (Bartol, 1978) have led some women to moderate their work goals and others to question the demands organizations make on women and men. A more radical voice is re-emerging, seeking change in the structures and practices of employment. This time far more of the women concerned are actually within the institutions they wish to transform.

With these developments, a new approach and greater self-confidence are appearing within feminism. Women are detaching themselves from seeing men as either oppressors or holders of prize possessions (Bardwick, 1979). This new phase is woman centered; it involves women honoring their own values and heritage (Gilligan, 1982; Miller, 1976). It means looking again at roles into which they have been socialized, particularly those to do with relationships and the family. Instead of seeing these roles as of low social worth because that is how a patriarchal society defines them, women are re-claiming their positive aspects (Friedan, 1982). In so doing, they no longer have to see themselves and society through men's eyes and are finding their own forms of expression, being and doing. Women are developing their own theories, reconstructing the world of knowledge (Spender, 1985), which has not only missed them out as content but has in its structures and methods also taken no account of their values (more of this in what follows).

Paradoxically, while reform feminism set in motion "progress" for women in the public world, recent developments have had more private impacts. For example, women attending low-cost, community-based assertion training courses have tapped suppressed sources of personal power. They have gone on to take new charge of their lives, not necessarily doing new things, but doing things differently. This orientation has been surprising and disappointing to people using traditional measures of "success" because they cannot point to larger numbers of women "getting to the top," but this orientation fits with women's renewed pride in their traditional domain, the "private" world (Gamarnikow et al., 1983).

This woman-centered view does not reject men but recognizes that the world they have created and perpetuated oppresses many of them too. Rather than being only facilitators to women, men are also developing their own gender awareness and exploring the often negative implications of stereotypes of masculinity (Canavan and Haskell, 1986; Simmons, 1986).

Feminism's offerings to career theory will differ depending on the phase of historical development from which they come. Reform feminism concentrated on helping women achieve the same career opportunities and experiences as men. More recent developments have begun to criticize established career practices, arguing that organizations have much to learn from women's more traditional, discontinuous life patterns. I identify strongly with these latest developments of feminism. They necessitate a *radical* approach to organizations: taking nothing for granted, looking critically at basic values and assumptions and identifying where, however subtly, they define male as positive and female as negative. The aim of these processes is to develop new social and organizational foundations that value women and men equally. At the same time, developments must be *re-visionist*[1] (Callaway, 1981; Rich, 1972), not rejecting the heritage we have but looking for the functions and creative potential of female and male patterns of being, especially drawing from archetypal levels of understanding to go beyond the limits of social stereotypes. This understanding is a source for our "imaginative power of sighting possibilities and thus helping to bring about what is not (or not yet) visible" (Callaway, 1981). Radical critique and re-visionist rebuilding strands intertwine throughout this chapter. The former prompts precautionary suspicion of established definitions of "career" as these have been developed in organizations dominated by men's experiences, needs and life patterns. Re-vision means respecting, rather than rejecting, aspects of women's development that

have not conformed to traditional notions of career. It means seeing their possibilities and integrating the values on which they are based into emerging theory.
These themes will be explored throughout the rest of the chapter.

Some of the ideas I shall develop are not purely the province of feminism. Many
connect with reformulations in career theory (e.g., Arthur and Lawrence, 1984)
and with "new paradigm" academic approaches (Lincoln and Guba, 1985; Reason
and Rowan, 1981; Schwartz and Ogilvy, 1980), which take account of the current
re-emergence of female values in society (Capra, 1982). Career theory itself is
obviously aware of gender issues, especially the potentially negative effects of
stereotypes on women's careers (e.g., Lessor, 1984). But the roots of this chapter
are importantly different. It takes as its heart the valuing of women, their experience and female values. This is not to idealize any of these, for feminism is
also now acknowledging and exploring the potentially destructive elements of
the female principle.

FEMALE VALUES AND SOCIAL POWER

I shall now develop two broad, complimentary aspects of feminism as a ground
for appreciating the individual in context and as a base for looking again at career
theory. The first framework distinguishes between basic human qualities and
identifies some as more typically associated with women and others as more
typically associated with men. This level of theory is psychological; its purpose
is to re-claim the female pole from the negative associations it has been assigned
in a patriarchal society. The second aspect takes a social, structural view of
society. It starts with the assertion that Western society has been dominated by
men and male values and looks at some of the implications for the structuring
of knowledge, work and career theory.

Potential human characteristics

Many studies have been able to prove that women are much the same as men
[e.g., see Bartol (1978) for a review on leadership behavior], and their findings
have been used to argue for women's acceptance in organizations. But there is a
growing appreciation in diverse literatures that women and men are *also and
significantly* different and that these differences have relevance to life in organizations, what we mean by "equality" and so on (Gallos, Chapter 6).[2] In broad
terms, women represent a different range of potential human characteristics from
those of men. Socialization has played some part in establishing and maintaining
this difference but is only part in the story. If we look to more physiological and
archetypal analyses, we find that men and women are grounded in (but not
exclusively shaped by) different fundamental patterns. These are expressed especially clearly in the Chinese concepts of yin and yang (Colegrave, 1979; Cooper,
1981). Here I shall use the labels "female values" and "male values" with similar
associations.

Theorists who are now developing these concepts are essentially revising theories of adult psychology and development to include or separately consider
women. Attention has particularly been paid to the importance of relationships
to women's sense of identity. Traditional psychology has valued independence

(see most basic course texts) and considered "relational identity" as inferior, overdependent and somewhat unhealthy. Feminist theorists are re-claiming and asserting the value of this contributor to a self-concept (Gallos, Chapter 6). Gilligan (1982), for example, concludes from various research projects that women speak "in a different voice" from men. She sees two moral systems co-existing side by side. The male moral system views the world in terms of rights and principles that can be defended and used as the basis for decision making. The female system perceives life as a network of social relationships with the individual at its center. Right and wrong become relative and pragmatic, dependent on the situation. Miller (1976) presents a similar analysis, noting that the distinctive qualities women can access have traditionally been devalued in society. She calls particularly for the re-valuing of affiliative behavior.

A dichotomy I have found particularly helpful for exploring differences and similarities between men and women is that of Bakan (1966). Its base is not feminist, but it speaks to and incorporates many of feminism's issues. I shall develop this schema in some detail here because it provides a robust and complex foundation from which to examine gender. In Marshall (1984) I have used it to build a model of male and female styles of being and as a sense-making framework for understanding the experiences of women managers. Loden's (1985) distinction between masculine and feminine management styles has many similarities.

Bakan (1966) distinguishes two fundamental tendencies or principles of human functioning that he calls "agency" and "communion." In essence they are basic coping strategies for dealing with the uncertainties and anxieties of being alive. Agency is an expression of independence through self-protection, self-assertion and control of the environment. Communion is the sense of being "at one" with other organisms; its basis is integration. The agentic strategy reduces tension by changing the world about it; communion seeks union and cooperation as its way of coming to terms with uncertainty. While agency manifests itself in focus, closedness and separation, communion is characterized by contact, openness and fusion.

Agency achieves control by projecting difficulties outside the self. Bakan sees this as a sequential process. First, "liked" and "disliked" material are distinguished and the latter projected onto a person, group, object or concept in the environment, which is then devalued because of its associations. Individuals maintain a sense of control by screening out and repressing any feedback from the environment or their own emotions, which threaten the stability they have achieved. These techniques facilitate focused, directed action. The individuals are however vulnerable to the extent that their initial classification leaves areas of uncertainty outside their control. Only by moving to a further stage of "beholding" or encountering what they have repressed, which requires paradoxically setting aside their original anxiety, can they reach true mastery and full understanding.

Communion is not a modality of sequenced stages; it functions as a continuous realm of possibility. Communion's main strategies for dealing with the world are acceptance and personal adjustment. Its perception is naturalistic, reflecting the experienced patterns and contexts of the environment, and is minimally guided by prior analytic classifications. Openness to the environment produces intense personal, subjective impacts. These provide an extra, emotion-based dimension of sensing that contributes to understanding. Communion does not try to stabilize its environment but expects and accepts change and adapts.

Bakan's work is dense with associations of the two principles through science, religion and psychotherapy. Agency emerges as a principle of doing, activity, wanting to be judged by concrete achievement, entering into "contracts" defined in fixed terms of time and money and so on. There are obvious associations here with employment and with predominant concepts of career. In contrast, communion is better described as "being." Tolerance and trust are its characteristic manifestations; it works through non-contractual cooperation, showing forgiveness rather than exacting retribution if the other party contravenes expectations.

Both principles of being have their degenerative tendencies. Agency can become overcontrol, destruction of the environment, repression of uncertainty and all but manageable emotions. Communion can be penetrated, flooded and eventually destroyed by external forces or can move at their behest with no voice or direction of its own.

Bakan links agency with maleness through physiological data and mortality statistics and similarly associates femaleness with communion. The tendencies are potential complements rather than alternatives. Any individual is grounded in the tendency of its biological sex but has access to the other. Maturity means integrating the two tendencies in a relationship that maintains the distinctiveness of each (Colegrave, 1979). This conception of adult development has close similarities with Jung's concepts of anima, animus, individuation and self-actualization. It is an asymmetrically patterned notion of androgyny (Marshall, 1984). Implied in Bakan's work and supported by other sources are two further distinctions between the male and female principles of relevance to this chapter. The first is that women's journey of development is typically more inwardly oriented than that of men. Johnson (1977) depicts the archetypal journey of male development as the hero's quest, moving out to face challenges in the environment, leading later to inner growth. Woman's journey is more typically inward, toward her own core, learning from encounters in the inner world (Eichenbaum and Orbach, 1982; Perera, 1981). The second distinction is that the male principle is more closely associated with time, with linear progress in a given direction, and the female principle with space and a more cyclic pattern of change and transformation. The symbols of an arrow and a spiral represent them, respectively, in many ancient and modern mythologies (Mellor-Ribet, 1986; Woodman, 1982) and offer different potential models of life development.

Bakan closes his work by asserting the pressing need for "agency mitigated by communion." He speaks for individuals and a society rooted in agency. For those based in communion, and many women in employment are, despite their patriarchal upbringing, I have suggested the path of "communion enhanced by agency" (Marshall, 1984). In this formulation, communion can draw on agency to supplement, protect, support, aid, focus and arm it.

This model of human development re-values traditional female characteristics, strips them of stereotypic assumptions and sets them alongside male characteristics as equals and complements to which any individual has potential access (e.g., in relation to career development).

Social structure

The preceding analysis is idealized in its assumptions of equality. A second major strand of feminism recognizes the historic inequalities of power between male and female values, agency and communion. Although these inequalities are being pointed to and challenged, they still constitute much of the deep structure of Western society, its languages and its institutions.

The structural characteristics of patriarchy are well documented (e.g., Figes, 1970; Millett, 1972; Mitchell, 1966). How these are perpetuated through the operation of dominant and muted groups in society generally (Miller, 1976; Spender, 1980), and through elitism and uncertainty avoidance in organizations (Kanter, 1977), has also been analyzed. Work in this area demonstrates the power of social and organizational cultures to maintain themselves, even in the face of powerful forces for change. Increasing the numbers of women in organizations does not in itself, therefore, affect the predominance of male values.

The social dominance of male values is particularly important to the assumptions and formulations of career theory in two related areas: the construction of knowledge and definitions of "work."

Knowledge. Feminism represents a fundamental critique of knowledge as it is traditionally constructed (Gamarnikow et al., 1983; Marshall, 1985; Mitchell and Oakley, 1986; Spender, 1985). It challenges its *contents*, pointing out that knowledge has largely been constructed by and about men. "Knowledge" thus either leaves women out or stereotypes and devalues their experience. For example, social scientists have identified independence as "good," healthy, development and behavior. In consequence, interdependence has become labeled as inferior, inadequate and certainly unlikely to be worthy of promotion. Feminist writers challenge this polarization and argue for the potential benefits of collaborative, affiliative behavior in organizations (Gilligan, 1982; Miller, 1976).

Feminism also criticizes the *forms* of established knowledge: its preoccupation with seeking universal, immutable truth, failing to accept diversity and change; its categorization of the world into opposites, valuing one pole and devaluing the other; its claims of detachment and objectivity; and the predominance of linear, cause-and-effect thinking. These forms reflect male, agentic, experiences and strategies for coping with uncertainty. By shaping academic theorizing and research activities, they build male power and domination into the structures of knowledge (Gallos, Chapter 6; Roberts, 1981). One of feminism's most important activities is that of affirming the personal nature of knowledge making (e.g., Stanley and Wise, 1983). Thus it constitutes also a critique of traditional research *methods.* Career theory has its essence in patriarchal values and forms of knowledge making. Developments of theory extend its concepts, but the assumptive core remains the same. For example, the self-asserting individual remains the unit of evaluation; linear time underpins thinking despite some attention to phases; careers are largely assessed objectively, using socially visible markers such as hierarchical organizational level and against competitive notions of "success." Also career theory is rooted in a limited definition of work.

Work. Various writers, not only feminists, contend that some work is designated as more important by the rituals of employment – hours of compulsory attendance, centralized location of activities away from the home and the value placed on continuity of employment and commitment, for example. Pym (1980) suggests that these rituals all too often disguise the fact that no "real" work (i.e., those activities that generate goods and services) is being done. More specifically, feminist analyses such as those of Novarra (1980) and Rose (1986) argue that work traditionally identified as "men's" is a largely contrived and artificial activity, in contrast with "women's work," which arises "from the bedrock of necessity – these things cannot be left undone if the human race is to survive and life is to be tolerable." Yet housework and caring tend not to be counted as work or to be attributed the (social) importance of being paid.

The rituals of employment help to exclude child-bearing women, particularly from senior jobs. Work is constructed to suit men's life pattern in a society of divided, stereotyped roles. The part work has come to play in men's lives has agentic associations. This one aspect of life, perhaps because it offers more opportunities for control than do other areas, is often depicted in the literature as giving the whole of life meaning. Sofer (1970) says: "Through the commitment to the line of work the person has become committed to a particular social and personal identity. Investment in a particular line of work is simultaneously investment in a particular identity" (p. 48).

IMPLICATIONS FOR CAREER THEORY

From a feminist perspective we need then to re-vision career theory because it is rooted in male values and based on disguised male psychology; it neglects or devalues the feminine. New theories of career must give equal value to male and female aspects of being. This is necessary to accord women equality in all areas of life and to develop the potential of the female principle in society, including its significance as an aspect of men's identity. We therefore need to take models of women's psychology to the heart of career theory. Recent developments have modified its basic arrow design; we now need to re-create the core.

This work cannot be undertaken half-heartedly because we are always in the shadow of patriarchy's impressive power to shape and re-shape society in its image. Inequalities of power are still embedded in the deep structure of society and in its organizations and academic activities. We may *think* we are making changes, only to find that our new ideas and practices have been shaped by the culture as it was and so replicate fundamental assumptions we sought to escape (Lundberg, 1985; Marshall and McLean, 1985). Creativity will be needed to move beyond the dominant, male culture into new patterns and possibilities, which draw on the still tentative and fragile female principle. For example, in recognizing that some careers are non-hierarchical can we also challenge the norm of hierarchical thinking at the heart of career theory?

There are also practical implications of current inequalities of social power for women that will cycle back to affect career theory. Many women, even those in senior positions, currently define themselves as marginal in organizations. They experience the environment as "hostile" to their qualities and values (Marshall, 1984). Some of these women want to change the organizations they join *and* to hold on to their alternative visions. Many find that instead they become tired, worn down; some leave. At a recent national (U.K.) conference entitled "Asserting the Female Perspective," many of the sixty women participants described their needs to *stay* marginal, to maintain their fundamental suspicion of organizations and the values they embody. These people want to remember their roots as women and their muted social status and not to join the dominant group leaving society unchanged.[3] This attitude could be interpreted as negative ambivalence and lack of commitment. It can also be construed differently, accepted and taken seriously. The challenge will be to create employee development practices and career theory which have room for healthy scepticism and do not call it organizational disloyalty.

One central theme of new theorizing should be the reuniting of split dichotomies: work and the rest of life, male and female principles, conceptual understanding with other forms of knowing, particularly emotional intelligence, and so on. This can only be achieved meaningfully if we find ways to attribute value to opposites and diversity, working from communion to *accept* rather than from agency to value one pole above another.

In the remainder of the chapter I present my ideas for the re-visioning of career concepts, particularly exploring what an appreciation of communion might contribute and contrasting this with theory's current base in agency. I shall illustrate the possibilities proposed with case material from women at middle and senior organization levels in the retailing and book publishing industries (Marshall, 1984). The implications and further questions for career theory are arranged under five highly interrelated headings; at this stage in conceptual development some are more fully elaborated than others.

Doing and being: action and inaction

In Bakan's and similar typologies communion is characterized as *being* and agency as *doing*; in this lies a paradox for those "pursuing" careers. Agency engages in idealizations and tries to change the environment to match its own preconceived images. Doing is directed by internal, personal objectives. Communion is not inactivity in comparison, but its activity emerges from radically different roots – from its open contact with and appreciation of the environment. This orientation of "being" is contextually motivated. Prior awareness and acceptance of the world as it is results in action that is in tune with the surrounding context but is not conceptually premeditated. In a commentary to Wilhelm (1972), Jung captures this paradoxical essence as "the art of letting things happen, action through non-action." Action based in communion may be highly appropriate as a result. It also risks being too thoroughly shaped and distorted by the environment.

Career theory so far is largely based on notions of movement. Job moves, whether upward or sideways, have come to stand for development, carrying an assumption that outer development leads and determines inner development. Even when arguing for less hierarchically oriented careers, Evans (1986) calls for job moves every two to three years to avoid stagnation. Katz (1979), in his research on socialization, found that employees became unresponsive to task characteristics after about five years in a particular job. He suggests that people should be moved to maintain their usefulness to the company. From a feminist perspective we can take a fresh look at these findings and suggestions. They pay attention to outward, relatively quickly achieved, visible development. Learning and growth can also come from inner *deepening*, either of particular capabilities or of the integrity of the whole person. This may require a period of concentrating development energy inward, toward the self, during which individuals make no major contributions to the organization but simply perform satisfactorily in their current position. Eventually, paradoxically, they can then become more useful, reaching new levels of competence.

An expanded appreciation of the symbiosis between outward and inward development is required. Organizations concentrate on formal employee development. They need to allow more space for the individual's own process of maturation to guide his or her path, often doing their work subconsciously and sometimes temporarily disrupting public identity. From physics, Prigonine and Strengers (1984) offer us the notion of dissipative structures, the descent into chaos from which a new, higher level of order emerges. Many of the more impactful processes of individual development have these qualities and are much messier and time demanding than the cognitively aware, incremental shape of formal training. Accepting these other aspects of growth into organizations requires more tolerance of any individual's range of qualities and phases around the basic pattern which gives their personality stability.

Perera (1981) has made a significant contribution to understanding the meanings of non-action in women's lives. Using conceptual analysis and case material from her work as a Jungian analyst, she affirms the importance of allowing and living through periods of depression and standstill. She sees these as offering the potential for major learning through re-integrating subdued or repressed aspects of identity. The creative but potentially destructive Medusa aspect of the feminine seems particularly relevant to modern women (Whitmont, 1983).[4] We can see these processes of development in research data. For example, Hennig and Jardim (1978) found that, without exception, their sample of twenty-five women who made it to senior management had had a moratorium on career development in mid-career. They attended to more "feminine" interests; some married. This reclaiming of their femaleness was significant for both self *and career* development. A comparative sample of managers who did not take time out in this way did not progress beyond middle management levels.

Our concepts need, then, to develop a dual appreciation of movement and stillness, flow and pause and how these interrelate. This may mean valuing "stagnation" – perhaps better called incubation or regeneration – learning its lessons and creative potential.

Independence–interdependence

The agentic principle works through self-assertion, emphasizing its independence and competing with others for resources, rewards and importance. Projecting focused pre-conceptions onto the world and using cause-and-effect thinking, agency holds itself responsible for outcomes, claiming them as its own achievements. From this perspective, "success" is demonstrable and individual. Organization promotion systems focus on the individual and reward them for these perceived impacts. I recently filled out a form applying for promotion in my university. Against any joint publications I had to give an indication of my share of the responsibility. Writing alone is seen as more valuable than working with others, and within a colleague relationship the parties are cast into competition.

Communion sees itself, including its actions, as part of a wider context of interacting influences. It tends not to assume personal accomplishment when events turn out favorably and is certainly less likely to be able to identify its contribution. This may be significant but largely invisible and difficult to disentangle because work has been largely pursued through influence, by shaping environments for others or in mutually empowering relationships. Action based in communion may therefore go unrewarded by formal organizational systems. This has potentially negative consequences for the individual drawing on communion (and for the organizational culture), although public acclaim was probably not their primary intention.

Integrating communion with agency will require a radical re-vision of the value systems against which we judge good performance. Contributing to wider community interests – affiliative behavior – needs to be set alongside independent achievement and identifiable works as a desirable quality.

Phases: sequential and cyclic

Career theory is already moving away from a basically linear formulation toward notions of phases reflecting changing life development needs (Evans and Bartolome, 1980; Levinson, 1978). Feminism asks it to move further and to bring together the archetypally female spiral and the archetypally male arrow as two core, interrelated patterns.

The linear career view is shifting toward a scheme of *sequential* stages. Development is largely cumulative, each phase building on the achievements or conflict resolution of its predecessor in continual improvement. Development is acquisitive; once something has been gained, it should be retained. "Backward" as a direction has negative connotations. Theoretically a range of career possibilities are being recognized, but many are depicted as "failure," however generously put, because the organizational hierarchy still looms large as the value system within which choices are made and success judged.

Female values offer career theory a more *cyclic* interpretation of phases, based in notions of ebb and flow, of shedding and renewal. These are important counterpoints to the cumulative, building metaphor developed in the preceding. They involve giving something up, letting achievements go, in order to create anew and differently. This requires considerable faith that future creativity will be possible and an ability to embrace and engage with uncertainty. For many women this approach translates into a commitment to continual personal development (Loden, 1985), for which career theory needs to find a more positive space. For example, women approach many training activities with a fundamental openness to change. They bring their whole lives into review and expect to be transformed by the event. Many men, in contrast, present themselves as organizational people looking for specific learnings but believe that the core of who they are is unchangeable, quoting as justification the Jesuit dictum, "give me a man 'til he's seven and he will be mine for life" (Stewart and Marshall, 1982). It is part of a more cyclic view of development sometimes to go backward, to recapitulate steps made before, although they will be different each time and offer new learning because of their different place in the life pattern.

We can learn more about cyclic phases from the diversity of women's current life patterns. They are combining employment, marriage and motherhood in a wide variety of combinations and sequences, often appearing to start afresh as they give up status in one arena to take on a novice role in another. From this perspective, the connecting thread is the individual's life, not a building image of increasing social status. A next phase may appear wholly discontinuous from its predecessor, perhaps because the individual is working on muted or repressed characteristics that now require development. Rather than building on strengths, their move will be motivated by growing toward wholeness and integration.

Managers I studied (Marshall, 1984) used their own notion of phases to explain how they directed energy between different life areas. They might limit their social life as they learned a new job or mark time at work when personal issues were more important to them. Phasing was also part of seeing themselves in relationship, of taking into account the affiliative aspects of identity that emerge so strongly in new theories of female psychology. These may be relationships at home, suggesting that it may sometimes be valuable to see the family as the unit of career development. One manager had moved to a new location, suspending her career progression temporarily, while her partner took on major new responsibilities. A woman returning to work after raising a family was being told "it is your turn now" by husband and children. They organized and largely took over the housework to give her space to start her new career phase.

Entering a new career cycle is also sometimes prompted by a sense of responsibility to wider contextual needs. Someone may take on a task, for example a trades union post, to serve the community, benefiting unexpectedly themselves. But if the new direction does not resonate, however subconsciously, with the individual's own life issues, altruism and attunement can be misguided. Recently I have met several women managers who are wondering whether to apply for the next job up, typically head of a major department. They have been pressured to apply and believe themselves well capable of doing the job. They do not, however, for one reason or another, really want it. The crowning twist in their dilemma is that no woman has held the prestigious post before, and they are the only one qualified to do so in the near future. If they refuse, they believe other women will be viewed less favorably. These women are taking on the symbolism that they represent all women and their rights. Only if living out this fate satisfies some need of their own does it seem that they and their cause can ultimately benefit. To analyze their situation further requires a detached assessment of their motivations so that their identity does not get lost in their concern for women generally.

Theoretically we can affirm cyclic life patterns and the different paths of individual growth they might foster. But accommodating these within organizations will challenge many basic career assumptions and practices, such as links between age and organizational status and expectations that career development runs to and can be judged against relatively fixed time scales. The practices of assessing "high potential" early in an individual's work life and of defining older people who are not moving upward as "plateaued" become unnecessarily restrictive if people are capable of major growth and career change throughout their lives.

Taking cyclic notions seriously leads us toward more complex and diversity-allowing models of engagement between individuals and organizations. This will require re-vision of how people are judged as organization members; most employee developers do not approve of people concentrating energy outside the company and interpret multi-stranded life patterns as lack of organizational and career commitment. Both parties will need to develop their skills of management and negotiation to engage in new possibilities.

Whole lives and part lives

The expanded notion of career developed here takes the individual's whole life as its base. Whatever specific paths a person follows, they make sense within this framework of meaning. In this sense, too, there may be phases of ebb and flow, moving between concentration on the part and attention to the whole. Women managers I interviewed (Marshall, 1984) usually gave priority to "leading a balanced life," continually paying attention to, and adjusting their distribution of time and energy to achieve, life meaning outside as well as inside employment. At times some had let one life area take them over. Several younger, single managers had done this reluctantly; their competent work identity had dominated, and they had felt ill at ease and underdeveloped socially. Paradoxically, once they accepted the imbalance, they found that their work identity provided a base for the rest of their lives; they developed a new social confidence, less tied to stereotypes of femininity than the ideals they had previously pursued.

Traditional career theory and practice follow patriarchy's value system and see the individual selectively through employment's eyes, missing much of the richer picture. Wanting a balanced life challenges traditional definitions of career as the major source of identity. Also many people want to move away from the stereotype of life long, full-time employment in one company, on which career theory still largely draws, and toward more flexible and diverse work patterns. These developments challenge reliance on "commitment" as a desirable employee characteristic and suggest that we need to expand our definitions of relevant experience to include that gained in home and community activities, outside artificial boundaries of valuable work. Further theoretical attention is therefore required to the relationship of employment to other life areas, as always taking critical note of any assumptions of relative importance.

Career planning: through agency and communion

Agentic career planning seeks control, certainty and predictability. Much of the prescriptive literature on careers is about directing one's journey, presenting the right image, making short-term choices in the service of long-term aims and so on. This perspective is future oriented and goal dominated; status on retirement is a marker of life achievement. Agency-based individuals have strategies and shape their career, making assessments of how "far" they can get in the other world of employment. Goals are identified largely in terms of organizational status and financial reward and so are in limited supply. The majority of people must adjust to achieving less than they hoped.

Communion offers an alternative basis for "planning" and for judging the value of career. Its keynotes are flexibility, openness to opportunities and right timing as the person and appropriate environment meet. This process is not usually change seeking but change accepting. Individuals must be prepared for transformation, to lose and gain definitions of self as they both adjust to the environment and take up its challenges. Communion is essentially present oriented, concerned with the next appropriate step when choices are made rather than looking beyond. People may have "dreams" but hold them lightly, using them as visions of possibility rather than as aspirations that have to be realized. Many of the women I interviewed described their preferred style as learning through engagement, becoming wholly immersed in a particular task or job. While this was happening, they were thoroughly satisfied. Only when they were no longer stimulated or learning would the realization of their next needs crystallize, leading them outward to seek new challenge. Paradoxically, this focus largely on job, for which women have long been criticized, had led to satisfying and organizationally successful careers.

By balancing directing and accepting approaches to planning, individuals can attempt to accommodate their own life rhythms within the frameworks of employment. At times they will need challenge and stimulus, at others space and opportunities to follow the flow wherever it leads. They can, perhaps, use agentic strategies to facilitate growth through communion by creating their own pauses for renewal and reappraisal rather than feel driven toward disillusion or burnout.

In an increasingly complex world, the process approach of "readiness" and adaptability that female forms offer provides a valuable complement to more directive, goal-oriented strategies of career development. Re-visioning notions of planning could have many repercussions for theory and practice. For example, placing greater emphasis on development through immersion in a particular job might help reduce the hierarchical pull in judging the success of a career.

INTEGRATING FEMALE VALUES INTO CAREER THEORY

In the areas of development of career theory already noted, the repeated challenge has been to incorporate female values into a so far largely male base. This will involve re-visioning the contents, structures and methods of career theory – the three core aspects of knowledge making over which patriarchy has exerted so much control (see the preceding). In this concluding section I shall look in turn at these three aspects. In doing so, I am choosing to point initially to theoretical concerns rather than those of organizational practice because how we make new theory is vitally important. What frameworks we develop for understanding and assigning value to individuals and organizations can either set limits to or expand their variety, creativity and potential.

The previous section was concerned mainly with the *contents* of career theory. It argued for being, inaction, interdependence and engagement to be set alongside doing, action, independence and detachment as aspects of employee competence. The individual's whole life was set at the heart of re-visioned career theory. Drawing on archetypal female values, notions of cyclic phases, recapitulation and continual potential for transformation contributed a model of persons creatively weaving their life. This contrasts with traditional career theory's concentration on one aspect of life, viewing development as sequential and cumulative, a model of identity building. Organizations need to be able to welcome members following either model or combining the two.

Unless the *structures* of career theory also change, however, forms based in female values will merely be added on to a growing list of career possibilities, and male values will maintain their fundamental dominance. To achieve more than this, we must move away from hierarchical thinking, from splitting the world into opposites and valuing one pole above the other, and toward a flexible, multi-stranded value system. A first step toward the change in deep structure required is to recognize the forces that keep current theory and practice in place (Marshall and McLean, 1985). Hierarchies are frameworks for order; established through agentic processes of projection, they become standards outside ourselves, and so supposedly objective, for judging relative social worth and distributing resources and power. In career theory they help organizations rank people in relation to one another, individuals to chart their path through anxiety-producing choices and theorists to identify success. They serve our needs for coherence, certainty and control. To re-vision career theory, we must become more tolerant of change and flexibility, more adaptive and more accepting of diversity and difference. This will often feel like engaging with chaos. This need for flexibility, for understanding multiple realities simultaneously, applies as much to academics as to practitioners. Often theory represents our defence against anxiety, meeting our needs for security and conformity. In theory development we can respond with agentic control, communal openness or some combination of the two. Here is one of the greatest challenges!

We need to develop the conceptual sensitivity and language to map and value the range of considerations informing an individual's life choices, including health, personal growth, affiliation, challenge, creativity, opportunities to influence, geographical location and so on as well as financial reward and social status. Perhaps the notion of heterarchy (Schwartz and Ogilvy, 1980) has something to offer theoretically. A heterarchy has no one person or principle in command. Rather, temporary pyramids of authority form as and when appropriate in a system of mutual constraints and influences. The childhood game of paper, stone and scissors provides a simple illustration: paper wraps stone, stone blunts scissors, scissors cut paper. There is no fixed hierarchy, but each is effective, and recognized, in its own realm. In this way different values can take primacy in an individual's career pattern at different stages. Drawing on a multi-stranded value system, theory can appreciate these changes in priority. This means moving away from concern with outcomes – job achieved, skills developed – and toward a more process-based model, looking at the nature and quality of choice making, paying due respect to being and becoming as well as doing.

This chapter also calls for re-vision in the *methods* of career theory, some of which is already happening because of other theoretical trends. This involves moving away from organizations and society judging the individual from the outside using socially defined criteria of success and towards self-assessment, including criteria setting and personal responsibility; individuals negotiating their needs with organizations. To understand these processes, we shall need to engage in collaborative forms of inquiry, in which participants become co-researchers and sense makers (Reason and Rowan, 1981).

Feminism is a living and lived-out perspective. What it means to notions of career is currently being developed in people's lives as well as academically. This chapter has been only a beginning. Its ideas should next be taken into research, working in depth with women and men on their individual and joint processes of career and life creation. One of the tests of the adequacy of emergent theorizing will be whether it attributes equal value to female and male principles, to communal acceptance and agentic control.

NOTES

1 The hyphenated form is used in this chapter to emphasise the careful attention – always looking, and then *looking again* – necessary in such processes.
2 I am concerned about a new wave of feminist writing that concentrates on women and men's differences and sees these purely as biologically based, inherent. More acknowledgment of differences is currently necessary to balance the recent emphasis on similarities, but neither approach should exclude the other. See Segal (1987) for more on the dangers of explanations solely in terms of inherent sexual differences.
3 It is not my intention to devalue the experiences and achievements of women who have developed and are developing careers along more traditional lines – after all, that is what I have done! Rather, I think we now have the opportunity to expand the range of choices for men and women by bringing female values more explicitly into organizations. But this is not the pursuit of uniformity, in any form.
4 Whitmont identifies Medusa as "the abyss of transformation, the seemingly chaotic riddle that woman is to herself and to the puzzled man she leads to the dread of unpredictability and seeming emptiness and depression and annihilation" (p. 141). Perera (1981) believes that many women brought up in patriarchical society need to integrate this "goddess of the underworld" into their psyches as an important developmental stage.

REFERENCES

Arthur, M. B., and Lawrence, B. S. (1984). Special issue on environment and career. *Journal of Occupational Behaviour, 5* (1), 1–81.
Bakan, D. (1966). *The Duality of Human Existence.* Boston: Beacon.
Bardwick, J. M. (1979). *In Transition.* London: Holt, Rinehart and Winston.
Bartol, K. M. (1978). The sex structuring of organizations: a search for possible causes. *Academy of Management Review,* October, pp. 805–815.
Bridenthal, R., and Koonz, C. (eds.) (1977). *Becoming Visible: Women in European History.* Boston: Houghton Mifflin.
Callaway, H. (1981). Women's perspectives: research as revision. In P. Reason and J. Rowan (eds.), *Human Inquiry.* Chichester: Wiley.
Canavan, P., and Haskell, J. (1986). The great American male stereotype. *Women in Business Conference.* London, May. Organized by Management Centre Europe, Brussels.
Capra, F. (1982). *The Turning Point: Science, Society and the Rising Culture.* London: Wildwood House.
Colegrave, S. (1979). *The Spirit of the Valley: Androgyny and Chinese Thought.* London: Virago.
Cooper, J. C. (1981). *Yin and Yang: The Taoist Harmony of Opposites.* Wellingborough, Northants: Aquarian.
Davidson, M., and Cooper, C. L. (1983). *Stress and the Woman Manager.* Oxford: Robertson.
Eichenbaum, L., and Orbach, S. (1982). *Outside In . . . Inside Out.* Harmondsworth: Penguin.
Eisenstein, H. (1984). *Contemporary Feminist Thought.* London: Allen & Unwin.
Evans, P. (1986). Managing career development. In A. Mumford (ed.), *Proceedings of World Congress on Management Development.* London, June.
Evans, P., and Bartolome, F. (1980). *Must Success Cost So Much?* London: McIntyre.
Figes, E. (1970). *Patriarchal Attitudes.* New York: Stein and Day.
Friedan, B. (1963). *The Feminine Mystique.* New York: Dell.
Friedan, B. (1982). *The Second Stage.* London: Joseph.
Gamarnikow, E., Morgan, D. M. J., Purvis, J., and Taylorson, D. (eds.) (1983). *The Public and the Private.* London: Heinemann.
Gilligan, C. (1982). *In a Different Voice: Psychological Theory and Women's Development.* Harvard: Harvard University Press.
Greer, G. (1970). *The Female Eunuch.* London: MacGibbon and Kee.
Hennig, M., and Jardim, A. (1978). *The Managerial Woman.* London: Boyars.
Johnson, R. A. (1977). *He: Understanding Masculine Psychology.* New York: Harper & Row.
Kanter, R. M. (1977). *Men and Women of the Corporation.* New York: Basic Books.
Katz, R. (1979). Time and work: towards an integrative perspective. In B. Staw and L.

Cummings (eds.), *Annual Review of Research in Organizational Behavior*, Vol. 2. Greenwich, CT: JAI.

Lessor, R. (1984). The case of women flight attendants. *Journal of Occupational Behaviour*, 5,(1): 37–52.

Levinson, D. J. (1978). *The Seasons of a Man's Life*. New York: Ballantine.

Lincoln, Y. S., and Guba, E. F. (1985). *Naturalistic Inquiry*. Beverly Hills, CA: Sage.

Loden, M. (1985). *Feminine Leadership*. New York: Times Books.

Lundberg, C. C. (1985). On the feasibility of cultural intervention in organizations. In P. J. Frost, L. F. Moore, M. R. Louis, C. C. Lundberg, and J. Martin (eds.), *Organizational Culture*. Beverley Hills, CA: Sage.

Marshall, J. (1984). *Women Managers: Travellers in a Male World*. Chichester: Wiley.

Marshall, J. (1985). Feminism as a critique of knowledge. In M. Pedler and T. Boydell (eds.), *A Guide to Materials on Women and Men in Organisations*. Sheffield, United Kingdom: Manpower Services Commission.

Marshall, J., and McLean, A. (1985). Exploring organisational culture as a route to organisational change. In V. Hammond (ed.), *Current Research in Management*. London: Pinter.

Mellor-Ribet, E. (1986). Group processes: toward a female perspective. Ph.D. Thesis. University of Bath.

Miller, J. B. (1976). *Toward a New Psychology of Women*. Boston: Beacon.

Millett, K. (1972). *Sexual Politics*. London: Abacus/Sphere.

Mitchell, J. (1966). Women: the longest revolution. *New Left Review*, 40.

Mitchell, J., and Oakley, A. (eds). (1986). *What is Feminism?* Oxford: Blackwell.

Novarra, V. (1980). *Women's Work, Men's Work*. London: Boyars.

Perera, S. B. (1981). *Descent to the Goddess: A Way of Initiation for Women*. Toronto: Inner City Books.

Prigonine, I., and Strengers, I. (1984). *Order Out of Chaos: Man's New Dialogue with Nature*. London: Heinemann.

Pym, D. (1980). Towards the dual economy and emancipation from employment. *Futures*, 12(3).

Reason, P., and Rowan, J. (eds.) (1981). *Human Inquiry*. Chichester: Wiley.

Rich, A. (1972). When we dead awaken: writing as re-vision. *College English*, 34(1), 18–25.

Roberts, H. (1981). *Doing Feminist Research*. London: Routledge & Kegan Paul.

Rose, H. (1986). Women's work: women's knowledge. In J. Mitchell and A. Oakley (eds.), *What is Feminism?* Oxford: Blackwell.

Schwartz, P., and Ogilvy, J. (1980). *The Emergent Paradigm: Changing Patterns of Thought and Belief*. Analytical report no. 7, Values and Lifestyles Program. Menlo Park, CA: SRI International.

Segal, L. (1987). *Is the Future Female: Troubled Thoughts on Contemporary Feminism*. London: Virago.

Simmons, M. (1986). Undoing men's gender conditioning – A Key Issue for Men as Leaders. In A. Mumford (ed.), *Proceedings of World Congress on Management Development*. London.

Sofer, C. (1970). *Men in Mid-Career*. Cambridge: Cambridge University Press.

Spender, D. (1980). *Man Made Language*. London: Routledge & Kegan Paul.

Spender, D. (1985). *For the Record: The Making and Meaning of Feminist Knowledge*. London: Women's Press.

Stanley, L., and Wise, S. (1983). *Breaking Out: Feminist Consciousness and Feminist Research*. London: Routledge & Kegan Paul.

Stewart, R., and Marshall, J. (1982). Managerial beliefs about managing: implications for management training. *Personnel Review*, 11(2), 21–24.

Watzlawick, P., Beavin, T. M., and Jackson, D. D. (1967). *Pragmatics of Human Communications*. New York: Norton.

Whitmont, E. C. (1983). *Return of the Goddess*. London: Routledge & Kegan Paul.

Wilhelm, R. (1972). *Confucius and Confucianism*. London: Routledge.

Woodman, M. (1982). *Addiction to Perfection*. Toronto: Inner City Books.

14 Reciprocity at work: the separate, yet inseparable possibilities for individual and organizational development

MICHAEL B. ARTHUR AND KATHY E. KRAM

INTRODUCTION

The title of this chapter includes several terms central to this chapter. First, we are interested in how career processes produce both individual and organizational outcomes. Second, we subscribe to developmental views of both the individual and the organization, paying separate attention to each party. Third, we are concerned with how work arrangements transmit influence from individual to organization, and vice versa. Fourth, we explore the notion of reciprocity, that is, what individuals and organizations give back in return for what they draw from one another.

Our overall purpose is to examine how patterns of individual–organization interaction support or hinder individual and organizational developmental outcomes as a basis for further theory building and research. Our examination will incorporate recent ideas on developmental stages, transitions, and strategic choice and political behavior as they apply to both individuals and organizations. A central question is, how can reciprocity between the two parties contribute to the future possibilities for individuals – and so their careers – and organizations – and so their further evolution?

Our definition of the *career* is that adopted for this volume, namely, the evolving sequence of a person's work experiences over time. This incorporates all organizational members and offers a "moving perspective" (Hughes, 1958) of how work unfolds. However, our ideas about *development* are more particular and heavily influenced by recent views of "developmentally normal" patterns of adult development (Kram, 1985; Levinson et al., 1978; Levinson, 1984)[1] and comparable views on organizational development (Greiner, 1972; Quinn and Cameron, 1983; Wholey and Brittain, 1986). We see development in terms of normative, but not inevitable, sequences of either individual or organizational needs. More specifically, development is defined here as the ongoing adaptation of either individuals or organizations to predictable changes in their own needs over time. With regard to reciprocity, we are also interested in the adaptation of individuals and organizations to one another and the developmental consequences for each party that result.

The sections that follow begin by applying a concept of reciprocity to a three-stage model of the individual career and from this providing an account of successive individual needs and associated behaviors. The relevance of these behaviors is then considered in the light of stage-based views of organizational development, from which a framework for matching individual and organizational

292

needs is proposed. The prospects for individual–organizational reciprocity are seen to be dependent on the prevailing developmental stage of each of the two parties. Also, individual and organizational complexity are each seen to involve interdependence among each party's needs as development takes place. The second major section draws on separate models for understanding individual–organization fit at micro- and macrolevels of analysis. For both individuals and organizations, two separate forms of dysfunction, or lack of fit, are identified. The third section draws on preceding discussion to present a model of interaction between individual and organizational needs along with six propositions to guide further research. The propositions bring together what are presently separate threads of individual and organizational theory as they apply to developmental stages, transitions, and strategic choice and political behavior. The chapter closes with a plea for further research to recognize the simultaneity of individual and organizational development and the interdependence between the developmental needs of each party.

THE NOTION OF RECIPROCITY

Our notion of reciprocity derives from Barnard and Simon's inducement–contribution model (March and Simon, 1958; Simon, 1976). This postulates that the separate outcomes of organizational inducements to individuals and individual contributions to organizations must each be satisfactory for an effective and continuing individual–organization association. Thus reciprocity, as used here, refers to the extent to which individual and organizational needs are separately and simultaneously met.[2]

The Barnard and Simon model underlies subsequent work on the psychological contract (Argyris, 1960; Levinson, 1962) and, notably through Schein's (1978, 1980) further work, has already influenced existing career theory. However, emergent views on matching individual and organizational needs have been more particular about individual development (e.g., Arthur, 1984; Schein, 1980; Wanous, 1980). In considering reciprocal effects, this chapter attends to both individual and organizational development.

Reciprocity and the career

Adult development and career development perspectives from various sources have illuminated predictable individual tasks at successive career stages and throughout the life course (Erikson, 1957, 1968; Gould, 1978; Hall and Nougaim, 1968; Jaques, 1965; Levinson et al., 1978; Ortega y Gassett, 1958; Schein, 1978; Sofer, 1970; Super, 1957; Vaillant, 1977). Recent work on mentoring and developmental relationships has added to our understanding of these tasks and their associated individual needs (Clawson, 1980; Kram, 1985, 1986; Kram and Isabella, 1985; Lindholm, 1982; Missirian, 1982; Phillips-Jones, 1982; Thomas, 1986; Zintz, 1988). Young adults launching new careers, for example, frequently find coaching, counseling and role models in relationships with senior colleagues that enable them to develop competencies, self-confidence and a professional identity. More experienced adults, in contrast, as they approach middle career and beyond, can find mentoring junior colleagues a way to satisfy generative needs that tend to emerge at this stage.

There is a convergence of views on how individual needs change as careers unfold. Much of this convergence can be captured by seeing the individual career as three consecutive stages, each of around fifteen years duration. In the discussion that follows, *early career* is viewed as usually ending in the early to mid-thirties, *middle career* usually lasting until the middle to late forties, and *career maturity* going on to around the early or middle sixties. However, we acknowledge there can be wide variations from this normative view.[3]

Most of the work done emphasizes the shifting individual needs associated with the preceding stages. However, the same sources also suggest associated individual behaviors if needs are being met. In keeping with this chapter's concern with reciprocal effects, both individual needs and their associated behaviors are reviewed.

Early career

During the early career years, a young adult is faced with the major tasks of developing job competence and an initial occupational identity. Simultaneously, the person is usually learning the ropes of the organization, developing a life structure apart from the family of origin and preparing the ground for the predictable career decisions that lie ahead (Dalton, Thompson, and Price, 1977; Hall, 1976; Levinson et al., 1978; Schein, 1978). Each of these tasks can be facilitated through work arrangements, and especially through the interest, guidance and support of a mentor and other more experienced colleagues. Jobs should provide opportunities for the individual to learn, to demonstrate competence, to experience acceptance and protection and to have access to role models for future career choices. Consistent with other accounts, we call the dominant individual need of the period *exploring*.

In return for their early career experiences, people frequently offer the organization a high level of energy for work, a "youthful vitality" (Levinson et al., 1978), even displays of "passion and heroism," although these exertions are still conditional and not rooted in any necessary or inflexible identification with the work role (Ortega y Gasset, 1958; Sofer, 1970). The essential concern is with "*doing*" (Jaques, 1965, p. 508) and demonstrating competencies in occupational or technical roles rather than in subtler ways grounded in personal or administrative experience (e.g., Dalton and Thompson, 1986; Sofer, 1970). This high level of energy for work is usually accompanied by optimism and a willingness to trust organizational and occupational seniors (Sofer, 1970). The creativity associated with this energy is of a "precipitative" form, that is, "intense and spontaneous, and comes out ready made" (Jaques, 1965). We call the behavior associated with this period *exuberance*.

Middle career

During the middle career years, individuals have generally got their early explorations behind them and developed some focus on the career goals to pursue. Clear on their "career anchors" (Schein, 1978), they are most concerned about personal advancement, advancement typically spanning both work and community. In seeking external recognition, they usually want greater autonomy from senior colleagues and responsibility over junior ones. The overall purpose of these behaviors is to seek out opportunities to be visibly successful on the organization's – and therefore their own – behalf (Hall, 1980; Levinson et al., 1978; Osherson, 1980; Schein, 1978). Jobs mediate between individuals and their organizational contexts (such as the nature of promotional opportunities, rewards and assignments) to shape the exposure and recognition sought. The dominant individual need of the period can be appropriately called *advancing*.

In return for satisfactory middle career experiences, people's central concerns with "climbing the ladder" and gaining greater acceptance by the "tribe" they have come to associate with (Levinson et al., 1978) can foster an intense desire for organizational success. However, this desire is conditional on the opportunity for members to associate their own advancement – for example, in social rank, income, power or fame – with organizational achievement (Levinson et al., 1978). Supervision of other employees is sought but is again provisional on the members' judgment of the personal rewards to be obtained (Kanter, 1983). Creativity is also offered on similar, even if implicit, conditions. We call the emergent behavior associated with this period *directedness*.

Career maturity

Finally, during the mature career years,[4] individuals are generally faced with the tasks of securing and maintaining their emergent status, experiencing continued affirmation of their work and passing on the benefits of their learning and experience to others (Erikson, 1968; Kram, 1985; Kram and Julesa, 1978; Levinson et al., 1978). In order for these tasks to be successfully accomplished, job arrangements must provide feedback from peers and superiors that one's contributions continue to have significance, opportunities to actively mentor succeeding generations and an eventual chance to prepare for retirement by sharing anticipations of this major life transition with trusted peers (Kram & Isabella, 1985). Since there are dual components of taking care of self as well as others, we label the individual need associated with the preceding *protecting*.

The outer manifestation of career maturity emerges from people who have attended to both sides of the major mid-life dichotomy between self-absorption and generativity (Erikson, 1968). Thus, there is – and we address this from the organization's perspective – a fundamental concern that the skills and knowledge developed so far continue to be relevant, accessible and useful. Provided people's own status is assured, there will be a desire to extend a sense of caring toward younger generations and to offer them the benefit of earned experience (Baird and Kram, 1983). Supervision of others is not now conditional on any quid pro quo for further external achievement but rather can extend into deeply felt acts of mentoring (Kram, 1985; Levinson et al., 1978). The creativity associated with this period is of a "sculpted" kind, involving constructive resignation to the limitations of any new work, and of getting things done in the environment (Jaques, 1965). We call the emergent behavior associated with this period *stewardship*.

We do not view these needs and behaviors over time evolving and receding in strict sequence. Rather, consistent with Erikson (1957, 1968), Levinson (Levinson, 1984; Levinson et al., 1978) and other developmental theorists, we see these needs as building on one another. Previous needs are neither forgotten nor altogether neglected but become integrated into the still-developing person. We also see differences in emphasis and timing of these needs accounting for certain reported differences between male and female development (Bardwick, 1980; Gilligan, 1982; Gutek and Larwood, 1987), allowing for a greater degree of individual diversity (Bailyn, 1984) and accommodating varying age distributions in organizational settings (Lawrence, 1987).[5] Thus, beyond the immediate question of which need dominates lies a subtler one about the interdependence between the three career needs described. From this vantage point the three needs of exploring, advancing and protecting provide a framework for considering the emerging *complexity* of individual needs as the career unfolds.

Reciprocity and organizational evolution

From Barnard and Simon's inducement–contribution standpoint (March and Simon, 1958; Simon, 1976), the distinction drawn in the preceding between individual needs and behaviors is crucial. Organizations offer inducements in attempts to meet individual needs. Similarly, individuals offer behaviors in attempts to make contributions to organizations. Exploring, advancing and protecting were proposed to reflect major needs for individual development. Thus, a further question to be asked is how well do the behavioral counterparts of exuberance, directedness and stewardship respond to predictable *organizational* needs? And beyond, how much can a developmental view of organizations be portrayed through these descriptors?

For a first answer to these questions we can call on the individualistic view embraced by Barnard and Simon (e.g., Simon, 1976) that sees organizational needs emerging from the interplay among individual members. This suggests that organizational needs for exuberance, directedness and stewardship will stem from the behavior of organizational members as they pursue their own career needs.[6] A more precise argument from a similar starting position sees organizations having three essential core activities of (i) adapting to the external environment, (ii) achieving objectives, and (iii) maintaining themselves internally (Argyris, 1962, 1964). As we have envisioned it, exuberance is mostly about adaptation to the environment. Directedness, in contrast, is principally concerned with achieving objectives. Finally, stewardship is focused on maintaining the internal organization. Thus, exuberance, directedness and stewardship appear each to associate with one, and together to associate with all three, of the core activities that Argyris describes.

On the further question of organizational development, we can turn to a separate body of structuralist views on how such development takes place. A new organization emphasizes entrepreneurial activity (Adizes, 1979), adaptation to the external environment through raw innovation (Lyden, 1975) or "growth through creativity" (Greiner, 1972). In their integrative model Quinn and Cameron (1983) refer to an "entrepreneurial" stage – involving little planning but a significant emphasis on idea generation. As it was presented earlier, the notion of exuberance overlaps heavily with these ideas. Thus, we suggest that the exuberance need is most prominent at a first stage of organizational development.

Next, an organization moves to a second stage of "growth through direction" (Greiner, 1972). The emphasis is on producing results (Adizes, 1979) and developing a reputation (Lippitt and Schmidt, 1967). Quinn and Cameron (1983) see a "collectivity" stage that associates the external success of the organization with that of its members. These second-stage attributes overlap most closely with the previously described notion of directedness. We therefore suggest that directedness is usually prominent at a second stage of organizational development.

Beyond, Greiner (1972) describes a third stage of organizational "delegation," Adizes (1979) suggests "prime" and "maturity" organizational stages valuing stability and formalization and Lyden (1975) a "pattern maintenance" stage. Quinn and Cameron (1983) suggest a "formalization and control" stage, involving a stable structure, emphasis on maintenance, institutional procedure and conservatism. These thoughts in turn mostly overlap with our description of stewardship. We conclude that stewardship is likely to become emphasized at a third stage of organizational evolution.

A further stage of organizational evolution can be amalgamated for Greiner's (1972) later delegation, coordination and collaboration stages, calling for the interconnection between predominant qualities of previous stages. Quinn and Cameron (1983) call this the "elaboration of structure" stage, with continuing organizational adaptation and renewal as critical components. These views suggest that organizations – and so organizational complexity – can eventually be viewed in terms of interplay among the dominant characteristics of the first three developmental stages. In our terms, and analogously to our earlier discussion of individual needs, the organizational needs of exuberance, directedness and stewardship provide a framework for considering organizational complexity as the organization continues to evolve.

In sum, we are suggesting a matching framework of individual and organizational needs, with each successive need at one level of analysis having a reciprocal counterpart at the other. The framework responds to popular stage-based ideas about individual and organizational development. Moreover, eventual individual and organizational complexity can each be seen as emerging from the interplay between exploring, advancing and protecting needs on the one hand and exuberance, directedness and stewardship needs on the other.

Given the preceding framework, we need to appreciate that it is through interaction between individual and organization that development takes place. So far, we have built our ideas relying only on normative, and unidirectional, models of individual and organizational development. However, development is a relative term, and the pressure of organizational needs may have either a functional or a dysfunctional effect on an individual's development. Similarly, the pressure of individual needs may have either a functional or a dysfunctional effect on an organization's development. It is to this distinction beween functional and dysfunctional effects, at both individual and organizational levels of analysis, that we now turn our attention.

INDIVIDUAL AND ORGANIZATIONAL DEVELOPMENT

In the discussion that follows we draw on two approaches developed to consider the appropriateness of job arrangements and through them emphasize how individual–organization interaction can either enhance or detract from the separate outcomes for either party.[7] The first approach is a revision of Bailyn's (1984) model focusing on effective adaptation for the individual as a function of person–job fit. The second approach is derived from Walton's (1980) model concerned with effective adaptation for the organization that results from various forms of job design. Although developed separately and directed at different levels of analysis, the two models emerge as complementary to one another. For the first, we explore how job arrangements are likely to affect people differently, according to their career stage. For the second, we explore how responses from people at varying career stages are likely to produce different outcomes for the organization.

Interaction and individual development

At the individual level of analysis, Bailyn's focus is on the fit between a person's level of commitment on one hand and the degree of job challenge provided by the organization on the other. Writing from a standpoint calling for a new level of flexibility in employment arrangements, she uses these constructs as axes for her two-dimensional model of individual–organization career negotiation. Derived from the work of Csikszentmihalyi (1975), the model identifies an "area of fit" along a diagonal line between the two axes and sees individual growth or development over time as an outward shift along the prescribed diagonal path (Figure 14.1). The representation suggests two distinct areas where individual needs are not met. In the first, a person will experience boredom if he or she brings a level of commitment greater than the job challenge available. Conversely, a person will worry if a job demands more than he or she can give to the work situation.[8] If we bring our previous thinking to bear on this model, we can predict a series of different outcomes according to the developmental need under consideration.

For the particular individual need of *exploring*, fit will occur when organizational circumstances provide the person with commensurate opportunity. Thus, fit will occur if the organization allows for the pursuit of major individual tasks such as developing job competence and occupational identity and learning the ropes of the organization.

If, however, organizational circumstances are not responsive to the exploring individual's developmental needs, dysfunctional outcomes can be expected to fall into two categories. For example, if assigned tasks are uninteresting or if supervision is excessive, there will be little encouragement to build new competencies, and the formation of early occupational identity will be obstructed. Such circumstances will be likely to contribute to the level of boredom characterizing an individual's early career experiences. Alternatively, if assigned tasks are overwhelming and/or if relationships with seniors and peers do not provide appropriate guidance and support, the potential for failure – or the experience of failure – will result in considerable worry. In both these categories not only will the exploring need itself be frustrated, but so will foundational experiences critical to successful performance, adaptation and further career development (Berlew and Hall, 1966).

For the particular individual need of advancing, fit will occur when the organization provides a different kind of commensurate opportunity. Thus, fit will occur if the organization allows for the pursuit of major individual tasks such as earning promotion, expanding job possibilities or gaining external recognition of one's achievements.

If the organization is not responsive to the advancing need, job arrangements are likely to be inappropriate. If a person's job situation denies the opportunity for individual achievement or obscures recognition of that achievement by others, boredom is the likely outcome. Alternatively, if challenges are unrealistic or if

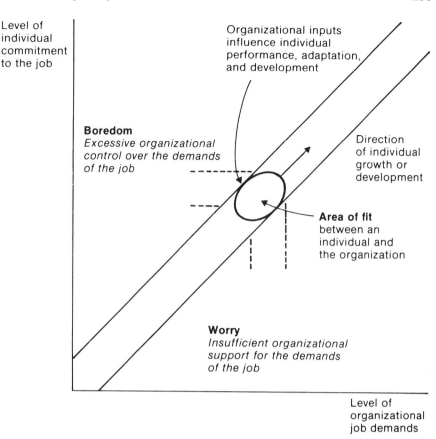

Figure 14.1. Individual–organization interaction at the individual level of analysis

superiors, peers and subordinates have high expectations but do not offer confirmation and recognition, worry is the likely outcome as doubts about competence and value to the organization will be magnified. This time, both kinds of mismatch will frustrate the individual's advancing need, and both will mean that vital career development functions, usually before or during the "mid-life transition" (Levinson et al., 1978), will be lacking.

For the particular individual need of protecting, fit will occur when there is yet a third kind of organizational opportunity. Thus, for a fit the organization will need to cater to the individual's own need for career maintenance as well as allow the individual to provide support to less experienced colleagues.

Career theory views suggest that people at this stage will not wish to be treated as if middle career counted for little, and competencies still had to be proven. Thus, boredom, as it is meant here, will occur if the individual does not come to be viewed as an established member of the organization, with an equivalent role to play. On the other hand, worry will occur if a person's potential contribution is discounted because of age-linked perceptions or associated attributions about educational or experiential obsolescence. The common outcome that the protecting need is frustrated this time brings with it a threat to the usual developmental tasks of career maturity and threatens individual performance and adaptation that is dependent on the integration of successive developmental needs up to that time (Vaillant, 1977).

In sum, the distinctions between exploring, advancing and protecting suggest differences in the way job fit is likely to occur for individuals. Corresponding differences apply for lack of fit, with the boredom–worry distinction offering a further level of refinement. In Csikszentmihalyi's (1975) original formulation, both boredom and worry, and therefore all six kinds of mismatch described in the preceding, can become manifest in the common symptom of individual *anxiety*. A prospective contribution of the career development perspective developed so far is to allow for this anxiety to be better understood.

Interaction and organizational development

When an organization is responsive to the career stage needs of individuals, it has the opportunity to benefit from the overall level of commitment it receives. In contrast,when an organization precipitates individual outcomes of boredom or worry, individual performance, adaptation and development will predictably suffer, and the organizational outcomes are likely to be dysfunctional. However, if we are to better understand the reciprocal nature of these organizational outcomes, we need to move to an organizational level of analysis. To do so, we draw from the work of Walton (1980, 1986), in turn derived from Etzioni (1961). Walton's focus, like Bailyn's, is also on the nature of jobs and further on how jobs can provide for high-commitment work systems. Walton's (1980) model also provides two axes for considering the appropriateness of job arrangements, but this time from the organization's perspective.

Our focus is now on the fit between the overall level of commitment brought by organizational members and the set of organizational job arrangements provided in response. The set of matched situations again falls within a diagonal band between the two axes, this time with an outward shift along the diagonal path representing organizational evolution or development. The revised model is shown in Figure 14.2 and, analogously to Bailyn's approach, there are again two separate areas of mismatch. In one area, job arrangements generally provide insufficient opportunity for members to respond to organizational needs. We call the resulting effect organizational *stagnation*. In the second area of mismatch, job arrangements generally make excessive demands of members on behalf of organizational needs. We call the resulting effect organizational *paralysis*.[9]

This time around, our thinking about development attends to organizational issues. Thus, for the particular organizational need of exuberance, fit will occur when job arrangements draw on the raw energy, vitality and concern with "doing" that certain members (usually those in early career) seek to supply.

When members are unable to respond appropriately to the organization's need for exuberance, two categories of outcomes are likely. In the first, the organization is denied the kind of energy to explore new or develop existing markets or even to maintain a presence in existing markets over time. In these circumstances organizational stagnation is a likely outcome. In the second outcome category, exuberance is likely to go unchecked. Youthful energy alone lacks the clarity of purpose or guiding experience to assure continuing success. Short-term achieve-

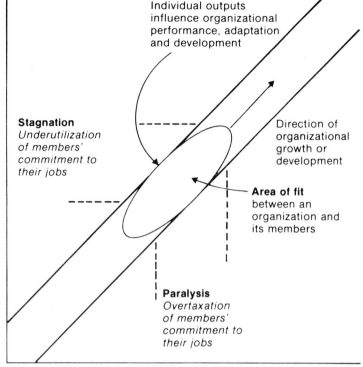

Figure 14.2. Individual–organization interaction at the organizational level of analysis

ments can fuel perceived competence and heighten the difficulty of more experienced voices being heard. In such circumstances organizational paralysis is likely. Stagnation and paralysis not only will frustrate a critical organizational need for exuberance, they will also interfere with normative evolution toward a second, more directed form of organizational growth (Greiner, 1972).

For the particular organizational need of directedness, fit will occur when job arrangements draw on associated desires for identification with, advancement through and achievement by the organization that certain members (usually those in middle career) seek to supply.

Problems will occur if job arrangements fail to serve the directedness need appropriately. For example, an organization can fail to develop the strategic opportunities open to it, so wasting distinctive strengths in new research or established goodwill. In such circumstances organizational stagnation can be predicted. Conversely, if directedness comes to dominate, it can be channelled into political – but not necessarily productive – goals of certain members (Ortega y Gasset, 1958). Lack of effective communication with either youthful creativity or senior experience can foster organizational paralysis. This time, both forms of mismatch will frustrate the organization's directedness need, and both will interfere with normative progression toward a third more decentralized stage of organizational development (Greiner, 1972).

For the particular organizational need of *stewardship*, fit will occur when job arrangements draw on desires to remain associated with what has been built, to reach out as mentors and role models to younger generations and to assure organizational continuity that certain members (usually in career maturity) seek to supply.

It is through job arrangements that organizations succeed or fail to incorporate these properties of stewardship. On the one hand, if job arrangements do not provide channels to draw on available wisdom and experience, stagnation is likely to occur. Stagnation is likely, in this sense, if *enaction*, or learning by doing, dominates as a form of organizational activity over *proaction*, involving the application of prior learning (see Miles and Randolph, 1980). A contrasting circumstance is when stewardship is allowed to operate unchallenged and without active questioning from junior members. Such a predominance of "top down dictates" (Kanter, 1983) allows little room for new questions and knowledge to influence the organization's course and implies paralysis in the sense meant here. Now, the unsatisfactory responses to the stewardship need will bring a third kind of threat to organizational development since normative progression toward further "elaboration of structure" (Quinn and Cameron, 1983) will be impeded.

Thus, the distinctions between organizational needs of exuberance, directedness and stewardship suggests differences in the way aggregate job fit is likely to occur for organizations. And, analogously to individuals, a corresponding argument applies for lack of fit at the organizational level, with the stagnation–paralysis distinction offering a further level of refinement. Again, we can expect these various kinds of mismatch to become manifest in overlapping ways. Insofar as these are not understood, we can expect them to translate into a general symptom of organizational *confusion*. As for individual anxiety, the intent of the perspective here is to allow for this organizational confusion to be better understood.

DEVELOPMENT AND RECIPROCAL EFFECTS

We now turn to build a composite picture of individual and organizational development. Central to this picture is a portrayal of reciprocal individual–organization effects not visible in stage-based models for any one party. We also identify different combinations of individual and organizational needs where reciprocity does not occur and the common symptoms of individual anxiety and organizational confusion are likely. Our discussion will lead on to consideration of individual and organizational transitions between adjacent stages and of the strategic and political behaviors associated with individual and organizational development.

The interaction of individual and organizational development

A matrix of alternative combinations of individual and organizational needs is shown in Figure 14.3. The vertical axis portrays the usual sequence of individual needs for exploring, advancing and protecting and the horizontal axis portrays the usual sequence of organizational needs for exuberance, directedness and stew-

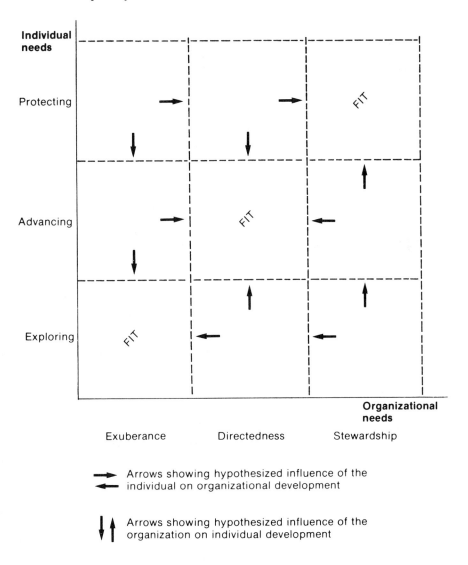

Figure 14.3. Hypothesized reciprocal effects of individual and organizational development

ardship. Each of the nine cells illustrates a different combination of circumstances. A similar formulation has been offered by Hall (1984, p. 173), but this discussion will go further by articulating the distinct properties of each combination.[10] The figure shows three combinations indicating individual–organization fit and six combinations indicating lack of fit. For the latter, horizontal and vertical arrows show the hypothesized influence of individual and organizational needs on each other. For example, an individual in career maturity and seeking to satisfy the protecting need is likely to press an organization toward greater stewardship.

Patterns of fit

The first section of this chapter, drawing on individual development (e.g., Hall and Nougaim, 1968; Levinson et al., 1978; Sofer, 1970; Super, 1957) and organizational development (e.g., Adizes, 1979; Greiner, 1972; Quinn and Cameron, 1983; Wholey and Brittain, 1986) theories, suggested that reciprocity between individual and organizational needs is likely when certain developmental circumstances combine. Thus, the combinations of individual–organizational needs represented by exploring–exuberance, advancing–directedness, and protecting–stewardship offer a prospective fit between individual and organization. The reasoning for fit will differ according to each of the three paired stages of individual and organizational development. These observations underlie Proposition 1. In passing, we can note that individual–organization fit, even when achieved, may not always be healthy. An individual may fail to anticipate the need to move on to a new developmental stage (Levinson, 1984). Or, an internal coalition may project a set of organizational needs consistent with its members' own needs as individuals but out of touch with the reality, or opportunity, of the organization's environment (Mintzberg, 1984).

Proposition 1. The fit between an individual and an organization is dependent on the matching of each party's developmental needs. Specifically, fit will depend on the degree of reciprocity between individual needs for exploring, advancing and protecting and respective organizational needs for exuberance, directedness and stewardship.

Emergent from the individual and organizational life stage theories are separate literatures on *transitions*. For individuals, these transitions involve letting go of successful adaptations made for one career stage and reaching on to the uncertainties of the next stage (Louis, 1980, 1982; Nicholson, 1984; Nicholson and West, Chapter 9). For organizations, the transitions involve predictable organizational crises (Greiner, 1972) or a revised "liability of newness" (Stinchcombe, 1965; Hannan and Freeman, 1984) as successive developmental stages are encountered. Thus, individuals need support and role modeling to help them negotiate personal career transitions, while organizations need the kind of leadership that helps them negotiate their further evolution. Bringing this thinking on individual and organizational transitions together suggests the need for regular adjustments in intraorganizational relationships.

Proposition 2. The maintenance of individual–organizational fit will involve accommodating changes in each party's needs over time. Specifically, these changes will involve successive incorporation and emphasis of exploring, advancing and protecting needs for individuals and of exuberance, directedness and stewardship needs for organizations.

Developmental views on individuals and organizations are also giving rise to separate literature on strategic choice (deciding what to do) and political behavior (acting on one's decisions). It has been suggested that individual needs influence a person's strategic thinking about his or her career and so the choice of political behavior to be adopted in organizational settings (Derr, 1986). Thus, for example, the political behavior adopted to serve the early career need of exploration – to try new things and be seen as enthusiastic – is likely to differ from that adopted for the middle career need for advancing – to prove one's abilities and be seen as successful. It has also been suggested that organizational needs influence strategic thinking about further organizational evolution (Gray and Ariss, 1985; Smith, Mitchell and Summer, 1985), which will in turn affect the political behavior directed toward members. For example, this political behavior toward members is likely to vary according to whether the organization is pursuing a "build," "hold" or "harvest" strategy (Gupta and Govindarajan, 1984) or defining its mission as a "prospector," "analyzer," "defender" or "reactor" (Miles and Snow, 1978). In turn, the level of exuberance, directedness and stewardship needed by the organization is likely to vary according to the strategy it adopts. For example, an organization with a prospector strategy is likely to have a higher need for exuberance to fulfill its entrepreneurial aspirations. Bringing the individual and organizational perspectives together, we can see the combination of individual and organizational strategies affecting the likely responses each affords the other.

Proposition 3. Strategic choice and political behavior on behalf of individuals and organizations will be affected by each party's separate developmental needs. Specifically, the distribution of individual needs for exploring, advancing and protecting and of organizational needs for exuberance, directedness and stewardship will contribute to the strategic choices and political behaviors adopted. Political behaviors, on behalf of the individual or the organization, will in turn influence the degree to which individual–organizational fit is maintained.

Patterns of deviation

On either side of the outward diagonal in Figure 14.3 are six combinations of individual–organizational needs that deviate from the patterns of reciprocity previously described. For example, the early career need for exploring is unlikely to be served if the person is asked to respond to an organizational need for stewardship, and vice versa. Drawing on the same theories of individual and organizational development cited for Proposition 1 but now focusing on the six combinations of predictable mismatch between individual and organizational needs, we can offer the following.

Proposition 4. Lack of fit between an individual and an organization will be dependent on the degree of mismatch between each party's developmental needs. Specifically, lack of fit will be dependent on a lack of reciprocity whereby individual needs for exploring, advancing and protecting are not matched against respective organizational needs for exuberance, directedness and stewardship.

To lead on to our next proposition, we draw once more on the literature on individual and organizational transitions and also on the second section of this chapter. Distinctions were drawn previously between individual boredom and worry and between organizational stagnation and paralysis. These guide us to view the sets of three combinations on either side of the diagonal in Figure 14.3 as separate from each other.

The first subset consists of the advancing–exuberance, protecting–directedness and protecting–exuberance combinations. In each of these the individual's needs can be viewed as developmentally ahead of those presented by the organization.

Our preceding analyses predict a twofold effect. The expression of organizational needs to the individual will call for behavior associated with a previous career stage and so threaten individual *boredom*, as the term is used in this chapter. Conversely, the expression of individual needs to the organization will call for behavior associated with a subsequent stage of organizational evolution and so threaten organizational *paralysis*.

The second subset, namely, the exploring–directedness, exploring–stewardship and advancing–stewardship combinations, implies an opposite set of circumstances where organizational needs can be viewed as developmentally ahead of those represented by the individual. The predicted twofold effect will now involve organizational needs calling for individual behavior associated with a subsequent career stage, threatening individual *worry*. Likewise, individual needs will be calling for organizational behavior associated with a previous stage of organizational evolution, threatening organizational *stagnation*.

If we relabel the forces promoting individual boredom and organizational stagnation as regressive forces (taking each party back through predicted developmental stages) and the forces promoting individual worry and organizational paralysis as progressive forces (taking each party forward through predicted developmental stages), we arrive at our next proposition. It allows for some further interpretation of recently observed associations between corporate strategy and either managerial characteristics (Gupta and Govindarajan, 1984; Gupta, 1986) or levels of career achievement (Slocum et al., 1985) since we can begin to consider alternative ways that these associations come into being. For example, Slocum et al. report a greater incidence of career plateauing in "defender" firms. We would ask: to what extent is this because of a satisfactory fit between individual protecting and organizational stewardship needs, or to what extent do individual protecting needs push the organization toward premature stewardship; or conversely, to what extent do organizational stewardship needs push members toward premature protecting?

Proposition 5. Attempts to correct for lack of individual–organization fit will invite competing demands from the other party. Progressive need demands from individuals will invite regressive responses from organizations. Similarly, progressive need demands from organizations will invite regressive responses from individuals.

Lastly, our proposition drawing on strategic choice and political behavior initiatives alerts us that trying to serve only one set of developmental needs – individual or organizational – will be problematic. In the absence of fuller understanding, people will go to great lengths to interpret their own behavior as satisfactory (Greenberger and Strasser, 1986); for example, a middle career person concerned with advancing could view an organization's expressed stewardship need as inappropriate, even if a product's maturity dictated otherwise. It is also likely to be problematic if differences are disguised through individual–organization ingratiation (Ralston, 1985); for example, if the middle career person projected false satisfaction in responding to the stewardship need of the organization. Similar relationship problems can occur when the organization's, rather than the individual's, needs are being projected. Regrettably, the preceding distinction between progressive and regressive forces suggests one party's meat may be another's poison. Attempts to bridge between individuals and organizations may be destined to falter as long as each party lacks an appreciation of the other's developmental circumstances. This view is supported by separate individual- (Veiga, 1983) and organizational- (Wagner, Pfeffer and O'Reilly, 1984) level findings on turnover and mobility.

Proposition 6. Strategic choices and political behaviors on behalf of either individuals or organizations, intended to correct for lack of individual–organization fit, are likely to be viewed as unhelpful by the other party. Attempts to improve individual–organizational fit are more likely to succeed when strategic choices and political behaviors are sensitive to both individual *and* organizational needs.

SUMMARY AND CONCLUSION

Central to this chapter has been a notion of individual–organizational reciprocity grounded in the earlier work of Barnard and Simon. We have sought to reconcile this with subsequent – and distinctly separate – views of individual and organizational development. From this emerged our three-step model of matching individual and organizational needs, involving exploring–exuberance, advancing–directedness and protecting–stewardship.

The concern with both individual and organizational parties leads to a new way of viewing how interaction between them can contribute to a range of developmental outcomes. We concur with other writers that outside an area of fit between individual and organization, each party is vulnerable to two distinct kinds of lack of fit. Thus, unsatisfactory individual outcomes of boredom and worry, enacted differently at each career stage, can underlie a common symptom of individual anxiety. Similarly, unsatisfactory organizational outcomes of stagnation and paralysis, dependent on the stage of evolution, can underlie a common symptom of organizational confusion.

Bringing these pictures together culminated in our framework for considering individual–organization reciprocity. This outlines a way of linking between the so-far separate literatures on individual and organizational development. Our framework also connects to subsequent but still largely separate works on individual or organizational transitions and on individual- or organization-centered strategic choice or political behavior. Finally, we have formulated a set of six propositions about reciprocal effects between individual and organizational levels of analysis. These propositions are concerned with the patterns of fit between individual and organizational needs, how fit can be affected by transitions and how fit can be affected by strategic choices and political behaviors. Three more propositions are concerned with patterns of deviation between individual and organizational needs, how deviation can be affected by transitions and how deviation can be affected by strategic choices and political behaviors. The six propositions are testable by reference to the hypothesized directions of reciprocal influence our framework suggests.

However, testing of the listed propositions calls for research designs that are complicated and longitudinal. This is because we want to investigate both individual and organizational development over prolonged time periods. The concern calls for methodologies at multiple levels of analysis, from in-depth qualitative analysis with individuals to large-scale survey activity with organizations. It also calls for comparative analyses allowing for the time-dependent outcomes of career stages and organizational evolution to be observed. Our research activities have not always responded to such challenges; instead, there has been a bias toward expediency (Kimberly, 1980) in the work undertaken. Yet, if we want to build a better understanding of individual–organization reciprocity, our research designs will have to be more ambitious.

We believe such an ambitious research agenda is necessary, for the course of this writing has led us to a clear and central conviction. It is that attempts at either individual or organizational development are likely to be dysfunctional for the other party *unless reciprocity is considered from the outset*. Therefore, it is essential to connect more fully between individual and organizational levels of analysis. We offer this brief exploration of individual–organizational reciprocity as a starting point.

NOTES

We are deeply grateful to Lotte Bailyn, Tim Hall, Barbara Lawrence, Bob House and various participants in the Careers Division workshop of the Academy of Management, 1986, for their comments on earlier drafts of this chapter.

1 Levinson et al.'s (1978) notion of predictable, sequential and interdependent developmental tasks in adulthood traces back to related positions taken by Erikson (1957, 1968) and Jung (see Campbell, 1971). These normative views are extremely useful for looking at overall careers; however, we also acknowledge that there is growing evidence of deviations from them. As we acknowledge later in the chapter, it is essential to take both normative views *and* reported deviations into account if we are to achieve more accurate understanding of developmental processes.

2 The definition of "reciprocity" is in turn dependent on a definition of *needs*, a term used by Schein (1978), although not by Simon (1976). A simplification of Atkinson's (1958, p. 597) definition suits us here, whereby a need is "a relatively enduring disposition ... to strive for a particular kind of goal-state or aim." The culture and strategy literature has made it quite clear that organizations have dispositions as well as people.

3 For example, people who change occupations need to return to certain developmental tasks characteristic of earlier years for others (Super, 1980), as do women returning to work at mid-life (Gallos, Chapter 6). Organizations can also influence the duration of each of the career periods (Lawrence, 1984).

4 Kram (1985) has previously used the labels of early, middle and late career. The distinctions here are similar, although in this present work transitional issues are de-emphasized, and adjustments have been made to align the three stages described with Ortega y Gasset's (1958) view of generations, so allowing a further link between micro- and macrolevels of analysis.

5 We also concur with Super (1980) that if a major shift of work activity is undertaken, there will be some necessary recycling through the stages noted. Sometimes such a major shift is termed a "career change," although such use is inconsistent with the notion of one life, one career adopted in this text.

6 Our argument does not imply individual needs are usually being met. As the power and influence literature tells us, individual needs are often projected onto others.

7 This discussion of individual–organization interaction embraces our previous writing on job relationships. Kram (1985) has proposed the idea of the *relationship constellation* as the set of relationships contributing to the psychosocial and career development of the person (Kram, 1985). Regarding organizational effects, Arthur (1985) has proposed that the set of relationship constellations, the constellation of constellations, be used as a way to think about the development of the organization. The discussion here incorporates these ideas on relationships as well as other factors such as job design, group norms, reward systems and so on that can also contribute to individual or organizational outcomes.

8 We have reverted to Csikszentmihalyi's original labels of boredom and worry. While

Bailyn used anxiety instead of worry, the earlier formulation suggests anxiety can occur for either kind of mismatch. As Tim Hall has pointed out, this becomes a particularly critical issue in career maturity, where plateaued employees can simultaneously report a lack of job challenge (and so boredom) as well as much anxiety about their career situations.

9 The axes on the Walton model are labeled type of member involvement and type of organizational role or role structure. Situations of mismatch are labeled as errors of managerial pessimism or errors of managerial optimism. At this stage of analysis, we do not wish to attribute the reasons for either of these outcomes to "managerial" anything. The adjective suggests an opinion about cause and effect that seems premature. Our use of the terms "stagnation" and "paralysis" is drawn from Hedberg (1981), and his suggestion that benevolent environments breed stagnation and hostile ones paralysis is very much consistent with the model presented.

10 Hall's (1984) model also shows a withdrawal or decline stage, for both individuals and organizations. We have chosen to simplify the version here by viewing both the individual and organization as vital entities. By the same token, our model does not address individual or organizational entry into the employment market. Separate literatures exist on each of these entry and withdrawal topic areas.

REFERENCES

Adizes, I. (1979). Organizational passages: diagnosing and treating life cycle problems in organizations. *Organizational Dynamics*, Summer, pp. 3–24.
Argyris, C. (1960). *Understanding Organizational Behavior*. Homewood, IL: Dorsey.
Argyris, C. (1962). The integration of the individual and the organization. In C. Argyris et al. (eds.), *Social Science Approaches to Business Behavior*. Homewood, IL: Dorsey, pp. 57–98.
Argyris, C. (1964). *Integrating the Individual and the Organization*. New York: Wiley.
Argyris, C. (1982). *Reasoning, Learning and Action*. San Francisco: Jossey-Bass.
Arthur, M. B. (1984). The career concept: challenge and opportunity for its further application. In M. B. Arthur, L. Bailyn, D. J. Levinson, and H. A. Shepard, *Working With Careers*. New York: Center for Research in Career Development, Graduate School of Business, Columbia University, pp. 3–24.
Arthur, M. B. (1985). Review of K. E. Kram: Mentoring at Work. *Administrative Science Quarterly, 30*, 454–456.
Atkinson, J. W. (1958). Thematic apperception measurement of motives within the context of a theory of motivation. In J. W. Atkinson (ed.), *Motives in Fantasy, Action and Society*. New York: Van Nostrand.
Bailyn, L. (1984). Issues of work and family in responding to social diversity. In M. B. Arthur, L. Bailyn, D. J. Levinson, and H. Shepard, *Working With Careers*. New York: Center for Research in Career Development, Graduate School of Business, Columbia University, pp. 75–98.
Baird, L., and Kram, K. (1983). Career dynamics: managing the superior/subordinate relationship. *Organizational Dynamics*, Summer, pp. 46–64.
Bardwick, J. (1980). The seasons of a woman's life. In D. G. McGuigan (ed.), *Women's Lives: New Theory, Research and Policy*. Ann Arbor, MI: The University of Michigan, Center for Continuing Education of Women, pp. 35–55.
Berlew, D. E., and Hall, D. T. (1966). The socialization of managers: effects of expectations on performance. *Administrative Science Quarterly, 11*, 207–223.
Campbell, J. (1971). *The Portable Jung*. New York: Viking.
Clawson, J. (198). Mentoring in managerial careers. In C. B. Derr (ed.), *Work, Family, and the Career*. New York: Praeger, pp. 144–165.
Csikszentmihalyi, M. (1975). *Beyond Boredom and Anxiety: The Experience of Play in Work and Games*. San Francisco: Jossey-Bass.
Dalton, G. W., and Thompson, P. H. (1986). *Novations: Strategies for Career Management*. Glenview, IL: Scott Foresman.
Dalton, G. W., Thompson, P. H., and Price, R. L. (1977). The four stages of professional careers – a new look at performance by professionals. *Organizational Dynamics*, Summer, pp. 19–42.

Derr, C. B., (1986). *Managing the New Careerists*. San Francisco: Jossey-Bass.

Erikson, E. H. (1957). Identity and the life cycle. *Psychological Issues, 1*(1), 1–177.

Erikson, E. H. (1968). *Identity, Youth and Crisis*. New York: Norton.

Etzioni, A. (1961). *A Comparative Analysis of Complex Organizations*. New York: Free Press.

Gilligan, C. (1982). *In a Different Voice*. Cambridge, MA: Harvard University Press.

Gould, R. (1978). *Transformations: Growth and Change in Adult Life*. New York: Simon & Schuster.

Gray, B., and Ariss, S. S. (1985). Politics and strategic change across organizational life cycles. *Academy of Management Review, 10*, 707–723.

Greenberger, D. B., and Strasser, S. (1986). Development and application of a model of personal control in organizations. *Academy of Management Review, 11*, 164–177.

Greiner, L. E. (1972). Evolution and revolution as organizations grow. *Harvard Business Review, 50*, 37–46.

Gupta, A. K. (1986). Matching managers to strategies: point and counterpoint. *Human Resource Management, 25*, 214–234.

Gupta, A. K., and Govindarajan, V. (1984). Business unit strategy, managerial characteristics, and business unit effectiveness at strategy implementation. *Academy of Management Journal, 27*(1), 25–41.

Gutek, B. A., and Larwood, L. (1987). *Women and Career Development*. Beverly Hills, CA: Sage.

Hall, D. T. (1976). *Careers in Organizations*, Pacific Palisades, CA: Goodyear.

Hall, D. T. (1980). Socialization processes in later years: can there be growth at the terminal level? In C. B. Derr (ed.), *Work, Family and Career*. New York, Praeger, pp. 219–233.

Hall, D. T. (1984). Human resources development and organizational effectiveness. In C. J. Fombrun, N. M. Tichy, and M. A. Devanna, *Strategic Human Resource Development*. New York: Wiley, pp. 159–181.

Hall, D. T., and Nougaim, K. (1968). An examination of Maslow's hierarchy of needs in an organizational setting. *Organizational Behavior and Human Performance, 3*, 12–35.

Hannan, M. T., and Freeman, J. (1984). Structural inertia and organizational change. *American Sociological Review, 49*, 149–164.

Hedberg, B. (1981). How organizations learn and unlearn. In P. C. Nystrom and W. H. Starbuck (eds.), *Handbook of Organization Design*, Vol. 1. Oxford and New York: Oxford University Press, pp. 3–27.

Hughes, E. C. (1958). *Men and Their Work*. Glencoe, IL: Free Press.

Jaques, E. (1965). Death and the midlife crisis. *International Journal of Psychoanalysis, 46*, 502–514.

Kanter, R. M. (1983). *The Change Masters*. New York: Simon & Schuster.

Kimberly, J. R. (1980). The life cycle analogy and the study of organizations. In J. R. Kimberly and R. H. Miles (eds.), *The Organizational Life Cycle*. San Francisco: Jossey-Bass, pp. 1–17.

Kram, K. E. (1985). *Mentoring At Work*. Glennview, IL: Scott Foresman.

Kram, K. E. (1986). Mentoring in the workplace. In D. T. Hall and Associates, *Career Development in Organizations*. San Francisco: Jossey-Bass, pp. 160–201.

Kram, K. E., and Isabella, L. (1985). Mentoring alternatives: the role of peer relationships in career development. *Academy of Management Journal, 28*, 110–132.

Kram, K. E., and Julesa, G. (1978). Anticipation and realization: a study of retirement. Unpublished research report. Yale University.

Lawrence, B. S. (1984). Age grading; the implicit organizational timetable. *Journal of Occupational Behaviour, 5*(1), 23–35.

Lawrence, B. S. (1987). An organizational theory of age effects. In S. Bacharach and N. DiTomaso (eds.), *Research in the Sociology of Organizations*. Greenwich, CT: JAI.

Levinson, D. J. (1984). The career is in the life structure, the life structure is in the career: an adult development perspective. In M. B. Arthur, L. Bailyn, D. J. Levinson, and H. Shepard, *Working With Careers*. New York: Center for Research in Career Development, Graduate School of Business, Columbia University, pp. 49–74.

Levinson, D. J., with C. N. Darrow, E. B. Klein, M. H. Levinson, and B. McKee (1978). *The Seasons of a Man's Life*. New York: Knopf.

Levinson, H. (1962). *Men, Management, and Mental Health*. Cambridge, MA: Harvard University Press.

Lindholm, J. (1982). Mentoring: the mentor's perspective. Cambridge, MA: Working Paper 1350–82, Sloan School of Management, Massachusetts Institute of Technology.

Lippitt, G. L., and Schmidt, W. H. (1967). Crises in a developing organization. *Harvard Business Review, 45*, 102–112.

Louis, M. R. (1980). Career transitions; varieties and commonalities. *Academy of Management Review, 5*, 329–340.

Louis, M. R. (1982). Managing career transitions: a missing link in career development. *Organizational Dynamics, 10*(4), 68–77.

Lyden, F. J. (1975). Using Parson's functional analysis in the study of organizations. *Administrative Science Quarterly, 20*, 59–70.

March, J. G., and Simon, H. A. (1958). *Organizations.* New York: Wiley.

Miles, R. E., and Snow, C. C. (1978). *Organizational Strategy, Structure, and Process.* New York: McGraw-Hill.

Miles, R. H., and Randolph, W. A. (1980). Influence of organizational learning styles on early development. In J. R. Kimberly and R. H. Miles (eds.), *The Organizational Life Cycle.* San Francisco: Jossey-Bass, pp. 144–182.

Mintzberg, H. (1984). Power and organizational life cycles. *Academy of Management Review, 9*, 207–224.

Missirian, A. K. (1982). *The Corporate Connection: Why Executive Women Need Mentors to Reach the Top.* Englewood Cliffs, NJ: Prentice-Hall.

Nicholson, N. (1984). A theory of work role transitions. *Administrative Science Quarterly, 29*, 172–191.

Ortega y Gasset, J. (1958). *Man and Crisis.* New York: Norton.

Osherson, S. (1980). *Holding On or Letting Go.* New York: Free Press.

Phillips-Jones, L. (1982). *Mentors and Proteges.* New York: Arbor House.

Quinn, R. E., and Cameron, K. (1983). Organizational life cycles and shifting criteria of effectiveness: some preliminary evidence. *Management Science, 29*(1), 33–51.

Ralston, D. A. (1985). Employee ingratiation: the role of management. *Academy of Management Journal, 10*, 477–487.

Schein, E. H. (1980). *Organizational Psychology*, 3rd ed. Englewood Cliffs, NJ: Prentice-Hall.

Schein, E. H. (1978). *Career Dynamics: Matching Individual and Organizational Needs.* Reading, MA: Addison-Wesley.

Simon, H. A. (1976). *Administrative Behavior*, 3rd ed. New York: Free Press.

Slocum, J. W., Cron, W. A., Hansen, R. W., and Rawlings, S. (1985). Business strategy and the management of plateaued employees. *Academy of Management Journal, 28*, 133–154.

Smith, K. G., Mitchell, T. R., and Summer, C. E. (1985). Top level management priorities in different stages of the organizational life cycle. *Academy of Management Journal, 28*, 799–820.

Sofer, C. (1970). *Men in Mid-Career.* Cambridge: Cambridge University Press.

Stinchcombe, A. L. (1965). Social structure and organizations. In J. G. March (ed.), *Handbook of Organizations.* Chicago: Rand McNally, pp. 142–193.

Super, D. E. (1957). *The Psychology of Careers.* New York: Harper & Row.

Super, D. E. (1980). A life-span, life-space approach to career development. *Journal of Vocational Behavior, 16*, 282–298.

Thomas, D. (1986). An intra-organizational analysis of black and white patterns of sponsorship and the dynamics of cross-racial mentoring. Ph.D. dissertation. Yale University, New Haven, CT.

Vaillant, G. (1977). *Adaptation to Life.* Boston: Little, Brown.

Veiga, J. F. (1983). Mobility influence during managerial career stages. *Academy of Management Review, 26*(1): 64–85.

Wagner, W. G., Pfeffer, J., and O'Reilly, C. A. III (1984). Organizational demography and turnover in top-management groups. *Administrative Science Quarterly, 29*, 74–92.

Walton, R. E. (1980). Establishing and maintaining high commitment work systems. In J. R. Kimberly and R. H. Miles (eds.), *The Organizational Life Cycle.* San Francisco: Jossey-Bass, pp. 208–290.

Walton, R. E. (1986). From control to commitment in the workplace. *Harvard Business Review, 63*(2), 76–84.

Wanous, J. P. (1980). *Organizational Entry*. Reading, MA, Addison-Wesley.

Wholey, D. R., and Brittain, J. W. (1986). Organizational ecology: findings and implications. *Academy of Management Review, 1*(3), 513–533.

Zintz, A. C. (1988). Effective mentoring of career-immobile women within corporate settings. Ph.D. dissertation. The Fielding Institute, Santa Barbara, CA.

15 Career improvisation in self-designing organizations

KARL E. WEICK AND LISA R. BERLINGER

We want to have certainties and no doubts – results and no experiments – without even seeing that certainties can arise only through doubt and results only through experiment.

C. G. Jung, 1978

To follow up a problem in the company library, to experiment with work methods, or to study new materials or markets should be working rights, not only for researchers and executives, but for all employees.

B. L. T. Hedberg, 1984

Doubt and experimentation have become institutionalized in self-designing organizations, which are social forms built to deal with rapid environmental change. These self-designing forms have distinctive properties that pose unique issues for people who build and study careers.

If we define careers as "the individually perceived sequence of attitudes and behaviors associated with work-related experiences and activities over the span of a person's life" (Hall, 1976, p. 4), then we know little about the experiences, activities, and perceptions that are created when a career unfolds in a flexible system where change is continuous, experiments are routine, and growth replaces advancement as a measure of success. We know little about what it means to have a career in a system that does not use traditional external markers to signify progress, advancement, and movement in some consistent direction. This chapter suggests a starting point from which researchers can explore career issues in self-designing organizations.

We first describe six characteristics of self-designing systems and then contrast these systems with others in the organizational literature that appear to be similar. Using these descriptions as background, we then propose that career paths in self-designing systems originate from subjective rather than objective sources. Having suggested that subjective careers connect a self-designing system, we conclude by suggesting that career development under these conditions requires sensitivity to five issues.

THE NATURE OF SELF-DESIGNING ORGANIZATIONS

The problem that self-designing organizations are designed to solve is how to take collective action in a continually changing environment that is evolving at a more rapid pace than in the past. The self-designing organization seeks to match the variety in a changing environment with increased variety in the organization.

313

In contrast to traditional organizations designed to face benevolent, slowchanging environments with standard operating procedures, skill specialization, and hierarchies, self-designing organizations face rapidly changing environments with improvisation, generalists, and networks. Self-designing organizations need variety in the organization because they cope by continually evolving as the environment evolves. Variety in the organization makes it more adaptable to continuous changes in the environment.

Traditional organizations change infrequently, but when they do change, the change tends to be revolutionary, uprooting, and disorienting. Discontinuity is a way of life in a traditional organization faced with a changing environment. Self-designing organizations, on the other hand, usually make small, frequent changes. While self-design may seem to be a radical form, in fact it is conservative and proceeds by continuous updating, incremental changes, and the institutionalization of a tradition of change that is built into culture and procedures. Continuous change is adaptive as long as environmental changes are not themselves massive and discontinuous. If environmental change becomes massive and unpredictable, self-designing organizations have no obvious advantage over traditional organizations other than the fact that their employees are more accustomed to change and may have more resources to deal with new problems. However, the vast majority of organizational environments do not change so fast or so dramatically that alert people completely miss early warnings of what is happening. Instead, most environmental change that looks dramatic in fact was signaled for some time, and it was a mixture of ethnocentrism, arrogance, self-absorption, and overestimation of distinctive competence inside the firm that led it to misperceive the accumulation of permanent change.

Characteristics of self-designing organizations

The logo of a self-designing organization might read Stability through Change. A commitment to change in a self-designing organization is associated with different attitudes, values, and characteristics than are found in a traditional organization. Self-designing organizations continually (1) redesign their processes, (2) value impermanence, (3) facilitate learning, (4) encourage meta-level analyses, (5) remove informational filters, and (6) focus commitment. We review these six properties briefly.

Redesign. The identifying characteristic of a self-designing organization is that its members continually redesign their organization and its processes. The members of a self-designing organization define their own problems, generate their own solutions, and evaluate and revise their own solution-generating processes (Hedberg, Nystrom, and Starbuck, 1976, p. 43). They experiment even when there is no urgency or demand to do so. They "discard even adequate old methods in order to try new ones, looking upon each development as an experiment that suggests new experiments" (Hedberg et al., 1976, p. 45). Self-designing systems ceaselessly question present assumptions and practices.

This preoccupation with design distinguishes the self-designing organization from other types of organizations where design is "widely thought to be outside the stream of routine activities" (Hedberg et al., 1976, p. 42). While most organizations consider the products and services they produce to be the principal outputs of the organization, fewer organizations also consider their designs, redesigns, and capacities for design as important outputs. As Torbert says, in describing the stage of collaborative inquiry in organizations, "its identity becomes lodged less in its current structure than in its capacity for restructuring" (Torbert, 1987). The same may be said for self-designing organizations in general.

Self-designing organizations can be distinguished from start-up entrepreneurial organizations. While an entrepreneur is a self-designer, start-up or entrepreneurial organizations seldom are. Self-designing organizations continuously tap the variety present in the organization in the service of redesign. But, although a start-up may be self-designing in its initial phase, once it is launched self-design ceases and people tend to stay with processes that have been successful in the past. An entrepreneurial organization may never be self-designing (if the entrepreneur is the only one who designs the processes in the organization) or it may start as a self-designing organization and evolve to a more traditional form.

Impermanence. While traditional organizations usually move toward stability and security, "a self-designing organization functions most smoothly if its ideology cherishes impermanence" (Hedberg et al., 1976, p. 43). The quality of impermanence in self-designing systems comes from the widespread beliefs that optimal responses are rare, good responses become obsolete quickly, and the accumulation of inertia is fatal: "The essence of all efforts to reduce organizational inertia is to induce organizations to act as if optimal is an impossible state" (Hedberg, Nystrom, and Starbuck, 1977, p. 177). One way that a self-designing organization promotes impermanence is that it is underspecified. An underspecified system must be filled in by the people involved in it. Since they fill it in in real time, it will tend to be more current and less burdened by antiquated practices imported from the past. Impermanence is evident in such things as time constraints on management contracts, zero-based budgeting, sunset procedures, job exchange schemes (Hedberg, 1981, p. 21), and limited planning and forecasting (Hedberg, 1984, p. 56).

Learning. Learning and exploration are also necessary features of a self-designing organization. Self-designing organizations institute the principle of evolutionary operation: "Routine interaction with the task environment should generate information about ways to improve performance" (Metcalfe, 1981, p. 503). Unless the individuals involved in the self-designing organization are willing to learn, the organization will not continue to redesign. Managers within a self-designing system are portrayed as arithmetic teachers whose success is judged by what their students do, not by what they do (Hedberg et al., 1977, p. 174). To the extent that managers are evaluated by how well their subordinates do, they will be more inclined to develop and facilitate their learning.

The emphasis on learning in a self-designing system means several things. For the individual it means "developing new attitudes and values, new competencies, new images of himself, and new ways of entering and conducting himself in social situations. As he faces new roles which bring new demands, it is from his repertoire of attributes and skills that he constructs and reconstructs himself to meet these demands" (Schein, 1971, pp. 266–267).

For the system, an emphasis on learning means that rather than spending 100% of every sixth year relearning some new position, people would spend 20% of their time in each of the preceding five years relearning a position that is then practiced during 80% of the sixth year while the remaining 20% is spent learning the next position (Hedberg, 1984, p. 57).

A system emphasis on learning can also take the form of job rotation, sabbatical leaves every five years taken inside the firm, and less use of outside consultants to suggest design changes (these come from internal sources) but more use of consultants to bring in new ideas that stimulate divergent thinking (Nemeth, 1986).

Meta-analyses. Virtually all descriptions of self-designing systems specify that at least two levels of awareness are necessary for successful adaptation. People have to become conscious of their consciousness in order to self-design. The basic idea is that a person has an experience, the person becomes conscious of the experience as an object to be analyzed (first-order awareness), and the person then becomes conscious of the ways in which the analyses themselves can be conducted (second-order awareness). Relearning, change, and redesign all require that basic assumptions be reviewed and often reformulated. This is the message of the distinction between single- and double-loop learning (Argyris and Schon, 1978), first- and second-order change (Watzlawick, Weakland, and Fisch, 1974), first-order and deutero learning (Bateson, 1972), operational and strategic plans (Metcalfe, 1981), and experience, consciousness, and comprehensiveness (Miller-Tiedeman and Tiedeman, 1985). As Beyer (1981) summarizes the issue, self-designing organizations require the formation of meta-ideologies and meta-values that call for some internal mechanisms to ensure that organizations keep changing (p. 195). Since individuals are the "internal mechanisms" that embody the meta-values and meta-ideologies, their ability to stand apart from experience, review it, and review the ways of reviewing is crucial both for survival and for effective performance within these settings.

Hall (1986, p. 348) has also emphasized higher order awareness as a key property of career development: "To be responsible for one's career in today's turbulent organizational environments, the employee needs new *career competencies*, not just job skills. These career competencies might be called 'metaskills' because they are skills in acquiring new skills. The most important metaskills are adaptability (routine busting), tolerance of ambiguity and uncertainty, and identity change."

Information filtering. Self-designing organizations need timely information about changes in their environments and their performances (Hedberg et al., 1977, p. 175). To get such information, these organizations reduce perceptual filtering and uncertainty absorption so that they can see more (Hedberg, 1981, p. 21). To reduce uncertainty absorption, organizations adopt flat hierarchies and local decision making, replace specialists with generalists so that specialist labels do not dominate perception, and as in the case of hospitals, often use diverse criteria to judge themselves (Hedberg et al., 1977, p. 175).

But, when uncertainty absorption is reduced, individuals can become overloaded and confused. As uncertainty increases, people receive more diverse data, their traditional categories leave larger unexplained residuals, and favorite views of the world are disconfirmed when unfiltered data no longer fit them. As a result, individuals become less sure of their views and themselves, which can be unsettling and disruptive of further processing. As uncertainty increases, there should be a stronger tendency for individuals to apply traditional categories but greater stress when they find that these categories fit less incoming data.

This cycle of stress can be especially dangerous in self-designing systems. It has been shown (e.g., Eysenck, 1982) that as stress increases, attention narrows, people pay attention to fewer things, and they fall back on more habitual ways of responding (i.e., they become more conservative and do more things that are appropriate for older environments they no longer face). These tendencies are especially threatening to self-designing systems because they gut the core resources that allow them to survive.

It is precisely those people who are able to dampen such typical stress reactions and experiment, learn, and evaluate despite such pressures who will be valued and advance in self-designing systems. Furthermore, overload from decreased filtering can be reduced if decision groups become more homogeneous, the costs of information search are raised, and informal communication is discouraged (Hedberg, 1981, p. 21).

Overload from decreased filtering can also be moderated if people act forcefully on the environment and take action that slows the change and imposes an interpretation on the change that is advantageous to the organization. For purposes of self-design, people can change either the external environment (Hedberg et al., 1976, p. 46, call this "manipulative" change) or the environment internal to the firm (Hedberg et al., 1976, p. 46, call this "adaptive" change). Self-designers can either design a niche that is suited to their identities and capabilities or design their identities to fit existing niches.

Perhaps lulled by the modifier "self," prescriptions for adaptation usually focus on redesign of self rather than on redesign of the environment. That emphasis is relatively harmless if investigators remember that "over time chains of intermingled adaptations and manipulations transform both an organization and its environment" (Hedberg et al., 1976, p. 47).

Commitment. Since the survival of a self-designing system depends on swift unlearning and relearning, commitment plays a key role because it can retard change. Commitment intensifies when people volitionally take irrevocable action and do so publicly (Salancik, 1977). Public, irrevocable, volitional acts are acts that have clearly occurred and clearly are the responsibility of specific people. This unequivocal linkage of people to actions puts pressure on people to justify those actions with which they are linked, which means that, once justified, the actions seem more sensible and less in need of change. Heavily justified actions can persist beyond the point where they are appropriate, as is demonstrated by Staw's (1982) important work on escalation.

While commitment can be valuable because intense action in the service of justification gets things done, it can also be a liability because it is a counterforce to change. This dilemma is especially keen in self-designing systems because these settings tend to maximize visibility, choice, and irrevocability.

For example, Hedberg's (1984) proposed design for a self-designing steelworks appears to encourage visible choices that are irrevocable. Actions are visible because most of them occur in home teams or in parliament rather than in isolation, dialectics are a prominent means of communication, most agreements are stated in public contracts, and work in progress is monitored by video equipment.

Actions are volitional in the sense that more people have a larger say in policy, employees are given more discretion over tasks and how they spend their time, representatives to parliament are elected rather than appointed, people can choose to do extra-credit activities, and the information system is designed to convey data that highlight choices people can make. Administrators, interestingly, should be the least committed people in the steelworks since they do what people tell them to do (low choice) and are instructed to work themselves out of their jobs (low irrevocability).

Finally, actions are irrevocable in the sense that the physical facilities, the production process, the products themselves, and the required participation embody decisions that cannot easily be changed.

Against this background, it is conceivable that a steelworks designed to have a strong capacity for self-design in reality could become heavily committed to its current structure by its form of governance and therefore be unable to imagine any design other than the one it now justifies vigorously. That possibility is a basic tension in self-design.

Whether the process of self-design inadvertently undercuts the intention to remain flexible depends on to what people are committed. If people are committed to the current structure, tasks, and products, then unlearning will be difficult. If, however, people develop commitment to the process of self-design rather than to its outcomes, then commitment will facilitate unlearning and relearning.

Distinctive emphases in self-designing organizations

To understand the self-designing system more fully, it can be contrasted with other forms discussed in the organizational literature.

A self-designing organization differs most sharply from the traditional form of organization. Traditional organizations contain a mixture of skill specialization, systematic coordination, clear objectives, and an unambiguous authority structure that is well adapted to stable, slow-changing, benevolent environments. In slow-changing environments, "ad hoc analyses can be replaced by standardized routines; routines can be multiplied, reduced to their essential elements, and then preserved in capital equipment and training programs; communications can be compressed with efficient codes; and responsibilities can be delineated precisely. Because they are designed for benevolent and relatively slow changing environments, today's organizations avoid debates and conflicts, and they impose rationality on activities" (Hedberg et al., 1977, p. 177).

The concept of a self-designing system resembles Driver's (1979) description of the transitory and spiral organizational culture. The transitory organization contains temporary teams and loose control by rules, grants autonomy, has transient, tent-like places of work, and treats employees as means to an end. The spiral organization is characterized by constant reassessment of products and needs with changes in output based on these reassessments, autonomous teams, self-determined control, rotation of assignments to expand job skills, rewards for creativity, dispersed work sites, and close attention to personal development.

Driver argues that individuals who themselves have transitory and spiral career concepts will be most satisfied and most productive if they work in organizations whose cultures embody the same concepts. Since most organizations have linear rather than transitory or spiral career cultures, the people best suited for self-design usually find themselves in organizations that neither understand nor appreciate their self-design skills.

A self-designing system also resembles an adhocracy (Mintzberg and McHugh, 1985), a prospector organization (Miles and Snow, 1978), a temporary system (Goodman, 1981), and an organic organization (Burns and Stalker, 1961). However there are subtle but important differences in emphasis between all four and the idea of self-design. These differences will be illustrated by contrasting the organic organization with one that is self-designing.

In an organic organization, the operating styles of managers vary freely, authority is rooted in situational expertise, there is "free adaptation by the organization to changing circumstances" (Khandwalla, 1977, p. 411), and on-the-job behavior accommodates both the situation and the personality of the person doing the work. The organic system is underspecified so people have to communicate in order to discover what they have to do and the resources they have to do it.

Despite the overlap between this description and characteristics described earlier, there are important differences.

First, the self-designing system is deliberately kept off-balance through inconsistent and incomplete design in the belief that low levels of contentment sharpen perception: "Ambiguous authority structures, unclear objectives, and contradictory assignments of responsibility can legitimate controversies and challenge traditions ... Incoherence and indecision can foster exploration, self-evaluation, and learning. Redundant task allocations can provide experimental replications, and partial incongruities can diversify portfolios of activities" (Hedberg et al., 1976, p. 45). Imbalance is not intentionally cultivated in organic systems.

Second, self-designing systems are suspicious of nonparticipant designers because designs brought in from the outside seldom fit complex internal systems. Furthermore, outsiders take so much time to invent designs that problems change while insiders wait for the invention. Finally, the mere act of defining a problem often sets solutions in motion, and this process is under the control of insiders. For these reasons, insiders are more wary of outsiders in self-designing systems than in organic systems.

Third, a self-designing system tends to see the environment as dynamic, benevolent, and filled with opportunities rather than as static, hostile, and filled with constraints (Hedberg et al., 1976, p. 48). These perceptions are consequential because they tend to be self-confirming. Organic systems tend not to have a distinct style of perceiving change or environments.

Fourth, self-designing systems treat self-doubt (Weick, 1979, pp. 224–228), and discrediting of prior knowledge (Weick, 1977) as normal reactions to the dual realities of ceaseless evolution and responses that quickly become dated. Organic systems spend less time reflecting on their own processes and place less value on the process of critical reflection. Nondefensive self-criticism is difficult, and it is only because self-designing systems are fully committed to impermanence, learning, and growth and fully designed to achieve it that they are able to treat criticism as an accomplishment rather than as an indictment.

Fifth, both self-designing systems and organic systems intentionally underspecify their properties, but underspecification is more targeted in self-design. Prescriptions for self-design specify that "self-designing organizations should have minimal amounts – that is just a little bit more than not enough – of the properties that characterize good and orderly organizations ... consensus, contentment, affluence, faith, consistency, rationality ... This would provide for enough frequent triggering, reasonably easy unlearning, sufficiently low trust in previous success, and enough slack resources to implement new strategies" (Hedberg, 1981, p. 22).

The corresponding prescription for organic systems is more global (Burns and Stalker, 1961, pp. 122–125) and states that there is a reasoned basis for underspecification, namely, the impossibility of adequate specification. The more task definition that is requested, "the more omniscient the management must be, so that no functions are left wholly or partly undischarged, no person is overburdened with undelegated responsibility, or left without the authority to do his job properly" (Burns and Stalker, 1961, p. 123). Since omniscience is limited in a world of bounded rationality, people in organic systems are responsible for specifying whatever they need to get their work done. While a self-designing system deliberately keeps the system alert and active by focusing on six specific sources of inertia and reducing them to minimal levels, organic systems encourage activity and alertness by a more general infusion of ambiguity.

Sixth, self-designing systems are more reluctant to use forecasts than are organic systems. Since opportunities often occur without warning, systems guided by forecasts often fail to notice them. Furthermore, forecasts retard updating because they trigger self-fulfilling prophecies, emphasize constraints, postpone action, become ends in themselves, exaggerate influences from past experience, and introduce inaccuracy. To forestall these problems, rapid adaptation is substituted for forecast-oriented designs (Hedberg et al., 1977, p. 174).

We should emphasize that these six differences are matters of degree. Taken together, however, they show that self-designing systems are distinguished by their preoccupation with continuous redesign such that most decisions are made to protect and exercise this capability.

CAREER PATHS IN THE CONTEXT OF SELF-DESIGN

With the preceding contextual information as background, we now focus on the central questions of this essay: What does it mean to survive, grow, and advance in a firm that is always changing? What does it mean to have a career amidst impermanence? In the words of Stumpf (1984, p. 207), "How can you establish career paths and do career planning in a firm where the paths will change if the organization is at all responsive to changes in its environment?"

The answer to be developed is that to survive in a self-designing system, people need to anchor their security in processes rather than states or structures (Hedberg, 1984, p. 58). Specifically, if people pursue processes rather than outcomes, competencies rather than titles, fulfillment rather than advancement, and roles rather than positions, they will accomplish career growth and, in doing so, will also become indispensible resources for the self-designing organization.

Subjective careers as organizational structure

To understand career dynamics in self-designing systems, one must first review a durable distinction in the career literature between objective careers and subjective careers. Objective careers are defined by a sequence of official positions, salary changes, formal statuses, and titles, all of which are publicly accessible and defined external to the person (Van Maanen and Schein, 1977). Subjective careers are defined by the specific experiences individuals have in official positions. These subjective experiences reflect changing aspirations, satisfactions, self-conceptions, and attitudes toward work. Success in a subjective career is often defined psychologically in terms of self-fulfillment, challenge, and satisfaction. The subjective career emphasizes self-direction and greater personal responsibility for the choices that are made. Those people who develop their subjective careers tend to engage in an "interminable series of experiments and explorations" that Hall (1976) has described as the Protean career.

For a person to be governed by the subjective career means that the adequacy of performance is defined by the person's own criteria of good performance, attitudes emphasize work satisfaction achievement and job involvement rather than organizational commitment and loyalty, identity is sought through activities that raise self-respect and heighten self-awareness, and adaptability is used as the measure of work experience (e.g., a person asks, what flexibility can I develop by doing these tasks and how can I maintain the flexibility I already have?)

The subjective career assumes special importance in self-designing organizations. This becomes clear when we recall a key property of traditional organizations. In a traditional organization, the external career is defined by positions in the organizational structure, and movement through this structure is often adopted by people as their subjective career. In self-designing organizations, however, typical markers of the external career such as titles, advancement up a hierarchy, and stable career paths are rare. In the absence of such external markers, the objective career dissolves, and in its place the subjective career becomes externalized and treated as a framework for career growth. Just as the ambiguity of a projective test gets resolved when a person imposes an idiosyncratic interpretation on equivocal graphics, the ambiguity of a self-designing system gets resolved when a subjective career is imposed to specify a meaningful structure and a plausible path through this structure.

Subjective careers as resources for self-design

If we assume that subjective careers generally incorporate themes of growth, skill development, and integration of more complexity, then when these subjective milestones are externalized, the system too will define growth as a career path. The system values and rewards growth because that is what the participants impose, value, and work toward. As the participants learn more while pursuing personal growth, the system also learns more.

An organization in which the subjective career becomes the objective career should show more cumulative learning, exploration, and change than an organization in which external career markers tied to existing structures become the subjective career. When the external criterion of movement through a hierarchy is internalized as a proxy for personal growth and development, people develop fewer new attitudes, competencies, or images of self. Since structures always lag behind environmental changes, people who treat movement through a structure as a sign of personal growth will gain less new knowledge of the environment outside of that structure or of themselves. When subjective careers get externalized, however, direct awareness of the current environment is more likely, as is more adequate coping.

Individual career growth furthers organizational self-design. People who are able to redesign themselves through new experience and new integrations of this experience provide the variety the system needs to match a changing environment. The self-designing organization can facilitate the development of subjective career paths by constructing nonlinear career patterns. Hall (1986) states: "An emerging model for continual career renewal is skill-based (not position-based) career paths. Here, advancement takes place in tasks and skills mastered rather than positions and levels attained" (p. 154). Employees would be moved through various jobs or projects so that they could experience different approaches, problems, and solutions. Some of the moves might be downward or lateral moves, but if the compensation system were based on skills mastered and not on the position and if these nontraditional moves were considered the norm in the organization, then the moves could be understood as growth opportunities rather than as advancement or demotion in traditional linear terms. Individuals would thus be encouraged to derive their security from the process of growth. This makes them flexible, inclined to learn, and more willing to experiment.

Patterning among subjective careers

A potential problem when differing individual career paths form the structure of a self-designing system is that these systems could become virtual anarchies when different people follow different career paths. There are several reasons why this is unlikely. First, pursuit of multiple career paths, especially when each path involves both growth in competence and higher level integrations of experience, expands the organization's capability to cope with a wide variety of environmental changes. Second, there is an orderliness and pattern to growth stages (e.g., Jung, 1978, pp. 15–16), which means that when people at the same growth stage pursue their own individual definitions of growth, there is considerable overlap in their assessments of where they are and what they need to develop next. Third, subjective careers are often socially constructed, which means that people build a consensual definition of what development and progression mean within a firm. This consensus reduces the variety of subjective careers that operate simultaneously. Fourth, the demographics of entry positions often ensure some homogeneity of personnel, which means that when managers encourage career growth, people will develop in a similar manner because they are at similar points in their development. And fifth, if we assume that organizations are loose federations of subcultures, then subjective careers are more likely to differ between subcultures than within subcultures. Again, the point is that there are limits to the number of different subjective careers that will be salient to serve as substitutes for objective careers.

CAREER DEVELOPMENT IN THE CONTEXT OF SELF-DESIGN

The self-designing organization is a unique setting in which structure is limited in the interest of faster change. Much of the structure that ties such organizations together (Van Maanen, 1977, p. 177) is a career structure built from externalized subjective careers. This structure places some unique demands on people if they are to cope with it, contribute to it, and develop identity, competence, and satisfaction within it. To undertake career development under these conditions, people need to do at least five things:

1. cultivate spiral career concepts;
2. decouple identity from jobs;
3. preserve discretion;
4. identify distinctive competence; and
5. synthesize complex information.

Cultivate spiral career concepts

As we saw earlier, an organization interested in self-design may develop either a spiral form or a transitory form. These two forms encourage complementary career orientations. A person with a spiral career orientation makes extensive use of information and develops a complex career plan that changes often and is affected by both work and nonwork experience. A spiral places high value on personal experience, which means that trial and error is an important source of information. This spiral develops an increasingly complex concept of self that is continually open to change and that incorporates multiple views of self. This person makes deliberate and substantial career movements every five to seven years in line with new integrations of new experiences.

A person with a transitory career orientation shifts activity frequently but less in response to new integrations of experience and a deepening self-concept and more in response to changes in personal contacts and opportunities. Transitory people may be either active, resembling an entrepreneur who keeps innovating activities, or passive, resembling a drifter who goes from job to job and cherishes the freedom to move on (Driver, 1979, p. 93).

Thus, the most straightforward answer to the question of how to survive in a company that is always changing is to develop a spiral career concept and, if that is not possible, develop a transitory career concept and try to make it more spiral. For the person who is already a spiral, the advice would be to model that career path to encourage self-design by others.

Decouple identity from jobs

To self-design, a person must view jobs as means, not ends. This is easier said than done because people treat jobs as an important part of identity, especially in American culture. When individuals intertwine their identities with their jobs, they will be reluctant to change jobs because change raises new questions about who they are. Miller-Tiedeman and Tiedeman (1984) suggest that people can decouple their identities from specific jobs by viewing any job as temporary and only a part of their careers (with other parts being comprised of family, hobbies, clubs, etc.). A small, temporary job is less likely to become the benchmark of identity.

If specific jobs are not a source of identity, other sources must be found. In self-designing organizations, identity is found in the context of the roles a person has already filled and also aspires to. For example, a university professor may think of his or her career in terms of positions (assistant to associate to full professor) or in terms of roles such as writer, researcher, or teacher. In this regard, professionalization more generally can help people decouple their identities from specific jobs since professional identity is grounded in skills and processes rather than specific jobs. Professional memberships also give people a reference group other than the people with whom they work. Besides encouraging variety (members of an organization interact with people from other organizations), professionalization makes it easier to separate identity from a specific job and therefore to change jobs. Professionalization can thus foster growth and self-design.

People can also decouple identity from specific jobs if they experiment with career identities (Weick, 1976). This is the career equivalent of galumphing or play (Weick, 1979, p. 248). When people play, they put their experiences into novel combinations and learn things that make them better able to cope with changing conditions in a self-designing system. This suggestion goes beyond Miller-Tiedeman and Tiedeman's (1984) suggestion that people should first discover what they want to be and, then, what they want to do will follow. Weick (1977) explains:

A pervasive assumption in creating any alternative design is that occupants can rearrange their activities and responsibilities, but not their identities . . . If the prescription to "be someone else" is used as a general framework for redesign, it relaxes the constraints imposed by fixed identities. The participants in the self-designing system can take liberties with self-definition and can try to construct a set of selves that they find more engaging, interesting, or efficient. (p. 38)

People can be encouraged to experiment with their own identities in a number of ways, including finding a new job or a second job, taking a leave of absence during which the individual does something completely different from his or her regular job, experiencing an extended stay at a survival camp such as Outward Bound, or engaging in role playing.

Preserve discretion

Discretion, freedom, and control are preconditions for continuous relearning. The dynamic operating here is illustrated by high-technology firms (Blotnick, 1984, pp. 122–123). If employees work in an area where there are few alternative employers, they tend to be cautious so they can keep the jobs they have. This caution puts a damper on both the individual's and the firm's ability to redesign.

High-technology enclaves such as Silicon Valley, Route 128 outside Boston, and Research Boulevard in Austin should be especially successful resisting this constraint on design for two reasons. First, when there are clusters of similar companies, there is direct competition among the companies themselves, which induces swift redesign. Second, an individual who works in a cluster company can easily go across the street and get an equally good job, which means that this individual feels less necessity to accept local ideas and is more willing to take risks. A high number of attractive alternative jobs encourages risk taking by individuals as well as closer attention to those risk takers by their employers in the interest of keeping them and reducing turnover. Both tendencies combine to accelerate redesign, adaptation, and receptiveness to innovation. Thus, the mere presence of alternative work settings may be sufficient to improve self-design, even if the alternatives are never exercised. It is this possibility that illustrates the importance of perceived freedom to self-design.

Freedom is more fully available in individual lives when commitment and the necessity to justify are low. While low commitment and low pressure to justify may result in satisficing performance, this is less crucial in self-designing systems than is the ease with which people can unlearn current practices. Effectiveness requires skill in managing commitment so that it can be increased in the interest of short-term performance but decreased in the interest of longer term unlearning and relearning.

Successful management of commitment often requires the development of career insight (London, 1983). As insight develops, people may discover that they have new choices they did not realize, that the effects of earlier actions are revocable, that their previous actions have been less visible than they thought, and that earlier choices were based on limited information, which means they really were not choices at all. All of these discoveries lower commitment, unfreeze prior learning, facilitate change, and restore discretion.

Identify distinctive competence

Individuals are valuable to the self-designing organization for the requisite variety that they bring to it. Ashby's principle of requisite variety "states that the variety within a system must be at least as great as the environmental variety against which it is attempting to regulate itself" (Buckley, 1968, p. 495). Self-designers, those individuals who are designing and redesigning the organization, are the source of the variety the organization uses to comprehend its environment.

Self-designers will be valuable to the organization to the extent that they have access to the distinctive sources of variety contained in their experience. Individuals have unique competencies, abilities, and expertise, but unless they are able to use their skills to generate new ideas, to build on the ideas of others, or to integrate seemingly disparate ideas, they cannot contribute to one of the primary outputs of a self-designing organization, its redesign. Having the desired skills is not enough. Individuals in self-designing organizations must be assertive enough to push their ideas and must be able to communicate the reasoning behind their ideas and hunches.

Self-designers must also be willing to follow hunches or intuition. When we say that a person has good intuition, we usually mean that he or she draws on a wealth of experience. Intuition that is grounded in personal experiences and personal theories allows the individual to transform fragmented information into a personally meaningful whole. The organization gets richer meanings than it would if it used societal meanings that are insensitive to individual experiences, preferences, and strengths. The individual also benefits because decisions that are personally grounded feel plausible and worth implementing. Experience is the key to intuition. The self-designing organization will value people who possess a wealth of experience and who can draw from that experience to benefit the organization.

Synthesize complex information

We also need to look at careers from the perspective of the organization itself and ask, what does the firm need to produce continuous self-design? Whatever the firm needs is what it will reward, and this in turn suggests what should be more and less successful career paths even when there is impermanence.

The following is speculative, but we suggest that the primary problem of a self-designing organization is not idea generation, but rather synthesis of the proposals that are made, gaining acceptance of the synthesis, and implementing the result while keeping people receptive to new experience. Everybody has ideas about how organizations can be improved, and more of those ideas should be visible in an organization designed to encourage such ideas. Thus, a self-designing organization is likely to be overloaded with ideas. Those who are able to manage this overload, cull it, and build syntheses where people can recognize their own inputs are likely to be influential in these organizations.

Thus, somewhat in contradiction to our earlier line of argument, we suggest that if an organization has been able to increase its capacity for self-design (e.g., it has been able to reduce its uncertainty absorption), it may face a problem of too much awareness. If that happens, those people who are able to organize this awareness will experience more growth and influence. Hedberg (1981, p. 21) suggests that overload can also be reduced by people who are able to integrate larger amounts of information and articulate larger visions that show how individual contributions have been accepted and fit together. There need not be a trade-off between quality and acceptance in group decision making if quality is defined as solutions that incorporate most of what was proposed. To build such solutions is an exercise that involves both symbolic management (Pfeffer, 1981) and cognitive complexity (Streufert and Swezey, 1986). The cognitive complexity is required to build the synthesis that incorporates much of what was proposed; the symbolic management is required to articulate the synthesis so that the components it has incorporated are visible to everyone.

CONCLUSION

We emphasize that the requirements we have proposed for career adaptation and growth in self-designing systems are difficult to implement. It is not as if everyone walking around could immediately fit into a self-designing organization. Mere self-realization does not ensure fit, nor does mere flexibility. To prepare oneself for a lifetime of learning and exploration is to become attached to processes rather than structures. Processes are harder to grasp, harder to count, harder to ascend, harder to change, and harder to accumulate. Since careers are so often defined as tangible possessions and accomplishments, a shift toward self-designing careers is neither easy nor are there many models for how to do it. We have suggested some possibilities for what life lived in self-designing systems might look and feel like in the hope that others can use these descriptions to move beyond them.

REFERENCES

Argyris, C., and Schon, D. A. (1978). *Organizational Learning*. Reading, MA: Addison-Wesley.
Bateson, G. (1972). *Steps to an Ecology of Mind*. New York: Chandler.
Beyer, J. M. (1981). Ideologies, values, and decision making in organizations. In P. C. Nystrom and W. H. Starbuck (eds.), *Handbook of Organizational Design*, Vol. 2. New York: Oxford, pp. 166–202.

Blotnick, S. (1984). *The Corporate Steeplechase*. New York: Penguin.

Buckley, W. (1968). Society as a complex system. In W. Buckley (ed.), *Modern Systems Research for the Behavioral Scientist*. Chicago: Aldine, pp. 490–513.

Burns, T., and Stalker, G. M. (1961). *The Management of Innovation*. London: Tavistock.

Driver, M. J. (1979). Career concepts and career management in organizations. In C. L. Cooper (ed.), *Behavioral Problems in Organizations*. Englewood Cliffs, NJ: Prentice-Hall, pp. 79–139.

Eysenck, M. W. (1982). *Attention and Arousal*. New York: Springer.

Goodman, R. A. (1981). *Temporary Systems*. New York: Praeger.

Hall, D. T. (1976). *Careers in Organizations*. Pacific Palisades, CA: Goodyear.

Hall, D. T. (1986). Breaking career routines: midcareer choice and identity development. In D. T. Hall and Associates, *Career Development in Organizations*. San Francisco: Jossey-Bass, pp. 154–155.

Hedberg, B. (1981). How organizations learn and unlearn. In P. C. Nystrom and W. H. Starbuck (eds.), *Handbook of Organizational Design*, Vol. 1. New York: Oxford, pp. 3–27.

Hedberg, B. (1984). Career dynamics in a steelworks of the future. *Journal of Occupational Behaviour, 5*, 53–69.

Hedberg, B. L. T., Nystrom, P. C., and Starbuck, W. H. (1976). Camping on seesaws: prescriptions for a self-designing organization. *Administrative Science Quarterly, 21*, 41–65.

Hedberg, B. L. T., Nystrom, P. C., and Starbuck, W. H. (1976). Designing organizations to match tomorrow. In P. C. Nystrom and W. H. Starbuck (eds.), *Prescriptive Models of Organizations*. Amsterdam: North-Holland, pp. 171–181.

Jung, C. G. (1978). The stages of life. In J. Campbell (ed.), *The Portable Jung*. New York: Penguin, pp. 3–22.

Khandwalla, P. N. (1977). *The Design of Organizations*. New York: Harcourt, Brace, and Jovanovich.

London, M. (1983). Toward a theory of career motivation. *Academy of Management Review, 8*, 620–630.

Metcalfe, L. (1981). Designing precarious partnerships. In P. C. Nystrom and W. H. Starbuck (eds.), *Handbook of Organizational Design*, Vol. 1. New York: Oxford, pp. 503–530.

Miles, R. E., and Snow, C. C. (1978). *Organizational Strategy, Structure, and Process*. New York: McGraw-Hill.

Miller-Tiedeman, A., and Tiedeman, D. V. (1984). To be in work: on furthering the development of careers and career development specialists. In N. C. Gysbers et al. (eds.), *Designing Careers: Counseling to Enhance Work and Leisure*. San Francisco: Jossey-Bass, pp. 91–192.

Miller-Tiedeman, A., and Tiedeman, D. V. (1985). Educating to advance the human career during the 1980s and beyond. *Vocational Guidance Quarterly*, September, pp. 15–30.

Mintzberg, H., and McHugh, A. (1985). Strategy formation in an adhocracy. *Administrative Science Quarterly, 30*, 160–197.

Nemeth, C. J. (1986). Differential contributions of majority and minority influence. *Psychological Review, 93*(1), 23–32.

Pfeffer, J. (1981). Management as symbolic action: the creation and maintenance of organizational paradigms. In L. L. Cummings and B. M. Staw (eds.), *Research in Organizational Behavior*, Vol. 3. Greenwich, CT: JAI, pp. 1–52.

Salancik, G. R. (1977). Commitment and the control of organizational behavior and belief. In B. M. Staw and G. R. Salancik (eds.), *New Directions in Organizational Behavior*. Chicago: St. Clair, pp. 1–54.

Schein, E. H. (1971). The individual, the organization, and the career: a conceptual scheme. *Journal of Applied Behavioral Science, 7*, 401–426.

Staw, B. M. (1982). Counterforces to change. In P. S. Goodman (ed.), *Change in Organizations*. San Francisco: Jossey-Bass, pp. 87–121.

Streufert, S., and Swezey, R. W. (1986). *Complexity, Managers, and Organizations*. Orlando, FL: Academic.

Stumpf, S. A. (1984). Adult career development: individual and organizational factors. In N. C. Gysbers et al. (eds.), *Designing careers: Counseling to Enhance Work and Leisure*. San Francisco: Jossey-Bass, pp. 190–215.

Torbert, W. R. (1987). *Managing the Corporate Dream: Restructuring for Long-Term Success.* Homewood, IL: Dow Jones-Irwin.

Van Maanen, J. (1977). Summary: towards a theory of the career. In J. Van Maanen (ed.), *Organizational Careers: Some New Perspectives,* New York: Wiley, pp. 161–179.

Van Maanen, J., and Schein, E. H. (1977). Career development. In J. R. Hackman and J. L. Suttle (eds.), *Improving Life at Work.* Santa Monica, CA: Goodyear, pp. 30–95.

Watzlawick, P., Weakland, J. H., and Fisch, R. (1974). *Change.* New York: Norton.

Weick, K. E. (1976). Careers as eccentric predicates. *Executive, 2,* 6–10.

Weick, K. E. (1977). Organization design: organizations as self-designing systems. *Organizational Dynamics,* Autumn, pp. 38–39.

Weick, K. E. (1979). *The Social Psychology of Organizing,* 2nd ed. Reading, MA: Addison-Wesley.

Weick, K. E. (1983). Contradictions in a community of scholars: the cohesion–accuracy tradeoff. *Review of Higher Education, 6*(4), 253–267.

16 *Organization career systems and employee misperceptions*

JAMES E. ROSENBAUM

INTRODUCTION

In large organizations, people often fail to see the institutional structures that affect their lives. Students are often unaware of the school structures that affect their careers in schools and in later life (Rosenbaum 1976, 1980a, 1980b), and employees and managers often do not see organizational practices that constrain their careers (Kanter 1977; Rosenbaum 1984). Why do these misperceptions occur? Their occurrence in diverse organizations seems to imply systematic causation.

This chapter investigates whether our conception of organization careers is defective and whether it creates these misperceptions. This chapter indicates the limitations of the dominant model of careers in American society, proposes an alternative, and presents empirical tests of the two. After examining how these two models are related to employees' misperceptions, this chapter considers the implications of mistaken models and misperceptions for organization policies and practices.

Employees' careers in organizations have been conceived in at least two ways.[1] The *individualistic* model, the dominant model of careers in the United States, contends that individuals are the main agents determining their job progress. The *structural* model views careers as "a structural aspect of an organization," and it contends that individuals' careers in organizations are structured by internal labor market structures, vacancy chains, and organization policies (Slocum 1974: 6). While each model has strengths, each also has serious limitations.

Formal structural models, such as internal labor market and Markovian models, are limited in not being easily related to individuals' attributes or their actual career paths, and these models sometimes require restrictive assumptions (Doeringer and Piore 1971; Milkovich et al. 1976; Nystrom 1981; Vroom and MacCrimmon 1968; White 1970). Another kind of structural model, based on organization policies, clearly delineates firms' intentions about recruitment, selection, and succession (Kellogg 1972; Schein 1978; Shaeffer 1972); but policies are not always accurate accounts of the ways career systems operate in actual practice. As noted in a previous review, some of these limitations could be overcome if structural models incorporated individualistic factors by analyzing organization career practices in dealing with individuals and by analyzing the different career trajectories of various employee groups (Rosenbaum 1987).

The present review approaches the issue from the opposite direction: identifying how individualistic models might be improved by incorporating structural factors. Individualistic models posit that careers are determined by individuals: Psycho-

329

logical models stress individuals' ability, motivation, or interests; economic models stress their rational choices; biological models stress their development and aging. However, while all these factors affect careers, they are still incomplete. They ignore structural factors that impinge upon careers.

Until now, efforts to integrate individualistic and structural models have been more like inventories of influences than like models of causal processes. They comprehensively identify many structural influences (Hall 1976; Schein 1978), but they are sometimes vague about the mechanisms of career systems or about their specific effects on employees' careers. A different synthesis is proposed here. The tournament model posits that organization career systems operate like a tournament in which individuals' histories of "wins" and "losses" define their future career opportunities, their incentives, and the organization investments they receive.

This chapter compares the individualistic and tournament models and tests them by empirical analyses of career patterns in a large corporation. We then review research on the accuracy of employees' perceptions of career systems, including the results of a new study, to explore how employees' misperceptions are related to these models. The chapter concludes that employees' perceptions must incorporate structural features (1) if employees are to perceive career options accurately and target career efforts optimally and (2) if firms are to make accurate ability-based promotions and keep their employees motivated.

INDIVIDUALISTIC MODEL OF CAREERS

Americans have an individualistic model of careers. Individualism can be defined in several ways. As distinct from Thoreau's individualism (individual withdrawal from society), the contemporary view comes from Social Darwinism (Sennett and Cobb 1972: 72). According to this view, individuals – by their own actions – are the main agents for determining their careers, and employers are highly responsive to individuals' efforts.

Individualism has many appealing features in our society. First, it is a strong norm. Indeed, it is so pervasive in American culture that it seems natural to see organizational careers in this way. Second, individualism suggests practical rules for behavior, and it inspires ambition. It directs employees' attention to actions they can take to improve their fate, and, even if it were only partly true, it enhances their motivation so that they are more productive. Third, its efficiency is justified by economic theories, which, as noted later, indicate that individualism fosters efficient allocation of investments in human resources.

By this view of individualism, careers depend on people knowing their own strengths and interests, but not on their knowing much about organizations or career systems. This belief is implicit in the practices of many career counselors. Guidance counselors do not spend much time giving clients information about the job world or career mechanisms (Ginzberg 1972). Guidance counselors focus on aptitude and interest tests (Strong 1943), as if individuals were in control of their careers. Some counselors also give advice on dressing for success, mentors, support groups, and networking; but this advice, although informative about the job world, still does not convey information about career patterns or structures. Counseling practices seem to assume that individuals' self-awareness and their actions are the main determinants of career success.

Of course, the information counselors give is important, and counselors often have great success with their individualistic approach. However, by ignoring career systems, counselors may encourage people to believe that career systems either don't exist or don't matter.

Similarly, organization career policies tend to be individualistic and ignore career system mechanisms. These policies blame employee problems on deficiencies in individuals, rather than on structural causes. For instance, concerns about unrealistic ambitions in early career (Gould 1978; Schein 1964) and low motivation in midcareer (Kay 1974; Levinson 1969, 1978; Miller 1976; Vaillant 1977) are viewed as individuals' maladies. Organizations treat such problems as if they arise from individuals, and they try to remedy these problems with programs to improve employees' attitudes. However, since these problems are concentrated in certain career periods, it is quite possible that they arise not from individuals but from organizations' career systems.

Even realistic job previews (Wanous 1975), which try to inform prospective employees about their career prospects, do not consider organization career systems. These previews mostly convey information about first jobs, not future career probabilities. Indeed, such information is often unavailable because most firms do not analyze advancement patterns or probabilities in their career systems. Yet employees need this kind of information about the career system for making realistic goals and career decisions.

Personnel managers also need information about career systems. Although individualistic analyses are adequate for understanding the staffing decision for a single job at one point in time, "large organizations must staff complex job structures; [and] several jobs and people must be considered at one time" (Nystrom 1981: 283). Human resource planning systems stress the need for broader perspectives (Burack and Gutteridge 1978; Sonnenfeld 1984), but conceptual models and empirical methods for analyzing career systems are inadequate at this time. Both employees and managers need to understand the career systems that arise in organizations.

Organization behavior research and theory on careers has often relied upon individualistic approaches and ignored career systems. In Hall's (1976) classic text on the topic, all but one of the chapters focus on individuals: individuals' career choices, individuals' career stages, individuals' performances, and so forth. There is only one exception, a chapter on redesigning organizations, and it differs from the other chapters in reviewing few studies and summarizing practitioner reports of firms' policies. This is not a deficiency of the text; it is an accurate reflection of the state of work in the field. More recently, research has begun to show how organization career structures may affect employees, and there is a growing awareness of the need to increase our understanding of these influences (Bailyn 1980; Baron 1984; Kanter 1977; Lawrence 1984, 1987).

STRUCTURAL INFLUENCES IN AN INDIVIDUALISTIC MODEL

Toward a structural version of the human capital model

In analyzing how individualistic models may be improved by adding structural features, this review focuses on the human capital model in economics. The human capital model is a detailed version of the individualistic model. It highlights both the strengths and problems of the individualistic model, and it shows how structural features may arise.

Just as classical economic theory posits that firms invest in physical capital (machines, factories, etc.) for future profits, the human capital model posits that people invest in their human capital (education, training, etc.) to improve their capabilities and their future careers (Becker 1964; Mincer 1974). According to the human capital model, people differ in ability, so their self-investments will produce different rewards. People invest in their human capital if they think they have enough ability to justify their investments (of time and tuition). The human capital model represents the most important feature of the individualistic ideal: People control the investments that affect their careers.

However, the following analysis identifies two problems with the human capital model, and it shows how these problems introduce structural features. First, in contrast with the human capital assumption that managers know their employees' abilities, we find that managers have insufficient information about employees' abilities, and they supplement their information by using structural indicators of ability, what theorists have called "signals" of ability (Arrow 1973; Spence 1974; Stiglitz 1975). Second, in contrast with the human capital assumption that individuals make the only investments in their careers (Mincer 1974), we find that firms also make investments in selected individuals, which may be much larger than individuals' self-investments and have much greater influence on career outcomes.

These two mechanisms, signaling and stratified investments, though phrased in terms of the human capital model, introduce major organizational constraints on that model. Instead of individuals controlling their own human capital, organizational practices control the detection and development of individuals' human capital. Although human capital principles are still the basic dynamic, they are constrained by organizational practices used to infer ability and allocate jobs and training.

To examine whether these speculations are correct, we must investigate several questions. First, do firms use signals for promotion decisions, and, if so, what signals are used? Second, do firms invest in training for employees' career advancements? These questions can best be answered by analyzing firms' actual practices.

Do firms use signals for promotion decisions?

Ability is an important component of human capital, and the human capital model assumes that employers know employees' abilities. However, there are reasons to doubt this assumption, especially in large organizations. Ability is not easy to identify and measure. Ability tests, the simplest ways to measure ability, are avoided because employers share society's mistrust of these tests. At best, tests measure "school-type" abilities that may not be pertinent to work performance; at worst, tests may be discriminatory (*Griggs v. Duke Power* 1971).

Supervisors' ratings are the most commonly used indicators of ability in workplaces (Campbell et al. 1970), but even these ratings are difficult to use in large organizations. Promotion committee members in a large corporation report several problems with using supervisors' ratings (Rosenbaum 1984). First, since more candidates get top ratings than can be promoted in most cases, supervisors' ratings are rarely sufficient. Second, ratings are difficult to interpret since top-rated candidates are often in incomparable jobs, are rated by different supervisors with different standards, and are known only by a few promotion committee members. Third, in the kinds of jobs that offer the most promotions (managerial and white-collar jobs), performance is difficult to measure and difficult to credit to particular members of a work group. Fourth, even direct supervisors often lack adequate information, as industrial psychologists have noted:

Direct information about subordinates' job behavior is often fragmentary; direct personal contact with subordinates may be minimal and restricted to a particular set of situations, depending on the nature of the job. Jobs themselves are incompletely understood, and specific duties may be inadequately described or entirely unspecified. (Feldman 1981, 128; cf. also Miner and Miner 1985)

Given the extensive problems of appraisal, how do managers make selections? Attribution theory and research suggest that people attribute qualities to others based on contextual factors, some of which are quite irrelevant. These processes tend to make supervisors' appraisals subject to a "ubiquitous halo" effect (Cooper 1981). Indeed, supervisors may even respond to cues of which they are unaware (Langer 1978; Nisbett and Wilson 1977), and this is supported by work on "automaticity" and "script processing" (Feldman 1981; Shank and Abelson 1977). Research suggests that certain cues, such as race, sex, dress, speech, and height, are particularly influential in making attributions (McArthur and Post 1977; Taylor and Fiske 1978).

Unfortunately, psychologists have not addressed another set of important cues: cues in the social structural context of employing organizations. Obviously, since most attribution research is done in laboratories, it is understandable that this research has ignored cues from organization structures. Do structural cues influence managers' appraisals?

In order to see how promotion committees deal with the problem of assessing promotion candidates, I interviewed a small sample of managers who had served on promotion committees in a large corporation (Rosenbaum 1984). Of course, the generalizability of these accounts is uncertain, but they are a reasonable starting point for investigating an issue that has received little study. The following points emerged from the interviews.

Since promotion committee members often do not know all candidates personally, promotion committees need other ways to compare candidates with equally high supervisor ratings. Respondents reported that in actual practice, promotion decisions are sometimes affected by objective labels and attributes that are thought to connote ability. For instance, just as educational credentials like MBA degrees and college status are commonly used to signal ability in hiring decisions (Spence 1974), educational credentials are sometimes used for the same purpose in promotion decisions, according to respondents (Rosenbaum 1984). Race, sex, and appearance were also mentioned. In addition, promotion committee members reported two aspects of employees' career history that were also used in inferring ability.

Past attainments. Individuals' past education and job attainments are interpreted as ability signals. An employee who started his career as a staff assistant in finance is viewed as more able than one who began as a staff assistant in personnel, who, in turn, is viewed as more able than a clerical assistant. Such inferences are not just prejudices about the value of various departments or jobs, they are based on "common knowledge" about the selectivity of these jobs. A more selective job can signal a previous decision about an individual's ability. Of course, many assumptions about the accuracy, persistence, and pertinence of the early decision are implicit in practices based on these inferences, and these assumptions are often unexamined and may not be warranted. But, although implicit and untested, these inferences seem to be widely shared among the managers interviewed.

Jobs are not the only attainments used as signals. As noted, high school and college degrees are sometimes used as ability signals. Many respondents also noted that graduates of high prestige colleges tend to be favored in promotion committee decisions. This influence has also been noted by other researchers (Karabel and McClelland 1983), although specific colleges may also have status effects, independent of the ability of their graduates (Rosenbaum 1981).

Career velocity. Promotion committee members report that in comparing candidates with equally high promotion ratings, employees are viewed as more capable if they have *rapidly advancing careers* or if they are *younger* than their peers in their status level. High-velocity advancements indicate that employees have quickly won many competitions, presumably because they are more capable. Managers in this firm frequently expressed this decision rule in the maxim: "The cream rises to the top." This kind of inference has also been indicated in other studies. Kanter (1977) notes that advancement opportunity could be inferred from the ratio of employees' attainments divided by their age (or tenure). Shrank and Waring (1983) and Dannefer (1984) note that employees who are young for their position are considered to be "ahead of schedule" and thus more able. Lawrence (1984, 1987) empirically documented these relationships in two firms, and she has presented a comprehensive conception of how age norms develop in organizations and how these norms affect employees' careers.

A recent meta-analysis affirms our contention that the age signal strongly affects supervisors' ratings, although it casts doubt on the validity of the age signal. Reviewing 40 samples from diverse studies, the meta-analysis finds that while productivity (measured objectively) increases with increasing age, supervisors' performance ratings tend to decline with age (Waldman and Avolio 1986). One interpretation is that age is such a strong negative signal that it negatively distorts supervisors' ratings, in spite of increased objective performances.

The age signal not only answers *when* selections can be made, but it also provides a scorecard. Even if competitions and their results are invisible, the age signal makes it easy to know at a glance how each employee has done in past competitions. It also specifies another feature of the selection system: One's competitors are in one's own age cohort.[2]

How do these signaling inferences arise? When asked to explain their inferences, managers report that they see careers as emerging from a Social Darwinian competition. Employees compete for career success, their career histories reveal their successes in past competitions, and only the most able can win several competitions. Of course, in our society, competitions are a common way to identify ability. Competitors are pitted against one another, and the Social Darwinian rationale dictates that winners have more ability. Organizations often stress competition in descriptions of their career systems, and employees commonly speak of career achievements in terms of athletic competitions. As one manager explained: "My endurance won out in the end, and I took the prize [of the promotion]." Endurance, sacrifice, and practice are common images in both athletic contests and organization competitions. Organizations sometimes go to great lengths to enhance competition: contests, motivation workshops, Horatio Alger inspirational notebooks, implicit competitions about staying long hours (Webber 1976). In some departments, like sales, competition is often explicit, including pep talks, posted scores, and public meetings to announce winners. Even in technical departments, employees are evaluated on their successful projects and jobs, and these may be publicly announced.

But regardless of whether competitions actually occur, the belief in competitions allows a manager to infer individuals' ability from their past job attainments. Thus, when ability is hard to measure, an employee's job history provides objective indicators that are interpreted as signals of ability. Employees in high status or demanding jobs are viewed as winners of past competitions and, consequently, as more able.

Of course, the generalizability of these accounts is uncertain since they pertain to only a single firm. Nonetheless, they are certainly no less plausible than the human capital model's assumption that promotion committees can accurately compare employees' abilities, which has not been empirically tested (and which conflicts with the results of Waldman and Avolio's meta-analysis).

Do firms invest in human resources?

The human capital model assumes that employees invest in themselves if they think their investments will improve their chances for future advancements. Self-investments preserve our open opportunity ideal since anyone willing to make sacrifices and take risks has the same chance to receive the possible benefits. However, the human capital model also assumes that firms exert no influence on the investments in individuals and on their future advancements. In reality, firms are not as passive as this.

While firms could let individuals make all the investments, firms have many reasons to invest in their employees.[3] In recent years, human resource planning (HRP) has been strongly advocated in the personnel literature. According to this view, human resources are assets, and firms should optimize their use of these assets. Firms should analyze their current work force, project their future human resources needs, devise career paths to fill projected needs, and devise developmental programs to prepare employees for this goal. The message has been effective, and HRP programs have been implemented in many organizations (Burack and Gutteridge 1978; Sonnenfeld 1984: 322).

Although HRP is often described as isolated programs, this understates their impact. Optimally, HRP programs affect all personnel decisions in the organization. Many diverse features of organizations – jobs, supervisors, and training programs – are seen as investment decisions; and these investments are directed to employees who are thought to have the most to offer the company. Human resource planning fosters selective investments in employees. Although the rationale for investing is similar to that in human capital theory – returns to investments – HRP directs that firms, not individuals, make the investments; so an individual's control is limited.

One implication of HRP is that firms will stop investing scarce resources in employees who are viewed as less able (i.e., those losing a competition). In effect, HRP assumes that *it is expensive to keep the doors of opportunity open* because as long as they are open, the firm is "wasting" scarce investments on "unproductive" people. Organizations can limit their investments by deciding that some individuals are no longer in contention. Indeed, if successive competitions increasingly winnow down the winners over time, firms can progressively reduce the numbers of employees receiving investments.[4]

In sum, two kinds of implementation difficulties make career systems differ from the individualistic model. Managers must infer ability in circumstances where information is inadequate, and they must invest in some employees, which may reduce the influence of employees' initiative and self-investments. These difficulties may be unavoidable, and our aim is not to criticize these practices. However, these practices suggest ways that unrecognized structural features can arise in career systems.

TOURNAMENT MODEL OF CAREER SYSTEMS

According to the previous sections, career systems tend to be sidetracked from their individualistic aims by structural elements such as ability signals and HRP investments. A structure of implicit competitions is imposed; wins and losses are signaled by age and career velocity; and "winners" (rapidly advancing people) receive most of a firm's human resources investments and are the only ones allowed to contend for the highest positions.

These selection practices, which fit neither individualistic nor structural models, are best described as a tournament. Tournaments are systems for selecting the most talented individuals by a series of progressively more selective competitions. Tournaments make selections at each stage, declare some winners, who then compete for the next higher level. People who lose a competition cannot compete with winners since it is inefficient to allow losers – who have been declared less able – to occupy the time and attention of supervisors and the challenging positions on primary career ladders. While early losers may subsequently attain similar positions as early winners, their early loss is a stigma that limits their future career possibilities. In some kinds of tournaments, losers may compete with other losers in a secondary tournament for lesser prizes.

While losing has permanent effects, winning is tentative – subject to later competitions. However, each win is an important statement about ability: It says that each winner has more ability than all losers at that stage of the tournament. In contrast with "round-robin" models in which cumulative win–loss records define one's standing and each victory adds only a small increment to their records (e.g., baseball during the main season), tournaments make each victory carry additional symbolic meaning. A victory connotes ability above *all losers* at that stage – including people one has never faced in competition.

However, career tournaments differ from sports tournaments in certain respects. First, performance is the sole criterion in sports tournaments but not in career tournaments. Because of difficulties of measuring performance, *signals also affect selections.* Second, since career competitions are not single events, but take place over time, *time itself affects selections.* Third, because of the long time between selections, firms can make *additional investments* in the winners at each stage. As the stakes increase at higher levels, firms make additional investments to *improve performance*, to *test* people's potential for higher jobs, and to *prepare* them for higher jobs. While the essential features of a tournament still apply, these distinctions make the tournament model more complex than sports tournaments: Variations in signals and investments affect one's chances in subsequent competitions. These variations mean that individuals at the same position can have somewhat different job histories, and these differences can affect their future careers.

The tournament model incorporates structural features into an individualistic model. By focusing on selections of individuals, the tournament model resembles individualistic models. Unlike structural vacancy models, the tournament model describes selection criteria and selection processes, and, unlike structural models with one-dimensional "job ladders," the tournament describes situations where individuals have career options. But the tournament model introduces structural features into individualistic models: It defines constraints on employees' career options at each stage of selections, and it describes how structural signals and HRP investments are allocated to individuals and influence future selections. While the human capital model implies that selections may be reversed (e.g., if an individual makes added self-investments), the tournament model suggests that losses are irreversible, negative signals have a lasting stigma, and the absence of company investments cannot be easily made up later. Contrary to the individualistic ideal, where the hero of a Horatio Alger story picks himself up, dusts himself off, and redeems himself after a loss, tournaments create a lasting stigma that limits future career possibilities.

Career systems do not always resemble tournaments, and we can better understand the tournament model by stating its assumptions and noting where it does not apply. The tournament model assumes that individuals differ from one another and that those with more "merit" rise. The tournament model does not apply to job ladders where everyone rises automatically, nor to caste systems that ignore individual merit. Second, the tournament assumes that information about individuals' abilities is imperfect, so that repeated competitions are needed to eliminate Type II errors (false positives). In situations where ability is thought to be accurately measured (e.g., state competitions in high-school mathematics), tournaments are unnecessary. Third, the tournament assumes that a person's history of past attainments counts. Unlike door-to-door sales, where your past success rate doesn't get you in the next door, tournaments occur in situations where one's past successes have important effects. Fourth, the tournament model assumes that information can be conveyed and interpreted accurately. In judging job applicants from other firms, employers often have difficulty interpreting people's job histories, so the tournament model is less likely to apply to inter-firm mobility than to intra-firm mobility, where past attainments are easily interpreted. Specifically, the tournament model is more likely to occur in firms that are *large* enough to offer varying career options and *old* enough to have stable interpretations of the meaning of individuals' job histories in the firm. Tournaments are less likely in small, young firms because of the lack of options and lack of consensus about the value of job attainments.

Obviously, some of the tournament's assumptions indicate potential shortcomings. Tournaments not only select inequalities; they can *create* inequalities. Tournaments make selections even if competitors' abilities are equal: There is only one winner in the Super Bowl, no matter how matched the teams are. Chance is an important element in all selections, and chance alone helps assure that someone wins the tournament, even when competitors are equal. Tournaments can introduce artificial distinctions between equivalent competitors.

Moreover, tournaments also risk introducing systematic biases. They allow structural features of a firm, which sometimes arise for reasons independent of individuals, to influence inferences about individuals' abilities and to determine their future careers. When the number of winners is predetermined, winners in one year may have less ability than those in the next, depending on the number of wins permitted each year and the number and quality of competitors in that year. In addition, if any past selections were based on non-ability criteria, the use of career history as ability signals will amplify these distortions in future selections. Meanwhile, changes in employees' performance may be less likely to be detected or to influence employees' careers. In effect, a career structure may arise.

Finally, since the competition avoids the important issue of selection criteria, the actual criteria for a victory may easily be corrupted. Tournaments assume that early wins signal ability, but quick decisions reduce the information available and increase performance sampling errors, so a few people will be selected and look like "heroes" (cf. March and March 1978). More often, however, tournaments probably have a strong capacity for reducing Type II errors (false positives) by repeated competitions, but tournaments are less good at reducing Type I errors (false negatives), for they allow no second opportunities for anyone losing a competition. Indeed, "seeded" and "double elimination" tournaments are variants used to reduce Type I errors.

Tournament career systems also define a new organizational status – ability status. In contrast with "job status," which confers rewards or prerogatives, "ability status" labels which individuals remain in the competition for advancement to the top. Although attainments in the job status hierarchy (job grades) affect inferences about one's ability status, the two are not the same. While job status automatically confers rewards or prerogatives, it confers ability status only if attained quickly or at a young age. Ability status is transient and contingent – a temporary status that requires reaffirmation by continued victories. Staying at the same high-status job for a long time conveys low ability status; low career velocity is seen as a failure to win competitions. Ability status crosscuts job status, and it must be continually proven. It can vanish if performance declines or if one stops advancing to higher positions (Rosenbaum 1986).

Tournaments embody the *economic rationality* of the human capital model: They posit that only employees with some likelihood of further advancement receive investments. However, recognizing that not only individuals – but also firms – make human capital investments, the tournament model stresses that firms determine career outcomes. The tournament goes beyond the human capital model in describing the larger structural context: how ability is determined, how selections are contingent on past history, and how firms' investments are structured.

CONFLICTING PREDICTIONS OF HUMAN CAPITAL AND
TOURNAMENT MODELS

Are careers structured like a tournament or are they unstructured? Do careers have predefined patterns or are careers responsive to changes of individual ability and effort as the human capital model implies? These questions can be examined in empirical tests.

Unfortunately, while the tournament makes clear predictions about career patterns, the human capital model does not. The human capital model does not deny career patterns; it only ignores them, so it is hard to test. No matter what form careers may take, the human capital model can "explain" them. Even if careers are patterned, the human capital model can provide a post hoc explanation in terms of employees' unmeasured abilities (while IQ tests may measure academic ability, productive ability at work is not easily measured). This is a handy escape clause for the human capital model, but it is also a serious weakness of this model.

In contrast, the tournament presents highly testable predictions about career patterns. Three predictions are considered here that are clear enough to be refuted if they are incorrect. The human capital model's predictions on these issues are also presented, based on the customary use of the model. These predictions are a reasonable statement of the way the human capital model is ordinarily used, and they represent an individualistic – anti-structural – approach. However, because of the unmeasurability of ability, the human capital model's predictions are less certain and could easily be modified by introducing new assumptions about ability.

Lasting effects of early selections

The tournament model contends that early selections determine which set of career branches an employee is allocated, and this, in turn, defines the employee's subsequent options. Tournament selection defines options irreversibly, so that even if employees subsequently overcome an initial loss and attain a later advancement, the early loss continues to have a lasting impact on their later careers. Moreover, these early-selection effects are independent of individual attributes. Horatio Alger types who seem to overcome early selections still do not have the same chances for subsequent advancement. This may be called the historical-effects hypothesis.

In contrast, the human capital model implies that early selections, per se, do not have lasting effects. It implies that Horatio Alger types will exist: Some people will overcome initial low origins or poor initial starting positions, and they will have the same chances of subsequent advancement as employees beginning in higher positions. Indeed, the human capital prediction was tested and confirmed by a study that found that unemployment after high school has little effect on youths' subsequent employment or earnings (Freeman and Wise 1982). Do early jobs in a firm have the same lack of effect on later careers within the firm?

Effects of age timetables

The tournament predicts that an employee is viewed as being in the competition for advancement from the time people normally enter the work force. If one doesn't enter the work force at the normal age, or if one chooses not to compete for advancement in one's first years at work, one is nonetheless judged as having failed to advance in the early tournament. Being over-age in a job implies that one is "behind schedule" (Neugarten and Datan 1973) and that one has lost earlier competitions – even if one wasn't competing for them. As a result, the tournament predicts that advancements sharply decline after a critical age.

In contrast, the human capital model implies no clear age timetables. While the human capital model implies gradual age declines (due to gradual declines in individuals' self-investments), it does not predict sharp declines. The denial of timetables is explicit in Markov models (McGinnis 1968; Sørensen 1975), which assume that mobility rates are independent of time (the stationarity assumption). Moreover, individualistic norms support this view. They imply that some people will be late bloomers, and mottos that "it's never too late" suggest a belief that ability can emerge late and advancements can occur late.

Effects of changing organization growth

The two models also differ in their predictions about how changes in organizational growth affect employees' careers. The tournament model implies that the most capable employees, who are already advancing as quickly as possible, cannot rise much more quickly when a firm grows (since they must await the next competition). Instead, when a firm grows, the tournament allows more people to be winners in each selection, and some early losers may have improved promotion chances. Similarly, when a firm shows decreasing growth, the tournament more sharply curtails the opportunity of less capable employees than it does for more capable ones.

In contrast, the human capital model assumes that the only limits on individuals' careers are inside themselves. As a result, capable people can benefit more from increased incentives than less capable people. Because they have more to gain or lose from increasing or decreasing organization growth, capable individuals' investments, and their resulting promotions, would be more responsive to changes in firms' growth or contraction than the investments and promotion of less capable individuals.

Again, we must stress that these predictions are not definitive tests of individualism or the human capital model, for the human capital model is difficult to refute. However, these predictions can show the relative usefulness of the two models in predicting career patterns.

EMPIRICAL TESTS

This section reviews evidence on the preceding issues. As noted, few studies have systematically analyzed actual career structures in organizations and addressed these issues. After summarizing evidence from previous research, I present the results from a study that focused on these issues. This study analyzed the personnel records of a large corporation (called ABCO) over a 13-year period. Although the detailed findings are presented elsewhere (Rosenbaum 1979a, 1979b, 1984), this review briefly summarizes some pertinent results. Four analyses were conducted: two longitudinal and two cross sectional. The longitudinal analyses followed employees' careers from 1962–75; the cross-sectional analyses study changes in career patterns over this period.

Lasting effects of early selections: longitudinal analyses of career paths

Stewman and Konda (1983) found that, among managerial staff of a state police organization, those promoted earliest tend to attain higher grades. Since that analysis did not control for individual attributes, we cannot know whether early selections, per se, have this effect. It would also be worth knowing whether similar relationships occur in organizations other than a state police bureaucracy.

My own research analyzed the career paths of an entering cohort over its first 13 years. The results indicate that early winners (employees receiving early promotions) have much more steeply advancing future career paths than early losers (employees who didn't receive early promotions). These diverging career paths closely resemble the tournament predictions. Although such patterns could be due to unmeasured employee attributes, multivariate analyses find that, even after controlling for many employee attributes (race, sex, tenure, entry age, education, and college selectivity – a proxy for ability) and for early earnings (a proxy for early human capital), early job attainments continue to have a strong and significant influence on later careers (Rosenbaum 1984, Chapters 2 and 6). Early losers are still behind 13 years later; indeed, they are even further behind. A one-level disadvantage in 1962 becomes a 1.36 level disadvantage in 1975 – even after controlling for individual attributes. Early selections have increasingly strong effects over those 13 years.

Moreover, early attainments (1962) have significant effects on later attainments (1975), after controlling for intervening attainments (1965) (Rosenbaum 1984, Chapter 6). These historical effects remain significant after controlling for employee attributes. Apparently, even employees who overcome an initial loss by their fifth year are still behind ten years later. In another firm, Forbes (1987) found that early promotions do not have significant effects, net of intervening attainments, but since only seven employees got early promotions in his sample, a lack of significance is not surprising. On the other hand, Forbes found significant effects by other early attainments: Number of previous moves and early favored positions have lasting significant effects, net of intervening positions. Taken as a whole, Forbes's findings mostly support the historical-effects hypothesis underlying the tournament model.

In both studies, late bloomers and Horatio Alger types who appear to overcome early career deficiencies (in early attainments, job moves, or early favored positions), still never catch up with people who started higher. These analyses provide unusually strong evidence against the human capital model and clear support for the tournament model. Of course, the human capital model's escape clause still applies; this study could not control for all aspects of human capital, nor could any study. Nonetheless, the tournament model's predictions are supported, and the human capital model's predictions are not.

Effects of age timetables

A number of observers have noted an age break in careers around age 40 (Martin and Strauss 1959; Sheehy 1976; Sofer 1970). Spilerman's (1977) analysis of the 1970 Census found that occupational shifts within industries (which often denote promotions) decline after age 40 in some occupations, suggesting the possibility of wide generalizability of the age 40 timetable. As noted, Shrank and Waring (1983) and Dannefer (1984) have noted that employees who are young for their position are considered to be ahead of schedule and thus more able. Some systematic analyses of age distributions in organizational hierarchies have noted patterns suggesting that there was an important division at the age of 40 (Lawrence 1987; Stewman and Konda 1983). However, analyses of promotion rates are necessary to permit clear inferences on this issue.

In the ABCO study, promotion rates were plotted as a function of age. Separate analyses were conducted for employees with and without college degrees (BAs and non-BAs) in each of three separate levels in the firm's authority hierarchy. Results indicate that BAs face clear career timetables: The promotion rates of foreman-level BAs drop precipitously after age 35, and those over age 39 are rarely or never promoted. In contrast, non-BAs face different career timetables: Their initial promotion rates are much lower, but their promotions continue through much older ages (Rosenbaum 1984, Chapter 3). These age effects remain even after controlling for years of tenure in the company. Contrary to the human capital model, late-blooming BAs would appear to have no chance to advance in this system. Although we cannot know whether any BAs actually had late emerging abilities, it is remarkable that no BAs advanced after age 39 in several periods, but many non-BAs did. Although the human capital model could explain this as indicating different patterns of human capital emergence, multivariate analyses controlling for many aspects of human capital (tenure, education, college selectivity, and early earnings) find that age continues to have a significant effect. The tournament provides a much simpler explanation – that early selections distinguish the career paths of the two groups.

Effects of changes in organization growth

Cross-sectional analyses of age–promotion curves were run for three periods: 1962–5, 1965–9, and 1969–72, periods of modest growth, increased growth, and declining growth, respectively. The results indicate that, consistent with predictions of the tournament model, the most favored group (young BAs) gained little from increased growth and lost little from declining growth, while the next most favored group (older BAs and young non-BAs) gained and lost more than other groups (Rosenbaum 1984, Chapter 3). More detailed multivariate analyses reach the same conclusion: The most favored group (young BAs from high status colleges) gained and lost little, and the next most favored groups (from lower status colleges) gained and lost more from changes in growth (Rosenbaum 1984, Chapter 7). Again, the tournament model prediction is supported, and the human capital prediction is not.

THEORETICAL IMPLICATIONS OF THESE FINDINGS

These findings were not predicted by the human capital model. Although the human capital model could explain these findings after the fact, it doesn't predict the structural patterns in these findings, nor does it explain them very well. It could attribute career changes to changes inside individuals (the natural emergence of "ability") or to changes in individuals' investments, but these changes are not easily measured, and the model does not explain why these changes occur.

These findings are predicted and explained by the tournament model. The tournament explains the timing of selections, the creation of ability signals, and their later impact on careers. Indeed, even if career patterns arose from the natural emergence of ability, ability seems to "naturally emerge" by the tournament's rules, perhaps because managers expect ability to fit the tournament model. This is quite reasonable. Managers seeing these career patterns might reasonably conclude that ability could be inferred from an employee's career velocity and age. This inference would make these career patterns – regardless of their origin – into dependable signals of ability, and use of these signals would create a career structure – even if one had not previously existed.

One other theoretical model must be considered. Social-psychological models stress the interaction between individuals and social-situational influences. Such models overcome some – but not all – limitations of the human capital model. Berlew and Hall (1966) propose that an organization's initial expectations for employees determine the level of challenge that the organization offers them, and employees' performance will tend to rise to this level of challenge. The model portrays a dynamic interplay between individuals and social settings. Challenge improves employees' performance, which, in turn, encourages firms to pose higher challenges. In contrast, "routine performance, even when no more than that is expected, is not generally rewarded, [and successfully meeting low] expectations will not bring about internalization of high performance standards or [confer] feelings of success" (Berlew and Hall 1966: 208).

Analyzing longitudinal data on managers' careers, Berlew and Hall (1966) find that early company expectations are indeed correlated with employees' later performance and career success. These findings are seen as support for their model: Early high expectations lead to early challenges that socialize managers to better performance.

The Berlew–Hall findings are similar to those of Rosenbaum (1984) and Stewman and Konda (1983). Early expectations (in the Berlew–Hall study) and early selections (in the previous studies) have similar effects and are probably related. In addition, the Berlew–Hall model of job challenge as "socialization" is similar to the tournament model of job challenge as "investments in winners." The two models and the two sets of findings are highly comparable in some respects.[5]

However, the two models suggest different interpretations of career patterns. Because the Berlew–Hall model lacks a conception of social structure, this model attributes the importance of early selections to constraints in individuals' development: "A critical period for learning, a time when the trainee is uniquely ready to develop or change ... never again will [a manager] be so 'unfrozen' and ready to learn as he is in his first year" (Berlew and Hall 1966: 222). In contrast, the tournament model asserts that career systems – not individuals – become increasingly "frozen" over time. In a tournament, the "critical period" is the time span that organizations allow before assigning negative ability labels to employees and withdrawing further investments and challenges.

Simply put, the conflicts between these two models are questions about causation. Does an individual's ability to benefit from challenge vanish over time or does the challenge from the environment vanish? *Is the critical period an attribute of individuals or an attribute of career systems?*

These questions have practical implications. If the critical period is in the person, then a person in an unchallenging first job will be socialized to poor performance and less capable of high performance *in any future job*. In contrast, if the critical period is in the system, then the person's future performance will be impaired *only in this particular system*. If people move to a new firm where no one knows the stigma of their first jobs, they begin with a clean slate with no serious impairment to second and third jobs. They can be late bloomers if the career system gives them a chance. Unfortunately, we have no research to indicate which process actually occurs.

In sum, individualistic models have many strengths, but they also have serious limitations. The human capital model portrays the reward–sacrifice trade-offs people must consider in their investment decisions, and the Berlew–Hall model portrays the dynamic features of the interaction between environmental challenge and individual performance. But neither model accounts for many features of careers reviewed here. In contrast, the tournament model explains which individuals receive early job challenges, why the firm encourages these investments, why they tend to be made early, what influences they have on later careers, and what influences persist over periods of increasing and decreasing organizational growth. Human capital and psychological models have not adequately addressed such issues.

Individualism is a central premise of society's norms, firms' policies, and psychological and economic theories. Yet promotion committee practices and the findings on career patterns discussed suggest that structural features are introduced into career decisions. These structural features make careers of some employee groups more rigidly patterned and less responsive to increasing and declining growth than individualistic models would suggest.

DO EMPLOYEES' PERCEPTIONS INCORPORATE STRUCTURAL INFLUENCES?

Individualism assumes that people see their careers accurately and understand the factors that affect their future career advancements. Career counselors reflect this assumption: They help individuals explore their own interests or develop their skills, but they rarely impart information about organizational factors that affect careers. The implicit assumption is that such information is unneeded. The same assumption arises in formal models. The human capital model assumes that people are well-informed, for informed choices are necessary if people are to make the correct human capital investments.

However, structural models propose that employees' careers are affected in ways that are more difficult for them to observe, thus the accuracy of their perceptions becomes an important empirical and theoretical issue. Moreover, if people base their perceptions on individualistic norms, they will be even more likely to miss seeing any structural factors constraining their careers. Consequently, it may be useful to re-examine our assumptions about informed choice and to review studies that compare employees' perceptions with actual career systems.

The accuracy of employees' career perceptions has rarely been questioned by research. This neglect is not surprising. After all, employees spend 2000 hours every year in their workplaces, and they spend much of that time talking about promotions and trying to figure out how promotions are decided. Despite their extensive efforts, accurate perceptions are difficult. While employees see some promotions in a large organization, they cannot see them all, so they don't get the whole picture. Even the information they have is hard to integrate since they must not only recall events over a long period of time, but they must also adjust for the possible effects of different kinds of individuals, supervisors, jobs, and historical conditions. Unfortunately, individuals' perceptions are ill-suited to such multivariate analyses. It is hardly surprising that employees' discussions of this topic often conclude with the vague statement, "It's all politics," a statement that attributes all promotion decisions to idiosyncratic causation.

The problem is compounded because social norms strongly define the ways things *should be*, and these norms tend to distort perceptions. Social norms tend to make individual success stories appear more salient than failures, regardless of the actual frequency of successes and failures. Indeed, some success stories may even be myths. Organizations often have their own local versions of Horatio Alger stories, with a few individuals epitomizing the mailroom-to-executive ideal. Even if these stories are not exaggerated, their high salience gives them undue importance and makes it difficult for employees to figure out how much advancement opportunity is actually available.

Furthermore, inaccurate perceptions are encouraged when organizations present misleading official policies about their practices. Official personnel policies are sometimes ambiguous or misleading about the ways advancement opportunities are determined (Rosenbaum 1984; Shaeffer 1972). While exemplary careers are stressed, constraints on career paths are downplayed, presumably to avoid dampening motivation. As a result, official renditions of organizational careers are sometimes evasive or misleading. Indeed, in one company, reports to outsiders admitted the existence of career tracks that were denied by the firm's internal policy statements (Shaeffer 1972).

While the preceding discussion leads us to expect misperceptions, the degree of misperceptions discovered in research is still remarkable. Chinoy (1955) reports that most automobile workers in his study initially expected rapid promotions, and only over the course of time did they figure out that promotions were very unlikely. Moreover, misperceptions are not restricted to workers. Goldner's (1970) study of a large manufacturing firm found that only about half (51.8%) of the middle managers expecting promotions actually received a promotion in the following five years. Evidently, even many middle managers do not accurately perceive their promotion chances.

Although self-reports about one's own promotion chances may also be explained as wishful thinking, research suggests that managers misperceive career systems, too. Kanter (1977: 132) observes that managers had a "general lack of clarity" about career tracks. For slowly advancing employees, "awareness of being stuck came ... indirectly," and even fast-track employees learned about it only gradually in "strange and devious ways" (Kanter 1977: 133). Kanter attributes misperceptions to the fact that information was hard to get. "It was often denied by vice-presidents that officer material was judged so low down the ranks" (Kanter 1977: 113). Peers also had diverse reasons for avoiding the topic. Employees on the fast track did not discuss it because they didn't want competition, while those who were stuck felt it was too embarrassing to admit. The lack of official information was accompanied by a lack of informal discussion among peers.

Indeed, even high-level managers may not perceive the career system accurately. Analyzing personnel records in a large corporation, Vroom and Mac-Crimmon (1968) found that employees in finance and marketing had much greater promotion chances than those in other departments. These findings were a complete surprise to managers, including a senior personnel manager who immediately took steps to change these practices (Vroom, personal communication). However, while Kanter and Vroom document the existence of misperceptions, they provide no quantitative indication of how common they are. For that, we must turn to more recent research.

Lawrence (1987) proposed a series of hypotheses about employee perceptions about age effects tested in an electric utility and an electronics firm. Comparing employees' perceptions of the age distribution in each level with the actual distribution, she found that employees' perceptions regress to the mean; employees do not see both ends of the age range. Employees were especially likely to miss seeing older employees in lower levels. This finding may indicate that employees implicitly believe that everyone rises out of these levels before they get old, a belief epitomized in the individualistic ideal, though strongly contradicted in the reality described in Lawrence's studies (1983; 1987). Lawrence's analyses provide unambiguous evidence that employees hold mistaken views about the career system.

Rosenbaum's (1984) longitudinal analyses of ABCO, already reported, permit dynamic analyses of career moves that aren't possible with the cross-sectional data that is usually available. Recently, Rosenbaum (1989) compared employees' perceptions of the career system with the reality of the career system as indicated in the personnel records. Interviews with 163 men and women in the two lowest levels of management compared career realities with employees' perceptions of their own opportunities and of the career system. This work is still ongoing and has not yet been published, so it will be reported here in more detail than is customary for a review.

Do employees accurately perceive age barriers? As noted, after age 39 virtually none of the foreman-level BAs were promoted in any three-year period, including the period immediately preceding the interviews, 1975–8.[6] Since the interviews were conducted in 1978, a period of no growth (when management ranks were actually being cut), managers should have expected that the age 39 barrier would continue to operate. Yet while foreman-level BAs over age 39 had no realistic chance of promotion, 37% ($n = 8$) of them thought their promotion chances in the next six years were 50% or better. Similarly, while less than 5% of non-BAs over age 39 were promoted in the two most recent periods (1972–5; 1975–8), most who were interviewed (58%; $n = 12$) thought their promotion chances in the next six years were 50% or better. Similarly, in lower-management levels, while less than 2% of BAs and non-BAs over age 39 were promoted, 42% ($n = 12$) of BAs and 20% ($n = 15$) of non-BAs thought their promotion chances were 50% or better in the next six years. Obviously, substantial proportions of these employees have plans that won't be realized.

Although these analyses are more detailed than Goldner's, the same problem of interpretation remains: Do these expectations actually reflect "wishful thinking"? We can avoid this interpretation by asking employees about their perceptions of the career system itself. Of course, these perceptions may also be distorted by hopes, but they have a less personal referent.

Employees were asked "Is there any age after which practically no promotions are made from foreman to lower-management? What age?" A substantial proportion (42.2%, $n = 154$) of employees denied that there was any such age barrier. Employees in foreman level were more likely to deny it than employees in the higher level (46.7% versus 35.4%, $n = 92, 62$). For BAs, for whom the age barrier was most prominent, the denial of age barriers declines regularly with age, both in foreman level[7] and in lower management.[8] Evidently, employees are increasingly likely to see the barrier as they approach it and after they pass it.

Thus, we find a surprisingly large degree of misperceptions of age barriers. As one might expect, these barriers are more likely to be seen at higher levels and by older employees in each level. However, many employees who are past the age of promotions still expect promotions. This doesn't seem to be merely a matter of wishful thinking about their own prospects, for many employees' descriptions of the career system indicate a lack of awareness of age barriers. Although we cannot be certain how much wishful thinking affects these results, the group most motivated to deny age barriers – employees over age 39 – are less likely to do so. Inexperience, rather than motivated denial, seems to account for these misperceptions.

Employees seem to be guided by the individualistic ideal that no barrier *should* exist, so they continue to deny the existence of age barriers until their experiences convince them to the contrary. Obviously, too few studies exist to permit definitive conclusions about generalizability, and some of the findings of my study involve too few cases for significant conclusions, particularly for the smaller age subgroups. Nonetheless, these few studies all point to the same conclusions: Employees may not perceive their career options accurately and may not have an accurate view of the career system in their organizations.

IMPLICATIONS OF IGNORING STRUCTURAL INFLUENCES

If employees don't see the age barriers associated with the tournament structure, their work efforts are likely to be poorly timed. In a system conceived as individualistic, people are assumed to be making free and informed decisions about their careers. This assumption is crucial for fairness: A tournament would not be fair if some competitors didn't know the rules of the game. The assumption is also crucial for efficiency: If competitors randomly choose when to exert their top performance, without knowing the tournament's timetables, then the winners may not be the most talented – they may only be the ones who happened to have the fewest distractions at the crucial time. Misperceptions may undermine the legitimacy and efficiency of career systems.

According to the preceding review, even high-level personnel managers may hold these misperceptions. Obviously, their misperceptions could have extensive repercussions. Managers could misinterpret personnel problems and formulate counterproductive policies. Our analysis has described a career system in which structural incentives encourage inappropriate motivation at certain times in employees' careers. The problems are exacerbated if high-level managers fail to see these structural incentives and misinterpret these problems, for example, by blaming individuals for the outcomes that the firm's incentives encourage. Some examples follow.

Unrealistically high ambitions in early career

Employers often complain about the excessive career expectations of young employees, especially those with MBAs. They blame youth or colleges for these excesses: Young people are too impatient and colleges convey unrealistic expectations. In a newspaper article about a low-prestige business college, a professor boasted, "MBAs are a dime a dozen, and they are too expensive. Our graduates don't expect private offices. They are happy to get a partitioned office and the chance to show their abilities." Obviously, this professor is happy to exploit a common stereotype about MBAs. But is the stereotype true?

Are youths and colleges solely responsible for excessive career expectations? Do organizations contribute in any way to these problems? The present analysis suggests that firms do encourage these high expectations by the way they design careers. Firms encourage fast-track employees to believe that they are "high-potential people" and that they are entitled to extra training, challenge, visibility, and rapid advancements. Firms sometimes intentionally encourage MBAs to have high expectations in order to retain these valued employees, but these expectations may outgrow reality to such an extent that they create discontent.

"Ruthless opportunism" at the expense of the firm

MBAs are sometimes accused of ruthless selfish pursuit of their personal career goals, even at the expense of their jobs, peers, and firms. They may make decisions that increase their personal reputation, even at the expense of the long-term good of the firm. Such behavior has been described as a form of opportunism in which investments are made for short-term benefits at the expense of long-term ones (Williamson 1975). In interviews with managers at ABCO, I frequently heard such accusations, and some managers implied that MBA programs teach such behavior.

"Ruthless Opportunism" is not listed as a course in any MBA program I've seen (although it may be listed under some other title). But ruthless opportunism may be a part of the hidden curriculum of career systems in organizations. Indeed, if career systems are based on the tournament rule – that employees must keep advancing quickly to stay in contention for top management – then employees are trapped in an incentive structure that severely punishes investments that provide long-term payoffs and slow career advancements. This message, hidden in the career system, would be a strong incentive for ruthless opportunism.

Midcareer crisis and "cooled" motivation

The midcareer crisis has been seen as an individual problem. Some accounts describe the midcareer crisis as an inevitable stage in adult development (Gould 1978; Levinson 1978). Some even hint that it arises from biological or psychological roots occurring in all cultures and in all historical eras (Sheehy 1976). With such a view, many large organizations have developed expensive psychotherapeutic programs to cure valued employees of their midcareer crises.

However, if organizations' career systems offer sharply declining incentives in midcareer, then the career structure itself may *create* the declining motivation that typifies the midcareer crisis. As long as career systems provide sharply declining incentives for employees' motivation in midcareer, they will encourage the attitudes associated with the midcareer crisis, and expensive psychotherapeutic strategies will be ineffective (cf. Lawrence 1980; Rosenbaum 1979c).

Moreover, the midcareer transition may even be more difficult because of employees' misperceptions. Employees' misperceptions foster unrealistically high aspirations in early career, and, as a result, employees will invest more of their efforts in trying to fulfill their unrealistic plans. The eventual disappointment conveys a message of wasted efforts and makes the blow more severe.

A Machiavellian might advocate deception to encourage these misperceptions. After all, misperceptions may raise motivation and productivity in early career by keeping young employees from knowing the futility of their goals. However, even Machiavelli realized that deceit could be counterproductive if its long-term costs outweighed immediate benefits. Employees' unrealistic plans may take their toll in the following 10 years, with repercussions that may endure for the remaining 30 years of the worklife of these employees. Moreover, the fact that many managers are affected by these unrealistic plans means that these misperceptions are poisoning the motivation of employees who are placed in positions requiring special trust and loyalty. Even for a Machiavellian, the cost–benefit ratio is against deception.

CONCLUSION: INCORPORATING STRUCTURE INTO POLICIES
AND PERCEPTIONS

This review suggests that careers must be conceived more broadly. Individualism has many virtues, and it may even be the best model for many purposes, but it is not sufficient to describe many career-related phenomena in organizations. We have noted some ways that structural influences enter into career selections. Unfortunately, these influences are rarely incorporated in career research, in organization policies, or in employees' career plans.

As long as we keep seeing careers solely through individualism's blinders, we will fail to notice important aspects of careers. *Individualism is not wrong, but it is incomplete.* It ignores systematic features, and it doesn't even encourage us to look for them. Alternative perspectives permit – indeed force – us to notice aspects of careers that we may overlook with our customary individualistic models. If our career models incorporate structural features, employees are more likely to perceive career options accurately and to target their efforts optimally, and firms are more likely to select their best talent and keep their employees motivated. In addition, personnel analysts will be more able to diagnose employee problems correctly and treat them effectively, and organization career policies will be more able to encourage valued behavior and foster motivation.

Our discovery of the limits of individualism does not mean that individual action is ineffectual; indeed, the reverse may be true – recognition of structure may reduce fatalistic attitudes. In any competition, people must know the rules by which they will be judged. Choices must not only be free; they must be informed. Without information, people will make free choices that fail to advance their aims, and they will pursue impossible goals or activities unrelated to their goals, while ignoring possible alternatives. Uninformed choices will result in repeated frustrations, which, being poorly understood, will lead to fatalistic resignation.

While tournaments impose some structural constraints that define the rules of the game, they do not eliminate the influence of individuals' initiatives. If the tournament model helps employees become aware of age timetables, then employees will make more informed choices. And if the tournament model helps organizational planners to be sceptical about making tightly constricted career timetables, then planners may design more humane and more efficient career systems.

NOTES

This work benefited enormously from the detailed, thoughtful comments of the three editors, Tim Hall, Mike Arthur, and Barbara Lawrence. The main editor of this chapter, Barbara Lawrence, deserves special credit, and my deep appreciation, for her extensive suggestions that greatly improved this chapter. In addition, I received helpful suggestions from many participants when this paper was presented at the careers workshop at the 1986 Academy of Management meetings. I particularly want to thank Lotte Bailyn, Paul Nystrom, and Jim Stoner. I also wish to thank the Center for Urban Affairs and Policy Research at Northwestern University for its support of this work.
1 Hall (1976:4) reviews various definitions of careers. The present chapter focuses on objective careers, and employees' perceptions of them, and does not consider subjective careers, which are stressed in Hall's preferred definition.
2 Although allowing past career history to affect future careers has some plausibility, it risks introducing systematic biases, as we note later.
3 The customary assumption in human capital theory – that firms won't invest in general training for employees because they will lose them in turnover – is partly true: Firms do have much turnover of the employees receiving these investments. But, if turnover is a problem, firms increase their compensation packages to retain these employees. Economists may wonder how they justify paying so much, but firms can easily envision a very high value to the people it calls "high-potential people," "water-walkers," and "top-management material," so enormous expenditures are easily justified. The many general training programs offered by employers have been noted in the recent Carnegie report, *Corporate Classrooms* (Eurich 1985).
4 Of course, HRP downplays the difficulties of inferring who is less able, the possible morale costs of not investing in these employees, and the ultimate outcome of such a system: Ending investments makes losses irreversible.
5 Berlew and Hall's measures of performance were global ("the company's overall appraisal" and outsiders' ratings), not specific (e.g., an immediate supervisor's performance rating), so labeling effects of signals may have affected "performance" measures.
6 The single exception was the 1965–9 period of unusually high growth; cf. Rosenbaum 1979b.
7 Age barriers are denied by 57.1, 44.0, and 37.5% in successively older age groups – under 30, 30–39, over 39; n = 14, 25, 8.
8 Of college-educated lower managers 26.9% were under age 40 and 18.2% of older ones denied an age limit ($n = 26$, 11).

REFERENCES

Arrow, K. J. (1973). Higher education as a filter. *Journal of Public Economics*, 2, 193–216.
Bailyn, L. (1980). The slow-burn way to the top: some thoughts on the early years of organizational careers. In C. B. Derr (ed.), *Work, Family and the Career: New Frontiers in Theory and Research*. New York: Praeger.
Baron, J. N. (1984). Organizational perspectives on stratification. In R. Turner (ed.), *Annual Review of Sociology*, Vol. 10. Palo Alto, CA: Annual Reviews.
Becker, G. (1964). *Human Capital*. New York: Columbia University Press.
Berlew, D. E., and Hall, D. T. (1966) The socialization of managers: effects of expectations on performance. *Administrative Science Quarterly*, 11, 207–223.
Burack, E. H., and Gutteridge, T. G. (1978). Institutional manpower planning: rhetoric versus reality. *California Management Review*, 20(3), 13–22.
Campbell, J. P., Dunnette, M. D., Lawler, III, E. E., and Weick, L. E. Jr. (1970). *Managerial Behavior, Performance, and Effectiveness*. New York: McGraw-Hill.
Chinoy, E. (1955). *Automobile Workers and the American Dream*. New York: Random House.
Cooper, W. (1981). Ubiquitous halo. *Psychological Bulletin, 90*, 218–244.

Dannefer, D. (1984). Adult development and social theory: a paradigmatic reappraisal. *American Sociological Review, 49*, 100–116.

Doeringer, P., and Piore, M. (1971). *Internal Labor Markets and Manpower Analysis*. Lexington, MA: Heath Lexington Books.

Eurich, N. P. (1985). *Corporate Classrooms: The Learning Business*. Princeton, NJ: Carnegie Foundation for the Advancement of Teaching.

Feldman, J. M. (1981). Beyond attribution theory: cognitive processes in performance appraisal. *Journal of Applied Psychology, 66*, 127–148.

Forbes, J. B. (1987). Early intraorganizational mobility: patterns and influences. *Academy of Management Journal, 30*(1), 110–125.

Freeman, R., and Wise, D. A. (1982). *The Youth Labor Market Problem*. Cambridge, MA: Harvard University Press.

Ginzberg, E. (1972). Toward a theory of occupational choice: a restatement. *Vocational Guidance Quarterly, 20*, 169–176.

Goldner, F. (1970). Success vs. failure: prior managerial perspectives. *Industrial Relations, 9*, 453–474.

Gould, R. L. (1978). *Transformations: Growth and Change in Adult Life*. New York: Simon & Schuster.

Griggs v. Duke Power Co., 1971.401 U.S. 424.

Hall, D. T. (1976). *Careers in Organizations*. Pacific Palisades, CA: Goodyear.

Kanter, R. M. (1977). *Men and Women of the Corporation*. New York: Basic Books.

Karabel, J., and McClelland, K. (1983). The effects of college rank on labor market outcomes. Paper presented at the Annual Meetings of the American Sociological Association, Detroit, September.

Kay, E. (1974). *The Crisis in Middle Management*, New York: American Management Association.

Kellogg, M. (1972). *Career Management*. New York: Amacom.

Langer, E. J. (1978). Rethinking the role of thought in social interaction. In J. H. Harvey, W. J. Ickes, and R. F. Kidd (eds.), *New Directions in Attribution Research*, Vol. 2. Hillsdale, NJ: Erlbaum.

Lawrence, B. S. (1980). The myth of the midlife crisis. *Sloan Management Review, 21*(4), 35–49.

Lawrence, B. S. (1983). The age grading of managerial careers in work organizations. Ph.D. dissertation. Sloan School of Management, MIT, Cambridge, MA.

Lawrence, B. S. (1984). Age grading: the implicit organizational timetable. *Journal of Occupational Behaviour, 5*, 23–35.

Lawrence, B. S. (1987). An organizational theory of age effects. In S. Bacharach and N. DiTomaso (eds.), *Research in the Sociology of Organizations*. Greenwich, CT: JAI.

Levinson, D. J. (1978). *The Seasons of a Man's Life*. New York: Knopf.

Levinson, H. (1969). On being a middle-aged manager. *Harvard Business Review, 47*, 51–60.

McArthur, L. Z., and Post, D. I. (1977). Figural emphasis and person perception. *Journal of Experimental Social Psychology, 13*, 520–535.

McGinnis, R. (1968). A stochastic model of social mobility. *American Sociological Review, 33*, 712–722.

March, J. C., and March, J. G. (1978). Performance sampling in social matches. *Administrative Science Quarterly, 23*, 434–453.

Martin, N. H., and Strauss, A. L. (1959). Patterns of mobility within industrial organizations. In W. L. Warner and N. H. Martin (eds.), *Industrial Man*. New York: Harper & Row, pp. 85–101.

Milkovich, G. T., Anderson, J. C., and Greenhalgh, L. (1976). Organizational careers: environmental, organizational and individual determinants. In L. Dyer (ed.), *Careers in Organizations*. Ithaca, NY: School of Industrial and Labor Relations, pp. 17–30.

Miller, N. (1976). Career choice, job satisfaction and the truth behind the Peter principle. *Personnel, 53*, 4–19.

Mincer, J. (1974). *Schooling, Experience, and Earnings*. New York: National Bureau of Economic Research.

Miner, J. B., and Miner, M. G. (1985). *Personnel and Industrial Relations*. New York: Macmillan.

Neugarten, B., and Datan, N. (1973). Sociological perspective on the life cycle. In P. B. Baltes and K. W. Schaie (eds.), *Life Span Developmental Psychology: Personality and Socialization.* New York: Academic, pp. 53–69.

Nisbett, R. E., and Wilson, T. D. (1977). Telling more than we can know: verbal reports on mental processes. *Psychological Review, 84,* 231–259.

Nystrom, P. C. (1981). Designing jobs and assigning employees. In P. C. Nystrom and W. H. Starbuck (eds.), *Handbook of Organizational Design,* Vol. 2. New York: Oxford University Press, pp. 272–301.

Rosenbaum, J. E. (1976). *Making Equality: The Hidden Curriculum of High School Tracking.* New York: Wiley-Interscience.

Rosenbaum, J. E. (1979a). Tournament mobility: career patterns in a corporation. *Administrative Science Quarterly, 24,* 220–241.

Rosenbaum, J. E. (1979b). Organizational career mobility: promotion chances in a corporation during periods of growth and contraction. *American Journal of Sociology, 85,* 21–48.

Rosenbaum, J. E. (1979c). Organizational careers and life cycle stages. Paper presented at the Annual Meetings of the American Sociological Association, Boston, August.

Rosenbaum, J. E. (1980a). Track misperceptions and frustrated college plans: an analysis of the effects of tracks and track perceptions in the National Longitudinal Survey. *Sociology of Education, 53* (April), 74–88.

Rosenbaum, J. E. (1980b). Social implications of educational grouping. In D. C. Berliner (ed.), *Annual Review of Research in Education.* Washington, DC: AERA, pp. 361–404.

Rosenbaum, J. E. (1981). Careers in a corporate hierarchy: a longitudinal analysis of earnings and level attainments. In D. J. Treiman and R.V. Robinson (eds.), *Research in Social Stratification and Mobility,* Vol. 1. Greenwich, CT: JAI, pp. 95–124.

Rosenbaum, J. E. (1984). *Career Mobility in a Corporate Hierarchy.* New York: Academic.

Rosenbaum, J. E. (1986). Institutional career structures and the social construction of ability. In J. G. Richardson (ed.), *Handbook of Theory and Research for the Sociology of Education.* New York: Greenwood, pp. 139–172.

Rosenbaum, J. E. (1987). Structural models of organizational careers: a critical review and new directions. In R. L. Breiger (ed.), *Social Mobility and Social Structure.* New York: Cambridge University Press.

Rosenbaum, J. E. (1989). Employees' perceptions of an organization career system. Unpublished paper. Department of Sociology, Northwestern University.

Schein, E. H. (1964). How to break-in the college graduate. *Harvard Business Review, 42,* 68–76.

Schein, E. H. (1978). *Career Dynamics: Matching Individual and Organizational Needs.* Reading, MA: Addison-Wesley.

Sennett, R., and Cobb, J. (1972). *Hidden Injuries of Class.* New York: Random House.

Shaeffer, R. (1972). *Staffing Systems: Managerial and Professional Jobs.* New York: Conference Board.

Shank, R., and Abelson, R. P. (1977). *Scripts, Plans, Goals, and Understanding,* Hillsdale, NJ: Erlbaum.

Sheehy, G. (1976). *Passages: Predictable Crises of Adult Life.* New York: Bantam.

Shrank, H. T., and Waring, J. M. (1983). Aging and work organizatons. In M. Riley, B. Hess, and K. Bond (eds.), *Aging in Society: Selected Reviews of Recent Research.* Hillsdale, NJ: Erlbaum, pp. 53–69.

Slocum, W. (1974). *Occupational Careers.* Chicago: Aldine.

Sofer, C. (1970). *Men in Mid-Career.* London: Cambridge University Press.

Sonnenfeld, J. A. (1984). *Managing Career Systems: Channeling the Flow of Executive Careers.* Homewood, Ill: Irwin.

Sørensen, A. B. (1975). The structure of intragenerational mobility. *American Sociological Review, 40,* 456–471.

Spence, A. M. (1974). *Market Signaling: Information Transfer in Hiring and Related Processes.* Cambridge, MA: Harvard University Press.

Spilerman, S. (1977). Careers, labor market structure, and socioeconomic achievement. *American Journal of Sociology, 83,* 551–593.

Stewman, S., and Konda, S. L. (1983). Careers and organizational labor markets: demographic models of organizational behavior. *American Journal of Sociology, 88,* 637–685.

Stiglitz, J. E. (1975). The theory of "screening," education, and the distribution of income. *American Economic Review, 65,* 283–300.

Strong, E. K., Jr. (1943). *Vocational Interests of Men and Women.* Stanford, CA: Stanford University Press.

Taylor, S. F., and Fiske, S. T. (1978). Salience, attention, and attributions: top of the head phenomena. In L. Berkowitz (ed.), *Advances in Experimental Social Psychology,* Vol. 11. New York: Academic.

Vaillant, G. E. (1977). *Adaptation to Life.* Boston: Little, Brown.

Vroom, V. H., and MacCrimmon, K. R. (1968). Toward a stochastic model of managerial careers. *Administrative Science Quarterly, 13,* 26–46.

Waldman, D. A., and Avolio, B. J. (1986). A meta-analysis of age differences in job performance. *Journal of Applied Psychology, 71*(1), 33–38.

Wanous, J. P. (1975). Realistic job previews for organizational recruitment. *Personnel, 52* (April), 50–60.

Webber, R. A. (1976). Career problems of young managers. *California Management Review, 18,* 19–33.

White, H. C. (1970). *Chains of Opportunity.* Cambridge, MA: Harvard University Press.

Williamson, O. 1975. *Markets and Hierarchies.* New York: Free Press.

17 Blue-collar careers: meaning and choice in a world of constraints

ROBERT J. THOMAS

> We all have skills. Whether we use them in this plant is the question.
>
> *Auto worker quoted by R. J. Thomas 1988*

Should we bother with blue-collar careers?

Answer 1: No. Blue-collar workers don't have careers, they have jobs. Jobs involve limited tasks and responsibilities. Jobs tend not to be connected to an ascending staircase (i.e., as in the normative model). At best, they make sense as "work histories," not as careers like professionals or managers have.

Answer 2: Yes. But toss out the normative, achievement-oriented model of careers. Develop instead an inclusive perspective that transcends the color of the collar and, in the process, seeks similarity in work experience over time while helping to explain differences. Insert an objective definition or a set of dimensions that allow for horizontal as well as vertical mobility, that contrast externally defined tasks or responsibilities with internally generated rationales for a history of jobs, and that introduce parallel sequences, like adult development, life cycles, or family stages.

It is tempting to go with the first answer and be done with the topic. After all, despite the persistent theme of human resource development in the management literature, few organizations subscribe in practice to the idea that low-level, non-supervisory employees have or even want careers. Certainly most organizations provide reasonably clear steps or gradations in jobs that can be construed as paths of upward mobility. But quite often the training necessary for climbing the organizational staircase is inadequate or inaccessible, external credentialing is required, or some other obstacle (e.g., family, ability, individual preference) intervenes to make the staircase look like a series of cliffs each separated by a deep crevasse.

Yet, accepting that answer would only confirm an incorrect assumption: The only work experiences and sequences worth examining are vertical ones. Thus, the second answer is tempting.

The second answer has the merit of including a host of intervening variables to explain why not all careers are vertical and why all work experiences over time should be viewed as careers. For example, Van Maanen and Schein (1977) include as careers horizontal progressions from less central to more central positions in an organizational stratum or function. Van Maanen and Barley (1984) suggest that "occupational communities" offer an alternative to organizationally mandated hierarchies for acquiring a sense of status and achievement. They add that even in the absence of opportunities to construct occupational communities, blue-collar workers can fashion "themes" around the most boring work and thus

354

make sense of (or at least accommodate themselves to) careers that are neither particularly vertical nor horizontal.

The disadvantage of this approach is that it hollows out the core concept. If anything is a career, we must either establish a descriptive taxonomy of careers – vertical, horizontal, stagnant, plateaued, cyclical, parabolic – or dispense with the term. While the latter option might displease the reader, it is not altogether unattractive.

Though lacking the courage to junk the concept (at this point at least), I will suggest that there is a third answer. We *should* bother with the concept of a blue-collar career for two reasons. First, in contrast to what the normative concept of a career implies, blue-collar workers do indeed accumulate skills (general and specific) over time and are concerned about the meaning of their work experiences. Yet, many make sense of their work experiences in ways that are undetectable if normative criteria are employed. Instrumental attitudes toward work (i.e., work as a means to other ends), work as a game or contest, investment in the social relationships that work provides, and/or turning work into a form of self-expression will be identified as ways in which people adjust themselves to the realities of restricted opportunities. In this regard, I advocate borrowing from the second answer to amend the first.

Second, in order to avoid the indeterminacy of the second answer, we must place blue-collar careers in a context. The context I propose emphasizes the interplay between (1) societies and organizations as a structure of positions into which individuals are inserted and out of which identifiable social classes (and, by extension, classes of careers) are formed and (2) the perceptions, strategies, and behaviors people fashion in response to the structures they encounter. Thus, I will suggest, blue-collar careers are real, identifiable experiences characterized by real and, from the perspective of the overall structure, necessary constraints to vertical mobility. As such, they are distinguishable from, but inextricably linked to, white-collar, managerial, and professional careers. But, in order to avoid the excessively deterministic tone of the structural perspective, I will suggest that blue-collar workers often adopt strategies for coping with limited opportunities similar to those in white-collar jobs whose careers have stopped moving upward. Thus, the auto worker trapped on the assembly line may seek engagement in the informal social system of the shopfloor in much the same fashion as the engineer who has plateaued (or *has been* plateaued) within a firm may divert his or her attention to office politics or the company softball team.

The arguments in this chapter will be presented in three parts. In Part 1, I will consider separately three levels for analyzing the processes that shape blue-collar work experiences over time. I will suggest that the *social milieu of class*, the *organizational arrangement of occupations*, and *labor market segmentation* singly and then jointly limit career opportunities and, in turn, influence individual and group behaviors in response to those career opportunities. In Part 2, I will present an argument for conceptualizing jobs as coordinates in a three-dimensional space defined by Part 1. I will then proceed to analyze worker behavior as a response to that structure. In particular, I will emphasize the importance of status hierarchies in the workplace in both limiting *and* engaging the energies of blue-collar workers. In Part 3, I will briefly consider the implications of these arguments for the future development of career theory.

PART 1: A MULTI-DIMENSIONAL VIEW OF BLUE-COLLAR
CAREERS

There is truth to the old saw that "where you begin determines where you'll end up." By contrast to what I will suggest is the individual-centered analysis of careers, I will begin with broader social and economic processes that structure career opportunities and experiences for blue-collar workers. I begin at some remove from the individual not because individual experiences or explanations are unimportant but (a) because "careers" are not simple aggregations of individual choices and (b) because individuals rarely command the resources to consciously and purposively fashion their careers at work. Starting from a structural perspective and moving toward individuals (i.e., their experiences and their methods for making sense of those experiences) necessarily orients the analysis toward limitation in choice, rather than structures being viewed as the product of aggregated choices. Yet, this starting point is critical for two reasons. First, much of the work that has defined the field of career theory has begun with the individual as the relevant unit of analysis – and subsequently aggregated across individual experiences to talk about career paths and career anchors (cf. Schein, 1978). As a consequence, choice (especially individual choice) has come to play a critical role in explaining how and why people end up doing what they do. External factors, such as family ties and roles, aging, and adult development processes, help cast careers as developmental phenomena, but they tend also to offer only passing reference to the social and economic structures that filter people into careers and constrain or delimit career opportunities over time. Even the useful analytical distinction between external and internal careers (Van Maanen and Schein, 1977) refers largely to the discrepancy between what organizations offer and what *individuals* value. The very ethnographic studies of work that have provided important insights about what individuals value have only rarely attempted to make linkages with social or economic processes *outside* the workplace. Thus, we may learn a great deal about the dynamics of work and informal organization in a given shop or office, but we fail to learn about how the political economy of the community, the company, or the industry shape the environment in which work and social relationships are carried out.

By contrast, I will emphasize the important filtering and delimiting roles played by social and economic processes, particularly as they provide a measure of stability and continuity in the construction of blue-collar careers.

Second, I want to urge a critical re-examination of theories that explain the employment strategies of blue-collar workers on the basis of *individual choices* spurred by *individual needs or preferences*. Choice has constituted an important variable in social sciences that start with (or seek to affirm) market-based models of societies and organizations (cf. Parsons, 1937). Market-based models basically argue that, in modern industrial systems based on marketized exchange of goods and services, neither traditional (e.g., property-based) nor class-based factors intervene in the distribution of opportunities (or rewards). For example, mobility within society must be based on some normally or randomly distributed characteristics, for example, intelligence, ambition, skill, dexterity. These characteristics can be either innate or acquired. If innate (such as physical strength, musical ability, aptitude with respect to some other activity), their presence need not be explained as a product of some social process; they simply *are*. If acquired (such as education, special skills acquired through training, or development of ambition), they are assumed to be available to *all* members of the group in question. This latter set of assumptions leads to the conclusion that the place of blue-collar workers (in organizations and in society) is a product of their lack of innate abilities and/or their choice(s) *not* to acquire socially or organizationally valued skills, certifications, and so on. If there does appear to be a non-random or skewed distribution of innate and achieved abilities, it must be explained from the point of view of either *biological, non-social and therefore ahistorical factors* (e.g., sex, race, individual psychology, genetic mishap) or *cultural, and/or historical factors* that influence people *not* to excel (e.g., the culture of poverty thesis). Thus, the traditional pyramid of society and of organizations (in terms of income, prestige, status, and power) is *legitimated* by the assumption of choice – the very thing that most needs to be explained.

Unsophisticated but popular interpretations of needs theories provide persuasive accompaniment to the market-based theories of choice (cf. Friedman and Friedman, 1982). Whereas market-based theories suggest "utility maximization" (which can include preference for home and family life, stability and security in employment as against "risk-taking," or power-oriented behavior) as a generic process that can explain the widely differing work histories of workers and managers, needs theories suggest that people employ different weighting schemes to help them choose when confronted by alternative work/career options. Thus, those with "lower-order" needs (safety, security, etc.) "choose" to focus on satisfying them via "jobs" (since jobs generally involve less responsibility, higher supervision, less direct connection between one's performance and the organization's well-being).

Viewed from the apex of the organizational/societal pyramid, therefore, the bottom appears to be populated by people whose existence and plans are conditioned by their fixation with basic needs, the origin of which is *psychological* (and thus usually not social) and *individual* (and thus not organizational). The process of personnel selection, so important in determining the future opportunities of employees, therefore is *constrained* by the needs and choices of employees and *ameliorative* in the sense that it serves to match human beings with tasks that make the most of their abilities.

In this chapter I place more emphasis on the role of externally imposed constraints on the experiences of blue-collar workers than I do on individual characteristics when referring to the process of choice. Three categories of external factors are relevant: the social milieu of class, the organizational structuring of jobs, and labor market segmentation. All three, I will argue, are related. Figure 17.1 broadly depicts the relationships with which I am concerned and the individual and group responses that issue from them (discussed in Part 2). In the following section I will indicate how they affect career shapes and possibilities and why it is necessary to use their points of overlap to explain the behaviors of blue-collar workers.

Social milieu of class

By contrast to the view of American society as an "open-class" system, a structural perspective from sociology seeks to explain the relative stability of income distributions and occupational structures. Different approaches to the study of in-

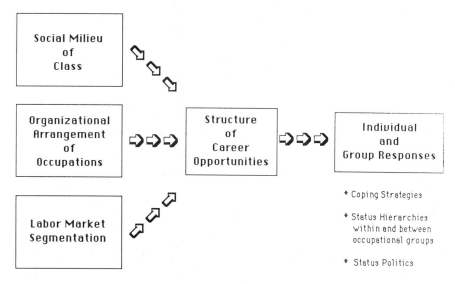

Figure 17.1. Schematic diagram of multi-dimensional framework

come and occupational stratification, of course, use different criteria for describing the nature of class. The most straightforward distinction between approaches can be built off Wright's (1981: 3–18) distinction between "gradational" and "relational" theories.

Gradational theories, following Max Weber's (1976) sociological translation of economic theory, emphasize markets as the principal devices for acquiring and distributing economic resources. People acquire skills and/or capital, sell or trade them in a marketplace, and the outcome of their market transactions is a hierarchy of income and economic resources. Grouping people by income level offers a rough approximation of a "class system." However, relationships between income classes are indirect at best: They are ranked vis-à-vis one another by means of their relationship to a common process (the market) and their relative possession of valued skills and resources. Thus, as the market mediates economic transactions, it also mediates relationships between different income groups.

Relational theories, following in broad terms Marx's political economy, emphasize relationships between classes based on the positions people occupy in the production of social and economic goods. The division of the population into those who own and/or control capital, equipment, and machinery and buy labor versus those who have only their labor to sell constitutes the most fundamental social and economic relationship and the relationship out of which social classes are formed. Differences in income are, at best, approximations of class. Thus, although levels of skill and/or education may offer some additional explanation or specification for the distribution of income, they are secondary to the ownership/nonownership of capital. More important in the analysis of blue-collar careers, these classes are inextricably bound: They presuppose one another. Those who sell their labor create the value(s) that materially support the owners of capital and their (managerial) staffs; working people create value and support those whose job it is to sustain the relationship, for example, managers and supervisors, as well as owners and executives.

The contrast between these two approaches would be ideological, at best, if it were not for their very different implications for the process of choice as it applies to work experiences over time. Gradational theories imply that open class systems are open by virtue of the availability of the various "escalators" for movement between classes. Education, for example, constitutes an essential prerequisite for social and economic movement, especially as it tends to be positively valued as a device for enhancing an individual's "marketability." Opportunity to partake of universal education is a key ingredient in the market-based, gradational models and, in like fashion, decisions to forego education also represent "choices" made.

Relational theories, however, tend to discount the escalator effect of education. From this perspective the universal availability of education (e.g., through a public educational system) does not necessarily imply equality of educational opportunity (cf. Bowles and Gintis, 1977; Ryan 1974; Spaeth, 1976; Willis, 1981). Enormous variations in the quality as well as the content of education exist within the public system, and the gulf between public and private educational systems further undermines the role played by education in social and economic mobility. The continued use of informal tracking systems in high schools as well as the uneven distribution of "cultural capital" (e.g., access to theater, the arts, classic literature) between school districts in different areas results in different *classes* of students and, with them, different *classes* of career/employment options for students (Jencks, et al., 1972, 1979). To put it simply, the relational approach argues that there is working-class education and non-working-class education.

Beyond the contribution of education to the process of stratification, gradational and relational theories differ on the broader role of class milieu in preparing for a life of work. By class milieu, I refer to the network of social and cultural institutions that characterize people of different occupational, educational, and income levels. Though gradational theories acknowledge differences in culture and experience between, for example, the poor, the middle class, and the wealthy, those experiences are only separated by a matter of time and achievement. That is, a black woman raised in an inner-city tenement or an immigrant can, with education, effort, and time, acquire the style, the appearance, and the mannerisms of wealthy suburbanites. The process of acculturation may take more than one generation, but it is nonetheless possible. The relational theories, while acknowledging the slim possibilities for individual upward mobility, emphasize the essential stability of the distinct classes themselves and the generally low level of true social and economic mobility (cf. Domhoff, 1967; Hauser, et al., 1975; Wright, 1981, 1985). Culture and class are tightly linked – both through external constraints like those associated with stratification of educational opportunity and educational quality and through internal processes, for example, the different worldviews that develop in different social and cultural milieu (cf. Komarovsky, 1962; Sennett and Cobb, 1972; Willis, 1981; Sabel, 1982).

Rubin's (1976) study of working-class families illustrates the processes through which the social milieu reinforces class boundaries. Rubin's interviews reveal that many working-class men find themselves stuck in dead-end jobs, in organizational structures that do not yield to their (real or fantastic) desires for self-expression, and in economic positions in which the vagaries of business cycles (when combined with low or non-transferable skills) create the constant threat of job loss. Finding their desires for personal growth stifled by jobs that offer limited opportunity for creative activity and little incentive for personal invest-ment, many men seek to achieve a measure of authority, self-expression, and dominance in the home. Their frustration at work can contribute to negative behaviors at home: alcohol abuse, consumerism, family violence, and sexual dys-function. Low evaluations of husbands by wives are a product of husbands' strug-gles to earn enough to keep the family afloat and the fact that wives, as much as husbands, are propelled to measure husbands' performance in terms of their vision of the American dream.

Working-class women, including those who work outside the home, find them-selves trapped in a double sense: Household chores circumscribe their social in-teractions outside the home; and their low "social worth" is determined by the status of housewife and by their husband's economic and occupational fortunes (Hartmann, 1976; Oakley, 1976; Willis, 1981). Often their social experiences have been limited further by the fact of pregnancy – "getting caught" – at an early age and having to live with the consequences.

Working-class children, as Rubin and others (e.g., Steinitz and Solomon, 1986) have shown, often live in a world bounded by frustration and insecurity. The household environment – which can alternately demand subordinance on chil-dren's part or lay off on children the unreachable dreams of parents – can easily be oppressive. In an effort to "escape" the home, children engage in freedom-seeking behavior: getting jobs in order to make an indepenent living, street life, early sexual experimentation, alcohol, and substance abuse. "Getting caught" is one way in which the cycle is reproduced. Add to these the fact that working-class and poor neighborhood schools tend, disproportionately, to direct these chil-dren into trade schools (if any post-secondary education is recommended at all), and there is a clear link to inequalities in labor market "preparedness."

The net result of differences in class milieu is a process both of contracting choice and differential preparation for work. It is not to deny the possibility for "upward" social and economic mobility over the life cycle of an individual or a group, but, more importantly, it emphasizes an essential stability in class struc-ture. Thus, blue-collar careers are fashioned within an environment of constrained opportunities.

Organizational arrangement of occupations

A second factor that must be reckoned with in analyzing blue-collar careers is the arrangement of occupations within and between organizations. Simply put, choice in one's line of work is severely affected by the way organizations construct and link jobs. Despite the lure of craft or trade as a means to provide individual autonomy (cf. Chinoy, 1955), the growth of modern industry and the large-scale corporation has brought with it the dominance of organizations in the construction and arrangement of jobs (Piore and Sabel, 1984: ch. 2).

The growth of organizationally constructed occupations has been attributed to the necessity for large-scale business enterprises to render controllable and/or more efficient tasks formerly controlled by social groups (via guilds or fam-ilial structures) – or to arrange for the accomplishment of tasks brought about by new developments in product or process technology (cf. Bendix, 1974; Chandler, 1962; Clawson, 1980; Ginzberg, 1982; Hounshell, 1984; Noble, 1984; Pollard, 1960; Tausky, 1983). Implicit in this depiction is an alteration in the purpose that informs the organization of work: from the satisfaction of localized needs in a restricted economic environment to the satisfaction of organizational (shareholder, owner, corporate) needs in an environment of pervasive competition; from a "social" division of labor in which ties of custom and culture dominate the learning and practice of a craft to an "industrial" division of labor in which the owners of capital and equipment designate the methods and techniques of work (Marx, 1976: chs. 14 and 15); and from custom or trade understood as both a complete work activity and a communal status to occupation as "partial craft" with a looser connection to one's social standing in the community.

This "mass production" approach to the arrangement of work is not, of course, complete. Sinecures of craft-dominated production systems continue to exist even within the most rationalized of organizations (cf. Blauner, 1964; Piore and Sabel, 1984; Stinchcombe, 1959; Tausky, 1983). Yet, the fact that the bulk of jobs available to young people entering the labor market are "partial crafts" means that the arrangement of occupations within organizations will be crucial in determining the nature of their careers as blue-collar workers. Whether ladders or lines of occupations exist will be a central factor, independent of the ambitions any individual employee may have in confronting a life of work. Thus, the way in which organizations structure, arrange, and/or compartmentalize tasks into occupations constitutes an important constraint on the choices facing blue-collar workers.

To render these considerations more explicit, it is useful to contrast different explanations for why occupations are arranged the way they are. To do so, I again contrast the gradational (and market-based) theories with the relational approach. In the gradational scheme, organizations represent rational hierarchies of skill and responsibility. Akin to the open class system that surrounds them, strata within organizations are linked by reference to external measures – for example, education, skill, and ambition. Thus viewed, organizations are devices for accomplishing shared goals but characterized by the necessity for linking differentiated activities (i.e., organic activities). One's position in the organizational structure is largely determined by the skills, abilities, and ambitions one brings to bear. Though organizations will value (or evaluate) skills differently depending on the economic environment in which they operate, the presumption is that organizations must compete in the market for those skills (or, better put, the market for individuals with those skills). Thus, all who aspire to greater reward and/or responsibility are theoretically equal competitors for open positions. This competition applies at all levels within the organization, even when the prerequisites for mobility involve going outside the organization for the appropriate training or certification of expertise.

The relational approach, by contrast, emphasizes the centrality of occupations (i.e., partial crafts) and discontinuous ladders of skill and responsibility to the maintenance of organizational control (cf. Braverman, 1975; Edwards, 1979; Hill, 1981; Zimbalist, 1979). The very principle of fragmenting and rearranging craft into partial craft represents a process through which control for organizational leaders is made possible. The industrial division of labor represents less a revolution in favor of rationality in work organization than a displacement in power to control job content (and outcomes) in favor of those who own equipment and tools as against those who lack the resources to effectively and separately compete as producers. Lacking complete knowledge of the production process, blue-collar workers' activities are subject to managerial control. The "de-skilling" of the work process renders the activities of workers controllable – and thereby rational from the perspective of those whose job it is to manage complex operations. Thus, occupations are the product of managerial efforts to render predictable the efforts of producers.

From this perspective, blue-collar work is most rational when it effectively facilitates the translation of labor as a potential to work into products. Given that all any employer purchases when he/she hires someone is that person's potential to work, then the primordial managerial problem is turning that potential effort into real outcomes, be they auto parts or typewritten letters. By rendering tasks more routine and predictable, outcomes should be more predictable and measurable (against, e.g., a theoretical maximum).

The net result for blue-collar workers, particularly in large-scale manufacturing enterprises, is a varied array of occupations, the bulk of which are characterized by a low level of skill and discretion. Jobs may be linked by sequence or by similarity of task, but frequently they are divided both vertically and horizontally. Levels of skill may be evident within an organizational hierarchy, but even then they are often loosely linked. For example, mastering the skills associated with mounting a carburetor on an engine manifold does not lead implicitly (or explicitly) to the more skilled job of tuning the carburetor on a finished engine. Indeed, mounting a carburetor bears greater resemblance to installing a headlight.

The flattening of skill hierarchies reduces opportunities for upward mobility in terms of skill and, quite often, pay. This process is exacerbated by the tendency of most organizations to limit investments in the training that might foster a more articulated skill hierarchy. As Nollen (1984) has shown, the corporate approach to training has tended to be cyclical, at best. American companies, by contrast to the Japanese for example (cf. Cole, 1979; Thomas and Shimada, 1983), tend (1) to invest in training for blue-collar workers during periods of rapid technological change and (2) quite often invest only in those segments of the labor force (i.e., maintenance workers) that are most skilled to begin with. The hesitancy to invest derives from what the relational approach points to as a desire on the part of management to reduce uncertainty through the replacement of manual labor with machines (cf. Noble, 1984; Shaiken, 1985). Additional concern derives from the difficulty of accounting for the contributions of training to the economic performance of the firm. Lacking more generally is a belief that investment in human resources affects the organization's competitiveness, especially in an environment in which competitors are perceived to gain advantage through the use of labor-saving technology.

To suggest that most business organizations do not prize articulated promotional ladders for blue-collar workers is not to suggest that managers have been alone in creating the limited opportunity structures. American industrial unions, particularly those in the basic industries, have pursued a policy of "job control" unionism (Dunlop 1948) aimed at maximizing job security and worker protection from arbitrary management action regarding labor allocation. The emphasis on seniority, flat wage structures, and detailed job classifications provides greater security and solidarity to the membership, but, at the same time, it limits opportunities for the construction of clear-cut promotion ladders. Job classes, for the purposes of administering a complex seniority system, emphasize the importance of non-skill factors (such as shift preferences and horizontal distinctions between jobs) and thus orient workers and managers alike to bureaucratic regulations rather than tightly linked steps in skill acquisition.

Equally important, the union emphasis on solidarity in its membership buttresses a well-developed barrier between hourly, blue-collar work and salaried managerial positions. The development of a professional managerial group, already well entrenched in the opening decades of the 1920s (cf. Bendix, 1974; Chandler, 1962, 1977), raised obstacles to the simple movement of organizational members upward in the hierarchy of status and power. Emphasis on the scientific basis of managerial practice – evidenced in the popularity of that segment of Frederick Taylor's ideas – created a clear distinction between those who conceived production plans and those who executed them. And, while it was possible in the 1920s for an employee to cross the divide between labor and management, the construction of various criteria for management status – particularly high school and then college diplomas – have reduced the possibility for such transitions today. Unions contributed to the process by insisting that the line between hourly and salaried status was a hostile border: Leaving the ranks of blue-collar work was, at best, to be construed as leaving a community of peers and, at worst, as a denunciation of the union itself.

Thus, the ways in which organizations construct and arrange occupations and the role unions have played in circumscribing them leave the bulk of blue-collar workers a fairly narrow range of alternative careers among which to choose. Choosing a "line of work" does not necessarily carry with it a set of clear expectations about mobility and accumulation of skills and status. Choosing an organization in which to work offers no guarantees about being able to move up as a result of dedicated effort. And, crossing the line between labor and management, although perhaps providing some hope of increased reward and status, carries with it the necessity of severing social ties with the group from which one came.

Thus, instead of viewing organizations as simple pyramids of skill and responsibility, the relational approach emphasizes the rather formidable boundaries between blue-collar and white-collar work and between occupation (or partial craft) and craft. It emphasizes the primordial division between classes of career and, at the same time, provides a different perspective on the principles guiding the arrangement of blue-collar occupations: Occupations are partial crafts because their occupants must be controlled if organizational goals are to be achieved.

Segmentation of labor markets

In recent years, labor market theory has been expanded in an attempt to develop explanations for a number of problems long ignored by neoclassical economics: for example, the persistence of poverty, differential levels and types of employment for different population groups (especially blacks, women, and Hispanics), the creation of different career trajectories for members of the traditional working class, and variation in employment opportunities and jobs by organizational type (Gordon, 1972). Averitt (1968) and Bluestone (1970) proposed dual and tripartite models of economic organization, claiming that the division of the economy into different kinds of enterprises – differentiated along the lines of size, market share, and capitalization – had resulted in radically different opportunity structures for workers (as represented in job structures in different types of organizations). They counterposed, for example, the relative affluence of workers in heavily unionized, large-scale firms with the low wages and unprotected positions of workers employed by less substantial, nonunion enterprises.

Doeringer and Piore (1975), looking much more closely at the employment and training practices developed by those large-scale firms, argued that the traditional notions of labor market operation had been undercut by the appearance of a division between internal and external labor markets. Internal labor markets, they contended, had evolved within many large enterprises, especially those located in basic industries like steel and auto, into administrative structures designed to shelter firms from the vagaries of external labor market operation (especially the difficulty of acquiring skilled labor in the external labor market), and to provide workers with a measure of protection from competition with outside labor market participants. They further noted that internal labor markets resulted from the construction of durable relationships between management and organized labor, that is, collective bargaining seniority systems had pushed for the creation of bureaucratic rules and procedures for the allocation of union members into slots within the organization. The upshot of internal labor market construction was the creation of barriers to entry into some of the more highly rewarded occupations in the overall economy. Entry-level positions were concentrated at the lower ranks of the blue-collar hierarchy, and reward systems (especially non-wage benefits such as insurance and pensions) were oriented toward maximizing stability in the individual firm's labor force.

Later research has resulted in a more elaborate theoretical approach to the relationship between economic organizations and labor markets. "Dual labor market" and "segmented labor market" theories (cf. Gordon, Edwards, and Reich, 1982; Edwards, 1979, for the most detailed models) draw attention to the relationship between economic segmentation among firms, segmentation in labor markets, and divisions within the working class. The thrust of their arguments can be summarized in the following propositions:

1. Since the 1920s, the economy has been increasingly segmented into two categories of firm: *core* (large-scale, highly capitalized and oligopolistic) enterprises and *peripheral* (small-scale, less capitalized and competitive) enterprises.

2. The dominant position of core enterprises has been brought about in part by their increasing market shares and in part by their development of more and more productive forms of work organization.

3. The introduction of more productive forms of work organization resulted in higher levels of concentration of workers in large, mechanized firms, a greater capacity on the part of those workers to view themselves as a collectivity, and the expression of common worker interests in the form of unions and union contracts.

4.   The size and scale of core enterprises, combined with the increasing militance of workers, necessitated the development of new forms of control within those organizations. Traditional mechanisms of control (manifested in paternalism, strong foremen, and economic coercion) were undermined by the increasing size and complexity of the organizations and had to be replaced (in the post–World War II era) by technical forms of control (manifested in the greater subdivision of tasks and machine pacing coupled with wage increases tied to higher productivity).

5.   The increasingly organization-specific character of many occupations within the core enterprises, the higher level of educational training (or credentialing) required to fill white-collar positions, and the creation of new, service-oriented enterprises, required not only new techniques for management but also new forms of control over employees – resulting in the rise of "bureauractic" control systems, organized principally around the administrative structures for labor allocation Doeringer and Piore refer to as internal labor markets.

6.   These factors in combination have resulted in an economic landscape characterized by one hill and a number of hillocks – with core enterprises constituting the hill in terms of their economic leverage, their share of the labor force, and their impact on the economy, and peripheral firms constituting the hillocks, with their lesser levels of organizational complexity, fewer employees, lesser technological sophistication, and less extensive job opportunities.

Accompanying economic segmentation has been a roughly parallel segmentation of labor markets (depicted in Figure 17.2). The segmentation of organizations into core and peripheral enterprises brings with it rather substantial differences in occupational structures and employment opportunities. Core firms, while employing more advanced technologies of production, also offer greater employment stability and security, higher wages, and, to some extent, more extensive opportunities for upward occupational mobility for blue-collar workers – though the latter may occur more through the proliferation of titles than an articulation of skill "steps" in a job ladder. Core enterprises are more likely to employ internal labor market procedures for allocating labor and filling vacancies. Peripheral enterprises, by contrast, rely extensively on external labor markets for employees and are pressed, by virtue of operating in far more competitive environments, to economize on investments in labor. Thus, they seek to tap labor markets in which they do not have to compete with core enterprises in terms of wages, benefits or employment security. Not surprisingly, they must also economize in the techniques of production, relying on intensive but low-cost, low-skilled labor as a substitute for capital equipment and higher-cost labor.

In broad terms, labor markets are segmented two ways: by skill level (to be discussed later) and by enterprise. The notion of a massive and relatively undifferentiated market for labor – central to the gradational perspective – is replaced by a hierarchy of markets, labor needs, and employment opportunities. Being located in one market or another, or skill level within a market, will have serious consequences for an individual's work experiences over time. Likewise, returning to the issue of groups *created* by similarities in position and experience, the nature

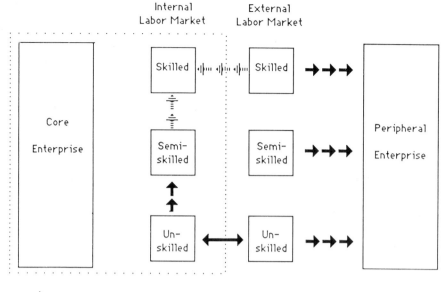

Figure 17.2. Segmentation of labor markets and organizations

of group interaction will be directly influenced by skill level, organization type, and market position.

PART 2: MAKING SENSE OF CAREERS AND JOBS

Within the framework developed to this point, a distinction has been made between three factors that affect blue-collar careers: social milieu of class, organizational structures, and labor market segmentation. Jobs exist at the intersection of those factors: That is, jobs are coordinates in that three-dimensional space. Although an individual may, in changing jobs, move out of one plane into another, the tendency is for an individual to occupy adjacent jobs on a line within a single plane. Moving between planes generally requires a significant change in *qualification* (e.g., from semi-skilled to skilled work), in *organization* (e.g., from a small firm with few opportunities for accumulation of skill to a larger one with a more articulated skill ladder), or in *labor market position* (e.g., from a labor market with an excess supply of competitors to a shortage of competitors).

Using jobs as coordinates in a three-dimensional space, it is possible then to discuss careers (as a sequence of jobs over time) for blue-collar workers and the ways in which career behaviors are structured. In Table 17.1 I use the job types discussed earlier in combination with the presence or absence of internal labor

Table 17.1. *Career opportunities in relation to skill level, organization type, and labor market structure*

Job type	Core enterprise Internal labor market	Peripheral enterprise: no internal labor market
Unskilled	Low potential for movement into semi-skilled job, or Moderate potential for movement between unskilled jobs	Dead-end
Semi-skilled	Low to moderate potential for upward movement into skilled job, or Moderate potential for movement between semi-skilled jobs	Low to moderate potential for movement into skilled job, or Dead-end
Skilled	Moderate to high potential for movement into lower management, or Lateral movement into equivalent job in another firm	Low to moderate potential for movement into lower management, or Lateral movement into equivalent job in another firm

markets (a surrogate for organizational structure) to depict the kinds of opportunity structures commonly available to blue-collar workers.

Looking across the columns in Table 17.1, it is clear that, in theory at least, the opportunities for some movement up a hierarchy of skill, reward, and/or responsibility are more likely in an internal labor market (ILM) setting than in a non-internal labor market setting. Yet, the existence of an ILM is no necessary guarantee that opportunities will be available, especially as regards entry-level positions. Comparing down the columns, opportunities for vertical movement are greater for those with greater skills. The volume of opportunities is likely to be greater and of two types: into blue-collar positions of greater skill/reward or into lower levels of management. Thus, we get three general types of career: dead-end/low opportunity for advancement (unskilled in ILM, unskilled and semi-skilled in non-ILM), moderate opportunity for advancement (semi-skilled in ILM and skilled in non-ILM), and a high opportunity for advancement (skilled in ILM).

Making sense of constrained opportunities

I will now argue that, following the relational perspective, the constraints on opportunities for advancement and self-expression through work require blue-collar workers to make sense of careers in ways that are quite often tangential to those of the organizations that employ them. That is, incompleteness in work activities, limited visions of the relationship between one's work and overall organizational products or goals, and limited returns on investment in one's job all create the objective conditions for indifference and alienation. These outcomes are not simply the product of an inalterable structure of technology or market influence but are instead systemic, that is, part and parcel of an economic system that is fueled by private and restricted ownership of the means of production. The boundaries constructed between blue-collar and managerial positions may be legitimated by means of educational criteria and the demand for technical knowledge, but the primordial task of management remains the organization and control of the activities of blue-collar workers.

Yet, by contrast to those proponents of the relational perspective who argue that alienation can or will lead to resistance to managerial control or revolutionary activity (cf. Braverman, 1975, or Edwards, 1979), I will argue that alienation or rejection is only one way in which workers respond to the limitations inherent in blue-collar careers. More commonly, blue-collar workers cope with their situations by focusing on status hierarchies in the workplace (i.e., positions of esteem or discretion vis-à-vis other blue-collar workers) or on goals to be achieved through work, rather than in work. An activity common to both coping strategies, however, is the transformation of work into a form of contest, involving other workers, managers, or both.

Opportunity structures and coping strategies

In a setting offering limited opportunities for advancement in terms of skill, reward, or responsibility, blue-collar workers must develop coping strategies with which to make sense of their situation. Unskilled workers in dead-end jobs, the most clear-cut case, are bounded by a lack of incentive to invest in their jobs. Desires to earn more or to acquire greater skills are often tempered by perceived opportunity costs: to wit, the costs associated with moving between organizations in search of training programs; the costs of lost income and their impact on other, often familial, responsibilities; and the chances for securing better employment in a labor market with many potential competitors. The perceived costs, not surprisingly, increase with age and familial responsibilities. Paradoxically, the costs associated with leaving a dead-end job in an internal labor market setting may in fact be higher than leaving a similar job in a non-ILM setting: The generally higher pay and more extensive benefits associated with ILMs raise the stakes for leaving a dead-end job.

In a setting offering moderate opportunities for advancement, other obstacles may exist. As Doeringer and Piore (1975) point out, the semi-skilled worker may find him or herself frozen in place by virtue of discontinuities in what would otherwise appear to be linked jobs. For example, bureaucratic boundaries between semi-skilled and skilled jobs are often buttressed by extensive qualifications criteria – such as apprenticeships involving long periods of training and reduction in seniority levels (e.g., having to start the seniority clock over if one is to move to a skilled position). Unless a shift to a skilled trades apprenticeship is made early in one's career, the costs associated with that shift may prove great enough to preclude the move.

The other avenue for advancement, into lower-level management (quite often to the position of first-level production supervisor) carries with it important risks. They involve abandonment of a workplace social network built around an important commonality in status – becoming part of a very different milieu. The costs associated with such a move can be great: loss of intimacy in dealing with former workmates, coping with enormous role conflict, and facing the relatively higher levels of stress in return for low chances of advancement beyond a supervisor's position (especially given the credentialization of management). For skilled workers, as Sabel (1982: ch. 3) argues persuasively, the choice is acute: Many pride themselves on having the ability to conceive and execute intricate tasks and treasure the responsibilities that entails; yet, occupying a purely supervisory position strips the skilled worker of his or her ability to directly participate in the practice of craft. Thus, for skilled workers at least, the appeal of higher pay and responsibility can be effectively muted by the loss of opportunity to practice (demonstrate) mastery of one's craft.

Faced with a future of work in which opportunities/incentives for advancement in an organizational hierarchy are limited or blocked, blue-collar workers must nonetheless make sense of their careers in ways which, if not psychologically self-destructive, are engaging in some fashion. Various coping strategies have been examined by researchers and are worth reviewing here.

Instrumentalism. Quite simply, work becomes a means to other ends, such as material rewards, retirement, or greater opportunities for one's offspring. Levels of involvement in the work process and organizational goals decline with the realization that opportunities are low and/or costs of shifting are high (cf. Goldthorpe, Lockwood, Bechhoffer, and Platt, 1968; Kanter, 1977).

The instrumental approach explains how workers put up with dead-end jobs in general, but it requires a measure of elaboration. In particular, the broad notion of instrumentalism disguises other strategies for enduring limited opportunities, for example, the behavior of some workers who might otherwise be eligible for upward movement in skill or responsibility but who forsake those opportunities to protect a labor market position. Many writers in the past decade, for example, have identified the ways in which organizations segregate certain categories of workers (such as women) into specific strata of jobs (cf. Blau and Jusenius, 1976; Hartmann, 1976; Kanter, 1977; Thomas, 1985). The organizational advantages are relatively clear: If lower wages can be paid to a disadvantaged group of employees (and movement into the positions they occupy can be restricted by their identification with the low-status group), then those jobs can be protected from claims to higher wages or greater benefits. But, taking as an example the case of women factory workers in the internal labor market of a unionized auto company, another and not necessarily contradictory explanation emerges: Many women in low-skilled jobs hesitate to leave them even when opportunities arise because they risk losing the security associated with seniority. For women who must work to support a family, and act as homemaker as well, the risk associated with leaving a dead-end job is loss of security (seniority) in the job. Thus, an instrumental approach to work may also imply a set of responsibilities *external* to the job that preclude efforts at advancement even when opportunities are available.

Tourism. Another coping strategy, related to instrumentalism but involving movement between jobs at a given skill level rather than stability in a job, can be called "tourism." The term has been used by Pape (1964) to describe the job-changing behavior of nurses who seek diversity within an otherwise routinized job by changing work settings at various intervals. The term can, however, be used more broadly to characterize the careers of unskilled and semi-skilled workers who respond to the lack of opportunities for advancement in an organizational hierarchy by touring between jobs in search of diversity of experience. For workers in an ILM setting, this can involve availing oneself of the administrative procedures of the ILM to sample various jobs in an effort to alleviate the boredom that sets in with mastery of a restricted task. In research in the auto industry, I found considerable evidence of such shifting among unskilled and semi-skilled workers (cf. Thomas, 1988). Several workers explained it as the only alternative to boredom available within a setting where pay levels varied little.

For many workers in a non-ILM setting, similar strategies may develop, although the potential costs of organization changing are higher. Again, however, the general labor market position of unskilled and semi-skilled workers argues against such movement, that is, it is more difficult to sample jobs between organizations when there exists a greater stock of potential competitors for those positions in the external labor market. Nonetheless, touring between jobs represents a way in which skills can accumulate and, perhaps, be employed by a worker in ways that are more satisfying than simply turning a job into a means to satisfy other ends.

Cycles and games. Two other strategies for coping involve temporal dimensions to the work experience. In the absence of a relatively clear-cut trajectory to a career, people often focus their attention on the short- and medium-term events and relationships that characterize the work setting (cf. Van Maanen, 1977). One approach is temporal in nature, involving a pattern or web of activities that occurs within a set time period, whether a day, a week, a pay period, or a cycle of events over a longer interval. The other approach relates more to the social structure of the workplace, in particular a "struggle for place" within the status hierarchy of the workplace. Both approaches involve engagement in the job and the social organization of the workplace on their own terms, that is, in terms of what *is* going on not what *might be* going on.

In the absence of a visible set of steps in one's career ladder, or job ladder within an organization, or in one's work, cycles of activity become useful benchmarks for making sense of career, organization, and job. They can be measured in terms of days or weeks or months of service, pay periods (which culminate in one of the few visible rewards/rationales for doing one's job), or in time lines of activity within one's work setting (e.g., stock days, sale days, and inventory days in a retail establishment; new model introductions, re-tooling, and close-outs in an auto factory; or the cycle of the school year for bus drivers). Cycles of activity provide an approximation to variety in the work task that the job itself might not require and thus become a surrogate for other, more visible accomplishments. The acquisition of a five-year or a ten-year seniority pin (adorned with one or two diamond chips, respectively) are concrete manifestations of accomplishment for an airline mechanic who cannot otherwise point to anything he has produced over five or ten years. The creation of a time line to provide a benchmark to one's accomplishments can be a far shorter duration, as well. Roy's (1958) classic article on "banana time" notes that the construction of arbitrary events in an otherwise invariant environment helps engage people – establishing informal ceremonies and rituals that substitute for other accomplishments at work.

Another approach uses time as a central feature, but instead of time serving as a surrogate for accomplishment, time is instead something that itself must be overcome. Garson (1975), chronicling the responses of blue-collar workers to routinized jobs, notes that games are often highly creative constructs for "passing the time." Women working in jobs as diverse as fish fileting, lip-gloss manufacturing, and ping-pong paddle assembly alternately "race" through their work in an attempt to beat a personal record in a given task, "space out" or work with their eyes closed to see how much they can do without making a mistake, and converse with workmates (often against company policy) to make the time pass.

Games can, however, be far more important symbolic devices for dealing with the power structure at work. Reflecting on earlier studies of "restriction of output," Burawoy (1979) argues that games at work can constitute a terrain of contest between workers and managers. In the idiom of the machine shop, "making out" constituted a contest between workers and managers over the piece rates associated with various machining tasks. To make out was to master a given job and piece rate so that the rate could be made or beaten in a regular work shift. Assignments that were easily done failed to challenge machinists; likewise, rates that could not be met were abandoned as unacceptable. Finding the middle ground between challenges that are too small or too great involved negotiation between workers and lower levels of management. Although workers might defy organizational policy by building a "kitty" of completed pieces to be added to the next day's tally, they did not overtly defy the piece-rate practice; rather, they sought to carry on the game of making out with a fair set of rules. Low-level supervisors were occasionally induced to conspire with workers against higher management in order to alter, eliminate, or even subvert policies that rendered the rules for making out unfair or impossible to follow.

Games, thus constructed, involve much more than an effort on the part of workers to soldier or get something for nothing. Rather, games become devices for inserting challenge and therefore interest into otherwise meaningless chores. Games pass the time, but they also provide benchmarks of activity and a means by which to make sense of the work experience.

Status hierarchies at work

Even in the absence of a career marked by clearly defined ascending steps in an organizational or professional hierarchy, blue-collar workers both confront *and* create hierarchies that mediate the work experience. Status hierarchies can be broadly defined as distinctions in status and prestige within the social web of the workplace. They *confront* workers as levels of skill and authority imposed from the outside (e.g., by management) in the form of differentiated occupations and a stratified distribution of titles, rewards, and benefits. But, as suggested earlier, they need not be imposed only by management: Other groups, such as skilled trades sections with union backing, may impose apprenticeships and other devices designed to restrict access to a category of positions in either an internal or an external labor market. Status hierarchies can, however, also be *created* by workers as they evaluate the relative desirability and prestige of positions in the workplace. In some instances, worker evaluations parallel the status hierarchy imposed from the outside: Skill distinctions or differentiated levels of discretion and technical prowess may constitute the basis for according prestige to a ladder of positions or to individuals occupying those positions. Thus, the more experienced and/or capable co-workers will be accorded higher status in the social system of the workplace. In other instances, however, different yardsticks may be used: for example, perceived danger associated with different jobs (cf. Gouldner, 1954), willingness of individuals to resist or challenge managerial authority (Zimbalist, 1979), capacity to garner free time by circumventing management rules and regulations regarding performance of a job (Burawoy, 1979), or the ability to dispense favors or work-related benefits to co-workers with or without management involvement (Garson, 1975).

In both instances, status hierarchies in the workplace act to *engage* blue-collar workers in a set of pursuits that can produce valued outcomes even in the absence of the rewards associated with traditional notions of career. Although it is important to recognize that this "struggle for place," as Sabel terms it, can diminish the chances for unified worker opposition to a limited opportunity structure, it can also serve as the basis for worker resistance to managerial efforts to alter the distribution of tasks and responsibilities. By contrast to the relational perspective that foresees a long-term diminution of distinctions among categories of workers through the process of de-skilling and with that process the forging of a uniform worldview among workers, I draw attention to the way distinctions are created by *workers* and made the object of contest. And, by contrast to the gradational perspective, I draw attention to the ways that status hierarchies at work can constitute important bases of resistance to the alleged technical rationality of managerial control.

Status politics and careers at work

In an effort to explain the varieties of workers' politics, Sabel (1982) introduced a very important set of distinctions in his concept of "careers at work." Careers at work constitute for Sabel the subjective response of workers to the objective conditions of production – the unfolding of an individual's worldview through a series of experiences at work over time.

To appreciate the multi-dimensionality of status politics, it is useful to consider each of the categories of blue-collar worker presented earlier, beginning with the skilled craftsman. First, becoming a craftsman involves a learning process in which the individual enters a community already stratified internally along the lines of prowess (Sabel, 1982: 138–177; Schrank, 1978; Thomas, 1985; Van Maanen and Barley, 1984). Apprentices are differentiated from journeymen and masters both in terms of time in the craft and in terms of knowledge, expertise and, indeed, creativity. Second, becoming a craftsman involves acquiring status vis-à-vis those who are not craftsmen. To some extent, craftsmen forge their privileged position by attempting to restrict the access of other workers to the trade (cf. Whyte, 1961; Bonacich, 1976). Lengthy apprenticeships and selective entry regulate the supply of craftsmen and , simultaneously, establish a discontinuity between craftsmen and others (Van Maanen and Barley, 1984). Creating and enforcing scarcity in the supply of craftsmen bolsters the position of craftsmen even within internal labor markets. Such activities also create the basis for contention between categories of blue-collar worker within the same organization (company *or* union). In the automobile industry (cf. Goode, 1976), for example, craftsmen are alternately reviled for their relatively greater influence in the union (e.g., their ability to veto a contract) and envied for their privileged position in the process of production (e.g., contractually forbidding other workers from doing routine maintenance and appearing to be less subjected to direct supervision because their jobs are not as narrowly defined or mechanically paced).

Third, becoming a craftsman involves acquiring status vis-à-vis those who are one's organizational superiors. By acquiring and protecting control over the content of work activities, craftsmen seek to insulate themselves from managerial interference. Insistence on the sanctity of time-honored traditions of craftsmanship represents a way to maximize individual discretion and autonomy in the face of management efforts to reduce dependency on this category of blue-collar worker. Thus, to the extent that craftsmen are capable of sustaining exclusiveness and control, they acquire a measure of *organizational* status – status bearing a resemblance to that of management in their ability to both conceive and execute tasks (cf. Blauner, 1964).

It is this very multi-dimensionality of status politics that, as Sabel points out, leads craftsmen to look upon non-craftsmen with a measure of disdain – akin to what Thompson (1968) characterized as the distinction between honorable and dishonorable labor in 19th-century Great Britain. But, it also leads them to fiercely resist co-optation by management in terms of the power structure of the industrial enterprise. Faced with challenges from "below" – that is, from non-skilled workers who wish access to control over work activities and discretion in the approach to one's work – craftsmen can act very conservatively and refuse to cooperate (cf. Thomas, 1988). Faced with managerial efforts to undercut craft control via new technology or even more flexible work practices (e.g., polyvalent skilling), craftsmen can exhibit great solidarity, occasionally framing their interests in terms of the "demise" of craftsmanship. Faced with broad challenges to the livelihood of both craft and non-craft workers – for example, full-scale factory automation or managerial demands for across-the-board concessions – craftsmen can join hands with all segments of blue-collar workers and characterize the process as class struggle.

For semi-skilled workers with plant or even process-specific skills, the struggle for place proceeds within more restricted confines but nonetheless engages workers in cross-cutting contests. Their position within an organizationally defined status hierarchy is far more contingent on external control of work activities; management specifies the technology in which workers are versed. Thus, as Sabel (1982) notes, their labor market position is far less secure than that of the craftsmen; managers may choose to substantially change the equipment and processes they employ and thus render redundant or obsolete the skills of machine operators. Yet, their contingent position does not preclude semi-skilled workers from seeking the status of craftsmen – through claims to special (though restricted) knowledge of how *their* machines behave – and thus challenging the positively valued position of the craftsmen in the status hierarchy of the workplace (Liker and Thomas, in press). Nor does it preclude them from seeking to distinguish themselves from unskilled workers, for example, in referring to assembly-line workers as robots or grunts.

As in the case of the skilled craftsmen, the multi-dimensionality of status politics may lead semi-skilled workers into different stances under different circumstances. When faced with the opportunity to acquire greater status by means of more discretion in work – as has occurred with the emphasis in some companies on a system of multi-skilling to replace job classifications – semi-skilled workers may forge temporary alliance with management to restrict the dominion of the skilled trades (cf. Parker, 1984). Faced with the possibility of skill obsolescence or de-skilling through new technology, they may make alliance against unskilled workers – particularly when the unskilled workers are new entrants in the labor market, such as blacks, women, or workers in non-unionized and/or rural environments (cf. Bonacich, 1976). Faced with a generalized challenge to job security, they may define class as the basis for solidarity, thus forsaking (perhaps only temporarily) the status hierarchy of the workplace as the central terrain of contest.

For unskilled workers, engagement in the broader status hierarchy of the workplace is determined by the extent to which the occupations they perform are linked to the acquisition of skills, for example, the chances of moving into semi-skilled or skilled positions. As Sabel (1982) suggests, they may aspire to a position of greater prestige and/or discretion (what Sabel refers to as the "would-be craftsmen"), but achieving those positions quite often involves overcoming *both* organization and group-imposed obstacles. Not having attempted to enter the trades at an early stage in their individual careers – or having been denied access by virtue of ethnic, gender, or racial exclusion – unskilled workers must adopt a strategy for coping with restricted opportunities. Strategies such as instrumentalism, tourism, and/or gaming have been mentioned already.

However, to suggest that coping strategies are necessary is not to imply that status hierarchies do not engage the energies of unskilled workers. Rather, it is to suggest that, to the extent that pursuit of status in the broader hierarchy of the workplace is limited, unskilled workers can become enmeshed in a far more immediate dimension of status politics: status in and among the body of unskilled workers. Industrial sociologists and ethnographers alike have provided an enormous literature on informal organization and interaction in a wide variety of workplaces. Many, particularly those concerned with the lived experience of blue-collar work, have emphasized the ways in which symbolic differences in status give meaning and continuity to what otherwise might appear to be highly routinized, undifferentiated, and unfulfilling jobs. Van Maanen's (1974) studies of police, Gouldner's (1954) comparison of mining and factory work, Whyte's (1962) research in restaurants, among others, point to the remarkably complex and engaging rituals and practices in which people who spend thousands of hours together participate. Terkel (1977) and Schrank (1978), in reflecting on the work lives of blue-collar employees, both point to the ties of friendship, familiarity, and reciprocal obligation that deter many blue-collar workers from seeking alternative and more rewarding jobs *and* that provide a measure of personal fulfillment in the absence of such opportunities.

The significance of status hierarchies at work can be demonstrated in two, admittedly personal, examples. One involved relationships among drivers working for a relatively small charter bus company in southern California. As a new (but experienced) bus driver, I was confronted by a status hierarchy based largely on length of employment. Despite the fact that hourly wage levels varied by only 10% between new and old employees, seniority was symbolically important for several reasons: it represented a kind of veteran status since the company's principal client was the city's court-ordered desegregation program; it represented endurance since the company's owners made a practice of demanding driving times in excess of FTC regulations; and it represented a form of progression since the senior drivers had worked their way from driving the oldest and most dilapidated equipment to the newest and most comfortable. As it turned out, four of the eight most senior, and higher status, employees were women. After a very short time in the job and notwithstanding my protestations to the contrary, I learned that I was considered a rookie among my fellow employees and would only improve my position in the bus yard through a demonstration of perseverance and humility. Before long, and against my better judgment, I found myself yearning for acceptance, coveting the new, shinier buses, and anxiously awaiting the arrival of someone lower on the totem pole than I. After a year of driving (and the accumulation of my own "war stories" and a less dilapidated bus), I could look with pride on my accomplishments and feel loss at leaving a position of some prestige among my peers.

The second example involves work in connection with a study of the industrialization of agriculture (Thomas, 1985) and further emphasizes the mediating effect of status hierarchies. As part of that research I spent time working as a lettuce harvester in a large agribusiness firm in California. The harvest crew I joined was composed of thirty workers distributed into the various stages of the harvest: cutting, plastic-wrapping, and packing lettuce heads in the field. As a newcomer, I was put to work as a cutter – someone who walked behind a large, mobile conveyor machine, stooped to cut the heads and placed them on the machine to be wrapped and packed by people who rode on the machine. Cutting was an onerous job – involving the equivalent of over a thousand toe-touches a day – and the wrapping and packing jobs looked luxurious by comparison. According to company policy, vacancies in the packer and wrapper positions were filled by seniority. However, as one fellow cutter found out much to his chagrin, much more than seniority was involved. When one of the wrappers failed to show up for work one day, this fellow climbed onto the wrapper's chair and began working. I noted several other workers stare at him and mutter under their breaths and assumed that he had broken the seniority policy. It was not until someone referred to him as a "queer" that I noticed that even though there were male and female cutters and packers, there were only female wrappers. The distribution of men and women in those jobs was not, as I had initially surmised, coincidental. Over time I came to learn that the wrapping jobs were considered the least strenuous of jobs in the harvest and were "given" to women by the men out of deference to their alleged frailty. When I finally did "move up" to a packer's job, I was made part of the crew's elite (as a man and as a packer) and took pride in looking down on the others.

Both these examples, circumscribed as they are, nonetheless point to the ways in which status hierarchies in even the least challenging work environment provide channels of accomplishment. The accomplishments may be seen as trivial when viewed from the outside (or from within an air-conditioned office), but they do have meaning to those inserted into the complex of social relationships that exist at work. Those relationships engage and, to a considerable extent, structure the experiences of blue-collar workers – even to the point of creating informal norms and allegiances that simultaneously *shield* workers from organizational superiors (as in the case of output restriction or gaming) and *cement* workers into jobs that offer few if any intrinsic opportunities for personal growth or intellectual development.

PART 3: CONCLUSIONS AND IMPLICATIONS FOR CAREER
THEORY

Through the course of this chapter I have attempted to demonstrate the utility of a multi-dimensional framework for analyzing blue-collar careers. Central to this project is an appreciation for the integrity of each level of analysis – social and economic, organizational, group, and individual – alongside an effort to integrate levels into a relatively coherent whole. The framework has been illuminated through the use of contrasting theoretical perspectives – market-based/gradational and relational – with the hope that ideas in conflict may generate more insight than rote acceptance of one or another model.

The principal weakness of the framework proposed is its failure to specify an adequate means for fully integrating the levels of analysis into a coherent whole. This dilemma derives, at least in part, from the implicitly interactive process through which work experiences are shaped. Rather than rest with the assumption that careers are a matter of individual choice – as if choice were an entirely unrestricted process – I have suggested ways in which the range of choices and the content of the choices are themselves affected by factors well beyond individual control and, in some instances, beyond individual awareness. Conversely, the choices people make do come to constitute patterns of behavior and benchmarks for others faced with similar situations – a body of group experience and symbolism that serves as a guide to acceptable behavior and that may come to be regarded as "common sense" within a class of similarly situated people. In this regard, I have attempted to avoid representing blue-collar workers as passive objects manipulated by social structures and agents of social control.

Though the framework offers only vague beginnings for understanding the interaction between the various levels (from the structural to the individual), it should be sufficient to steer career theorists away from entirely individual-centered analyses. Obviously, this is not a new warning (cf. Van Maanen and Barley, 1984), but it is one that ought to be taken most seriously in light of new developments and research findings in several areas. The following are two of the most prominent.

New technologies and skill requirements. With the advent of microprocessor-controlled production equipment, greater attention is being paid to the kinds of skills needed by industrial organizations (cf. Davis and Taylor, 1976; Shaiken, 1985). Although few studies have detailed the impact of these new technologies on job structures (cf. Hunt and Hunt, 1983; Chen et al., 1984), two trends appear to be emerging: (1) The organizational importance of skilled labor, particularly in service and repair, will increase, and organizations and/or public agencies will have to provide adequate training opportunities and clear career incentives to provide an adequate supply of skilled workers; and (2) the rationalization of formerly semi-skilled work, including clerical and office workers in addition to the more traditional machine operator, will threaten to further divide unskilled from skilled employment.

Business strategy and labor relations will also directly affect the employment of new technologies and, by extension, the shape of work opportunities and career structures for blue-collar workers. Whether anyone (business, government, or union leaders) follow Piore and Sabel's (1984) advice and initiate a return to "craft" or small-batch custom production systems, the employment of flexible manufacturing systems will require substantial reform of the customs and practices of training and labor allocation. The cost of pursuing this strategy will include a re-examination of both the politics of status hierarchies among blue-collar workers as discussed in this chapter and a challenge to the bureaucratic stipulations of union contracts (Kochan, Katz, and McKersie, 1986).

Quality of work life and human resource management. Partially as a result of the perceived superiority of Japanese human resource management techniques and partially because of unresolved questions of worker alienation, quality of work life (QWL) programs have received considerable attention in recent years (cf. Kanter, 1983; Simmons and Mares, 1982, among a host of others). Yet, in the absence of adequate consideration of career-related concerns among blue-collar workers, many of the QWL efforts have floundered. As Thomas (1988) has shown, QWL programs rapidly devolve into very limited housekeeping endeavors when they fail to offer opportunities for workers to deepen their involvement in basic operating decisions and extend their influence beyond fragmented, specialized jobs. Even when autonomous work groups are fashioned to decentralize work responsibilities, they often stall when the authority to affect decision making does not match the increase in group and individual responsibilities (Parker, 1984).

In order for flexible, participative, and cooperative programs of production management to succeed, far greater attention has to be paid to the types of jobs being constructed and the kinds of challenges they pose to existing status hierarchies and management practices. Discontinuous skill ladders and turf battles between workers of different skill levels – as well as Taylorist managerial assumptions – will require substantial rethinking if QWL and human resource management practices are to be anything more than reincarnated (and short-lived) fads.

REFERENCES

Averitt, R. (1968). *The Dual Economy.* New York: Norton.
Bendix, R. (1974). *Work and Authority in Industry.* Berkeley: University of California Press.
Blau, F., and Jusenius, C. (1976). Economists' approaches to sex segregation in the labor Market. *Signs, 1,* 181–199.
Blauner, R. (1964). *Alienation and Freedom.* Chicago: University of Chicago Press.
Bluestone, B. (1970). The tripartite economy: labor markets and the working poor. *Poverty and Human Resources Abstracts, 5,* 15–35.
Bonacich, E. (1976). Advanced capitalism and black–white relations in the United States: a split labor-market interpretation. *American Journal of Sociology, 41,* 34–51.
Bowles, S., and Gintis, H. (1977). *Schooling in Capitalist Society.* New York: Basic Books.
Braverman, H. (1975). *Labor and Monopoly Capital.* New York: Monthly Review Press.
Burawoy, M. (1979). *Manufacturing Consent.* Chicago: University of Chicago Press.
Chandler, A. D. (1962). *Strategy and Structure.* Cambridge: MIT Press.
Chandler, A. D. (1977). *The Visible Hand.* Cambridge: Harvard University Press.
Chen, K., Eisley, J., Liker, J., Rothman, J., and Thomas, R. (1984). *Human Resource Development and New Technology in the Auto Industry.* Paris: OECD.
Chinoy, E. (1955). *Automobile Workers and The American Dream.* New York: Random House.
Clawson, D. (1980). *Bureaucracy and the Labor Process: The Transformation of U.S. Industry, 1900–1920.* New York: Monthly Review Press.
Cole, R. E. (1979). *Work, Mobility and Participation.* Berkeley: University of California.

Davis, L., and Taylor, J. C. (1976). Technology, organization and job structure. In R. Dubin (ed.), *Handbook of Work, Organization and Society*. Chicago: Rand McNally.

Doeringer, P., and Piore, M. (1975). *Internal Labor Markets and Manpower Analysis*. Lexington, MA: Heath.

Domhoff, G. W. (1967). *Who Rules America?* Englewood Cliffs, NJ: Prentice-Hall.

Dunlop, J. (1948). The development of labor organization. In R. Lester and J. Shister (eds.), *Insights into Labor Issues*. New York: Macmillan.

Edwards, R. C. (1979). *Contested Terrain*. New York: Basic Books.

Friedman, M., and Friedman, R. (1982). *Free to Choose*. New York: Avon.

Garson, B. (1975). *All the Livelong Day*. New York: Doubleday.

Ginzberg, E. (1982) The mechanization of work. In Scientific American, *The Mechanization of Work*. San Francisco: Freeman.

Goldthorpe, J., Lockwood, D., Bechhoffer, F., and Platt, J. (1968). *The Affluent Worker: Industrial Attitudes and Behavior*. Cambridge: Cambridge University Press.

Goode, B. (1976). The skilled trades: reflections? In B. J. Widick (ed.), *Auto Work and Its Discontents*. Baltimore: Johns Hopkins University Press.

Gordon, D., Edwards, R., and Reich, M. (1982). *Segmented Work, Divided Workers*. New York: Cambridge University Press.

Gordon, D. M. (1972). *Theories of Poverty and Underemployment*. Lexington, MA: Heath.

Gouldner, A. (1954). *Patterns of Industrial Bureaucracy*. Glencoe, IL: Free Press.

Hartmann, H. (1976). Capitalism, patriarchy and job segregation by sex. *Signs, 1*, 137–169.

Hauser, R., Dickinson, J., Travis, H. P., and Keffel, J. N. (1975). Structural changes in occupational mobility among men in the United States. *American Sociological Review, 40*, 585–598.

Hill, S. (1981). *Competition and Control*. Cambridge, MA: MIT Press.

Hounshell, D. (1984). *From the American System to Mass Production, 1900–1932*. Baltimore: Johns Hopkins University Press.

Hunt, H. A., and Hunt, T. (1983). *Human Resource Implications of Robotics*. Kalamazoo, MI: Upjohn Institute.

Jencks, C., Bartlett, S., Corcoran, M., Crouse, J., Eaglesfield, D., Jackson, G., McClelland, K., Mueser, P., Olneck, M., Schwartz, J., Ward, S., and Williams, J. (1979). *Who Gets Ahead? The Determinants of Economic Success in America*. New York: Basic Books.

Jencks, C., Smith, M., Acland, H., Bane, M., Cohen, D., Gintis, H., Heyns, B., and Michelson, S. (1972). *Inequality: A Reassessment of the Effect of Family and Schooling in America*. New York: Harper.

Kanter, R. (1977). *Men and Women of the Corporation*. New York: Basic Books.

Kanter, R. (1983). *The Change Masters*. New York: Simon & Schuster.

Kochan, T., Katz, H., and McKersie, R. (1986). *The Transformation of American Industrial Relations*. New York: Basic Books.

Komarovsky, M. (1962). *Blue Collar Marriage*. New York: Vintage.

Liker, J., and Thomas, R. J. (in press). The prospects for human resource development in the context of technological change. In D. F. Kocaglu (ed.), *Handbook of Technology Management*. New York: Wiley.

Marx, K. (1976). *Capital*, Vol. 1. New York: International Publishers.

Noble, D. (1984). *Forces of Production*. New York: Knopf.

Nollen, S. (1984). Changes in working patterns and their impact on education and training. Report presented to the Centre for Educational Research and Innovation, OECD, Paris.

Oakley, A. (1976). *Women's Work*. New York: Vintage.

Pape, R. (1964). Touristry: a type of occupational mobility. *Social Problems, 11*(4), 336–344.

Parker, M. (1984). *Inside the Circle: A Union Guide to QWL*. Boston: South End.

Parsons, T. (1937). *The Structure of Social Action*. New York: McGraw-Hill.

Piore, M., and Sabel, C. (1984). *The Second Industrial Divide*. New York: Basic Books.

Pollard, S. (1960). *The Genesis of Modern Management*. New York: Vintage.

Roy, D. (1958). Banana time: job satisfaction and informal interaction. *Human Organization, 18*(4), 158–168.

Rubin. L. (1976). *Worlds of Pain*. New York: Harper & Row.

Ryan, W. (1974). *Blaming the Victim*. New York: Avon.

Sabel, C. (1982). *Work and Politics: The Division of Labor in Industry.* New York: Cambridge University Press.

Schein, E. H. (1978). *Career Dynamics.* Reading, MA: Addison-Wesley.

Schrank, R. (1978). *Ten Thousand Working Days.* Cambridge, MA: MIT Press.

Sennett, R., and Cobb, J. (1972). *Hidden Injuries of Class.* New York: Vintage.

Shaiken, H. (1985). *Work Transformed.* New York: Holt, Rinehart and Winston.

Simmons, J., and Mares, W. (1982). *Working Together.* New York: Knopf.

Spaeth, J. (1976). Cognitive complexity: a dimension underlying the socioeconomic achievement process. In W. Sewell, R. Hauser, and D. Featherman (eds.), *Schooling and Achievement in American Society.* New York: Academic.

Steinitz, V., and Solomon, E. (1986). *Starting Out.* Philadelphia: Temple University Press.

Stinchcombe, A. (1959). Craft and bureaucratic administration of production. *Administrative Science Quarterly, 4,* 168–187.

Tausky, C. (1983). *Work and Society.* Itasca, IL: Peacock.

Terkel, S. (1977). *Working.* New York: Pantheon.

Thomas, R. J. (1985). *Citizenship, Gender and Work.* Berkeley: University of California Press.

Thomas, R. J. (1988). Participation and control: a shopfloor perspective on employee participation. In R. Magjuka (ed.), *Annual Review of Research in the Sociology of Organizations.* Greenwich, CT: JAI.

Thomas, R. J., and Shimada, H. (1983). Human resource management and labor relations. In R. Cole and T. Yakushiji (eds.), *U.S. and Japanese Auto Industries in Transition.* Ann Arbor, MI: Center for Japanese Studies.

Thompson, E. P. (1968). *The Making of the English Working Class.* New York: Vintage.

Van Maanen, J. (1974). Working the streets: a developmental view of police behavior. In H. Jacob (ed.), *The Potential for Reform of Criminal Justice.* Beverly Hills, CA: Sage, pp. 53–130.

Van Maanen, J. (1977). Experiencing organization: the meaning of careers and socialization. In J. Van Maanen (ed.), *Organizational Careers: Some New Perspectives.* New York: Wiley.

Van Maanen, J., and Barley, S. (1984). Occupational communities: culture and control in organizations. *Research in Organizational Behavior, 6,* 287–365.

Van Maanen, J., and Schein, E. (1977). Improving the quality of work life: career development. In J. R. Hackman and J. L. Suttle (eds.), *Improving Life at Work.* Santa Monica, CA: Goodyear, pp. 30–95.

Weber, M. (1976). *Economy and Society.* Berkeley: University of California Press.

Whyte, W. F. (1961). *Men at Work.* Homewood, IL: Dorsey.

Willis, P. (1981). *Learning to Labour.* New York: Columbia University Press.

Wright, E. O. (1981). *Class Structure and Income Determination.* New York: Academic.

Wright, E. O. (1985). *Classes.* London: New Left Books.

Zimbalist, A. (1979). *Case Studies on the Labor Process.* New York: Monthly Review.

18   A political perspective on careers: interests, networks, and environments

JEFFREY PFEFFER

The careers literature, like much of the literature in organizational behavior (Pfeffer, 1982), is dominated by a perspective that focuses on the individual or organization in isolation and argues either implicitly or explicitly from an efficiency-oriented or value or goal attainment perspective. Thus, individual career choices are presumed to reflect individual goals, needs, personality, or interests (Hall, 1976: Ch. 2), and the applications literature deriving from such a focus is oriented to self-assessment and self-discovery procedures to enhance individual career planning (Crites, 1973; Hall, 1976: Ch. 2; Strong, 1943). The organization's task is seen as one of defining the relevant abilities, which derive from the technical requirements of work, devising screening and selection systems to pick the most able applicants and then devising training programs, job rotation, and promotion ladders that motivate and retain as well as develop skills in the work force (Hall, 1976: Ch. 6; Schein, 1977; Schneider, 1976). The applications-oriented literature developing from this perspective focuses both on the analysis of jobs in terms of skill requirements and task attributes (McCormick and Tiffin, 1974; Schneider, 1976: Ch. 2) and on screening procedures (e.g., Bray and Grant, 1966; Hall, 1976: Ch. 4), promotion and job rotation practices (Katz, 1982; Pelz and Andrews, 1966; Wellbank et al., 1978), and training and socialization efforts (e.g., Bass and Vaughan, 1966; Berlew and Hall, 1966; Morgan, Hall, and Martier, 1979; Van Maanen, 1982) to produce a motivated and skilled work force.

The purpose of this chapter is to propose an alternative perspective on understanding careers and career processes. Although individual choices and strategies are important and efficiency concerns do have some role in explaining organizational arrangements and individual decisions, the current preoccupations overlook some important considerations for understanding careers and career processes. This chapter develops a more political and sociological focus, arguing for the importance of interests, environments, and networks. This perspective alters both the questions asked and the analysis used to answer them.

A POLITICAL PERSPECTIVE

The distinction between a political approach and other perspectives on careers is not based on presumptions of rationality. As Granovetter (1985) has argued, rationality is often a reasonable first approximation for understanding behavior, and in any event, the political perspective itself often assumes rational, conscious, and foresightful action. Rather, the distinction revolves around the role of power and influence in decision making, the basis for decisions, and the role of interests in organizations.

380

The political perspective maintains that there are multiple and distinct interests in organizations, each pursuing its own, occasionally parochial objectives (Pfeffer, 1981). Decisions result from the interplay of these interests, with the more powerful actors or interests able to get more of what they want (March, 1966). Power or political activity is used in decision making primarily when there is conflict among interests and when the issue being decided is critical (Pfeffer, 1981; Salancik and Pfeffer, 1974). There are a number of other approaches that argue, in contrast, that it is reasonable to assume that organizations behave "as if" they were single actors pursuing interests of efficiency (Winter, 1975), or in other words, "efficiency drives out power" (Williamson and Ouchi, 1981). There are yet other approaches to analyzing organizations that question the purposefulness and strategic nature of both of these accounts, emphasizing instead the random and serendipitous nature of organizational activity (e.g., Cohen, March, and Olsen, 1972; March and March, 1978; March and Olsen, 1976).

To this point, many tests of the political perspective have developed measures or indicators of subunit or interest group power and then related those measures to some organizational outcome such as resource allocations (e.g., Hills and Mahoney, 1978; Pfeffer and Leong, 1977; Pfeffer and Moore, 1980; Pfeffer and Salancik, 1974; Provan, Beyer, and Kruytbosch, 1980; Salancik and Pfeffer, 1974). Yet another set of studies have inferred a political outcome by relating who benefits to the characteristics of those making the decision. Thus, for instance, Pfeffer, Salancik, and Leblebici (1976) reported that National Science Foundation grant allocations tended to favor those institutions represented on the advisory panels more in less paradigmatically developed scientific fields, while Pfeffer, Leong, and Strehl (1977) found that publication in journals tended to more closely correspond with the institutional representation on editorial boards in fields with less developed paradigms. Politics has been inferred from the correlation of the affiliations or identities between decision-making bodies and recipients, controlling for other factors, as well as from examining the effect of indicators of subunit power on decision outcomes, again with other factors presumably controlled. Although the distinction between political and other decision-making models is, at times, difficult to demonstrate empirically (Chaffee, 1980), nevertheless, the underlying conceptual premise is clear. There is a presumption of different interests, and evidence for a political perspective derives from studies that indicate the effect of interests on allocation outcomes that cannot be accounted for by rational, efficiency, or bureaucratic standards. This is an important point to recall in the discussion that follows in this chapter.

In studies of the political perspective, interests have most often been identified with distinct organizational subunits such as academic departments (Hills and Mahoney, 1978; Pfeffer and Moore, 1980; Pfeffer and Salancik, 1974) or departments of firms (Hinings et al., 1974; Perrow, 1970). However, particularly when studying careers, it is important to remember that interests are not limited to formal organizational units. Interests may be defined along class or demographic lines as well, with one of the more important demographic distinctions involving gender. Gusfield's (1957) account of the Women's Christian Temperance Union provides an example of differences defined along demographic cohorts, with consequences for succession and the welfare of the organization. Kanter's (1977) work as well as the extensive literature on sex segregation (e.g., Baron and Bielby, 1985) and wage discrimination (Madden, 1985) indicate that gender is also a significant distinction among groups in organizations. And, of course, the class perspective argues that classes reproduce themselves and continue to occupy powerful positions. The literature from this perspective has focused on processes including network building (Domhoff, 1974), the acquisition of cultural capital (DiMaggio, 1982) such as social skills and knowledge of high culture, and credentialling (Collins, 1979), which facilitate this process. Thus, class and demographic interests, as well as formal subunits, must be considered in analyzing the politics of careers.

It is also clear that interests do not lie entirely within the organization's boundaries. Pfeffer (1981: Ch. 5) has talked about involving outside interests in coalitions. Certainly, one cannot consider the politics of careers without considering the actions of interests that are partly outside the organization, including the efforts of unions to advance certain economic interests and often to reduce differentiation and wage dispersion, the efforts of both the state and national governments to regulate employment, wages, and hours, and the actions of professional associations, including personnel professionals, licensing bodies, and compensation and human resource consultants, which contribute to the diffusion and thus the homogeneity of certain practices as well as to the development and enforcement of specific ways of managing careers.

The political perspective is very much concerned with the effect of power on decisions and thus with the issue of why some subunits or interests have more power than others. The perspective is also quite concerned with strategies for the exercise of power (e.g., Pfeffer, 1981). In both of these instances, the political perspective invokes the ideas of networks and the importance of the environment.

From where do interests and their relative power come? Hickson et al. (1971) suggest that power accrues to those actors that can best cope with uncertainty emanating from the environment. Salancik and Pfeffer (1974) suggest that those actors that can best deal with the problem of extracting resources from the environment come to have comparatively more influence (see also Pfeffer and Salancik, 1978: Ch. 9). Thus, one cannot understand the power of a given group or, for that matter, how groups come to be defined and identified without reference to the environment. For example, Baron, Dobbin, and Jennings (1986) have argued that the intervention of the government in employment relations during World War II helped personnel professionals gain power. The state made manpower planning, skills inventories, and personnel record-keeping required and more critical. After the war, personnel professionals sought to maintain these practices, invoking the interests of enhanced labor relations and productivity. The war and the state intervention in labor relations that accompanied it were instrumental in redefining the role of personnel management and in causing a discontinuous change in the use of bureaucratic control procedures (Edwards, 1979).

Power is developed and implemented through networks of relations (Pfeffer, 1981). Indeed, Burt (1982, 1983) has developed a measure of power based on network concepts. Granovetter (1985, 1986) has argued that social relations are embedded in networks in that one's access to information and influence depends importantly on to whom one is connected. Note that in studies that have examined the effect of social similarity or institutional similarity on decisions (e.g., Pfeffer et al., 1976; Salancik and Pfeffer, 1978), the effect of networks of relations on the operation of decision processes to overcome other bases for making choices is implicit.

Because of the concern for power and its acquisition, use, and effects on decisions, the political perspective focuses attention on the environment as a source of power and on networks as both sources of power and a critical mechanism through which influence gets accomplished. These concepts, along with the concept of interests, define and distinguish the political approach to organizational analysis.

In the next sections of this chapter, we explore the implications of a political approach for understanding the following aspects of careers and organizational career systems: hiring, internal labor markets and promotion patterns, the division of labor and job classifications, wages, and succession. In that discussion, we focus on careers primarily from an organizational perspective because power and politics exist in larger social structures and, indeed, emerge only within and through such structures. The approach taken here sees the concept of career as structural, embedded in organizations subject to both efficiency pressures and the force of power and interests.

THE POLITICS OF HIRING

There are no careers, at least for the vast majority of the U.S. work force that is employed by others, without jobs, and one does not have a job unless and until one is hired. Thus, we begin at the beginning in our analysis of the politics of careers – with the process of being hired. There are three elements of the hiring process that are highlighted – recruiting and job search, the standards that are set, and the actual matching or selection process. Who gets hired depends on the sources and methods of recruiting, on the standards and criteria that are developed for particular positions, and finally, on the particular selection standards used in the matching process.

It is likely that the interests that are important in this stage of careers are defined along demographic lines. Kanter (1977) has written about "homosocial reproduction," and many others have documented the fact that similarity is both an important basis of attraction (e.g., Berscheid and Walster, 1969) and a mechanism for resolving uncertainty (Pfeffer, Salancik, and Leblebici, 1976; Salancik and Pfeffer, 1978). The issue is who is to be recruited into the organization, and what matters about the "who" is their similarity to those already in place, in terms of gender, class, educational background, and age cohort (e.g., Ryder, 1965). Thus, the study of the politics of hiring becomes a study of how and under what conditions people already in the organization are able to affect the process to ensure reproduction of the organization so as to favor their interests.

Recruiting and job search

To be hired, it is necessary that the individual know about the organization and that the organization know about the individual. Thus, we need to understand the choice of recruiting sources. Granovetter (1974) has provided one of the few studies of the process of recruiting in a study of the labor market in the Boston area. He found that impersonal sources of recruiting, such as agencies and advertisements, were used more in the case of technical as contrasted with managerial jobs and for jobs that were lower paying. Granovetter's results indicate that jobs that are higher in uncertainty (managerial jobs and jobs that pay more because they entail more responsibility) are filled more through the operation of personal networks, through contacts between people in the organization and potential recruits. Granovetter (1973) has also indicated that very often the ties that constitute these networks are "weak," in the sense of being based on casual acquaintance rather than on family connections or years of contact. Granovetter (1974) also found that jobs found through personal contacts tended to be liked better by incumbents, probably because they had better information through the personal network on which to make their job choice decision.

Of course, who one knows depends on where one is and has been, both locationally (Huckfeldt, 1983) and organizationally (Granovetter, 1986). Because contact networks are themselves structured by economic, gender, educational, and age distinctions, it is scarcely surprising that the recruiting process tends to facilitate homosocial reproduction and the populating of organizations by people like those already there. Baty, Evan, and Rothermel (1971) observed that there were clusters of movement among business school faculty so that people with degrees or jobs in a set of places tended to move primarily to other places within that set. It is likely that this structured movement is produced not only by selection but also by recruiting practices, in which people tend to follow lines of movement that have been established by prior people and organizations tend to look to previously used recruiting sources with which they are familiar. Indeed, this is explicitly recognized by people on both sides of the labor market. Thus, organizations often try to hire someone from a certain school or academic program to develop a link to that program and to facilitate future recruiting; similarly, alumni from programs (or from organizations) become sources to be consulted for those seeking to find new positions, with a natural tendency to follow previously developed paths.

This is a plausible line of argument, but it requires specification in several directions. Uncertainty has been asserted to be an important element producing the use of personal contact networks in recruiting (e.g., Granovetter, 1974; Kanter, 1977; Salancik and Pfeffer, 1978). But, other dimensions of the job environment may also be important. In particular, the arguments about the effect of scarcity and criticality on the use of power (Salancik and Pfeffer, 1974) suggest that networks will be used more in conditions of scarcity of either positions or applicants and that networks and social similarity will be more important in filling positions that are more critical or important. A second issue is the basis along which networks become defined and formed. Similarity in age, social class, gender, and educational background do not always perfectly covary, and we need to understand under what circumstances each becomes a relatively more important basis for defining networks and social similarity. One likely possibility is that the factor that helps discriminate among candidates is the one that is used – in a group of all male applicants of approximately the same age, school ties and social class may be comparatively more important. Some of the factors such as gender and age have more physical manifestations and thus define similarity immediately and without detailed knowledge of the person; others, such as educational background and the possession of cultural capital, become known only with some effort and over time. That would suggest that the choice of others similar on more subtle dimensions would be more likely to be observed in contexts in which the recruiting goes on for a longer period and in which the investment in the recruiting process, on both sides of the transaction, is greater. It seems clear that we need many more examinations of the clusters of personnel movement across organizations and a more systematic examination of the choice of sources of recruiting channels.

Hiring standards

Once identified, prospective applicants are evaluated according to some set of hiring standards. Many organizations have educational credential requirements, have minimum or maximum age requirements, give written or unwritten tests, or use other forms of screening. With respect to hiring standards, two questions can be posed: (1) what determines the degree of organizational selectivity and (2) what particular standards or ways of screening are used?

Examining variation in organizational selectivity across a sample of establishments in the San Francisco Bay area, Cohen and Pfeffer (1986) found that selectivity was related both to some technical factors such as the degree of technological change, the amount of training, and the tendency to promote from within (which would suggest that need for workers who would be qualified for promotion) and to the presence and potency of two organizational interests, personnel departments and labor unions. Cohen and Pfeffer (1986) found that the presence of a personnel department was positively associated with selectivity, net of other factors, and that the higher the proportion of the work force that was unionized, the less selective was the organization. Cohen and Pfeffer suggested that it was in the interests of the personnel department to be more selective, as the administration of hiring standards was an activity often left to that department, and the imposition of hiring standards would give the department more power in the organization. Unions would oppose hiring standards, particularly those administered by employers, as such screening might be used to weed out applicants with pro-union leanings and would legitimize skill differentials and differential treatment not based on seniority that is antithetical to union values.

The Cohen and Pfeffer study examined overall selectivity, but it would also be important to examine factors that influence which particular standards or which criteria tend to get used. In the recruiting of MBA graduates, for example, some consulting firms give the applicants cases to be analyzed, while others do not. Of course, one possibility is always that different degrees of selectivity and the choice of different criteria reflect actual differences in the technical nature of the work. Such an explanation must always be considered and is likely to be partly valid. Yet, it is also the case that selection criteria operate with differential effect on different groups. We would suggest that criteria and standards are derived at least partly as the result of a contest among interests in the organization, each seeking to put in place procedures that will tend to favor the obtaining of more people like those in that group. In any event, it is important to move beyond the assumption of the technical rationality of selection standards and practices to treat them as dependent variables to be examined as the consequence of both technical and political forces.

The politics of selection

The question of who gets chosen is more than the application of formal hiring standards, which do not exist in every case and which, in any event, often still leave a pool of applicants available. As in the case of recruiting, the prediction is that similarity is an important basis of the final choice, particularly under conditions of uncertainty. The literature on interviewing, for instance (e.g., Baskett, 1973; Frank and Hackman, 1975), suggests that the similarity between the interviewer and the interviewee affects the evaluation of the applicant. Salancik and Pfeffer (1978), in an experimental study, found that the choice of a similar other was greater when there was more uncertainty about the choice because the applicants were about equal in formal attributes and when information about the applicants and who made the decision was to be kept secret.

One of the interesting issues is how organizations and job applicants signal to each other their degree of similarity. Consider, for example, the case of a class of Stanford or Harvard MBAs recruiting for positions in consulting or investment banking. On most of the formal criteria, the people are almost equal, having already been highly selected on the basis of ability, motivation, and achievement. Having gone to training sessions on how to write resumes, how to interview, and indeed, how to dress, many of them have, compared to the population as a whole, highly developed and similar interviewing and recruiting skills. And, each faces the task of conveying the simultaneous impression that he or she is at once part of and similar to the school and the employing organization but also different enough and distinct enough to be worth pursuing as compared to the numerous other, similar applicants. This is a task of impression management worthy of Goffman (1971), and how it is accomplished is an important research issue. The methods of study that will need to be used will probably have to be observational and more qualitative, as the messages and signals being conveyed are at once subtle and complicated.

Again, similarity is not the only basis for choice, although in informal interviews with both recruiters and applicants, the idea of "fit" is mentioned extraordinarily frequently. As in the case of recruiting, we need to know what other attributes are important in what circumstances and also how the possession of such characteristics gets communicated. For instance, if upper class background is an important attribute (Pfeffer, 1977a,b), how does one communicate possession of such a background? Cultural and social capital (DiMaggio, 1982; Weber, 1968) gets expressed, it is likely, through conversation, and dropping hints about where one has been and what one has seen and has had the opportunity to do. The analysis of such conversations would be a fruitful area for understanding this process of matching.

Particularly at higher organizational levels, selections involve much more than tests of competence but also entail tests for whether those being selected are in basic agreement with the goals and philosophy of the leaders. Thus, Helmich and Brown (1972) observed that outside succession at the top management level was accompanied by more turnover in the executive's role constellation. Those being selected were either former associates of the new CEO or else others that could be relied on to provide support and to behave and make decisions in ways consistent with the new strategy and direction. One need only look at Iacocca bringing in ex-associates from Ford to help him run Chrysler to see a familiar case example of this phenomenon.

There are, of course, variations in the extent to which this hiring of one's former associates is done. It is probably more common at higher organizational levels, such as boards of directors where there is a premium placed on loyalty and the uncertainty involved in the tasks makes objective selection less feasible or desirable. An interesting issue to explore would be not only the correlates of homosocial reproduction but also its consequences for the organization. Are executives who bring in loyal and trusted colleagues more effective, or do they suffer from the consequences of groupthink (Janis, 1972) that may result from surrounding oneself with like-minded individuals? The effects, of course, may vary depending on the turbulence or degree of change in the environment and the need for the organization to respond to new circumstances. Certainly, new selection biases represent one of the ways in which organizations change. When a new interest or group (marketing, women, MBAs, or whatever) takes over, it uses its enhanced power to ensure that new hires are similar in the relevant background characteristics. Thus, new people are brought in and a new perspective on the organization and its issues comes to occupy more and more positions in the organization – perhaps until that power becomes institutionalized, the organization fails to adapt, and the process begins anew (cf. Pfeffer and Salancik, 1978).

MOBILITY STRUCTURES: INTERNAL LABOR MARKETS
AND JOB CLASSIFICATIONS

Once inside the organization, employees are assigned to specific positions with specific titles. They then face mobility prospects that depend not only on their own ability and motivation but also on the place of their specific job in job ladders and the overall status system of the organization. Some organizations promote primarily from within; others hire extensively from outside. Ceteris paribus, one's mobility chances inside an organization are enhanced by its having promotion from within policies, as one then competes against a smaller number of candidates. One's chances are also better if the organization is growing (Stewman and Konda, 1983) and if one's entering cohort was comparatively small [for this argument on a societal level, see Easterlin (1980)]. Mobility prospects are affected not only by whether or not there is an internal labor market, but also by whether or not one's own position is in such a labor market (e.g., Carroll and Mayer, 1986). The comment "that is a dead-end job" implies that it does not lead to higher, more responsible, or better paying positions. Some jobs prepare one for other jobs, and others do not. This has to do not only with the objective nature of the job, but also with what kind of career ladders and relationships among jobs the organization has defined. It is an interesting example of the individualistic, astructural bias in much of the mobility and careers literature that almost without exception, studies of mobility focus on individual attributes rather than the person's position and its place in the overall job structure.

If mobility prospects are affected by whether or not the organization has an internal labor market (Doeringer and Piore, 1971) as well as by whether or not one's job is in a ladder leading to higher level positions, then it is important to understand both the determinants of internal labor market arrangements as well as the factors affecting the shape and scope of career ladders. To this point, there has been only limited attention to these questions, both of which have political elements in their answers.

Pfeffer and Cohen (1984) examined the determinants of the extent of internal labor market practices in a sample of almost 300 organizations in the San Francisco Bay area. They found that such practices, including promotion from within and hiring from the outside only in a few, limited positions, were positively related to the organization's having a personnel department, to its being a branch establishment, to the degree of technological change and training provided, and to its being in the core sector of the economy. Internal labor market arrangements were negatively related to the percentage of the work force covered by collective bargaining. As in the case of hiring standards, the influence of two important interests, personnel professionals and unions, is evident.

In analyzing the structure of jobs and whether or not jobs are placed in job ladders, there is some evidence for the importance of the politics of gender. Baron, Davis-Blake, and Bielby (1986) analyzed job ladders in 100 establishments in California. At the establishment level of analysis, they found that the presence of job ladders tended to be positively related to size, to being linked to a larger establishment, to the provisions of establishment-specific training, and to being in the manufacturing sector. Internal labor market practices were negatively related to the use of unit technology and to the percentage of professional, technical, and managerial jobs. Their study did not replicate the Pfeffer and Cohen finding of the negative effect of unionization. However, further analysis by the authors indicated that establishment-level factors only basically distinguished between those places with any internal labor market practices and those with none and did not correlate well with the degree of internal opportunity.

Baron et al. (1986) then proceeded to analyze the place of jobs in career ladders at the job level of analysis, examining as dependent variables things such as whether or not a job was in a career ladder, whether or not the job was on the bottom of such a ladder, and whether or not the job was dead-end (in other words, had some prospects for mobility). They found that in larger organizations, jobs were more likely to be in job ladders, and in unionized organizations, jobs were less likely to be in ladders. Baron and his colleagues also observed that "women's jobs are significantly less likely to be in job ladders. Moreover, among jobs in ladders, men's jobs were . . . somewhat less likely to be dead-ended" (1986: 265).

The Baron et al. (1986) results are quite consistent with political perspective on career mobility. Note that their findings indicate that the structure of opportunity depends on the strength of various labor market interests such as unions and professional, technical, and managerial workers as well as on gender. The Baron et al. measure of union strength is basically dichotomous, and no effort was made to explore the correlates of the extent of gender-based structuring of job opportunities. One might certainly expect that at some point, there would be enough women in an organization, particularly if they occupied higher level positions, to change the job structure to overcome some of the biases that retard women's mobility. Indeed, one might examine the effect of numbers of persons of various demographic groups on the place of jobs occupied primarily by those demographic groups in organizational career ladders. And in a similar fashion, one could examine career ladders leading into higher level positions as they varied by department, with the prediction being that more powerful departments would have career ladders that led more to higher level organizational positions.

Baron and Bielby (1986) also studied a related phenomenon, the proliferation of job titles or how finely jobs are classified. Once again, the effect of interests was observed. They found that the presence of unions reduced job title proliferation while the presence of personnel specialization increased the number of titles, controlling for other factors such as organizational size and technology. They found that personnel specialization was particularly strongly related to job title proliferation outside of the manufacturing sector. Job titles are important for, among other things, people are paid according to the title of the job they hold. Baron and Bielby (1986) suggested that one of the factors motivating a proliferation of job titles is the desire to give different names to jobs being done by both men and women, so that the jobs being done primarily or exclusively by women can be paid less. Indeed, this issue is the foundation of the comparable-worth debate as well as being the object of wage discrimination suits.

As in the case of hiring standards, we see the operation of interests, such as personnel professionals, unions, and the politics of gender, acting to affect the development of job structures, job title proliferation, and internal labor market arrangements. The studies cited clearly have examined only a few of the possible interests that might affect the structuring of opportunity within organizations. There are significant demographic groups besides those defined by gender, as noted previously, and there are other important interests besides unions and personnel professionals. How job opportunities are structured by educational group, by age and tenure, and by department are also important considerations in understanding how interests operate to affect career mobility in organizations.

THE POLITICS OF WAGES

How much different individuals get paid for working in different positions and why are two of the more important questions associated with understanding careers from either an organizational or an individual point of view. The functional theory of stratification (Davis and Moore, 1945; Huaco, 1970) suggests that positions are compensated more if special skills or education are required because incremental rewards are necessary to attract the most qualified people and to induce them to invest in education and training. This approach is similar to that of human capital theory (e.g., Becker, 1962; Mincer, 1964), which argues that in order for people to invest in additional education, there must be some return to that education. In a similar fashion, training or work experience that provides additional skill must be compensated, or else some other organization would hire away the individual and obtain the benefits of that skill.

The political perspective would suggest that wages are a resource and, like other resources, are allocated at least in part on the basis of the power of various interests. This would be particularly the case if we considered relative wages or the wages paid to some group or position compared to some other. Examining wage progression in a university, Moore and Pfeffer (1980) reported that more powerful departments were able to get larger wage increases for their faculty, controlling for other factors such as departmental size and quality. One might predict that controlling for other factors that also affect wages, the wage level would be comparatively greater for those persons who were in more powerful departments. And one would predict that the ratio of wages across departments would be more favorable for those departments that were more powerful. In other words, the ratio of the wage of faculty in physics to faculty in English would be higher in those settings in which physics had comparatively more power and English comparatively less. Similar comparisons could be made, of course, across departmental salaries in other types of organizations as well.

Pfeffer and Davis-Blake (1987) have argued that higher wages accrue to those departments that are the most critical and that criticality varies by contextual factors. Examining the relative wages paid to six college administrative positions, they found that the salaries paid to positions such as admissions director and director of development, comparatively more important in private settings, were higher, controlling for other factors, in those settings. Conversely, the salaries paid to positions such as athletic director and the director of community services (which includes extension), more important in public settings, were compensated comparatively more highly in public universities. Thus, conditions of the environment affect the power of units and positions, and this power is, in turn, reflected in relative wages.

One could also examine the politics of wages using demographic groups as defining distinct interests. So, one might ask how the proportion of long-tenured persons affects the share of compensation received by such people or how the proportion of persons with certain educational backgrounds, race, or sex, affects returns to those characteristics. In the case of tenure, it is likely the structure of compensation, including the amount paid in benefits such as retirement and medical plans, as well as the economic returns to tenure may be affected by the organization's work force composition.

The returns to social origins, or the politics of class within organizations, is a neglected but nevertheless important issue. Pfeffer (1977a,b) found that even after controlling for other individual characteristics, there were effects of socioeconomic origins on wages. Such effects were smaller for persons with advanced business degrees as contrasted with those with just undergraduate degrees and were smaller for persons working in manufacturing, in line positions, and in larger organizations. Pfeffer argued that returns to social origins were greater when the uncertainty of evaluating job performance was higher or when such origins directly contributed to job performance, as in positions in which access to high-status networks were critical. Useem and Karabel (1986), examining mobility solely among senior managers, found that social origins were less important for persons who had advanced business degrees. There seems to be some indication that formal credentials or the possession of cultural capital offer alternative ways of advancing in one's career.

Why and how wages and wage increases are allocated – by department, by demographic group, by gender, and by class – are important issues to be explored. The political perspective focuses attention on issues of relative compensation by interest group and causes us to ask the question, why do some get more than others? Power and its sources and how it is exercised provides a part of that answer.

THE POLITICS OF SUCCESSION

Intwined with the issue of who gets how much is the issue of who gets chosen for promotion, or the politics of succession. As Zald (1965) noted some years ago, succession, particularly at higher administrative levels, is a political event. In those cases where one's predecessor did not die or retire, the politics of succession is often associated with the politics of replacement, or how people leave organizations. For there to be a vacancy, there must have been an event that created that vacancy.

Replacement is associated with poor performance in business firms (Allen and Panian, 1982; James and Soref, 1981; Salancik and Pfeffer, 1980), sports teams (Allen, Panian, and Lotz, 1979; Brown, 1982; Gamson and Scotch, 1964; Grusky, 1963), and labor unions (Kahn, Lang, and Kadev, 1986). The question is how does the power position of the leader affect the likelihood and speed of replacement when the organization's performance is poor. The answer seems to be that power, which accrues to owners, to persons with long tenure, or to persons with substantial share ownership or control of the board of directors, retards replacement when organizational performance is poor. Involuntary replacement is a political act, and power must be mustered to remove the incumbent. To the extent that the incumbent's power is greater, he or she has enhanced staying power. Variables such as the proportion of outside directors, the extent of the incumbent's ownership interests, and the form of organization are all relevant. Although confined primarily to studies of top management replacement or the replacement of the head coach or manager in sports teams, there is absolutely no reason why the same kinds of arguments could not be used to explore the replacement of persons in other positions in the hierarchy. In academic settings, it is probably harder to replace a dean or department head in a powerful unit, and the same is likely to be true for business firms. Sources of power for these lower level managers might include ties to constituencies or powerful interests inside or outside the organization, share ownership, and their ability to embarrass or otherwise cause difficulty for those seeking to do the replacement. A superb example of this latter factor from the political sphere is provided by the case of Robert Moses (Caro, 1974), who was able to forestall the wishes of numerous political leaders who would have liked to see him out of his many offices and commissions.

Assuming a vacancy has occurred, for whatever reason, then the issue becomes who is chosen to fill it. That the choice of a person represents something about the power of the interests symbolized and represented by that individual is so clear that, in some cases, the choice becomes constrained by that very fact. Thus, for instance, in the choice of associate deans at the Graduate School of Business at Stanford, care is taken to ensure that no single group is represented too much in the office of the dean and that the various paradigms or perspectives each have their spokesperson. By the same token, representation in the higher levels of management has been argued to be an indicator of the power of departments or other units (Pfeffer, 1981) and is likely to be one of the consequences of power held by particular interests. Indeed, this is so much the case that almost no empirical research has been done to test these assertions. Although representation on university committees, an indicator of power, was examined in relation to the ability of academic departments to bring in outside funds (Salancik and Pfeffer, 1974), neither these authors nor others that we know of examined the composition of high-level executive positions in either universities or other organizations as reflecting the power of interests to place their representatives in such critical positions.

Even if the effect of power on succession is as clear-cut as it seems, there remain some interesting issues to be explored. First, it has been quite a while since someone argued publicly for an individual's candidacy for a position by asserting that the person was favored by powerful interests, at least outside of the explicitly political realm. Thus, candidacy and advocacy is always masked and legitimated, and other, more objective and rational-appearing criteria are asserted. How does the use of power in shaping succession get accomplished in all of this talk? Again, there are important insights to be gained from a more detailed, fine-grained analysis of the processes by which power gets used to favor a position and the conversational and interactional processes involved.

Second, the connection between departmental or interest group power and succession is probably not the same in all settings. It is important to understand the conditions under which power translates into succession fairly reliably and those in which it does not. Even more importantly, what are the consequences of all of this for the organization? Some years ago Pfeffer and Salancik (1978: Ch. 9) argued that power was a wonderful mechanism for aligning the organization with its environment. Since power was associated with the ability to solve critical contingencies or to provide critical resources, and power was, in turn, related to succession that in turn was related to the decision premises used in and by the organization, the argument was made that the operation of power and politics ensured the organization would be led by people and groups best able to handle the organization's pressing issues. Indeed, Salancik and Pfeffer (1977) argued that the operation of power and politics was important to the organization's success for just this reason. None of these assertions tying the operation of power to succession and adjustment to environmental contingencies has, in fact, been adequately tested. So, there is the question of to what extent succession actually reflects considerations of power and the second question of the consequences of this for the organization.

CONCLUSION

Although developing a complete political theory of careers is beyond the scope of this chapter, we can briefly sketch the outlines of such an approach. A political approach to careers recognizes, first, the fundamental primacy of interests. It thus becomes one of the tasks of research adopting such a perspective to identify the dimensions along which political cleavages occur and, indeed, to explore and explain why these have become important dimensions. As an example, one cannot possibly read the literature on wages, job ladders, mobility, and recruitment without being confronted with the importance of gender. One of the important tasks for research is to not only document the profound effects of gender on structuring opportunity, but also to explore why this dimension, as contrasted with some others, has come to have the importance that it does. The first task of a political theory of careers is to identify interests and to explore how and why they have come to be defined as they have.

Second, a political perspective on careers would then seek to explore how interests, and their relative power, structure opportunity, wage relationships, and succession in organizations. Throughout, of course, such an approach needs to be compared with predictions derived from theories emphasizing efficiency or economic rationality as well as the technical requirements of work and how it is structured. This means continuing the task of developing indicators of power and exploring how power in organizational career systems develops as well as seeking to explore the effects of power on wages, mobility, recruitment, and succession.

Since power is derived at least in part from the organization's environment and is developed and exercised through networks, the political perspective tends to focus our attention on factors occurring outside as well as inside the organization and on structural features of interaction. The current careers literature is, at times, almost naive in its single-minded emphasis on the primacy of individual needs, goals, and values and the treatment of individuals in isolation from one another. Concepts such as cohorts (Pfeffer, 1983; Stewman and Konda, 1983) and network ideas that emphasize the interconnections among people, both in helping each other as in recruitment and in the zero-sum competition for status and promotions, are essential.

It is also clear that the political perspective presents a description rather than a prescription for organizational careers. One is struck in reading much of the careers literature by its applied, prescriptive focus. How do we find, develop, move, train, and socialize the right people to fit the organization's requirements is the emphasis in much of this literature. Yet, in neglecting the realities of how careers are structured, recruiting gets accomplished, and wages get set, the prescriptions may be less valid as well as less usable than they might otherwise be. By focusing on how careers are affected by political elements, we can develop an approach to the analysis of careers that is at once more consonant with reality and more able to comprehend and consequently deal with that reality.

REFERENCES

Allen, M. P., and Panian, S. K. (1982). Power, performance, and succession in the large corporation. *Administrative Science Quarterly, 27*, 538–547.
Allen, M. P., Panian, S. K., and Lotz, R. E. (1979). Managerial succession and organizational performance: a recalcitrant problem revisited. *Administrative Science Quarterly, 24*, 167–180.
Baron, J. N., and Bielby, W. T. (1985). Organizational barriers to gender equality: sex segregation of jobs and opportunities. In A. S. Rossi (ed.), *Gender and the Life Course*. New York: Aldine, pp. 223–251.
Baron, J. N., and Bielby, W. T. (1986). The proliferation of job titles in organizations. *Administrative Science Quarterly, 31*, 561–586.
Baron, J. N., Davis-Blake, A., and Bielby, W. T. (1986). The structure of opportunity: how promotion ladders vary within and among organizations. *Administrative Science Quarterly, 31*, 248–273.
Baron, J. N., Dobbin, F. R., and Jennings, P. D. (1986). War and peace: the evolution of modern personnel administration in U.S. industry. *American Journal of Sociology, 92*, 350–383.
Baskett, G. D. (1973). Interview decisions as determined by competency and attitude similarity. *Journal of Applied Psychology, 57*, 343–345.
Bass, B. M., and Vaughan, J. A. (1966). *Training In Industry: The Management of Learning*. Belmont, CA: Wadsworth.
Baty, G., Evan, W., and Rothermel, T. (1971). Personnel flows as interorganizational relations. *Administrative Science Quarterly, 16*, 430–443.
Becker, G. (1962). Investment in human capital: a theoretical analysis. *Journal of Political Economy, 70* (Suppl.), 9–44.

Berlew, D. E., and Hall, D. T. (1966). The socialization of managers: effects of expectations on performance. *Administrative Science Quarterly, 11,* 207–223.

Berscheid, E., and Walster, E. H. (1969). *Interpersonal Attraction.* Reading, MA: Addison-Wesley.

Bray, D. W., and Grant, D. L. (1966). The assessment center in the measurement of potential for business management. *Psychological Monographs, 80,* whole no. 625.

Brown, M. C. (1982). Administrative succession and organizational performance: the succession effect. *Administrative Science Quarterly, 27,* 1–16.

Burt, R. S. (1982). *Toward a Structural Theory of Action: Network Models of Social Structure, Perception, and Action.* New York: Academic.

Burt, R. S. (1983). *Corporate Profits and Cooptation: Networks of Market Constraints and Directorate Ties in the American Economy.* New York: Academic.

Caro, R. A. (1974). *The Power Broker: Robert Moses and the Fall of New York.* New York: Knopf.

Carroll, G. R., and Mayer, K. U. (1986). Job-shift patterns in the Federal Republic of Germany: the effects of social class, industrial sector and organizational size. *American Sociological Review, 51,* 323–341.

Chaffee, E. E. (1980). *Decision Models in University Budgeting.* Ph.D. dissertation. Stanford University, Palo Alto, CA.

Cohen, M. D., March, J. G., and Olsen, J. P. (1972). A garbage can model of organizational choice. *Administrative Science Quarterly, 17,* 1–25.

Cohen, Y., and Pfeffer, J. (1986). Organizational hiring standards. *Administrative Science Quarterly, 31,* 1–24.

Collins, R. (1979). *The Credential Society.* New York: Academic.

Crites, J. O. (1973). *Theory and Research Handbook, Career Maturity Inventory.* Monterey, CA: McGraw-Hill.

Davis, K., and Moore, W. E. (1945). Some principles of stratification. *American Sociological Review, 10,* 242–249.

DiMaggio, P. (1982). Cultural capital and school success: the impact of status culture participation on the grades of U.S. high school students. *American Sociological Review, 47,* 189–201.

Doeringer, P. B., and Piore, M. J. (1971). *Internal Labor Markets and Manpower Analysis.* Lexington, MA: Lexington.

Domhoff, G. W. (1974). *The Bohemian Grove and Other Retreats: A Study in Ruling Class Cohesiveness.* New York: Harper & Row.

Easterlin, R. A. (1980). *Birth and Fortune: The Impact of Numbers on Personal Welfare.* New York: Basic.

Edwards, R. C. (1979). *Contested Terrain: The Transformation of the Workplace in the Twentieth Century.* New York: Basic.

Frank, L. L., and Hackman, J. R. (1975). Effect of interviewer–interviewee similarity on interviewer objectivity in college admission interviews. *Journal of Applied Psychology, 60,* 356–360.

Gamson, W. A., and Scotch, N. R. (1964). Scapegoating in baseball. *American Journal of Sociology, 70,* 69–76.

Goffman, E. (1971). *Relations in Public.* New York: Basic.

Granovetter, M. (1973). The strength of weak ties. *American Journal of Sociology, 78,* 1360–1380.

Granovetter, M. (1974). *Getting a Job: A Study of Contacts and Careers.* Cambridge, MA: Harvard University Press.

Granovetter, M. (1985). Economic action and social structure: the problem of embeddedness. *American Journal of Sociology, 91,* 481–510.

Granovetter, M. (1986). Labor mobility, internal markets, and job matching: a comparison of the sociological and economic approaches. In R. V. Robinson (ed.), *Research in Social Stratification and Mobility,* Vol. 5. Greenwich, CT: JAI, pp. 3–39.

Grusky, O. (1963). Managerial succession and organizational effectiveness. *American Journal of Sociology, 69,* 21–31.

Gusfield, J. R. (1957). The problem of generations in an organizational structure. *Social Forces, 35,* 323–330.

Hall, D. T. (1976). *Careers in Organizations.* Pacific Palisades, CA: Goodyear.

Helmich, D. L., and Brown, W. B. (1972). Successor type and organizational change in the corporate enterprise. *Administrative Science Quarterly, 17,* 371–381.

Hickson, D. J., Hinings, C. R., Lee, C. A., Schneck, R. E., and Pennings, J. M. (1971). A strategic contingencies' theory of intraorganizational power. *Administrative Science Quarterly, 16,* 216–229.

Hills, F. S., and Mahoney, T. A. (1978). University budgets and organizational decision making. *Administrative Science Quarterly, 23,* 454–465.

Hinings, C. R., Hickson, D. J., Pennings, J. M., and Schneck, R. E. (1974). Structural conditions of intraorganizational power. *Administrative Science Quarterly, 19,* 22–44.

Huaco, G. A. (1970). The functionalist theory of stratification. *Inquiry, 9,* 215–240.

Huckfeldt, R. R. (1983). Social contexts, social networks, and urban neighborhoods: environmental constraints on friendship choice. *American Journal of Sociology, 89,* 651–669.

James, D. R., and Soref, M. (1981). Profit constraints on managerial autonomy: managerial theory and the unmaking of the corporation president. *American Sociological Review, 46,* 1–18.

Janis, I. L. (1972). *Victims of Groupthink.* Boston: Houghton Mifflin.

Kahn, S., Lang, K., and Kadev, D. (1986). National union leader performance and turnover in building trades. *Industrial Relations, 25,* 276–291.

Kanter, R. M. (1977). *Men and Women of the Corporation.* New York: Basic.

Katz, R. (1982). Managing careers: the influence of job and group longevities. In R. Katz (ed.), *Career Issues in Human Resource Management.* Englewood Cliffs, NJ: Prentice-Hall, pp. 154–181.

McCormick, E. J., and Tiffin, J. (1974). *Industrial Psychology,* 6th ed. Englewood Cliffs, NJ: Prentice-Hall.

Madden, J. F. (1985). The persistence of pay differentials: the economics of sex discrimination. In L. Larwood, A. H. Stromberg, and B. A. Gutek (eds.), *Women and Work, An Annual Review,* Vol. 1. Beverly Hills, CA: Sage, pp. 76–114.

March, J. C., and March, J. G. (1978). Performance sampling in social matches. *Administrative Science Quarterly, 23,* 434–453.

March, J. G. (1966). The power of power. In D. Easton (ed.), *Varieties of Political Theory.* Englewood Cliffs, NJ: Prentice-Hall, pp. 39–70.

March, J. G., and Olsen, J. P. (1976). *Ambiguity and Choice in Organizations.* Bergen, Norway: Universitetsforlaget.

Mincer, J. (1974). *Schooling, Experience, and Earnings.* New York: Columbia University Press.

Moore, W. L., and Pfeffer, J. (1980). The relationship between departmental power and faculty careers on two campuses: the case for structural effects on faculty salaries. *Research in Higher Education, 13,* 291–306.

Morgan, M. A., Hall, D. T., and Martier, A. (1979). Career development strategies in industry: where are we and where should we be? *Personnel, 56* (March/April), 13–20.

Pelz, A., and Andrews, F. M. (1966). *Scientists in Organizations.* New York: Wiley.

Perrow, C. (1970). Departmental power and perspectives in industrial firms. In M. N. Zald (ed.), *Power in Organizations.* Nashville, TN: Vanderbilt University Press, pp. 59–89.

Pfeffer, J. (1977a). Toward an examination of stratification in organizations. *Administrative Science Quarterly, 22,* 553–567.

Pfeffer, J. (1977b). Effects of an MBA and socioeconomic origins on business school graduates' salaries. *Journal of Applied Psychology, 62,* 698–705.

Pfeffer, J. (1981). *Power in Organizations.* Marshfield, MA: Pitman.

Pfeffer, J. (1982). *Organizations and Organization Theory.* Marshfield, MA: Pitman.

Pfeffer, J. (1983). Organizational demography. In L. L. Cummings and B. M. Staw (eds.), *Research in Organizational Behavior,* Vol. 5. Greenwich, CT: JAI.

Pfeffer, J., and Cohen, Y. (1984). Determinants of internal labor markets in organizations. *Administrative Science Quarterly, 29,* 550–572.

Pfeffer, J., and Davis-Blake, A. (1987). Understanding organizational wage structures: a resource dependence approach. *Academy of Management Journal, 30,* 437–455.

Pfeffer, J., and Leong, A. (1977). Resource allocations in united funds: examination of power and dependence. *Social Forces, 55,* 775–790.

Pfeffer, J., Leong, A., and Strehl, K. (1977). Paradigm development and particularism: journal publication in three scientific disciplines. *Social Forces, 55*, 938–951.

Pfeffer, J., and Moore, W. L. (1980). Power in university budgeting: a replication and extension. *Administrative Science Quarterly, 25*, 637–653.

Pfeffer, J., and Salancik, G. R. (1974). Organizational decision making as a political process: the case of a university budget. *Administrative Science Quarterly, 19*, 135–151.

Pfeffer, J., and Salancik, G. R. (1978). *The External Control of Organizations: A Resource Dependence Perspective*. New York: Harper & Row.

Pfeffer, J., Salancik, G. R., and Leblebici, H. (1976). The effect of uncertainty on the use of social influence in organizational decision making. *Administrative Science Quarterly, 21*, 227–245.

Provan, K. G., Beyer, J. M., and Kruytbosch, C. (1980). Environmental linkages and power in resource-dependence relations between organizations. *Administrative Science Quarterly, 25*, 200–225.

Ryder, N. B. (1965). The cohort as a concept in the study of social change. *American Sociological Review, 30*, 843–861.

Salancik, G. R., and Pfeffer, J. (1974). The bases and use of power in organizational decision making: the case of a university. *Administrative Science Quarterly, 19*, 453–473.

Salancik, G. R., and Pfeffer, J. (1977). Who gets power – and how they hold on to it: a strategic-contingency model of power. *Organizational Dynamics, 5*, 3–21.

Salancik, G. R., and Pfeffer, J. (1978). Uncertainty, secrecy, and the choice of similar others. *Social Psychology, 41*, 246–255.

Salancik, G. R., and Pfeffer, J. (1980). Effects of ownership and performance on executive tenure in U.S. corporations. *Academy of Management Journal, 23*, 653–664.

Schein, E. H. (1977). Increasing organizational effectiveness through better human resource planning and development. *Sloan Management Review, 18*, 1–20.

Schneider, B. (1976). *Staffing Organizations*. Pacific Palisades, CA: Goodyear.

Stewman, S., and Konda, S. L. (1983). Careers and organizational labor markets: demographic models of organizational behavior. *American Journal of Sociology, 88*, 637–685.

Strong, E. K., Jr. (1943). *Vocational Interests of Men and Women*. Stanford, CA: Stanford University Press.

Useem, M., and Karabel, J. (1986). Pathways to top corporate management. *American Sociological Review, 51*, 184–200.

Van Maanen, J. (1982). Boundary crossings: major strategies of organizational socialization and their consequences. In R. Katz (ed.), *Career Issues in Human Resource Management*. Englewood Cliffs, NJ: Prentice-Hall, pp. 85–115.

Weber, M. (1968). *Economy and Society*. New York: Bedminster.

Wellbank, H. L., Hall, D. T., Morgan, M. A., and Hamner, W. C. (1978). Planning job progression for effective career development and human resources management. *Personnel, 55* (March/April), 54–64.

Williamson, O. E., and Ouchi, W. G. (1981). The markets and hierarchies program of research: origins, implications, prospects. In A. H. Van de Ven and W. F. Joyce (eds.), *Perspectives on Organization Design and Behavior.* New York: Wiley-Interscience, pp. 347–370.

Winter, S. G. (1975). Optimization and evolution in the theory of the firm. In R. H. Day and T. Groves (eds.), *Adaptive Economic Models*. New York: Academic, pp. 73–118.

Zald, M. N. (1965). Who shall rule? A political analysis of succession in a large welfare organization. *Pacific Sociological Review, 8*, 52–60.

19 Rites of passage in work careers

HARRISON M. TRICE AND DAVID A. MORAND

There is a comparison between the ritual way major life stages are negotiated in
small-scale societies and our own poverty of effective rites of passage – Western
culture is lacking in effective mechanisms for socialization.

Colin Turnbull, 1984

Entering into a trade, marrying, growing old and aging, are also celebrated . . .
after the phrase of Van Gennep, they have come to be called *rites of passage*, rites
of transition.

Everett Cherrington Hughes, 1958

In essence, a work career can be conceptualized as a series of transitions from
one role to another within an organizational or occupational social system (Barley,
Chapter 3; Hall, 1976). The fact that work careers are comprised of sequences of
roles is often obscured by alternative conceptualizations that emphasize career's
more unitary connotations as a calling, vocation, or professional pursuit. Yet, if
we take seriously the idea that a career consists of a sequence of roles, the question
of just how the transitions between these roles are accomplished takes on an
importance in its own right. Indeed, the study of the social and psychological
mechanisms that enable individuals to transit across roles proves to be quite a
critical area of investigation.

Hence, this chapter suggests that the role transitions encompassed by work
careers, these "turning points" (Hughes, 1958:11), are central to careers and that
they pose crucial problems to anyone seriously interested in understanding how
careers work. An anthropological model known as rites of passage [Van Gennep,
1960, (1909)] is used to show that major transitions are managed ceremonially
across three universal stages of separation, transition, and integration. Although
the literature on work careers makes occasional mention of it (Hall, 1976:137;
Van Maanen, 1977), Van Gennep's rites of passage seems to have been largely
overlooked in thinking about both organizational and occupational careers; such
an omission is unfortunate for rites of passage are central to work careers, and
the rites of passage model can cast a wealth of light onto career studies.

The conceptualization of role transitions, as comprised of some form of separation from the old role, of transition, and of incorporation into the new role, has
been widely recognized since it appeared in the work of Lewin (1947), and more
recently in that of Schein (1961, 1971, 1979).[1] Lewin's work captures elements
common to all change processes, and his three stages of unfreezing, changing,
and refreezing conceptually parallel the separation, transition, and incorporation
phases of rites of passage. Nevertheless, in their respective applications these
two models diverge significantly. Lewin's stages, for instance, have most consistently been used to model the psychological processes involved in attempts to

397

influence individual beliefs, attitudes, and values. In contrast, a rites of passage model, while not denying the fundamental psychological processes involved, also incorporates a more macro, sociological perspective. In this sense, rites of passage are well-established ceremonial events that manage major role transitions within a social system. Rites of passage explicitly entwine a sociological perspective in that they enlist significant others in the organization or occupation to serve, as it were, as the supporting cast for the social drama. Even more broadly, a rite of passage serves as a signaling device, publicly signifying to the wider social group that a role transformation is occurring.

Given these prefatory remarks, this chapter will first define rites of passage and then will apply this anthropological model to modern organizations and occupations. A number of examples of rites of passage in modern organizations and occupations will be provided, including how training programs function as rites of passage. Lastly, the implications of the model for further career theory, research, and applications will be explored.

GENERIC FEATURES OF RITES OF PASSAGE

Rites of passage in modern life fall into the general category of ceremonial phenomena that Moore and Myerhoff (1977) call "secular ritual." These two anthropologists see such rituals as collective ones, as "especially dramatic attempts to bring some particular part of life firmly and definitely into orderly control," but without involving mystical, unseen spirits as was the case within more tribal, simple cultures. Thus,

secular ceremonials can present unquestionable doctrines and can dramatize social/moral imperatives without invoking the spirits at all. If the realm of the religious and the realm of the sacred are not treated as co-terminous, then it is possible to analyze the ways in which ceremony and ritual are used in the secular affairs of modern life to lend authority and legitimacy to the positions of particular persons, organizations, occasions, moral values, views of the world, and the like (Moore and Myerhoff, 1977:3).

Three distinct rites make up the passage ceremony: rites of separation, rites of transition, and rites of integration. Rites of separation act to detach passengers, often physically as well as symbolically, from their former roles and to move them into the transitional, "betwixt-and-between" phase. During this transitional period, former statuses and roles are symbolically stripped away, and the rite puts newcomers in an ambiguous state in which they pass through experiences that have few if any features of past or approaching conditions. Finally, rites of integration consist of collective actions that function to actually incorporate newcomers into their new roles. In effect, the incorporation phase consummates the transition.

At first blush these three phases seem to be deceptively simple. That is, there is a beginning, a middle, and an end to the role transition. Van Gennep's contribution, however, was to observe "just how similar are the beginnings, middles and ends of an extraordinarily wide range of rituals . . . [he] emphasized that these similarities are not random analogies, but part of a single, general phenomenon" (Huntington and Metcalf, 1979:8). Van Gennep [1960:191 (1909)] puts the process in the following words:

Our interest lies not in the particular rites but their essential significance and their relative positions within ceremonial wholes – that is, their order . . . Their positions may vary, depending on whether the occasion is birth or death, initiation or marriage, but the difference lies only in matters of detail. The underlying arrangement is always the same. Beneath a multiplicity of forms, either consciously expressed or merely implied, a typical pattern always recurs: *the pattern of rites of passage.*

In other words, there is a general structure underlying a vast array of rites that function to move persons from one role to another and that accompany them in unavoidable or important events such as pregnancy, childbirth, the onset of sexual maturity, the entry into a craft, and death. In essence, then, there are basically two social statuses involved in all the transitions where rites of passage occur – the old one and the new one. And the social processes that move a person from one status to another are uniform across the myriad of rites that occur worldwide. Thus rites of passage are not merely relics of preliterate, savage, tribal life; they also occur in modern life. Our interest here is in the specific role they play in the work careers of many present-day workers.

At this juncture, a remaining point to note about rites of passage is that they, as do practically all cultural elements, simultaneously generate both technical and expressive outcomes. Another way of stating this is to consider that these rites serve to both "do things" and "say things" (Leach, 1968:523). This very basic duality of function may be illustrated by considering the functions of eating. While food provides us with physiological sustenance, acts of eating invariably become laden with expressive, ceremonial meaning; what, when, how, and with whom we eat are matters of no small significance. Or, similarly, while clothing achieves certain technical ends, such as protection from the elements, our choice of clothing is heavily laden with manifold expressive meanings. The color, the cut, the perceived expense of the clothing we wear – all these elements convey social, expressive meanings to those around us. Even if we do not intend or desire to express particular meanings with our clothing, meanings will invariably be attributed to what we wear; others will tend to make expressive interpretations concerning our choice of clothing.

This technical/expressive distinction proves quite germane to an analysis of rites of passage in modern organizations because although as intendedly rational entities modern organizations emphasize primarily technical functions, the expressive consequences of actions will nevertheless prove to be powerful and pervasive forces. The further ramifications of this technical/expressive distinction will be discussed later in this chapter.

RITES OF PASSAGE IN ORGANIZATIONS

Chester Barnard (1938:180) caught the modern functions of rites of passage in work organizations when he observed that

ceremonials of investiture, inaugurations, swearing-in, induction, and introduction, are all essentially appropriate methods of making known who actually fills a position and what the position includes as authority. In order that these positions may function it is often necessary that the filling of them should be dramatized . . . to inculcate the sense of organization.

Separation

Rites of separation seem to be essential in the entry process in order to facilitate the newcomers in "letting go" their current statuses and roles. Louis (1980:231), for example, insists "that unfreezing, moving away, or letting go is a necessary preliminary step in effecting change at both individual and group levels." Schein (1978:95) writes of the "unlearning" process that must take place as MBA students moved from the student role into managerial positions. For example, they had to unlearn their reluctance to deal with other people and to be involved in the "selling," "compromising," and "politicking" necessary to get their ideas adopted. It seems likely that the rigorous interviewing and selection processes (Pascale, 1984; Trice et al., 1969) that many companies use serve an unfreezing function, setting the stage for recruits to accept the idea that it is not selling out if they are politicking to get their ideas utilized. In a similar vein, companies have increasingly come to use line managers to interview managerial candidates, rather than using specialists from personnel and human resources departments (Pascale, 1984); managers take promising candidates to dinner and "tell it like it is." In some instances there are two, even three, rounds of such interviews for all recruits that are hired, and, salary negotiations may take place *after* acceptance of an offer. These actions facilitate the "changing from" process of leave-taking and entry into an actual passage.

The separation phase of unlearning and letting go is well illustrated in rather extreme form by military organizations. In Navy boot camps within an hour after arrival

the new recruit is told to remove all his civilian clothes, his jewelry, religious medals, etc., and place them, along with wallet, comb, key ring, and the like into the shipping box that has been given him. He stands there nude and wraps and addresses the box containing the accouterments of his civilian identity. When finished he proceeds through a line in which he is issued his naval attire (Zurcher, 1967:91).

During the paper processing prior to this stripping process, the recruit is still called "Mr."; following it he becomes a "boot" because the leggings he wears do resemble actual boots. The shaved head completes the separation process. Moreover, the recruit cannot talk with non-recruits, cannot leave the physical isolation of the base, and suddenly must do practically everything in some form of mass formation that contrasts dramatically with the freedom of individual movement experienced in the immediate past. In officer training in the U.S. Coast Guard some additional moves facilitate separation: The new recruit discovers that it is taboo to discuss personal wealth or background and, further, he cannot receive any additional money from home (Dornbusch, 1954). For the "boot" Zurcher (1967:91) concludes: "there he and his company mates stand in their ill-fitting, stiff dungarees, arms still burning from shots, heads cold and itching from the haircut, tired, lonely and lost." No one would doubt that powerful separation processes have occurred.

Transition

The second phase, transition, is characterized in classical terms by liminality (Turner, 1969), a state of limbo in which the newcomer is marginal, experiencing a state of not being in his or her old role, or, for that matter, in the one toward which the passage is leading him or her. It is an unstructured and ambiguous state of "betwixt-and-between." Many tribal versions of this liminal period are marked by the initiates' names being taken from them; each is merely called by some generic phrase that refers to a neophyte category (Turner, 1970:358). In effect "they are no longer classified and not yet classified." One could think of them as being "sociologically naked" since nakedness is a mark of the newborn. When these rites are collective, as they often are, strong comradeship comes from the experience of passage together, and a sense of equality permeates the neophytes.

In many situations this comaraderie transcends rank, age, kinship, and accomplishment. "Each for all, and all for each" rapidly becomes the sentiment. All, in effect, experience the common processes that grind them down "to be fashioned anew and endowed with additional powers to cope with their new station in life" (Turner, 1970:362). Recruits in police academy training experience this sense of comaraderie even years after they enter the police force. Cohorts in graduate schools discover deep friendships that grow and flourish from the liminal comradeship of going through common rites of transition together. Other examples of elaborate rites of transition are commonly found in the training of recruits into dangerous and anxiety-producing occupations, such as the military (Bourne, 1967), police (Van Maanen, 1973), firefighters (McCarl, 1976), doctors (Becker et al., 1961), and even missionaries (Wilson, 1981).

Debasement experiences, in one way or another, tend to characterize the transition period of rites of passage. They reinforce separation rites by requiring the abandonment of old responses and by underscoring the need to acquire new roles and responses. In short, they act "to open up" the newcomer to the influences of the organization. Schein (1971:8) coined the phrase "up-ending experiences." These were "deliberately planned or accidentally created circumstances which... upset... some of the major assumptions the new man holds about himself, his company, or his job." Ritti and Funkhouser (1977:5) provide a cogent example from modern work life, although here the situation is an individual, not a collective one. Stanley, a new junior-level manager, had to walk all the way around the building from the parking lot – and then walk all the way back through the plant to get to his office. He discovered, however, that there was a door, a loading gate presided over by a security guard, at the back of the building located between his office and his car. Stanley felt reassured, but quickly learned that only those on his supervisor's list could use the door. A forthright inquiry with the boss's secretary established the fact that Stanley would be informed when, and if, he got on the list. In the meantime, he trudged back and forth everyday, rain or shine – four times if he went out to lunch. Months later his boss asked him into his office for his semi-annual review. During this session he told Stanley about a raise for him, and, incidentally, that he was putting him on "the list"; "just tell the guard who you are." At the end of the day he confidently went to the guard, told him his name, and in a few seconds was at his car. This is an example of a mildly debasing experience that set the stage for full membership in the organization. Stanley was liminal until he got on his boss's list.

Similarly, Schein (1978:106) describes how the strategy of bosses initiating brand new engineers was to deliberately arrange up-ending experiences. The strategy was to get the new employee deeply involved in some task that "violates his or her expectations about self or the organization in order to teach certain realities quickly and dramatically. For example, an engineering manager gave every new graduate entering his group the task of analyzing a circuit that should not work, but did. When the recruit said it would not work, he was shown that it did and was asked to explain why. Rare was the newcomer that could explain the matter, leaving them chastened and skeptical of their education. Again, youthful, new professors, frequently find themselves facing large, unresponsive classes of freshmen. The experience is usually a shock. It drives home the university's need to sensitize the newcomer to its needs for teaching as well as research – a point largely missing from the research-oriented Ph.D. education experienced in graduate school. Pascale's (1984:30) summary of these liminal experiences catches their flavor: "You may know a lot, but as far as this organization is concerned you are in kindergarten."

Incorporation

The last stage, that of incorporation into new roles, seems often to be missing from rites of passage in modern-day work places. At least the relevant literature typically fails to describe many instances of these rites. An exception is Pascale's description (1984:30) of how successful companies put new managerial recruits into the field and give them "carefully monitored experience" following rites of transition. Although not explicitly labeled as such, this is clearly an incorporation ritual.

In a managerial training program observed by Trice, Belasco, and Alutto (1969:47), trainees who had been at an assessment and training center were brought back to the plant where a brief induction rite was held during a shutdown of the production processes. The production superintendent gave a short speech emphasizing the rigors of the retraining that the recruits had just received. He then read the names and new positions of each of the new managers, thus formally assigning them their new statuses and powers as "bosses." A cocktail party in honor of the new managers took place in a management club nearby that evening; spouses and other managers were invited. This final event clearly was intended to communicate that the new members were a part of the management group and so were their spouses.

Just how often rites of integration such as these, into new roles and new groups, actually occur as a part of rites of passage in workplaces is obviously unknown. "There is, however, every reason to believe that rites of passage are as important now as they have always been for our social and psychological well-being. Indeed, given the fragmented, confusing, complex, and disorderly nature of modern experience, perhaps they are more important" (Myerhoff, 1982:129).

Effective rites of passage may be lacking at the opposite pole of organizational life, namely, that of organizational death. Harris and Sutton (1986) studied "parting ceremonies" that arose in response to the impending death of eight very different kinds of organizations. Although the classical breakdown into Van Gennep's three stages did not explicitly emerge in the analysis, the function of these ceremonials was clearly one of facilitating the passage of employees from the dead organization into a transition period. In this sense these parting ceremonies comprised the separation phase for organizational members. Names attached to these rites graphically indicated their overall function: "the last supper," "the last hurrah," "the wake," and the "final party."

According to the researchers "organizational death packs an emotional wallop," one that calls for emotional support from outside the individual psyche. A number of devices were used in attempting to bring the experience into some form of orderly control. For example, exchanging names and addresses, mutual sadness and anger, and the presence of former members who had already left helped members gracefully break their current social bonds with the organization. Sharing food and drink, not just "snacks," but meals, symbolized a sense of common grief and sadness and an open expression of these emotions. Alcohol use helped to produce, for a brief period at least, a sense of community and primary groupness. In short, the parting ceremonies provided a sanctioned setting where members could openly grieve together for the death of their organization.

In addition, these parting ceremonies were the occasion for the telling of "summary" stories about the organization, stories that caught up the organization as employees recalled it. When combined with other stories, these provided a "social system schemata" for the parting members. Also, discussions of causes of the organization's death during the ceremony provided an opportunity to firm up a casual explanation for the demise in individual members' minds. Additional features helped members face the realities of role transitions – by talking with those former members who have already made successful transitions to new roles, the soon-to-be displaced members began to cope with the transition they inevitably faced.

OCCUPATIONAL RITES OF PASSAGE

Entrance into many occupational cultures displays, often in a classical manner, the social consequences associated with Van Gennep's rites of passage. Occupational career and organizational career are not, of course, mutually exclusive concepts; many occupational careers do unfold primarily within organizational settings. However, to consider occupational careers as a mere subset of careers in organizations would be misleading; these two arenas for career development are best depicted as a Venn diagram of two intersecting circles. While for many occupations, such as public school teacher or police, the area of intersection will be large, the use, here, of occupation as a distinct analytic lens is intended to focus the reader's attention on a set of socializing phenomena that merit attention in their own right (see Van Maanen and Barley, 1984). In general, occupations probably engage in more discernable socialization efforts, and in more rites of passage, than do organizations.

Lortie (1968) contrasts the two extremes – presence and absence of rites of passage in occupational entry – by comparing the socialization of professors with that accorded to public school teachers. He concludes that ordeals experienced in graduate school and leading to the professoriate contain phases that resemble the puberty rites often found in tribal life, whereas the entry process into public school teaching is without such a ritualized domain. "Progress [for the professor] calls for clearing a series of hurdles such as course examinations, language tests, general examinations, and completion of a dissertation." Lortie cites research on doctoral students, conducted by Douglas T. Hall (1968), that shows that the gaps students felt between themselves and their professors had narrowed significantly after the general examinations for the doctoral degree, in contrast to one month prior to the examinations (Lortie, 1968:254). The rites of incorporation that operate in a specific university, to confer tenure on a new assistant professor five or six years later (Trice and Beyer, 1984b), complete the socialization into the occupation via specific rites of passage. And, since the academic discipline (occupation) plays a predominant role in the tenure decision process for assistant professors, the occupation continues to exert socializing influences even within one specific university or college.

According to Lortie (1968:256), the entry process into public school teaching stands in sharp contrast. Practice teaching is in no way an ordeal, student teachers are eased into teaching gradually and easily. Although there are instances during practice teaching that might be seen as ordeals, these are individual experiences that in no way involve peers in simultaneous, collective experiences. Apparently "sink or swim" is an "apt description of the young teacher undertaking his full time teaching responsibility" (Lortie, 1968:258). Consequently the feeling that one has become a teacher seems to be an individual attainment, not the requirements of a well-organized occupational group. Consistent with these socialization experiences is the tradition of public teaching as a role for males in transit to more lucrative positions and prestige rewards, or, if female, to marriage and family life.

Vaught and Smith (1980) have provided a detailed description of the occupational rites of passage of miners. For the new worker, the separation phase of passage is symbolized in a profound and impressive manner by the "portal" to the mine, which marks a boundary between the old life on the outside and the new one to be experienced far below. The new recruit, of necessity, must put on new, standard overalls, mining belt, boots, and other accouterments of the occupation, including a bright orange hat, dinner bucket, and lamp. The newness of this equipment spotlights the newcomer, and during the first trip down the "slope" – and for a period thereafter – he is subject to a variety of indignities: "beating the hat, pulling the recruit's lamp cord and belt, kicking dents in his shiny new dinner bucket, and generally calling attention to the trappings of the occupation." These serve to remind the new worker that he is now a member of a "select" group that inhabits a different world, and that they will soon be occupying a new status:

Crowded into the man-trip, personal space invaded and freedom of movement restricted by the close proximity of other workers, they are lowered into an environment that is noisy, dark, dusty, and illuminated only by shifting beams from miners' cap lamps. They are in truth "new men" . . . they are now dependent upon these boisterous strangers to lead them around and show them what to do. (Vaught and Smith, 1980:166–167)

This separation phase is further characterized by three or four shifts during which the newcomer will be ignored, but occasionally discussed as if he were not present.

The transition phase commences with a "filling out" period during which older miners become very inquisitive about the newcomer's private life, what he did before coming to the mine, what he does on the outside – and every detail that the initiate can be made to divulge. From this information older miners form opinions about potential reliability, loyalty, beliefs about mining, and capacity to control tempers when frustrated. Nicknames are typically given to the recruit during this period, coming from a gaffe or mistake, from some peculiar personal trait, or from some "stunt" or incident in which he has been involved. These are usually very colorful: "Big Coon," "Jackhouse Jones," "Smooth Mouth," "Maggot Mouth," "Plunger Lip," and "Dynamite" are examples. These are symbols of being in another world where outside names do not count. Vaught and Smith (1980:168) cite Lucas to the effect that "many miners may work together for years without knowing each other's real name."

The rite of "making a miner" usually occurs two or three weeks after a recruit's first shift, and it marks the end of transition. This phase consists of asking if the newcomer "has been made a miner." Obviously not, must be the answer, whereupon he is grabbed and held down while an older miner administers "several swats" to the posterior with a clapboard. This process is repeated enough to satisfy all units who feel constrained to beat the newcomer ("smacked him pretty good"). They force him to submit to a humiliating degradation of self, confronting him with the solidarity of the group and forcefully impressing upon him the fact that he must give deference to group will.

Rites of incorporation for miners are blatantly gross, body-centered games that occur during the first year. "Whippings," "getting some ass," apparently were common as were "greasings" and "penis games." Greasing was carried out by several members of a unit by grabbing the victim unannounced, removing his trousers, and coating his genitals with grease, followed by throwing of handfuls of rock dust on the greasy genitals. An example of a penis game was the "pretty pecker" contest during which mock judges were chosen who then proceed to evaluate the genitals of five or six of the new men, choosing one as the "prettiest."

Rites of passage for police officers offers nothing as gross or physical, yet the outlines of the three phases of rites of passage are nevertheless there. The ubiquitous police academy acts to separate out and isolate the police recruit; the basic idea is to strip the rookie of past habits so that he or she can be made fit for the role of police officer. Harsh and arbitrary discipline characterizes the regimen along with a ritualistic attention to detail, rigorous physical training, and constant hazing (Van Maanen, 1973). During the in-between, transition period much technical information and occupational self-imagery is imported. Harris (1973) analyzed the basic content of the training of one large police academy as it represented this transition period, and he reported it broke down into three major facets: defensiveness, professionalization, and depersonalization. Recruits were trained to be constantly alert to the possibility of danger and to be very suspicious of most situations. The term "professional" was used to instill a positive image of responsible, independent commitment, while "depersonalization" imparted a view of occupational self as seeing the public in a detached and categorical manner, rather than individually and emotionally.

Incorporation occurred in the rituals of graduation and in the first experiences as a rookie. Often this involved a harsh exposure to the realities of specific patrols. Where hazardous, dangerous duty assignments are differentially available, the new recruits may get a significantly larger number of them, further extending the incorporation phase of the rites of passage (Jermier, 1982). That is, incorporation into the occupation becomes thoroughly symbolized by repeated sharing of constant danger with established occupational members. Applebaum (1984) has reviewed this process among, for example, soldiers, high-steel workers, and longshoremen.

Finally, it is important to realize that rites of passage, as cultural forms dealing with symbolic role journeys, can also function to effect an exit from an occupation.[2] Green (1965:62), for example, describes the use of prescribed auctioneering rituals in a rite of transition among maritime craft occupations just prior to World War II. When an old-timer died, his expensive, often ornate tools were meticulously auctioned off one by one to fellow union members. Since symbolically his tools were his most concrete representation of himself, their dispersion among members expressed his transition to a new role, that of deceased union brother. All the proceeds from the auction were publicly presented to the deceased's family at a union meeting, further symbolizing his final entry into the role of dead union member.

McCarl (1984) was a participant observer of an elaborate retirement dinner that, even more emphatically than the maritime craft's auctions, acted as a rite of passage at the end of a career. He carefully recorded a complicated retirement dinner during which a firefighter ate his last meal with his fellow firefighters, following which he was without a doubt a "retiree." This was the last rite in a chain of increasingly elaborate food events that marked the career of a firefighter: After a rookie finished his probationary year, he arranged and served a probationer's dinner to other members of his company; when he advanced into officer rank (to sergeant, for example), he organized a somewhat more elaborate promotional dinner for the members of his company.

The most prominent feature of this retirement dinner analyzed by McCarl was the inclusion of a verbal "roast" during which the audience and speakers confronted the retiree with many of his past misdeeds and indiscretions, and generally reviewed his overall performance as a firefighter. But these roasts were intermingled with verbal compliments and expressions of respect and appreciation. In essence, there was considerable ambivalence built into the entire rite. Moreover, the critical context also provided an opportunity to criticize the hierarchy in which the occupation functioned. There was also considerable license to engage in personal insults and affronts and other forms of verbal attack. During the actual verbal roast, stories, observations, and evaluation of the retiree's actual performance are "aimed point blank at the retiree who is expected to respond when his portrait is misrepresented" (p. 408). He did so six different times during the roast, and in the midst of banter, raucous humor, and innuendo about blacks and women becoming members of the occupation.

At the end of the dinner, the retiree appears publicly in front of his fellow firefighters as no longer a firefighter. At the same time he is forced into isolation from the others and must realize the inevitable change that is happening before his, and others, eyes. He has been put into a liminal position during which he was pummeled, insulted, and subjected to criticism. This served as a transition rite for him, and the dinner had moved him "symbolically from being a member of the group to a new non-active status as a retired fire fighter, resigned to his new role as it had been anticipated throughout his career" (p. 417).

Occupational rites of passage, if moderately successful, produce an internalization of occupationally based beliefs and behaviors that reduce the need for surveillance and discipline. The repeated expectations of significant others in one way or another induce taken-for-granted beliefs and behaviors that have their roots in occupational socialization. Thus in the absence of sanctions and often against self-interests, occupational members may act according to the major components of their socialization. Obviously, this adherence varies widely with the strength of the socialization and with the organizational structure in which an employee practices his or her other occupation.

TRAINING AND RITES OF PASSAGE

Training programs often involve several distinct rites in sequence; indeed they have many of the features of rites of passage. Yet, in line with comments previously made in this chapter, the functions of training tend to be evaluated and understood in light of technical, as opposed to expressive, criteria (see Trice and Roman, 1973). Thus, for example, while a training program may transmit to individuals specific knowledge on a discrete set of skills, training also engenders a set of more tacit, expressive social outcomes. Such expressive outcomes of training must be examined to fully appreciate how these programs function as rites of passage.

Take, for example, an instance of a managerial training program in a Japanese bank (Rohlen, 1973). The training at the Uedagin bank consisted of an unusual amalgam of events. In the rite of separation, trainees and their parents attended an entrance ceremony, during which the president of the bank gave a speech congratulating the parents on raising such fine children, and reassuring the trainees and their families that taking a job at this bank was like joining a large family that takes good care of its members. The rites of transition included a two-day trip to a nearby army camp where the trainees were subjected to some of the rigors of basic training: Marching under the direction of a sergeant and sweating their way over obstacle courses, they wore castoff army fatigues that symbolized their shared lowly status. They were told that a large company required a high degree of order and discipline, that military training was the best way to teach this, and they accepted this explanation. Periodically, they were also taken to a Zen temple for a two-day session in meditation and other Zen practices. Here they were also subjected to a strict regimen that included tasteless gruel for meals and a whole series of rituals that had to be meticulously observed.

A twenty-five-mile marathon walk held at the end of the training acted as a rite of incorporation. Trainees were told to walk the first nine miles together in a single body, the second nine in designated groups, and the last seven alone and in silence. Past trainees monitored their conformity to the rules and tempted them with cold drinks, which they were not allowed to accept. The first phase, walking and talking together was relatively pleasant. During the second phase, intergroup competition emerged, leading the trainees to escalate their pace even though competition had not been encouraged. The result was that many trainees could not stand the pace and had to drop out. The final phase of the walk was very painful and difficult; any who finished took great personal pride in that accomplishment. Rohlen suggests that the marathon walk taught the values of perseverance, self-denial, and rejection of competition as the route to collective accomplishment. In addition to all of the ordeals mentioned, the trainees were expected to study bank operations and pursue a variety of other scheduled activities; every day except Sundays were filled with fourteen hours of supervised activity. Rohlen reported that similar in-company training rites were employed by as many as one-third of all medium and large Japanese companies with apparently successful consequences in terms of employee productivity and commitment.

When training is viewed from the standpoint of this example, it becomes clear that the expressive outcomes of training may be as prominent – possibly even more so – than the technical outcomes. Considerable applied research and observations about managerial training has supported the concept that both technical and expressive outcomes may result, and that the expressive – the cultural outcomes – may be very prominent. Chen and Rossi (1980), for example, point out that evaluation research in general tends to overlook outcomes other than those that narrowly focus upon official technical goals. Trice and Roman (1973:11) put this approach to training evaluation as follows:

There may be many desirable unanticipated consequences of training that are not detected by evaluations. It could easily be that no results are achieved on the formal, technical goals, yet the indication of ceremonial results could justify the entire effort, i.e., if persons think of themselves as supervisors and are defined by others as such, they may act more effectively than if this were not the case. In short, "ceremonial payoffs" should always be looked for regardless of what other approaches might be used.

In a rigorously controlled evaluation of supervisory training this did indeed turn out to be the case. Using three control groups and an experimental group, randomly sampled, the study demonstrated that the technical outcomes of training on newly recruited managerial trainees were relatively unimportant, but the "side effects," the unanticipated outcomes, were significant (Belasco and Trice, 1969a,b). In a qualitative field study of the same phenomenon, Trice, Belasco, and Alutto (1969:47) concluded that neither "testing nor training achieved any of their explicit goals," but that members of management strongly believed that the testing and training program for new supervisory recruits prepared them to be effective, and as a consequence, the selection, testing and training program persisted. One outcome was the latent effects of these programs on "insiders," that is, those already a part of management. Despite the relative ineptitude of the content of the training, it nevertheless reduced the anxieties of current management about how to keep the organization adequately and competently staffed. In addition, these programs acted on insiders to reinforce their positive perceptions and commitment to the organization's culture. That is, "sophisticated selection and training increase the value of organizational memberships, not only for the new initiate, but also for the currently employed organizational member" (Trice et al., 1969:46).

An additional finding was that the lengthy supervisory training program studied provided a comaraderie by which newcomers shared similar problems – a form of "supervisors anonymous" that persisted for years; it seemed to indicate that the organization genuinely cared and knew about them; it symbolized the importance of supervisors and supervision, and that training that has difficulty, rigor, and high expectations – even failures – has true value in generating organization commitment and making the role truly attractive.

In a management training program observed (Trice and Beyer, 1985) recruits selected from rank and file employees were physically removed from their normal work settings into assessment centers where they were tested and evaluated for two weeks. The first phase communicated both to the participants and to the audience (other members of the organization) that the recruits had been identified as candidates to receive additional powers and that they were going to be carefully screened and tested to be sure they were worthy to actually assume these new powers. Meanwhile, they were separated from their old statuses as a sign and indication that they would no longer have these statuses in the future, if they were selected for the new status. In this particular rite, the scientific trappings of extended testing symbolized the rationality that is valued in managerial cultures in general (Feldman and March, 1981; Trice, Belasco, and Alutto, 1969). Testing helped to provide a "rational" basis on which candidates could be certified as worthy to exercise additional powers.

Subsequent research and observation have borne out and refined these findings. Van Maanen (1975), in a longitudinal study, found that formal training in a police academy for a large city police force produced rather irrelevant and weak technical outcomes; however, the expressive outcomes of the training were found to be highly consistent with the occupational ideologies of autonomy, pragmatism, and "don't rock the boat." Similarly, Rosenthal and Mezoff (1980:105) observed that "surprisingly, the ceremonial effects of training may represent a more potent change agent than the intended effects of training," and went on to describe how the conduct of training sessions "off site" maximized the opportunity to develop organizational bonds with trainees. That is, "space speaks; by employing an off-site facility, the organization is sending the message that this training counts and *you* (the participant) matter to this organization." Guyot (1977, 1978) has also reinforced this general point.

Recently, Pascale (1984:30) concluded from looking at "winner" companies that the socialization of neophyte managers tended, in part, to be in the form of experiences and training "calculated to induce humility and to make him question his prior behavior, beliefs, and values. By lessening the recruit's comfort with himself, the companies hoped to promote openness toward their own values and norms." This sounds remarkably like the transition phase of rites of passage, especially since the humility induced is brought on by long hours of intense work that carry the recruit close to his or her limits. As a consequence "everyone has so much work to do that he doesn't have time to see people outside the company or re-establish a more normal social distance from co-workers." Somewhat like T-group training, an exceptionally marginal environment is staged in which the trainee is outside the normal life, and is cut off from her or his past and future. It seems that "if entry into an organization is a result of success in a series of difficult trials, then membership in that system must be valuable" (Trice et al., 1969:46). Gordon (1979:23) may well have summarized the processes in management training by saying that they are the "organization's rough equivalent of a Bar-Mitzvah."

But it should also be pointed out that the expressive consequences of training can be dysfunctional for the organization even though it is functional as a rite of passage for an individual member. That is, the ceremonial effects of training can be so consuming within the organization that it is blinded to environmental forces that directly impinge upon it and to which it must adapt in order to survive. A dramatic example of this dysfunction comes from the training of U.S. ground forces in Hawaii just prior to the Japanese attack on Pearl Harbor. In an effort to train troops for internal sabotage and native Japanese uprisings on the islands, Lt. General Walter C. Short, and to a lesser extent, Admiral Husband E. Kimmel, focused intensive training efforts on tactics to prevent and contain such eventualities. General Short became "tremendously preoccupied with training for its own sake ... He got so wrapped up in the training business that he could not see the other issues at stake ... He was so busy honing his own blade that he forgot its sharpness mattered little unless it was ready to hand." (Prange, 1981:729). So, at the time of the Japanese surprise attack, mobile guns had no ammunition and were not in field positions. Radar installations were understaffed and their reports were ignored. All training had focused upon internal subversion. The ceremonial effect of the training was one of reassurance and certainty.

SOME IMPLICATIONS

At this juncture it should be reiterated that the definition of rites of passage encompasses both their sociological as well as their psychological aspect. That is, that while the phases of the rites of passage do function to transform the psychological identity of a focal individual, to be comprehensively understood, these rites must be viewed more broadly in their role as social-ceremonial activities. Rites of passage, in their classic form, are visible, public events that derive much of their transformative potential due to the effects they yield upon a whole company of social actors. In this sense roles are provided by, and sustained by, those with whom we interact; no psychological role transformation will be successfully maintained if it is not reinforced by others around us. In a somewhat broader sense rites of passage function to uphold the normative status of careers in an organizational or occupational collectivity. For, if an individual – whether this be the focal individual or an onlooker – is to have a vision of a career as an expected sequence of events, then socially recognized role transformations must exist.

There is substantial evidence to suggest that rites of passage occur in work careers as the necessity to change from role to role occurs, and that they appear in a near classic form as well as in instances where they are far less distinct. This is a quite crucial point to note, yet it may also seem puzzling, for if rites of passage are so central to careers, how may they also be considered indistinct at times? There are two broad explanations for this. One asserts that rites of passage are, in fact, firmly in place, but for various reasons they may be difficult to observe. The second explanation derives from the fact that many modern organizations and occupations are relatively young or else they exist in turbulent and uncertain environments; thus, a high degree of novelty or uncertainty may inhibit the emergence of rites of passage in their classic form.

Regarding the first category of explanation, it is important to consider that rites of passage may be difficult to initially observe or delineate. In this connection it should be recalled that because passage ceremonies often function in an expressive rather than a technical capacity, they may be difficult to initially grasp or observe. Additionally, while the three stages may very well exist in a classic and pronounced form, they are often found to be dispersed across space or time, hence, rendered problematic to locate. For instance, rites of passage may involve both the occupation and the organization in a sequential fashion; that is, the separation phase may take place within the framework of the occupation, while the transition and incorporation phases occur primarily within the control and direction of the work organization.

An example of this is found in a recent study done by the first author (Trice, 1987) of occupational choice among seniors in a professional school in a northeastern university. Trice found that the majority of methods available for securing jobs upon graduation were those vigorously put forward by the school itself. The professional school went to great lengths to help the senior realize that he or she must "let go" of student life. At the very beginning of their senior year students became quite aware of the activities of the placement office, which aggressively pursued seniors giving them an opportunity to "bid" on job opportunities, to attend various seminars on what it was like to be separated from school, and go into an actual workplace. In addition, the school urged seniors to come to "senior day" during which it made very clear the nature of their separation from the school. Instead of relying upon the commencement ceremony of the entire university, the school conducted its own graduation ceremonies that further underscored the process of leave-taking from the present school and of moving into a new workplace within the larger system. Further data from graduating seniors of the last two years suggested that the rites of transition occurred in the company to which they were recruited, and within which they were hired. In addition, it also appeared that the rites of incorporation also occurred there. Consequently, on the basis of these empirical indicators, it seems that rites of separation are occurring in a different milieu than the rites of transition and incorporation, but all three within the same overall system.

Additionally, rites may exist, but in a truncated fashion. Sensitivity groups, also known as T groups, were at one time quite a popular form of training. Yet, they became known for their failure to maintain the gains achieved during the training itself after participants returned to their respective organizations. This was undoubtedly due to the fact that while T groups engendered powerful separation and transition rites, the integration of returning employees was weakly ceremonialized. It is worth noting that what are rites of passage for some individuals do not always function as such for similar others. Telephone company workers, for instance, still report that there is no second chance to go to the assessment center and the failure rate at assessment centers is high.

Further, rites of passage may lack salience because roles involved are poorly ceremonialized. It seems relevant to observe that the literature offers little evidence that rites of passage occur in mid-career. Though the study of careers has been quite inattentive to rites of passage, it may well be the case that mid-career rites do actually occur but are unrecorded. Glaser and Strauss (1971) conclude that persons going through mid-career passages often do so alone. It may be the case that these mid-career expressions are pale facsimilies, at best, of any aspects of the rites of passage process. Such observations suggest that there may be inevitable and important role passages that occur in work lives that are largely devoid of any of the features of rites of passage. Or, it may be that the role transitions involved in mid-career may not be sufficiently important in overall life stresses and events.

Where role transitions appear to be weak or vague, it may on the surface seem that they should be strengthened. Indeed, an implication of this review is the distinct possibility that rites of passage may act as emotional supports for individuals who face implacable role and status changes during their careers. Ceremony and social gatherings surround important passages in most cultures. However, when these status passages are unceremonialized or poorly ceremonialized "they are much more likely to involve bizarre behaviors" (Eaton, 1980:38) than if well-defined rites of passage are associated with the transition. It seems reasonable to assume that "ceremonies of status passage are an implicit recognition of, and attempt to control these potential instabilities – to guide the individual into the proper role, introduce him or her to the appropriate role audience and solidify their mutual bonds, and permanently remove the former roles from the social identity."

Research on the life event stresses that occur in normal populations equates these stressful events with status passage of one kind or another (Holmes and Rahe, 1967). Sokol and Louis (1984), for example, equate the career transition literature and the life events adaptation literature. That is, the role transitions involved in career changes typically involve life event stresses that require extraordinary demands of both physical and psychic energy. Moreover, a considerable amount of research further suggests that newly ill persons, both mentally and physically, experience much higher amounts of stressful life events in conjunction with their new illnesses (Dohrenwend and Dohrenwend, 1974). It is a reasonable hypothesis to predict that the intensity of the illnesses accompanying role transitions would be inversely related to the quality and completeness of the rites of passages accompanying the transition.

A closely related implication of this review is the extent to which – either in occupations or organizations – individual commitment is positively enhanced by experiencing rites of passage. It has been observed that middle managers seem to be devoid of the experiences that accompany rites of passage. Based upon their study of middle managers, Schrier and Mulcahy further state that most middle managers "do not make it to top management and resign themselves to a career of being 'betwixt and between': a guy is sixty years old and has lost every battle along the way and says 'fuck it' and waits until retirement . . . Liminality is inherently stressful and protracted liminality is protractedly stressful." (1988:148)

This brings to mind an observation made by Beckhard (1977:150) concerning the "disaffection in the ranks of middle management [that] is growing. I do not believe that it is widespread, at least not yet. But I do believe that it is most prevalent among the most effective and innovative managers in their 40s – the very people on whom top management counts to carry on the business." Such observations make the question about the cogency of rites of passage a very real one. To what extent do persons develop loyalties, attachments, and commitments of energies, time, and effort without going through such rites, regardless of what point in their careers the role transition occurred? In short, why confine the important benefits that can be gleaned from rites of passage to new recruits? Other rites of passage can be devised so that existing members can also be indoctrinated through them with the new values and ideologies of the new role. They could be used, for example, to mark any changes in status – perhaps as persons are promoted, or pass from one skill level to another within a grade. Unfortunately, at present, rites of passage seem to be relatively neglected as a means of instilling new sets of values and beliefs into current members.[3] One of the reasons middle-aged employees have problems remaining involved in work is that, not only are promotions at an end, but formal rites of passage, for example, training programs, are no longer provided. Also, one reason organizations may have difficulty incorporating women is that existing rites of passage, such as the miners' rites, are explicitly sexist. Thus, bringing women into men's jobs, or vice versa, is difficult because it necessarily disrupts rites of passage that have strong meanings for the participants.[4]

Other observers have expressed similar concerns about the extent to which work provides self-identity and the sense of involvement and commitment to work. For example, Van Maanen (1977:176) observes that

it [work] may provide . . . the single most important sense of identity for individuals living in modern industrial societies. Yet it is also clear that there are many careers that do not appear to offer much aid in so far as the construction of a positive self-image is concerned (and the number of these careers may well be growing).

On the face of it, rites of passage apparently act to inculcate a sense of identity and commitment to careers. It seems virtually impossible – but exceptions are obviously the rule – for individuals to experience these rites without being more involved, committed, and identified with occupation, organization, or both, than prior to experiencing them.

Yet to propose carte blanche that rites of passage are intrinsically good is shortsighted. A simple transposition from description to prescription is problematic because, despite many functional values of rites of passage, it is likely that they could be dysfunctional in a variety of ways. Despite their stabilizing influence, they are nevertheless forces of the status quo. At the individual level, rites can set up a custodial view of the organization or occupation, such that individuals are unreceptive to change. At the organizational level, rites can also act to discourage change and innovation, particularly at a time when the organization may be facing competition and even extinction, when the need for innovative styles is obviously paramount. Thus, rites of passage in their traditional form may well stymie the flexibility necessary to make adaptations to a turbulent environment.

In essence, the most frequently advanced objection to rites of passage and to other cultural forms for that matter is that organizations will be regimented. Yet such rites arise so frequently in workplaces it is doubtful that managers can be effective in suppressing them. Rather, it seems likely that they are mutable and can be made more amenable to change. Although rites of passage are used in tribal societies to ensure that people will behave in traditional ways in the roles into which they are moving, there is no inherent reason why variations on these rites cannot also express new ways of acting in traditional roles or cannot be used to prepare or move persons into entirely new roles. Such a conceptualization is reflected in Van Maanen and Schein's (1979) model of organizational socialization. They propose that certain socialization processes will engender role innovation, particularly processes that involve, among others, informal, random, and disjunctive mechanisms.

In this vein, the record does not bear out that distinct rites of passage stymie innovativeness. Pascale (1985) argues persuasively that many of the companies who socialize most extensively are the ones that have lasted over many generations – at least prima facie evidence of sufficient innovation to cope with the changing environment. Consider for example 3M or Bell Labs. Both socialize newcomers extensively, but both are highly innovative, and they remain so by fostering social rules that reward innovation. Nevertheless the question of conformity and of reduced individual autonomy – in a culture where it has been elevated to a position of a sacred norm – is a real one. In such conditions the implications of rites of passage can be highly conflictual. In essence, the individual is socialized into a condition where he or she is less free to make choices and thereby may be deprived of the autonomy that many people believe is necessary in managing and cultivating careers. But, again, the empirical evidence does not suggest that this is necessarily the case in modern corporations and unions. Pascale (1984, 1985) consistently points out examples in which rites of passage are relatively prominent, but within which there is retained wide latitude for divergence in opinions and behavior. He points to IBM, Proctor and Gamble, Morgan Guaranty Trust, and to Bain and Company as examples in which rites of passage have occurred but have not stymied the individuality of the persons who have experienced them.

On balance, it seems reasonable to argue that the presence of rites of passage in careers is more functional than it is dysfunctional. As a consequence there is probably a need to explore how to encourage and cultivate them in career sequences. One point seems clear beyond a doubt: Even in modern, secular societies, and in "rational," instrumental work organizations, they seem to naturally appear in one way or another. On this assumption, the question becomes how to design them in such a way that their functional features predominate in career process, while their dysfunctional aspects are attenuated. Perhaps the best place to begin would be to become much more aware of their presence, how potent they are, and how they might be adapted to the organization's dynamic ebb and flow of change pressures. Relative to the latter, rites of passage could be encouraged when the need is to stabilize and conserve following adaption to change, while they could be weakened and muted during periods when the organization faces inordinate change. Although too simplistic, such suggestions nevertheless can initiate the consciousness raising that is obviously necessary in order that the macro, structural dimensions of careers can be more often incorporated into their study.

NOTES

1 Although Lewin's (1947) work is more widely recognized and extensively cited, Van Gennep's (1909) work does predate that of Lewin. However, there is no evidence to suggest that Van Gennep's formulations directly influenced Lewin.
2 This mention of exits may conjure up in the reader's mind the ceremonial aspects of firing, demotion, and so on – in short, rites of degradation. Indeed, such rites of degradation are pertinent to the study of careers. For the interested reader, Trice and Beyer (1984a) have published a typology of rites often seen in the workplace, including rites of passage, rites of degradation, rites of enhancement, rites of renewal, rites of conflict reduction, and rites of integration.
3 There is some evidence that such mid-career rites are utilized in Japan. A recent 60 Minutes broadcast (1987) showed Japanese mid-level managers, in their thirties, forties, and even fifties, undergoing a thirteen-day program of "self-improvement" that in many respects resembles a rite of passage.
4 We are indebted to Professor Barbara S. Lawrence for these last two points.

REFERENCES

Applebaum, H. (1984). Work in Market and Industrial Societies. Albany: State University of New York Press.
Barnard, C. (1938). The Functions of the Executive. Cambridge, MA: Harvard University Press.
Becker, H. S., Geer, B., Hughes, E. C., and Strauss, A. (1961). Boys in White: Student Culture in Medical School. Chicago: University of Chicago Press.
Beckhard, R. (1977). Managerial careers in transition: dilemmas and directions. In J. Van Maanen (ed.), Organizational Careers: Some New Perspectives. New York: Wiley, pp. 149–160.
Belasco, J., and Trice, H. M. (1969a). The Assessment of Change in Training and Therapy. New York: McGraw-Hill.
Belasco, J., and Trice, H. M. (1969b). Unanticipated returns of training. Training and Development Journal, July, pp. 12–17.
Bourne, P. G. (1967). Some observations on the psychosocial phenomenon seen in basic training. Psychiatry, 30, 187–196.
Chen, H-T., and Rossi, P. H. (1980). The multi-goal, theory-driven approach to evaluation: a model linking basic and applied science. Social Forces, 59, 106–122.

Dohrenwend, B. S., and Dohrenwend, B. P. (eds.) (1974). *Stressful Life Events – Their Nature and Effects.* New York: Wiley.

Dornbusch, S. (1954). The military academy as an assimilating institution. *Social Forces, 33* (May), 316–321.

Eaton, W. W. (1980). *The Sociology of Mental Disorders.* New York: Praeger.

Feldman, M. S., and March, J. G. (1981). Information in organizations as signal and symbol. *Administrative Science Quarterly, 26,* 171–184.

Glaser, B. G., and Strauss, A. L. (1971). *Status Passage.* Chicago, Aldine-Atherton.

Gordon, G. E. (1979). Looking from the outside in: management/executive development programs from the employer's viewpoint. *Exchange: The Organizational Behavior Teaching Journal,* Fall, pp. 23–25.

Green, A. (1965). American labor lore: its meanings and uses. *Industrial Relations, 4,* 51–68.

Guyot, J. F. (1977). Prescription drugs and placebos: a new perspective on management, *Personnel Journal, 54* (May/June), 67–72.

Guyot, J. F. (1978). Management training and post-industrial apologetics. *California Management Review, 20,* 84–93.

Hall, D. T. (1968). Identity changes during the transition from student to professor. *School Review, 76,* 445–469.

Hall, D. T. (1976). *Careers in organizations.* Pacific Palisades, CA: Goodyear.

Harris, R. (1973). *The Police Academy: An Inside View.* New York: Wiley.

Harris, S. G., and Sutton, R. I. (1986). Functions of parting ceremonies in dying organizations. *Academy of Management Journal, 29*(1), 5–30.

Holmes, T. H., and Rahe, R. H. (1967). The social readjustment rating scale. *Journal of Psychosomatic Research, 11,* 213–218.

Hughes, E. C. (1958). *Men and Their Work.* Glencoe, IL: Free Press.

Huntington, R., and Metcalf, P. (1979). *Celebrations of Death.* New York: Cambridge University Press.

Jermier, J. M. (1982). Ecological hazards and organizational behavior: a study of dangerous urban space–time zones. *Human Organizations, 41* (Fall), 198–207.

Leach, E. R. (1968). Ritual. *International Encyclopedia of the Social Sciences, 13,* 520–526.

Lewin, K. (1947). Frontiers in group dynamics: concept, method, and reality in social science: social equilibria and social change. *Human Relations, 1,* 5–47.

Lortie, D. C. (1968). Shared ordeal and induction to work. In H. Becker, B. Geer, D. Riesman, and R. S. Weiss (eds.), *Institutions and the Person.* Chicago: Aldine, pp. 252–264.

Louis, M. R. (1980). Surprise and sense making: what newcomers experience in entering unfamiliar organizational settings. *Administrative Science Quarterly, 25,* 226–251.

McCarl, R. S. (1976). Smokejumper imitation: ritualized communication in a modern occupation. *Journal of American Folklore, 81,* 49–67.

McCarl, R. S. (1984). You've come a long way – and now this is your retirement. *Journal of American Folklore, 97*(386), 393–422.

Moore, S. F., and Myerhoff, B. G. (1977). Secular ritual: forms and meaning. In S. F. Moore and B. G. Myerhoff (eds.), *Secular Ritual.* Assen, Amsterdam, The Netherlands: Van Gorcum, pp. 3–25.

Myerhoff, B. G. (1982). Rites of passage: process and paradox. In V. Turner (ed.), *Celebration.* Washington, DC: Smithsonian Institute, pp. 109–135.

Pascale, R. (1984). Fitting new employees into the company culture. *Fortune, 109*(11), 28–40.

Pascale, R. (1985). The paradox of "corporate culture": reconciling ourselves to socialization. *California Management Review, 27*(2), 26–41.

Prange, G. W. (1981). *At Dawn We Slept: The Untold Story of Pearl Harbor.* New York: McGraw-Hill.

Ritti, R. R., and Funkhouser, G. R. (1977). *The Ropes to Skip and the Ropes to Know: Studies in Organizational Behavior.* Columbus, OH: Grid.

Rohlen, T. P. (1973). Spiritual education in a Japanese bank. *American Anthropologist, 75,* 1542–1562.

Rosenthal, S. M., and Mezoff, R. (1980). How to improve the cost–benefit ratio of management training and development. *Training and Development Journal, 34*(12), 102–107.

Schein, E. H. (1961). *Coercive Persuasion.* New York: Norton.

Schein, E. H. (1971). Organizational socialization and the professor of management. In D. A. Kolb, I. M. Rubin, and J. M. McIntyre (eds.), *Organizational Psychology: A Book of Readings*. Englewood Cliffs, NJ: Prentice-Hall, pp. 1–15.

Schein, E. H. (1978). *Career Dynamics: Matching Individual and Organizational Needs*. Reading, MA: Addison-Wesley.

Schein, E. H. (1979). Personal change through interpersonal relationships. In W. Bennis et al. (eds.), *Essays in Interpersonal Dynamics*. Homewood, IL: Dorsey, pp. 129–162.

Schrier, D. A., and Mulcahy, F. D. (1988). Middle management and union realities: coercion and anti-structure in a public corporation. *Human Organization*, 47(2), 146–150.

60 Minutes, "How to succeed in business." CBS Productions. New York. January 11, 1987.

Sokol, M., and Louis, M. R. (1984). Career transitions and life event adaptations: integrating alternative perspectives on role transition. In A. Vernont and E. van de Vliert (eds.), *Role Transitions: Explorations and Explanations*. New York: Plenum, pp. 81–93.

Trice, H. M. (1987). Critical factors operating among university students in their occupational choices. Working Research Paper No. 26. School of Industrial and Labor Relations, Cornell University.

Trice, H. M., Belasco, J., and Alutto, J. A. (1969). The role of ceremonials in organizational behavior. *Industrial and Labor Relations Review*, 23 (October), 40–51.

Trice, H. M., and Beyer, J. M. (1984a). Studying organizational cultures through rites and ceremonials. *Academy of Management Review*, 9(4), 653–669.

Trice, H. M., and Beyer, J. M. (1984b). Employee Assistance programs: blending performance-oriented and humanitarian ideologies to assist emotionally disturbed employees. In R. G. Simmons (ed.), *Research in Community and Mental Health*, Vol. 4. Greenwich, CT: JAI, pp. 245–297.

Trice, H. M., and Beyer, J. M. (1985). Using six organizational rites to change cultures. In R. H. Kilman, M. J. Saxton, and R. Serpa (eds.), *Gaining Control of the Corporate Culture*. San Francisco: Jossey-Bass, pp. 370–399.

Trice, H. M., and Roman, P. M. (1973). *Evaluation of Training: Strategy, Tactics and Problems*. Madison, WI: American Society for Training and Development.

Turnbull, C. (1984). Interview with Colin Turnbull. *Omni*, June, pp. 87–90, 124–134.

Turner, V. W. (1969). *The Ritual Process*. Chicago: Aldine.

Turner, V. W. (1970). Betwixt and between: the liminal period in rites of passage. In E. A. Hammel and W. S. Simmons (eds.), *Man Makes Sense*. Boston: Little, Brown, pp. 354–369.

Van Gennep, A. (1960) [1909]. *Rites of Passage*. Chicago: University of Chicago Press.

Van Maanen, J. (1973). Observations on the making of policemen. *Human Organizations*, 32 (Winter), 407–417.

Van Maanen, J. (1975). Police socialization: a longitudinal examination of job attitudes in an urban police department. *Administrative Science Quarterly*, 20, 207–228.

Van Maanen, J. (1977). Experiencing organization: notes on the meaning of careers and socialization. In J. Van Maanen (ed.), *Organizational Careers: Some New Perspectives*. New York: Wiley, pp. 15–49.

Van Maanen, J., and Barley, S. (1984). Occupational communities: culture and control in organizations. In B. Staw (ed.), *Research in Organizational Behavior*, Vol. 6. Greenwich, CT: JAI, pp. 287–365.

Van Maanen, J., and Schein, E. H. (1979). Toward a theory of organizational socialization. In B. Staw (ed.), *Research in Organizational Behavior*, Vol. I. Greenwich, CT: JAI, pp. 209–264.

Vaught, C., and Smith, D. L. (1980). Incorporation and mechanical solidarity in an underground coal mine. *Sociology of Work and Occupations*, 7(2), 159–167.

Wilson, W. A. (1981). *On Being Human: The Folklore of Mormon Missionaries*. Logan, UT: Utah State University Press.

Zurcher, L. A. (1967). The naval recruit training center: a study of role assimilation in a total institution. *Sociological Inquiry*, 37(1), 85–98.

20 Pin stripes, power ties, and personal relationships: the economics of career strategy

JAY B. BARNEY AND BARBARA S. LAWRENCE

The study of careers is an important component of microeconomic theory. Careers, after all, are closely linked to the structure and function of labor markets, and labor markets constitute a major factor of production considered in virtually all microeconomic theories of the firm (Bain, 1956; Chamberlin, 1933; Hirschleifer, 1980). Although considerable economic research focuses on careers, relatively little of this work provides insights for individual employees. When an employee wishes to be successful by organizational criteria,[1] what should he or she do? This chapter develops a model of individual career strategy based on modern microeconomic theory, discusses the individual and organizational implications of this model, and proposes research questions for further study.

We begin by briefly reviewing neoclassical labor market theory. The perfectly competitive labor markets suggested by this theory offer employees little control over their career destiny. However, many economists recognize that labor markets rarely meet the conditions of perfect competition, and we next discuss several models that relax some of the restrictive conditions of perfect markets. These theories do not focus on prescription, but they do provide clues that point toward career strategies. Further, they cover many topics examined in noneconomic career research, including the processes by which employees search for and choose jobs, the ways in which employment relationships are managed, the personal and organizational investments that employees and firms make in careers, and the broader meaning of careers for society and the economy. Finally, building on the ideas provided by these economic theories, we propose a tentative model of individual career strategy, and discuss the implications of this model for individuals, organizations, and future career research.

THE ECONOMICS OF CAREERS

Economic theory recognizes labor as a key factor of production. Thus, microeconomists are interested in how firms acquire the labor output of individuals and what price must be paid for this labor (Hirschleifer, 1980). Much of the early economic work on labor markets (Knight, 1921) explores these questions beginning with the assumption that labor markets are perfectly competitive. Several conditions must hold for perfectly competitive labor markets to exist. First, no firm can hire a relatively large proportion of employees available in its labor market. Second, there must be no costs associated with searching for or switching jobs. This assumes that both firms and potential employees possess perfect in-

417

formation concerning the structure of the labor market. Third, potential employees must be homogeneous with respect to their skills and capabilities, or equivalently, all the jobs filled in a market must require identical skills. Finally, firms make decisions that maximize profits, and individuals make decisions that maximize utility. This assumes that both firms and individuals make rational decisions with respect to decision-making goals.

Manual labor in Southern California provides an example of a labor market that approximates the conditions of perfect competition. Each weekday morning, several hundred manual laborers gather at a corner in West Los Angeles. Employers looking to hire workers for a single day drive to this corner, and, by raising a hand, indicate the number of jobs available and the hourly rate. No single "firm" hires a relatively large proportion of employees in this market. There are virtually no special skills in doing manual labor; thus, potential employees are homogeneous from the point of view of employers. Finally, search and switching costs are nearly zero because no real or implied long-term contracts exist. Laborers are paid, typically in cash, for their day of work, and the process repeats itself the following day.

Perfectly competitive labor markets provide individual employees with little opportunity to develop or implement career strategies. In a market where employment decisions depend solely on the supply and demand for labor, employees exert no control over the probability of getting hired, receiving higher wages, or obtaining promotions. Career strategies can only occur when employment decisions depend on differences in individual skills and capabilities. By definition, such markets are imperfectly competitive. Thus, microeconomic discussions of neoclassical labor markets hold limited value for developing a model of individual career strategy.

Research suggests that few labor markets approach perfect competition. A number of economists relax some of the restrictive conditions of perfect competition, and their work provides important insights on what employees can do to be successful within an organizational context. We next review this literature, focusing on four topics relevant to individual career strategies: job search, human capital and market signaling, the employment relation, and implicit contracts.

Job search

The initial task for individuals seeking to obtain, and then manage, a career is to choose a particular job with a particular company. In discussing the matching of people and jobs over time, economists recognize the individual costs incurred while choosing and changing jobs within and across firms. Thus, this literature relaxes the second condition of neoclassical labor markets by assuming that costs exist for both searching for and switching jobs.

Beginning with a seminal paper by McCall (1970), microeconomists have treated the job search process as a problem of decision making under uncertainty. Unemployed individuals are presumed to be searching for a new job, typically with a known probability of success (Kormendi, 1979) or with a known probability of success discovered over time (Lippman and McCall, 1976; 1979). However, while the success of this search acquires a known probability, the duration of the search usually remains unknown. The most important search cost is foregone income during the search. Thus, the task facing individuals in these models is to trade off the likelihood of obtaining a better (higher paying) job at some uncertain point in the future against the ongoing costs of continuing the search.

These classic job search models have been criticized because their assumptions are unrealistic. First, they assume that individuals are currently unemployed, and the task at hand is to find re-employment. Research by Granovetter (1973, 1974) and others (Hall, 1982; Johnson, 1978; Jovanovic, 1979; Mincer and Jovanovic, 1981; Randolf, 1983) shows that many job changes do not include a period of unemployment. If employees conduct a job search while employed, they do not incur the major cost of searching: the loss of current income. Second, the models assume that unemployed individuals know the probability that they will obtain a new job, and thus that they make purely rational calculations in deciding to continue the search or to take a job. Neither assumption seems valid in real job search situations. People rarely know the probability of obtaining a new job, and even under the best of circumstances, it remains questionable whether people make decisions purely on "rational grounds" (Nisbett and Ross, 1980). Finally, classical search models fail to specify the process by which a job search takes place. Typically, people are members of many social networks, and these networks provide important sources of job and career information, thus reducing the search costs (Granovetter, 1973, 1974).

Boorman (1975) proposes a model that partially addresses these criticisms. Boorman suggests that employees are embedded within a social network of close friends and acquaintances and that the probability of obtaining a job depends on these various contacts. Following Granovetter (1973, 1974), Boorman models the situation in which managers enjoy close personal relations (strong ties) and acquaintances (weak ties) and concludes that, under most reasonable assumptions, weak ties provide a higher probability of generating information that leads to employment than strong ties. The rationale for this conclusion turns on the number of weak ties an individual can maintain. Because it takes considerably more time and emotional commitment to maintain close relationships (strong ties), individuals generally maintain more weak ties than strong ties. The higher frequency of weak ties offsets the probability that if a strong tie has information about a job, he or she will almost certainly share that information with a job searcher.

Job search theories make at least two suggestions for individual career strategies. First, individuals seeking a new job either within or outside an organization should assess the potential search costs and decide what costs they are willing to bear. More generally, managing one's career is likely to entail significant personal costs. Ultimately, the benefits of such actions must be carefully weighed against these costs. Second, individuals should attempt to reduce their search costs as much as possible by utilizing the job and career information available from friends and acquaintances. Social networks, and the personal relationships they represent, thus become an important factor in managing individual careers.

The employment relation

Where job search models focus on the process by which individuals are matched with specific jobs and firms, research on the employment relation focuses on the development of the relationship between a firm and its employees. This work stretches neoclassical labor market conditions further than job search theories.

Here, in addition to lost current income, changing jobs includes the costs of modifying and perhaps abandoning complex social relations between employer and employee. Neoclassical labor market theory assumes that the relationship between a firm and its employees is a simple short-term contract with terms and conditions established by supply and demand. In contrast, research on the employment relation assumes complex social connections between employer and employee. Much of this literature follows the lead of Simon (1961) who saw the employment relation as fundamental to understanding a broad range of organizational processes.

Work on employment relations covers many important questions concerning organizations, including why firms exist (Williamson, 1975), what the boundaries of a firm are (Barney and Ouchi, 1986; Walker and Weber, 1984), and how firms are organized (Alchian and Demsetz, 1972; Armour and Teece, 1978). Williamson's analysis (1975, 1979; Williamson, Wachter, and Harris, 1975) of the employment relation provides the basis for his transaction cost approach to economic analysis. For Williamson, economic transactions are managed through different transaction governance mechanisms, depending on the underlying characteristics of a transaction. The two broad classes of governance mechanisms cited by Williamson (1975) are markets and hierarchies, although numerous governance mechanisms that fall somewhere between markets and hierarchies have also been described (Barney and Ouchi, 1986; Ouchi, 1980; Williamson, 1979).[2]

A hierarchically governed employment relationship is the type of employment relationship most often thought of in the study of careers (Schein, 1978; Sonnenfeld, 1984). Individuals employed in this type of a relationship typically have some sort of a boss and have granted this boss (or bosses) legitimate but limited authority to direct their actions within the firm. Williamson describes this type of relationship as an incomplete contingent claims contract, for at the time an employee joins the firm, his or her duties are only partly specified. Firms utilize such incomplete contracts because the costs of writing and enforcing a complete contract covering an employee's entire career with the firm are prohibitive. As long as neither the firm nor the employee engage in activities inconsistent with the implicit psychological contract (Kotter, 1973) that underlies their relationship, the relationship continues.

At the other extreme, in situations where the costs of monitoring an employee's contract are low, a market-governed employment relationship is more efficient. The labor market for manual laborers discussed earlier provides an example in which the employment relation between employees and firms is market in character. Such employment relations may occur where the job being accomplished is relatively routine or easily measurable, and when employees have no implicit or explicit long-term commitments to a firm. Employers manage this employment relation through complete contingent claims contracts, where all employee obligations and compensation are specified a priori. Clearly, such relationships cannot be complex. If they were complex, it would be difficult to specify all conditions of the relationship within a contract. Moreover, if this employment relation evolved in ways not anticipated when the contract was written, both the firm and the employee might be subject to opportunistic actions of the other party.

Williamson's (1975, 1979) analysis focuses primarily on the choice between market and hierarchical means of governing the employment relationship. Alchian and Demsetz (1972), on the other hand, focus on the character of organizational hierarchies. They begin by observing that teams of employees can be more productive than employees working independently. The role of management within this model is not to increase team production directly but to create settings in which teams can realize their own productivity.

However, teamwork creates its own set of problems. In particular, as long as it is relatively difficult and costly to detect the shirking of individuals on a team, then a strong incentive for free-riding exists (Arrow, 1974; Olson, 1965). This incentive suggests that teams will not be maximally productive because all individuals will, to some extent at least, shirk their work responsibilities.

The obvious solution to this free-riding problem is for the team to hire an individual to monitor the actions of team members. This monitor ensures that shirking does not take place, that the overall performance of the team improves beyond the cost of employing the monitor, and that everyone is better off. Unfortunately, the hired monitor also has strong free-riding incentives and will shirk if left unchecked. Who then, monitors the monitor?

Alchian and Demsetz's (1972) solution suggests that, ultimately, this situation requires monitors who monitor themselves; more specifically, monitors without incentives to engage in free-riding. These monitors turn out to be classic entrepreneurs (Knight, 1921) because they enjoy the property rights (Demsetz, 1967) to the residual productivity of the teams they monitor. Such individuals do not need monitoring because they hold a direct interest in reducing shirking, for shirking reduces their wealth and income (Jensen and Meckling, 1976). Thus, for Alchian and Demsetz, the analysis of the employment relationship remains closely linked to the entrepreneurial function in an economy, and the property rights associated with that function (Fama and Jensen, 1983).

While Alchian and Demsetz apply their economic analysis of the employment relation to developing organizations, Hirschman (1970) focuses on this relationship within firms experiencing difficult economic times. For Hirschman, employees have three classes of responses to such difficulties. The first response is exit: Employees abandon the troubled organization for more secure firms with better opportunities. Neoclassical labor market analysis would end here because it assumes that labor migrates, free of switching and transfer costs, to its highest valued use (Hirschleifer, 1980).

However, Hirschman suggests that employees have two additional options that violate neoclassical assumptions. The first of these Hirschman calls voice. Voice is the process by which employees describe their concerns and suggestions to supervisors. Voice is only possible when the managerial system of a particular firm allows or encourages upward communication (Ouchi, 1980; Peters and Waterman, 1982). If neither exit nor voice are possible, then only loyalty remains.

Loyalty means that employees neither leave nor express their concerns when a firm is having difficulties. Notice that loyalty is not necessarily a positive expression of commitment to a firm. In contrast to traditional definitions of commitment (Mowday, Porter, and Steers, 1982), loyalty means employees are willing to stay. It does not mean they identify with the firm or exert additional efforts on behalf of the firm. Employees' loyalty simply results from the lack of other options, namely, the inability to engage in either exit or voice.

Research on the employment relation makes a major contribution to career strategy by helping define those aspects of careers under an individual's control. First, relationships between employers and employees are complex and fragile social contracts. Employees can exert some influence but can never acquire control over these relationships. Thus, the outcomes of career management are at best uncertain. Second, employees acquire no control over the context of the employer–employee relationship. For example, when the demand for an employee's services limits his or her external career options, this forecloses the employee's option to exit. Management style may also limit an employee's ability to utilize voice. Neither market demand nor management style are under the control of individuals seeking to influence their careers.

Human capital and market signaling

Human capital is the sum of an individual's experiences and training (Becker, 1964). Incorporating human capital into labor market theory relaxes the third condition of perfectly competitive labor markets. Here, employees are no longer assumed to be homogeneous with respect to their skills and capabilities. Work in this area examines the different kinds of investments that employees and firms can make to enhance the employee's value to the firm, and thus the firm's performance. A wide variety of human capital assets has been studied, including education, training, on-the-job experience, and fit within the organization's career structure (Becker, 1964; Rosenbaum, 1984; Spence, 1973).

Human capital theory identifies two types of assets in which firms and employees may be able to invest: general human capital and specific human capital. General human capital includes skills, training, or education that possess value in virtually all work settings. Literacy is, perhaps, the best example of general human capital. Literacy allows an employee to engage in a wide variety of transactions that hold economic value within and across work settings. Specific human capital, on the other hand, includes skills, training, experience, or education that possess value in a restricted set of work settings. Firm-specific human capital holds economic value only within a given firm. Examples might include a foreman's skill in getting the best out of a specific group of auto workers or an engineer's knowledge of a firm's unique and proprietary technology. The smaller the range of transactions in which these skills allow an employee to engage, the more specific the human capital.

Human capital theory suggests that employers make employment and promotion decisions by matching the firm's need for general and specific human capital with the employee's investments. Although this explanation of employment decisions begins to outline the kinds of investments individuals can make in their careers, it does not explain the process by which such investments produce career outcomes. Spence's (1973, 1974) work on market signaling, which is closely linked to human capital theory, focuses on this process.

Spence proposes that an individual's human capital influences employment and promotion decisions only if these assets can be observed by employers. If an employer misperceives an individual's skills and abilities, then the career decision is based on incorrect asset information. Unfortunately, many of the skills and abilities of interest to employers are not easy to observe accurately. These skills and abilities include important human capital assets such as creativity, ability to motivate others, and willingness to do a good job.

How then do employers distinguish good employees from bad ones? Spence suggests the answer lies in the "signals" that employers observe. Signals are "activities or attributes of individuals in a market which by design or accident, alter the beliefs of, or convey information to, other individuals in the market" (Spence, 1974: 1). Human capital investments become signals when employers believe a relationship exists between the human capital asset in question and the observed investment. Such relationships develop because individuals with the human capital asset tend to have an easier time investing in the observed signal than people without the asset. For instance, some people find it easier to make investments, such as advanced degrees or technical training, than others. Thus, employers tend to perceive level of education, reputation of academic institution, and specialized technical training as signals of an employee's human capital assets.[3]

This brief summary of human capital and market signaling theories makes several interesting suggestions for individual career strategies. First, this literature suggests that individuals identify and invest in human capital valued by the organization in which they hope to succeed. For example, Japanese firms are well known for requiring successful employees to gain experience in jobs that cross all functional areas within the firm (Ouchi, 1981). Individuals who desire employment in this type of firm should emphasize their general human capital. They should take a broad spectrum of business courses during school and write resumes that show their experiences in diverse business settings. In contrast, many American firms keep their successful employees within a single functional area. Individuals who desire employment in this type of firm should emphasize their specific human capital. They should focus their training in one area of interest, say marketing or finance, take summer jobs related to that area of interest, and prepare a resume that emphasizes the consistency and depth of their training in this area.

Second, this literature suggests that employees invest in human capital that can be observed easily. Thus, if a student gains admission to several colleges and universities, given no other constraints, he or she should attend the school with the best reputation. Similarly, if an employee can choose between several job assignments, he or she should select the assignment whose completion produces the most visible economic value to the firm.[4]

Implicit contracts

Many of the insights developed in research on job search, the employment relation, human capital, and market signaling have been integrated into a single area known as implicit contract theory (Azariadis, 1975; Azariadis and Stiglitz, 1983; Baily, 1974; Gordon, 1974). Indeed, implicit contract theory has become an important arena within economic research. However, implicit contract theory connects the functioning of labor markets with the functioning of the economy as a whole (Friedman, 1968; Lucas, 1973). Given this macroeconomic emphasis, implicit contract theory provides limited additional insights for career strategy. However, it does suggest why an individual's career strategy is not independent of the career strategies of others within the organization.

The labor market described in implicit contract theory possesses many of the attributes cited in previous literatures. Whereas the neoclassical model envisions a decentralized and impersonal market – where firms make labor demand decisions unilaterally, and where workers make labor supply decisions unilaterally

– implicit contract theory envisions a market in which demand and supply decisions are made jointly between firms and employees. Employer–employee relationships are negotiated and bilateral. According to Rosen (1985: 1145), labor markets are more like marriage markets than they are like stock markets.

The negotiated relationship between firms and employees is presumed to take the form of a contract (Fama and Jensen, 1983; Jensen and Meckling, 1976). The concept of contract employed here is very general (Williamson, 1979). A contract need not be written down or formal, yet it can still be an important determinant of employee and firm behavior. These contracts have several functions. The most important is to specify how the value and utilization of investments shared by employees and firms will be distributed under various states of nature. Following Williamson (1975), under conditions of no uncertainty, it will be possible to specify all future states of nature in a complete contingent claims contract. However, under uncertainty (the more common case), contracts may only specify the mechanisms through which the distribution of investments will be decided, that is, through a hierarchy (Williamson, 1979) or some other means (Ouchi, 1980).

Another important feature of implicit contract theory is that the wages established through negotiating employment contracts implicitly include payments by employees of insurance premiums during good times, and the receipt of indemnities in bad times (Abowd and Ashenfelter, 1981). These wages are equilibrium payments based on the numerous independent decisions made by employees and employers. Thus, in some sense, firms "overpay" employees when the supply of employees outstrips current demand, and they underpay employees when demand outstrips supply. In this manner, the stability of employment is increased, despite historical fluctuations in the business cycle (Abowd and Ashenfelter, 1984).

Many of these insights about the structure and function of labor markets are abstract, divorced from the concerns of individuals looking to manage successful careers. Yet, this research does point to a characteristic central to understanding career strategy. Wages, payments, and the implicit contracts negotiated with employees reflect the numerous independent choices made by employees and employers. In this sense, the career decisions made by one set of individuals partly define the context of career decisions made by others. Thus, career choices depend on the analysis of both an individual's human capital assets, and on the human capital assets of others. Signaling investments must be considered in the context of signals created by others. Search choices depend on the search choices of others. That the context of career management is itself partly the result of career management is an important point in developing a model of individual career strategy.

A MODEL OF INDIVIDUAL CAREER STRATEGY

As we have suggested, the economic literature bears directly on career strategies within organizations. However, despite these applied observations, microeconomic research on careers does not, by itself, constitute an economic model of individual career strategy. The main reason microeconomic theories of labor markets resist translation into applied career models rests with the level of analysis employed by economists. Economists have been interested in the structure and functioning of labor markets as a whole, rather than in the experiences of individual employees within the labor market. Thus, following Williamson (1975), microeconomics has yet to exert a major impact on applied career theories because it is not sufficiently micro in orientation. In other words, microeconomics still does not facilitate analysis of *individuals'* careers within and between firms. A prescriptive model of individual career strategy requires moving the level of analysis to individual employees and considering how employees' actions influence their success within internal and external labor markets.

The first task in developing a model of individual career strategy is to define the boundaries within which we develop the model and specify our assumptions. The model is applicable to all organizational careers, the formally defined sets of related jobs that employees may hold within an organization. The characteristics that define these jobs as related include the type of task performed, the historical mobility patterns of individuals within and not outside this set of jobs, and some criteria that define status differences, such as salary, seniority, increased task choices or responsibilities, and promotions. Thus, we use the external as opposed to the internal definition of an organizational career (Van Maanen and Schein, 1975).

We develop a model of individual career strategy, illustrate it with managerial careers as the example, and focus on internal labor markets (cf. Doeringer and Piore, 1971). Although many organizational careers exist, the familiarity of the managerial career – its job characteristics, mobility patterns, and status criteria – make it a useful example for this initial discussion. The model, however, applies equally well to other organizational careers such as flight attendants, engineers, hotel managers, or steel workers.

Organizational criteria provide individuals with many definitions of success. For instance, many contemporary organizations now include lateral and cross-functional moves in addition to promotional moves as criteria for success. In the managerial career example, we define success as promotion within the career hierarchy. We acknowledge that many promotion criteria exist over which managers exert little or no control. For instance, managers exert little or no control over the number and timing of positions available (Pfeffer, 1983; Spilerman, 1977; Stewman and Konda, 1983; White, 1970), the normative career patterns or ages that may influence promotion decisions (Lawrence, 1987, 1988; Martin and Strauss, 1956; Rosenbaum, 1984; Sofer, 1970) and the external labor market for such positions (Hirschman, 1970). However, because this model attempts to evaluate promotion criteria over which individuals do exert some control, we assume that the former promotion criteria hold constant across managers competing for the same position.

The second task in developing such a model is to specify its prescriptive objectives. With some seriousness we titled this chapter "Pin Stripes, Power Ties, and Personal Relationships" to portray the realistic range of individual career strategies within organizations. One objective of a prescriptive model could be to allow managers to identify and implement career strategies within this range that guarantee promotion. Although managers might like such a model, it seems unlikely that it would be valid, except under the narrowest of conditions. Subordinate managers can influence but not control a superior's promotion decisions. Thus, developing a model that leads to promotion with a probability of one is an unrealistic objective.

The model presented here has a more modest objective. This model examines career strategies that improve a manager's promotion chances above the random probability of promotion. The random probability of promotion is analogous to normal economic performance in the neoclassical microeconomic theory of the firm (Barney, 1986a; Hirschleifer, 1980; Porter, 1980). Thus, the random promotion probability provides a base level against which to measure improvement in promotion chances. In a purely random promotion model, N managers at level i are considered for n positions, where $n < N$. The promotion probability in this random model is simply n/N.

Building on the human capital and market signaling models, managers attempt to improve their promotion chances above a random level by making investments in their human capital. Individual career strategy therefore consists of choosing which human capital investments to make and which to avoid. The impact of these investments on promotion chances depends on the perceived value of the investments within the organization and on the number of other managers who make the same investment.

Organizationally perceived value

The perceived value of a career investment is the economic value added to the firm by the investment, as perceived by top management in that firm. We assume that the higher the perceived value of a career investment, the more it increases an individual's promotion chances. Typically, managers make career investments at some time, t_1, to enhance promotion chances at a later time, t_2.[5] This time lag introduces uncertainty into the impact of career investments on promotion chances. People and organizations change over time. Thus, an investment perceived as valuable at t_1 may not be seen as valuable at t_2. If t_1 and t_2 are quite close together in real time, then relatively little uncertainty exists concerning the likelihood that career investments at t_1 will be perceived as valuable at t_2.

The uncertainty of the promotion outcome at t_2 associated with a career investment also depends on the specificity of the investment at t_1. In general, the more specific the investment, the less likely that the investment will possess perceived value at t_2, and thus the greater the uncertainty of the promotion outcome associated with the investment. Such firm-specific human capital investments remain valuable only as long as the underlying attributes and characteristics of the firm change little between t_1 and t_2. For instance, knowledge of a firm's culture is likely to remain a valuable asset over long periods of time because organizational culture usually evolves slowly (Barney, 1986b).[6] In contrast, because general human capital investments retain value in virtually all settings, the uncertainty of the promotion outcome associated with these investments at t_2 is very low.

Number of individuals who make the investment

In addition to the perceived value of an investment, the number of managers who make the investment also influences the impact of career investments on promotion chances. Consider the case in which all managers believe an investment possesses perceived value, and, as a result, virtually all managers at a given level in the organization make the investment. Such investments do not differentiate one manager from another, thus the promotion chances associated with the investment revert to the random promotion level. On the other hand, if only a few managers make the investment, then these few managers have, other factors being equal, greater promotion chances than managers who have not made the investment.

The number of managers who make a specific human capital investment depends both on the number who make the investment at t_1 and the ease with which those who did not make the investment at t_1 can make the investment between t_1 and t_2. Market signaling theory suggests that capable managers and managers with greater social or financial resources experience greater ease making these investments. However, less capable managers and managers with lesser social or financial resources may also make the same investments, although at higher personal cost. It is important to note that success does not care about personal cost. In the old tale about the tortoise and the hare, the hare was the superior runner, but the tortoise eventually won the race. What counts in promotion competitions is that those who make promotion decisions directly observe the signals produced by an individual's career investments.

Certain career investments are difficult to duplicate, no matter how capable the manager. For example, mentor relationships require the time and mutual interest of both the superior and subordinate. Such relationships are difficult to establish and maintain, especially if the mentor already holds a position of influence. Individual managers who establish and maintain personal relationships with an influential mentor before he or she acquires a position of influence hold a sustained advantage over those managers who do not have such relationships. The literature suggests that this sustained advantage results in increased promotion chances for subordinates (Kram, 1985). Other examples of difficult-to-duplicate career investments include years of experience in a business specialty and ground-floor experience in a new technology. Any time the ability to make a career investment depends on being in "the right place at the right time," the career investment is difficult to duplicate.

Strategic career investments

These two dimensions, the likelihood that a career investment will possess perceived value at t_2 and the number of managers who make this investment, can be brought together into a single model. As shown in Table 20.1, simplifying each dimension into two categories (high and low likelihood, high and low numbers) suggests four different types of career investments that managers can make.[7] Each of these investments exerts a different impact on promotion chances.

Type I career investments (low likelihood/low numbers) include investments that (1) are unlikely to possess perceived value at t_2 and (2) relatively few managers make. Examples of Type I investments include training in a narrow technological field, experience in a highly specialized business function, and developing a relationship with a particular mentor. In all three cases, the specificity of the investment is such that, in a wide variety of situations, the investment would not possess perceived value at t_2. The technology in question may turn out to be a dead end, the business function may not be important, and the mentor may get fired. The frequency of these investments will be relatively low because relatively few managers will be in a position to obtain the kind of training or to develop the kind of relationship necessary to make these investments.

Table 20.1. *An economic model of individual career strategy*

Likelihood of organizationally perceived value at time of promotion decision (t_2)	Number of managers who make the investment	
	Low	High

Low	*Type I*
	Training in a narrow technology
	Experience in a specialized
	  business function
	Relationship with a mentor
		Type II
		Membership on a task force or
		  committee
		Being a good citizen, e.g.,
		  arranging social functions,
		  handling bureaucratic details

High	*Type III*
	An MBA degree from a
	  prestigious school
	Membership on a committee of
	  critical importance to the firm
		Type IV
		The right clothes
		The right hair style
		A college education

Type II career investments (low likelihood/high numbers) include investments that (1) are unlikely to possess perceived value at t_2 and (2) many managers make anyway. Perhaps the best example of Type II investments is task force or committee memberships in research universities. In such universities, faculty members widely acknowledge research as the major promotion criterion. Faculty agree that committee work exerts only a minor impact on promotion chances. Nevertheless, a significant amount of committee work goes on, involving large numbers of faculty. The likelihood of this work improving promotion chances is small, but the frequency with which faculty engage in this work is relatively high.

Type III career investments (high likelihood/low numbers) include investments that (1) are likely to possess perceived value at t_2 and (2) that few managers make. In some firms, MBAs from prestigious business schools may be an example of this type of investment. For instance, a Harvard MBA provides a signal of a manager's intelligence, assertiveness, and general management training. Further, because the Harvard Business School restricts entry, relatively few managers possess this degree. A second example of a Type III career investment is membership on a committee of critical importance to the organization. The organization places tremendous value on this committee work, thus the investment holds high perceived value. Further, only a small group of managers get selected to participate on such a committee, thus the number of managers who make the investment is low.

Type IV career investments (high likelihood/high numbers) include investments that (1) are likely to possess perceived value at t_2 and (2) many managers make or could make rapidly. Examples of Type IV investments include clothes (pin stripes or power ties), hair style, and college education. In some firms, an MBA degree is beginning to take on the attributes of a Type IV career investment. Many Type IV strategies appear obvious and mundane. By definition they have high perceived value and everyone can invest in them. However, such investments are still significant.

INDIVIDUAL AND ORGANIZATIONAL IMPLICATIONS

Individual implications

If an employee wishes to be successful by organizational criteria, what should he or she do? In a world of zero costs, employees should engage in all four types of career investments. However, time, energy, and monetary limitations place investment constraints on all employees. Thus, employees must make choices. Consistent with our previous discussion, employees should choose strategies that provide the greatest increase in chances for a desired success over the probability of random success.

We begin with Type IV investments (high likelihood/high numbers). The failure to engage in these investments can reduce success chances below the random success level. If everyone within the firm values some human capital asset, and if virtually all employees make this investment, then failure to make the investment marks an employee as lacking the full set of human capital assets required for success.

Although failure to engage in Type IV investments can hurt an employee, engaging in these investments does not improve success chances above the random success level. Employees who engage in Type IV investments make themselves the same as other employees in the firm. Strategies that do not distinguish between employees result in random success chances. For instance, the very popularity of "dress for success" books (cf. Kennedy, 1986; Wavada, 1986) reduces the impact of dressing for success on promotions to the base or random level.

Unlike Type IV investments, failure to engage in Type III investments (high likelihood/low numbers) does not reduce success chances below the random success level. Since so few people possess the human capital assets that result from Type III investments, failure to engage in these investments places employees in a large, basically homogeneous job pool. Successes from this pool occur through random success processes.

On the other hand, engaging in Type III strategies can substantially enhance success chances. By definition, such investments possess perceived value to the firm at t_2, and few employees can duplicate these investments. Thus, employees who distinguish themselves in this manner, increase their success chances considerably over the random success level.

Type I investments (low likelihood/low numbers) are similar to Type IV strategies in that employees who fail to engage in Type I investments do not reduce their success chances below the base level. Type I investments, on the other hand, *may* substantially enhance success chances if these investments turn out to possess perceived value at t_2. Indeed, valuable Type I strategies have the same success chances as Type IV strategies. Unfortunately, Type I investments involve considerable risk. The likelihood that Type I strategies will possess no perceived value at t_2 is high. If this occurs, then the investment exerts no impact on success chances at t_2. And, given this career outcome, the personal costs in time, training, and commitment may be quite high.

Finally, Type II investments (low likelihood/high numbers), if they possess perceived value at t_2, exert the same impact on success chances as Type IV investments. That is, omitting Type II investments reduces success chances below the random success level; however, engaging in these investments does not increase success chances above the random success level. If Type II investments turn out not to possess perceived value at t_2, then neither engaging in them nor omitting them exerts any impact on success chances.

In summary, the message for employees from this analysis is quite clear. First, employees should engage in Type IV investments. Failure to make these investments almost certainly jeopardizes success chances. Second, if employees can engage in Type III strategies, then they should, for such strategies exert a nearly certain positive impact on success chances. Third, employees should engage in Type I investments if such investments do not interfere with Type IV or Type III efforts. A positive success outcome is possible from Type I investments, but such outcomes are less certain than those from Type III investments. Finally, employees should only expend efforts in Type II investments if it does not interfere with any other career investments. Type II investments may reduce success chances below the random success level, but the probability of this occurring is relatively low. Even if Type II strategies do turn out to possess perceived value in a firm, they cannot raise success chances above a random selection level. A safe approach with respect to Type II strategies is to monitor them closely, and if it appears that they may turn into Type IV investments, to go ahead and make the necessary investment to protect against the loss of success chances.

Organizational implications

If employees engage in these career strategies, what are the implications for organizations? The model suggests that employees make investments based on the perceived value of the investment. However, investments that hold perceived value for career success do not necessarily hold real economic value for a firm. Thus, the first organizational implication of the model is that organizations need to identify the career investments necessary for economic success and make sure that formal and informal reward structures imbue these investments with perceived value. This seems an obvious suggestion (Kerr, 1975). However, organizations often operate in ways that do not support their economic interests.

A group of research and development engineers, interviewed by the second author, provides an example of such human resource mismanagement. In this firm, engineers get recognition by "troubleshooting" – solving last-minute problems under deadline pressure. Successful troubleshooters are valued highly, and engineers feel such activities contribute more to career success than research and development innovation. Yet, although short-term problem solving is important, the long-term economic success of the firm depends on research and development innovation. Thus, from the employees' perspective, the organization provides more perceived value for activities that have less real economic value.

This example suggests that organizations may not always be aware of the formal and informal reward structures perceived by employees. Thus, a second organizational implication of the model is that good human resource management must include not only a clear knowledge of the career investments necessary for economic success but an ongoing assessment of employees' perceptions of the relative value of different career investments. Employees' perceptions frequently get lost in organizations, either through everyday inattention or through grand plans administered by top management. Yet, these perceptions determine how employees are likely to invest their energies. Thus, an accurate understanding of how employees perceive the formal and informal reward structure is necessary if organizations hope to avoid rewarding employees for career investments that add little economic value.

These first two implications suggest that organizations should maintain a fit between the perceived value of career investments and the real economic value of such investments (cf. Nystrom, 1981). However, different organizations have different economic goals, and the fit between career investment strategies and economic value depends on these goals. Firms that require a heterogeneous labor pool and management skills should reward employees for investing in Type I and Type III career strategies. This should produce a group of employees with a large variety of skills and capabilities. This variety should enable the firm to respond quickly to new technological opportunities, which is consistent with the generalist strategy discussed by Hannan and Freeman (1977).

On the other hand, firms engaging in a specialist strategy (Hannan and Freeman, 1977) may find the heterogeneity created by Type I and Type III investments difficult to manage. These firms might find rewarding employees for Type IV investments more consistent with the firms' strategic objectives. This reward structure should produce a group of employees with relatively homogeneous skills and capabilities, which is more consistent with the specialist approach.

RESEARCH QUESTIONS

The review of labor market theories at the beginning of this chapter suggests two economic assumptions about human behavior. First, people have perfect information on labor markets; and second, knowing this information, people make rational decisions. Our model of individual career strategy within organizations relaxes the first assumption but not the second. The model does not assume that employees obtain perfect information concerning top managements' view of the perceived value of career investments; however, the model does assume that employees make rational decisions, that is, decisions that provide employees with the highest chances of career success. The implications of these two assumptions for the model raise theoretical and research questions concerning reward structures and individual career investments within organizations.

The first assumption suggests that employees accurately perceive the investments that top management believes hold perceived value within organizations. Relaxing this assumption generates several sets of questions. First, how do career investments acquire perceived value? It seems likely that this occurs through both formal and informal channels. Formally, career investments are likely to acquire perceived value through the organization's reward structure. For instance, licensing regulations may state that an Electrician I needs to pass an examination before promotion to Electrician II. Thus, the examination probably becomes a Type IV career investment. Informally, career investments are likely to acquire perceived value through informal contracts that evolve from social relationships. Thus, a supervisor might recognize the unpaid, extra hours put in by a bank clerk to meet deadlines with a special gift or bonus at the end of the year. If the bonus gets paid, or if the extra effort is remembered at performance review time, the bank clerk's extra hours probably represent a Type III career investment.

Although the formal investments that acquire perceived value may be relatively easy to identify, the informal investments are not perceived so easily. Thus, a second area of research might be to describe the perceived career investments within a firm. What types of perceived career investments exist? Do all employees perceive such investments similarly or do "subcultures" exist across which employees' perceptions differ? Are perceived career investments similar across organizations within the same industry or do they differ dramatically? These questions partly address issues concerning "why things get done" in a firm. Thus, this research may contribute to studies of organizational culture, in which "what it takes to survive around here" (Louis, 1983; Van Maanen and Barley, 1983) remains a central concern.

Given that the career investments of perceived value within an organization are known by human resource personnel or "objective" outsiders, a third set of questions surrounds the accuracy with which employees perceive these investments. We know from previous research (Lawrence, 1987, 1988; Rosenbaum, 1984; Rosenbaum, Chapter 16) that employees frequently misperceive the formal structures within their organizations. Thus, it seems likely that employees will misperceive both the formally and informally defined perceived value of career investments. Significant questions on this topic include: What types of investments do employees tend to perceive accurately? When employees misperceive investments, what types of judgment biases do they exhibit (cf. Tversky and Kahneman, 1974)? What are the implications of these misperceptions for individuals? For organizations? When the actual perceived value of career investments changes, for instance as the result of mergers or new management teams, how rapidly do employees' perceptions adjust?

If successful employees are proactive, and if they succeed because they assess the perceived value of career investments accurately, where do they get their accurate perceptions? Do they possess individual attributes that make them better at such assessments or are they "taught the ropes" by successful mentors? Along these lines, we know that groups are often better at assessing complex situations than individuals, thus another possibility is that strong peer groups (Kram and Isabella, 1985) help employees make more accurate assessments of what career investments hold perceived value.

A final set of questions relaxes the second assumption that all employees make rational career decisions. Even when employees identify the perceived value of investments accurately, not all employees invest in successful strategies. Why is it, for instance, that some faculty members consistently overinvest in activities, such as committee work, that universities clearly state have little perceived value for promotions? One possibility is that employees' needs for positive reinforcement exceed the time span required for some investments. The positive rewards accrued from research occur after long periods of career investment, whereas committee work provides more short-term satisfactions. Another possibility is that the organization's career investments of perceived value do not fit the employee. For instance, if an employee's career anchor (Schein, 1978) is stability, then the employee may feel uncomfortable or unable to make entrepreneurial investments of high perceived value. In addition, the investments this employee makes are likely to depend on the extent to which he or she is risk neutral, risk averse, or risk seeking (Rosen, 1985).

Answering these questions links the economic model of individual career strategy with the career investments in which employees actually engage and shifts the model from a primarily prescriptive orientation to a prescriptive and descriptive research tool.

CONCLUSION

Careers have been a major focus of research in microeconomics. Yet, the implications of this work for how individuals should manage their own careers remain obscure. Periodically, work on job search, employment relations, human capital, and market signaling has suggested prescriptive insights. However, the bulk of related economics research continues to be descriptive and mathematically abstract. Implicit contract theory exemplifies this approach to studying careers.

Our effort has been to take the widely scattered prescriptive insights from these theories and organize them into a simple model that suggest how individuals should manage their careers. The model suggests that career choices must be evaluated relative to their future perceived value within the firm and the number of other employees who make the same choices. Specific kinds of career choices possess predictable implications for the success chances of individual employees.

The arguments presented here also suggest important limits on individuals' ability to manage their careers. Uncertainty, linked with the ability of others to duplicate human capital investments, limits the impact of these investments on chances for success. Moreover, the broader social and economic context within which career management efforts unfold have been shown to constrain career management discretion. The interplay of these constraints with individual discretion continues to be an area of promising research effort.

Finally, the model provides a useful framework for examining how reward structures influence career-related employee behavior within organizations. By describing what employees should do to obtain career success within organizations, the model encourages organizations to consider the differences between what employees believe are valued career investments and what investments the organization would like to be valued. Thus, the model provides a stimulus for ongoing efforts to understand both individual attainment within organizations and the effectiveness of organizational reward structures.

NOTES

We gratefully acknowledge the comments of Mike Arthur, Tim Hall, and the participants in the 1986 Careers Division Preconference Workshop, National Academy of Management Meetings.

1 The definition of success used throughout this chapter refers only to how well an employee does by organizational criteria of success. Thus, for managers, success may mean promotions, whereas for blue-collar workers, success may mean assignment to the best jobs and working hours.

2 Between relationships governed by hierarchy and relationships governed by markets, there exist many employment relationships where incomplete contingent claims contracts are still employed, but where the relationship in question is still largely arm's length in character. The relationship between firms and outside consultants, advertising agencies, and some sales representatives (Anderson and Schmittlein, 1984) all fit into these categories.

3 Of course, signals do not always provide accurate information. For instance, age norms within organizations may provide signals to employers about employee performance. Employees who are young for their career level are more likely to be seen as hot shots,

whereas employees who are old for their career level are likely to be viewed as over-the-hill. These stereotypical signals guide employment decisions, even though the signal may be inaccurate for a given employee. Older women may have difficulty returning to the labor force, not because they are women but because their age provides a signal that employers interpret, often inaccurately, as "too old to be good at this kind of work" (Kanter, 1977; Lawrence, 1987, 1988; Rosenbaum, 1984).

4 These career strategy examples mirror Kanter's (1977) observations within a large corporation of how individual's acquire power, the ability to get things done. Career success within an organizational context requires this type of power. Interestingly, Kanter suggests that individuals involved in extraordinary, visible, and relevant activities acquire power. This result supports our contention that, in fact, signaling strategies do help individuals become successful. Employees who engage in and do well at extraordinary, visible, and relevant organizational activities do well within their careers because such activities provide easily observable human capital signals of "the ability to get things done" to employers.

5 We recognize that even during one time period, employees are not always certain of what the organization values. However, we assume that their ability to assess perceived value during time 1 is at least as good as, and probably better than, their projection of perceived value at some later time 2.

6 This assumes that firms experience no dramatic changes in their economic environment, leadership, or ownership, all of which may exert a dramatic impact on culture.

7 In fact, these dimensions represent continua, with ranges from 0 to 100% likelihood, and from 0 to N managers, where N equals the managerial population. However, we simplify the model here to contrast the differences between types of career strategy.

REFERENCES

Abowd, J., and Ashenfelter, O. (1981). Anticipated unemployment and compensating wage differentials. In S. Rosen (ed.), *Studies in Labor Markets.* Chicago: University of Chicago Press, pp. 141–170.
Abowd, J., and Ashenfelter, O. (1984). Compensating wage and earnings differentials for employer determined hours of work. Unpublished manuscript. Department of Economics, University of Chicago.
Alchian, A. A., and Demsetz, H. (1972). Production, information costs, and economic organization. *American Economic Review, 62,* 777–795.
Anderson, E., and Schmittlein, D. C. (1984). Integration of the sales force: an empirical examination. *Bell Journal of Economics, 15*(3), 385–395.
Armour, H. O., and Teece, D. J. (1978). Organization structure and economic performance: a test of the multidivisional hypothesis. *Bell Journal of Economics, 9,* 106–122.
Arrow, K. J. (1974). *The Limits of Organization.* New York: Norton.
Azariadis, C. (1975). Implicit contracts and underemployment equilibria. *Journal of Political Economy, 83*(6), 1183–1202.
Azariadis, C., and Stiglitz, J. (1983). Implicit contracts and fixed price equilibria. *Quarterly Journal of Economics, 98*(3), 1–22.
Baily, M. (1974). Wages and employment under uncertain demand. *Review of Economic Studies, 41*(1), 37–50.
Bain, J. S. (1956). *Barriers to New Competition.* Cambridge, MA: Harvard.
Barney, J. B. (1986a). Organizational culture: can it be a source of sustained competitive advantage? *Academy of Management Review. 11,* 656–665.
Barney, J. B. (1986b). Strategic factor markets: expectations, luck and business strategy. *Management Science. 32,* 1231–1241.
Barney, J. B., and Ouchi, W. G. (1986). Information cost and the organization of transaction governance. Unpublished manuscript. Graduate School of Management, University of California at Los Angeles.
Becker, G. (1964). *Human Capital.* New York: Columbia University Press.
Boorman, S. A. (1975). A combinatorial optimization model for transmission of job information through contact networks. *Bell Journal of Economics, 6,* 216–249.
Chamberlin, E. H. (1933). *The Theory of Monopolistic Competition.* Cambridge, MA: Harvard.

Demsetz, H. (1967). Toward a theory of property rights. *American Economic Review, 57,* 347–359.

Doeringer, P., and Piore, M. (1971). *Internal Labor Markets and Manpower Analysis.* Boston: Heath.

Fama, E. F., and Jensen, M. C. (1983). Separation of ownership and control. *Journal of Law and Economics, 26,* 327–349.

Friedman, M. (1968). The role of monetary policy. *American Economic Review, 58*(1), 1–17.

Gordon, D. F. (1974). A neo-classical theory of Keynesian unemployment. *Economic Inquiry, 12*(4), 431–459.

Granovetter, M. S. (1973). The strength of weak ties. *American Journal of Sociology, 78,* 1360–1380.

Granovetter, M. (1974). *Getting a Job: A Study of Contacts and Careers.* Cambridge, MA: Harvard University Press.

Hall, R. E. (1982). The importance of lifetime jobs in the U.S. economy. *American Economic Review, 72*(4), 716–724.

Hannan, M. T., and Freeman, J. (1977). The population ecology of organizations. *American Journal of Sociology, 82,* 929–964.

Hirschleifer, J. (1980). *Price Theory and Its Applications,* 2nd ed. Englewood Cliffs, NJ: Prentice-Hall.

Hirschman, A. O. (1970). *Exit, Voice, and Loyalty: Responses to Decline in Firms, Organizations, and States.* Cambridge, MA: Harvard University Press.

Jensen, M. C., and Meckling, W. H. (1976). Theory of the firm: managerial behavior, agency costs, and ownership structure. *Journal of Financial Economics, 3,* 305–360.

Johnson, W. R. (1978). A theory of job shopping. *Quarterly Journal of Economics, 92*(2), 972–990.

Jovanovic, B. (1979). Job matching and the theory of turnover. *Journal of Political Economy, 87*(5), 972–990.

Kanter, R. M. (1977). *Men and Women of the Corporation.* New York: Basic Books.

Kennedy, M. M. (1986). *Glamour Guide to Office Smarts.* New York: Ballentine.

Kerr, S. (1975). On the folly of rewarding A, while hoping for B. *Academy of Management Journal, XX,* 769–783.

Knight, F. H. (1921). *Risk, Uncertainty, and Profit.* Boston: Houghton Mifflin.

Kormendi, R. C. (1979). Dispersed transactions prices in a model of decentralized pure exchange. In S. A. Lippman and J. J. McCall (eds.), *Studies in the Economics of Search.* Amsterdam: North-Holland, pp. 53–81.

Kotter, J. (1973). The psychological contract: managing the joining-up process. *California Management Review, 15,* 91–99.

Kram, K. E. (1985). *Mentoring at Work: Developmental Relationships in Organizational Life.* Glenview, IL: Scott Foresman.

Kram, K. E., and Isabella, L. (1985). Mentoring alternatives: the role of peer relationships in career development. *Academy of Management Journal, 28,* 110–132.

Lawrence, B. S. (1987). An organizational theory of age effects. In S. Bacharach and N. DiTomaso (eds.), *Research in the Sociology of Organizations,* Vol. 5. Greenwich, CT: JAI, pp. 37–71.

Lawrence, B. S. (1988). New wrinkles in the theory of age: demography, norms, and performance ratings. *Academy of Management Journal, 31,* 309–337.

Lippman, S. A., and McCall, J. J. (1976). The economics of job search: a survey. *Economic Inquiry* (Parts I and II), *14,* 155–189, 347–368.

Lippman, S. A., ard McCall, J. J. (eds.) (1979). *Studies in the Economics of Search.* Amsterdam: North-Holland.

Louis, M. R. (1983). Culture: yes; organization: no! Unpublished manuscript. Presented at the National Academy of Management, Dallas, August 1983.

Lucas, R. E., Jr. (1973). Some international evidence of output–inflation trade offs. *American Economic Review, 63*(2), 326–334.

Martin, N. H., and Strauss, A. L. (1956). Patterns of mobility within industrial organizations. *Journal of Business, 19,* 101–110.

McCall, J. J. (1970). Economics of information and job search. *Quarterly Journal of Economics, 84,* 113–126.

Mincer, J., and Jovanovic, B. (1981). Labor mobility and wages. In S. Rosen (ed.), *Studies in Labor Markets*. Chicago: University of Chicago Press, pp. 21–64.

Mowday, R. T., Porter, L. W., and Steers, R. M. (1982). *Employee–Organization Linkages: The Psychology of Commitment, Absenteeism, and Turnover*. New York: Academic.

Nisbett, R., and Ross, L. (1980). *Human Inference: Strategies and Shortcomings of Social Judgment*. Englewood Cliffs, NJ: Prentice-Hall.

Nystrom, P. C. (1981). Designing jobs and assigning employees. In P. C. Nystrom and W. H. Starbuck (eds.), *Handbook of Organizational Design*, Vol. 2. New York: Oxford University Press, pp. 272–301.

Olson, M. (1965). *The Logic of Collective Action: Public Goods and the Theory of Groups*. Cambridge, MA: Harvard University Press.

Ouchi, W. G. (1980). Markets, bureaucracies, and clans. *Administrative Science Quarterly*, *25*, 129–141.

Ouchi, W. G. (1981). *Theory Z*. Reading, MA: Addison-Wesley.

Peters, R., and Waterman, R. (1982). *In Search of Excellence*. New York: Harper & Row.

Pfeffer, J. (1983). Organizational demography. In L. L. Cummings and B. Staw (eds.), *Research on Organizational Behavior*, Vol. 5. Greenwich, CT: JAI, pp. 299–357.

Porter, M. E. (1980). *Competitive Strategy: Techniques for Analyzing Industries and Competitors*. New York: Free Press.

Randolf, W. C. (1983). Employment relationships: till death do us part? Ph.D. dissertation. State University of New York at Stony Brook.

Rosen, S. (1985). Implicit contracts: a survey. *Journal of Economic Literature*, *23*, 1144–1175.

Rosenbaum, J. E. (1984). *Career Mobility in a Corporate Hierarchy*. Orlando, FL: Academic.

Schein, E. H. (1978). *Career Dynamics: Matching Individual and Organizational Needs*. Reading, MA: Addison-Wesley.

Simon, H. (1961). *Administrative Behavior*, 3rd ed. New York: Free Press.

Sofer, C. (1970). *Men in Mid-Career: A Study of British Managers and Technical Specialists*. Cambridge: Cambridge University Press.

Sonnenfeld, J. (1984). *Managing Career Systems: Channeling the Flow of Executive Careers*. Homewood, IL: Irwin.

Spence, A. M. (1973). Job market signaling. *Quarterly Journal of Economics*, *83*, 355–374.

Spence, A. M. (1974). *Market Signaling: Informational Transfer in Hiring and Related Screening Processes*. Cambridge, MA: Harvard University Press.

Spilerman, S. (1977). Careers, labor market structure, and socioeconomic achievement. *American Journal of Sociology*, *83*, 551–593.

Stewman, S., and Konda, S. L. (1983). Careers and organizational labor markets: demographic models of organizational behavior. *American Journal of Sociology*, *88*(4), 637–685.

Tversky, A., and Kahneman, D. (1974). Judgment under uncertainty: heuristics and biases. *Science*, *185*, 1124–1131.

Van Maanen, J., and Barley, S. R. (1983). Cultural organization: fragments of a theory. Unpublished manuscript. Sloan School of Management, Massachusetts Institute of Technology.

Van Maanen, J., and Schein, E. H. (1975). Improving the quality of work life: career development. In *Improving Life in Organizations*, monograph series. Washington, DC: U.S. Department of Labor.

Walker, G., and Weber, D. (1984). A transaction cost approach to make or buy decisions. *Administrative Science Quarterly*, *29*(3), 373–391.

Wavada, J. E. (1986). *Yup the Organization: How to Succeed in Business with Savvy, Smarts, and Style*. New York: Franklin Watts.

White, H. C. (1970). *Chains of Opportunity*. Cambridge, MA: Harvard University Press.

Williamson, O. E. (1975). *Markets and Hierarchies: Analysis and Antitrust Implications*. New York: Free Press.

Williamson, O. E. (1979). Transaction cost economics: the governance of contractual relations. *Journal of Law and Economics*, *22*, 233–261.

Williamson, O. E., Wachter, M. L., and Harris, J. E. (1975). Understanding the employment relation: the analysis of idiosyncratic exchange. *Bell Journal of Economics*, *6*, 250–278.

21 Rhetoric in bureaucratic careers: managing the meaning of management success

DAN GOWLER AND KAREN LEGGE

> In career research, we have often operated as if there were some specific content of human action, an already objectivized world; but, in fact, there is not.
> *A. Collin and R. A. Young, 1986*

INTRODUCTION

The point of departure for this chapter is provided by Weigert (1983:316), who, when discussing biographies and careers, comments that

> to make sense, a biography must be sustained by a social structure that renders the story plausible (Berger 1967; McLain and Weigert 1979). Storytellers are important sustainers of the social structures that provide a meaningful context for the grunts and groans of life. In a bureaucratically organized society, the structures accept individuals as holders of prearranged careers. The faded pictures behind the idea "career" are of a wagon on a path or a runner on a racetrack. The commonsense notion of a career restricts it to highly visible occupations such as law, medicine, politics, or sports. In a bureaucratically organized society, however, the term *career* is appropriately applied to all members.

Our choice of these comments has been influenced by their direct reference to the construction of meaning in social contexts, which clearly reflects an emerging stance toward the study of careers (Arthur and Lawrence 1984; Collin and Young 1986; Van Maanen 1977). However, as indicated by the opening quotation, *we find it fruitful to modify the suggestion that a given social structure in some way determines the form and meaning of careers*. Instead, we argue that *the rhetorical construction of careers is not only determined by our social environments, but also creates and legitimates them*. In other words, we adopt an interpretive socio-linguistic approach to these issues, where the "storyteller" as rhetorician actually enacts his or her social environment.

We develop and illustrate this argument through the discussion of three major themes: (i) the dominance of bureaucratic organization and control, (ii) careers and the rhetoric of bureaucratic control and (iii) careers as reputations and the aggrandizement of management. But before elaborating upon these issues, it is necessary to clarify what we mean by "an interpretive socio-linguistic approach" to the study of careers.

LANGUAGE, IDEOLOGY AND RHETORIC

Throughout this chapter we assume the terms "socio-linguistic approach," "language," "ideology" and "rhetoric" to be inextricably intertwined. Thus, following

437

Kress and Hodge (1979:5), we regard "socio-linguistic" as involving the study of language in social interaction – for communicable perception has to be coded in language; only what has a name can be shared. *Language* comprises systems of categories and rules that frame fundamental assumptions about the world. Furthermore, by treating some distinctions as crucial and ignoring others (as the clichéd comparison between the number of Inuit and English words for "snow" illustrates), language imposes its own grid on experience. Indeed, social anthropologists (Douglas 1966, 1975; Leach 1964, 1976) have illustrated how the relationship between categorization and the framing, foregrounding and backgrounding of meaningful experience reveals the moral order of society. As Jayyusi (1984:45) states, categorizations can be made to function simultaneously as inferences, descriptions and judgments.

Now, if *ideology* is defined as sets of ideas involved in the framing of our experience, of making sense of the world, expressed through language (Abercrombie, Hill and Turner 1984; Fowler and Kress 1979; Trew 1979), then language is "ideological" in two senses. It is both the means through which ideologies are expressed and also embodies ideology – as is only too clear in sexist and racist language (see, e.g., Spender 1980). *Rhetoric* is the art of using language to persuade, influence or manipulate (Culler 1981:189; Eagleton 1983:205; Hunter 1984:1). And so, in our view, when used rhetorically, language asserts ideology (Parkin 1975:116).

Our position, then, as Eagleton (1983:60) would put it, reflects the "linguistic revolution" of the twentieth century: "that meaning is not simply something 'expressed' or 'reflected' in language: it is actually *produced* by it."

The very word "career" and commonly used definitions of the term illustrate this position. As Arthur and Lawrence (1984:1) point out, the term derives from the Latin *carraria,* meaning a road or carriageway. Embodied in the concept of "road" are ideas about direction, for example, that the road should lead somewhere, that it provides a link between places, that it exists to facilitate movement between places. Additionally, it suggests intention and purposive behavior, with the further connotation of "getting somewhere," which is not a surprising allusion in social systems that idealize achievement (Gowler and Legge 1983; Offe 1976). Thus, the very word "career" itself has multiple facets of meaning, which are variously illuminated in everyday speech. Let us look at Crompton and Sanderson's (1986:2) observation that

career is a term that we would use in a fairly loose fashion to describe *the construction and/ or determination of adult life experience* . . . However, *in everyday language* and much of industrial sociology – the notion of "career" refers to a continuous period in the labour force, with the same or different employment or seeking work, during which the individual does his or her best to make rational decisions which advance their employment career. (emphasis added)

It should be noted that these comments rhetorically evoke a variety of positive meanings: "best," "rational," "advance," "construction," and "seeking," which by association convey the desirability of a career over and above the surface meaning of the sentences employed. For us, then, this quotation fulfils several purposes: It defines careers in terms of experience while simultaneously providing an example of a written rhetoric arguing the centrality of career in life's experience. Furthermore, the reference to "the construction and/or determination of adult life experiences to the external and internal worlds allows us to highlight the duality of human structures, such as careers, and their "structuration" through language as a series of "reproduced practices" (Giddens 1976:161). Just as language is both constituted by human agency yet at the same time is the medium of this constitution, so people construct careers through language, by assigning meanings to their actions, and use these constructs to interpret and express the experiences that provide the stimulus for such constructions (cf. Van Maanen 1977:18). As Kress and Hodge (1979:5) point out, the part played by language in the "social construction of reality" (Berger and Luckmann 1967) is crucial; for

language fixes a world that is so much more stable and coherent than what we actually see that it takes its place in our consciousness and becomes what we think we have seen. And since normal perception works by constant feedback, the gap between the real world and the socially constructed world is constantly being reduced, so that what we do "see" tends to become what we can say.

In this chapter, we focus on the ways in which rhetorical language constructs careers that reflect and reproduce the ideology of bureaucratic organization in British and American society. As explained in the preceding, we emphasize rhetorical language not only because it is doubly charged with ideological form and content but because *its high symbolic content allows it to reveal and conceal but above all develop and transform meaning.* Rhetoric privileges metaphor in its construction of meaning (Culler 1981:189), and metaphor – which communicates the unknown by transposing it into terms of the known – can act as an "innovatory inaugural force" (Culler 1981:189). Thus, our perceptions and constructions of career change radically when it ceases to be presented as a ladder or path and, for example, is alternatively characterized in terms of a rat race or an uphill struggle.

To elaborate this point, *rhetoric heightens and transforms meaning by processes of association, involving both evocation and juxtaposition.* For instance, within the structure of a rhetorical statement, the word "career" may be used to evoke thoughts and feelings conventionally attributed to other words, for example, reputation. Or, by juxtaposition, career and, say, reputation may become associated, as when a person's reputation is used to justify the offer or denial of promotion (Crossman 1979:459). Consequently, as a result of association, evocation and juxtaposition, a process of transformation may occur, where one word is used synonymously with another – as when career and reputation become conflated. Consequently, a particular career transition may be described as a move to a "graveyard of reputations" (and, by implication, to the "death" of a career). In this example, the transformation is completed and enhanced by metaphor. As Parkin (1975:119) observes, "Through rhetoric, people have licence, so to speak, to explain and evaluate the causes and consequences of social relations, sometimes to the point of distortion. Rhetoric is thereby dynamically involved in their organisation and perpetuation."

Finally, Arthur and Lawrence (1984:3) state that an individual's experience of career and the meanings he or she attributes to it "cannot be understood without reference to the environment in which it takes place." While we would not see "environment" in such concrete terms (cf. Smircich and Stubbart 1985:726), we consider that the "reproduced practices" of bureaucracy generate the dominant set of meanings that shape people's understandings and experience of career in the societies under consideration here. These meanings are expressed through what we have termed "the rhetoric of bureaucratic control" (Gowler and Legge 1983).

THE DOMINANCE OF BUREAUCRATIC ORGANIZATION AND CONTROL

It is now a commonplace notion that emergent with the rise of bureaucratic forms of social organization came attendant ideas and images that have provided us with a calculus for containing a heavily charged set of meanings about work, life and success. For example, when discussing the rituals of employment, Pym (1982:223–4) asserts:

Bureaucratic organizations now dominate employment. The case against the alienating features of bureaucracy is well-documented. But our relationships with this abstract parent to which we owe much of our material well-being is not simple. Success not failure has led to its excess and individually we demonstrate a remarkable ability to dissociate our own actions from those excesses. *Over organization comes from underestimating the extent to which our upbringing and education train us to think bureaucratically.* We are all bureaucrats now. (emphasis added)

Additionally, Smircich (1985:57) observes:

It is clear that the Western world has elevated organization and management to the status of cultural values. A trip to a bookstore quickly reveals our fascination with organizations and careers, and our preoccupation with managing them. We understand and make sense of our lives with reference to the concepts of organization and management. These concepts are filters through which we experience our lives and know ourselves. (emphasis added)

Indeed, it has even been claimed that the pervasive effect of bureaucratic organization has given rise to a particular personality and behavior. For example, when discussing the problems accompanying the introduction of matrix organizations, Argyris (1967) argues that the traditional pyramidal structure has produced a characteristic pattern of "bureaucratic" behaviors, for example, conformity, mistrust, lack of risk taking and so on, that inhibit change.

It is not surprising given this degree of pervasiveness that the conventional concept of a career – implying intra- and inter-organizational "progress" – also reflects notions about bureaucratic structures (Arthur and Lawrence 1984:2). But for us the significant issue is that along with the rise of so-called rational forms of organization there also emerged a characteristic type and ideology of control. This may be illustrated in Weber's (1946, 1947) classic statements about the ideal typical bureaucracy and, of course, in subsequent elaborations by a veritable host of academic commentators. For the purposes of this chapter, however, we draw attention to four views of control, that is, *hierarchy, accountability, achievement and membership,* that litter this literature:

The organisation of offices follows the principle of *hierarchy;* that is, each lower office is under the *control* and supervision of a higher one. (Weber 1947:331, emphasis added)

Every official in this administrative *hierarchy* is *accountable* to his superior for his subordinates' decisions and actions as well as his own. (Blau and Meyer 1971:191, emphasis added)

The achievement principle is a prescriptive model of status distribution, providing *for formal organizations* in industrial societies the sole principle by which social status is legitimated, where status includes both differences in existing status and *changes of status by means of occupational mobility.* (Offe 1976:55, emphasis added)

Membership in hierarchical organizations may be viewed from four perspectives. One perspective, perhaps that of organizational leaders, seeks *members who contribute to achieving organizational goals.* This perspective values proficiency and economy in task performance. Any organizations which exist to provide goods or services must place high value on selecting and retaining members who are effective in providing the goods or services, or in facilitating the work of members who do. (Guion 1981:369, emphasis added)

As two other commentators sum it up:

Bureaucratic control is embedded in the social and organizational structure of the firm and is built into job categories, work rules, *promotion procedures*, discipline, wage scales, definitions of responsibilities, and the like. Bureaucratic control establishes the impersonal force of "company rules" or "company policy" as the basis for control. (Edwards 1979:131, emphasis added)

The Weberian structure has been built upon, rationalized, adjusted, twisted, and modified for the past forty years, but its essential assumptions still govern the *popular conception* of organizations and administrators, the training programs for administrators in our colleges and universities, the research that is undertaken in the field, the development activities that produce our most usable and used technologies, and *the way we talk about our work places.* (Clark 1985:51, emphasis added)

Importantly for the argument being developed here, Clark (1985:49–50) illustrates how this dominant bureaucratic paradigm is reflected and confirmed in a variety of familiar aphorisms, for example, "the buck stops here" and "authority should be commensurate with responsibility." Thus, everyday language has become the handmaiden of bureaucratic control in Western, industrialized societies. At the same time, the scientific management movement, as Merkle (1980:81) contends, continues to provide ideological fuel for the bureaucratic form of control.

Such statements as those quoted in the preceding illustrate the point that there exists *a dominant ideology of control* that shapes and is shaped by our experience of the world. We suggest that this is very evident in *both* the academic debate and everyday discussions about careers. In the following section, we show how "talk" about careers provides a semantic "conduit" through which such control is enacted. Just as notions of hierarchy, accountability, achievement and membership together construct a meaning of career in certain societies, so its enactment in these terms *reproduces* (Giddens 1976; Weick 1979) the practice of bureaucracy. We now consider how this is accomplished.

CAREERS AND THE RHETORIC OF BUREAUCRATIC CONTROL

Among those scholars entering the water margins of interpretive method, it is a commonplace belief that symbolic actions may only be rendered meaningful in terms of the system of meaning in which they occur. This is then said to require an intensive, social-anthropological knowledge of the local scene (Linstead 1985). However, while we accept that rhetoric enacts "specific forms of social life" (Eagleton 1986:169), there are generalized systems of meaning, such as those concerning the sanctity of human life, available to the social actor (which includes

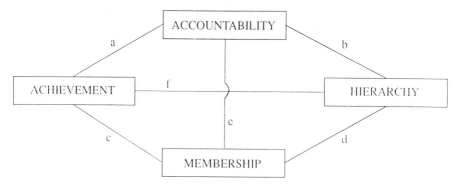

Figure 21.1. Themes in the rhetoric of bureaucratic control

the would-be analyst). They are so pervasive that one does not have to travel any distance for an example. Consequently, in addition to academic sources, we locate the rhetoric of bureaucratic control in the mundane environment of everyday communication, for example, managerial conversation and correspondence (Gowler and Legge 1983:206). In an attempt to conjure up the enacted environment of careers and, by association, reputation, in Figure 21.1 we identify four themes that illuminate the rhetoric of bureaucratic control.

We take the theme of accountability first. Several theorists have claimed that the accountability of conduct is a "distinctive characteristic of the human species and is bound up with the social character of language" (Semin and Manstead 1983:32) and that "the foundation of meaning. . .is the system of accountability" (Douglas 1980:71). In our culture, this "distinctive characteristic" is often expressed in terms of individual and/or collective *responsibility*. Careers and reputations are frequently framed in accounts of responsible behavior – a very poignant example being the account of Captain Oates's altruistic behavior in walking away from his companions (and so sacrificing his life) in order not to further slow down their return to safety on Scott's ill-fated polar expedition. Less dramatically, when talking about work and jobs, individuals often refer to the people, events and things for which they are or have been "responsible."

As illustrated in Figure 21.1, however, accountability is frequently associated or even treated as synonymous with achievement (see association a). A fine example of these meanings is provided in the closing lines of a letter to a well-known professional journal. The correspondent, who is commenting upon aspects of British industrial relations, concludes:

Experience teaches us that the *responsibility* for the *achievement* of sound employment policies, expanding prosperity and, more importantly, the prospects of our successors has never left *the boardroom*. (Taylor 1985:41, emphasis added)

This fragment of the rhetoric of bureaucratic control contains a universe of meanings that cannot be tracked here. But it should be noted that the direct attribution of responsibility alludes to the membership of a group of company directors placed at the top of a management hierarchy (see associations e, b and d). We have discussed elsewhere (Gowler and Legge 1983) that the configuration of meanings represented by associations a, b and e in Figure 21.1, that is, by accountability, achievement and hierarchy, are used to express and legitimize "the right to manage." Among other things, this is the buck-stops-here construction of a moral environment, where authority and responsibility are neatly conflated. But as Clark (1985:49) says of the aphoristic construction of reality, it may be that the buck never stops anywhere and that authority and responsibility are almost never congruous in an organization. Nevertheless, the letter quoted in the preceding shows how, like myth, the rhetoric of bureaucratic control helps to stitch up the ragged ends of an untidy world while providing a "frame" for our careers, that is, the meaningful construction of "adult life experiences" (Crompton and Sanderson 1986:28).

This issue of framing or the organization of experience (Bateson 1973; Goffman 1974) takes us to the theme of achievement, the very icon of careers. Thus, in Figure 21.1, we draw attention to a crucial aspect of this analysis. This is that our careers and reputations are socially constructed and evaluated as a form of achievement. In other words, we provide an acceptable frame of meaning for ourselves and others by the artful attribution of our attainments. Nowhere is this more in evidence than in those catalogues of success and failure, the managerial autobiography. For example, in Sloan's (1965:xxiv) treasure trove of rhetoric, he presents his achievements in the round as shareholder, executive and benefactor. He asserts:

Since joining the corporation I have been a substantial shareholder in it. For a long time I was one of its largest shareholders, with about 1 per cent of the common stock. Almost all of the fortune that this represents has gone and is going into the charitable foundation which bears my name, and from there into education and scientific research and other fields.

And with a swift elaboration of this confession, he continues:

Thus the shareholder's point of view is natural to me. I have always taken a strong stand for the shareholder, explicitly in such matters as representation on the board of directors and its committees, and the payment of dividends. Yet I have also considered myself as one of the breed that we now call the "executive." Management has been my specialization.

Now with due respect for a famous son of capitalism, here we see career, reputation and achievement framed in some of the dominant values of his society. For instance, we have self-evaluation constructed in terms of free enterprise, financial success, private benevolence and managerial expertise. Furthermore, Sloan's rhetoric, by conjuring up a systemic view of organization (through his involvement with *inputs*/shareholders, *transformations*/executives and *outputs*/ dividends) generates submerged understandings about the nature of organizational survival and growth. By implication, Sloan's image of career, he having reached the summit of one of the world's largest companies, takes on an aura of god-like achievement and accountability.

Achievement is also associated with hierarchy (see association f, Figure 21.1). In the following piece of fine rhetorical writing, Stuart-Kotze and Roskin (1983:3) provide a colorful and instructive example:

The modern history of management is a chronicle of striving to run organizations more effectively, of trying to achieve more with less, and attempting to increase output and returns continually. But if management has one underlying goal, it is to *achieve!* That's the name of the game, no matter how it's played. *No results mean no job in any position of significance*. Politics, power, wheeling and dealing, all eventually have to show some positive results for the organization if a manager wants to keep his or her job. It's achievement that gives power, and it's lack of it that saps power. When things turn bad staff and shareholders lose their loyalty to the management they once heaped with praise. (latter emphasis added)

In this quotation, however, it is possible not only to detect the association between hierarchy ("position of significance") and achievement but also to find others assumed in Figure 21.1. For example, there is an implicit link between membership ("job or no job") and achievement (association c). In other words, if people do not perform, they either lose their jobs or the loyalty of those that count, for example, "staff and shareholders." Looked at in this way, *achievement is construed here in terms of high performance earning the trust of significant others and the bestowal of a "good reputation."*

Taking a closer look at hierarchy, we find not only the organization of persons in graded ranks, each of which controls that below it, but also an organization or framing of meanings. In other words, hierarchy as the vertical division of labor is also the realization of a bureaucratized means of administration (Reed 1985:15) that represents the graded relations between individuals as *a natural state of affairs.* Consequently, for some, meaning is found in relations of domination and subordination. Careers and reputations are frequently expressed and evaluated in terms of the rank achieved in work organizations. For example, when discussing the topical issue of "career dynamics," Hall and Isabella (1985:22) write:

As organizations become flexible in having to adapt to new environments, they will need employees who are correspondingly flexible and adaptive. The more that employees can move up, down, laterally, and in and out to acquire and utilize important new skills, the more effective employees and organizations can be. And the more this movement is under the *joint control* of the employee and organization, the more effective organizations will be.

Similarly, Baird and Kram (1983:47) point out:

Research on the careers of engineers, scientists and professional managers has found that what one wants and needs from a job will depend on the person's career stage – that is, the jobs they have held, their current position, and the direction in which they are moving. This research has also found that individuals progress through particular career stages, each of which is characterized by unique dilemmas, concerns, needs and challenges. Because experience and maturing cause people to go through these career stages, and what they need from each other changes as they move through successive career stages, *it is important that they maintain a dynamic perspective on their superior/subordinate relationships.* (emphasis added)

In short, bureaucratic domination is not only seen to provide the most legitimate and rational mode of work (Meyer and Rowan 1977), but it also supplies the semantic scaffolding of our careers and reputations. In accounts of promotions, fast tracks, and moves to another floor, we see the enactment of the environment of bureaucratic control, where the preferred way to ensure accountability is to establish and maintain an appropriate hierarchy of power relations (association b, Figure 21.1) and performance (association a, Figure 21.1).

To complete this brief tour of the four themes identified, we turn to the question of organizational membership. Any "telling" of a career and any "puffing" of reputation is likely to make references to the organizations where "one has been." Our calendar of careers is marked off by organizational entrances and exits. *It is not enough to have "worked."* The sine qua non of a career constructed in terms of the rhetoric of bureaucratic control is that one has entered a contractual, rule-bound relationship with an organization, has entered employment, has become a member. But entries and exits are confined not only to the organization, but also to its constituent groups and rungs on the ladder. Promotion, for example, may be presented "as a step in the right direction" (up the hierarchy) as well as in terms of new responsibilities and membership of a different group (see associations e and d, Figure 21.1). Here a transition involves the understanding and acquisition of new codes and conduct.

This is the socialization approach to organizational membership. As Louis (1980:229–230) puts it: "Organizational socialization is the process by which an individual comes to appreciate the values, abilities, expected behaviors and social knowledge essential for assuming an organizational role and for participating as an organizational member." She goes on to point out that since each role transition, whether within or between organizations, involves socialization into new relationships and settings, this is a pervasive process throughout adult life. Furthermore, the competent social actor is able to cope with the surprises encountered in novel circumstances by individual and collective sense making.

This process of sense making, which provides the raw material of accounts about careers and reputations, is often shaped and punctuated by the rites of passage of organizational membership, "the most commonly recognized rites in modern society" (Trice and Beyer 1985:373). The study of rites of initiation reveals how becoming a member of a work organization involves the associations expressed in Figure 21.1. For example, when discussing the socialization of sailors on their first ship, Zurcher (1983:35) records that "new crew members are exposed to the formal role expectations in their assignments to shipboard jobs and to a place in the ship's hierarchy of official authority." In this fragment, it does not take too much analysis to uncover the themes of accountability and achievement, for example, in the reference to "role expectations" as well as in the direct allusion to hierarchy.

In summary, what we have attempted to do here is to offer some evidence of the rhetoric of bureaucratic control in the literature and conversation about careers and employment. In doing so and as mentioned in the introduction to this chapter, career and reputation have been semantically associated. For, if the rhetoric of everyday usage constructs career, we would suggest that it often does so through the building of reputation, that putative relative of achievement. It is to this neglected aspect of adult life experience we now turn.

CAREERS AS REPUTATIONS AND THE AGGRANDIZEMENT
OF MANAGEMENT

We have pointed out how the rhetoric of bureaucratic control – highlighting as it does the notions of hierarchy, accountability, achievement and membership – constructs the dominant meaning of career in our society. Career in everyday language is presented as achievement in "climbing the ladder" to the "top of the tree" in occupational settings, and the implicit social evaluation of such meanings is conveyed rhetorically by metaphor. Interestingly enough, even the attempts to question these images and/or realities have difficulty in escaping this system of representations, that is, ideology. For example, when discussing new directions in career management, Evans (1986:29) comments: "Most of our thinking about career development is confined by assumptions that this means providing a *hierarchical ladder for achievement* and advancement, rather than thinking in terms of the steady state or spiral career" (emphasis added). However, he concludes his article with the following suggestions:

The concept of a career as a spiral can be particularly suited to the needs of firms operating in an uncertain environment. The spiralist wishes to pursue a particular line of work for five to seven years, then spiral off into a related career – from engineering to the creation of one's business, later back into sales management, then into freelance consulting. Too often we fall into the trap of assuming that all talented individuals are looking for the ladders, and we focus our career management attention on those with the highest potential to climb the biggest ladders. But in the organisations of tomorrow there are likely to be fewer and fewer ladders.

It seems to us that even this prophecy about the shape of future careers and organizations still envisages *achievement* (talented individuals with potential) *embedded in a bureaucratic division of labor* (moving between specialist functions).

In the meanwhile, however, careers are portrayed in a metaphorical fugue of socio-organic images woven in space and time. For example, someone with a "successful career" is a "high flyer" who has survived the "rat race" and beaten competitors on the "fast track." Here the images are positive: of "ascent," "speed," and "winning." In contrast, the individual who has "no career" or is a "career failure" is often described negatively in terms of a "dead-end job," "dead wood," "passed over," "washed up" or "burnt out." Notably the images are frequently of death, decay and destruction – although by natural elements ("water" and "fire"), not by the socially validated perpetrator, the organization.

In bureaucratic organizations, an individual's progress depends crucially on the evaluation of his or her superiors. Hence managing a career or – in everyday language – "having a career at all" involves the development of a "high profile" and "targeting" it at those with the authority to "ease one's way up the ladder." In other words, it involves the construction of a reputation that will further one's career.

But this points to a paradox contained in the notion of reputation: It is both a possession and not a possession. Historically, the study of reputational blackmail is instructive. Hepworth (1975:15) points out that in the nineteenth century "good reputation," being regarded as "an increasingly significant mainstay of conventional order," began to merit "the protection of the courts." Reputational blackmail became perceived as a form of "moral murder" tricked out with all the imagery of financial extortion, for example, vampirism and blood letting, reflecting the extended significance of money in society (Hepworth 1975:22). In short, reputation became a *commodity* and, as such, a potential possession. But, the very fact that it might merit the protection of the courts points to its "vulnerability" (Hepworth 1975:15), a vulnerability stemming from its attributional quality: "A man's reputation is not a quality that he possesses, but rather the opinions which other people have about him" (Bailey 1971:4).

As a possession, with its connotations about good or bad behavior/performance, reputation has become a commodity, with a price in both community and labor market. Thus, managers are "head-hunted" by recruitment consultancies on the basis of their reputations, and "high fliers" are urged to become "effective in selling their ideas and themselves" (McCormack 1984:72). But, given the attributional quality of reputation, the value of the commodity (possession) is worthless (non-possession) unless the marketplace is prepared to buy it – to believe in the value of what is offered. McCormack (1984:71–2), in his best seller *What They Don't Teach You at Harvard Business School,* captures well the dual nature of reputation as both a personal quality and commodity when he juxtaposes ideas of impressing the boss with the need for individuals to sell their ideas and themselves.

We would suggest that rhetoric is used to mediate the paradox of reputation by "selling" it to a recipient in a form that he or she is prepared to buy, so maintaining and reinforcing a set of attributions. Consequently, individuals may shape their reputations by the rhetorical presentation of careers, particularly through the construction of curriculum vitae and the *verbal reconstruction of employment histories in selection and appraisal interviews:* by "putting one's best foot forward" (Goffman 1959). As Tedeschi and Reiss (1981) illustrate, these verbal strategies of impression management are complex and delicate, providing a wealth of material for attribution theorists.

The paradox of reputation may also be mediated *by relating and, at times, conflating its meaning with those of career, work and employment.* All these are things that people do not possess automatically (for they have to be given or achieved) but which they actually have. Thus, for many adults, especially men, their careers become their reputations – as is symbolized by the British honors system, which largely rewards reputation in occupational roles. This example is especially instructive because it shows how reputation symbolically may be secured: first, by conversion into a successful career and then into an honor actually "worn" as a medal, ribbon or title.

We return to such associations in what follows, but here it is necessary to draw attention to the proposition that most managers in bureaucratic organizations know something about reputations as careers. Furthermore, several commentators have suggested that the *"successful" manager is the one who manages the good opinions of others* (Gowler and Legge 1983; Heller 1972, 1985; Kotter 1977). And Tsui (1982:265) argues that now "organizations value the most reputationally effective managers" and suggests that

the reputation of being effective may be the most valid and reliable indicator for differentiating good from poor managers. Ultimately, *managerial effectiveness may be a matter of perceptual consensus* . . . It is conceived that the most reputationally effective manager will more likely contribute to the collective goals of the organization by being responsive to the needs of others and will come to be valued more highly in the social system. (emphasis added)

The representation of the manager as a master of social evaluation is now commonplace in the burgeoning literature on organizational power, politics and leadership (e.g., Pfeffer 1981a, b). This is also very evident in the fashionable literature on organizational culture and "excellent" companies (Deal and Kennedy 1982; Peters and Waterman 1982), where the rhetorical skill to persuade others appears to be at a premium.

Central to the argument presented here is the idea that we might profitably view "talk" about careers as the management of meaning, and we have illustrated how this manipulation is framed in terms of a dominant ideology of control. However, we now extend the case by showing the associations between meanings

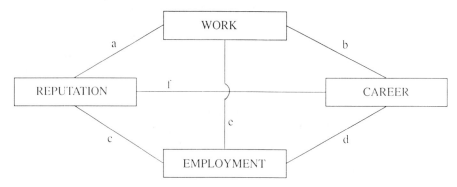

Figure 21.2. Career as reputation

embodied in everyday usage of concepts of reputation, work, employment and career (see Figure 21.2), linking these everyday connotations to the themes chosen to interpret the rhetoric of bureaucratic control.

This diagram represents the view that in contemporary market-oriented societies "employment" means a contractual arrangement whereby individuals are rewarded for work (see association a) *specified by some position in a formal organization, that is, in a hierarchy of roles and controls.* This is such a taken-for-granted relationship in the English language that "work" and "employment" have become synonymous terms, possibly confusing our understanding of the nature and impact of unemployment (Hartley 1980). For example, work outside this contractual relationship, not being conventionally rewarded by pay, becomes devalued and with it reputation, for example, one is "only a housewife" (see association a). When *non*-employment is experienced as *un*employment, the impact can be negative in the extreme. Fineman (1983:112), from his sample of white collar unemployed, reports their experience of being stigmatized, of being labeled as "inferior" by the employed. It is also to be observed, in Britain, that unemployed managers often seek to present themselves in terms of an erstwhile prestigious image: the freelance consultant. In short, the loss of employment has subjective and objective consequences for one's reputation. Conversely, employment, high material reward and reputation are often seen as naturally associated: "you get what (the person) you pay for" (association c). Moreover, it is not to stretch a point to claim that success and failure at work is used as *a measure of achievement.*

In theory, the concept of career should be as embedded in notions of work (association b) as of employment (association d). Appropriately, when reviewing various definitions of the term "career," Arthur and Lawrence (1984:1–2) conclude that the two themes that stand out are work and meaning to life as perceptions of identity – "I am what I do" become intertwined with those of vocation – "My life is my work." Van Maanen (1977:1) similarly appears to stress that *forms of work,* just as much as employment, can constitute the focus of a career, assuming such work serves as the point around which the individual organizes his or her life and derives its meaning. But we would suggest that the meaning individuals ascribe to such a career is generally framed in terms of shared social evaluations of work, which reflect social, cultural *and* economic values of society; for example, employment is often reputed to be more valuable than work and hence constitutes a "real" career (association f). Additionally, the association between reputation and career may involve ideas about being an *accountable member* of society.

Arthur and Lawrence (1984:2) succinctly put this social perspective when they comment that "the term 'career' should be applicable to anyone who works, and to any succession of work roles that a person may hold. *Yet social evaluation is an assumption about work that conflicts with that goal"* (emphasis added). Not surprisingly, then, if society evaluates career in terms of employment and, by association, in terms of the values pervading employment relationships, that is, those embodied in the rhetoric of bureaucratic control, the reputation of that category of persons who have been legitimately charged with the exercise of such control is elevated. Hence, as Martin (1983:17) claims:

The idea that managers are absolutely essential to organisations has been *persuasively incorporated* into almost every aspect of public and business administration. It has reached mythological proportions in the sense that *it has become part of the ideology of our society* . . . and (has) led to the aggrandizement of the role and functions of managers. (emphasis added)

Other contemporary writers have commented on this "rampant managerialism" (Anthony 1977:266), and Hales (1986:88) confirms this aggrandizement of management:

Arguments that the quality of management is decisive in both organizational and national economic performance presuppose that the exclusively "managerial" contribution to that performance is both tangible and identifiable. Claims for managerial authority inevitably rest not upon *de facto* status and power, but upon an implicit "job of managing" for which *authority is the necessary resource.* (emphasis added)

In claiming authority, managers are called upon to manage meaning (Bolman and Deal 1984; Deal and Kennedy 1982; Frost et al. 1985; Peters and Waterman 1982; Pfeffer 1981a, b; Pondy et al. 1983) and, in doing so, "manufacture consent" (Burawoy 1979) to their complete indispensability.

CONCLUSION

In this chapter, we have adopted the view that career may be treated in terms of a socially constructed environment, that is, where individuals and collectivities enact their "external conditions" through the experiencing and sense-making processes embedded in acts of communication (Gahmberg 1986:42) and, in particular, rhetorical language.

The notion of career expressed in such language, through asserting values and beliefs about hierarchy, accountability, achievement and membership, reproduces and develops an ideology of bureaucratic control (see Figure 21.1). This in turn both reflects and reinforces the values and beliefs of a market-oriented society (see Figure 21.2). As Presthus (1978:18) argues:

Administrators often try to reconcile the organization's interests with those of the individual, but they tend nevertheless to view human beings as instruments designed to achieve ends considered to be more important than those of any individual person. As a result, *collective values become the bench mark for evaluating and rewarding the individual. Humans, in effect, are made for the organization. They may succeed and prosper within it, but the organization, reflecting in turn the dominant values of society, always defines the terms of success.* (emphasis added)

Does all this mean that the concept of career cannot break free from the ideology of bureaucratic control? Probably, but perhaps not necessarily. First, it must be recognized that the process of enactment is inevitably elusive, and any fixity of meanings associated with career and reputations cannot be assumed. Indeed, Morgan et al. (1983:13) are correct when they remind us that

many patterns of symbolic construction have this contradictory character, created to express one pattern of meaning but reconstituted in the eyes of others to conform with other patterns of meaning. Many organizations consciously attempt to create complex symbol systems which are intended to signify the desirability of engaging in rigorous patterns of rational, instrumental and pragmatic action. Symbols reinforcing the pursuit of excellence, achievement, aggressiveness, competitiveness and intense commitment to organizational ends provide good examples here. While intended by management to symbolize the characteristics of success, and to encourage the pursuit of success, for some organizational members they may stand as a symbolic structure which expresses their perceived inferiority and inability to cope.

Such "patterns of symbolic construction" may resemble viewing those created by a kaleidoscope: The same pieces constitute similar but, in a sense, unique patterns for each person who gazes through the peephole. For every individual who perceives and celebrates career as a race to be won or a mountain to be climbed, in other words, who is likely to construct a career as a game to be enjoyed, there is another who disdains or fears the competing "rats" that run in the race and longs to have a career doing his or her own thing. Such an individual may then abandon an imagery that constructs career in terms of racing and achievement and reconstruct it in terms of never-ending purposelessness: career as a treadmill, the pressures of which can only be escaped by jumping off. Certainly, researchers, teachers and especially career counselors should bear it in mind that when we are dealing *in* language, it is necessary to remember that we are engaged in the process of creating meaning, not establishing any fixed meaning. This, incidentally, also applies to those making such caveats.

Second, if the announcement of the "demise of bureaucracy" (Bennis 1966:10) was premature, the advent of more flexible organizational forms (Atkinson 1984; Handy 1984) goes hand in hand with changing metaphors. For example, that of "career anchor" (evoking the desirability of fixity in a sea of change) is already passing from the academic (Schein 1978) to the practitioners' vocabulary. But while metaphor both enacts and enables new perceptions of the world, through making innovatory connections, the process is inevitably both incremental and tangential. For metaphor, like all language, constrains as much as it liberates, since it must rely on the existence of prior conventions that make understanding possible (Culler 1981:39).

Finally, we might most fruitfully look for changing conceptions of career by studying how rhetoric reflects, refracts and constructs the dominant values and beliefs of society, especially in terms of the themes outlined in Figure 21.1. Moreover, we make a special plea for the consideration of how rhetoric constructs career as reputation (see Figure 21.2), for this process highlights changing patterns of social evaluation. As Ball (1970:345) comments about these issues:

It is to such matters that we now turn: respectability as a rhetoric, as a patterned communicative strategy or tactic, having a regular dimensional structure within which specific meanings or content are manipulated by social actors in search of respectable appearances.

We emphasize this point because careers, however conceived, involve building an identity and face to the world. Indeed, we all have to dress our self and social esteem in a looking glass that is itself constructed in the act of reflection. As a master rhetorician reminds us, this is a delicate matter because

> The purest treasure mortal times afford
> Is spotless reputation; that away,
> Men are but gilded loam or painted clay.

(Richard II, I, i, 177)

REFERENCES

Abercrombie, N., Hill, S., and Turner, B. S. (1984). *The Penguin Dictionary of Sociology.* Harmondsworth: Penguin.
Anthony, P. D. (1977). *The Ideology of Work.* London: Tavistock.
Argyris, C. (1967). Today's problems with tomorrow's organizations. *Journal of Management Studies, 4,* 31–55.
Arthur, M. B., and Lawrence, B. S. (1984). Perspectives on environment and career: an introduction. *Journal of Occupational Behaviour, 5,* 1–8.
Atkinson, J. (1984). Manpower strategies for flexible organizations. *Personnel Management, 16*(8), 28–31.
Bailey, F. G. (1971). Gifts and poison. In F. G. Bailey (ed.), *Gifts and Poison: The Politics of Reputation.* Oxford: Blackwell, pp. 1–25.
Baird, L., and Kram, K. (1983). Career dynamics: managing the superior/subordinate relationship. *Organizational Dynamics, 11*(4), 46–64.
Ball, D. W. (1970). The problematics of respectability. In J. D. Douglas (ed.), *Deviance and Respectability.* New York: Basic Books, pp. 326–371.
Bateson, G. (1973). *Steps to an Ecology of Mind.* London: Paladin.
Bennis, W. G. (1966). *Changing Organizations.* New York: McGraw-Hill.
Berger, P., and Luckmann, T. (1967). *The Social Construction of Reality.* Harmondsworth: Penguin.
Berger, P. L. (1967). *The Sacred Company.* Garden City, NY: Doubleday.
Blau, P. M., and Meyer, M. W. (1971). *Bureaucracy in Modern Society,* 2nd ed. New York: Random House.
Bolman, L. G., and Deal, T. E. (1984). *Modern Approaches to Understanding and Managing Organizations.* San Francisco: Jossey-Bass.
Burawoy, M. (1979). *Manufacturing Consent: Changes in the Labor Process under Monopoly Capitalism.* Chicago: University of Chicago Press.
Clark, D. L. (1985). Emerging paradigms in organizational theory and research. In Y. S. Lincoln (ed.), *Organizational Theory and Inquiry: The Paradigm Revolution.* Beverly Hills, CA: Sage, pp. 43–78.
Collin, A., and Young, R. A. (1986). New directions for theories of career. *Human Relations, 11,* 837–853.
Crompton, R., and Sanderson, K. (1986). Credentials and careers: some implications of the increase in professional qualifications amongst women. *Sociology, 20,* 25–42.
Crossman, R. (1979). *The Crossman Diaries.* London: Magnum Books. (Version edited by A. Howard.)
Culler, J. (1981). *The Pursuit of Signs: Semiotics, Literature, Deconstruction.* London: Routledge & Kegan Paul.
Deal, T. E., and Kennedy, A. (1982). *Corporate Cultures.* Reading, MA: Addison-Wesley.
Douglas, M. (1966). *Purity and Danger.* London: Routledge & Kegan Paul.

Douglas, M. (1975). *Implicit Meanings: Essays in Anthropology*. London: Routledge & Kegan Paul.

Douglas, M. (1980). *Evans-Pritchard*. Glasgow: Fontana.

Eagleton, T. (1983). *Literary Theory: An Introduction*. Oxford: Blackwell.

Eagleton, T. (1986). *Against the Grain*. London: Verso.

Edwards, R. (1979). *Contested Terrain: The Transformation of the Workplace in the Twentieth Century*. London: Heinemann.

Evans, P. (1986). New directions in career management. *Personnel Management, 18*(12), 26–29.

Fineman, S. (1983). *White Collar Unemployment: Impact and Stress*. Chichester: Wiley.

Fowler, R., and Kress, G. (1979). Rules and regulations. In R. Fowler, R. Hodge, G. Kress, and T. Trew (eds.), *Language and Control*. London: Routledge & Kegan Paul, pp. 26–45.

Frost, P. J., Moore, L. F., Louis, M. R., Lundberg, C. C., and Martin, J. (eds.) 1985. *Organizational Culture*. Beverly Hills, CA: Sage.

Gahmberg, H. (1986). Symbols and values of strategic managers. In *Series A, Acta Academiae Oeconomicae Helsingiensis*. Helsinki: Helsinki School of Economics.

Giddens, A. (1976). *New Rules of Sociological Method*. London: Hutchinson.

Goffman, E. (1959). *The Presentation of Self in Everyday Life*. New York: Doubleday.

Goffman, E. (1974). *Frame Analysis*. Harmondsworth: Penguin.

Gowler, D., and Legge, K. (1983). The meaning of management and the management of meaning: a view from social anthropology. In M. J. Earl (ed.), *Perspectives on Management: A Multidisciplinary Analysis*. London: Oxford University Press, pp. 197–233.

Guion, R. M. (1981). Choosing members for organizations. In P. C. Nystrom and W. H. Starbuck (eds.), *Handbook of Organizational Design*, Vol. 2, *Remodeling Organizations and their Environments*. New York: Oxford University Press, pp. 358–381.

Hales, C. P. (1986). What do managers do? A critical review of the evidence. *Journal of Management Studies, 23*, 88–115.

Hall, D. T., and Isabella, L. A. (1985). Downward movement and career development. *Organizational Dynamics, 14*(1), 5–23.

Handy, C. (1984). *The Future of Work*. Oxford: Blackwell.

Hartley, J. (1980). Psychological approaches to unemployment. *Bulletin of the British Psychological Society, 33*, 412–414.

Heller, R. (1972). *The Naked Manager*. London: Barrie and Jenkins.

Heller, R. (1985). *The New Naked Manager*. London: Hodder and Stoughton.

Hepworth, M. (1975). *Blackmail: Publicity and Secrecy in Everyday Life*. London: Routledge & Kegan Paul.

Hunter, L. (1984). *Rhetorical Stance in Modern Literature*. New York: St. Martin's.

Jayyusi, L. (1984). *Categorization and the Moral Order*. London: Routledge & Kegan Paul.

Kotter, J. P. (1977). Power, dependence, and effective management. *Harvard Business Review, 55*(4), 125–136.

Kress, G., and Hodge, R. (1979). *Language as Ideology*. London: Routledge & Kegan Paul.

Leach, E. (1964). Anthropological aspects of language: animal categories and verbal abuse. In E. H. Lenneberg (ed.), *New Directions in the Study of Language*. Cambridge, MA: MIT Press.

Leach, E. (1976). *Culture and Communication: The Logic by which Symbols are Connected*. Cambridge: Cambridge University Press.

Linstead, S. (1985). Breaking the "purity rule": industrial sabotage and the symbolic process. *Personnel Review, 14*(3), 12–19.

Louis, M. R. (1980). Surprise and sense making: what newcomers experience in entering unfamiliar organizational settings. *Administrative Science Quarterly, 25*, 226–251.

McCormack, M. H. (1984). *What They Don't Teach You at Harvard Business School*. London: Collins.

McLain, R., and Weigert, A. J. (1979). Toward a phenomenological sociology of family: a programmatic essay. In W. R. Burr, R. Hill, I. Reiss, and F. I. Nye (eds.), *Contemporary Theories about the Family*, Vol. 2. New York: Free, pp. 160–205.

Martin, S. (1983). *Managing without Managers*. Beverly Hills, CA: Sage.

Merkle, J. A. (1980). *Management and Ideology: The Legacy of the International Scientific Management Movement*. Berkeley: University of California Press.

Meyer, J. W., and Rowan, B. (1977). Institutionalized organizations: formal structure as myth and ceremony. *American Journal of Sociology, 83*, 340–363.

Morgan, G., Frost, P. J., and Pondy, L. R. (1983). Organizational symbolism. In L. R. Pondy et al. (eds.), *Organizational Symbolism, Monographs in Organizational Behavior and Industrial Relations*, Vol. 1. Greenwich, CT: JAI, pp. 3–35.

Offe, C. (1976). *Industry and Inequality*. London: Arnold.

Parkin, D. (1975). The rhetoric of responsibility: bureaucratic communications in a Kenya farming area. In M. Bloch (ed.), *Political Language and Oratory in Traditional Society*. London: Academic.

Peters, T. J., and Waterman, R. H., Jr. (1982). *In Search of Excellence: Lessons from America's Best-Run Companies*. New York: Harper & Row.

Pfeffer, J. (1981a). *Power in Organizations*. Boston: Pitman.

Pfeffer, J. (1981b). Management as symbolic action: the creation and maintenance of organizational paradigms. In L. L. Cummings and B. M. Staw (eds.), *Research in Organizational Behavior*, Vol. 3. Greenwich, CT: JAI, pp. 1–52.

Pondy, L. R., Frost, P. J., Morgan, G., and Dandridge, T. C. (eds.) 1983. *Organizational Symbolism, Monographs in Organizational Behavior and Industrial Relations*, Vol. 1. Greenwich, CT: JAI.

Presthus, R. (1978). *The Organizational Society*, rev. ed. New York: St. Martin's.

Pym, D. (1982). Emancipation and organization. In N. Nicholson and T. D. Wall (eds.), *The Theory and Practice of Organizational Psychology*. London: Academic, pp. 213–235.

Reed, M. (1985). *Redirections in Organizational Analysis*. London: Tavistock.

Schein, E. H. (1978). *Career Dynamics: Matching Individual and Organizational Needs*. Reading, MA: Addison-Wesley.

Semin, G. R., and Manstead, A. S. R. (1983). *The Accountability of Conduct: A Social Psychological Analysis*. London: Academic.

Sloan, Jr., A. P. (1965). *My Years with General Motors*. London: Sidgwick and Jackson.

Smircich, L. (1985). Is the concept of culture a paradigm for understanding organizations and ourselves? In P. J. Frost, L. F. Moore, M. R. Louis, C. C. Lundberg, and J. Martin (eds.), *Organizational Culture*. Beverly Hills, CA: Sage, pp. 55–72.

Smircich, L., and Stubbart, C. (1985). Strategic management in an enacted world. *Academy of Management Review, 10*, 724–736.

Spender, D. (1980). *Man Made Language*. London: Routledge & Kegan Paul.

Stuart-Kotze, R., and Roskin, R. (1983). *Success Guide to Managerial Advancement*. Reston, VA: Reston.

Taylor, S. (1985). Unions not to blame. *Personnel Management, 17*(1), 41 (letters).

Tedeschi, J. T., and Reiss, M. (1981). Verbal strategies in impression management. In C. Antaki (ed.), *The Psychology of Ordinary Explanations of Social Behaviour*. London: Academic, pp. 271–309.

Trew, T. (1979). Theory and ideology at work. In R. Fowler, R. Hodge, G. Kress, and T. Trew (eds.), *Language and Control*. London: Routledge & Kegan Paul, pp. 94–116.

Trice, H. M., and Beyer, J. M. (1985). Using six organizational rites to change culture. In R. H. Kilmann, M. J. Saxton, R. Sherpa, and Associates (eds.), *Gaining Control of the Corporate Culture*. San Francisco: Jossey-Bass, pp. 370–399.

Tsui, A. S. (1982). A role set analysis of managerial reputation. In K. H. Chung (ed.), *Academy of Management Proceedings, 42nd Annual Meeting*. New York: Academy of Management.

Van Maanen, J. (1977). Experiencing organization: notes on the meaning of careers and socialization. In J. Van Maanen (ed.), *Organizational Careers: Some New Perspectives*. New York: Wiley, pp. 15–45.

Weber, M. (1946). *From Max Weber: Essays in Sociology* (translated and edited by H. H. Gerth and C. Wright Mills). New York: Oxford University Press.

Weber, M. (1947). *The Theory of Social and Economic Organization* (translated by T. Parsons and A. M. Henderson). New York: Free.

Weick, K. (1979). *The Social Psychology of Organizing*. Reading, MA: Addison-Wesley.

Weigert, A. J. (1983). *Social Psychology: A Sociological Approach through Interpretive Understanding*. Notre Dame, IN: University of Notre Dame.

Zurcher, L. A. (1983). *Social Roles: Conformity, Conflict and Creativity*. Beverly Hills, CA: Sage.

22 The internal and external career: a theoretical and cross-cultural perspective

C. BROOKLYN DERR AND ANDRÉ LAURENT

INTRODUCTION

While psychologists say that "people make careers," sociologists claim that "careers make people" and the career literature shows a dearth of cross-referencing between these two frames of reference (Van Maanen, 1977:8).

Indeed, theory and research on careers have developed along two dominant, independent and sometimes conflicting streams of thought over the last fifty years. As discussed by Gysbers (1984), these may be characterized as (1) primarily psychological in nature (e.g., self-development within a career, career motivation, career orientation) and (2) primarily sociological in nature (e.g., career paths and occupational streams, career stages within organizations, the nature of various occupations in society).

It has also been observed that traditional epistemologies that place stock in observable, structural, and measurable social facts are increasingly set in contrast to cognitive (often phenomenological) views that, focusing on language, sense making and symbolic processes, proceed from a premise that reality is largely socially constructed (Berger and Luckmann, 1966; Pfeffer, 1981:1–52). Examining the social reality of careers may in fact provide an opportunity to achieve some degree of integration between these contrasting perspectives.

As articulated in this volume by Barley (Chapter 3) on the Chicago School of Sociology, careers link individuals to the social structure by fusing the objective and the subjective, the observable facts and the individuals' interpretation of their experience. The dialectical nature of career dynamics calls for an epistemological framework that can address this ontological duality in a comprehensive manner.

It is suggested here that the concept of culture may actually provide such a framework. To the extent that "culture mediates between structural and individual realms" (Van Maanen and Barley, 1985:35), a cultural framework should help to couple a psychological or personal perspective of career with a sociological or organizational point of view. These two dimensions of career, which have been labeled in the literature as the internal and external career, will be presented here as inseparable and interactive elements in the social construction of career reality. As career dynamics is embedded in the cultural texture of social groups and institutions such as nations and organizations (Schein, 1984a), a cultural model of career dynamics will be proposed as an attempt to integrate different research traditions and to suggest new research directions.

THE INTERNAL AND EXTERNAL CAREER

Schein's (1975, 1978) development of the "career anchor" concept is a conceptual breakthrough in assessing career orientations. Briefly stated, Schein asserts that people begin their work lives (often as young adults in school) with certain ambitions, fears, hopes and illusions and through early work experiences uncover initial interests, motives, values and skills. Over time and with much more life experience, they gradually realize what they need and like, what they more deeply believe or value about work and life, what they are good at and what skills and abilities are critical to their work. These motives, values and talents gradually coalesce in a total career self-concept. That most people must spend on-the-job time to obtain the self-discovery information necessary to bring this career identity into focus is an important underpinning of the theory. Schein writes:

Talents, motives and values come to be inter-related into a more or less congruent total self-concept through a reciprocal process of learning to be better at those things we are motivated to do and value, learning to want and value those things we are good at, and avoid those things we are not motivated to do or do not value, resulting in loss of abilities or skills in those areas. (1982:2)

He goes on to point out that the career anchor is an "over-riding concern or need that operates as a genuine constraint on career decisions. The anchor is the thing the person would not give up if he or she had to make a choice" (1982:8). Moreover, Schein's research has uncovered several career anchors: managerial, technical/functional, autonomy, creativity, security, service, pure challenge, identity and life-style. Schein and Van Maanen (1977) postulate that one's self-definition of a career, or the *internal career,* is a person's own subjective idea about work life and his or her role within it.

Driver (1979, 1980, 1982) has also published seminal work on the idea of different career self-concepts or internal careers. Driver developed four diverse career concepts (linear, spiral, steady state and transitory), and he postulated that this internal career map is interdependent with certain cognitive styles, thus serving to guide an individual's long-term career choices.

Derr (1986) builds on Schein's and Driver's work and postulates five diverse internal career success maps: getting ahead, getting secure, getting free, getting high and getting balanced. He also discusses changes and major transitions of the internal career, asserting that while any career orientation is long term and basic (as opposed to short term and transitory), events may trigger shifts in the internal career map. These alterations of the internal career may occur not only due to major events at work, but also when events in one's personal life (e.g., a divorce or a mid-life crisis) provoke a change in our lifeview.

Other career theorists such as Super (1953) and Holland (1973) have advanced important theories of diverse personal orientations toward work. Super maintains that vocational self-concept is a part of total self-concept and maturity. Holland believes personality impacts vocational behavior, which in turn is influenced by various career opportunities and external events. Numerous scholars have linked individual career decision making to some definition of internal psychological needs or values (e.g., Allport, Vernon and Lindzey, 1960; Kuder, 1977; Roe, 1956).

Holland's model relating the personality to the external environment poses a conceptual counterpart to the internal career, or, in Schein's terms, brings forth the *external career:* the realities, constraints, opportunities and actual job sequences in the world of work. A crude way of differentiating the internal and the external career would be to conceive the former as primarily "subjective" and owned by the careerists and the latter as "objective" and reflecting a real world of constraints and opportunities in organizations and occupations.

The core of the internal career is the individual's career self-concept within the context of organizations and occupations; the core of the external career, however, is one's perception of the organizational and occupational context itself. A critical personal question regarding the internal career is "What do I want from work, given my perceptions of who I am and what's possible?" A companion question that illuminates the external career is "What's possible and realistic in my organization and occupation, given my perceptions of the world of work?"

However, both the internal and external careers can be considered psychological constructs and social typifications. While the external career is said to represent objective work realities, it is highly subjective in that it is influenced by our own perceptions of ambiguous, complex and fast-changing phenomena. Dealing with the historical roots of contemporary cognitive science, for example, Gardner (1987) captures the essence of this perspective while describing Kant's attempts to reconcile rationalism and empiricism: "[Objective reality] cannot be perceived directly: there is no privileged access to the thing itself (das Ding an sich). We must deal always with the phenomena – appearances – and not with noumena – the unknowable external world" (p. 58).

In their seminal work on the social construction of reality, Berger and Luckmann (1966) further describe the processes by which individuals objectify and typify their experiences:

I apprehend the reality of everyday life as an ordered reality. Its phenomena are prearranged in patterns that seem to be independent of my apprehension of them and that impose themselves upon the latter. The reality of everyday life appears already objectified, that is, constituted by an order of objects that have been designated as objects before my appearance on the scene. (pp. 21–22)

In the careers field, where our research is still in its infancy and where it is difficult to know what is really happening in fast-changing organizations and occupations, the work on social typifications is especially important. The internal career is obviously one's own subjective map, but the external career is likewise a construction and interpretation of selected external events and stimuli. Nevertheless, the usefulness of delineating these concepts (the internal and external careers) lies in differentiating two important foci of career dynamics: individual aspirations and occupational "realities." This framework stresses the dialectical nature of a career by locating it at the interface between the person and his or her work environment, while recognizing the careerist's perceptually constructed and individualistic view of the "realities" of work.

CAREER AND CULTURE

Kelly's (1955) personal construct theory argues that human conceptualization is the result of attempts to construct an unequivocal and predictable environing situation, and from this contemporary base a rich tradition of schema-oriented cognitive literature has developed to elucidate the foundations of individual behavior. Studying the impact of individuals, cultural anthropologists locate the foundations of individual behavior beyond the realm of the person. As noted by Kluckhohn (1951:960–961), "how the individual is oriented to his situation is, in the concrete sense, 'within' the actor, but not in the analytical sense, for modal orientations cannot, by definition, be determined from observing and questioning a single individual – they are culture."

In recent years, many students of organizations have adopted such a cultural perspective on social reality by focusing on the concept of organizational culture (Davis, 1984; Deal and Kennedy, 1982; Frost et al., 1985; Kilmann et al., 1985; Ouchi, 1981; Pascale and Athos, 1981; Peters and Waterman, 1982; Sathe, 1985; Schein, 1985). Smircich (1983), building on Geertz (1973), for example, views organizational culture as the product of a "commonly held fabric of meanings" and asserts that these meanings are available:

by analyzing the knowledge that individuals possess about their situations and by examining the understandings that the individual has of him or herself, the boss, colleagues, and the wider context within which the organization operates. (p. 162)

Another stream of organizational research has investigated the effects of the wider societal or national culture on the structuring and functioning of organizations (e.g., Maurice, Sorge, and Warner 1980).

By contrast, and with the notable and exemplary exception of recent work reported by Gerpott et al. (1988), much of the career literature has remained acultural or blindly unicultural, thus failing to account for either symbolic or cross-cultural issues in career dynamics.

It is our contention that a cultural and cross-cultural perspective of career dynamics may help to broaden our understanding of the socially constructed reality of careers.

For the purposes of this chapter, a closer consideration of Schein's culture model is appropriate. Schein (1984b, 1985) defines culture as the "basic assumptions and beliefs that are shared by members of an organization" (1985:8), and he discusses three levels of culture. The first level Schein labels "artifacts," which refer to the visible manifestations of a culture such as behavioral patterns, dress codes and the most obvious configurations of time and space. Artifact culture is easily observed but deciphered with difficulty.

The second level in Schein's cultural model is labelled "values." This refers to guiding beliefs, preferences or norms, the manifest or espoused values of a culture, for instance, its emphasis on achievement or affiliation, on competition or collaboration and on confrontation or avoidance of conflict. This level is more difficult to assess but can be partly inferred from the analysis of artifacts.

The third level or deep culture is termed "basic assumptions." These are the invisible, preconscious or unconscious, nondebatable, taken-for-granted, underlying cognitive structures that determine how group members perceive, think and feel. Basic assumptions confer meaning to manifest values and overt behavior and can be considered the fundamental assumptions about humankind, nature and activity that are patterned into cultural paradigms. Examples of such underlying assumptions are: time is limited, nature is there to be mastered and shaped by man and people can change their behavior at will. Such infrastructure is very difficult to uncover but, once unearthed, is highly meaningful in interpreting social reality. While artifacts may easily illustrate differences across cultures, the interpretation of such differences will require some understanding of these fundamental assumptions.

It is our contention that the basic assumptions of Schein's model can best be understood in terms of broad societal or ecological contexts such as national cultures. Such homogeneous contexts are formative through early educational experience, family patterns, institutional arrangements, religious experiences and language. Organizational cultures, while important, constitute an individual's "situation" and are less likely to exert such a profound effect or to impact people at such a deep level. On the other hand, organizational cultures may exert a substantial impact on the upper layers of the cultural edifice, that is, on behavioral norms and artifacts.

This cultural framework will be employed to approach the internal–external career construct. The internal career, we argue, is a personal and subjective map that operates at the basic assumption level. National culture is therefore basic and critical in influencing the internal career. Additionally, we believe that national culture influences the external career, particularly through the mediating effects of different organizational cultures.

Since both the internal and external dimensions of the total career concept are constructed views of reality and affected by the basic assumptions of a careerist, a career will have different meanings in different cultures and, therefore, evidence different dynamics. Considering culture as "the fabric of meaning" (Geertz, 1973; Smircich, 1983) undergirds these propositions.

The sections that follow present some preliminary evidence for the contention that internal and external careers are culturally derived concepts whose formulation is significantly shaped by national culture.

THE EXTERNAL CAREER

The external career includes perceived realities of the world of work (e.g., job market, demographics, obsolescence, opportunity structure). Important elements of the external career can therefore be studied by collecting and analyzing various perceptions regarding careers and how careerists are being managed by employing organizations. Collective perceptions by numerous informed observers about the same career opportunities and career realities generate consensual validity. Argyris (1982) points out, for example, that espoused theories of action (ideals) are validated as theories-in-use (realities) if they have been confirmed as such by numerous informed and experienced observers.

One important element of the external career is what the organization values and rewards in its employees. And this can be examined, according to the preceding line of reasoning, by asking knowledgeable informants how they perceive the determinants of career success in their companies. We can ask, for example, which employees' traits, attitudes or behaviors do they perceive as being particularly valued and rewarded by their companies?

Laurent (1981a) developed such an approach as a tool for the diagnosis of organizational cultures and later reconstituted the methodology in a comparative research instrument he applied in a multinational context. Other studies (Inzerilli and Laurent, 1983; Laurent, 1981b) have indicated the substantial impact of national cultures on basic conceptions of management, organization and work values, (Hofstede, 1980). It has been established that cultural differences in managerial assumptions are not mitigated by the corporate culture of large multi-national firms (Laurent, 1983).

In order to assess the validity of these findings as they apply to career success, a large U.S.-based multinational corporation was approached because of its high professional reputation in human resource management (Laurent, 1986). This corporation had for years implemented a standardized worldwide system for the multiple assessment of managerial potential and performance. The research objective was to assess whether this common administrative system would standardize managers' perceptions of career success criteria across various national affiliated companies. Laurent conducted open-ended interviews of a representative sample of 100 upper-middle managers throughout the corporation. Among other questions, all interviews included the following one: "In your view, what does it take to be successful at XY?"

Individual responses were systematically recorded, and these responses produced a list of sixty different items. This list was divided into two balanced lists of thirty items (to reduce cognitive overload) and developed into a survey questionnaire format. National samples of around fifty managers (matched according to education, job level, age, experience with the company and function) were then surveyed in five affiliated companies in France, West Germany, the Netherlands, the United Kingdom and the United States. The respondents were asked in a confidential survey to select and check from each list of thirty items those ten that they perceived as being most important in determining career success at XY.

Of the original sixty-item list, the following ten items were chosen most frequently by the overall group of 262 respondents:

Rank

1. Ambition and drive (82% selected this item).
2. Leadership ability (77%).
3. Skills in interpersonal relations and communication (75%).
4. Being labeled as having high potential (72%).
5. Managerial skills (69%).
6. Achieving results (69%).
7. Self-confidence (65%).
8. Creative mind (60%).
9. Ability to handle interfaces between groups (58%).
10. Hard work (58%).

These results represent the aggregate perception of the overall sample about employee characteristics valued by the company. A comparative analysis further revealed important differences between the five national groups in spite of the convergence that could be expected from a similar worldwide career system.

The most significant cross-cultural variations in the preceding top-ten criteria were the following:

1. While only 57% of the Dutch managers selected skills in interpersonal relations and communication as a most important determinant of career success, 89% of the British did.
2. Being labeled as having high potential was perceived as most important by 54% of the Germans as opposed to 81% of the French.

3. Achieving results had a high American score of 88% and a low French score of 52%. Similarly, 81% of the Americans selected self-confidence while only 42% of the French did.

4. Finally, creative mind was perceived as the top success criterion by the Germans (rank 1 among 60, checked by 77%) while it was seen as much less relevant by the French (rank 21, checked by 40%).

National differences of even higher magnitude were observed on many other criteria. For instance, *job visibility and exposure* provided the following spread:

	United Kingdom	United States	France	Netherlands	West Germany
Percentage of choice	73	71	38	30	18
Rank	5	8	23	26	41

The results of the study also indicated important differences as to the amount of consensus within each national affiliate. For instance, while six criteria were selected as most important for career success by more than 80% of the American managers, the corresponding figures were three criteria selected for the British, one for the Dutch and the French and none for the Germans. Thus the degree of perceptual clarity, fit and comfort with the overall career success culture of the firm was much higher for the American managers who were, of course, culturally closer to the system designers.

Laurent (1986:96) summarizes some of his findings concerning the German, the British and the French managers in the following way:

German managers, more than others, believed that creativity is essential for career success. In their mind, the successful manager is the one who has the right individual characteristics. Their outlook is rational: they view the organization as a coordinated network of individuals who make appropriate decisions based on their professional competence and knowledge.

British managers hold a more interpersonal and subjective view of the organizational world. According to them, the ability to create the right image and to get noticed for what they do is essential for career success. They view the organization primarily as a network of relationships between individuals who get things done by influencing each other through communicating and negotiating.

French managers look at the organization as an authority network where the power to organize and control the actors stems from their positioning in the hierarchy. They focus on the organization as a pyramid of differentiated levels of power to be acquired or dealt with. French managers perceive the ability to manage power relationships effectively and to "work the system" as particularly critical to their success.

Thus, collective perceptions of one aspect of the external career (i.e., career success from an organizational perspective) vary according to national culture in a single multinational corporation where the occupational, administrative and organizational contexts are similar. This finding raises two questions: Do the various managers simply view the same organization through their own cultural lenses and arrive at different subjective interpretations of reality? Or, do the various affiliates operate and reward differently within their cultural settings, indicating there is no objective multinational reality of career success – regardless of what head office desires or designs? The answer to both questions may be yes.

In another study of 150 European executives undertaken at INSEAD (the European Institute of Business Administration) (Derr, 1987), another collective perception of external career dynamics in major European firms was obtained. The inquiry asked the respondents to identify which kind of employees their companies most valued. In general, the executives reported that their companies attached the greatest value to future high-level general managers. However, there were some interesting variations on this theme according to the national origin of the company.

German firms relied more on formal authority and structure and, along with the Swiss, attached higher value to technical competence and functional expertise. The French companies valued most those managers who came from elite schools with strong technical backgrounds but who quickly became general managers (avoiding all appearance of remaining narrow technical specialists). The British attached great importance to recruiting and developing persons with a more classical education and broad general approach to management and were currently debating the value of MBA training as opposed to this broader orientation. The Swedish firms maintained a delicate balance between differentiating some as high potential candidates and future "leaders" with special developmental experiences versus adherence to strong cultural norms of equality, social democracy and collaboration where no individual is singled out for special treatment.

It seems clear that career success from the organizational point of view, whether assessed by the careerists or by the policymakers and career systems designers, is no more culture free than other facets of the management and organizational world. In fact, it may be important and useful to view the external career as a cultural artifact. What about the internal career?

THE INTERNAL CAREER

In the study at INSEAD mentioned, Derr also derived a list from career orientation theory (DeLong, 1982; Derr, 1980, 1986; Derr and Chilton, 1983; Driver, 1982; Schein, 1978, 1982) of thirty-six different ideas about career success. Respondents were asked to select twelve (i.e., one-third of the items) that were most important to them as indicators of career success. The respondents were also asked to circle those four items among the twelve checked that were considered the most important. The questionnaire format was modeled after the one used by Laurent. In Laurent's survey, however, the respondents were asked to check the items they perceived as being the most important determinants of career success in their company (i.e., external career perceptions). The Derr questionnaire asked respondents to report their *personal* definitions of career success rather than the company point of view (i.e., internal career orientations). The top ten items chosen from the list of thirty-six, weighted before being ranked in order to reflect the structure of choices in the instrument, are:

Rank

1. Being influential enough to get exciting and challenging assignments.
2. Being in the "inner circle" regarding important decisions.
3. Being able to influence events and policies in support of my values and philosophies.
4. Achieving a balance in my progress at work, in my relationships (family life, friendships) and in self-development activities.

5.   Being able to keep personal and professional life in equilibrium.
6.   Becoming a general manager (e.g., director, vice president).
7.   Working for a firm whose values are congruent with mine.
8.   Being able to sell my ideas to others.
9.   Using my creative talents.
10.   Creating new products, ideas, services or organizations.

A number of the top items that comprise the internal career are associated with upward mobility, power and influence (see ranked items 1, 2, 3, 6 and 8). Achieving some sort of balance between personal and professional life is also an important internal career objective (see ranked items 4 and 5). Furthermore, there is an entrepreneurial aspect to several of the top ten items (see items ranked 9 and 10).

According to Derr's theory (1986), there are five different internal career success maps: getting ahead (upward mobility), getting secure (company loyalty and sense of belonging), getting free (autonomy), getting high (excitement of the work itself) and getting balanced (finding an equilibrium between personal and professional life). A forced-choice instrument, the Career Success Map (CSM) questionnaire (see Derr, 1986:189–193), was administered to the respondents to further ascertain their career orientations. Figure 22.1 is a graphical representation of the career orientation differences of four European nationalities using the CSM questionnaire. The lower the mean score on a scale of 1–12, the less a group has that particular career orientation.

One surprising feature of these data is the extent to which the entire population has a getting-balanced orientation. In what would be predicted as a very getting-ahead group of respondents (high potentials in an exclusive executive development program), 29% had a predominantly getting-ahead profile, while 26% were judged to be primarily getting balanced. There are fewer getting-high (20%) internal career orientations in this sample and relatively few getting-secure (16%) and getting-free (9%) orientations.

Some of this overall getting-balanced profile may be explained by response bias. Many of the INSEAD executives surveyed had been away from home for several weeks at the time of taking the survey. They may have been missing their families. Several sessions prior to responding, they had also participated in a lecture on the subject of balancing personal and professional life, and this class may have influenced them.

Another possible explanation is that managers often see themselves as more balanced and family oriented than do their spouses, children or those who know them well (Burke and Weir, 1977; Renshaw, 1977). They might report these skewed self-perceptions in the questionnaire. Still, the possibility exists that many considered "high flyers" by their companies are really getting-balanced careerists in disguise. That is, their subjective internal career maps are disguised from their employers because they perceive that they would be punished were they to reveal their true intentions. Given the first opportunity, they may make a career choice that promotes their actual internal career orientations.

As an illustration, Derr conducted an in-depth career interview with a young German executive at INSEAD. This executive had already deferred his gratification through a Ph.D. and M.B.A. program. His spouse was in medical training in Germany. He had all the proper qualifications and profile to be classified a

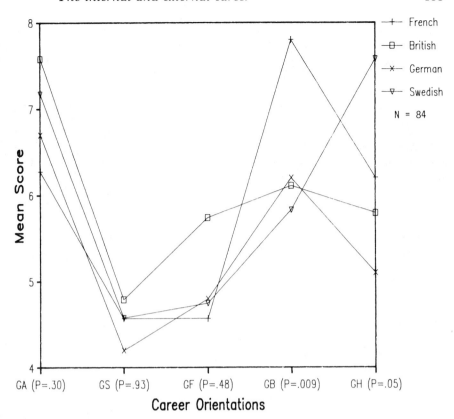

Figure 22.1. Career success map across four national cultures; statistics based on Kruskal–Wallis one-way analysis of variance test (abbreviations: GA, getting ahead; GS, getting secure; GF, getting free; GB, getting balanced; GH, getting high)

very high-potential executive. His plan, nevertheless, was to continue in his large German company, work hard for three to five years and establish himself, get located in the south of Germany (location of headquarters and key plants figured prominently in his choice of company) and then voluntarily plateau and become a balanced careerist. This plan was synchronized to correspond with his wife's medical training so she would be ready at the moment of his voluntary plateauing to establish a part-time practice. Together, once established, they would begin a family and spend much of their time in recreational pursuits. This person was quite sure that he did not want to work as hard as his father had done.

The other interesting point of the data presented in Figure 22.1 is the cross-cultural differences. The British and Swedes are significantly more getting-ahead oriented than are the French. The French, on the other hand, have a significantly higher getting-balanced orientation than the other national groups. Other clinical data indicate that the French, while working hard, view their time away from the workplace as sacred personal time and, hence, see themselves as more balanced. The big surprise is the Swedish data, where a more getting-balanced orientation would be predicted. Interviews reveal, however, that the respondents in this sample are from a small group of self-selected Swedish executives who choose to pursue the high-potential career track. One of the problems in Sweden is to find persons willing to opt for the high-potential track since this normally means being willing to relocate geographically and upset the spouse's career.

This cross-cultural analysis supports our contention that nationality is also a major factor influencing a person's internal career orientation. The basic assumptions of national culture, we argue, come from national or dominant subgroup experiences (e.g., common early childhood experience, educational systems, languages, religious experiences, geography), and these cultural assumptions are critical factors in influencing one's perspectives about life and work even though they are later influenced by real-world external career events and by corporate culture at the espoused values and norms and artifact levels.

Moreover, as pointed out in the preceding, nationality also influences how people perceive the external career. Thus, we see significant perceptual differences between national groups about what is important for career success within the same company.

Individuals may perceive the outside world (external career) according to their own cultural lenses and internal inclinations. Alternatively, individuals may also define their own subjective inclinations according to their assessment of the more objective cultural context. While the interaction between the internal and external careers is likely to work in both directions, the complicating factor is that the total career concept is defined both by the perceptual constructs of reality and by the larger cultural environment.

A CULTURAL MODEL OF CAREERS

Based on these research findings and the earlier theoretical discussion, it may be useful to propose a new model of career dynamics. This model serves to link together the careers perspective and the concept of culture. It also promotes understanding of how major culture variables interact with one another and, as such, may help guide future research. Figure 22.2 illustrates one component of our theoretical formulation: the levels of culture depth.

In this figure, the Schein culture model is drawn as a triangle to indicate that basic assumptions are at the foundation of culture and that artifacts, while important, are the more superficial layer. Espousing and subscribing to values and norms and speaking and behaving in certain ways are significant manifestations of culture, but they are not as profound a representation of the culture as are basic assumptions. In multinational corporations employees from all nations act out the part of the organizational culture, even changing through socialization some of their beliefs and values to correspond to those of the organization, but at the deepest level, they do not alter their fundamental assumptions about life and work.

Basic assumptions are mostly rooted in broad cultural settings such as nations. Common early childhood practices, language, religion and philosophy, geography, early education and educational systems and attitudes about work and life in the family of origin and the society are formative in determining the basic assumptions of a given culture. Values and norms and artifacts – while important,

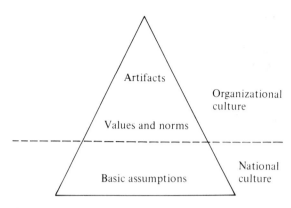

Figure 22.2. Levels of culture triangle

influential and key manifestations of basic cultural assumptions – emerge as differentiated translations and representations through different organizational histories. They are less deep or culturally embedded, more apt to change over time and more symbolic of social reality. Organizational culture usually operates at this artifact and values and norms level of the cultural edifice.

It is possible that the concept of national culture is most salient in countries with more common early childhood and formative patterns. In more heterogeneous countries, where common formative experience is less pronounced, one's religious or ethnic subculture may play an important basic assumptions function somewhat analogous to that of a more homogeneous national culture. Nevertheless, our research supports the proposition that nationality alone is a significant parameter in determining the internal career.

Figure 22.3 represents a second part of our theoretical formulation, namely, the factors that influence the role of culture in career dynamics. According to this model, national culture is the most determinant factor in influencing a person's internal career orientation through the shaping of basic assumptions. The internal career, as described earlier, represents an individual's basic assumptions about relating to the world of work.

National culture also impacts the culture of organizations by selecting and framing particular sets of organizational values, norms and artifacts that are consistent with its basic assumptions. Such perceived values, norms and artifacts related to the world of work in organizations and occupations constitute the individual's external career. Thus the external career is depicted as being directly influenced by organizational cultures that themselves mediate and differentiate the broader contextual effect of national cultures.

In summary, the model is meant to suggest that broad and deep ecological contexts like national cultures have a significant impact on career dynamics in two major ways. First, national cultures shape the individual's self-definition of a career – the internal career – through fundamental ideas about self and work that the individual acquires from early experience in families and schools – the prime carriers and reproducers of culture. National cultures shape the cultural filters of individuals so that they perceive the world of work – the external career – through the same cultural lenses as their compatriots. Second, national cultures

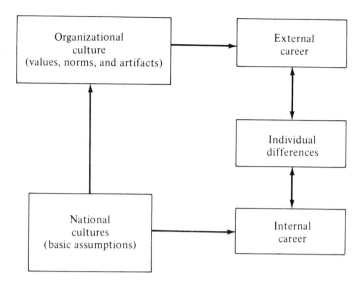

Figure 22.3. A cultural model of career dynamics

also shape the institutional context or design of work and the individual's perception of it – external career – through the norms, values and assumptions that the individual has already learned in the culture. Thus, careers link individuals to their cultures through their socialization experiences in various institutions. This may help us to understand that careers make people as much as people make careers.

The model is meant to be neither mechanistic nor deterministic. Broad cultural environments are differentiated into subcultures that provide the ground for the emergence of substantial variability among institutions and across individuals. There is also evidence that individuals socialized in a particular culture may adjust quite successfully to the requirements of other cultures. Thus French engineers, for example, whose internal career may have been strongly shaped by their national culture, may nevertheless be able to operate successfully within the context of an American organization's culture and appear to conform to the requirements of a U.S.-oriented external career. Alternatively, when multinational organizations seek to impose on their foreign subsidiaries career policies and practices that run counter to local values, local cultures find their own inventive ways of reinterpreting such requirements.

An important intervening variable in this model is "individual differences." While the concept of national culture as we are using it here is powerful in formulating career constructs, people are noted for their ability to make personal choices and deviate from family and cultural values. There are also many diverse personal experiences within any common context. Hence, it is important to recognize that both the internal and external careers are also influenced by individual differences.

Finally, the model intends to suggest a dynamic interaction between the internal and external career. The internal career is influenced by the external career in that persons from all walks of life cope and perform within organizational settings by changing aspects of their internal career or cognitive map to fit their perception of the requirements of the external career. Also, the internal career affects perceptions of reality and so impacts the external career. To show this relationship, the arrows in Figure 22.3 go in both directions between the internal and external careers, as linked by the intervening variable of individual differences. Career-oriented persons also change employers and even careers when their internal career (basic assumptions) become fundamentally threatened by the requirements of the external career. Therefore, one of the areas needing future research, as pointed out by Mihal et al. (1984) and Taylor and Prejor (1985), is coping with internal versus external career mismatches. It is important to understand that culture is a key variable in such coping and compromising.

We are proposing that careers cannot be understood in isolation from their cultural context. The concepts of internal and external career help to better articulate how the individual's constructed view of self in the world of work may be affected by different levels of culture depth. To say the least, we can anticipate that the very concept of career will have different meanings in different cultures. Yet this is still virgin territory in the garden of career theory.

CONCLUSIONS AND IMPLICATIONS

There are numerous practical implications of this model that are more appropriately elaborated elsewhere. Issues such as how to manage a culturally diverse work force are key concerns for multinational corporations. What is needed is a way to build on cultural and career similarities so that companies can manage effectively in the global economy of the future. On the other hand, how career policies and practices allow for cultural diversity is also a critical issue.

The more critical implications appropriate for this volume, however, are not oriented to practice but, rather, to career theory. At this juncture, our findings and theory yield several important propositions for further consideration.

First, while the "real world" of the career is not so neat as a simple dichotomy, it is useful to organize the careers field into the internal–external categories. Much of the literature about careers (career anchors, career orientations, personal vs. professional life, life stages, dual-career marriages) can be organized around individuals deciding and managing their internal career. Much of the organizational and occupational literature can come under the heading of the external career (career stages, career development systems, internal and external labor markets, career mobility, career planning models for organizations). Dividing career dynamics along these lines helps us to focus on the dialectical interplay between the person and the workplace over the span of time. Career theory currently vacillates between these two foci, and it may be useful to highlight the distinctions and attempt to understand their interaction.

Second, the discussion of culture helps us to focus on the very idea of "career." While some career literature brings forth examples of the meaning of a career to corporate managers and professionals, we have not explored enough what career means in diverse cultures: for example, in non-American or non-Western contexts, in certain definable subcultures (blacks, hispanics), for women, for skilled craftsmen or other kinds of laborers. If the concept of career carries across cultural boundaries, how do diverse cultures interpret this concept? What are the similarities and differences?

Third, our research puts forth the contention that both the internal and external careers are perceptual in nature and, as such, are heavily influenced by deep assumptions, values and perceptions (cultural lenses). This idea questions the concept of a more objective career reality. It lends credence to the theory of socially constructed realities in the career field and supports the proposition that the field is best understood as a symbolic representation of work patterns rather than as a more objective and systemic work reality. Also imbedded in this perspective is the idea that the internal career is more than the individual perspective. It also impinges on and influences organizational practices and systems (i.e., the external career).

Fourth, while the cultural model of career dynamics proposed one way of understanding variables in this conundrum of culture and career dynamics, additional research and theory is needed to help sort out conceptual causality and variable salience. What combination of various early childhood experiences constitute a strong national culture experience and, thus, greatly impact the internal career map? How powerful is organizational culture on one's internal career orientation and on one's basic assumptions? Do organizational cultures in more heterogeneous or fast-changing national cultures have a more salient and formative impact on the internal career than national culture? What about strong subcultures within national cultures: what role do they play in this model?

Fifth, the model and ideas in this chapter have implications for organizational change. One of the underpinnings of the change literature is the idea of intervention depth (Harrison, 1970). How deep must interventionists go in order to impact individuals and systems? Does it suffice, for example, to manage change at the artifact and perhaps the norms and values levels of culture, focusing change interventions on the organizational culture level? Do we inappropriately invade privacy and personal boundaries by attempting to socialize employees at the basic assumption level of culture, especially if they come from a different cultural fabric than those at the top? Or, to really affect change, do we need to intervene at the level of the internal career and basic assumption culture? If so, is it possible to intervene at these deeper levels or are we better off accepting diversity and utilizing contingency models of intervention?

Sixth, the direction of Hofstede's (1984) work is important here because he discusses national culture groupings and patterns. If we are able to group national cultures, we might come to better understand internal careers that are more or less compatible with basic assumptions of organizations. This might help us predict which corporate cultures and career development assumptions would best fit in what parts of the globe or where companies would need to vary their assumptions, policies and programs to better fit the various cultures. It is much more manageable to consider two or three different career management systems operating worldwide than a different one for each country in which the firm has employees.

Finally, it would be useful to differentiate, in future research, the relationship between national culture and the internal career in multinational versus national organizations. It may be that among those expatriates who opt to join MNCs (multinational corporations), many of whom welcome a chance to live abroad and experience cultures other than their own, are those who are less impacted by national culture per se and more open to cross-national or organizational cultures. That is, it is possible that research on national culture and internal careers when comparing MNC employees and employees of more local companies would reveal significantly different internal career maps. This leads us to want to explore in greater detail the salience of individual differences as an intervening variable in such research.

We conclude with a quotation that illustrates the oblique yet important status of the concept of culture:

> Culture is a blank space, a highly respected, empty pigeonhole. Economists call it "tastes" and leave it severely alone. Most philosophers ignore it – to their own loss. Marxists treat it obliquely as ideology or superstructure. Psychologists avoid it, by concentrating on child subjects. Historians bend it any way they like. Most believe it matters, especially travel agents. (Douglas, 1982:183)

From its diversity of meanings (Driver, 1982:24; Hall, 1976:4; Schein, 1978:1–3) the construct of career could well inspire a parallel quotation. Culture and career appear as important and interdependent concepts, but both are difficult to define operationally. Nevertheless, a theory of careers as it interacts with and upon culture is needed and will prove useful in enhancing our understanding of how people conceive of their work lives and act upon the array of opportunities and constraints presented to them by the world of work.

REFERENCES

Allport, G. W., Vernon, P. E., and Lindzey, G. (1960). *Study of Values.* Boston: Houghton Mifflin.

Argyris, C. (1982). *Reasoning, Learning and Action.* San Francisco: Jossey-Bass.

Berger, P. L., and Luckmann, T. (1966). *The Social Construction of Reality.* New York: Doubleday.

Burke, R., and Weir, T. (1977). Why good managers make lousy fathers. *Canadian Business,* November.

Davis, S. M. (1984). *Managing Corporate Culture.* Cambridge, MA: Ballinger.

Deal, T. E., and Kennedy, A. A. (1982). *Corporate Cultures.* Reading, MA: Addison-Wesley.

DeLong, T. J. (1982). The career orientations of MBA alumni. In R. Katz (ed.), *Career Issues in Human Resource Management.* Englewood Cliffs, NJ: Prentice-Hall, pp. 50–64.

Derr, C. B. (1980). More on career anchor concepts. In C. B. Derr (ed.), *Work, Family and the Career.* New York: Praeger, pp. 166–187.

Derr, C. B. (1986). *Managing The New Careerists.* San Francisco: Jossey-Bass.

Derr, C. B. (1987). Managing high potentials in Europe: some cross-cultural findings. *European Management Journal, 5* (Spring).

Derr, C. B., and Chilton, S. K. (1983). The career directionality of high school principals. *High School Journal, 67,* 11–19.

Douglas, M. (1982). Cultural bias. In M. Douglas (ed.), *In the Active Voice.* London: Routledge, pp. 183–254.

Driver, M. J. (1979). Career concepts and career management in organizations. In C. L. Cooper (ed.), *Behavioral Problems In Organizations.* Englewood Cliffs, NJ: Prentice-Hall, pp. 79–139.

Driver, M. J. (1980). Career concepts and organizational change. In C. B. Derr (ed.), *Work, Family and the Career.* New York: Praeger, pp. 34–41.

Driver, M. J. (1982). Career concepts: a new approach to career research. In R. Katz (ed.), *Career Issues in Human Resource Management.* Englewood Cliffs, NJ: Prentice-Hall, pp. 23–32.

Frost, P. J., Moore, L. F., Louis, M. R., Lundberg, C. C., and Martin, J. (eds.) (1985). *Organizational Culture.* Beverly Hills, CA: Sage.

Gardner, H. (1987). *The Mind's New Science: A History of the Cognitive Revolution.* New York: Basic.

Geertz, C. (1973). *The Interpretation of Cultures: Selected Essays.* New York: Basic.

Gerpott, T. J., Domsch, M., and Keller, R. T. (1988). Career orientations in different countries and companies: an empirical investigation of West German, British and U.S. industrial R&D professionals. *Journal of Management Studies, 25*(6).

Gysbers, N. (1984). Major trends in career development theory and practice. *Vocational Guidance Quarterly, 33*, 15–25.

Hall, D. T. (1976). *Careers in Organizations*, Santa Monica: Goodyear.

Harrison, R. (1970). Choosing the depth of organizational intervention. *Journal of Applied Behavioral Science, 2*(6), 182–202.

Hofstede, G. (1980). *Culture's Consequences*. Beverly Hills, CA: Sage.

Hofstede, G. (1984). The cultural relativity of the quality of life concept. *Academy of Management Review, 9*(1), 95–103.

Holland, J. L. (1973). *Making Vocational Choices: A Theory of Careers*. Englewood Cliffs, NJ: Prentice-Hall.

Inzerilli, G., and Laurent, A. (1983). Managerial views of organization structure in France and the U.S.A. *International Studies of Management and Organization, XIII*(1/2), 97–118.

Kelly, G. A. (1955). *The Psychology of Personal Constructs*. New York: Norton.

Kilmann, R. H., Saxton, M. J., Serra, R., and associates (eds.) (1985). *Gaining Control of the Corporate Culture*. San Francisco: Jossey-Bass.

Kluckhohn, C. (1951). Values and value orientations in the theory of action. In T. Parsons and E. A. Shills (eds.), *Toward a General Theory of Action*. Cambridge, MA: Harvard University Press.

Kuder, G. F. (1977). *Activity Interests and Occupational Choice*. Chicago: Science Research Association.

Laurent, A. (1981a). Perceived determinants of career success: a new approach to organizational analysis. In Trebesch, K. (ed.), *Organizational Development in Europe*. Berne and Stuttgart: Haupt.

Laurent, A. (1981b). Matrix organizations and Latin cultures: a note on the use of comparative research data in management education. *International Studies of Management and Organization, X*(4), 101–114.

Laurent, A. (1983). The cultural diversity of western conceptions of management. *International Studies of Management and Organization, XIII*(1/2), 75–96.

Laurent, A. (1986). The cross-cultural puzzle of international human resource management. *Human Resource Management, XXV*(1), 91–102.

Laurent, A. (1987). A cultural view of organizational change. INSEAD Working Paper.

Maurice, M., Sorge, A., and Warner, M. (1980). Societal differences in organizing manufacturing units: a comparison of France, West Germany and Great Britain. *Organizational Studies, 1*(1), 59–86.

Mihal, W. L., Sorce, P. A., and Compte, T. E. (1984). A process model of individual career decision making. *Academy of Management Review, 9*, 95–103.

Ouchi, W. G. (1981). *Theory Z*. Reading, MA: Addison-Wesley.

Pascale, R. T., and Athos, A. G. (1981). *The Art of Japanese Management*. New York: Simon & Schuster.

Peters, T. J., and Waterman, R. H., Jr. (1982). *In Search of Excellence*. New York: Harper & Row.

Pfeffer, J. (1981). Management as symbolic action: the creation and maintenance of organizational paradigms. In L. L. Cummings and B. M. Staw (eds.), *Research in Organizational Behavior*, Vol. 3. Greenwich, CT: JAI, pp. 1–52.

Renshaw, J. R. (1977). He can't even manage his own family. *The Wharton Magazine*, Winter, pp. 42–47.

Roe, A. (1956). *The Psychology of Occupations*. New York: Wiley.

Sathe, V. (1985). *Managerial Action and Corporate Culture*. Homewood, IL: Irwin.

Schein, E. H. (1975). How career anchors hold executives to career paths. *Personnel, 52*(3), 11–24.

Schein, E. H. (1978). *Career Dynamics*. Reading, MA: Addison-Wesley.

Schein, E. H. (1982). Individuals and careers. Technical Report 19, Office of Naval Research.

Schein, E. H. (1984a). Culture as an environmental context for careers. *Journal of Occupational Behavior, 5*, 71–81.

Schein, E. H. (1984b). Coming to a new awareness of organizational culture. *Sloan Management Review, 25*, 3–16.

Schein, E. H. (1985). *Organizational Culture and Leadership.* San Francisco: Jossey-Bass.
Schein, E. H., and Van Maanen, J. (1977). Career development. In J. R. Hackman and J. L. Suttle (eds.), *Improving Life At Work.* Santa Monica: Goodyear, pp. 30–95.
Smircich, L. (1983). Studying organizations as cultures. In G. Morgan (ed.), *Beyond Method.* Beverly Hills, CA: Sage, pp. 160–173.
Super, D. E. (1953). A theory of vocational development. *American Psychologist, 8,* 185–190.
Taylor, N. B., and Prejor, R. G. L. (1985). Explaining the process of compromise in career decision making. *Journal of Vocational Behavior, 27,* 171–190.
Van Maanen, J. (1977). *Organizational Careers: Some New Perspectives.* New York: Wiley.
Van Maanen, J., and Barley, S. R. (1985). Cultural organization fragments of a theory. In P. J. Frost, L. F. Moore, M. R. Louis, C. C. Lundberg, and J. Martin (eds.), *Organizational Culture.* Beverly Hills, CA: Sage, pp. 31–53.

PART III

Future directions for the development of career theory

Introduction to Part III

Now the basic groundwork has been done. Whereas Part I captures the field as we know it and Part II offers some new perspectives, Part III presents some samples of what might be made of the interplay among the ideas so far presented.

Three major scholars, each sympathetic to our endeavors to advance career theory, were asked to take the material in the first two parts and let their own thinking take its own creative course. There was a basic agreement that each writer would take primary responsibility for, but not be restricted by, a single level of analysis: the individual (Bailyn), the organization (Nystrom, joined by McArthur), and the society (Kanter). In the spirit of the exercise to allow the ideas to develop freely, no further guidelines were given. The result is three quite different chapters. What is common, however, is that each chapter offers a powerful demonstration of what can be made of the "land and materials" from Parts I and II.

In Chapter 23, Bailyn looks principally at the individual's experience of career processes and develops implications for career practice as well as theory. Bailyn stresses two complications in the study of careers: that the career is an interstitial concept and that career theory needs also to serve as a guide for applying the knowledge it conveys. From these she develops an argument that the immediate context of work, the acknowledgement of discontinuity, and the character of subjective experience are major issues for future career studies. After illustrating the complex interaction among these issues, she concludes that future career studies will require a new vision of organizational life, one that is both more flexible and more humane and that transcends traditional career rules and assumptions. The message for career scholars is to support the increased diversity of individuals in the work force that can help bring this new vision about.

A quite different perspective is taken by Nystrom and McArthur (Chapter 24). The purpose of their chapter is systematic theory building. Nystrom and McArthur make a detailed analysis of the concepts covered in each chapter and then systematically document the relationships (both implicit and explicit) the chapter posits between each set of the hundreds of variables included in the chapters in Parts I and II. Then, based on this exhaustive analysis of all the relationships in this handbook, they make observations about the current and desired future state of career theory. Thus, the chapter encourages readers to form their own cross-disciplinary insights based upon Nystrom and McArthur's organization of the conceptual material in the handbook.

For our closing chapter, Kanter examines careers by raising our sights one level of analysis beyond most handbook chapters. She suggests that career structures should be examined not only as individual, group, organizational, and oc-

475

cupational phenomena, but also as societal phenomena. At this level of analysis important questions concerning the economic and social performance of nations can be examined. After describing three principal opportunity forums that create career structures – bureaucratic, professional, and entrepreneurial – Kanter describes how such structures may exert a profound influence on national concerns. For instance, it seems possible that the structures underlying political careers shape how a country's decision makers resolve important issues, such as national industrial policy, by encouraging some solutions and constraining others. The author concludes by generating a series of questions concerning the causes and consequences of the three career structures, their evolution, and the impact of mixed structures on a broad range of organizational, political, and societal issues.

There will be no afterword to Part III. Instead, we leave it for the spirit of inquiry exemplified by all the handbook authors to be joined by its readers. We have presented career theory as a changing landscape, and we most sincerely invite you to join in its further cultivation.

23 Understanding individual experience at work: comments on the theory and practice of careers

LOTTE BAILYN

In a precursor to this volume (Arthur and Lawrence, 1984), the editors set out the needs for a multi-disciplinary approach to the study of careers that takes into account the environments in which careers unfold. Reaching such a goal, they observed, was limited by the fact that the study of careers "has received by far the most attention from the psychological perspective" (p. 4).[1] In this volume, therefore, they have called on experts with less individually oriented perspectives to augment the story and thus provide a more extended view but also a less focused one. We already know from previous attempts to pull together the thinking on careers how complex such an undertaking is (Law, 1981; Sonnenfeld and Kotter, 1982; Van Maanen and Schein, 1977); and we know the intricately contextual and descriptive requirements of a meaningful career theory (Collin and Young, 1986; Schein, 1986; Van Maanen, 1977). These difficulties are even more apparent in the present volume.

So how, in a concluding chapter to this handbook, might one say something useful about careers and career theory? The chapters are so varied that one is tempted to accept Thomas's (Chapter 17) passing suggestion to forget about the concept of career altogether. Let some people talk about adult life development in relation to work, family, and self; let others worry about how social structures are both determined by and yet constrain the actions of people; let some concern themselves with non-traditional groups now entering the labor force: women, minorities; and let still others analyze organizational processes in a multitude of ways: economically, politically, rhetorically, humanistically. If the concept of career is to represent the communality among all these ideas, is it left with any meaning?

I believe it is, if one concentrates on what actually happens to people directly and concretely involved in the world of work: what they do, how they are treated, and how they react to these experiences. But even with such a more narrow focus, there are complications involved in the study of careers. First, "career" is an interstitial concept, residing somewhere between an individual and a collective level of analysis. Second, the study of careers, more than many other social science topics, requires a theory that is more than a codification of knowledge. Such theory also needs to serve as a guide to applying knowledge, and it should point to ways of changing organizational life so as to enhance people's experiences at work (cf. Arthur et al., 1984).[2] That these two issues introduce complications is highlighted by Bell and Staw (Chapter 11), who point out that in recent years theoretical discussions have tended to emphasize characteristics of the social environment

477

in explanations of career outcomes, whereas career development programs have continued to stress the importance of individual initiative.[3]

What I shall do in this chapter, therefore, is to outline some of my thoughts on how the study of careers might deal with these issues. In particular, I shall discuss three points: (1) work careers in context; (2) the dynamics of work careers; and (3) the distinction between the external, objective and the internal, subjective career. I will draw, where relevant, on the chapters in this handbook, but I make no attempt to summarize their contents.

The outline of my argument can be stated briefly. First, in studying careers, one cannot deal only with individual traits or individual development since there are important contextual determinants of people's work experiences. In particular, it is the *immediate context of work* that needs detailed analysis if one is to combine understanding with constructive application. Second, since careers evolve over time, their study cannot be convincingly conceived in static terms. And the dynamic aspects of highest theoretical and practical import are likely to be those that acknowledge *discontinuity*, not only those that seek to explain stability. Finally, for a realistic understanding of people's experiences at work, context by itself is not sufficient. Differences among people must play a key role, and the differences that matter are not only external attributes but also the character of their *subjective experience*.

THEORETICAL PERSPECTIVES ON CAREER

Careers in context

The editors have adopted a person's emerging set of work experiences over time as the "shared" definition of career. This definition anchors the concept in both time and space (cf. Arthur, 1984; Van Maanen, 1977). It is a definition that sees careers as residing in people, not in organizations or occupations. But, as is evident from a number of the chapters, there is an equally compelling case to be made for a definition that locates careers in the wider context within which individual work histories (Nicholson and West, Chapter 9) unfold. Both the individual and the contextual perspective provide useful material, but they need to be combined, for careers depend on the interaction of individual agency and the constraining or enabling aspects of the social context.

As far as the individual perspective is concerned, there is much in these chapters that points to fruitful directions. One needs to be alert to people's ascribed characteristics such as race and gender (Gallos, Chapter 6; Thomas and Alderfer, Chapter 7); their educational level and expectations (implicit in Thomas); their abilities and personal characteristics (Bell and Staw; Betz, Fitzgerald, and Hill, Chapter 2; Dalton, Chapter 5); and the role of work in their total lives (Gallos; Marshall, Chapter 13; Sekaran and Hall, Chapter 8). One needs to be aware, also, that there will always be differences among people, even among those in homogeneous social groups and in highly similar occupational positions. As I will argue later, only if one combines social attributes with more individualized and personal orientations can one gain the understanding necessary to deal realistically with people's work experiences.

As to the contextual level, the preceding chapters illuminate the importance of many aspects of the working situation: from the job and its reward structures

(Thomas), to organizations with their career systems, rules, and rhetoric (Barney and Lawrence, Chapter 20; Gowler and Legge, Chapter 21; Rosenbaum, Chapter 16), to the larger economic and social environment as part of a national culture (Derr and Laurent, Chapter 22; Pfeffer, Chapter 18; Sonnenfeld, Chapter 10). Choice here should center on the immediate work situation of the people one is studying. For it is here that there is the greatest leverage for change and hence the most realistic link to practice. It is here, also, that the interaction between people and their environment is most readily observable. Further, the more distant social, economic, and cultural environment is reflected in this immediate situational context.

Such an interactive view of career is often advocated. But in order for it to be put to use, it needs to inform both research and practice. It requires multi-level research using an individual as well as a collective level of analysis; and these levels must be integrated without fallacious inferences from one to the other (Falter, 1978). What this means concretely is that one cannot generalize from the study of a specific situation to the experiences of the people in it; nor can one assume that any context-free analysis of people will make it possible to assess their reactions to a particular set of working conditions. So one is forced into a messier, descriptive and contextually-specific research mode (cf. Arthur and Kram, Chapter 14; Bailyn, 1977a; Betz, Fitzgerald, and Hill; Nicholson and West; Thomas).

Further, the emphasis on contextualized knowledge leads to a different view of career development from that currently practiced. It is now clear, as evidenced by this handbook, that career outcomes may not be responsive to individual effort because the nature of the work setting defines, to a great extent, the limits of such action. Nor, frequently, is learning to know oneself – one's abilities, interests, and values – sufficient for effective career development; one must also be able to decipher the career rules at work in the organization (cf. Barney and Lawrence; Nicholson and West; Pfeffer; Rosenbaum; Van Maanen, 1980). The individual, on the other hand, is not a passive onlooker in this process (Bell and Staw; Dalton; Thomas). And it is the bringing together of individual attributes with the immediate work context that will improve practice and enhance understanding.

Dynamics of work careers

Every investigator would agree that "career" is a dynamic concept and, ideally, should be looked at over time – hence the frequent call for longitudinal research designs. No longer is one-time fit, implicit in the previous emphasis on vocational choice, seen adequate in view of what we know today (Betz, Fitzgerald, and Hill). But there is less consensus on whether to emphasize continuity and stability in careers or discontinuity and change.

In general, research has emphasized continuity. We know, for example, how embedded the meaning of any point in a career is in the trajectory of that career over time (cf. Bailyn, 1980). Such stability may reside in the themes or retrospective reconstructions of experience (Van Maanen, 1977), in a person's ever more clearly emerging self-concept (Schein, 1978; Super, 1963), or in organizationally or culturally defined career structures (Lawrence, 1984; Rosenbaum). Further, there are convincing theories to explain this stability (cf. Barley, Chapter 3; Gowler and Legge).

The emphasis on stages of development (Arthur and Kram; Cytrynbaum and Crites, Chapter 4; Dalton; Gallos; Sekaran and Hall) is seemingly more concerned with change. But there are some theoretical difficulties with this idea. First, given the diversity in modern complex society, developmental theories, almost by definition, have to universalize experiences that only fit a modal group (cf. Gallos; Marshall; Thomas and Alderfer). Also, by identifying the requirements of any particular stage, such theories may inadvertently reinforce processes that lead more to rigidity than to flexibility since we know that fit at any given stage may make it more difficult to adapt to a subsequent stage (Arthur and Kram; Latack, Chapter 12; Maas and Kuypers, 1974; Sekaran and Hall).[4] So even here, the emphasis is more on stability and continuity. It is only when the discussion shifts to the organizational world itself that one gets the vision of the self-designing career (Weick and Berlinger, Chapter 15), which is specifically geared to continuous flexibility and change.

The explicit study of transitions (Barley; Nicholson and West; Trice and Morand, Chapter 19) is one way to shift the focus away from an emphasis on stability. Also, at the organizational level, one can look for possible sources of unanticipated directions of action, as for example in the play of conflicting interests (e.g., Pfeffer; Thomas and Alderfer). And at the individual level one can look for deviations from modal patterns. In other words, it seems important to confront our dominant theories with real life exceptions to their pronouncements. In a rapidly changing world, such "leading edge exemplars" are more likely to provide usable knowledge for the future than are generalizations based on current norms.

So, for example, caution is indicated about defining the early career needs of future managers on the basis of understanding how the careers of currently successful managers have evolved. Prescriptions for the future that are based on a direct translation from knowledge of the present assume that what is is what has to be (cf. Brown, 1984). Such a direct translation also risks interpreting all change as developmental and unrelated to historical changes in the social and cultural demography of the work force.[5] We need a different link between theoretical inferences drawn from current data and conclusions reached about how to apply this knowledge (cf. Gallos). Obviously, the study of existing patterns must continue. One cannot think realistically about the future without understanding the past and present, particularly not without understanding the constraining forces on change. But the value of this understanding for practice will only be evident when the focus shifts from the theory to the real problems that people confront as organizational employees. And this requires the ability to translate our understanding of current organizational processes into designs for new forms that better fit the needs of an increasingly diverse work force.

A number of the chapters in this handbook enhance the theoretical understanding of the forces, both psychological and social, that reinforce the status quo, but how to use this knowledge for change is more elusive. Some hints are available. They range from explicit awareness of constraints (Arthur and Kram; Pfeffer; Rosenbaum), to reconsideration of the definition of key concepts (Gallos; Gowler and Legge), to better management of transition processes (Nicholson and West; Trice and Morand). How actually to effect such change will require extensive local knowledge of the people and procedures involved.

Differentiating the internal from the external career

The definition of "career" adopted for this handbook does not specify whether the career should be looked at subjectively as the internal meaning given to it by the individual or objectively from an external point of view – that of the employer perhaps or the researcher or social planner. This is an old issue in career theory. It was already well stated in the early writings of the Chicago school and has been reiterated by researchers in that tradition (cf. Van Maanen and Schein, 1977) as well as in some of the chapters here (e.g. Barley; Thomas), which explicitly differentiate the career as an objective work history from the ever-changing subjectively imputed meanings and themes (Hughes's "moving perspective" (Hughes, 1937:413) by which people make sense of their lives (see also Watts, 1981).

In many aspects in the study of people, it is of course necessary to distinguish an externally defined reality from a person's perceptions of it, as evident, for example, in the chapter dealing with stress (Latack). The study of stress has also been contextualized and has its subjective and objective side. The external reality of stress, however, is different from the objective side of career because the external career is part of the social control of society, culturally bound and rhetorically reinforced. It is part of the institutional order. To ignore this external aspect, therefore, or to accept it uncritically is to miss a crucial part of the story. But the internal is also necessary because human action and interaction can affect the social structures in which they occur.[6] The key question, of course, is how to combine these two sides of the career.

On the whole, it is easiest to presume that external definitions coincide with internal ones. It is instructive, for example, to note how readily one falls into the presumption that upwardly mobile careers are experienced as successful even when one's adopted definition specifically denies such a connection. So, how can one best deal with the internal career? Not idiosyncratically, individual by individual – at least not for research and theory. Rather, what is required is an aggregation of individual data that reflects differences in subjective meanings. It is my sense that such aggregation would result in what one might call *orientational categories,* which can then be related to the social categories that both determine and are defined by the larger social context.

Such orientational categories deal with subjective meanings. They classify people according to individual predispositions that specifically deal with the topic at hand: according to their career anchors (Schein, 1978), for example, or their levels of occupational commitment (Bailyn, 1984). They are taxonomies based on individual actors' wants, plans, and commitments. They contrast with social categories, which classify people according to certain ascribed characteristics (e.g., gender or race) or according to the social positions they occupy (e.g., blue-collar workers or managers). The chapters by Gallos, Thomas, and Thomas and Alderfer are examples of the social level of aggregation. They provide crucial insights into the broad structural issues that set the bounds for individual action. And some of the chapters based on an individual perspective (e.g., Bell and Staw; Betz, Fitzgerald, and Hill) deal with orientational categories. But the critical need is to combine the two in any given study.

Let me indicate what can be gained by such a combination by starting with the wealth of information in the chapters dealing with social aggregations of current concern: women (Gallos; Marshall); minorities (Thomas and Alderfer); and blue-collar workers (Thomas). These chapters bring new perspectives to the understanding of careers. They highlight vividly the effect on individuals of restricted opportunity; they point out the diversity of styles by which a given occupation can be approached; and they underline the dysfunction of the homogeneous and single model presumed by most occupational and organizational career structures. They draw attention to the assumptions underlying current employment practices (cf. Bailyn, 1984). But they do not relate these insights to differences in individual orientations and thus are unable to specify how to improve the faulty career practices they have identified.

It would be a mistake, for example, to assume that all members in a particular social category share the modally identified subjective orientations. Such a presumption might lead to setting up organizational procedures that deal differently with different social groups, which not only goes against our professed views on equality of opportunity but presumes a homogeneity within social groupings that is as misleading as the presumed homogeneity based on a modal group (cf. Keller, 1986). What is needed, rather, is more of a statistical model. Yes, there may be systematic mean differences between social groups, but there is also enough variety within each group to provide significant overlap between them. Therefore, if one is to link such new knowledge to improvements in practice, it is not sufficient to catalog mean differences. Rather, one needs to identify those attributes that best account for these differences and needs to do so across social groupings, both traditional and new. Concretely, this means that one must combine social categories with orientational ones and must look as closely at "deviant" combinations as at modal ones.

For example, in one of my own studies (Bailyn, 1987) I found that in a closely matched sample of male and female engineers (divided by the social category of gender), the women experienced their careers very differently from the men even though in external aspects they were nearly identical. The women engineers had less self-confidence and had a less integrated view of their work and non-work lives. Though interesting, this mean difference needs to be pursued further by looking for particular orientations or ways of relating to work that account for it. An example comes to mind from a much older study based on a male professional sample. There I found a similar difference between accommodative men – those for whom family concerns take priority over work issues (a small minority) – and non-accommodative men (Bailyn, 1977b). Accommodation is a career orientation, part of the subjective career. If it were found to account for the difference in experience between male and female engineers, one would be led to a very different understanding of the original finding. One would be forced to consider the relation of accommodation to the work place rather than to continue focusing on sex differences. And thus one would be led to ask why technically trained employees, both men and women, with serious commitments to their private lives as well as to their work have difficulties with current organizational practice.

Such an approach enables one to go beyond the detailing of differences between men and women in the work place and helps identify the dynamics that underlie them.[7] This is not to deny that there may be key differences between the sexes that affect their career behavior (cf. Rossi, 1985) or that gender is a social category that defines opportunities and constraints (Gallos; Marshall;

Sekaran and Hall). But, by shifting the focus to career procedures in relation to individual differences in subjective orientations, we may be able to identify more accurately the locus of organizational constraints – a first step in trying to change them.

The inclusion of orientational differences is a way of bringing the internal career into our research. It is critical in any study of socially defined groups that hopes to have an impact on practice. Methodologically, such an approach requires the use of what I once called *proximate variables* (unpublished memo). Such variables are not distant and abstract but lie close to the phenomenon one is trying to study. They mirror the particular context in which the phenomenon occurs and deal with people's experiences of that context. They provide meaning to statistical associations and allow a more realistic understanding of the causal dynamics behind research findings. To go back to the example of differences in experience between men and women: a number of the chapters in this handbook (Gallos; Marshall; Sekaran and Hall) give convincing evidence that gender is important for the understanding of careers. And, by the specific and separate inclusion of women in research samples, one is beginning to amass a number of differences in career issues between men and women. What an emphasis on proximate variables implies is that one must go beyond such findings and look for orientational characteristics – correlated with a person's sex, at least at this point in historical time – that help explain these distinctions. Accommodation was a first suggested candidate. It is possible, also, that accommodation is a more proximate expression of Bakan's distinction between agency (independence, self-assertion) and communion (interdependence, fusion), analyzed in the chapter by Marshall, which itself is a more proximate categorization than gender (see also Sampson, 1988).[8]

The use of proximate variables introduces orientational categories into research designs. They must be combined with the social categories to which people belong – both in the organization and in society (cf. Thomas and Alderfer) – and with the tasks and structures that define the constraints and opportunities of the work setting. It is at this intersection that one finds the link between the internal and external career.

An example

As a concrete example of the complex interactions among context, dynamics, and internal–external distinctions, let us consider the experience of high-level organizational employees who use computers to work part of the regular work week at home. This is not yet a common practice – indeed, there is a great deal of resistance to it from both professional employees and their managers. But there are a few situations that provide data useful for understanding what is involved in this new work place phenomenon and what would be required to allow it to occur more easily.

Clearly, there are individual issues here: self-discipline is the one most often mentioned, though it also requires the ability to provide one's own structure of time and space and to forge a personal bridge between work and private life. Even more important, there are general cultural constraints, which have to do with the meanings of "office" and "home" and with their separation as part of the organization of industrial society (Perin, 1988) as well as with the importance of visibility to the pursuit and management of high-level careers (cf. Gowler and Legge). All of this is critical for an understanding of the general resistance to this pattern of work. But it is only from the experiences of particular groups of people whose work follows aspects of this pattern that one really learns what is going on.

Thus, among property professionals in an oil company whose base was moved from office to home as a result of a divisional reorganization, one group made the transition with relative ease; the other group has continued, even after a number of years, to suffer. The reason for the difference lies in the details of the tasks of these groups. The group whose work requires frequent, particularized contacts with many different groups is much more handicapped by the withdrawal of traditional office support than the group whose contacts are more standardized in form. Both groups had professional training and both groups were used to working autonomously and independently in a field environment. But this small difference in task requirements created an entirely different response to an organizational change (Bailyn, 1988). Hence the need to study in detail the immediate work context.

Further, a comparison of home-based with office-based systems developers, employees of the same company, indicates clear differences between the two groups in their career dynamics and in the subjective meaning of the career (Bailyn, in press). The home-based group consists primarily of women with children, eager to keep up their skills while at the same time giving priority to family needs.[9] They opt, therefore, for a more slowly evolving career, with the result that they are in fact more experienced and more competent in the work they do than are their office-based counterparts. And, for most of them, the internal meaning of career resides in the actual technical work – its challenge and its potential for providing a sense of achievement. The subjective meaning of career for most of the office-based group, in contrast, resides in the organizational hierarchy and the possibility of moving up into less technical but more lucrative positions.

The two groups of systems developers also exemplify the importance of looking at "deviant" groups, for there are some office-based workers (men as well as women) who share the modal orientation of the home-based group. Upon closer investigation of this small group, it turns out that they are prevented from mixing office and home as a work place by company policy – not written company policy, but policy as enacted in the interactions of management and the personnel department. So a manager who had arranged with an employee to take equipment home a few days a week in order to cut down on commuting difficulties, was told by his personnel representative:

This is not a precedent we wish to set at this time; let the employee move to the home-based group, where the management of remote people is well understood.

It is this kind of specific data that is needed to understand the conditions that preclude the introduction of work place innovations.

Summary

I have stated that careers must be viewed in the context of the immediate work situation within which they unfold. It makes little sense, therefore, to theorize about careers in general without understanding the occupational, organizational, or task requirements of the work entailed in that career. Further, careers must be viewed dynamically since needs and orientations change over a person's life span in response to changing personal and family circumstances. And, I propose, such changes will require discontinuity during the course of a career. Finally, and most important, the subjective, internal meaning of the career must be juxtaposed with its external more objective characteristics. Thus personal meanings, though affected by the social categories to which one belongs, cannot be inferred solely from those categories. It is important, also, to consider orientational categories.

LOOKING TO THE FUTURE: WHAT NEXT?

When one considers the implications of this view of careers for organizational procedures, one realizes that it requires a new model of organizational life, one that is more flexible than the traditional hierarchical one and more humane – less constraining and more supportive of individuality. The outlines of such a model emerge from a number of chapters in this handbook, which envision, implicitly if not explicitly, a radical transformation: a "re-vision" (Marshall) of the assumptions underlying the management of people and a redefinition of "work" and "career" and what it means to be successful in life (see also Gallos; Gowler and Legge; Weick and Berlinger).

The organizing principle of the new vision is geared to long-run adaptability more than to short-run efficiency (Weick and Berlinger). It gets its impetus from the needs of a rapidly changing technological, social, and economic environment as well as from "non-traditional" people (cf. Bailyn, 1984; Dalton; Gallos; Marshall; Sekaran and Hall; Thomas and Alderfer) – from individuals with expectations and orientations different from those who have traditionally occupied key organizational and occupational positions.

Such a vision is a model in the sense of an "ideal type." It does not describe an existing reality but rather sets out an internally consistent system centered on a particular objective (Checkland, 1981). Its purpose is to allow one to assess a given situation in terms of its divergence from the model and thus to permit inferences as to the kinds of changes needed to approximate more closely the "ideal" state.

So, what are the career rules necessary to support this vision? Their essence seems to be to foster a "culture of diversity" (cf. Bailyn, 1984; Gallos; Marshall; Thomas and Alderfer; Weick and Berlinger) by sanctioning discontinuity and variety in the external career, which then allows for greater diversity in the meanings assigned to these work experiences – in the internal or subjective career (cf. Nicholson and West; Thomas). Such a career system must be based on reciprocity between individual and organizational needs (Arthur and Kram). It must rely on temporary structures, on work assignments geared to generalizing rather than specializing skills, and on flatter hierarchies that devolve responsibility locally (Sekaran and Hall; Weick and Berlinger). And it must guard against the rigidity produced by organizational procedures that assign an ability status, or level of potential, in a relatively permanent way (cf. Rosenbaum; Sonnenfeld). In the long run what this means is that careers will have to become discontinuous, organized into independent segments (Bailyn, 1984). Underlying such a notion is an emphasis on flexibility and change rather than on stability, which will require a "re-vision" of timetables and age-specific notions of career stages (Marshall; Rosenbaum).

Managerial processes necessary to effect such change are closer to the principles of interdependence (Gallos; Marshall) and self-design (Weick and Berlinger) than they are to autonomous agency and bureaucratic hierarchy (cf. Dalton; Sampson, 1988).[10] They need to be geared less to regulation and more to "appreciation" (Gadalla and Cooper, 1978): to depend more on openness to new possibilities in people and in situations than on pre-set procedures anchored in traditional assumptions (Gallos; Marshall; Weick and Berlinger). Help to transcend these received traditions can come from the increased diversity in the work force, at least as long as that diversity is allowed to play itself out and is not fettered by too much homogeneity in rules and assumptions.

CONCLUDING NOTE

I have outlined some of my ideas on careers and how they are best studied and managed. In this process I have been stimulated by this handbook. I conclude, therefore, with what, in my opinion, are the most important lessons that emerge from its chapters. First, they introduce a more complex view of reality, away from static, overly abstract, and homogeneous attempts to understand people's careers at work. Second, they warn against prescriptions based on oversimplified assumptions about current functioning. Finally, they present a vision of the future against which to assess current practice.

These are the conclusions that seem most relevant to me. Even if others disagree with their specific content, I hope that they indicate the generativity of the previous chapters and thus show that a major purpose of this handbook has been served.

NOTES

I am grateful for the helpful comments made on earlier drafts by the editors, particularly Michael Arthur, and by Bernard Bailyn, Marie Jahoda, Deborah Kolb, Edgar Schein, Robert Thomas, and John Van Maanen.

1 The possibility that psychological dominance is based on a cultural bias in U.S. research is raised in the conclusion to that volume (Schein, 1984) as well as in a contrast between American and British career research (Collin and Young, 1986).

2 In other words, we want our knowledge to be "usable": "to achieve intended consequences in the world of practical affairs" (Argyris, 1985:79–80).

3 Underlying this individualistic approach to practice is the presumption of a basic convergence of values and norms between individual and organization and sufficient individual resources to exercise personal control. But such circumstances are only selectively met in actuality (Brown, 1982) and reflect a middle class, especially a managerially defined, reality (cf. Schein, 1986; Thomas).

4 One of the consequences of fit is that it breeds rigidity and may make it more difficult to respond flexibly if conditions should change. This has been shown, also, in research on technical careers (Katz, 1982; Pelz and Andrews, 1976). A similar disclaimer on the value of matching organization design to prevailing contingencies has been made by Child and Kieser (1981).

5 It is for this reason, also, that longitudinal research is not the panacea it is often assumed to be for the study of the dynamics of careers.

6 Derr and Laurent have a similar view of the internal career but define the external one

very differently: "The core of the internal career is the individual's career self-concept within the context of organizations and occupations; the core of the external career, however, is one's perception of the organizational and occupational context itself ... both the internal and external careers can be considered psychological constructs." As such, they are talking of two different aspects of the individual's perspective – the one of one's career orientations, the other of the opportunities one faces. This is very different from the double perspective implied in the present section, where the distinction depends on a differentiation between the meaning attributed to career issues (orientations or opportunities) from the inside, by the person, or defining them from an external "outsider" perspective, as serving the organization or society at large.

7 A similar discussion on the social category of race can be found in Thomas and Alderfer.
8 The particular choice of proximate variables will reflect the disciplinary inclinations of the researcher. So, e.g., Kanter (1977) – a sociologist – uses the opportunity structure in an organization as a proximate variable for sex in her analysis of differences in work behavior. Further, it should be said that the contextual level of analysis can also be viewed from both an objective and a subjective, more "proximate" side (cf. Lawrence, 1984; Rosenbaum; Stebbins, 1970).
9 That these data come from England and that a similar experiment with American women of equal training was not successful is another example of the contextual embeddedness of work place phenomena – in this case in cultural differences in the priorities of women (see also Derr and Laurent).
10 There are a number of interesting commonalities between certain of the chapters in this handbook. One of the more intriguing is that between the Weick and Berlinger chapter on the self-designing career and the ones by Gallos and Marshall on women. Is an organization based on principles of communion – of "being" and "caring" – a self-designing organization? Is it possible that people whose dominant mode is communion will fit more easily into such organizations than do those whose behavior is guided more by agency?

REFERENCES

Argyris, C. (1985). Making knowledge more relevant to practice: maps for action. In E. E. Lawler, A. M. Mohrman Jr., S. A. Mohrman, G. E. Ledford Jr., T. G. Cummings, and Associates (eds.), *Doing Research That Is Useful for Theory and Practice*. San Francisco: Jossey-Bass.
Arthur, M. B. (1984). The career concept: challenge and opportunity for its further application. In M. B. Arthur, L. Bailyn, D. J. Levinson, and H. A. Shepard, *Working With Careers*. New York: Center for Research in Career Development, Columbia University.
Arthur, M. B., Bailyn, L., Levinson, D. J., and Shepard, H. A. (1984). *Working With Careers*. New York: Center for Research in Career Development, Columbia University.
Arthur, M. B., and Lawrence, B. S. (eds.) (1984). A special issue on environment and career. *Journal of Occupational Behaviour*, 5(1), 1–81.
Bailyn, L. (1977a). Research as a cognitive process: implications for data analysis. *Quality and Quantity, 11*, 97–117.
Bailyn, L. (1977b). Involvement and accommodation in technical careers: an inquiry into the relation to work at mid-career. In J. Van Maanen (ed.), *Organizational Careers: Some New Perspectives*. London: Wiley.
Bailyn, L. (1980). The "slow burn" way to the top: some thoughts on the early years in organizational careers. In C. B. Derr (ed.), *Work, Family, and the Career: New Frontiers in Theory and Research*. New York: Praeger.
Bailyn, L. (1984). Issues of work and family in organizations: responding to social diversity. In M. B. Arthur, L. Bailyn, D. J. Levinson, and H. A. Shepard, *Working With Careers*. New York: Center for Research in Career Development, Columbia University.
Bailyn, L. (1987). Experiencing technical work: a comparison of male and female engineers. *Human Relations, 40*, 299–312.
Bailyn, L. (1988). Freeing work from the constraints of location and time. *New Technology, Work and Employment, 3*, 143–152.

Bailyn, L. (in press). Toward the perfect workplace? The experience of home-based systems developers. *Communications of the ACM.*

Brown, R. (1982). Work histories, career strategies and the class structure. In A. Giddens and G. Mackenzie (eds.), *Social Class and the Division of Labour: Essays in Honour of Ilya Newustadt.* Cambridge: Cambridge University Press.

Brown, R. (1984). Working on work. *Sociology, 18,* 311–323.

Checkland, P. (1981). *Systems Thinking, Systems Practice.* Chichester: Wiley.

Child, J., and Kieser, A. (1981). Development of organizations over time. In P. C. Nystrom and W. H. Starbuck (eds.), *Handbook of Organizational Design,* Vol. 1. Oxford: Oxford University Press.

Collin, A., and Young, R. A. (1986). New directions for theories of career. *Human Relations, 39,* 837–853.

Falter, J. W. (1978). Some theoretical and methodological problems of multilevel analysis reconsidered. *Social Science Information, 17,* 841–869.

Gadalla, I. E., and Cooper, R. (1978). Towards an epistemology of management. *Social Science Information, 17,* 349–383.

Hughes, E. C. (1937). Institutional office and the person. *American Journal of Sociology, 43,* 404–413.

Kanter, R. M. (1977). *Men and Women of the Corporation.* New York: Basic.

Katz, R. (1982). Managing careers: the influence of job and group longevities. In R. Katz (ed.), *Career Issues in Human Resource Management.* Englewood Cliffs, NJ: Prentice-Hall.

Keller, E. F. (1986). How gender matters: or, why it's so hard for us to count past two. In J. Harding (ed.), *Perspectives on Gender and Science.* London: Falmer.

Law, B. (1981). Careers theory: a third dimension? In A. G. Watts, D. E. Super, and J. M. Kidd (eds.), *Career Development in Britain.* Cambridge: Hobsons.

Lawrence, B. S. (1984). Age grading: the implicit organizational timetable. *Journal of Occupational Behaviour, 5,* 23–35.

Maas, H. S., and Kuypers, J. A. (1974). *From Thirty to Seventy: A Forty-Year Longitudinal Study of Adult Life Styles and Personality.* San Francisco: Jossey-Bass.

Pelz, D. C., and Andrews, F. M. (1976). *Scientists in Organizations: Productive Climates for Research and Development,* rev. ed. Ann Arbor: Institute for Social Research, University of Michigan.

Perin, C. (1988). The moral fabric of the office: organizational habits vs. high-tech options for work schedule flexibilities. Sloan School of Management Working Paper No. 2011-88, MIT.

Rossi, A. S. (1985). Gender and parenthood. In A. S. Rossi (ed.), *Gender and the Life Course,* New York: Aldine.

Sampson, E. E. (1988). The debate on individualism: indigenous psychologies of the individual and their role in personal and societal functioning. *American Psychologist, 43,* 15–22.

Schein, E. H. (1978). *Career Dynamics: Matching Individual and Organizational Needs.* Reading, MA: Addison-Wesley.

Schein, E. H. (1984). Culture as an environmental context for careers. *Journal of Occupational Behaviour, 5,* 71–81.

Schein, E. H. (1986). A critical look at current career development theory and research. In D. T. Hall (ed.), *Career Development in Organizations.* San Francisco: Jossey-Bass.

Sonnenfeld, J., and Kotter, J. P. (1982). The maturation of career theory. *Human Relations, 35,* 19–46.

Stebbins, R. A. (1970). Career: the subjective approach. *Sociological Quarterly, 11,* 32–49.

Super, D. E. (1963). Self concepts in career development. In D. E. Super, R. Starishevsky, N. Matlin, and J. P. Jordaan (eds.), *Career Development: Self-Concept Theory.* New York: CEEB.

Van Maanen, J. (1977). Introduction: the promise of career studies. In J. Van Maanen (ed.), *Organizational Careers: Some New Perspectives.* London: Wiley.

Van Maanen, J. (1980). Career games: organizational rules of play. In C. B. Derr (ed.), *Work, Family, and the Career: New Frontiers in Theory and Research.* New York: Praeger.

Van Maanen, J., and Schein, E. H. (1977). Career development. In J. R. Hackman and J. L. Suttle (eds.), *Improving Life at Work: Behavioral Science Approaches to Organizational Change*. Santa Monica: Goodyear.

Watts, A. G. (1981). Career patterns. In A. G. Watts, D. E. Super, and J. M. Kidd (eds.), *Career Development in Britain*. Cambridge: Hobsons.

24 *Propositions linking organizations and careers*

PAUL C. NYSTROM AND
ANGELINE W. MCARTHUR

How do organizations affect careers? And how do careers affect organizations? This integrating chapter begins to answer these questions by setting forth 155 propositions. We extracted or refined these propositions by thoroughly searching the chapters in Parts I and II of this handbook.

Given the editors' laudable aim to focus this handbook on theory rather than on measurement issues or practical applications, this chapter engages in theory building. Theories evolve as scholars develop propositions. Preferably, these propositions will specify sequential or determinant laws of interactions between continuous variables rather than merely delineating categories (Dubin, 1978).

The hundreds of variables mentioned in the previous chapters emanate from a diverse array of theories rooted in different academic disciplines. Authors address divergent issues, they use partially incompatible terminologies, and they anchor their endeavors in partially inharmonious values and beliefs. In the past, career theory has been fractionated (Schein, 1986; Sonnenfeld and Kotter, 1982), with scholars in each academic discipline tending to ignore ideas about careers developed by scholars in other disciplines. This chapter seeks integration between disciplines that contribute to our understanding of careers. To foster this integration, our chapter articulates propositions and arrays them in ways that we think will enable readers to form their own cross-disciplinary insights. We hope that this chapter will serve as a useful reference source for doctoral students and faculty who conduct research about careers.

PROPOSITIONS

Tables 24.1–24.4 contain propositions that treat organizational attributes as the independent variables or determinants and treat career attributes as the dependent variables or outcomes. Tables 24.5 and 24.6 reverse the roles of the organization and career variables relative to Tables 24.1–24.4, with careers becoming the causes of organizational outcomes.

Each table groups propositions according to similarities in the independent variables. Three of the categories – organizational strategies, structures, and processes – underlie well-known theories of organizational design (Chandler, 1962; Galbraith, 1977; Mintzberg, 1979). Such contingency theories assert that organizational strategies determine which type of organizational structure will be most appropriate. The chosen structure determines, in turn, which types of organizational processes will be most appropriate. A fourth category, labeled conditions here, subsumes the familiar idea of environments, but it also encompasses conditions or states of affairs inside an organization. To some extent, this fourth category called conditions also serves as a residual category containing those ideas that do not fit under the three categories labeled strategies, structures, or processes.

Chapter authors occasionally stated ideas explicitly in propositional form. The editors had urged authors to state propositions when revising their drafts. In many cases, however, the propositions contained in our tables should more appropriately be regarded as having been translated, explicated, or inspired by some statement. Few propositions were extracted verbatim. In accordance with a wise academic norm, we accept responsibility for any errors of interpretation. Whenever necessary, variables were restated in ways that facilitate comparisons across chapters. Also, variables stated originally as categories were converted to continuous-type variables instead.

When a handbook author cites other work in conjunction with a proposition, then those additional references appear after the colon following the chapter author's name. Chapter authors' names appear in italics.

Reasonable people may disagree about the placement of some propositions into one table rather than another. Propositions have been grouped into tables simply to facilitate comparisons of similar ideas. Our concern in this chapter focuses on the propositions per se, not on their groupings into tables.

Each proposition implies a causal arrow. For instance, the first proposition in Table 24.1 states that promotional opportunities vary positively with organizational growth. The causal implication is that higher growth rates create more promotional opportunities; lower growth rates imply fewer promotional opportunities. This proposition emerged in the chapters by Pfeffer and by Rosenbaum.

Careers as dependent variables

Strategies. The 11 propositions in Table 24.1 concern independent variables commonly regarded as organizational strategies. Organizational growth, downsizing, mergers, and acquisitions all alter an organization's size, so size has been categorized here as an associated strategy variable. One could argue that size is an attribute of organizational structure (Meyer, 1972), but other projects such as the Aston studies (Pugh et al., 1969) classify size as a contextual variable rather than as a structural one. Core versus peripheral firms reflects a host of strategic choices that position an organization into one of two segments of the economy. Core firms operate in oligopolistic markets by becoming large and highly capitalized (Gordon, Edwards, and Reich, 1982). Peripheral firms operate in competitive markets and tend to remain smaller. Propositions state, for instance, that core firms tend to pay higher wages than do peripheral firms.

Structures. The 43 propositions in Table 24.2 involve independent variables normally classified as organizational structures or characteristics associated with organizational structures. Independent variables are arrayed in a continuum that begins with entire organizations and ends with attributes of jobs.

Processes. Authors suggested many more propositions about how organizational processes affect careers than about all other organizational independent variables

Table 24.1. *Propositions about the effects of organizations' strategies upon careers*

Organizations as independent variables	Sign	Careers as dependent variables	References
Organizational growth	+	Promotional opportunities	*Pfeffer:* Stewman and Konda, 1983 *Rosenbaum:* Rosenbaum, 1984
Downsizing	+	Career stress	*Latack:* Kram, 1985
Mergers and takeovers	+	Career stress	*Latack*
Mergers and takeovers	+	Frequency of transitions	*Latack*
Organizational size	+	Acquisition of transferable skills	*Sonnenfeld:* Oster, 1979; Ryan, 1984; Sadowski, 1982
Organizational size	+	Compensation levels	*Sonnenfeld:* Masters, 1969; Oster, 1979; Ryan, 1984; Sadowski, 1982; Stolzenberg, 1978 *Thomas:* Averitt, 1968; Bluestone, 1970
Organizational size	+	Promotional opportunities	*Sonnenfeld:* Oster, 1979; Ryan, 1984; Sadowski, 1982
Organizational size	−	Radical career moves	*Nicholson and West:* Brett, 1984
Core vs. peripheral firms	+	Wage levels	*Thomas*
Core vs. peripheral firms	+	Employment security	*Thomas*
Core vs. peripheral firms	+	Promotional opportunities	*Thomas*

combined. Table 24.3 offers 72 propositions about the impacts of organizational processes. Independent variables appear in a logical flow that begins with recruitment of new organizational members and ends with power politics.

Conditions. The residual category labeled organizational conditions contains seven propositions that do not fit well in Tables 24.1–24.3. The conditions listed in Table 24.4 can be regarded as states of affairs capable of varying and thereby affecting careers. Independent variables in Table 24.4 start with internal conditions and end with external conditions.

Careers as independent variables

Careers become the independent variables and organizations become the dependent variables in Tables 24.5 and 24.6. Career variables that deal with any aspect of mobility appear in Table 24.5. All other career variables not pertaining to mobility topics appear in Table 24.6.

Mobility. The ten propositions in Table 24.5 concern careers as mobility phenomena (Nystrom, 1981). For example, the first proposition states that more promotion opportunities lead to higher quality of the work force. Note that only one proposition suggests an impact of career mobility on organizational performance.

Table 24.2. *Propositions about the effects of organizations' structures upon careers*

Organizations as independent variables	Sign	Careers as dependent variables	References
Pyramidal structure	+	Conformity	*Gowler and Legge:* Argyris, 1967
Pyramidal structure	–	Risk taking	*Gowler and Legge:* Argyris, 1967
Hierarchical forms	+	Success defined as upward mobility	*Marshall*
Hierarchical levels	+	Upward mobility	*Thomas*
Hierarchy level	+	Conformity	*Bell and Staw*
Job level	+	Accuracy of career system perceptions	*Rosenbaum:* Goldner, 1970
Hierarchical skill levels	+	Pay-increase opportunities	*Thomas*
Professionalization	+	Job mobility	*Weick and Berlinger*
Departmental power	+	Salary levels	*Pfeffer:* Moore and Pfeffer, 1980
Self-design in organization	–	External career markers	*Weick and Berlinger*
Incomplete organizational design	+	Learning	*Weick and Berlinger:* Hedberg, Nystrom, and Starbuck, 1976
Sequential technology	+	Lateral mobility	*Sonnenfeld:* Vardi, 1980; Vardi and Hammer, 1977
Mediating technology	+	Upward mobility	*Sonnenfeld:* Vardi, 1980; Vardi and Hammer, 1977
Mediating technology	+	Interfirm mobility	*Sonnenfeld:* Vardi, 1980; Vardi and Hammer, 1977
Technological change	+	Skill obsolescence	*Dalton:* Dalton and Thompson, 1971; Dalton, Thompson, and Price, 1977
Internal labor market permeability	+	Turnover	*Sonnenfeld*
Internal labor market permeability	–	Short-term personal goals	*Sonnenfeld:* Williamson, 1975
Internal labor market permeability	–	External labor market competition	*Thomas:* Doeringer and Piore, 1975
Internal labor market permeability	–	Employment security	*Sonnenfeld*
Bureaucratic boundaries	–	Promotion opportunities	*Thomas:* Doeringer and Piore, 1975
Cohort size	+	Turnover	*Sonnenfeld:* Stewman and Konda, 1983
Cohort size	–	Promotion opportunities	*Sonnenfeld:* Stewman and Konda, 1983
Fragmentation of job structure	–	Occupational choices	*Thomas*
Job ladders	–	Turnover	*Sonnenfeld:* Baron and Bielby, 1980
Capped job structure	+	Job-switch rate	*Thomas*
Capped job structure	+	Lateral mobility	*Thomas*
Dead-end jobs	+.	Antisocial behavior away from work	*Thomas:* Rubin, 1976
Autonomy	–	Learned helplessness	*Bell and Staw*
Autonomy	–	Stress	*Latack:* Latack, Aldag, and Josephs, 1986
Autonomy	+	Satisfaction	*Bell and Staw:* Hackman and Oldham, 1980

Table 24.2. *(cont.)*

Organizations as independent variables	Sign	Careers as dependent variables	References
Decision latitude	–	Stress	*Latack:* Karasek, 1979
Ambiguity	–	Conformity	*Bell and Staw:* Mischel, 1977; Snyder and Ickes, 1985
Job simplification	+	Conformity	*Dalton:* Argyris, 1964
Job simplification	+	Absenteeism	*Dalton:* Argyris, 1964
Job simplification	–	Risk taking	*Dalton:* Argyris, 1964
Job challenge	+	Self-efficacy	*Nicholson and West:* Brousseau, 1983; Frese, 1982; Kohn and Schooler, 1983; Mortimer and Lorence, 1979
Job challenge	+	Skills	*Arthur and Kram:* Bailyn, 1984; Csikszentmihalyi, 1975
Job challenge	–	Boredom	*Arthur and Kram:* Bailyn, 1984
Job pressures	+	Intensity of development crises	*Cytrynbaum and Crites:* Cytrynbaum, Lee, and Wadner, 1982
Feedback	–	Stress	*Latack:* Latack, Aldag, and Josephs, 1986
Job criticality	+	Administrative salary	*Pfeffer:* Pfeffer and Davis-Blake, 1986
Union job control	+	Job security	*Thomas*
Union job control	–	Promotion opportunities	*Thomas*

Other career variables. A list of 12 propositions involving career variables other than mobility appear in Table 24.6. Three of these propositions predict that organizations will be affected by career variables pertaining to various stress factors.

A comparison of Tables 24.5 and 24.6 with Tables 24.1–24.4 reveals two striking differences. The first difference concerns magnitudes: Tables 24.5 and 24.6 contain only about one-fifth the number of propositions set forth in Tables 24.1–24.4. Clearly, the careers literature provides many more ideas about the effects of organizations upon careers than about the effects of careers upon organizations. Second, the organizations variables listed in Tables 24.5 and 24.6 constitute a surprisingly different set than those contained in Tables 24.1–24.4. Thus, phenomena that scholars consider as organizational determinants of careers differ substantially from those considered as organizational outcomes of careers.

In addition to the bivariate relationships between organizations and careers shown in Tables 24.1–24.6, organizations or career variables might also serve as moderators. A search of the chapters for moderators yielded only two such propositions. Barney and Lawrence suggested that the negative relationship of labor market fluctuations and employment stability is moderated positively by organizational wages levels. Cytrynbaum and Crites suggested that job satisfaction and organizational productivity only exhibit a strong positive relationship after the beginning of the maintenance stage of adult life.

Table 24.3. *Propositions about the effects of organizations' processes upon careers*

Organizations as independent variables	Sign	Careers as dependent variables	References
Scope of recruitment	+	Work force heterogeneity	*Pfeffer:* Granovetter, 1986; Ryder, 1965
External recruitment	+	Turnover of co-workers	*Pfeffer:* Helmich and Brown, 1972
Realistic job previews	+	Socialization	*Sonnenfeld:* Kotter, 1973; Wanous, 1980
Entry standards	+	Valued membership	*Trice and Morand:* Trice, Belasco, and Alutto, 1969
Personnel practices	+	Hiring selectivity	*Pfeffer:* Cohen and Pfeffer, 1986
Selection	+	Work force heterogeneity	*Bell and Staw:* Miner and Estler, 1985
Personnel testing	+	Legitimacy of new occupants	*Trice and Morand:* March and Feldman, 1981; Trice, Belasco, and Alutto, 1969
Placement errors	–	Job performance	*Betz, Fitzgerald, and Hill:* Dawis and Lofquist, 1984
Official qualification criteria	–	Promotion opportunities	*Thomas:* Doeringer and Piore, 1975
Use of educational credentials	–	Promotion opportunities	*Thomas*
Market employment relationship	+	Shirking	*Barney and Lawrence:* Arrow, 1974
Hierarchical employment relationship	+	Organizational commitment	*Barney and Lawrence:* Williamson, 1975
Signal-based personnel decisions	+	Investment in signals	*Barney and Lawrence:* Spence, 1973
Gender-defined jobs (women)	–	Promotion opportunities	*Pfeffer:* Baron, Davis-Blake, and Bielby, 1986
Socialization practice	+	Organizational commitment	*Trice and Morand:* McCarl, 1984
Socialization practices	+	Conformity	*Bell and Staw:* Katz and Kahn, 1978; Thompson, 1967; Van Maanen and Schein, 1979
Socialization practices	+	Sense making	*Gowler and Legge:* Louis, 1980 *Nicholson and West:* Nicholson, 1988
Socialization practices	+	Accuracy of career aspirations	*Betz, Fitzgerald, and Hill:* Wanous, 1980 *Trice and Morand*
Organizational rites	+	Cohort cohesiveness	*Trice and Morand:* Turner, 1970
Organizational rites	+	Ease of role transitions	*Trice and Morand:* Harris and Sutton, 1986; Zurcher, 1967
Rites of passages	–	Employee illness	*Trice and Morand:* Dohrenwend and Dohrenwend, 1974
Stories and myths	–	Accuracy of career system perceptions	*Rosenbaum:* Rosenbaum, 1986
Employment rituals	–	Job opportunities for women	*Marshall:* Pym, 1980
Debasement practices	+	Readiness for change	*Trice and Morand:* Schein, 1978
Debasement practices	+	Unlearning	*Trice and Morand:* Schein, 1978
Early identification of potential	+	Age discrimination	*Marshall*

Table 24.3. *(cont.)*

Organizations as independent variables	Sign	Careers as dependent variables	References
Early identification of potential	+	Gender discrimination	*Marshall*
Early identification of potential	+	Career expectations	*Rosenbaum:* Rosenbaum, 1986
Organizational career planning	+	Regularity in status transitions	*Barley:* Strauss, 1959
Selective organizational investment in human capital	–	Upward mobility of others	*Rosenbaum:* Rosenbaum, 1986
Specificity of human capital investment	+	Uncertainty of promotion	*Barney and Lawrence*
Investment-to-promotion time lag	+	Uncertainty of promotion	*Barney and Lawrence*
Training	+	Organizational commitment	*Trice and Morand:* Rohlen, 1973; Trice, Belasco, and Alutto, 1969
Training	+	Role adjustment	*Nicholson and West:* Nicholson, 1988
Training	+	Legitimization	*Trice and Morand:* Belasco and Trice, 1969
Training	+	Employee productivity	*Trice and Morand:* Rohlen, 1973; Trice, Belasco, and Alutto, 1969
Knowledge of results	+	Learning	*Dalton:* Dill, Hilton, and Reitman, 1962
Recognition of achievements	–	Boredom	*Arthur and Kram*
Counseling	+	Preparation for job change	*Nicholson and West:* Nicholson, 1988
Sponsorship	+	Upward mobility	*Dalton:* Becker and Strauss, 1956
Mentoring	+	Career development	*Dalton:* Clawson, 1980
Racial disparity in mentoring	+	Initiation time	*Thomas and Alderfer:* Kram, 1985
Supervisory support	+	Satisfaction	*Latack*
Supervisory support	–	Stress	*Latack:* Beehr, 1985
Excessive supervision	–	Skills	*Arthur and Kram:* Bailyn, 1984; Csikszentmihalyi, 1975
Excessive supervision	–	Occupational identity	*Arthur and Kram:* Bailyn, 1984
Excessive supervision	+	Boredom	*Arthur and Kram:* Bailyn, 1984
Excessive supervision	+	Worry	*Arthur and Kram:* Bailyn, 1984
Objective performance standards	–	Socially ascribed salaries	*Pfeffer:* Pfeffer, 1977a,b
Rewards unrelated to performance	–	Competence development	*Dalton:* Dalton, 1959
Individual-based rewards	–	Collaboration	*Marshall*
Organizational signals (past attainment; career velocity)	+	Upward mobility	*Rosenbaum:* Dannefer, 1984; Lawrence, 1984; Shrank and Waring, 1983
Tournament rules	+	Persistence in differential promotion rates	*Rosenbaum:* Rosenbaum, 1986
Tournament rules	+	Ability status	*Rosenbaum:* Rosenbaum, 1986
Seniority rules	+	Promotions rejected	*Thomas*

Table 24.3. *(cont.)*

Organizations as independent variables	Sign	Careers as dependent variables	References
Age norms	+	Feelings of asynchronism	*Sekaran and Hall:* Rosenbaum, 1984
Age barriers	–	Promotional opportunities	*Rosenbaum*
Racial barriers	–	Promotional opportunities	*Thomas and Alderfer*
Cooling-out policies	–	Stagnation	*Barley:* Clark, 1960; Faulkner, 1973; Goldner, 1965; Martin and Strauss, 1959
Cooling-out policies	+	Commitment of plateaued employees	*Barley:* Clark, 1960; Faulkner, 1973; Goldner, 1965; Martin and Strauss, 1959
Dangerous assignments	+	Shared values	*Trice and Morand:* Applebaum, 1984; Jermier, 1982
Shared information on jobs	–	Skill obsolescence	*Sonnenfeld*
Shared information on jobs	–	Unfair discrimination	*Sonnenfeld*
Participatory career development practices	–	Stress	*Latack*
Career incentives	–	Mid-career crisis	*Rosenbaum:* Lawrence, 1980
Employment security practices	+	On-the-job learning	*Sonnenfeld:* Williamson, 1975
Employment security practices	+	Commitment	*Sonnenfeld:* Walton, 1985
Fringe benefits	+	Work force stability	*Thomas:* Doeringer and Piore, 1975
Upward communications encouraged	+	Voice	*Barney and Lawrence:* Hirschman, 1970; Ouchi, 1980
Symbol management	+	Career coherence	*Gowler and Legge*
Activity cycles	–	Boredom	*Thomas*
Norms of individualism	–	Accuracy of career system perceptions	*Rosenbaum:* Rosenbaum, 1979
Power politics	+	Involuntary turnover of executives	*Pfeffer:* Allen and Panian, 1982; Zald, 1965

DOMAIN MAPS

Tables 24.7 and 24.8 map the organizations–careers domain by showing the frequencies of relationships discussed in the earlier chapters. Organization variables are classified as strategies, structures, processes, and conditions. Career variables are classified either as mobility variables or as other variables describing some attribute of careers. For instance, the first cell entry in Table 24.7 indicates that five propositions link organizational strategies as determinants of career mobility.

Table 24.7 reveals that organizational processes and structures have received much more attention than organizational strategies or conditions as determinants of careers. By contrast, Table 24.8 reveals that more propositions about career

Table 24.4. *Propositions about the effects of organizations' conditions upon careers*

Organizations as independent variables	Sign	Careers as dependent variables	References
Long-term organizational uncertainty	+	Stress	*Latack*
Organizational crisis	+	Turnover	*Barney and Lawrence:* Hirschman, 1970
Organizational change	+	Internal career map shifts	*Derr and Laurent:* Derr, 1986
Organizational inflexibility	+	Turnover of women	*Gallos*
Idea overload	+	Promotion of synthesizers	*Weick and Berlinger:* Hedberg, 1981
Organizational performance	–	Involuntary management succession	*Nicholson and West:* Allen and Panian, 1982; Brown, 1982; Grusky, 1963
Degree of unionization	+	Wage levels	*Thomas:* Averitt, 1968; Bluestone, 1970
Degree of unionization	–	Hiring selectivity	*Pfeffer:* Cohen and Pfeffer, 1986

Table 24.5. *Propositions about the effects of career mobility upon organizations*

Careers as independent variables	Sign	Organizations as dependent variables	References
Promotion opportunities	+	Quality of work force	*Sonnenfeld:* Oster, 1979; Ryan, 1984; Sadowski, 1982
Upward mobility	+	Organizational investments in person	*Rosenbaum*
Desire for rapid promotion	+	Short-term organizational goals	*Rosenbaum*
Spiral careers	+	Self-design in organization	*Weick and Berlinger:* Driver, 1979
Technical careers	–	Organizational control	*Barley:* Van Maanen and Barley, 1984
Skill-based careers	+	Organizational adaptability	*Weick and Berlinger:* Hall, 1986
Involuntary management succession	–	Organizational performance	*Nicholson and West:* Allen and Panian, 1982; Brown, 1982; Grusky, 1963
Vacancy rates	+	Cohort competition	*Sonnenfeld:* White, 1970
Proximity to boundary passage	+	Organizational innovation	*Dalton:* Schein, 1971
Ease of changing employment	+	Organizational innovation	*Weick and Berlinger:* Blotnick, 1984

determinants focus on organizational conditions as the dependent variables. Note that Table 24.7 contains 135 propositions with careers as dependent variables, whereas Table 24.8 contains only 20 propositions with careers as independent variables. When careers are treated as dependent variables, much less attention has been directed to career mobility than to other career variables. Some scholars

Table 24.6. *Propositions about the effects of other career variables upon organizations*

Careers as independent variables	Sign	Organizations as dependent variables	References
Job stress	+	Organizational rigidity	*Weick and Berlinger:* Eysenck, 1982
Job stress	−	Productivity	*Latack*
Job stress	+	Health care costs	*Latack*
Work–family role overload	−	Productivity	*Sekaran and Hall:* Sekaran, 1986
Cohort cohesiveness	+	Informal social network	*Trice and Morand:* Turner, 1970
Compensation	+	Quality of work force	*Sonnenfeld:* Oster, 1979; Ryan, 1984; Sadowski, 1982
Acquisition of transferable skills	+	Quality of work force	*Sonnenfeld:* Oster, 1979; Ryan, 1984; Sadowski, 1982
Employee shirking	+	Number of supervisors	*Barney and Lawrence:* Alchian and Demsetz, 1972; Jensen and Meckling, 1976
Organizational commitment	−	Organizational change	*Weick and Berlinger:* Salancik, 1977; Staw, 1982
Organizational commitment	−	Surveillance of employees	*Trice and Morand:* McCarl, 1984

Table 24.7. *Frequencies of propositions about the effects of organizations upon careers*

Organizations	Careers		Totals
	Mobility	Other	
Strategies	5	6	11
Structures	13	30	43
Processes	16	57	73
Conditions	4	4	8
Totals	38	97	135

Table 24.8. *Frequencies of propositions about the effects of careers upon organizations*

Careers	Organizations				Totals
	Strategies	Structures	Processes	Conditions	
Mobility	3	1	2	4	10
Other	1	1	3	5	10
Totals	4	2	5	9	20

have admonished others to conceive of careers broadly and not solely as vertical movement within hierarchies (Becker, 1952; Van Maanen and Barley, 1984). Clearly, many of the authors in this handbook do define careers in widely encompassing ways. Indeed, the boundaries between career variables and organizational behavior variables appear quite fuzzy at this point in the evolution of career theory.

Dynamics

To determine the degree of stability or dynamism exhibited by current career theory, revised chapters were compared with the original versions. The 15 chapters initially available to us had yielded 158 propositions. A reanalysis of these 15 chapters after revision approximately two years later yielded 152 propositions. However, beneath this net change of only 6 propositions, a much greater degree of change occurred. Authors added 25 propositions that had not appeared in the original versions, and they deleted 31 propositions when revising their chapters. Career theory seems to be in a state of flux; career theory certainly does not appear stagnant or moribund.

FUTURE RESEARCH

Tables 24.7 and 24.8 could be interpreted as maps to help guide future research. Some of those cells containing few or no propositions may be fertile areas worthy of greater exploration.

Readers can scan Tables 24.1–24.6 to look for missing variables. At first, it may seem difficult to notice gaps when confronted with an almost bewildering list of variables. Which missing variables one notices depends partially on one's interests. Yet, pondering missing variables may lead readers to identify important gaps deserving future research. For instance, note the absence of well-known organizational strategies such as product diversification, market leadership, vertical integration, innovation, or emphasis on low costs. Organizational strategies may prove more informative as moderators than as independent variables. Note the absence of well-known structural variables such as decentralization, flexibility, formalization, divisionalization, technological changes, knowledge intensiveness, or automaticity. An organization's conditions could include the stage in the life cycle, the degree of managerial ownership, and the environmental dimensions of dynamism, complexity, and munificence.

One would hope that future research moves beyond considering only two variables at a time. The dyadic relationships presented in Tables 24.1–24.6 form basic building blocks that can and should be assembled into larger models. Constructing such multivariate models will enable researchers to specify contingencies and constraints. Combining related two-variable propositions may occasionally expose logical contradictions between heretofore separate ideas. Building multivariate models will also facilitate cross-disciplinary research. For instance, astute readers will note that the same or very similar variables appear in propositions developed by different authors, often working in different academic disciplines. Linking their propositions into causal models may stimulate new research ideas by recognizing model misspecifications, particularly by identifying missing variables that ought to be included.

Three general prescriptions for future research seem warranted. First, scholars should state their ideas explicitly as propositions, using continuous-type variables rather than categorical ones whenever possible. Second, scholars should consider specifying contingency models rather than the prevalent universal models. Third, scholars should consider casting organizational variables into the role of moderators.

As you read the chapters in Parts I and II, you may see somewhat different ideas, may extract slightly different propositions, or may classify variables in different ways than those presented here. No matter! Our fundamental point remains valid: Scholars will advance career theory if they develop propositions and link them together to create models.

REFERENCES

Alchian, A. A., and Demsetz, H. (1972). Production, information costs, and economic organization. *American Economic Review, 62,* 777–795.
Allen, M. P., and Panian, S. K. (1982). Power, performance, and succession in the large corporation. *Administrative Science Quarterly, 27,* 538–547.
Applebaum, H. (1984). *Work in Market and Industrial Societies.* Albany: State University of New York Press.
Argyris, C. (1964). *Integrating the Individual and the Organization.* New York: Wiley.
Argyris, C. (1967). Today's problems with tomorrow's organizations. *Journal of Management Studies, 4,* 31–55.
Arrow, K. J. (1974). *The Limits of Organization.* New York: Norton.
Averitt, R. (1968). *The Dual Economy.* New York: Norton.
Bailyn, L. (1984). Issues of work and family in responding to social diversity. In M. B. Arthur, L. Bailyn, D. J. Levinson, and H. A. Shepard, *Working With Careers.* New York: Center for Research in Career Development, Graduate School of Business, Columbia University.
Baron, J. N., and Bielby, W. T. (1980). Bringing the firms back in: stratification, segmentation, and the organization of work. *American Sociological Review, 45,* 737–765.
Baron, J. N., Davis-Blake, A., and Bielby, W. T. (1986). The structure of opportunity: how promotion ladders vary within and among organizations. *Administrative Science Quarterly, 31,* 248–273.
Becker, H. S. (1952). The career of the Chicago public school-teacher. *American Journal of Sociology, 57,* 470–477.
Becker, H. S., and Strauss, A. (1956). Careers, personality, and adult socialization. *American Journal of Sociology, 62,* 253–263.
Beehr, T. A. (1985). The role of social support in coping with organizational stress. In T. A. Beehr and R. S. Bhagat (eds.), *Human Stress and Cognition in Organizations: An Integrated Perspective.* New York: Wiley.
Belasco, J., and Trice, H. M. (1969). *The Assessment of Change in Training and Therapy.* New York: McGraw-Hill.
Blotnick, S. (1984). *The Corporate Steeplechase.* New York: Penguin.
Bluestone, B. (1970). The tripartite economy: labor markets and the working poor. *Poverty and Human Resources Abstracts, 5,* 15–35.
Brett, J. M. (1984). Job transitions and personal and role development. In K. Rowland and J. Ferris (eds.), *Research in Personnel and Human Resource Management,* Vol. 2. Greenwich, CT: JAI, pp. 155–185.
Brousseau, K. R. (1983). Toward a dynamic model of job–person relationships: findings, research questions, and implications for work system design. *Academy of Management Review, 8,* 33–45.
Brown, M. C. (1982). Administrative succession and organizational performance: the succession effect. *Administrative Science Quarterly, 27,* 1–16.
Chandler, A. D., Jr. (1962). *Strategy and Structure.* Cambridge, MA: MIT Press.
Clark, B. R. (1960). The "cooling out" function in higher education. *American Journal of Sociology, 65,* 569–576.

Clawson, J. (1980). Mentoring in managerial careers. In C. B. Derr (ed.), *Work, Family and the Career*. New York: Praeger.

Cohen, Y., and Pfeffer, J. (1986). Organizational hiring standards. *Administrative Science Quarterly, 31*, 1–24.

Csikszentmihalyi, M. (1975). *Beyond Boredom and Anxiety: The Experience of Play in Work and Games*. San Francisco: Jossey-Bass.

Cytrynbaum, S., Lee, S., and Wadner, D. (1982). Faculty development through the life course. *Journal of Instructional Development, 5*(3).

Dalton, G., and Thompson, P. (1971). Accelerating obsolescence of older engineers. *Harvard Business Review, 49* (September/October), 57–67.

Dalton, G. W., Thompson, P. H., and Price, R. (1977). The four stages of professional careers – a new look at performance by professionals. *Organizational Dynamics, 6*, 19–42.

Dalton, M. (1959). *Men Who Manage*. New York: Wiley.

Dannefer, D. (1984). Adult development and social theory: a paradigmatic reappraisal. *American Sociological Review, 49*, 100–116.

Dawis, R. V., and Lofquist, L. H. (1984). *A Psychological Theory of Work Adjustment*. Minneapolis: University of Minnesota Press.

Derr, C. B. (1986). *Managing the New Careerists*. San Francisco: Jossey-Bass.

Dill, W. R., Hilton, T. L., and Reitman, W. R. (1962). *The New Managers*. Englewood Cliffs, NJ: Prentice-Hall.

Doeringer, P., and Piore, M. (1975). *Internal Labor Markets and Manpower Analysis*. Lexington, MA: Heath.

Dohrenwend, B. S., and Dohrenwend, B. P. (eds.) (1974). *Stressful Life Events – Their Nature and Effects*. New York: Wiley.

Driver, M. J. (1979). Career concepts and career management in organizations. In C. L. Cooper (ed.), *Behavioral Problems in Organizations*. Englewood Cliffs, NJ: Prentice-Hall, pp. 79–139.

Dubin, R. (1978). *Theory Building*, rev. ed. New York: Free Press.

Eysenck, M. W. (1982). *Attention and Arousal*. New York: Springer-Verlag.

Faulkner, R. R. (1973). Career concerns and mobility motivations of orchestra musicians. *The Sociological Quarterly, 14*, 334–349.

Frese, M. (1982). Occupational socialization and psychological development: an underemphasized research perspective in industrial psychology. *Journal of Occupational Psychology, 55*, 209–224.

Galbraith, J. R. (1977). *Organization Design*. Reading, MA: Addison-Wesley.

Goldner, F. H. (1965). Demotion in industrial management. *American Sociological Review, 30*, 714–724.

Goldner, F. H. (1970). Success vs. failure: prior managerial perspectives. *Industrial Relations, 9*, 453–474.

Gordon, D., Edwards, R., and Reich, M. (1982). *Segmented Work, Divided Workers*. New York: Cambridge University Press.

Granovetter, M. (1986). Labor mobility, internal markets, and job matching: a comparison of the sociological and economic approaches. *Research in Social Stratification and Mobility*, Vol. 5. Greenwich, CT: JAI, pp. 3–39.

Grusky, O. (1963). Managerial succession and organizational effectiveness. *American Journal of Sociology, 69*, 21–31.

Hackman, J. R., and Oldham, G. R. (1980). *Work Redesign*. Reading, MA: Addison-Wesley.

Hall, D. T. (1986). Breaking career routines: midcareer choice and identity development. In D. T. Hall and Associates, *Career Development in Organizations*. San Francisco: Jossey-Bass.

Harris, S. G., and Sutton, R. I. (1986). Functions of parting ceremonies in dying organizations. *Academy of Management Journal, 29*, 5–30.

Hedberg, B. (1981). How organizations learn and unlearn. In P. C. Nystrom and W. H. Starbuck (eds.), *Handbook of Organizational Design*, Vol. 1. New York: Oxford University Press, pp. 3–27.

Hedberg, B. L. T., Nystrom, P. C., and Starbuck, W. H. (1976). Camping on seesaws: prescriptions for a self-designing organization. *Administrative Science Quarterly, 21*, 41–65.

Helmich, D. L., and Brown, W. B. (1972). Successor type and organizational change in the corporate enterprise. *Administrative Science Quarterly, 17,* 371–381.

Hirschman, A. O. (1970). *Exit, Voice, and Loyalty.* Cambridge, MA: Harvard University Press.

Jensen, M. C., and Meckling, W. H. (1976). Theory of the firm: managerial behavior, agency costs, and ownership structure. *Journal of Financial Economics, 3,* 305–360.

Jermier, J. M. (1982). Ecological hazards and organizational behavior: a study of dangerous urban space–time zones. *Human Organization, 41,* 198–207.

Karasek, R. A. (1979). Job demands, job decision latitude and mental strain: implications for job redesign. *Administrative Science Quarterly, 24,* 285–308.

Katz, D., and Kahn, R. L. (1978). *The Social Psychology of Organizations,* 2nd ed. New York: Wiley.

Kohn, M. L., and Schooler, C. (1983). *Work and Personality.* Norwood, NJ: Ablex.

Kotter, J. P. (1973). The psychological contract: managing the joining up process. *California Management Review, 15*(3), 91–99.

Kram, K. E. (1985). *Mentoring at Work.* Glenview, IL: Scott, Foresman.

Latack, J. C., Aldag, R. J., and Josephs, B. (1986). Job stress: determinants and consequences of coping behavior. Working paper, Ohio State University.

Lawrence, B. S. (1980). The myth of the midlife crisis. *Sloan Management Review, 21*(4), 35–49.

Lawrence, B. S. (1984). Age grading: the implicit organizational timetable. *Journal of Occupational Behavior, 5,* 23–35.

Louis, M. R. (1980). Surprise and sense-making: what newcomers experience in entering unfamiliar organizational settings. *Administrative Science Quarterly, 25,* 226–251.

McCarl, R. S. (1984). You've come a long way – and now this is your retirement. *Journal of American Folklore, 97*(386), 393–422.

March, J. G., and Feldman, M. S. (1981). Information in organizations as signal and symbol. *Administrative Science Quarterly, 26,* 171–186.

Martin, N. H., and Strauss, A. (1959). Consequences of failure in organizations. In W. L. Warner and N. H. Martin (eds.), *Industrial Man.* New York: Harper & Row.

Masters, S. H. (1969). An interindustry analysis of wages and plant size. *Review of Economic Statistics, 51,* 341–345.

Meyer, M. W. (1972). Size and the structure of organizations: a causal model. *American Sociological Review, 37,* 434–441.

Miner, A. S., and Estler, S. E. (1985). Accrual mobility: job mobility in higher education through responsibility accrual. *Journal of Higher Education, 56,* 121–143.

Mintzberg, H. (1979). *The Structuring of Organizations.* Englewood Cliffs, NJ: Prentice-Hall.

Mischel, W. (1977). The interaction of person and situation. In D. Magnusson and N. S. Endler (eds.), *Personality at the Crossroads: Current Issues in Interactional Psychology.* Hillsdale, NJ: Erlbaum.

Moore, W. L., and Pfeffer, J. (1980). The relationship between departmental power and faculty careers on two campuses: The case for structural effects on faculty salaries. *Research in Higher Education, 13,* 291–306.

Mortimer, J. T., and Lorence, J. (1979). Work experience and occupational value socialization: a longitudinal study. *American Journal of Sociology, 84,* 1361–1385.

Nicholson, N. (1988). The transition cycle: a conceptual framework for the analysis of change and human resources management. In K. M. Rowland and G. R. Ferris (eds.), *Research in Personnel and Human Resources Management,* Vol. 5. Greenwich, CT: JAI.

Nystrom, P. C. (1981). Designing jobs and assigning employees. In P. C. Nystrom and W. H. Starbuck (eds.), *Handbook of Organizational Design,* Vol. 2. New York: Oxford University Press, pp. 272–301.

Oster, G. (1979). A factor analytic test for the theory of the dual economy. *Review of Economic Statistics, 61,* 33–39.

Ouchi, W. G. (1980). Markets, bureaucracies, and clans. *Administrative Science Quarterly, 25,* 129–141.

Pfeffer, J. (1977a). Toward an examination of stratification in organizations. *Administrative Science Quarterly, 22,* 553–567.

Pfeffer, J. (1977b). Effects of an MBA and socioeconomic origins on business school graduates' salaries. *Journal of Applied Psychology, 62,* 698–705.

Pfeffer, J., and Davis-Blake, A. (1986). Understanding organizational wage structures: a resource dependence approach. Unpublished paper. Graduate School of Business, Stanford University.

Pugh, D. S., Hickson, D. J., Hinings, C. R., and Turner, C. (1969). The context of organizational structures. *Administrative Science Quarterly, 14,* 91–114.

Pym, D. (1980). Towards the dual economy and emancipation from employment. *Futures, 12*(3).

Rohlen, T. P. (1973). Spiritual education in a Japanese bank. *American Anthropologist, 75,* 1542–1562.

Rosenbaum, J. E. (1979). Tournament mobility: career patterns in a corporation. *Administrative Science Quarterly, 24,* 220–241.

Rosenbaum, J. E. (1984). *Career Mobility in a Corporate Hierarchy.* New York: Academic.

Rosenbaum, J. E. (1986). Institutional career structures and the social construction of ability. In J. G. Richardson (ed.), *Handbook of Theory and Research for the Sociology of Education.* New York: Greenwood, pp. 139–172.

Rubin, L. (1976). *Worlds of Pain.* New York: Harper & Row.

Ryan, P. (1984). Job training, employment practices, and the large enterprise. In P. Osterman (ed.), *Internal Labor Markets.* Cambridge, MA: MIT Press, pp. 191–230.

Ryder, N. B. (1965). The cohort as a concept in the study of social change. *American Sociological Review, 30,* 843–861.

Sadowski, P. (1982). Corporate training investment decisions. In G. Menseh and R. Niehaus (eds.), *Manpower Planning and Technological Change.* New York: Plenum.

Salancik, G. R. (1977). Commitment and the control of organizational behavior and belief. In B. M. Staw and G. R. Salancik (eds.), *New Directions in Organizational Behavior.* Chicago: St. Clair, pp. 1–54.

Schein, E. H. (1971). The individual, the organization and the career: a conceptual scheme. *Journal of Behavioral Science, 7,* 401–426.

Schein, E. H. (1978). *Career Dynamics: Matching Individual and Organizational Needs.* Reading, MA: Addison-Wesley.

Schein, E. H. (1986). A critical look at current career development theory and research. In D. T. Hall and Associates, *Career Development in Organizations.* San Francisco: Jossey-Bass, pp. 310–331.

Sekaran, U. (1986). *Dual Career Families.* San Francisco: Jossey-Bass.

Shrank, H. T., and Waring, J. M. (1983). Aging and work organizations. In M. Riley, B. Hess, and K. Bond (eds.), *Aging in Society: Selected Reviews of Recent Research.* Hillside, NJ: Erlbaum, pp. 53–69.

Snyder, M., and Ickes, W. (1985). Personality and social behavior. In G. Lindzey and E. Aronson (eds.), *Handbook of Social Psychology,* 3rd ed., Vol. 2. New York: Random House.

Sonnenfeld, J., and Kotter, J. P. (1982). The maturation of career theory. *Human Relations, 35,* 19–46.

Spence, A. (1973). Job market signaling. *Quarterly Journal of Economics, 83,* 355–374.

Staw, B. M. (1982). Counterforces to change. In P. S. Goodman (ed.), *Change in Organizations.* San Francisco: Jossey-Bass, pp. 87–121.

Stewman, S., and Konda, S. L. (1983). Careers and organizational labor markets: demographic models of organizational behavior. *American Journal of Sociology, 88,* 637–685.

Stolzenberg, R. M. (1978). Bringing the boss back in: employer size, employee schooling, and socioeconomic achievement. *American Sociological Review, 43,* 813–828.

Strauss, A. L. (1959). *Mirrors and Masks.* New York: Free Press.

Thompson, J. D. (1967). *Organizations in Action.* New York: McGraw-Hill.

Trice, H. M., Belasco, J., and Alutto, J. A. (1969). The role of ceremonials in organizational behavior. *Industrial and Labor Relations Review, 23,* 40–51.

Turner, V. W. (1970). Betwixt and between: the liminal period in rites of passage. In E. A. Hammel and W. S. Simmons (eds.), *Man Makes Sense.* Boston: Little, Brown, pp. 354–369.

Van Maanen, J., and Barley, S. R. (1984). Occupational communities: culture and control in organizations. In B. Staw and L. L. Cummings (eds.), *Research in Organizational Behavior*, Vol. 6. Greenwich, CT: JAI, pp. 287–365.

Van Maanen, J., and Schein, E. H. (1979). Toward a theory of organizational socialization. In B. M. Staw and L. L. Cummings (eds.), *Research in Organizational Behavior*, Vol. 1. Greenwich, CT: JAI.

Vardi, Y. (1980). Organizational career mobility: an integrative model. *Academy of Management Review, 5,* 341–355.

Vardi, Y., and Hammer, T. H. (1977). Intraorganizational mobility and career perspectives among rank and file employees in different technologies. *Academy of Management Journal, 20,* 622–634.

Walton, R. E. (1985). Toward a strategy of eliciting employee commitment based on policies of mutuality. In R. E. Walton and P. R. Lawrence (eds.), *HRM: Trends and Challenges*. New York: Harper & Row, pp. 35–67.

Wanous, J. P. (1980). *Organizational Entry*. Reading, MA: Addison-Wesley.

White, H. C. (1970). *Chains of Opportunity*. Cambridge, MA: Harvard University Press.

Williamson, O. E. (1975). *Markets and Hierarchies: Analysis and Antitrust Implications*. New York: Free Press.

Zald, M. N. (1965). Who shall rule? A political analysis of succession in a large welfare organization. *Pacific Sociological Review, 8,* 52–60.

Zurcher, L. A. (1967). The naval recruit training center: a study of role assimilation in a total institution. *Sociological Inquiry, 37*(1), 85–98.

25 Careers and the wealth of nations: a macro-perspective on the structure and implications of career forms

ROSABETH MOSS KANTER

On a street near my house, a car is parked with a provocative pro-peace bumper sticker: "One nuclear bomb can ruin your whole career."

Arresting as that sentiment is, it does point to a neglected issue in most writing about careers – the relationship between careers, a phenomenon conceptualized at the individual and occasionally the organizational level, and major events or consequences at the societal level.

Of course, it is hard to deny that cataclysmic or history-shaping events have important consequences for employment and thus for careers – war, famine, drought, international monetary crises, scientific discoveries that launch new professions, technological breakthroughs such as the invention of the telephone or microprocessor, civil rights movements, labor battles, or even a wave of corporate takeovers. But it is harder to find, in the literature about careers, the more subtle connections between careers and economic, social, or political issues within that society. And practically non-existent is any attention to the ways in which the structure of careers in a society, via the organizations that help form them, might play a role in outcomes for whole societies – for example, in aggregate health of the population or in the productivity or job creation capacity of the economy.

Differences in career structures might indeed be related to differences in the wealth of nations.

The nature of career opportunity throughout a society surely bears on such macro-level issues as the comparative economic and social performance of nations – as seen in numerous attempts to relate the superior productivity or product quality of certain Japanese firms to the system of "lifetime" career advancement within a single firm (e.g., Ouchi, 1981). At the same time, societal-level variables, including the availability of investment capital or the rules governing industries and professions, just as clearly play a role in enlarging, limiting, or shaping opportunity. Labor economists have provided excellent cross-national comparisons of the impact of government employment policies on job availability and job mobility (e.g., Osterman, 1988). Yet, analysts of careers have largely neglected the macro-issues associated with careers. There is little in the way of conceptual frameworks for identifying what is significant about career forms that may vary across organizations and across societies, with implications for both the wealth of nations and the wealth of individuals.

In this chapter I offer a first step in the exploration of the macro-organizational issues surrounding careers. By design, I raise questions rather than answer them; I propose connections and speculate about relationships rather than prove them.

506

I begin by challenging common assumptions about the relationship of careers to organizations, deepen the analysis by defining three principal career forms that can vary across societies (bureaucratic, professional, and entrepreneurial), and then consider the implications of this perspective. While this handbook pulls together the best present knowledge about careers, most chapters in it are still largely limited to micro-views based on an implicit model of bureaucratic careers that take place within employing organizations. Thus, by enlarging the conceptual base, I hope to make it possible to move career theory to the macro-level.

CAREERS AND ORGANIZATIONS

In industrialized societies, paid work – and therefore careers in which paid work is a component – tends to be organizationally mediated. This is not to say, however, that all careers are formed by employment relationships with organizations, as most of the chapters in this volume unfortunately imply. Instead, employment is only one of the ways in which organizations help form careers.

Among the major career functions performed by organizations are:

- Educating and credentialing – providing the evidence that a person is "qualified" to perform certain tasks, which then provides access to opportunity.
- Brokering or mediating between individuals and opportunities – as in recruiting firms, employment services, communication services (help-wanted and situation-wanted ads in newspapers), and talent agencies for actors, writers, and other performers.
- Employing – providing paid work on a temporary or permanent, short-term or long-term, full-time or part-time, task-specific or diffuse basis.
- Protecting and enhancing – ensuring that incumbents in work situations or career lines enjoy advantages over non-incumbents (as in professional associations that gain a legal monopoly over provision of certain services) or gain the power to improve their status (as in collective bargaining through unions).
- Regulating – setting the terms or conditions under which employment is provided.
- Funding – providing the capital to enable individuals to work independently or start businesses, as is done by such financial entities as banks, venture capital firms, and government lending agencies.

The full analysis of careers in an organizational and societal context, then, requires examining more than simply how employers offer opportunities or how individuals select among work options and job sequences. We also need to take into account the nature of decisions made in and by schools, employment agencies, communication media, unions, professional associations, and financial institutions – all connected, in turn, to institution-shaping or constraining decisions made by local and national governments. For example, it is widely held that the growth in the number of entrepreneurs in the United States in the past ten years is a direct function of the availability of more venture capital, in part influenced by more favorable capital gains tax laws passed in 1978.

An important macro-issue is how career-forming functions shift across organizations over time, and how the division of labor among organizations varies across economies and societies. In a complex society, many specialized organizations arise to provide one or more career services; such functions as education, to take the most obvious example, take place in independent organizations formed for that purpose, rather than in the context of an employment relationship. Numerous businesses form simply to provide career services. At the same time, there are circumstances under which large employing organizations also take over career-forming functions from specialist organizations – as "corporate classrooms" arise to conduct MBA-level advanced management education along with technical skills training, or as employers attempt to wrest the "protection" function from unions through employee councils, or as corporations form internal venture funds to put employees into business.

Attention should be paid to the nature of the organizations that play a role in forming careers, and to the relationships among them across societies. For example, in the United States career brokering is largely handled by private organizations on a fee basis or as a service to employers, while in other countries (e.g., West Germany) the government plays a larger role (Osterman, 1988), as a service to individuals. Are these organizational differences associated with the relative smoothness of transitions between the roles that form a career?

We should also examine the relative importance of formal organizations versus informal social networks for each career-forming function, another issue that varies across societies. Social networks clearly help to attach individuals to opportunities – in helping the person find a job, as Granovetter (1974) demonstrated, but also in publicizing a reputation that causes the job to come to the person, as in the word-of-mouth referrals that bring patients to physicians. Social networks can also be the source of education, of unofficial credentialing (as occurs in reputation bestowal within corporations), of protecting (as occurs when a group of influential friends writes a letter protesting a negative tenure decision), and even of funding (as entrepreneurs collect investment capital from their family and friends). In the United States, it appears that many career-forming functions are handled via social networks, in contrast to the greater activity occurring through formal organizations in European countries or in Japan – but this observation itself suggests a hypothesis about national differences that can be tested, and then examined, for its consequences.

Thus, the relationship of careers to organizations needs to be conceptualized in much broader fashion than is common to date. With the awareness that employment is only one of the ways that formal organizations shape careers, researchers can investigate a broader territory – a territory that considers all of the forms careers take, whether embedded in employing organizations or not.

THE THREE PRINCIPAL CAREER FORMS

There are three principal forms of opportunity from which career patterns derive: bureaucratic, professional, and entrepreneurial.

These labels do more than simply define different types of *work;* they are the organizing principle around which a career logic unfolds – the incentives for continuation, the nature of opportunity, the path to increased rewards.

In the sections that follow I will describe the ideal typical patterns that bear examination for their societal origins and societal consequences. In any society, in any historical period, we should then be able to examine the kinds of work organized by each career form and the implications for performance.

THE STRUCTURE OF BUREAUCRATIC CAREERS

Bureaucratic careers are defined by the logic of *advancement*. The bureaucratic career pattern involves a sequence of positions in a formally defined hierarchy of other positions. "Growth" is equated with promotion to a position of higher rank that brings with it higher benefits; "progress" means advancement within the hierarchy. Thus, a "career" consists of formal movement from job to job – changing title, tasks, and often work groups in the process. Indeed, these very characteristics were at the heart of Weber's original definition of bureaucracy.

In the typical bureaucratic career, all of the elements of career opportunity – responsibilities, challenges, influence, formal training and development, compensation – are closely tied to rank in an organization. Indeed, this – of all three major types – is the quintessential organizational career for which employment by an organization is a necessity for the administrative/bureaucratic job to have any meaning at all. There would be no such thing as a bureaucratic career without a structure of ranks and grades, defining by level who can do what and who can get what. For example, eligibility for membership on governing bodies may be tied to level, with an untested assumption that those who have attained higher levels have proven their qualifications simply by virtue of attainment of that level, as Rosenbaum (Chapter 16) pointed out. Or pay may be tied to rank through a job grading system, very common in American corporations, and because there is a ceiling on how high salaries can go within ranks – regardless of performance – then the person must be promoted, must advance to a "higher" position in order to make more money.

In industrialized nations, a large proportion of the "employed" are subject to the bureaucratic career logic. Even for those blue-collar workers with limited or non-existent advancement potential, such as those Thomas (Chapter 17) describes, their life chances are defined by the realities of hierarchy – and therefore, without advancement to a higher job, their earnings, influence, challenge, and voice are constrained. Women in clerical positions face a similarly "stuck" bureaucratic career.

The structuring of career incentives in the bureaucratic pattern serves to induce those eligible for higher ranks to seek them. It thus encourages a proliferation of ranks and grades – sufficient distinctions so that there is apparent "progress" at sufficient temporal intervals. It also encourages weak attachments to task or work group, since movement is the name of the game, but strong attachments to organization, since ultimate financial and political rewards will only come with sticking it out long enough.

This pattern best describes administrative/managerial careers in very large oligopolistic corporations and the civil service in the mid-twentieth century. It is the implicit model in much of the writing about internal labor markets and vacancy chains (Doeringer and Piore, 1971; Stewman and Konda, 1983; White, 1970). But it does not describe the nature of careers for craftspeople or for professionals employed in those same large organizations. This model also does not adequately describe the nature of careers within very small organizations and within rapidly growing newer organizations (Kanter, 1984) or careers for the self-employed, the independent professional, or the entrepreneur.

It may even have diminishing value in describing careers even within large American organizations. There are many indications that the dominance of this career structure as the model American type is already declining in the wake of corporate downsizing, hierarchy flattening, and work innovations that simulate professional situations (such as self-managed work teams and "pay-for-knowledge" systems) and entrepreneurial situations (such as gainsharing, new venture units, and profit-based bonuses). Even managerial work itself is "professionalizing," meaning that managers have technical skills transferable across organizations, recognized apart from hierarchical status, and with opportunity decoupled from promotion within a single organization.

Yet most career theory still uses the bureaucratic pattern as its foundation (witness this volume), and some practitioners are busily trying to simulate this kind of pattern for employed professionals through such devices as "dual promotion ladders." But we should not assume a priori that the bureaucratic pattern best describes all careers or even organization careers – either for most employees or for most organizations.

The bureaucratic type had its moment of historical dominance in the United States with the rise of the large twentieth-century industrial corporation based on mechanical technologies, American hegemony, and a certain labor force. As other nations come to the fore, as the global marketplace and international competition expands, as technology becomes more complex and more rapidly changing, as women and minorities seek access to the better jobs, and as growth slows (or reverses) in traditional industries, then it is harder to sustain the assumptions on which the bureaucratic pattern was based. For example:

- A limited pool of competitors for higher positions, with the "losers" accepting their place, thus permitting a pyramidal distribution of people and maintenance of the legitimacy of hierarchy;
- continuing organizational growth, so that opportunity could be offered through expanding the width of the pyramid; and
- continuing employment security, so that eventually, over the lifetime, rewards foregone now would be received later, at higher ranks.

Instead, professional and entrepreneurial career forms may be better suited to the "self-designing organizations" (Weick and Berlinger, Chapter 15) that seem to fit an uncertain and turbulent environment where innovation is a key to economic success (Kanter, 1983).

THE STRUCTURE OF PROFESSIONAL CAREERS

The logic of professional career structures is defined by craft or skill, with monopolization of socially valued knowledge the key determinant of occupational status, and "reputation" the key resource for the individual.

Career "growth" for professionals does not necessarily consist of moving from job to job, as it does for bureaucrats, and "advancement" does not have the same meaning. Instead, those on professional career tracks may keep the same "title" and the same nominal "job" over a long period of time.

Opportunity in the professional form, then, involves the chance to take on ever-more demanding or challenging or important or rewarding assignments that involve greater exercise of the skills that define the professional's stock-in-trade. "Upward mobility" in the professional career involves the reputation for greater skill. Note that age grading – or an organizationally determined career timetable in general – is much less relevant in this career form, except for those occupations where broad age-related features such as "youthful athletic prowess" or the "wisdom of experience" are assumed to be associated with skill. For example:

- The career of a dentist in private practice in the United States may involve doing nominally the same thing for a lifetime, but continuing to get better and better, thus attracting more interesting patients with more interesting (and higher fee) problems.
- The career of a baseball player may involve growing in reputation and being traded across teams, with a compensation advantage at each move, until skills begin to decline (at which point he might switch to an entrepreneurial career, as defined later, trading on his name).
- The career of an actress may consist of growing in skill and public acclaim, allowing her to choose more exciting productions to join, commanding higher prices for each.

Of course, in these examples reputation and skill are intermingled and not necessarily correlated – one of the problems in professional careers. Also, societies with a bureaucratic bent could attempt to "bureaucratize" any of these occupations, defining employment possibilities by hierarchical grade – for example, "actress grade 1" licensed for only certain kinds of productions. But still, the general logic of the professional career form holds.

"Stuckness" in a professional career, then, means a cap on the chance for skill growth – for several structural reasons beyond limitations of individual ability. There may be limited range or socially recognized differentiation built into the core craft, as is the case with electricians. There may be excessive specialization, which limits access for some to important, "growthful" assignments, either because individuals "won" only a limited piece of the problem or because others can keep them out. This is the case both for nurses in hospitals and for production workers whose skill growth is limited by minute job classifications.

Professional careers are not automatically based in single organizations, though there is clearly a range within this category from those that are highly organizationally embedded (e.g., engineers and teachers) to those that are weakly organizationally embedded (e.g., physicians in private practice affiliated with hospitals but not "employed" by them). As I shall indicate later, the professional "community" may be a more important organizing factor in the professional career model than the employing organization.

Since some professional careers are only weakly connected to employing organizations, they are more strongly connected to other kinds of career-forming organizations than either bureaucratic or entrepreneurial careers. There is a direct relationship here. Indeed, two criteria that sociologists use to identify "professionals" are primarily organizationally based: Long periods of schooling or apprenticeship resulting in formal or informal certification; and the existence of associations that certify professionals, protect their marketplace value by setting entry standards and guidelines for compensation and fighting off the claim of others to do similar work (a fight occurring among American psychiatrist, psychologist, and social worker associations today over who can conduct psychotherapy), define standards of conduct, and ensure continuing education or continuing conformity to professional standards. Some U.S. professional associations with high proportions of employed rather than independent professionals may also take on the appearance and function of unions in bargaining collectively with employers on behalf of their members. But even so, it is the shared knowledge of members – shared skill or craft – that forms the basis for association, rather than the common employer.

Professional careers exhibit weak loyalty to particular employing organizations. As occupations "professionalize," they not only command greater remuneration for services because of their enhanced collective reputation and the skill monopoly they gain through their associations, but they also exhibit a weaker attachment to employers, except perhaps for firms of fellow professionals. Indeed, firms of fellow professionals, such as law firms, management consulting firms, or firms of architects and designers, can flourish precisely because of portable skills that can be exercised on behalf of many different organizations rather than dedicated to one.

Professional careers are thus defined by the greater cross-organizational mobility of professionals, in contrast with bureaucrats or entrepreneurs. "Have reputation, will travel."

For certain kinds of independent professionals, organizations arise for the specific purpose of career management – such as talent and literary agencies for actors, entertainers, and writers or sports law firms for athletes. Opportunity-matching organizations include nurses' registries for private-duty nurses and (a relatively new development in the United States) temporary agencies supplying accountants, lawyers, and other professionals. There is also an American cross-employer portable pension fund that was developed over 60 years ago on the premise that college professors may work for many employers over their career – Teachers Insurance Annuity Association/College Retirement Equities Fund. As the bureaucratic career model (assuming mobility within single firms over the lifecycle) breaks down in an era of corporate restructuring, it has been proposed that similar funds be established for other workers (Choate and Linger, 1986).

The professional career's reliance on reputation stands in great contrast with the anonymity of the bureaucrat. And the determination of career fate by fellow professionals through peer review also stands in great contrast to the determination of a bureaucrat's fate by hierarchical "superiors" (a ridiculous label anyway since it refers to decision-making rights and may have nothing at all to do with whether bosses are "superior" in skill). The mobility of the professional career depends upon establishing an external marketplace value that is reputation based. This reputation is conferred by others – by peers (as in reviewers for professional journals or Pulitzer Prize boards or Cannes Film Festival voters or Deming quality award selectors in Japan) or sometimes by "fans" or "constituents" whose "votes" select the "best." "Star" creation is a hallmark of professional career dynamics. It serves, certainly, to increase opportunity dramatically for those so chosen, but it also serves to confer professional status on the entire occupation, by indicating that there are high objective standards attained by the best practitioners – standards that exist independently of what specific organizations will tolerate. Thus Deming Awards for quality in Japan help professionalize blue-collar industrial work by making clear that there are universal quality standards.

There is ample room within this definition for discrimination within professional careers, but the very identification of "objective" standards makes it harder to sustain the same kinds of discrimination possible in bureaucratic careers, where social acceptability may be treated as a legitimate selection criterion, and selection decisions often do not have to be justified. Thus, women and minorities more often succeed in those areas where visible standards are clearest and where reputations need to be performance based.

The peer review component of professional careers has been so strong in the United States, at least, that for a long time professionals were not permitted to advertise. Instead, the other-conferred reputation (through publishing or referrals, e.g.) substituted. Entrepreneurs, of course, can and must advertise their offerings; they are alone in the marketplace.

Professional career opportunity – growth in knowledge or skill and therefore access to ever-more-important problems, with the greater rewards that ensue – is also possible for employees of large organizations, although the dominance of the bureaucratic model has made it difficult, often, to see this. But in an increasing number of circumstances, the bureaucratic career model has been challenged in favor of more professional career structures. Why should teachers have to become administrators in order to earn more or have their greater mastery of their field acknowledged? Why should skilled craftworkers in factories face a salary ceiling if there are still more ways they could contribute within their current job title? Why is a proliferation of hierarchical "levels" reflected in changing job titles necessary to motivate performance in the United States if Japanese organizations are more productive with many fewer levels and classifications?

One of the attractions of offering professional opportunity is that it is inherently less limited than bureaucratic opportunity, in that "growth" is not dependent on either the widening of the pyramid or heightening of the hierarchy or on someone else moving out of a position. Hence, its attraction in times of slower economic growth or awareness of the costs of excessive hierarchy. Furthermore, professional opportunity involves setting high performance standards and incentives to master them – another attraction in competitive economies.

Some of the changes in the organization of work occurring in the United States and Canada, sometimes derivatives of models used in Japan, West Germany, and Scandinavia, thus involve attempts to substitute professional career structures for bureaucratic ones – increasing professional opportunities for growth. One good example is the pay-for-knowledge system (Lawler, 1981; Lawler and Ledford, 1985; Tosi and Tosi, 1986). This system provides individual incentives for employees to rapidly upgrade their performance.

The system used by one manufacturing company is heavily team based and "professionalized" (Kanter, 1987a). Teams have responsibility for all aspects of production: operating the machinery, working with suppliers, inspecting the product for conformance to quality standards, and keeping records. With this kind of responsibility, it clearly helps every member of the team to have highly skilled colleagues capable of fully sharing the load.

New employees are hired by the work team after extensive interviewing, and a training coordinator (also a team member) develops a five-year career plan for how the new employee will progress in skill. This planning is important to the team because other team members will have to provide coverage for the employee's job while he or she is attending training programs. (In one plant, the work team hired some "temps" because they planned to have two people out for personal computer training.)

Pay grows as the newcomer moves from entry to full team member. There are small pay increments for time served, through the first two years, but the real increases occur as the new team member progresses through as many as several dozen "skill blocks." The skill blocks move from general orientation (learning the plant, operating hand tools, the simplest jobs, etc.) to on-the-job and classroom training to learn all aspects of one production process. Advanced operating skills involve knowledge of more than one process. The multi-skills requirement adds such skills as machine maintenance, quality control, and – one of the payoffs in terms of "self-management" – problem-solving and leadership skills. All of this may occur within five years. By contrast, under the former system in the same plant, it took five years just to move from sweeper to helper to process operator for one process, with no training or responsibility for problem solving.

All in all, pay-for-skill is a clever approach. It stresses individual responsibility but does not have the drawbacks of other pay-for-performance systems that pit team member against team member in contention for the highest ratings. Because there is no limit to the number of people who can reach the highest pay levels, there is little formal inducement to maintain a monopoly of skills or withhold training from newcomers in order to preserve a superior position. It creates a community of nominal peers with a broad range of skills who decide among themselves how best to deploy those skills. Gone are the trappings of hierarchy, from job classifications and grading systems to stacks of supervisors.

A system like this also runs counter to the goal many neo-Marxist critics attribute to modern corporations: to "de-skill" jobs so as to keep more people confined to lower pay levels and to make it easier to accommodate turnover, ensuring that a reasonable proportion of the work force is always new and thus always paid at lowest rates (Braverman, 1974). The effects of de-skilling keep the total wage bill low. So how does an organization "justify" in economic terms doing the opposite? Productivity improvements and savings, because of a better work environment that better utilizes human skills, more than pay for the additional costs of higher average wages on the shop floor (Kanter, 1986).

As more employers see the advantages, it is likely that more non-managerial work will shift from bureaucratic to professional models.

A PROFESSIONAL CAREER SUBTYPE: POLITICIANS

Elected officials or career politicians – from members of city councils to Prime Ministers and Presidents (but not the civil service) – do not fit neatly into any of the three career structure types I have identified, in part because the dynamics of selection, the process of matching individual to opportunity, and the subsequent opportunity available after office-holding are so different. (For example, a union member may begin as a worker paid by a company, then "rise" by election to local union office.) This incumbency as an elected official then opens up the possibility of advancement through the administrative hierarchy of the international union, thus returning the person to a bureaucratic track.

Political scientists have examined these issues, but career theorists have paid practically no attention – despite the clear importance of government actions in the fate of other social institutions. For example, there has been a great deal of debate in the United States recently over the desirability of a national industrial policy, in light of the apparent advantages Japan gets from the policies of the Ministry of Trade and Industry. Or the welfare policies of Scandinavian countries are contrasted with their absence in the United States. Is there a connection between the ability of a country to form such policies and the typical career structure for elected officials?

In the United States, the career structure for politicians comes closest to fitting the professional model for the following reasons:

- The person's fate is a function of his or her reputation, not of the office itself. While the office may affect current tasks, responsibilities, and influence, it does not predetermine the next job. (In a recent Democratic primary election for the U.S. Senate, among those running were a U.S. Congressperson, a state representative, and a member of the City of Boston School Board.)
- There is only a weak (if any) linkage between the political career and the structure of specific organizations. There may be an official hierarchy of offices within any particular government bureaucracy (e.g., from Secretary of State to Lieutenant Governor to Governor of Massachusetts), but the decision to move a person between them generally lies beyond the bounds of the bureaucracy, and with respect to other government entities, there is no hierarchical connection (e.g., the Governor of Massachusetts is not "above" the Mayor of Boston, a fact the Mayor is more than willing to remind the Governor of, frequently).
- The political career involves movement across organizations, with title or current position often bearing limited relationship to the next office the person may attain and "job-hopping" across levels of government the rule rather than the exception. Richard Nixon was Vice President of the United States, then lost a race for President, and lost a race for Governor of California, before being elected President.
- There are timetables for office-holding (terms of office legally specified in advance) but not for individual mobility. Indeed, longer incumbency in a particular office may be seen as deepening professional skills and therefore as making the person even more suitable for other professional opportunities – why Michael Dukakis could be taken more seriously as a possible Presidential candidate after being elected to a third term as Governor of Massachusetts. And some people make a life-time career out of a single political office, such as the U.S. Congress, "growing" during this time the way professionals "grow" – in the respect of one's colleagues and therefore the challenging problems one is given to tackle (committee assignments).

Political careers, while largely professional, also have some elements in common with the last type, the entrepreneurial form.

THE STRUCTURE OF ENTREPRENEURIAL CAREERS

The third major career pattern is the entrepreneurial one. The term "entrepreneur" has come to be associated with the formation of an independent business venture or with the ownership of a small business, but these meanings are too restrictive. Instead, an entrepreneurial career is one in which growth occurs through the creation of new value or new organizational capacity. If the key resource in a bureaucratic career is hierarchical position, and the key resource in a professional career is knowledge and reputation, then the key resource in an entrepreneurial career is the capacity to create valued outputs.

Thus, for Kenneth Olsen, founder and chairman of Digital Equipment Corporation in 1955, career "growth" has involved no changes of title or job or position; yet, he has greatly increased his power, remuneration, and responsibilities by growing the organization to much larger size – and reaping a direct return from the economic value he has created. This entrepreneurial career pattern is not restricted to the single founder. It occurs for everyone in the same organization who "stays in place" but grows the territory for which he or she is responsible. Recently formed and rapidly growing businesses often offer entrepreneurial careers in many areas to many people. In a small financial firm, the director of auto industry projects began with three people, and then, as the business grew, she found herself managing several layers across several cities, with a bonus tied to the profits of her area.

Instead of moving UP, those in entrepreneurial careers see progress when the territory grows BELOW them – and when they "own" a share of the returns from the growth.

In the bureaucratic career pattern, limits on advancement can cause whole categories of workers to be "stuck" – low in opportunity, barred from further progress. In the entrepreneurial pattern, people get "stuck" because the business (or the territory they are growing) fails to grow. Thus, sole proprietors of a Mary Kay Cosmetics distributorship or Mom-and-Pop corner candy store owners share the entrepreneurial career pattern with Olsen of Digital – except his career was high in opportunity, while theirs may be low.

The risk of entrepreneurial careers is certainly greater than that of bureaucratic careers or even of professional careers. The essence of bureaucratic careers is security, in return for which people will sometimes take a lower wage than they might receive if they were in business for themselves. Professionals have taken on the mantle of skill or knowledge that commands a price in the marketplace. Entrepreneurs have only what they grow. But then, they can also capture a much higher proportion of the returns if they succeed.

Freedom, independence, and control over not only one's tasks (as the professional supposedly has) but also one's organizational surroundings, are associated with the entrepreneurial career, accounting for some of its attractions. But so is greater uncertainty about the future, about how the career will unfold. The bureaucratic career is more predictable.

The entrepreneurial career pattern thus offers many of the elements often found to be associated with motivation for high productivity: control over one's work, ability to set one's own pace, the joy of seeing something emerge out of nothing, monetary rewards tied directly to what one has accomplished. When entrepreneurial careers are embedded in organizations, they have the additional virtues of reducing fixed labor costs – because pay varies with how much people actually bring in. Hence, salespeople paid on commission often have entrepreneurial careers. Even though "employed" by large organizations and subject to the direction by managers, they grow their own territory and reap the rewards thereof – a condition both highly motivating in a potentially frustrating occupation like selling and risk reducing for the employer, who does not have to pay unless there are results. It is often hard to get top salespeople to leave the entrepreneurial track; the bureaucratic pace of a managerial career seems unappealing.

Some American corporations are trying to establish the entrepreneurial pattern as an alternative both for individual careers and for business growth. Within otherwise traditional corporations, including AT&T and Eastman Kodak (Kanter, 1987b), special venture participants can earn a return, just like founder-owners do, on the marketplace performance of their product or service. While this alternative is still relatively rare (only 6.9% of 1,618 AMA member organizations in a 1984 American Management Association survey had special venture funds or entrepreneurial opportunities – Goodmeasure, 1985), interest is growing.

Typically, such schemes allow people to start a business with the support of the parent company. They are paid a base salary, generally equivalent to their former job level, and they are asked to put part of their compensation "at risk"; their percent "ownership" is determined by the part they put at risk. This then substitutes for any other bonuses, perquisites, profit-sharing, or special incentives they might have been able to earn in their standard job. Sometimes the return is based solely on a percentage of the profit from their venture; sometimes it comes in the form of internal "phantom stock" pegged to the parent company's public stock price.

Payout may occur at several intervals in the development of the venture, and not simply after the 7 to 12 years it can take to earn a profit in a new venture. "Milestone bonuses" for meeting established targets may be used, with further incentives added for timeliness – if you're late, the payoff goes down (Kanter, 1989).

A progressive airline offers several examples of the new work incentives. As a base, all employees (called "managers," as in "flight manager" for pilot) are on salary (generally somewhat below industry norms) and own substantial blocks of stock. Then, every crew that successfully completes a flight and closes the books on it perfectly (e.g., all on-board ticketing receipts accounted for) gets an immediate cash payment within 45 minutes of turning in the money and paperwork. Crews also get a share of the profits from the food and beverage concession: They "buy" the cart, stocked to their order, and then sell it on board.

Among other things, the prospect of this cash is designed to keep everyone flying on crews at least part of the time, including the executives, and reduce status differentials based on job position. The funds for the bonus supposedly come from reduction in errors (like bad checks) and the labor-saving because crews are now doing the paperwork themselves. (Interestingly, this program makes the pilots' pay-out dependent on the effectiveness of the flight attendants – a potentially interesting power dynamic, even in a team-conscious company that would deny the legitimacy of such concepts as "status reversal.") The next step for the airline: Make each region an independent profit center, with the crews running the routes in and out of it as though it were their own business, with compensation based on profits.

A much smaller step toward opening entrepreneurial career options to workers in bureaucratic career systems involves partial employee ownership (Blasi, 1988; Rosen, Klein and Young, 1985) and gainsharing. These programs offer earnings, growth, and opportunities for influence in place, without the bureaucratic need to change jobs.

In theory, gainsharing is a simple idea. Employees should share in the gains from any contributions they make to improving the company's performance. In practice, the term "gainsharing" refers to a cluster of programs with some features in common: sharing with groups (as against subjective judgments or flexible criteria), and always involving at least the hourly work force (as against only salaried managers and professionals). The unit whose performance is the basis for the gain to be shared may be the whole organization, large subdivisions of it, or single facilities. What's important is that the whole group benefits from overall performance.

All of the variants of gainsharing plans are quite compatible with the presence of unions, and all are found in both union and non-union environments. Data on how many organizations use gainsharing and how many employees participate in programs are difficult to come by, but by 1984, 11% of the 1,618 organizations in the AMA membership survey cited earlier had some sort of gainsharing in operation (Goodmeasure, 1985).

If bureaucratic opportunity is inherently limited because it is tied to the availability of "openings" in higher-level positions, entrepreneurial opportunity is not only expansible but also more likely to bring paybacks, in the form of value added, to the organization or the community.

IMPLICATIONS

This kind of framework can help point the way to better macro-theories of careers as well as to integration of macro- and micro-views, by enabling us to consider the following kinds of issues. Each of the patterns may be examined for their causes and consequences, virtues and drawbacks, at the organizational and societal levels.

At the *organizational level:* What difference does it make to an organization to have varying proportions of careers defined by each of the types? What are the managerial requirements if an organization is dominated by professional-type careers rather than bureaucratic-type careers? How does this change organization design, job design, the nature of incentives, the informal social patterns and "culture?" How is organizational performance influenced by choices of career systems – such as bureaucratic versus entrepreneurial? Some McDonald's stores are managed by paid employees on their way up in a bureaucratic career, whereas others are managed by entrepreneurs who own franchises; what happens differently as a result of these career system differences? And what "causes" these organizational choices of career form – strategic vision, business necessity, labor market conditions, or simply imitation of peers?

At the *societal level:* What are the aggregate economic consequences of career forms and of their mix in a society? Recently the United States was referred to as a "job creation machine" in comparison to Western European nations because more new jobs were created in the 1980s; Birch (1981) has demonstrated that small organizations, and by implication, entrepreneurs, produced most of them. Does this mean that a higher proportion of entrepreneurial careers could be a factor in greater economic growth? Certainly, the trend among American corporations toward reducing layers of management as a step in achieving greater profitability and "shareholder value" indicates a hypothesis that an extension of bureaucratic career incentives reduces economic performance. Similarly, the causes or correlates of national differences in career structures can be examined – such as the factors accounting for the dominance of bureaucratic careers and the relatively peripheral nature of entrepreneurial careers in France compared with the United States. Career forms can also be tied to political activity – such as the predominance of company-based unions in Japan, where the dominant career form seems to be bureaucratic, or the importance of professional (skill-defined) unions across a wide spectrum of occupations in Scandinavia, associated with a professionalization of many occupations through "workplace democracy" programs and a diminution of managerial status gradations.

• Mixed patterns – for example, part-bureaucrat, part-professional, part-entrepreneur – as well as the relationship between career groups, may be examined for the tensions and contradictions they engender, as individuals and organizations attempt to marry seemingly incompatible principles.

For example, in Western societies, professional careers may be mixed with either bureaucratic elements – as employed professionals are provided with "career ladders" engendering changes of title, status, and decision-making responsibility – or entrepreneurial elements – as independent professionals also form and run organizations. How well does the growth and utilization of professional skills combine with either of the other career logics? Observations suggest that particular tensions arise in each combination. The bureaucratic–professional mix may dilute the incentive for the professional to keep growing in skill or may divert attention from craftsmanship to the politics of upward mobility, with a diminution of independent professional judgment in the process. Similarly, the entrepreneurial–professional mix may raise questions; when a lawyer who is also building a law firm makes a recommendation, is this based on the best professional judgment or on the hope of bringing in more business? Or, to take another kind of example, when a large corporation dominated by the logic of bureaucratic careers establishes a new venture unit with entrepreneurial career incentives, what conflicts arise? My own recent research points to several tensions. Those whose career opportunity is bureaucratic often resent the high immediate earnings potential of their former peers whose opportunity is now entrepreneurial. The mix of types creates conflicts. And managers and professionals often misunderstand one another because their careers are driven by a different logic (Raelin, 1986).

• The notion of individual career transitions can be enlarged to encompass transitions among career forms – the passage from professional to bureaucrat, from bureaucrat to entrepreneur, and so forth.

For example, considerable attention has been devoted to the problems of the transition from professional to bureaucrat, when talented professionals (such as engineers), skilled in behaviors appropriate for the professional role (such as rapid exercise of technical judgment), move into management where they may need instead to coach and delegate to others – and pay attention to movement into another job if they want to stay "on track" in a bureaucratic ascent. What about other transitions across career forms? What limitations does experience in one kind of career track – such as corporate manager – create for effective performance in another career form with a different logic – such as independent entrepreneur?

What happens when corporate employees are given the opportunity to start ventures (become entrepreneurs) inside their parent corporation? Is it easier to move in certain directions than others – for example, from professional to manager rather than in the reverse direction? What accounts for the relative effectiveness of these individual shifts in career form?

• Career pattern transitions can also be examined at the collective or group level, as the typical patterns in a society shift, or as groups involved in one or another pattern wax and wane in power.

For example, the social organization of an entire occupational category may shift over time, dramatically reshaping the career form associated with plying that trade. Some occupational groups thus shift in career from independent professional careers to bureaucratic careers as paid employees, as happened to certain skilled crafts in the early industrial era or, today, to physicians increasingly employed by multi-facility health care corporations (Starr, 1983). What causes such a change? How is it effected? With what consequences? In the health care case, does the exercise of professional skills change?

CONCLUSION

This kind of analysis opens the way toward comprehending and conceptualizing the societal consequences of career systems and career forms. Most of the career literature, including the chapters in this book, looks at career from the perspective of the individuals involved; a small sub-section examines careers in terms of consequences for organizations. Now clearly it makes a great deal of difference to people if opportunities are open or closed, if the chance to gain and use certain skills is available, if work possibilities lead them in some directions rather than others – and this emphasis on consequences for individuals keeps the career field more people centered than some other branches of management and organization theory. It can also make a difference to organizations if career systems help match people with skills to jobs with responsibilities in a smooth fashion or if the other assumed functions of good human resource management systems are carried out effectively.

But in addition, career forms also have macro-economic, macro-political, and macro-social consequences. At the societal level, the social organization of careers may be associated with the level and kind of productive capacity and economic output of that society, with its level and kind of political conflict, and with the aggregate well-being of its citizens. Career issues are thus implicated in the current debate over the competitiveness of nations – their ability to grow in a global economy. The wealth of nations, after all, rests on how the efforts of people are channeled into jobs. And *careers* as well as jobs matter at the societal level because behavior in *today's* work – and thus the choices made, the decisions taken – is often a function of the expectations for *tomorrow's* work.

REFERENCES

Birch, D. L. (1981). Who creates jobs? *Public Interest, 65,* 3–14.
Blasi, J. (1988). *Employee Ownership: Revolution or Ripoff?* Cambridge, MA: Ballinger.
Braverman, H. (1974). *Labor and Monopoly Capital.* New York: Monthly Review Press.

Choate, P. (1986). A new approach ensuring retiring income. *Business and Health, 4*(1), 12–13.

Choate, P., and Linger, J. K. (1986). *The High-Flex Society: Shaping America's Economic Future.* New York: Knopf.

Doeringer, P. B., and Piore, M. J. (1971). *Internal Labor Markets and Manpower Analysis:* Lexington, MA: Heath.

Goodmeasure, Inc. (1985). *The Changing American Workplace: Alternatives in the 1980's.* New York: AMA Membership Publishing Division.

Granovetter, M. (1974). *Getting a Job: A Study of Contacts and Careers.* Cambridge, MA: Harvard University Press.

Kanter, R. M. (1983). *The Change Masters.* New York: Simon & Schuster.

Kanter, R. M. (1984). Variations in managerial career structures in high-technology firms: the impact of organizational characteristics on internal labor market patterns. In P. Osterman (ed.), *Internal Labor Markets.* Cambridge, MA: MIT Press.

Kanter, R. M. (1986). The new workforce meets the changing workplace: strains, dilemmas, and contradictions in attempts to implement participative and entrepreneurial management. *Human Resource Management, 25,* 515–537.

Kanter, R. M. (1987a). The attack on pay. *Harvard Business Review, 65*(2), 60–67.

Kanter, R. M. (1987b). From status to contribution: some organizational implications of the changing basis for pay. *Personnel, 64*(1), 12–37.

Kanter, R. M. (1989). *When Giants Learn to Dance.* New York: Simon & Schuster.

Lawler, E. E. III (1981). *Pay and Organizational Development.* Reading, MA: Addison-Wesley.

Lawler, E. E. III, and Ledford, G. E. (1985). Skill-based pay: a concept that's catching on. *Personnel.* September, pp. 30–37.

Osterman, P. (1988). *Employment Futures: Reorganization, Dislocation, and Public Policy.* New York: Oxford University Press.

Ouchi, W. G. (1981). *Theory Z: How American Business Can Meet the Japanese Challenge.* Reading, MA: Addison-Wesley.

Raelin, J. A. (1986). *The Clash of Cultures: Managers and Professionals.* Boston, MA: Harvard Business School Press.

Rosen, C. M., Klein, K. J., and Young, C. M. (1985). *Employee Ownership in America: The Equity Solution.* Lexington, MA: Lexington Books.

Starr, P. (1983). *The Social Transformation of American Medicine.* New York: Basic Books.

Stewman, S., and Konda, S. L. (1983). Careers and organizational labor markets: demographic models of organizational behavior. *American Journal of Sociology, 88,* 637–685.

Tosi, H., and Tosi, L. (1986). What managers need to know about knowledge-based pay. *Organizational Dynamics, 14*(3), 52–64.

White, H. (1970). *Chains of Opportunity: Systems Models of Mobility in Organizations.* Cambridge, MA: Harvard University Press.

Name index

Abdel-Halim, A. A., 252
Abegglen, J. C., 10, 190, 207
Abelson, R. P., 53, 333
Abercrombie, N., 438
Abowd, J., 424
Abraham, K. G., 209
Abramson, J., 111, 119, 120, 123, 125
Adams, J., 183 .
Adams, J. M., 111
Adelson, J., 115, 167
Adizes, I., 296, 297, 3304
Adler, S., 233, 235
Alban-Metcalfe, B., 190
Alchian, A. A., 420, 421, 499
Aldag, R. J., 258, 493, 494
Alderfer, C. P., 16, 30, 84, 134, 145, 146,
    147, 148, 153, 154, 261, 478, 480, 481,
    482, 483, 485, 487, 496, 497
Allen, A., 234, 235
Allen, M. P., 192, 391, 497, 498
Allen, R. W., 241
Allport, G. W., 234, 455
Almquist, E. M., 133, 146
Alutto, J. A., 252, 402, 495, 496
Alvarez, R., 148
America, R., 134
Amernic, J., 34
Amis, M., 196
Anderson, B., 134
Anderson, C. R., 258, 260
Anderson, E., 433
Anderson, H. P., 207
Anderson, N., 43, 60
Anderson, R. A., 269
Andrews, F. M., 102, 380, 486
Andrisani, P. J., 162, 238
Angle, H. L., 241
Anthony, P. D., 449
Applebaum, H., 405, 497
Aranya, N., 34
Argyris, C., 11, 13, 18, 21, 102, 192, 293,
    296, 316, 440, 458, 486, 493, 494
Ariss, S. S., 305
Armour, H. O., 420
Arnold, J., 184, 193
Arnott, C. C., 162

Aronson, E., 252
Arrow, K. J., 332, 421, 495
Arthur, M. B., xvi, 8, 9, 13, 14, 16, 19, 21,
    84, 228, 278, 293, 309, 437, 438, 439,
    440, 448, 449, 477, 478, 479, 480, 485,
    494, 496
Asch, S. E., 237
Ashenfelter, O., 424
Assouline, M., 34
Astin, A. W., 33, 66, 127
Athos, A. G., 457
Atkinson, J., 450
Atkinson, J. W., 308
Averitt, R., 364, 492, 498
Avery, R. W., 47
Avolio, B. J., 334
Azariadis, C., 423

Bailey, F. G., 446
Baily, M., 423
Bailyn, L., 10, 16, 48, 49, 103, 159, 162,
    163, 176, 204, 260, 296, 297, 298, 331,
    475, 479, 481, 482, 484, 485, 494, 496
Bain, J. S., 417
Baird, L., 137, 295, 444
Bakan, D., 116, 279, 280
Ball, D. W., 450
Baltes, P. B., 69
Bamberger, J., 111
Bandura, A., 265, 268
Barak, A., 34
Bardwick, J. M., 72–73, 78, 82, 111, 114,
    117, 118, 119, 120, 121, 122, 166, 167,
    168, 171, 176, 277, 296
Barley, S. R., 10, 18, 20, 48, 53, 57, 58, 59,
    61, 84, 354, 372, 376, 397, 403, 432, 454,
    480, 481, 496, 497, 498, 500
Barnard, C., 399
Barnett, R. C., 111, 113, 165, 169, 261
Barney, J. B., 230, 420, 426, 479, 495, 496,
    497, 498, 499
Baron, J. N., 58, 60, 190, 208, 211, 331,
    381, 382, 388, 389, 493, 495
Bartol, K. M., 276, 278
Bartolome, F., 11, 159, 163, 171, 260,
    285

Subject index

abilities: human capital model, 332; and job performance, 29; supervisor ratings, weaknesses, 332–333; tournament model, 336; trait-factor, theory, 28–29, 32
ability requirements, congruence, 32
ability status, 338
ability tests, 332
absenteeism, 494
academy model, 215–218
accommodation, 482
accountability, 440–445, 449
achievement: bureaucratic organizations, 440–445; effect on organizations, 241–242; and language, 438; personality disposition, 238; women, 123
adaptability, 288
adaptation: self-designing organizations, 316–317, 324; subjective careers, 321
adhocracy, 319
adjustment, see career adjustment
adult development: and career adjustment, 66–85; and career development theories, 82–84; gender differences, 78–82, 166–168, 280–281; theories, 70–82; and women, 112–114, 118–123
adult socialization, 94–95
advancement, bureaucratic careers, 509
advancement need, 295, 298, 303–307
"adverse impact," 29
affective disposition, 233, 239
affiliative behavior, 279, 285
affirmative action, 147–149
age factors: coping response, 261, 265; and performance, 97; transitions, 76–78, 80
age timetable, 339–342, 497; career systems, 334, 339–342; employee perceptions, 346–347; professional careers, 511; supervisors' ratings, 334
agency, 279–280
agentic career planning, 287
aggrandizement, 445–449
airline pilot study, 45
alienation, 100–101
ambiguity: career effects, 494; self-

designing systems, 321; versus structure, organizations, 237–238
ambivalence, 89–90, 98–106
"analyzers," 217–219
anomie, 101
anonymity, 512
anthropology: career concept viewpoint, 10; and rites of passage, 397–398
anxiety, career mismatch, 300
archetypes, 280
artifact culture, 457, 464–469
assembly-type technologies, 213
assertion training, 277
assignment flow, 215
asynchronism: age norms, 497; definition, 164–165; dual-career couples, 159–178; and timing, 171–172
AT&T, 517
attachment: sex differences, development, 79–80, 115; theories of, women, 117–118
attainments, 333–334
attitudes: and career transitions, 187; and personality, 238, 244; self-efficacy role, 244; situational vs. dispositional theory, 233–248; two-career couples, 162–163
attraction-selection- attribution model, 36
attribution theory: and promotions, 333; reputations, 447
authority, 449
autonomy: career anchor, 93, 99; consequences, 493; gender differences, 167; and rites of passage, 413; stress factor, 258, 493
avoidance coping, 261

Bain and Company, 413
baseball team model, 215–218
basic assumptions culture, 457, 464–469
behavior control, 242–247
Bell Labs, 413
Bennington study, 186
bereavement model, 183–184
bias, 338
biculturalism, 136–137
biodata, 36

537